THE COLONIAL PERIOD OF AMERICAN HISTORY

THE SETTLEMENTS
I

PUBLISHED ON THE
LOUIS STERN MEMORIAL FUND

THE COLONIAL PERIOD

OF

AMERICAN HISTORY

BY

CHARLES M. ANDREWS

FARNAM PROFESSOR OF AMERICAN HISTORY, EMERITUS
YALE UNIVERSITY

THE SETTLEMENTS

I

NEW HAVEN · YALE UNIVERSITY PRESS

LONDON · HUMPHREY MILFORD · OXFORD UNIVERSITY PRESS

———

First Published, June, 1934
Second Printing, May, 1935
Third Printing, September, 1935
Fourth Printing, November, 1936
Fifth Printing, December, 1937
Sixth Printing, June, 1941

TO

E. W. A.

WHOSE UNSELFISH LOYALTY OF MANY YEARS
HAS MADE POSSIBLE THE WRITING OF THIS WORK

CONTENTS

PREFACE

IN considering the plan to be followed in fashioning this work—which I think it worthwhile to begin whether I am able to finish it or not—I have had no intention of adding another account to the existing histories of the thirteen original colonies. I have been convinced for many years that to place the colonies in their rightful historical setting and so to discover what our colonial history is all about, it would be necessary to reëxamine the evidence from a vantage point other than that usually taken, to view them not from within, as is commonly done, but from without, with the movement constantly forward, following the natural course of historical development, and disregarding all preconceptions based on later events. For this purpose I have approached the subject from the English end, from the land whence the colonists came and of which they were always legally a part, and have broadened the scope of my inquiry to include all England's colonial possessions in the West that were founded in the seventeenth century. I have done this because I believe that final conclusions must always rest upon the experiences England had with all, not a part, of her colonies. That some of these colonies remained British while others became American does not, historically speaking, enter in as a determining factor.

The point of view thus taken gives to the colonial period of our history a new aspect and a new perspective. It brings the mother country into the forefront of the picture as the central figure, the authoritative and guiding force, the influence of which did more than anything else to shape the course of colonial achievement. This point of view gives prominence also to the place which the colonies occupied as factors in England's expansion, to their position for one hundred and seventy-five years as members of a growing island kingdom that was gradually widening into empire, and to their status during all these years as subordinate and dependent communities legally subject to the executive authority of the sovereign power across the seas. It shows that, interesting and important as the colonies are in their individual traits and peculiarities and in their relation to the later history of the United States, their standing as colonies and not as independent states is the fact of greatest significance to the scholar—the key to the whole colonial situation.

Unfortunately, in the past, the absorbing interest of Americans in their own side of the story has tended to obscure and relegate to the background this cardinal feature of our early history. Writers of the older generation made no progress in their attempt to understand England's influence on colonial affairs or to fathom the depths of her colonial policy. Their attitude was rather that of the antagonist and critic than of the understanding scholar with a desire to be better informed. They never seemed willing to believe that England's relations with the colonies was determined by nothing more sinister than an instinctive and self-protective effort to ensure her own national stability and security as against her Continental competitors and was in line with her own best interest, as the men of the eighteenth century saw it. These older writers did not take into account the fact that for England to have sacrificed her welfare to that of the colonies—even had she thought her policy was doing them an injury, as she did not—would have been considered by her statesmen and merchants an act of national suicide, which no sovereign power in the history of the world, least of all the United States of America, has ever been willing to commit.

Further observation discloses the fact that the seventeenth century is the century of settlement and of organization on the governmental side only, and that England did not formulate any well-defined or consistent commercial and colonial policy until that century was nearing its close. Then with settlement completed and the colonies firmly established, and the revolution of 1689 ushering in an era of relative peace among those at home who for many years had been at odds over constitu-

tional and religious issues, England awoke to the importance of
her colonies as necessary sources of strength in her own struggle for leadership in the field of national and maritime rivalry.
Under the stimulus of this conviction she consolidated her previous commercial and mercantile experiments into a definitive
programme and set up a fairly effective machinery for its enforcement.

Herein lies the fundamental difference between the seventeenth and eighteenth centuries of our history. The seventeenth
century shows us an English world in America, with but little
in it that can strictly be called American; the eighteenth everywhere presents to the view an Anglo-American conflict. On one
side is England endeavoring to transform the private colonies
into royal dependencies and to bring them all into a uniform
system of administration—efforts begun in the seventeenth century but never at any time fully completed; to put into operation her acts of trade and navigation; to utilize the colonies as
sources of strength and profit to herself according to the principles of mercantilism; and to find some way of centralizing
her authority in America, an attempt that failed owing to colonial opposition. On the other side are the colonies themselves,
with marked individual and sectional differences that made
coöperation difficult and union practically impossible, each
moving forward in its own sphere toward a popular and local
management of its own affairs, through the growth to prominence and leadership of its representative assembly. These colonies were not only resisting England's policy of control and
challenging frequently the claims of the royal prerogative, but
were putting into practice certain ideas regarding government,
law, land tenure, and finance that were not in accord with
English precedent and usage. In these conflicts and divergences
of the eighteenth century are to be found the beginnings of
American history properly so called, and in the struggle that
arose between England's imperial aims after 1763 and the demand of the colonies for a recognition, as an accomplished fact,
of their self-governing status are to be found the first causes of
our Revolution.

Thus the colonial period of our history is not American only but Anglo-American, and therein lies its misfortune and one of the reasons for the neglect that has dogged its path. American writers, except in an incidental way, have ignored the English side of the story, because it was English and therefore out of their range if not beyond their ken; while English writers, unfamiliar, as a rule, with the history of the American continental colonies, have left them severely alone, because these colonies having withdrawn from their allegiance to the British crown were no longer a matter of concern to those in England who were working in the colonial field. There are and have been within recent years noteworthy exceptions to this statement of the case, but in the main it is correct. The time must come, however, when this duality of interest will be regarded as a necessary part of the stock in trade of every serious writer on the subject who deals with it in a fair-minded and comprehensive way, and not until that time has come will this long and eventful period of our country's past receive its merited treatment as history unalloyed and find proper recognition not merely as a phase preliminary to our own career as a nation, but also as an integral part of English and Continental history in an era of colonization and commercial and maritime aggrandizement.

C. M. A.

New Haven,
  December, 1933.

THE COLONIAL PERIOD OF
AMERICAN HISTORY

THE SETTLEMENTS
I

THE COLONIAL PERIOD OF
AMERICAN HISTORY

CHAPTER I

THE AGE OF DISCOVERY

TO the maritime states of Europe that bordered on the Atlantic Ocean in the seventeenth century the lands beyond the western seas were as real a frontier as ever were the regions beyond the Alleghenies to the people of the colonial and national periods in America itself. These European states were old settled communities, each with a vigorous past. They had emerged from the conditions of their medieval life and were becoming modern—powerful monarchies with boundaries that were fairly well defined and governments that were taking on more and more a centralized form. In the thirteenth century industry and commerce had been subordinate interests in a world that was largely agricultural and feudal, the affairs of which were controlled in the main by the local communities—boroughs, towns, manors, and communes; but in the sixteenth century these interests were rapidly becoming the concern of the state. Louis XI in France and Henry VII in England saw in trade and commerce the future strength of their kingdoms and became kings of the merchants, encouraging the accumulation of capital and furthering by means of treaties with other states the welfare of those who were engaged in trade beyond the borders. This centralization of control in matters that involved the exchange of commodities and the production of wealth was accompanied by the faint stirrings of a national spirit, for people were widening the range of their patriotism and were taking part and pride in something more comprehensive than the affairs of their local towns, manors, and parishes.

The rise to prominence of these compact and aggressive monarchical states along the Atlantic seaboard was in part the result of territorial consolidation. Earlier ambitions—feudal and imperial—had driven medieval kings, princes, and lesser lords to undertake conquests—as in the case of the English kings in France, French kings in Italy, and Spanish kings in Germany—that had no other immediate purpose than to support feudal claims or to further family aggrandizement. As long as such aims were merely feudal and hereditary, no strongly built centralized governments, within fixed areas of contiguous territory could come into existence. But during the sixteenth century, after a long transitional period, a series of able and virile men, contending with feudal pretensions at home and imperial claims abroad, succeeded in gathering into their own hands the reins of power. Gradually there arose the maritime states of western Europe, a congeries of monarchies, ready to compete with each other for the advantages that the world had to offer beyond their own boundaries.

France under her absolutist kings was widening the area of her control and centralizing her administration and her law. England, ceasing to yearn for influence and territory on the Continent, was continuing the work begun by Edward IV and Henry VII of setting her own house in order and, having lost Calais in 1557 and given up Dunkirk in 1663, was concentrating her resources upon her own island kingdom. Spain was finally brought under the rule of Ferdinand and Isabella and their successors, and Portugal, breaking loose from Spain in the fourteenth century, was consolidating her monarchy under her first king John and was preparing the way for the activities of her greatest hero, Henry the Navigator. Holland, which during the Middle Ages had been dominated by the feudal ambitions of outside rulers, began under the emperor Charles V to rid herself in some measure of old-time rivalries among the local communities and to progress toward a stronger federal unity. Revolting against the reactionary policy of Philip II of Spain, this group of petty provinces—known as the Low Countries or the Netherlands—won its independence in the early seventeenth century and received formal recognition as a separate state at Westphalia in 1648. Thus Portugal, Spain, Holland, England, and France—states bordering on the Atlantic Ocean and the North Sea—were attaining to a political unity and self-consciousness each of its own; and in its own way and in its own time each was to take advantage of the opportunities that its maritime location offered.

As local practices and interests gradually were subordinated to the larger welfare of the state as a whole, certain other impulses became effective. Habits and customs underwent important changes as the earlier feudal provincialism, bred of an agricultural and farming environment with its limited supply of the luxuries of life, was broken in upon by the influx of the products and ideas of other civilizations and other climes. Trading activities with the East had begun with the Crusades, and in the thirteenth and fourteenth centuries there had been brought to the West commodities and usages that were destined to influence, in a constantly accelerating degree, the daily existence of the western European peoples. The lust for trade had been growing for two centuries and a half, and through the intermediation of the Venetians and the leaguers of the Hanseatic towns and by routes partly overland and partly by water, there had been distributed through the West a more or less regular supply of tropical and semi-tropical goods and merchandise. The western states bordering on the Atlantic developed no merchant marine of their own, for in this early period the carrying trade was monopolized by the cities of the Mediterranean, the Baltic, and the North Sea.

To further this trade capital was necessary. The resources of the old landed classes, which were dependent for their support on the proceeds of their manorial estates, were wholly inadequate to meet the demands of commerce and colonization. Land, which constituted the wealth of the feudal lords, was indivisible and immobile, and it was not until a flexible capital came into being, capable of adapting itself to all kinds of business enterprise, that trade and commerce could be undertaken on a profit-making scale. The beginnings of an accumulated capital can be traced to the later period of the Crusades. Then it was that credit and banking, finding their origin in the need of meeting the cost of crusading adventures, in the difficulty of transporting coin or bullion, and in the demand, felt particularly by the Jews, for security from rapacious barons, prepared the way for a rapid extension of mercantile activity. The banking experiments of the Italian cities, the wide European transactions of the "Lombards," the bold financial enterprises of the Fuggers and their rivals the Welsers of Augsburg in southern Germany, the banking systems of Nuremberg, Antwerp, Lyons, and Amsterdam, the commercial spirit of the Huguenots of La Rochelle, Bordeaux, and Paris, made possible the utilization of capital for military, political, and commercial purposes and laid the foundations of the commercial and colonizing era. Modern financial technique dates from the period of the Renaissance,[1] which ushered in the modern era of capitalism.

1. Of recent years an extensive literature has appeared upon the subject of capital, banking, and credit, as important factors in history, particularly in the field of com-

As demand increased and capital became available, there sprang into existence great numbers of new industries, many of which were dependent on the raw materials from abroad that were worked up in the cities of the West. Refining, distilling, dyeing, the higher grades of weaving, the making of silks as well as of woolens, of glassware and steelwork, began to absorb the energies of western craftsmen. The planting of such industries was a capitalistic undertaking, demanding money, labor, and the protection of the state.

With the growth of capital came the demand for profit and a surplus. The old idea of subsistence farming was passing away. Old methods of agriculture were undergoing transformation. Field systems were replaced by enclosures, lands were rented out to farmers, the tenantry were no longer bound to the soil, and bondage as an economic factor was ceasing to exist. The manor was breaking up and the new commercial and industrial opportunities were little by little absorbing the laborers, scattered in the process of manorial transformation. As the old system disintegrated and the commercial and industrial activities increased, new openings for profit were sought in every direction. Men no longer raised what they wanted to eat or made what they wanted to use and to wear. They cultivated to sell, they manufactured for a market, and they were eager to start undertakings that would promise a return on their investments. Agricultural Europe was fast becoming a commercial Europe, in which capital and the need of capital, however obtained, was engaging the attention, not only of merchants and promoters but of kings and statesmen as well. Traditions, practices, and legal rules were heritages of the past and were to persist for generations to come, for feudal ideas and incidents were to remain inherent in the social and legal order long after the system itself had become moribund as a

merce, discovery, and colonization. Beginning with Ehrenberg's great work on the Fuggers, 1896, 3d ed. 1922, a series of volumes and articles has been issued chiefly from the pens of Jakob Strieder, *Studien zur geschichte kapitalischen organisationsformen,* 1914, 2d ed. 1925, *Zur genesis des modernen kapitalismus,* 1904, and *Jacob Fugger der Reiche,* 1926; and Henri Sée, "Rémarques sur l'évolution du capitalisme et le système coloniale," "L'évolution du capitalisme en Angleterre," and "Le grand commerce maritime et la système coloniale"—all in the *Revue de Synthèse histoire.* Sée's most recent treatise and the best for our purpose is *Les Origines du capitalisme moderne,* 1926. Ehrenberg's work, much abbreviated, has been translated and issued as *Capital and Finance in the Age of the Renaissance, a Study of the Fuggers,* 1928. For further German literature on the subject see "Recent Work in German Economic History," *The Economic History Review,* I, 341–342, R. H. Tawney, "Bibliography," *ibid.,* IV, 336–356, and for a general review, Weber, *General Economic History,* 1926.

vital institution. The environment was still feudal and society was still organized on a feudal basis. At that time nationalism, as we understand it, was unknown.

One of the most profitable trades in which the merchants of central and western Europe were interested was that with the Levant, at the eastern end of the Mediterranean, where terminated the caravan routes from Arabia, Persia, Mesopotamia, and the farther East. The commodities obtained were spices—such as ginger, cinnamon, pepper, cloves, mace, and nutmegs; drugs—such as camphor, rhubarb, and aloes; and various other articles—such as silks, cottons, gums, dates, sugar, currants, prunes, dyewoods, and wines.[1] The routes—an overland network of roads through central Europe and a combination of land and waterways via the Mediterranean, including a thoroughfare north from Marseilles by way of Lyons—varied in difficulty, so that when one was stopped another could be used. Owing to various changes of political control in Europe, the land routes, as time went on, tended to become less available and those by way of the Mediterranean ending in Syria and Egypt to attain increasing importance. Genoa and Venice furnished the carriers and traded directly with the Turks as middlemen, the attitude of whom was not one of hostility, except in so far as they excluded foreigners from monopolizing the land trade from the Levant eastward, for the simple reason that it was to their advantage to profit from the tolls exacted.

There were ups and downs to this trade but no serious stoppage, except in times of war and pestilence. The cities of the central Mediterranean—Florence, Amalfi, Genoa, and particularly Venice—grew rich at the business, and the people of the western maritime states obtained their supplies through them. This trade never ceased, for though it dwindled it never stopped entirely at any time before its revival in the sixteenth century. The traffic by way of Egypt and Syria was never seriously molested by the Turks before the conquest of Egypt in 1516, a quarter of a century after Columbus discovered America. The economic decay of the Levant was due, not to Turkish control of the region from the Black Sea to Lower Egypt, but to a new competition, that of the Portuguese who rounded the Cape of Good Hope in 1488, and the discovery of a cheaper route to and from the

1. Epstein, *The Levant Company*, ch. I; *The Mariner's Mirror*, XII, 150, 164; Crouse, *Quest of the Western Sea*, pp. 3–4.

East for all long distance supplies.[1] The supremacy of Venice was overthrown by the exploitation of the passage to India by the Portuguese, English, and Dutch. The all-sea route made unnecessary the breaking of bulk between India and England and saved the payment of expensive dues to the Turks and other Asiatic peoples through whose territories the former caravan lines ran.

Thus that which undermined the Levantine trade and destroyed the commercial supremacy of the cities of the Mediterranean was not Turkish oppression but Portuguese enterprise. The Portuguese, seeking religious conquest in northern Africa instead of the Holy Land, united the medieval enthusiasm of the crusader with the secular ambitions of a young monarchy looking for territorial enlargement and opportunity for trade and profit. The leader of this new activity in the field of expansion was Prince Henry of Portugal, son of John I, crusader and navigator, 1394–1460, who stood, as did Dante at the beginning of the Renaissance, a representative of the medieval spirit ushering in a new era in European progress. In his ardor for the advancement of the faith Prince Henry, almost unwittingly, gave an impulse to forces that had been gathering for a century and paved the way for a great intellectual and commercial revolution. It has been well said that he appeared "in an age when the European world was suffering from failure and exhaustion"; that "he rendered vital service to the civilization from which have sprung the progressive states, the universal commerce, the liberal society, the humanized and open-eyed intelligence of modern life."[2]

Portugal, which in its beginnings was a small duchy dependent on Castile, was the first of the seaboard states to undertake voyages of any distance into the Atlantic Ocean. These pioneer ventures were the resultant of many earlier activities—the Crusades, which aroused curiosity and increased wants; the reports of travelers to the East,

---

1. Lybyer, "The Ottoman Turks and the Routes of Oriental Trade," *English Historical Review*, 1915, pp. 578–588; "The Influence of the Rise of the Ottoman Turks upon the Routes of Oriental Trade," *Report*, American Historical Association, 1914, I, 127–133. Professor Lybyer's suggestive articles might well be enlarged and to some extent revised. The main conclusions appear sound, that the Turks not only did not obstruct trade but were the only Levantine power that encouraged it. Some of the evidence, particularly that based on western prices, is not conclusive. Only one commodity, pepper, is selected and the data presented proves little. A wider variety of Eastern products might well be chosen and studied through a longer period of time.

2. Beazley, "Prince Henry of Portugal," *American Historical Review*, XVI, 11–24; XVII, 252–267. See also Prestage, *The Portuguese Pioneers* and *Portugal: a Pioneer of Christianity* (1933).

which though often fabulous stirred men's souls to new ambitions; the revival of a knowledge of geography through the renewed study of the writings of Ptolemy and Strabo; a growing familiarity with the arts of navigation acquired in the waters of the Mediterranean; increased skill in the charting of waters and the building of ships; and a marked improvement in the making of the compass and other nautical instruments—conditions all of which made inevitable a more extended experimentation than had ever been tried before, and that too in the only quarter available, the open Atlantic. As southern Spain was still in the hands of the Moors, Portugal rather than Spain commanded the waters outside the Straits of Gibraltar, and it was a no more difficult task to navigate these waters and to coast southward along the African shores than it had been to buffet the waves of the great inland sea. It was no accident that Portugal was the first in the field of discovery and colonization. She was independent, fairly well united politically, and ably governed. Her external relations in the fifteenth century, particularly with England, were favorable. Because her coast at no point had an eastern outlook she had never been drawn into the Mediterranean trade, and having concerned herself only with northern Africa she had of necessity become proficient in the building of ships. Also because she lay outside the Straits and faced the Atlantic, she was familiar with some of the needs of an ocean-going commerce. Prince Henry in the entire course of his adventurous life scarcely ventured out of sight of land and entered upon no voyages that were more dangerous or more novel than those which had already been made in the Mediterranean and the Baltic; but he pointed out the direction that others were to follow and committed his small but energetic state to a new policy of commercial expansion.

There had been, of course, early attempts on the part of others than the Portuguese to penetrate this outer world. The Genoese had searched for an Indo-African waterway in 1291; the Catalans had sought for a "river of gold" in 1396; and the French had set foot on the Canaries in 1402. Even the Portuguese themselves are said to have discovered these islands while Prince Henry was still a boy. But it was not until 1415, when the prince himself led an expedition of a strongly crusading character across the Straits against the Moorish town of Ceuta, that a movement was begun which was destined to be continuous and permanent. The popes, Martin V and Eugenius IV, following the precedent set by their great predecessor Urban II, the spiritual promoter of the First Crusade, issued bulls in 1418 and 1436, calling on the sovereigns of Christendom to aid the Portuguese in the extermination of the infidels, and after 1442 Prince Henry himself made a similar appeal for coöperation in his plans of discovery and conquest. But these entreaties met with no response. The days of a general crusading movement were over, and except for the assistance of a few foreign seamen, who enlisted under his banner, Henry was compelled to pursue his task alone. No one, even for the love of Christ, would help him in his efforts.

But while thus eager to play the part of a spiritual warrior, advancing the boundaries of the great medieval church of which he was a faithful son, Henry never forgot the interests of his own kingdom, the foundations of which had been laid by his father, John I. His capture of Ceuta was a political conquest as well as a victory over the unbelievers, and to the end of his life he labored for the "honor of the kingdom" as well as for the "exaltation of the faith." To make the victory over the Muslims more secure and to obtain for Portugal outposts of colonization, he sent his mariners to explore the western islands—Madeira, the Cape Verde, and, finally, the Azores; and in order to broaden the trade of the young kingdom he sought for Guinea as a source of new riches and a market for Portuguese goods. He lived long enough to see his navigators round Cape Bojador (1433) and reach Senegal (1435) and Sierra Leone (1446), where the slaves and gold dust of a new field of exploitation enhanced the prosperity of the Portuguese people and the exchange of Portuguese products brought wealth into Portuguese pockets. Gradually as the significance of these undertakings began to be understood, the crusading aspects of Henry's labors became less conspicuous, and conquest and trade, territory and profit attracted more and more the attention of the Portuguese people. Before his death in 1460 Prince Henry himself was subordinating his zeal as a crusader to the more insistent demands of trade and commercial profit.

Thus Prince Henry the Navigator, beginning his public career in the medieval school of the crusader, finally emerges, after nearly half a century of unwearied devotion to Portugal's welfare, as the exponent of a new national and even international enterprise. He sought success not in the old world of the Mediterranean but in the new world of western Africa and the Atlantic. His was not a limited vision. He pictured a greater Portugal overseas, supreme in a sphere of her own, mistress not only of lands but of waters also, and the guardian of new trade routes and markets. He stimulated others to give reality to his dreams and aroused a new spirit among venturesome men of his own people to engage in trading voyages—often plundering raids—and to widen the scope of Portuguese authority and the opportunities for mercantile exchanges. Under Alphonso V, Portuguese navigators entered the Gulf of Guinea (1455), crossed the equator (1471), and discovered the Congo (1482). In 1488 Diaz rounded the Cape of Good Hope; in 1497-1498 Vasco da Gama made his way to India; and in 1521 Magellan, in the interest of Spain, circumnavigated the globe. These were the events that broke the monopoly of the Mediterranean cities, substituted the Atlantic for the Mediterranean as the scene of commercial activity and rivalry, ushered in an era of oceanic competition among the maritime states of the West, and transferred the leadership in trade and commerce from the cities of the old world to the oceanic states of the new. It was not the Turks who were responsible for the discovery of a new route to India. Rather was it the discovery of a new route which was more direct and less troublesome, that led to the decline of the eastern trade by way of the Levant and released the West from dependence on the Arabian and Persian caravans. That the Portuguese were in India, tapping the sources of the spice supply, which had formerly come to England by way of Aleppo and Alexandria, and so controlling that supply to England's disadvantage, explains why, in Elizabeth's reign nearly two centuries later, the Levant Company was chartered and the traffic revived between the western states of Europe and the eastern shores of the Mediterranean. The Portuguese monopoly was the starting point in that long series of treaties in the seventeenth and eighteenth centuries with England that brought Portuguese foreign trade finally under English control.[1]

While the Portuguese were pursuing their course along the western coast of Africa, circumstances were preparing the way for still bolder ventures to the westward. When Columbus began his career[2] the route to India had not been opened, but other contributory fac-

1. Shillington, "Beginnings of the Anglo-Portuguese Alliance," Royal Historical Society, Transactions, 2d series, XX, 109–132.

2. Columbus was born in Genoa, not later than 1451, of humble parents, and spent his young manhood as a wool carder and trader, possibly taking part in trading voyages in the central waters of the Mediterranean. He can have had no education during these early years and was probably illiterate when he left Genoa for Portugal about 1475, apparently with the object of advancing his fortunes by connecting himself with merchants interested in the wool trade, at that time carried on largely with

tors were at work foreshadowing the discovery of a new continent. The Portuguese occupation of the Azores, from 1443 to 1447, islands lying far out in the ocean three hundred leagues west from Portugal, was a bold and hazardous achievement, the like of which had not been known up to that time, and by 1460 the farthermost of the islands had been reached and a western outlook obtained from a point a third of the way across the Atlantic. Columbus was familiar not only with the work of the Portuguese navigators but not impossibly with the Vinland voyages of the Northmen also, and we know that he had come into touch with the exploits of the seamen of Bristol, the most noted port in that day of the English speaking race, who had been voyaging in a northwesterly direction by way of the Shetlands and Iceland. These Bristol men were finding that there were trade winds blowing southward and westward, rendering almost inevitable, as we see it today, under the navigating conditions of that time, a landfall somewhere in the Caribbean or Brazil. Columbus, the child of his age, was responsive to all the influences that were turning maritime and mercantile minds to an interest in the existence of possible lands beyond the seas. He was intensely religious and eager to convert any newly found pagans to Christianity. He was concerned also, as far as he could be, with the profit-making aspects of his voyage and sought for gold as well as for converts. He was ambitious to expand the territory of those whom he served and always took care to lay claim in the name of the king of Spain to each new island that he found. Thus his underlying motives were much the same as those of Henry the Navigator.

Some doubt has arisen as to the object that Columbus sought when, in 1492, he set out from Palos on his famous first voyage to the west. According to the current view it is commonly believed that he was seeking a shorter route to India than that which Portu-

England and Spain. In this interest he visited Madeira, the Azores, the Guinea coast, and Iceland and became informed regarding the activities of the Portuguese and the sailing and trading ventures of the Bristol merchants. No satisfactory reconstruction of the events of his life during the years before his first voyage is possible, for the essential facts are few and all of them in dispute. The latest and best account of his voyages, with admirable maps, is that of Cecil Jane, in his edition published by the Argonaut Press, *The Voyages of Christopher Columbus, being the Journals of his First and Third, and the Letters concerning his First and Last Voyages, to which is added the Account of his Second Voyage written by Andres Bernaldez. Now newly Translated and Edited, with an Introduction and Notes,* by Cecil Jane. Illustrated with five maps, 1930. Controversy is still current as to where Columbus was born and whether or not he was a Jew, but the issues are relatively unimportant.

gal was opening around the Cape of Good Hope; that inasmuch as the demand for tropical goods was rapidly increasing and the merchants of the day were growing impatient of the long and tedious passage to the south and east, Columbus proposed to reach the islands of Asia by sailing west; that he had become convinced, partly by a study of certain writings on geography and cosmography and partly by correspondence with a Florentine physician, Paolo Toscanelli, from whom he is said to have received a map and an encouraging letter, that a new route could be found; and that having reached the West Indies, he believed he had succeeded in his quest and had discovered Asia and Cypangu or Japan.

This statement of the case is now challenged and the counter opinion advanced that Columbus had no other purpose than to find new lands or islands to the westward, as the Portuguese had already found the Azores and the Madeiras. Regarding the existence of such lands he had long been gathering information, and in 1479 had visited Porto Santo, one of the Madeira islands, and searched the papers of his father-in-law, Bartholomew Perestrello, who had received the island by charter from Prince Henry, thus familiarizing himself with what knowledge the Portuguese had obtained up to that time. From this knowledge and from the experience he had gained in his contacts with the navigators of the day, he "sensed" the existence of more islands in the Atlantic lying beyond the Cape Verde and the Azores and to find these was the main object of his famous expedition. Whether this conclusion be ultimately accepted or not it in no way detracts from the renown of the great discoverer. To believe in the existence of lands unknown, to go in search of them in tiny vessels on an uncharted ocean, and to find the very lands that he went out to seek is evidence of genius of a very high order.[1] At the time Spain was in the full flush of her victories over the Moors, having recovered her lands by the subjugation of Gra-

1. The proponent of the new version of the Columbus voyage is Henri Vignaud, who summed up the investigations of many years in his most important work, *La tradition Colombienne et la découverte de l'Amérique*, 1911 (translated as *The Columbian Tradition on the Discovery of America*, 1920). A résumé of the controversy may be found in *History*, April, 1922. Vignaud's work was reviewed, on the whole adversely, by Beazley in *The Geographical Journal*, 56, pp. 416–418, and by Biggar in *Report*, American Historical Association, 1912, pp. 97–104. G. E. Nunn, *Geographical Conceptions of Columbus* (American Geographical Society, *Research Series* 14), though not discussing the main question, believes that Columbus, whom he calls "one of the foremost sailors of the world in an age of sails," set out to go to Asia and in his fourth voyage thought that he had actually reached that continent. *The*

nada, the last surviving Moorish stronghold in the Iberian peninsula, which fell in 1492, six months before Columbus started on his voyage. But through the discoveries of Columbus she gained her first title to lands in the New World and became a serious competitor with Portugal for leadership in the territories out of Europe in America and Asia.

The Portuguese and Spanish discoveries were made in an age, when the universal or international claims of pope and emperor were still living realities to the kings and princes of western Europe, and when the authority of the ecclesiastical organization, to which all western Christians belonged, was accepted without reservation as a force in temporal as well as spiritual affairs. Though the papacy in secular matters was losing its influence, and modern states, modern knowledge, and the beginnings of an international understanding were pushing their claims, it was still to all seeming in the plenitude of apostolic power. The crusading spirit still governed men's minds and the conversion of the heathen and the infidel was still a duty resting upon the human soul. Since the days when Adrian IV had presented Ireland to Henry II of England, the pope had always advanced claims to newly discovered lands, and at this juncture, when faithful sons of the church were acquiring titles to territories of unknown extent, he took advantage of the opportunity and extended in a remarkable and far-reaching form his papal jurisdiction and sanction. On January 5, 1455, Nicholas V issued a bull

Map of Christopher Columbus, which the great navigator is believed to have shown the Spanish monarchs in 1491, in support of his plans, has been issued in colored facsimile, half size, with a French and English text, under the editorship of Charles de la Roncière, 1924. M. de la Roncière thinks that the map demonstrates the truth of Vignaud's contention. Dr. E. L. Stevenson, our American cartographical expert, says that "the early maps do not, in general, support the assertion that it was the belief of the early visitors to the New World that they had reached the coast of Asia. On the contrary, with rare exceptions, they believed they had found new lands, new and hitherto unknown regions." (Letter to the *New York Times,* October 15, 1923.)

Vignaud also denied vigorously the authenticity of the Toscanelli letter (*Toscanelli and Columbus. A Critical Study.* 1902), and his conclusions on this point have met with somewhat more favor. There are those, however, who think that Vignaud would have done better to have let the Toscanelli letter alone, as it had nothing to do with Columbus, who never said a word about the Florentine cosmographer and did not need his advice. Columbus's latest biographer, Cecil Jane, is conservative on all these points. All agree that the Columbus story is full of anachronisms and contradictions, and that to accept Vignaud's conclusions is to raise almost as many problems as these conclusions are supposed to have solved.

authorizing Alphonso V of Portugal to reduce to servitude all infidel communities, saracen or pagan, and to take possession of their countries. Soon afterward he issued another bull praising the work of Prince Henry and granting to Alphonso "all that had been or should be discovered, south of Cape Nun and Cape Bojador toward Guinea," as a perpetual possession, threatening to excommunicate all intruders. On June 21, 1481, Sixtus IV granted to the Portuguese all lands from Cape Bojador *ad Indos.*

The control which Portugal thus obtained of the African coast was strengthened by the treaty of Alcaçova with Spain, that is, with Castile, in 1479. By this treaty she retained full right of navigating and making discoveries along the coast of Africa and of possessing all known islands, except the Canaries, which were formally ceded to Castile, under whose sovereignty they were destined to remain, as Castile expanded into Spain, down to the present day. Thus Portugal was confirmed in her exclusive right to the route, which, a few years later, her navigators were to follow into the Indian Ocean and that, too, thirty-seven years before Selim captured Egypt from the Mamelukes.

With the return of Columbus from his first voyage the rivalry between the two monarchies broke out anew, because the king of Portugal claimed the new-found lands as his own on the ground that the recent discoveries came within the scope of the concessions made by the papal bull of 1455 and confirmed by the treaty of Alcaçova. In this crisis the sovereigns of Castile and Aragon, in their turn, looked to the papal authority for a defense of their rights. They appealed to Alexander VI, a Spanish pope, native of Valencia, who in 1493 issued four bulls granting the privileges that Spain desired and drawing a line of demarcation between the possessions of the two powers in the sphere of the Atlantic. They were not formal bulls but papal briefs or letters, acts of papal sovereignty in favor of Spain, to whom Alexander felt greatly indebted. The bull of May 3, 1493, *Inter caetera,* made no reference to a dividing line, but the draft of May 4, which was issued as the second bull, *Inter caetera,* early in June, is the instrument which is properly known as the Bull of Demarcation. It granted to Ferdinand and Isabella the islands and continental lands, discovered and to be discovered, not only in the West but in the South and in the direction of the Indies, and it established a line of demarcation that was not to be passed by the subjects of any other prince, for purposes of trade or otherwise. That line was to run one hundred leagues to the west and south of the Cape Verde islands.[1]

This bull did not satisfy Spain, because she wanted definite mention of India. The omission was remedied by the fourth bull, that of September 26, granting the Spanish monarchs all the regions gained by sailing south and west even until India might be reached, thus greatly extending the sphere of Spain's colonial possessions. This action, in turn, angered Portugal, who was thereby denied the opportunity of taking advantage of the trade winds blowing toward the southwest and of the south flowing Brazil current and the east flowing Antarctic current. The pope refused to alter his decision and the dispute was finally settled by a compromise. Spain was willing to make concessions, and at a meeting of Spanish and Portuguese ambassadors, June 7, 1494, a treaty was drawn up—the treaty of Tordesillas—whereby the line was revised to the advantage of Portugal and removed to a point three hundred and seventy leagues west of the Azores, thus making it possible later for Portugal to occupy Brazil as a Portuguese possession. This treaty was formally sanctioned, twelve years later, by a bull of Julius II.

This famous division, the first determination of spheres of influence in history, was almost the last imperial or international act of secular sovereignty performed by the papacy. In fact it is probable that the papal act was largely formal, as there is reason to believe that neither the papal chancery nor the pope had any say in the matter, except to give to the decision the papal sanction. In all probability that decision originated in the Spanish chancery.[2] This line of demarcation, which conveyed a monopoly of possession upon two colonizing powers to the exclusion of all others, was never accepted by the remaining maritime governments, who paid no attention to the ban thus placed on their colonial ambitions. England, soon to repudiate the supreme jurisdiction of the Holy See, deemed it an infringement on her royal sovereignty and only three years afterward sent out John Cabot on a voyage of discovery. France, under Francis I, in despatching Jacques Cartier to the St. Lawrence

1. Van der Linden, "Alexander VI and the Bulls of Demarcation," *American Historical Review*, XXII, 1–20; XIV, 775, Gottschalk, *The Earliest Diplomatic Documents in America*, where the bulls appear in excellent facsimiles; Davenport, *European Treaties bearing on the History of the United States*, I, which contains the texts of all these documents from 1455 on, with admirable commentary and bibliographies.

2. Van der Linden, pp. 17, 20.

a little later, told Spain very frankly that the sun gave warmth to her people as well as to others and that she "much desired to see Adam's will to learn how he had partitioned the world." The line was never satisfactorily determined even in the West, for the Portuguese, into whose hands fell the eastern part of Brazil, were constantly crossing the western line in South America, where the boundaries were not fixed until the eighteenth and nineteenth centuries.

In the East the situation was even more complex and troublesome. There is no certainty that the line was intended to circle the globe, though some have thought that one object of Magellan's voyage was to discover whether or not the rich-bearing Spice Islands or Moluccas lay within the Spanish sphere. Portugal insisted that these islands were on the extreme eastern boundary of her own possessions, and the dispute was not ended until Charles V, king of Spain as well as emperor, happening to be in need of money, sold to Portugal, in 1529, in the face of strong opposition from the Spanish cortes, his right to the Moluccas, which he claimed by virtue of Magellan's discovery, and accepted a line drawn seventeen degrees east of the islands. Thus the Moluccas were retained within the Portuguese field. On the other hand, the Philippines, also on the Portuguese side of the line but within the range of Magellan's discovery of 1521, went to Spain by a decision reached in 1750 to annul the demarcation line entirely. This decision was reached after years of conflict and controversy, following deliberate and successful attempts at peaceful conquest and colonization, which began with the Legazpi expedition of 1564. After Spain had annexed Portugal in 1582, joining that kingdom to herself in a personal union under a common king, the other maritime states vehemently protested against this method of bargaining in the East Indies. The Danish minister declared that his master, the Danish king, "could not take account of the papal division of the East Indies between Spain and Portugal, which was the only foundation these countries had for their asserted rights." Drake in 1579 did not hesitate to enter these waters, though the English did not become dangerous competitors till the founding of the East India Company in 1600. The Dutch, however, enemies of Spain in Europe, early flouted the Spanish-Portuguese pretensions and sent fleets to the East in 1595–1596, and their East India company, founded in 1602, became an aggressive and dominant factor there in the seventeenth century. Its captains and merchants extended their trade, captured Portuguese territory, and laid the foundations of the present colonial power of Holland in the East. Thus the Eastern situation was finally cleared up, not by papal bulls but by strategy and force. After Portugal obtained her freedom from the Spanish ascendancy in 1640, England entered into such relations with her as to reduce greatly her commercial importance, and the rivalry between Spain and Portugal in the East was supplanted by the greater rivalry between England and Holland. The treaty of Lisbon, February 13, 1668, between Spain and Portugal, following a political revolution in the latter country, was of great significance to England in that it preserved the integrity of the smaller power and checked the aggrandizing tendencies of its more important rival. This agreement, which guaranteed Portugal's right to territories and trade in America, Asia, and Africa, made possible the Methuen treaty of 1703, which to all intents and purposes placed Portuguese trade and commerce under English control.[1]

Important as is the line of demarcation in explaining the whys and wherefores of many colonial boundaries and possessions of the present day, and essential as it is to a proper understanding of many events in early colonial history, it is no less explicit in establishing a fundamental principle underlying the accepted law of nations. The bull of Alexander VI, in asserting the rule that all lands discovered and to be discovered, not belonging to a Christian prince, became the property of the king under whom the discovery was made, established the modern right of discovery. At the same time it gave sanction to a dictum, of great consequence to the colonial history of the ensuing three centuries, that a mother country has a complete monopoly of the trade of its own colonies. That these rules would have governed the conduct of the maritime states of the west, in their policies toward their new possessions, even if the papacy had not intervened, is more than likely. They had their origin not in the papal but in the Spanish mind, and so represent the principles that the legal authorities of that day were more or less obliged to accept in order to give a semblance of order and regularity to the colonizing process. Rights of possession had to rest on some definite understanding, and the right of discovery, vague as it often was and the

    1. Bourne, Historical Introduction to Blair and Robertson, The Philippine Islands, pp. 24–80; Foreman, The Philippine Islands, pp. 28–31; Robertson, "Legazpi and Philippine Colonization," Report, American Historical Association, 1907, I, 143–155; Prestage, The Diplomatic Relations of Portugal, 1640–1688. Shillington and Chapman, Commercial Relations between England and Portugal, and Davenport, European Treaties, I, II, contain all the most important texts.

cause of endless disputes, was as sound a doctrine as could have been found in an age when half a dozen European powers were competing for the lands of a new world.

During the forty years that followed the return of Columbus from his first voyage, the waters of the northern Atlantic must have been crossed and recrossed many times by venturesome seamen in their small craft, some for purposes of exploration and some for the more prosaic business of catching fish. Columbus made three more trips to the West Indies between 1493 and 1503, coursing among the islands and touching South America at a single point near the mouth of the Orinoco. John Cabot for England reached Newfoundland, and in a second voyage with his son, Sebastian, may have gone as far southward as Florida; the Corte Reals and Fagundes for Portugal did the same; Gomez for Spain entered the St. Lawrence and coasted along the shores of Maine; and de Gonneville for France reached Brazil and Verrazano the region from Florida northward. How early fishermen made their way across the ocean to cast their lines and nets in the waters off Newfoundland and the adjoining Gulf of St. Lawrence can never be known, but that fishing boats from Portugal, from the Basque seaports of Spain and France, from La Rochelle and the harbors of Brittany and Normandy were there in considerable numbers before 1530 is known from unimpeachable testimony.[1] To those we may add Devonshire men from the West Country of England, whose interest in the banks of Newfoundland was to exercise for nearly three centuries a profound influence upon the history of that part of the English world. And even at this early date French privateers were continually engaged in preying upon the Spanish colonies and Spanish shipping, waylaying fleets, sacking towns, carrying off booty, and leaving little but wreckage behind. French sea dogs anticipated those of England by more than half a century.

The discovery by France of a suitable field for colonial enterprise began with the advent of Jacques Cartier, a captain of St. Malo, sent by Francis I, then in the heyday of his golden age, to secure a part of the wealth of gold and precious stones in which the New World was thought to abound. Cartier in two voyages of 1534 and 1535

1. St. John's in Newfoundland had become the center of the codfishery as early as the beginning of the sixteenth century, *Revue Historique,* X, 534. Roberval found "seventeene Shippes of fishers" there in 1542, some of which were Portuguese. Something will be said upon this subject in later chapters.

discovered the St. Lawrence, the "river of Hochelaga," and explored its course as far as Montreal.[1] The country was largely unknown and the French had the field practically to themselves; but eminently successful as they were as explorers, they failed in their first attempt at serious colonization. Like others of that and a later day, they sought a mysterious kingdom of gold, where people lived in towns and dressed like Europeans, where vegetation was tropical, and where mines were rich in gold, copper, and diamonds. The third voyage, that of 1541, which was led by Cartier and Sieur de Roberval, a Norman knight and a good deal of a freebooter, was a colonizing venture, with an eye to "diamonts" and "golde ore." Cartier sailed from St. Malo in 1541, with five ships, but Roberval did not get away from La Rochelle till the following year. Then in three ships, carrying a queer mixed crew of both sexes, 200 in number, including a few criminals released from prison, as well as masons, carpenters, priests, and a group of gentlemen-adventurers, he started on April 16, 1542, and reached St. John's, Newfoundland, in June. There he was joined by Cartier and his company, who, either wearying of the delay or, according to Roberval, "moved as it seemeth with ambition because they would have all the glory of the discovery of those parts themselves, without taking their leaves, stole privily away and departed home for Bretaigne." Roberval, continuing in his quest, landed on the site of the modern city of Quebec, which was not founded until 1608 by Champlain. Cartier had built a fort there during his year in Canada, and there established his colony, himself setting out later on an expedition to discover the mythical "Saguenay." With nothing to show for his effort Roberval returned to France in the autumn of 1543, with what remained of his colonists, wasted by disease and starvation.[2] This bold attempt left no trace behind, except, as M. de la Roncière points out, it furnished romantic material for one of the tales in the Heptameron of Margaret of Navarre and was possibly one of the sources from which Rabelais drew inspiration for his account of Pantagruel's peregrinations.

French activities from Labrador to Brazil, were most conspicuous during the first half of the sixteenth century, when the glories of the

1. Biggar, *The Precursors of Jacques Cartier, 1497–1534; The Voyages of Jacques Cartier; A Collection of Documents Relating to Jacques Cartier and the Sieur de Roberval* (Publications of the Public Archives of Canada). Lives of Cartier by Baxter and de la Roncière.

2. The documents are all given in Biggar's *Precursors.*

reign of Francis I shed lustre upon his name but left a legacy of debt to his successor. Under Henry II and his sons, religious dissension and civil wars weakened France and added to the financial distress which rendered the monarchy incapable of spending either money or energy upon exploration and colonization. Therefore it was not until Champlain began his great work in the early years of the next century (1604-1618) that the foundations were laid of the New France in America that was to play such a vital part in our colonial history.

England's claim to lands in the New World rested upon the discoveries of John Cabot, made at about the same time with the third voyage of Columbus. Cabot, a Genoese by birth but a Venetian by adoption, had settled in England's leading maritime city, Bristol. His son Sebastian, of colonizing fame but less certain veracity, was born in Venice.[1] John Cabot was familiar with the first discoveries of Columbus and like him aspired to do for England what the greater Genoese had done for Spain—to discover new islands and to increase the resources of the kingdom with profit to himself. In March, 1496, he received from Henry VII a grant similar to that which Columbus had received from Ferdinand and Isabella, giving to him as vassal and lieutenant of the king all lands that he should find west, east, and north, and a monopoly of the commerce of the region, in return for which he was to pay one-fifth of all his gains to the crown. He sailed in 1497—the exact day is uncertain and unimportant—and succeeded in reaching land somewhere in the neighborhood of the Gulf of St. Lawrence, perhaps the island now called Cape Breton. Of his second voyage, made in February of the next year, little more is known than that it may have extended considerably farther south toward Florida. Just where he went or whether he ever returned are details that have never been ascertained. The voyage upon which England's title rests is that of 1497, during which North America was discovered. In the first patent to Cabot power is granted to find

1. A definitive study of the Cabot question is by James A. Williamson, *The Voyages of the Cabots and the English Discovery of North America under Henry VII and Henry VIII. Illustrated with thirteen Maps* (The Argonaut Press, 1929), which almost for the first time treats the subject dispassionately and with an historian's regard for evidence. For the first time, too, we have an honest and adequate account of Sebastian Cabot, who in these pages appears as a living personage, compacted of a variety of good and bad qualities. The book is not designed for popular consumption, but offers, as the editor himself says "a tough exercise for the critical faculties." The editor's introduction follows instead of precedes the texts, covering pages 119-284.

countries "which before this time have been unknown to all Christians," a phrase which some have thought to indicate a possible recognition of Spain's claims to the southward, for while east, west, and north are mentioned in the charter, south is omitted. At first England seems tacitly to have accepted Spain's sphere as extending south of the 44th degree of northern latitude, but as time went on and the great freebooting expeditions of Elizabeth's reign followed, one after another, her attitude changed, and after 1576, a peaceful policy toward Spain gave way to one of open hostility. Even in 1562 Sir William Cecil told the Spanish ambassador that "the Pope had no right to partition the world and to give and take kingdoms to whomsoever he pleased," and in 1580 the English government declared that it could not acknowledge the Spanish monopoly claim to the new world, "either because of donations from the pope or because of occupations touching here and there upon those coasts, building cottages, and giving names to a few places; that by the law of nations such occupations could not hinder other princes from freely navigating those seas and transporting colonies to those parts where the Spanish did not actually inhabit; that prescription without possession availed nothing."[1] Henceforth, England and English seamen paid little or no attention to the Spanish pretensions, and the enmity between the two countries lasted, with but a brief intermission, 1604-1625, down through the period of the Commonwealth and the Protectorate to 1659, when the treaty of the Pyrenees brought a temporary peace to Europe. The abiding hostility for Spain and the organized opposition among the merchants and mariners of England to her control of the Caribbean and adjoining waters are conspicuous features of the early history of English colonization in America. The rivalry with France and the disputes that arose therefrom over French claims belong to the eighteenth century.

England's earliest interest in exploration lay, not unnaturally, to the northwest, and began with the effort to find a northwesterly pas-

1. Williamson, writing of the attitude of James I toward colonial territory, says, "He was prepared, on paper at least, to respect Spanish territory effectively occupied, but not to respect any claims of preemption of unexploited lands based upon prior discovery or upon the bulls of Alexander VI." *The English in Guiana*, p. 77.

Thomas Scott's *An Experimental Discoverie of Spanish Practices, or the Counsell of a well-wishing Souldier for the Good of the Prince and State* (1623) was designed to stir up popular feeling against Spain in 1623, by denying Alexander VI's right to give America to Spain, as it was not his to give, either by divine or by human right, and by asserting that Spain could claim no more by conquest than she had conquered.

sage around to Cathay. Such an effort was to be expected of English seamen, and was directed in part by the voyages of the Northmen, who had settled in Iceland and Greenland, and in part by the geography of the region, where a series of islands—Shetland, Faroe, and Iceland—made long voyages possible. The location of these islands was favorable to navigating experiments and the currents made possible an easy drift southward from the northernmost point reached on the coast from Hudson Bay to Labrador. Voyages in this direction resulted in no actual discoveries until the time of Cabot, who must have gone in the wake of his predecessors following the route of the Northmen and connecting with the south-flowing Arctic current, which brought him to the mouth of the St. Lawrence. Others pursued in part the same course—Frobisher, 1576–1578, Davis, 1585–1587; and after the turn of the century, from 1602 to 1632, financed by the two greatest trading companies of the day—the East India and the Muscovy—a series of navigators penetrated the waters of the Arctic region.[1] It was the Muscovy Company in 1607 that sent Henry Hudson on the voyage leading to the discovery of Hudson Bay. A little later London merchants—the Adventurers for the Northwest Passage—who had already been interested in Frobisher's voyage, supported Captain Luke Fox in his search for the northwest passage and at the same time the Merchant Venturers of Bristol

1. This will-of-the-wisp, the northwest passage to India and its fabled wealth, drew men into these northern waters for another century and a half, until the search for the entrance to Cathay, at times through Hudson Bay and at times through Davis Strait, merged into the wider exploration of the polar regions and the North Pole in the nineteenth and twentieth centuries. To find a passage to the South Sea, by way of Virginia's rivers, was one of the objects of the Virginia Company of London, for interest in the Northwest Passage was very keen at the time of the settlement of Virginia. In a letter from John Chamberlain to Sir Dudley Carleton, May 11, 1612, the former speaks of "a little treatise on the Northwest passage," which he had written, and of Sir Dudley Digges (member of the East India Company and author of *The Defence of Trade, in a letter to Sir Thomas Smyth,* 1615) as a great undertaker in this new discovery and "wonderfully possessed with the opinion and hope of that passage." In the forties of the next century, Arthur Dobbs, later a governor of North Carolina, took an active part in the search, sending Henry Ellis, himself later a governor successively of Georgia and of Nova Scotia, on a voyage thither (Ellis, *A Voyage to Hudson's Bay, by the Dobbs Galley and California, in the years 1746 and 1747, for discovering a North West Passage,* London, 1748, French translation, 1750), the net result of which was the proof that the passage did not lie through Hudson Bay. This voyage did not, however, disabuse men's minds of belief in the existence of the passage. The chief outcome of the earlier efforts was the founding of the Hudson's Bay Company and the Greenland Company and the development of the whaling and seal fisheries.

raised a stock and despatched Captain Thomas James on the same venturesome quest.[1]

While these hardy seamen were pursuing their dangerous courses to the northwest, others were attempting to find their way to Cathay by sailing to the northeast. In 1553, a group of London merchants, organized as a company for trade, sought new markets in the unknown northern and northeastern seas. On the advice of Sebastian Cabot, they sent Hugh Willoughby and Richard Chancellor, with three ships, on a voyage of exploration around the North Cape. Willoughby met with disaster and perished with his companions and crew, but Chancellor, weathering the storm that drove Willoughby to seek a fatal refuge on the coast of Lapland, landed at the mouth of the Dwina and made his way southward to Moscow, through the dominions of the Czar. There he was well received by Ivan IV and was able to prepare the way for a commercial connection between England and Russia. Hence arose the Muscovy Company, perhaps the first example of a trading company of the joint-stock type. This company entered into business relations with Russian subjects, by way of the White Sea and the Dwina River. With agencies as far south as Moscow and the Volga, they extended their enterprises to Kazan and Astrakhan and on to the Caspian Sea. In 1558 Anthony Jenkinson, one of the most energetic travellers of his day, and at the time in the employ of the Muscovy Company, penetrated as far south as Persia and east as far as Bokhara.[2]

1. The Merchant Venturers of Bristol raised a stock wherewith to send Captain James on his voyage, and sought for a patent. Charles I promised to give one, with equal liberties of trade as were granted to the Merchant Adventurers of the City of London for the same purpose. But the Bristol men were wary and refused to take out a patent (which was an expensive proceeding) until the discovery of the passage had been made. James sailed in the *Mary*, May 31, 1631, a month after Fox and Bruton had started on their expedition. The latter returned October 31, 1631, but James was gone sixteen months, not reaching Bristol until September, 1632. The account of his voyage (*The Dangerous Voyage of Captain James*) was printed in 1633, a new edition in 1740, and a third, edited by R. B. Bodilly, R.N., in 1928. In the New York Public Library may be found the "Letter Book of the Merchant Venturers of Bristol," which is concerned chiefly with the preparation for this expedition. The whole subject has been well treated by Crouse in his *In Quest of the Western Ocean* (1928), and for the earlier period by Manhart in *The English Search for the Northwest Passage in the time of Elizabeth* (1924). An excellent popular life of Frobisher has been written by William McFee (1928), with five maps which picture the world these navigators thought they lived in, while the book itself contains an admirable characterization of the conditions under which the seamen of that day labored, the vessels they sailed in, the hardships they endured, and the badly balanced diet from which they suffered many ills.

2. *Travels of Anthony Jenkinson*, with map, Hakluyt Society, I. An excellent ac-

The third group of English navigators and explorers branched out in three directions, the earliest voyages taking a southwesterly line toward Newfoundland and the coast of Maine. The fishermen were first in this field, and during Elizabeth's reign ships from the West Country, that is, from Bristol and the seaport towns of Devonshire, were going there every year, to the number of at least fifty, and were even attempting settlement. It is quite possible that in their search for new fishing grounds they coasted farther southward than the Newfoundland banks, perhaps along the shores of Nova Scotia and New England. We know that in 1579 and 1580 two voyages were made in Maine waters and that in 1583 Sir Humphrey Gilbert, idealist in the field of discovery, took possession of Newfoundland and St. John's in the name of the queen.[1]

The second movement, southward toward the Chesapeake and Virginia, is marked by Raleigh's famous attempts to plant colonies at Roanoke in Pamlico Sound, which gave to the state of North Carolina the name of its capital and fastened the name "Virginia" upon the whole region. Three voyages are associated with Raleigh's name, that of 1584, led by Amadas and Barlowe, that of 1585, led by Grenville and Lane, and that of 1587, led by John White—the lost colony. There is, as we shall see later, a close connection between these Raleigh ventures and the first permanent settlement of the English in Virginia made in 1607, for Raleigh's last attempt was to found a true colony, composed of men, women, and children, under a well conceived form of government. But the time was not yet ripe for colonization and Gilbert and Raleigh's efforts came to naught as had those of Cartier and Roberval before them.

The last movement southward was toward the northern coast of South America, that long stretch of tropical land, as yet unoccupied by either Spaniard or Portuguese, which extended from the Orinoco to the delta of the Amazon—the Wild Coast or Guiana. Here was the southern location of that wonderful land of El Dorado, which the king of France seems confidently to have expected Cartier to discover in North America, comparable to the similar lands which Cortez had found in Mexico and Pizarro had found in Peru. Be-

count of Jenkinson may be found in the *Dictionary of National Biography,* and pictures of Jenkinson and other Englishmen at the Russian court and city in Graham, *Ivan the Terrible* (1932).

1. Gosling, *History of Labrador;* Prowse, *History of Newfoundland;* Sabine, *Report on American Fisheries;* Slafter, *Sir Humfrey Gylberte,* Prince Society.

cause Cortez had come upon a great city standing in a lake in Mexico and had won fame and huge booty by storming it, men of his time and for generations after would not give up the hope of winning another and perhaps greater "Tenochtitlan." Cartier heard stories which led him to believe in the existence of such a city on the St. Lawrence; others sought for one in the region of the Rio Grande under the name of "Gran Quivera";[1] while still others in the southern continent, in the region of the Orinoco and the Amazon, marched, fought, starved, and in large numbers died in the frantic search for the city built of gold and therefore "Dorado." For more than half a century Spaniards from the north, northeast, and east explored the immense river valleys of the Amazon and the Orinoco and their innumerable tributaries, and forced their way through the widespread land of forests and swamps, seeking fabled mines and mythical empires. Here in the year 1595 Raleigh entered upon the "discoverie of the large rich and bewtiful empyre of Guiana," of which he was to write so glowing an account, and implanted in his mind those memories of the golden harvest, so seductively pictured in his narrative, that drove him twenty-two years later to enter upon his second and tragic attempt to find the mine, of which his lieutenant, Keymis, had told him—the mine of Manoa, the chief city of the Ingas. This famous expedition, a desperate gambler's game, brought him no gold from the valley Americapana, but only death on the scaffold in England. The terrors and sufferings of those in the Arctic north, who sought a route to India by way of the northwest passage, find their counterpart in the heroic, reckless, and fruitless endeavors of those in the tropical south, who risked their lives amid the dangers of the treacherous Guiana hinterland in search of the El Dorado of their dreams. At that time the quest for the one was as hopeless as the quest for the other.[2]

No colonies resulted from these various voyages and freebooting

1. The "Gran Quivera" is still a subject of investigation. The latest work, *Quivera,* by Paul A. Jones (1930) tells the story in a popular way, locating "Quivera" as near as may be and following the line of Coronado's march. The book is full of color and is picturesquely written.

2. Markham, *Expeditions into the Valley of the Amazon,* Hakluyt Society, 1859; Williamson, *The English in Guiana;* Harlow ed. *The Discoverie of the large and bewtiful Empire of Guiana by Sir Walter Raleigh.* Harlow thinks that Raleigh undertook the expedition of 1595 for the purpose of achieving some spectacular success in order to regain the favor of Queen Elizabeth, and that in so doing he took a gambler's chance (pp. xcviii, civ–cv). Williamson, who devotes a chapter to "Ralegh's

expeditions of the Elizabethan period and the reason is not far to seek. Before the days of the Virgin Queen, England had been too poor to engage in colonization and too weak to risk an encounter with Spain. Victory over the hated enemy had first to be won before colonization could be undertaken successfully. The passions that stirred men's souls were not born of a desire for peaceful expansion, they were brewed in the crucible of hate for Spain, for the spoiling and destroying of the Spaniards, "lyms of Antichrist," as they were still called in 1620. During the years from 1580 to 1596 these passions were at their height and until their intensity had been relieved by the breaking of the Spanish power, men could not be persuaded to turn aside from pursuing the quarry to engage in the more prosaic business of finding permanent homes. During these years every expedition that set forth from English shores took on a semi-piratical form, seeking booty, capturing cities and ships, or otherwise wreaking a crusader's vengeance upon the despoilers of the world's peace. Even those who aimed at trade and settlement or sought to rescue the lost colonists of Roanoke felt it a part of their stern but patriotic duty to "spoil the Egyptians," even while engaged upon errands of mercy or seeking legitimate profit. Making war with Spain and not the planting of colonies was the driving force that determined the direction of Elizabethan activities, at least in the waters of the northern Atlantic, and for seventy years after the Armada this war was relentlessly pursued, not by kings but by valiant captains, merchants, and trading companies, as an accepted part of the parliamentary and Puritan programme, until the menace of Spanish domination was removed and England had obtained a permanent hold upon some of the richest parts of the declining Spanish empire.

Raleigh stood at the beginning of a new era and saw the dawn of the coming day. He never appreciated or understood the difficulties of the colonial problem or envisaged the part that colonies were to play in England's later career, nor was he ever tenacious enough of purpose to follow any scheme to the end that success demanded. He was never imbued with the loftiness of design or the singleness of resolve that characterized the efforts of Calvert or Penn, or even of Shaftesbury, and as later events were to show, the transplanting

Last Voyage" finds it difficult to avoid the conclusion that Raleigh regarded the alleged mine "as a bribe wherewith to tempt the wisest fool in Christendom to unlock the gates of the Tower" (p. 78).

and successful uprearing of a colony in America demanded something more than the equipping of ships and the transporting of colonists. In order to assure permanent occupation there were required the religious zeal of Pilgrims and Puritans, the continuous and persistent efforts of the Calverts, the Penns, and the Carolina proprietors, and above all the wealth and organized coöperation of the capitalistic classes of England. Gilbert and Raleigh were members of the small landed class of the feudal type, lords of manors which furnished meagre revenues from tenancies and leases. Even when, as in Raleigh's case, these resources were supplemented by the returns from lucrative and secret privateering ventures, from a systematic robbery of England's enemies at sea, and from other money-making methods in which "rapacity was matched by a consummate skill in lying,"[1] they proved altogether insufficient to meet the expense of promoting settlement overseas. The colonization of America required not only the support of those who were lords of the soil, freebooters at sea, and favored courtiers of the queen, but also the active participation of the rich bourgeoisie—a class hardly existent at the beginning of the Tudor period, but one rising rapidly into political and commercial importance—ready to invest their reserves of capital in any form that offered of profit-bearing enterprise. This financial middle class began its influential career when it acquired the lands of the church under Henry VIII, and in so doing supplanted the impoverished nobility which had been broken and ruined by the wars of the Roses the century before.[2]

1. Harlow, Introduction to Raleigh's *Discoverie*, p. xxx.
2. Liljegren, *The Fall of the Monasteries and the Social Changes in England leading up to the Great Revolution* (1925); Gretton, *The Middle Classes*.

CHAPTER II

ENGLAND'S COMMERCIAL ACTIVITIES

FOR England the period after 1550 was one of steadily pro-gressing commercial expansion. Owing partly to the growth of a national spirit and pride and a desire to share in the wide-spread sea-going activity of the day, and partly to the example of Portugal, with its stirring naval and trading experiences in the East, and of Spain with its no less heroic search for treasure rather than trade, Englishmen of the time were gradually respond-ing to a new ardor and a new ambition. Though slow to awaken to the importance of overseas advantages, they now saw what two neighboring monarchies were doing and were eager to participate in the opportunities which the old and new worlds were offering to all comers. Before 1580 many obstacles of serious import stood in the way. Political and religious controversies—products of the reforma-tion in England—had absorbed time, energy, and resources; eco-nomic and social changes, due to the decay of feudalism and the consequent displacement of population, had raised new domestic issues, incident to a period of industrial transition and a shifting of the center of political gravity from the local bodies to the central government; as yet wealth hardly existed in masses abundant enough to meet more than local and present needs; and geographi-cal knowledge and familiarity with the ocean routes were still insuffi-cient to encourage distant voyages or to arouse interest in dangerous expeditions to unknown lands. Englishmen found large parts of the world market already controlled by foreigners and closed to their merchants, and saw journeys westward blocked by the barriers of a forbidding continent and those southward rendered difficult by the dominant control of Portugal and Spain.

But the situation was fast bringing its own remedy. The last days of the Venetian mastery of England's carrying trade were drawing to a close. From 1509 to 1518 no Venetian fleet visited England's shores and the trade steadily declined until in 1532 the Venetian Flanders Galley sailed from Southampton for the last time.[1] Indi-

---

1. Rawlinson, "The Venetian Flanders Galleys, 1327–1532," *The Mariner's Mir-ror*, XI. England's trade with Venice began about the middle of the thirteenth cen-

vidual Venetian merchants continued to deal with England for some years to come, but even their enterprise came to an end with the wrecking of a Venetian vessel off the Isle of Wight in 1587. The special privileges of the Hanseatic League were cancelled by Elizabeth in 1578, and through the activities of a small group of London merchants—the monopolistic Merchant Adventurers, fast rising into prominence—the Hansards were expelled in 1597 and the next year the Steelyard, the Hanse station on the banks of the Thames, was handed over to the City of London. Though later the leaguers attempted to recover a part of their privileges, this event was symbolic of the fact that at last the English had obtained the entire direction of their own foreign commerce. The Merchant Staplers, oldest of England's trading companies, the members of which went to and fro, exporting raw wool to the Continent, were passing away. Calais, their chief staple town across the Channel, was seized by the French in 1557. Antwerp, also an entrepôt for English wool, was sacked in 1567 and again in 1585. As a commercial satellite of the Continent, England was gradually severing the ties that kept her in a state of commercial dependence.

Local and private traders had already begun to organize themselves under that form of consolidated enterprise known as the "company," and for a century and a half had been promoting commerce by methods of this sort. As a rule, these companies were incorporated bodies, receiving charters at the hands of the crown and in some instances having their privileges confirmed by act of parliament. During the years from 1555 to 1698, when the "company" was the prevailing form of organized enterprise, these bodies controlled every variety of progressive business undertaking—domestic, foreign, and colonial—and there was scarcely an industry or a part of the world in which they were not active. They carried England's trade into remote corners of the globe; they aided private ventures, such as the search for the northwest passage; and they were responsible for the beginning of the colonizing movement in America.

Before 1606 five chief companies had come into existence, two of which had their origin in medieval times. The oldest of all in its antecedents, but not the oldest as an incorporated body, was that of the Merchant Adventurers. For two or three centuries there had existed in the leading ports of England various local or municipal

tury. In 1317 Venice organized the famous trading fleet known as the "Flanders Galley," which visited ports both of England and the Continent.

organizations, the "merchant adventurers," as they were called, a
name that came to be specifically identified with those engaged in
commerce with the Low Countries and Germany, each group trading individually on its own account, in the interest of its own particular municipality. The oldest of these groups was the Merchant
Adventurers of York, founded in 1357, licensed by Edward III and
incorporated in 1578. This body, reorganized as a chamber of commerce, still flourishes and its picturesque hall has recently been
restored.[1] Next among the survivors of today are the Merchant Adventurers of Newcastle-upon-Tyne, 1547, Bristol, 1552, and Exeter,
1557.[2] Those which have disappeared are the Merchant Adventurers
of Southampton, who coöperated with Sir Humphrey Gilbert in
1582,[3] Chester, 1553, and Hull. Probably there were many such
groups of merchants in the various ports of England, east and south
and southwest, in origin fraternities, afterward gilds or trade committees, the members of which, often if not always, went in person
to sell their cloths at one or other of the annual port-marts in the
Low Countries—Antwerp, Middleburg, Flushing, or Amsterdam.
Later they employed apprentices or independent merchants for the
purpose. Each group had its hall, that of York being the oldest
extant in England today, its rules of membership, its privileges, and
its ways of doing business, and was the ruling force in the political
as well as the commercial life of the community.

Most important of all was a group of merchants in the City of
London trading at Antwerp or Bruges. Prominent among them
were some of the members of the Mercers Company, who controlled
a fraternity dedicated to St. Thomas à Becket, which in the fifteenth
century had acquired property and built a gild house, first at Bruges
and then at Antwerp. Because of its efficiency this group of London
merchants commanded a monopoly of the trade with the Netherlands and in so doing shut out the members of the English municipal companies, who in order to continue their profitable trade in
cloth were obliged to pay a fee (a noble) and deal only through the

1. Sellers, *The York Mercers and Merchant Adventurers, 1356–1917* (Surtees Society, 1918); *The Merchant Adventurers of York* (1921).
2. Boyle and Denby, *Newcastle Merchant Adventurers* (1895); *American Historical Review*, IV, 678–683; Latimer, *History of the Merchant Venturers of Bristol*
(1903); Historical Manuscripts Commission, *Exeter*, pp. 40–41, 49–50, 203, 310, 349,
356, 395.
3. *Calendar State Papers, Colonial*, 1675–1676, §18; *Publications*, Southampton Record Society.

agency of the London group.[1] Inevitably the trade of the outports declined and that of the Londoners increased rapidly. The discontent thus fomented aroused the London group to demand a stronger legal position. In the end it was established as an organized body with definite regulations and an increase of powers. Incorporated in 1564, the London merchant adventurers became the Merchant Adventurers of London, in control of the cloth trade across the Channel and exercising their privileges and vested interests for the one purpose of maintaining their own monopoly, a very difficult task as they discovered. Though they were largely responsible for the expulsion of the Hanseatic Leaguers, they reaped only in part the fruits of that victory, for they were constantly confronted with interlopers on the one hand and the well-known Elizabethan opposition to monopolies on the other. This subject finally came up before the parliament of 1601, and it was in that year that John Wheeler, secretary of the company, wrote his defense of the organization in *A Treatise of Commerce,* one of the earliest tracts of the kind.[2] Wheeler's treatise clearly shows that the Merchant Adventurers were losing their control of the situation and that doubt was arising as to the necessity of their continuance. It also predicts the eventual withdrawal of the company from England, which took place a few years later.

Compelled to leave Antwerp in 1563, because of a decree of the Netherland government prohibiting the importation of woolen goods from England—the result of a trade dispute—the Merchant Adventurers sent their fleet first to Emden in Friesland and later, after the exploits of the Elizabethan sea dogs had seriously injured and at times completely stopped their trade with the Netherlands, to Hamburg, where they finally located in 1611 and where they

1. Note the request of the Merchant Adventurers of Newcastle-upon-Tyne in 1617, preferred to the "consideration of the Governor and Company of the Merchant Adventurers of London." The Newcastle merchants had asked permission of the Privy Council to exercise certain privileges of export and import. The Privy Council handed on the petition to the London Company. Historical Manuscripts Commission, *Eighth Report,* I, 268 b.

2. This well-known treatise has been recently reissued (1931), edited with an introduction and notes by George B. Hotchkiss of New York University. The introduction gives an account of Wheeler and the Adventurers, of the company's earlier career and relations with the Staplers and the Hanse, and in general of the trade policy of the period. The work was originally written to defend the Merchant Adventurers against the Hanseatic Leaguers, who were trying to recover their privileges, and against the government, which was inclined to doubt the usefulness of the company's monopoly.

were destined to remain for nearly two centuries, until 1807. There they played an important part in the commerce of Germany, and as the Hamburg (Hamborough) Company[1] came into frequent contact with many a colonial trader and merchant. Unlike the Merchant Staplers their domicile was located not in England, but across the Channel, and they were engaged in handling not raw wool but white cloth, undyed and unfulled, for distribution and sale on the Continent. In 1698 their monopoly was finally broken and cloth exporting was thrown open, interestingly enough the same year in which, by act of parliament,[2] the slave trade monopoly was abolished. Famous and picturesque though the Merchant Adventurers are, they were after all merely a body of merchants looking out for their own pocketbooks. They were without national character or purpose and can be said to have done but little for the enlargement of English commerce. In this respect they were distinctly less influential than were the other great trading companies of the day.[3]

Oldest of the companies to receive incorporation at the hands of the crown was the Muscovy or Russia Company, which obtained its

1. They were "commonly called the Hambrough Company" as early as 1670. Historical Manuscripts Commission, *Eighth Report*, I, 147 (§310). The treatise *Of a Free Trade*, by Henry Parker, Wheeler's successor as secretary, was written in Hamburg in 1647 and published in London in 1648. Professor Hotchkiss points out the odd fact that Parker never knew of Wheeler's earlier work.

2. 1 William and Mary, c. 32, §xii.

3. The place of the Merchant Adventurers in the history of English commerce has been the subject of revision at the hands of the late Professor Unwin, who in his *Studies in Economic History* and notably in his article "The Merchant Adventurers under Elizabeth," *Economic History Review*, I, 35–64 (a chapter in a forthcoming posthumous work, *A History of Commerce*), has made it abundantly evident that the Merchant Adventurers were in no way of national importance, but were only a private, privileged body with profit-making interests. Three special articles may be cited: Van Brakel, "Entwickelung und Organisation der Merchant Adventurers," in *Vierteljahrschrift für Social and Wirthschaftsgeschichte*, V, and Carus-Wilson, "The Origin and Early Development of the Merchant Adventurers Organization," *The Economic History Review*, IV, 147–176, for the early history; and for the later years at Hamburg, Halle, "Die Company of Merchant Adventurers und der Ausgang in Hamburg," *Internationale Wochenschrift für Wissenschaft*, April 8, 1908. Grey, *The Merchant Adventurers of London, 1600–1646*, is an excellent popular treatise, chiefly biographical and descriptive. One of the best accounts of the Merchant Adventurers is in Friis, *Alderman Cockayne's Project and the Cloth Trade* (1927), chs. I, II, with an excellent "List of Books." This elaborate work deals with Cockayne's attempt to break the monopoly of the cloth trade, which the Merchant Adventurers enjoyed, by the formation in 1614 of a company to dye and dress the cloth in England. Cockayne became the first governor of the new company. But the project failed, because the Dutch retaliated by buying their wool elsewhere and setting up looms for themselves. The Dutch effort, though proving in the long run unsuccessful, greatly injured the trade of the Merchant Adventurers.

charter in 1555 as the outcome of the Willoughby and Chancellor voyage and of Chancellor's negotiations with the czar, and began its long career as the importer of Russian commodities into England. It passed through many vicissitudes, was several times reorganized because of financial difficulties, gave up its spice trade with Persia after 1581, owing to the interference of the Cossacks, and lost its special trading privileges as a company in 1618.[1] It continued to exist as a mercantile body, but in all that concerned its original purpose was compelled to give way before the growing Dutch influence in Russia, where the Hollanders were slowly but surely driving out the English from the markets of that country. In 1649, so it is said, the czar angered by the execution of Charles I ordered all adherents of the parliamentary party to leave Russia,[2] but after 1660 the remaining members of the company gathered themselves together and set up a post at Archangel. They were never able, however, to recover their former position and in 1699 were deprived of their monopoly by act of parliament.[3] The company still has a legal existence, retaining its organization and exercising some of its functions.[4]

Third in point of age was the Eastland Company, an organization which traced its history back to the beginning of the fifteenth century (1404), for the purpose of carrying on trade with the cities of the Baltic. As trade in that quarter had proved in the long run unsatisfactory, on account of the powerful competition and even hostility of the foreigners, the rivalries of the merchants, and the control by the king of Denmark of the waters of the Sound, the entrance to the Baltic, the merchants sought the aid of the government. In 1578 they drew up a petition to the queen asking for a patent and a monopoly of the trade. To any of them, wherever doing business,

1. In *The Trades Increase*, by I.R. (London, 1615), the statement is made that even then "the Muscovy trade is about lost," only two ships instead of an earlier seventeen being engaged in it, the others having been scared away, p. 4.

2. Thurloe, *State Papers*, I, 131.   3. 10 William III, c. 6.

4. Cheyney, *History of England*, I, 311–342; Gerson, *Organization and early History of the Muscovy Company, passim;* Lubimenko, "Les relations diplomatiques de l'Angleterre avec la Russie au XVIe siècle," *Revue Historique*, CXL; "Les marchands anglais en Russie au XVIIe siècle," *ibid.*, CXLI; "The Correspondence of the First Stuarts with the Romanovs," *Transactions*, Royal Historical Society, 4 ser. I, 77–91; "The Struggle of the Dutch with the English for the Russian Market in the Seventeenth Century," *ibid.*, IV, 27–51; "England's Part in the Discovery of Russia," *Slavonic Review*, VI, 104–118. Madame Lubimenko says that the "discovery" of Russia was in reality not a discovery of a new land, because travellers had already visited and described it, but that it was the finding of a new route to the Muscovite state, *ibid.*, p. 107.

it was an advantage to have the government behind them and to the
government it was similarly an advantage to use the companies,
Eastland or other, as a convenient source of money loans and often
as an instrument of service in diplomacy, naval security, and war.
The charter was granted in 1579 and to the members of the company was given the monopoly of the Baltic trade.[1] The company
prospered, exporting chiefly English cloth and importing tar, hemp,
cordage, and other naval stores, but it suffered heavily from competition at the hands of Danes, Swedes, and Dutch, and was hard hit
by certain clauses in the navigation act of 1660. Its area of trade was
restricted because it could not do business with Narva, which was
controlled by the Muscovy Company, or with the cities of the southwestern Baltic coast, which were within the field of the Merchant
Adventurers. Consequently, it gradually dwindled in importance,
until in 1672 its monopoly was taken away and the trade thrown
open by statute.[2] Henceforward, the company, suffering from a decrease in the Continental demand for English woolens and from the
efforts which the British government made in the eighteenth century to procure its naval stores from the colonies, sank under the
weight of its many troubles and eventually ceased to exist.

The fourth of the great companies which were created for the
advancement of foreign trade in the sixteenth century was the Levant Company, founded for the purpose of reviving the moribund
traffic with the eastern Mediterranean. With the discovery of the all-
water route to India, Levantine activities had greatly diminished
and the commercial importance of Venice, Genoa, Florence, and the
free cities of Germany had steadily declined. But as the English
demand for such things as currants, pepper and other spices, alum
and other drugs had enormously increased and the control of the
Cape route, at first in the hands of Portugal and later of Spain, was
in the possession of the enemy, the need of another market than that
of Lisbon became imperative. During the fifteenth century a few
English merchant ships had ventured with cargoes into the Mediterranean, and in the sixteenth "divers tall ships," as Hakluyt calls
them, went from London, Southampton, and Bristol to the coasts

1. Cheyney, *History of England*, I, 342–348; Sellers, *Acts and Ordinances of the
Eastland Company*, Royal Historical Society, 1906, Camden Series 3, no. 11; Dear-
dorff, *English Trade in the Baltic during the Reign of Elizabeth;* Cunningham,
Growth of English Industry and Commerce, II, pt. I, 235–238.
2. 25 Charles II, c. 7, §v.

and ports east of Italy.[1] But it was not until 1575 that the revival of
the old traffic was seriously considered. Then the merchants of London sent an agent, William Harborne, by way of Poland to Constantinople, to obtain from the sultan trading concessions. Harborne
succeeded in his mission, and as a result Queen Elizabeth issued a
letters patent, dated September 11, 1581, erecting, though not formally incorporating, certain English and Venetian merchants as the
Turkey Company, she herself contributing to the success of the
undertaking by investing therein a part of her profits from Drake's
privateering exploit against the Spaniards. The company prospered
and two years later other merchants were given a patent as the Company of Merchants trading to Venice or the Venice Company, dealing chiefly in currants. From this time forward English intercourse
with the Mediterranean became frequent, and in order to give unity
and security to the trade there and to check rivalry and competition
—for the two companies were inclined to trespass on each other's
privileges—the old charters were allowed to lapse and a new charter
was issued, January 7, 1592, to a combination of old and new merchants, incorporated as the Governor and Company of the Merchants of the Levant or the Levant Company. Under the new arrangement the business became very profitable, but disputes arose
over the government's share of the returns, and in 1600 the charter
was annulled. Though renewed the same year, it expired on the
death of Elizabeth and in the disastrous disorganization of trade
that followed, the question was raised as to whether a limited company should be formed or the trade thrown open to others. The new
charter, issued in 1605, created a permanent organization, but conveyed no monopoly, and under this form of a trading company the
company continued to exist till 1825.[2]

Greatest of all the companies that came into existence before the
settlement of America was the East India Company, the antecedents
of which date back to 1579, when private missions were sent to the
East for the purpose of opening communication.[3] The Levant Company owed its origin to the Spanish-Portuguese monopoly of the

1. Rawlinson, "Early Trade between England and the Levant," *Journal of Indian
History,* II, 107–117.
2. Cheyney, *History of England,* I, 377–406; Epstein, *The Levant Company;* Row-
land, *England and Turkey, the Rise of Diplomatic and Commercial Relations.*
3. Hakluyt, *Principal Navigations,* V, 450–451, 464–505. The story of Ralph Fitch's
journeyings is well told in the *Dictionary of National Biography.*

Cape route, and the East India Company, started by members of the Levant Company and a by-product of it, furnished an opportunity for the use of capital, diverted from the Levant trade. Thus the English began the struggle of contesting in the East Indies the rapid advance of the Dutch—who in their turn were ousting the Portuguese—and so obtained a direct share in the drug, spice, opium, and calico trade in those parts.[1] English merchants, aroused by the menace of Dutch supremacy, petitioned the Privy Council for a charter of incorporation, and received it finally in 1600. This charter erected the company into a corporation under the name of the Governor and Company of Merchants of London trading into the East Indies, with full powers to be exercised under certain restrictions, and with the right of trafficking in all places where trafficking was possible, from the Cape of Good Hope to the Straits of Magellan, except in districts already in lawful and actual possession of a friendly Christian prince. The first governor was Sir Thomas Smith, later to become the head of the Virginia Company of London. At first the operations of the company lay largely within the island field, where the Dutch were already strongly intrenched, and resulted in interminable quarrels and disputes. Finally, in 1623, occurred the famous "massacre" of Amboyna, when a local Dutch governor seized and tortured and finally executed ten English traders who were doing business on the island under agreement with the States General of Holland. This "massacre," which aroused great indignation in England, was one of the causes of the century-long mercantile and naval warfare with the Dutch that followed. English merchants withdrew from the islands and concentrated their attention more and more on the mainland. During these years the waters of the Indian Ocean were the scene of conflicts, in which Malayan pirates, Portuguese, Dutch, French, and English vessels were all engaged.

The Portuguese in India were easier to contend with than were the Dutch in the archipelago. Passing through periods of financial stringency and economic depression, due to poor business methods and faulty administration, the East India Company emerged in 1657, after long debate as to the relative advantages of the regulated and the joint-stock systems with its various interests finally consolidated into a single joint-stock corporation under a new charter. From this

1. For the downfall of the Portuguese in the East, see articles by G. A. Ballard in *The Mariner's Mirror*, XII, 169–195, 264–288, 375–395.

time on, India became the chief scene of its activities. It had already
set up factories at Surat, Madras, Hooghly (Calcutta), and in 1667
at Bombay. The last named town and island had been acquired by
Charles II as part of the wedding dowry of his Portuguese wife, but
after four years of friction and inefficient management by the king
and his ministers it was given over to the company.[1] Gradually the
latter enlarged its field of operations and extended its trade from
Iraq and Persia on the west to Macao, Amoy, and Canton in China
and to Japan on the east. Its profits, running from twenty to forty
per cent, returned to those who had subscribed to the fund under
the new charter of 1657 their entire investment in eight years.

Endowed by the various charters it received—five from Charles II
alone, notably that of 1661—with large powers, such as the right to
acquire territory, contract alliances, control troops, coin money, declare war, and make peace, the East India Company during the
latter part of the seventeenth century, though legally only a private
corporation under the supervision and watchful care of the state,
became in fact a great political organization, exercising military, administrative, and judicial authority. Just as the Hudson's Bay Company was the starting point in the rise of the modern dominion of
Canada and the British South African Company of later date led to
wide extensions of British territory and British influence in southern
Africa, so the East India Company became in time the instrument
whereby India was transformed into a great dependency of the
British crown, destined, it may be, to become one of the self-governing dominions under a federative form. For two hundred and fifty
years the company continued its career, exploring, exploiting, developing, and ruling in India, not only amassing wealth but accumulating also a unique series of records, the ledgers of a first-rate
business house. Instructions from London, details of factory management, correspondence with agents and representatives, prices of commodities, rents of lands, reports on floods or treaties with native
princes—all were entered on its books and form the most valuable
sources of its history.[2]

1. Shafaat Ahmad Khan, "The Anglo-Portuguese Negotiations relating to Bombay,
1660–1667," *Journal of Indian History*, I, 419–570; "The Anglo-Portuguese Marriage
of 1662," *Hispanic American Historical Review*, X, 313–352.
2. Sainsbury, *Calendar of State Papers, Colonial, East Indies, China, Japan, Persia,*
five vols. to 1634; Continuation of the same, *Calendar of the Court Minutes,* by Ethel
Sainsbury, nine vols. to 1673; Birdwood and Foster, *The First Letter Book of the
Company;* Quaritch, *The First Letter Book;* Stevens, *Dawn of British Trade in the*

The five companies thus mentioned were only the most conspicuous among the many which were organized during these years for trade with the peoples of lands already settled and in different stages of advancing civilization. There were also a Spanish company and a French company and later attempts were made to establish a Canary company. Many a merchant was a member of more than one company or had money invested in many companies, so that his interests were widely distributed. Sir Thomas Smith was governor of no less than three companies, the Russia, the East India, and the French, and he was also one of the leading promoters of the Virginia Company and the Bermuda Company. He was one of the busiest and most enterprising of men in an age of active captains of commercial ventures, and his many connections brought him great wealth. Among those who promoted settlement in America were many who had office or investment in one or other of these companies, and even among the colonists themselves, there was occasionally one or more, as was the case with the Eatons of the New Haven colony, who had an interest in them as members and stockholders. Both Elihu Yale and Nathaniel Higginson were governors in Madras under the East India Company.

The centering of so much commercial business in London, during this period of rapid trading expansion, and the granting by charter to these companies of a monopoly of particular trades within a carefully defined territory raised two very important questions that were to play a conspicuous part in the commercial history of England during the seventeenth century. These were, first, the question of monopoly versus an open market, a subject which was hotly debated throughout the century and which finally led to the throwing open of the trade and the eventual downfall of the joint-stock system. Incidental to this, but of a lesser significance, was the question as to the

East Indies as recorded in the Court Minutes of the Company, to 1603; Birdwood, *List of General Records;* Danvers and Foster, *Letters Received,* six vols.; Foster, *Guide to the India Office Records,* 1600–1858; the same, *The English Factories in India,* fourteen vols. to 1669, *Early Travels in India, 1553–1679,* and *England's Quest of Eastern Trade* (1933); Rawlinson, *British Beginnings in Western India, 1579–1657* (early history of Surat); Khan, "The East India Trade in the XVII Century," *Journal of Indian History,* I, 1–27; Morse, *The Chronicles of the East India Company trading to China, 1634–1834,* five vols.; Khan, *Sources for the History of British India in the XVII Century* (1926); *Calendar of Persian Correspondence, being letters which passed between some of the Company's Servants and Indian Rulers and Notables,* five vols. to 1780. In 1682 the East India Company doubled its stock, its profit in 1679 having been 150 per cent, *Calendar State Papers, Domestic,* 1682, p. 242.

respective merits of the different forms of corporate organization. The second great issue, which aroused equally intense debate and at times great bitterness of feeling was the jealousy which the outports —Bristol, Exeter, Newcastle, Hull, York, and others—felt toward London, a city which, having been influential in bringing about the expulsion of the foreign merchants, was drawing the trade to itself and becoming rapidly not only a leader in commerce but also an important factor in determining governmental, that is, royal policy. The companies which we have mentioned had their origin in London and during the later years of the sixteenth century had succeeded in winning for that city a place of commanding leadership. Some of the outports—notably Bristol and York—mercantile centers that were older than London—resented the latter's determination to conduct business in her own interest and to frame regulations that were to her own advantage, and fought hard and long to stem the tide of London's advance. They were aided in the struggle, partly by the natural increase of trade, which in the seventeenth century brought them out of the decline upon which they had entered toward the end of Elizabeth's reign and placed them once more on the road to affluence and strength, and partly by their growing importance in the House of Commons, which was the successful opponent of the king and Privy Council in the constitutional conflict that was taking place. London had few members in the lower house, while the outports had many, and the London companies having obtained their charters from the king were more or less bound to support him by loans and influence. Mercantile affairs were not a major interest with the members of the house, who were largely of the country gentry, that is, of the landholding class, and therefore content to take the part of the outports against the Londoners, because in so doing they were supporting the parliamentarians against the king. The monopoly of the Russia, Eastland, Merchant Adventurers, Royal African, and other companies was taken away by acts of parliament and it was an act of parliament that brought to an end the era of the joint-stock ascendancy. Despite the passage of the navigation acts in the seventeenth century, the House of Commons was interested in commerce only so far as it was a useful instrument wherewith to increase England's political prestige and to further her financial solvency.

Thus far we have been concerned with companies that were active in the older and well-populated parts of the eastern world. But English merchants were looking in other directions also. Their eyes were upon Africa and America and upon the waters that extended in all directions from their own home shores, and they were ready for any adventure that would bring in a profit to themselves. Stimulated by the enthusiasm which, particularly after the fall of Portugal in 1582, was animating men of all classes with money to invest, they were eager to dispute with Spain whatever advantages might accrue from either trade or territory and to engage in enterprises, piratical or otherwise, that promised glory or success. Inevitably some of these enterprises were destined to prove speculative and short-lived. The forming of the Barbary, or Morocco, Company in 1585 and that of the Guinea Company three years later mark the beginning of that trade with the African coast which found its fulfilment in the Royal African Company of the next century. This latter company, first organized in 1662 as the Company of Royal Adventurers of England trading to Africa, and reorganized as the Royal African Company in 1672, possessed a complete monopoly until 1697, when by act of parliament the trade was thrown open the following year under certain conditions. Dissolved in 1747 it was again reorganized in 1750 and lasted until 1821. In 1765 the government, as the result of concessions made by France in 1763, erected the colony of Senegambia, and modeled its constitution on that of an American colony, a hybrid experiment which came to an end in 1783.[1]

Equally representative of the new spirit of mercantile adventure were the fishing companies organized to extend England's area of food supply, to increase her complement of seamen, and to compete with other fishing peoples, notably the Dutch. The latter, as pioneers in nearby waters, had won a complete control of the herring and deep sea fisheries and during the seventeenth century had resisted every attempt England made to compete with them in the North Sea and in the waters between Scandinavia and Greenland. The earliest effort was made in 1628, when the Greenland Company was chartered for the purpose of winning, if possible, the whale fishery.[2] In 1632 Charles I chartered the Association of the Fishery and in 1661 and later years Charles II brought into existence the Royal

1. Martin, *The British West African Settlements, 1750–1821*, which deals with the reorganized African company of 1750.
2. The Greenland Company was rechartered in October, 1693. For half a century it had been in a state of decay and its revival after a period of profitable activity under James I was the work of a group of men of London, among them Sir William Scawen and Peter Houblon.

Fishery Company.[1] But none of these expedients was successful, and during the century, despite acts of parliament, recommendations of committees, offers of free trade, and continued government support, the Dutch went on fishing in what Englishmen considered their own particular seas, even to the very coasts of England herself.

These and other similar companies were organized according to four different plans. The earliest was that of the regulated company, an enlarged edition of the city or trade gild, which in form was a kind of partnership, composed of a group of persons, incorporated by a royal letters patent, enjoying as individuals the monopoly of a certain trade. Each member on gaining admission to the company, by the payment of a heavy fine (hansa, a fee) and by passing a test demonstrating that he was "bred to the trade," was allowed to traffic under the rules of the company, with his own capital. In this class were the Merchant Staplers, the Merchant Adventurers, and the Eastland Company. The Royal African Company took this form from 1662 to 1672 and again after 1750. The method of incorporation and the manner of government was the same as that of the joint-stock company and there was always a great difference of opinion as to the respective merits of the two systems.

The second variety was the semi-joint-stock, a transitional form, in which there was no permanent joint or common stock, but a separate joint-stock for each venture. The most conspicuous example of this type was the East India Company during the first fifty years of its existence, but the plan was changed after the debate which lasted from 1650 to 1657 and the company was reorganized on a joint-stock basis.[2] The Muscovy Company seems at times to have taken this form and many other smaller undertakings were managed in this way, each expedition being financed by a different capital.

1. Elder, *The Royal Fisheries Companies of the Seventeenth Century*. Among the Associators of 1632 was the Earl of Arundel and Surrey. Captain John Mason was receiver and expeditor.

The fisheries question led to the famous dispute of 1615 between the Dutch, represented by Hugo Grotius, and the English with John Selden as their spokesman. Grotius maintained, in his *Mare Liberum*, that the sea was open to all; Selden, in his *Mare Clausum* (not printed till 1636), that the sea was subject to sovereignty as well as the land. This claim was essentially a Stuart pretension and was continued through the seventeenth century, directed primarily against the Dutch. It covered the four seas surrounding England, over which England claimed lordship. Fulton, *Sovereignty of the Seas*, pp. 521–522. Sir William Petty has an essay on this subject, *The Petty Papers*, I, xxxv–xxxvi, 219–242.

2. For this debate see Miss Sainsbury's *Court Minutes*, 1650–1657, and for a semi-joint-stock company, see *Calendar State Papers, Colonial*, 1675–1676, pp. 15–16.

The third variety was the most common and the most powerful of all—the joint-stock system. Such a form of organization was necessary in all large, expensive, and hazardous undertakings, where a very considerable amount of capital was needed for the building of better and more fully armed merchant ships, for the meeting of the heavy charges attendant on long voyages, and for the cost of extensive and difficult diplomatic negotiations, often including the maintenance of regular ambassadors of the crown.[1] The membership consisted of any one who was willing to subscribe to the joint-stock and it required no fees and no tests. The constitution of such a company was similar to that of a business corporation of today. From it gradually the old benevolent and fraternal elements of the gild were eliminated and the whole put on a strictly business basis. Under this system a majority of the members had little or no knowledge of the trade or of the way it was carried on and were chiefly interested, as are stockholders today, in dividends. The policy was shaped and the business carried on almost entirely by the governing body, upheld or restrained in times of emergency or difficulty by such of the shareholders as desired to attend the generality or court of the members, meeting usually four times a year. This form of organization was transferred to America and became the starting point in the development of the colonial system of government, not only in the royal colonies, beginning with Virginia, but in the corporate colonies as well. For instance, the main features of the government set up in Connecticut after 1662 and in Rhode Island after 1663 were of the joint-stock type. The Muscovy or Russia Company falls in this class for the period before 1623, after which it took a regulated form. The Levant Company was joint-stock at first, but was afterward reorganized as a regulated company. In the same group were the East India Company after 1657, the Royal African Company from 1672 to 1747, and the Hudson's Bay Company from the beginning.

In the fourth class may be entered all voluntary associations or partnerships, unincorporated and without legal standing, the members of which massed their capital in a joint-stock and traded as if they were chartered companies. The members were usually known as "associates" and the term probably dates from Elizabeth's reign.

1. For interesting contemporary statements of the reasons for incorporation in the case of a joint-stock company, see *English Historical Review*, 1916, pp. 542–543. The joint-stock concerned was that of the Canary Company.

We read of Sir Humphrey Gilbert's connection with Sir George Peckham, Sir Thomas Gerrard, and their Associates, of Rawdon and his Associates, Courteen and his Associates, Merrifield and his Associates, the Dorchester Associates or the New England Company—the predecessor of the Massachusetts Bay Company—the many Associates organized under the auspices of the Virginia Company of London, and the Associates of the Fishery. There were probably scores of such associations—not partnerships as commonly understood—formed in the seventeenth century before the Bubble Act of 1722 put an end to them, for it was common for merchants to join voluntarily in any promising undertaking and in so doing to avoid, if possible, the heavy expense of incorporation. One famous organization of this kind was that of Weston and his Associates, which aided the Pilgrims to cross the ocean in 1620. Voluntary joint-stocks were used in settling many of the early towns of New England, particularly in Connecticut, for the purpose of buying land of the Indians, with dividends returnable in home lots, arable, and pasture, distributed according to the amount of the subscriptions. Shares assigned by lot were frequently called "dividents" and the name has lingered on to the present day in local nomenclature. In 1644 the New England Confederation proposed to erect a joint-stock company, with a fund of from five to six thousand pounds, for trade with the Indians, but the project fell through.[1] How far the New England corporations had the legal right to erect minor corporations of their own that were other than voluntary associations is a matter of some uncertainty. In law a corporation cannot create a corporation.[2]

These various organizations, particularly active during the period from 1555 to 1720—the historic age of corporate enterprise in Eng-

1. *Plymouth Colony Records,* IX, 22–23; *Massachusetts Colonial Records,* II, 60, 138; Winthrop, *Journal* (Original Narratives of Early American History Series), II, 164.

2. On this point see J. S. Davis, *Essays in the Early History of American Corporations,* ch. I, and A. McF. Davis, "Corporations in the Days of the [Massachusetts] Colony," *Transactions,* Colonial Society of Massachusetts, I, 183–215. J. S. Davis calls attention to the fact that limited powers of incorporation, as of municipalities, could be delegated. The instances which he cites are all taken from the proprietary or feudal charters. No such powers were delegated to the governments of Massachusetts Bay, Connecticut, or Rhode Island, or to the Council for New England. No municipalities were incorporated in New England during colonial times, except in the case of the borough charter of Agamenticus by Gorges in Maine, though Massachusetts took upon herself to incorporate a trading company, a shoemakers company, and Harvard College, and Connecticut incorporated Yale College. Until 1650 Harvard was

land—laid the foundations of England's naval, maritime, and commercial greatness.[1] Their ancestry is traceable to the medieval borough and gild and they represent the transfer of the local mercantile methods of the towns and outports of England to the wider field of international trade. In the system of management, in the use of such terms as "fellowship," "brethren," "freeman," and the like, and in various aspects of their powers, privileges, proceedings, and the wording of their by-laws they disclose their fraternal and gild origin. The Merchant Adventurers of York started as a fraternity "in honour of the Lord Jesus Christ and the Blessed Virgin"; the Merchant Adventurers of London, as we have already seen, traced back to a fraternity dedicated to St. Thomas à Becket; members of the Virginia Company were "brethren" just as the members of Trinity House are today; the "freemen" of Massachusetts, Connecticut, and Rhode Island have a medieval origin, in that the term goes back by way of the trading company to the days when men had to be free of the gild in order to carry on their craft or their trade or to take part in the affairs of their borough. The colonial governments in New England represent the system of a trading company applied to the political organization of a state.[2]

governed by a president and board of overseers, possessed of quasi-corporate powers, but in that year by act of the general court of Massachusetts it was ordered that the "colledge in Cambridge" should be a corporation (*Massachusetts Colonial Records,* III, 195–196). The incorporation of Yale College was preceded by an act, passed by the general court of Connecticut, October, 1701, granting liberty to erect a "collegiate school." This act was enlarged in 1723 after the school had become established at New Haven and had been named after Elihu Yale. The present charter was issued in 1745 (Dexter, *Documentary History of Yale University,* 1701–1745).

1. No national government at this time, except the Spanish, was strong enough to undertake the task of developing overseas trade and colonization. The French, Dutch, Danish, and English East India companies were all private affairs, and exemplify Sir Charles Lucas's statement that the combination of private enterprise with supervision and control by the state, characteristic of England's colonial methods in the past, "has been the greatest of all factors in the making of the British Empire." *Overseas Enterprise,* pp. 35, 148.

2. Sellers, *The Merchant Adventurers of York; Virginia Company Records* (Kingsbury, ed.), I, 459, 489; Carr, *Select Charters of Trading Companies* (Selden Society), pp. xii, xx, xxii, xxiii, xlii, xlix. The early companies of English merchants traveling abroad were, like those concerned with industry at home, fraternally organized and concerned for the welfare of their members. Their members were brothers, they had oaths for officers and freemen and maintained a quasi-collegiate discipline. In the Muscovy Company the members were brothers and the company a fellowship. This company was first known as a "misterie and companie" and its first governor, Sebastian Cabot, was named as the "first and present governor of the same fellowship for life" and at his death the fellowship was "to choose one governor or two of them-

These companies were private concerns, standing for massed and regulated capital, but licensed and protected by the crown, not because they embodied any clear-cut, deliberate governmental policy, but because they were instruments that the state could use in widening the area of its political influence, in helping to fill the royal treasury, and aiding in the solution of many diplomatic, administrative, and fiscal problems.[1] Later these companies fell on evil times and, charged with stock-jobbing and speculation, particularly in connection with the South Sea mania, they were discontinued in large part for more than a century, until in 1825 the Bubble Act was repealed. But long before that time they had done their work for England. During the seventeenth century they were behind every important material advance that accompanied the expansion of the island kingdom across the oceans into the eastern and western worlds. The royal navy, the mercantile marine, foreign trade, and home improvements were all made possible because of the activity and courage of the sea-captains, the merchants, and the men with money to invest. On the one hand they provided funds for the equipment of the navy, the increase of the food supply, the reclamation of land, and the enlargement of credit; on the other, they became efficient agencies for the planting of colonies overseas. They were not the only agencies, by any means, in the promoting of settlement, because they were primarily interested in trade and profit and not in freedom of worship, the tillage of the soil, the building of permanent

selves in like manner as other worshipful corporations of London have used to assemble" (Hakluyt, *Principal Navigations,* II, 305–306). Early membership in these companies was that of the gild, due to sonship or apprenticeship, though later, in the joint-stock, this was changed to those holding shares in the common fund.

1. How far private enterprise, thus legalized and protected by the state, was beneficial in the long run is a subject that need not be discussed here. Little would have been accomplished in the first half of the seventeenth century, either in commerce or the settlement of colonies, had the state been left to take the initiative, for not only were the early Stuart kings too deeply immersed in affairs at home to interest themselves directly in such undertakings, but their treasury was far too empty to warrant any expenditure in overseas enterprise. As a pathbreaking instrument at this time the private company or promoter was indispensable. That the privately settled colonies had to give way eventually before an expanding state control was inevitable, as the state grew in wealth and power and gradually formulated a programme of its own, and as the needs of the whole overrode those of any of its parts. Hence arose in the history of the colonies the friction, ill-will, and endless complications that accompanied English expansion under the influence of mercantilist ideas. Private control was too often characterized by mismanagement, inefficiency, and inability to meet the problems that were raised as the colonies increased and their difficulties multiplied. Then it was that the state alone was able to handle so complicated a situation.

homes, or the acquisition of private estates from which an income could be derived. Consequently, the Puritan, the Roman Catholic, and the Quaker, and the many proprietors who sought lands, tenants, and rents in the New World have to be reckoned with. But even these were often stimulated by the promptings of the commercial spirit.

The period from 1603 to 1640 is characterized by an amazing ebullition of mercantile and financial activity in England, in other directions than those of trade with the European continent. While the great monopolistic companies were pursuing their course and reaping rich financial rewards, others with capital to invest and enterprises to promote were looking into the possibilities of the regions to the south and west. Some of these individual adventurers were engaged in single expeditions of their own to the West Indies, at times with only one or two ships, at times with a flotilla, and these expeditions were not merely prosaic business undertakings but often romantic wanderings, in which religious and patriotic zeal, conjoined with the sheer love of seafaring, gave an epic character to these odysseys of the ocean. At the beginning of the seventeenth century the islands of the Caribbean, which were unoccupied save by the Spaniards in the Greater Antilles, were resorted to by buccaneering seamen, who used them as convenient rendezvous for rest, refuge, and repair. They belonged to no one, at least by right of discovery and occupation, and were turned to useful account by Dutch, French, Swede, and Courlander, as the latter passed to and fro on their marauding expeditions.[1] Englishmen too were not only boldly pushing their way into the crowded harbors of the Levant and into the wider spaces and more dangerous waters of India and

1. One of the most picturesque gentlemen-marauders of this epic era was George Clifford, Earl of Cumberland, who either led or despatched twelve roving, semi-commercial, semi-piratical expeditions into Spanish and other waters between 1576 and 1598, seizing French, Spanish, and Portuguese vessels and returning with prizes and prisoners. The spirit which actuated his efforts is well indicated by the name of the ship, the *Scourge of Malice*, which was built for him at Deptford in 1595. In the Lambeth Palace Library, 250, 17, ff. 256–267, is a manuscript entitled, "All the Nyne Memorable Voyages made by the Righte Honorable George Erle of Cumberland to and from the king of Spaynes territoryes." John Sarracoll's account of one of the voyages is printed in Hakluyt, XI, 202, and that of the voyage of 1589 is in Monson's *Naval Tracts,* I, 226–239. There is an article on Cumberland, by J. K. Laughton, in the *Dictionary of National Biography* and a life by G. C. Williamson. It is known that the Earl of Warwick, when Robert Rich, was greatly stimulated by the accounts of Cumberland's activities and in his earlier enterprises intentionally followed Cumberland's example.

the Eastern archipelago, but they were lured also by the opportunities of the Caribbean and the Wild Coast to take what they could
from the lands and waters that had been assigned to Spain in the
demarcation bull of 1493. Some of these journeys were solely for
booty and plunder, led by men of high and low birth, of great
audacity and courage, who in large numbers frequented traffic routes
and who though suffering acute privation, imperiled Spain's monopoly in her part of the world. During the later years of the Elizabethan age the West was a world of corsairs not of colonists, for the
period was not favorable either to colonization or to the pursuit of
legitimate trade.

Side by side with the activities of pirate and buccaneer went the
scarcely more legitimate pursuits of a host of trading adventurers, to
whom the New World offered an opportunity for heavy returns on
a moderate investment. England had become too narrow a field to
absorb the rapidly accumulating capital, and even the companies,
trading with stocks that were large for their day in the older regions
of Russia, the Baltic, Morocco, the Levant, and the Far East, found
their legitimate spheres insufficient to engage all the available energies and wealth. Commercial expansion was the order of the day.
Even though aggressive traffic was brought to an end by the treaty
of 1604 with Spain, which closed English ports to Spanish prizes
and forbade the fitting out of vessels in English harbors, the merchants continued to indulge their enmity for Spain under the protection of foreign flags. Adventurers unable to sail from England
under a letter of marque—sometimes called a thieving letter—turned
to the Prince of Orange, the Duke of Savoy,[1] or the Prince of Cour-
land and, using the letter thus obtained almost as a screen for piracy,
went on as before, carrying their prizes into Dutch instead of English ports. Their ships were of small burden, medium in size but
swift and easily managed,[2] chiefly issuing from remote ports, such as

1. *Virginia Company Records*, II, 402, 407; Brown, *Genesis of the United States*,
II, 980; *William and Mary Quarterly*, XXII, 96; *Virginia Historical Magazine*, XV,
367.

2. The English ships of the late Elizabethan and early Stuart periods were built
after models by Sir John Hawkins, who was a practical shipbuilder with a marked
gift for diplomacy and "capable of connecting policy with strategy and strategy with
administration and ship design." He wanted ships that would be active and sea-
worthy, well gunned and easy to maintain, and suitable for oceanic warfare and
oceanic gunnery. Hawkins was not the grizzled sea dog, the heartless slave trader,
or the corrupt administrator that history in the past had made him out to be. J. A.
Williamson, *Sir John Hawkins, passim*.

those of Devonshire and Ireland. Among these merchant adventurers were the Reskeimers of Dartmouth, the Delbridges of Barnstaple, the Courteens of London and of Middleburg on the Continent—a prominent Dutch firm interested in English trade and colonization—and Ralph Merrifield and Marmaduke Rawdon, merchants of London, their partners and associates.[1] Conspicuous among them was Robert Rich, later Earl of Warwick, who sent out two ships, one the *Lion,* under Captain Thomas Jones in 1617, and the other, the *Treasurer,* under Captain Daniel Elfrith, in coöperation with Captain Argall of Virginia fame, in 1618. These vessels, probably designed originally for commercial ends, had extraordinary noncommercial careers. The voyage of Captain Jones, as the result of which Warwick got into trouble with the East India Company, was a piece of sheer banditry; the other, that of Elfrith, a roving voyage against Spain in the West Indies, which gave to Warwick, who was just entering upon his career as one of the most versatile men of affairs from 1604 to 1658, the doubtful glory of sharing with the Dutch the responsibility for bringing the first negroes to the American colonies.[2] After 1623 and the failure of the Spanish marriage, which brought to an end the peace with Spain, Englishmen once more sailed under their own flag. These men were not colonizers, but their activities prepared the way for colonization, for, as has been frequently said, every explorer and trader is potentially a promoter of commerce and settlement.

✓ The interest thus aroused in the West Indies was easily extended to Guiana and the Amazon, where the Spanish search for El Dorado had been going on at least since 1530.[3] The earliest English settlements, 1604–1606, were on the Wiapoco, the river that today bounds French Guiana on the east, and in 1609 Robert Harcourt sailed from Dartmouth and set up a colony there. But as he had embarked on this venture without legal sanction, he applied in 1613 for a royal

1. John Delbridge was an important member of the Virginia Company; the Courteens were among the most influential merchants and overseas traders of the day; Rawdon was identified with the settlement of Barbados. Doubtless the list of these merchant adventurers could be greatly extended.

2. For a brief account of the *Lion,* Bradford, *History of Plymouth Plantation* (Ford ed.), I, 276, note 4. For the *Treasurer,* Brown, *First Republic,* pp. 284–285, 311, 324–328; Historical Manuscripts Commission, *Eighth Report,* II, no. 261; *Acts of the Privy Council, Colonial,* I, §45. A thoroughgoing and reliable life of Warwick is greatly needed.

3. J. A. Williamson, *The English in Guiana;* Harlow, Introduction to Raleigh's *Discoverie,* and *Colonizing Expeditions to the West Indies and Guiana, 1623–1677.*

grant of that part of Guiana, which extended from the Amazon to the Essequibo. In making his application he recalled the fact that he had discovered this country "with great travaile and charge," he and his companions having resided there "for the space of three or four years last past," hoping "to plant with his Majesty's subjects, to the great benefitt of this kingdom by the increase of trade and the reducinge of that people to civility of life and Christianity."[1] The grant was made and Harcourt sent out a ship under a Captain Harvey, who had lived in the country for three years and was familiar with the difficulties ahead. Of the fate of the expedition we know nothing. A number of efforts were made in England to form a company, but at first these were brought to naught by Raleigh's unfortunate fiasco of 1617, in which both Harcourt and one Captain North, with whom at an earlier time he had undertaken a journey to the Amazon, were implicated. However, the project was carried out in 1619, when a second attempt was made and a patent secured, under the leadership of North, aided by a powerful group of men of estate, some of whom were Irish, including the earls of Arundel and Warwick.[2] But because of royal fears that the enterprise would arouse the hostility of Spain—since the patent included land that was clearly within the claims of Spain and Portugal—the charter was suspended in 1620 and a royal proclamation was issued enjoining the expedition.[3] In 1626 a new company was incorporated, the Company for the Plantation of Guiana, but the times were evil, war was in the air, and the venture failed. Though the royal enmity for Spain was revived after 1623, Charles I had no money wherewith to aid the promoters, and even the lure of the Amazon was not sufficient to attract investors, when safer and more promising opportunities lay nearer at hand. The company never had adequate financial support and came to an end in 1635.

The failure of settlement in the Amazon and Guiana regions is easily understood. Those who ventured there were preoccupied with the finding of gold and neither colonization nor trade held any

1. *Calendar State Papers, Colonial,* 1574–1660, p. 15; *Acts Privy Council, Colonial,* I, §3; Harcourt, *A Relation of a Voyage to Guiana* (ed. 1673, ed. by Sir Alexander Harris, 1928), with an appendix containing the additions made by Harcourt in the edition of 1623.

2. *Calendar State Papers, Colonial,* 1574–1660, pp. 18, 21, 23, 77, 78, 83; *Acts Privy Council, Colonial,* I, pp. 25, 26, 31, 35, 36, 37, 39. On Captain Roger North, *Virginia Company Records,* I, 433 and index.

3. *Acts Privy Council, Colonial,* I, §§55, 58.

interest for them. As Raleigh says in his *Discoverie,* "where there is store of gold, it is in effect nedeles to remember other commodities for trade." Gold, trade, tillage represent the three stages in the history of colonization, and the greatest of these, because fundamentally essential to permanence, is tillage. But not until well on in the seventeenth century did the production of sugar and the growing of tobacco make possible true colonization in the tropical and semi-tropical parts of the world. A few settlers remained in Guiana during these years when efforts were being made to finance a company in England; a few trading stations were established along the Guiana rivers; and as late as 1632 a project was set on foot to found a plantation between the Amazon and the Orinoco. But all these attempts had little other effect than to draw the islands of the West Indies within the sphere of England's colonizing ambitions. The expeditions of Leigh, Harcourt, and North failed in their immediate object, and England's permanent interest in Guiana really dates from the successful settlement made by Francis, Lord Willoughby of Parham, on the Surinam river in 1650 and 1652.[1]

Less foolhardy but equally adventurous were the ambitious plans for the opening up of Canada, Newfoundland, and the St. Lawrence to English trade. As early as 1610 a group of London and Bristol merchants had organized a company for the settlement of Newfoundland, of which an account will be given later, but more significant were the expeditions to Canada associated with the name of Kirke. As Harcourt and Raleigh had trespassed upon soil claimed by the Spanish king, so the Kirkes were trespassing on soil occupied by the subjects of the king of France where already French trading companies,[2] among them a few enterprising Basques, were active. In 1628, after war between England and France was resumed, a company—the Company of Adventurers to Canada—was organized for trade and settlement along the St. Lawrence and, under the leadership of Scottish-English adventurers, the Kirke brothers, Lewis, Thomas, David, and John—David being the general of the fleet and John the manager of the business in London—captured Quebec in 1629 and effected the first conquest of Canada.[3] The pro-

1. *Calendar State Papers, Colonial,* 1661–1668, §451.
2. Biggar, *The Early Trading Companies of New France.*
3. Kirke, *The First English Conquest of Canada,* a useful but somewhat old-fashioned work; Wrong, *The Rise and Fall of New France;* Brebner, *New England's Outpost,* ch. I; *Publications,* Massachusetts Historical Society, XII, 101–113; *Calendar State Papers, Colonial,* 1574–1660, pp. 103, 130.

moters of this company were determined to have a share in the trade for "beaver skins, wares, goods, and merchandize" and though they were much bothered by interlopers—among whom was Maurice Thompson, an influential London merchant interested also in the West Indies—who were "presuming to trade in those parts"; by the French merchants, whose goods they had seized; and by Exeter fishermen, whose fishing they had interfered with, they persisted in their efforts and made large profits. Among the adventurers was one William Berkeley,[1] afterward governor of Virginia, against whom, nearly fifty years later Bacon raised his famous rebellion. But Charles I soon brought the undertaking to an end. Concerned for his wife's dowry, he yielded to the demand of the French king, based on the voyages of Champlain, 1604–1608, and in the treaty of St. Germain-en-Laye, 1632, restored Canada to France reserving only certain rights of trade.[2] In consequence of this reservation, a patent was issued to the company "for the sole trade to the river and gulf of Canada and all places adjacent for thirty one years," and later, in 1636, the promoters received a private authorization from the king "to surprise and take . . . and after such taking to enjoy and possess," which shows that Charles I and his ministers were not above a manoeuvre that was closely akin to trickery. But affairs in England were in confusion and despite the English double-dealing, the French in the end proved too strong for the Company of Adventurers to Canada. Berkeley was sent to Virginia as governor in 1641. David Kirke, knighted for his freebooting enterprise, went as governor to Newfoundland, which had not been "restored" in 1632, and there ruled as a greedy autocrat, leaving many bitter memories behind. He turned Lord Baltimore out of his property at Avalon and seized the estate, for which Baltimore sued him in England, after his recall, and "laid him in prison." There he died, about 1654, the first conqueror of Canada, one hundred and thirty years before Wolfe's victory on the Plains of Abraham.

The period after 1604 was one of marked improvement financially in England, particularly in the outports, which had suffered a seri-

1. Among the docquets in the Crown office is one of a commission to Sir William Alexander, Jervas Kirke (the father), Robert Charleton, and William Barclay of London, to make a voyage into Canada for the purpose of trading in beaver wools and beaver skins, 1629. The same entry is to be found in Egerton, 2395, f. 25, where the name of George Kirke is added.

2. *Calendar State Papers, Colonial,* 1661–1668, §210; *Canadian Archives,* Report, 1912, pp. 27–34; Davenport, *European Treaties,* I, 313–323.

ous decline during the later years of Elizabeth's reign. It was a time of recuperation also from the depressing effects of the "boom in privateering," which had characterized the long drawn out struggle with Spain, for the freebooting of Elizabeth's reign had been bad for legitimate commerce, and the frequent reprisals on Spain's part had caused a stoppage of trade with the chief European countries. The political situation during the same years had been uncertain and the crown finances depleted, owing in large part to the heavy costs of the war, and this situation had been accompanied with an increase of taxation, which in its turn checked still further trading operations. There had been a series of bad harvests also, which led to higher prices; tillage was reported decayed and bread riots were frequent. There were several outbreaks of the plague, which at one time in London brought business to a standstill for nearly six months. The feeling of prosperity which had prevailed widely among the merchants from 1575 to 1586 was giving way to a sense of depression, and men, both in parliament and out, searching for and finding many ills, real and imaginary, placed monopolies among the first. The subject was prominent in the parliamentary debates of the period, particularly in the first parliament of James I.[1] But the peace with Spain of 1604 once more opened the markets and English commerce entered upon a new period of prosperity. Capital, no longer diverted to war expenditure, once more became available for legitimate investment, and money either came out of hoarding or increased in amount naturally with the expanding volume of business. Though James I had no commercial sense and consequently no commercial policy, and in fact exhibited little interest in economic questions of any kind, his Privy Council, which was almost the sole government agency in matters relating to trade and the plantations, gave support to the merchants, both in London and the outports, and the nobility and many lesser folk could usually be counted on to take shares in any undertaking that promised a financial return.[2]

1. Price, *The English Patent of Monopoly*. In *Alderman Cockayne,* pp. 145–149, Miss Friis discusses the subject of company organization and the monopoly debate and charges Gardiner (*History of England*) and Scott (*Joint-Stock Companies*) with "a complete misstatement" of the facts.

2. Châteauneuf, ambassador from France to England, said in a letter to Richelieu, 1629, that most of the members of the Privy Council were interested in navigation, plantations, and letters of marque and were partners and sharers in the captures that were made (*Canadian Archives,* report for 1912, p. 33). Among the privy councillors of that year were men whose names are prominent among those known to have been more or less concerned with colonization, such as the Earl of Arundel and Sur-

Long experience in privateering and exploration enabled the ship-builders to improve the sailing qualities of the merchant vessels and the sea-captains to acquire skill in the arts of seamanship and navigation. It is a noteworthy fact that many of the captains and the vessels under their command, which took part in the settlement of America, had already seen service in the Mediterranean or the West Indies before they were employed or chartered for the peaceful and harmless pursuit of carrying colonists to America. It was no fortuitous series of circumstances that led to the planting of Jamestown in 1607. Though the king, brought up as he was in Scotland, had no knowledge of the impulses that were at work among the English people and in his relations with the merchants was neither practical nor tactful, nevertheless the years from 1604 to 1619 were characterized by peace, prosperity, and confidence in England's future. During this period were taken the first steps toward the permanent colonization of the West.

rey, Pembroke, and Montgomery, Viscounts Dorchester and Falkland, and Sir Robert Naunton, Sir John Coke, and Sir Julius Caesar. The subscribers to the various stocks of the Virginia Company show the wide range of interest among the lesser folk.

CHAPTER III

FACTORS INFLUENCING COLONIZATION

BUT money and companies and prosperity, essential as they were, would not have gone far had not other influences been at work that were social and religious in character. Privateering and trade enlisted the energies of only a small part of the population of England—which at this time numbered not less than five millions of people—and engaged the attention of those only who were ready to face stormy seas and dangerous experiences or were willing to risk their lives and fortunes in the pursuit of wealth. Most of those who up to this time had crossed the ocean were prospectors for the gold which was always luring them on to penetrate the unknown, or else they were born fighters who preferred to amass their riches rather by deeds of valor against the Spaniard than by the more prosaic and peaceful activities of everyday life. Those that blazed the way, in like manner with the pioneers of the New World on its western frontier, were of the rough and ready sort, courageous and persistent, but turbulent, quarrelsome, and impatient, whose hands were better fitted for the sword than the plough.

Permanent colonization demanded a different type of recruit. It called for the common man as well as the adventurer, to whom life in old England had become, for one reason or another, joyless and burdensome, and who welcomed the opportunity that the new lands offered to better his worldly estate. Colonization demanded leaders and capital, but it demanded people as well—men, women, and children—to build homes, till the soil, and provide for the coming generations. Without colonists of this type, settlement was bound to be precarious and permanence was never assured. At the opening of the peace with Spain (1604) not a single colony of Englishmen had found place in either Asia, Africa, or America. Before the end of the century there were twenty colonies along the Atlantic seaboard and in the West Indies, peopled by nearly two hundred and twenty-five thousand human beings of all sorts and conditions, chiefly of English stock, engaged in building up communities of active, vigorous frontier life—towns, villages, farms, and plantations—and concerned with agriculture, industry, and commerce. This is an astonishing fact and points to forces at work in English society that were inducing a great migration and were bringing about an extraordinary enlargement of the English scene and expansion of English territory.

Conspicuous among the causes for colonization, in that it probably influenced the largest number of those who settled in North America, was the desire for land and an opportunity to make a home for wife and children. In the days of Elizabeth but a comparatively small part of England was available for tillage, and even that part had been considerably curtailed by the increase in sheep farming, the enclosure of the open fields and commons, and the conversion of tillable soil into pastures and plains. This transformation of rural life must have made a deep impression upon the popular mind and by just so much have loosened the ties that bound the country folk— normally a well-anchored social class—to the land of their birth. Arable land was growing scarce in the presence of the insistent demand for wool and efforts were being made in many directions to improve the situation. For a number of years a movement had been under way looking to the transmutation of moor, forest, and waste into more remunerative soil, by turning purprestures, assarts, and intakes into arable, draining the fenlands,[1] and irrigating where water was needed. In this effort private capital was being expended in reclamation projects that were authorized by parliamentary statute and were being carried on side by side with colonization during the seventeenth century. Many men, as, for example, Sir John Popham, were engaged in both enterprises, just as others, who were intimately concerned with settlement in America, were also deeply involved in trading undertakings in the East and elsewhere.

The lands thus reclaimed were trifling in extent as compared with the great reaches of a new continent and far more often benefited the landlord than the tenant. Not a project was set on foot looking to colonization in America that the promoters did not hold out the tempting inducement of land to those whom they wished to attract as prospective settlers. "With what content," reads a prospectus of 1622, "shall the particular person employ himself there when he shall

1. Vermuyden, *Discourse concerning the Draining of the Great Fennes* (1642); Dugdale, *History of Imbanking and Drayning* (1662); Dodson, *The Designe for the Perfect Draining of the Great Level of the Fennes* (1664).

find that for 12 10s adventure he shall be made lord of 200 acres of land, to him and his heirs forever. And for the charge of transportation of himself, his family and tenants he shall be allotted for every person he carries 100 acres more. And what laborer soever shall transport himself thither at his own charge to have the like proportion of land upon the aforesaid conditions and be sure of employment to his good content for his present maintenance."[1] "No man," said the Rev. Patrick Copland, in a sermon preached on April 18, 1622, "can justly say that this country is not capable . . . of all good things that the most opulent parte of Christendom do afford, neither are we hopeless that this country may also yield things of better value than any of these,"[2] and the Rev. Daniel Price, preaching from St. Paul's Cross, May 28, 1609, describes the New World as a country "not unlike to equalize . . . Tyrus for colors, Basan for woods, Persia for oils, Arabia for spices, Spain for silks, Narcis for shipping, Netherlands for fish, Pomona for fruit, and by tillage, Babylon for corn, besides the abundance of mulberries, minerals, rubies, pearls, gems, grapes, deer, fowles, drugs for physic, herbs for food, roots for colours, ashes for soap, timber for building, pastures for feeding, rivers for fishing, and whatsoever commodity England wanteth";[3] while the Rev. Mr. Simonds hopefully exclaims, "Let us be cheerfull to goe to the place that God will shew us to possesse in peace and plentie, a Land more like the Garden of Eden: which the Lord planted, than any part else of all the Earth."[4] Winthrop made the same appeal later, when in 1629 he endeavored to encourage the hearts of those whom he was urging to join in the voyage to Massachusetts Bay. "Why then [he wrote] should we stand striving here for places of habitation (where many are spending as much labour and coste to recover or keepe sometimes an acre or twoe of Land, as would produce them many and as good or better in another Countrie) and in the mean time suffer a whole Continent as fruitfull and convenient for the use of men to be waste without any improvement."[5]

1. *American Historical Review*, IV, 698.
2. Neill, *Memoir of Patrick Copland*, pp. 53–74.
3. Brown, *Genesis*, I, 313–314.   4. *Ibid.*, 289.
5. *Life and Letters of John Winthrop* (1864), p. 310. "Great pity is it," said Francis Higginson, "to see so much good ground for corn and for grass as any is under the heavens, to be altogether unoccupied, when so many honest men and their families in old England, through the populousness thereof, do make shift to live one by the other . . . As for wood, a poor servant may have more timber and fuel than

This appeal was made to every class and rank of men and was rarely omitted from the discourses and pamphlets that were issued to encourage settlement from 1607 to 1682. The small feudal land-owner and tenant farmer were alike discontented in England: one with the depreciating value of his landed estate and the dwindling returns from his tenancies; the other with the insufficiency of his acres for cultivation. Both were confronted with the changing con-ditions which were accompanying the breaking up of the medieval system of landholding, and the fall in the value of silver which was leading to the rise of prices. Decreasing profits from the soil, sta-tionary or falling rents, the difficulty of finding laborers and the unreliability and transient character of those that were obtained, the growth of luxury and the cost of living, the demand for better and more varied food, houses, equipage, and display—all these conditions tended to make the lower classes necessitous and the upper classes covetous and greedy. The tenantry resented the retention of the old feudal incidents and a land law which favored the landlords in all that concerned the use of the soil and the tenures by which it was held. They were growing impatient of feudal practices and pay-ments that made occupation uncertain and living precarious. They suffered from the encroachments of their lords upon their fields and commons, the passage of hounds and huntsmen over their cultivated acres, and heavy tithes, taxes, and rates. Laws of inheritance, con-veyancing, and tenure, still medieval, were to remain medieval for many generations to come, upheld by the lawyers and the courts. The heavy feudal burdens upon farmer and tenant, still living in something of a medieval atmosphere, made many a man long for the freer life of the New World, where land was plentiful and tenu-rial demands less likely to be imposed.[1] Thus land-hunger and the

could many a nobleman in England . . . And as for fresh water the country is full of dainty springs and some great rivers and some lesser brooks" (paraphrase in Young's *Chronicles of Massachusetts Bay*, pp. 242–254). Higginson's *New-England Plantation* (1630) is almost entirely taken up with alluring descriptions of the mate-rial advantages of New England, with only twelve lines at the end devoted to the "true Religion and holy Ordinances of Almightie God taught amongst us."

John Rolfe wrote from Virginia in 1616, "Seeing too many poor farmers in Eng-land work all the year, rising early and going to bed late, live penuriously, and much ado to pay their landlord's rent, besides a daily tasking and care to feed themselves and families, what happiness might they enjoy in Virginia where they may have ground for nothing more than they can manure, reap more fruits and profits with half the labour" (Historical Manuscripts Commission, *Eighth Report*, II, no. 208).

1. Sir Ferdinando Gorges and Sir Henry Spelman proposed in 1623 that a tenant

desire for a greater amount of property-freedom were among the powerful inducements that drove a restless awakening people to migration overseas. The bulk of the colonial population was of the artisan and tenant class, holding as a rule by some form of burgage or copyhold tenure. They became freeholders in America.

Imagination played its part. All classes of the population in cities and boroughs and notably along the eastern and southern coasts from East Anglia to the West Country were stirred to their inner-most souls by the visions of wealth and the tales of a sumptuously bountiful nature that were told by those who sent letters back from America or returned from ocean voyages thither. "It is the goodliest and most pleasing Territorie of the World," wrote Richard Lane to Hakluyt in 1585, "for the Continent is of a huge and unknown greatness," and a later writer, in pious rhapsody said that "such luxuriant plantie and admirable raritie of trees, shrubs, hearbs; such fertilitie of soyle, insinuation of seas, multiplicitie of rivers, safetie of ports, healthfulnesse of air, opportunitie of habitations, hopes in

belonging to any one of the patentees, to whom grants were made in New England, should not be allowed to "depart from the place where he is once planted, without lycence from his Land Lord" (*Proceedings,* American Antiquarian Society, 1867, p. 93); and the Massachusetts Bay Company in 1629 suggested that all who transported themselves to New England at their own charge and were not adventurers in the common stock "should, by way of acknowledgement to such from whom they receive their lands, become lyable to the performance of some service certaine dayes in the yeare, and by that service they and their posteritie after them to hold and inherit their lands, which wilbe a good meanes to enjoy their lands from being held in capite" (*Massachusetts Colonial Records,* I, 405). But in neither case was this last remnant of the old bondage, an example of which may also be found in Gorges' charter of 1639, ever enforced. Bradford, on his farm at Jones River in Plymouth Colony, 1647, had tenants, who owed him "rents and other dues" (*Plymouth Records,* II, 119), but whether this was a common practice at so early a date it is impossible to say. Another Plymouth colonist seems to imply that it was not, when he wrote "We are all freeholders, the rent day does not trouble us" (Young's *Chronicles of the Pilgrims,* p. 250), and George Cleeve of the Maine settlement said that "he would be a tenant to never a man in New England" (*Trelawney Papers,* p. 265). Roger Williams once wrote that "Land is one of the gods of New England," and Thomas Hutchinson, at a later date, remarked that "where there is one farm [in New England] in the hands of a tenant, there are fifty occupied by him who has the fee of it" (Hutchinson Papers, Massachusetts Historical Society). "Some persons," wrote Governor Francis Nicholson, at that time in Maryland, "taking up great quantities of land . . . is one great reason why the young English natives and servants, when they are free, leave these colonies and go Southward or Northward, for they are not naturally ambitious of being Landlords and not Tenants" (*Maryland Archives,* XXIII, 87–88). There is a curious token or coin extant for the year 1647, which bears the inscription, "In Virginia land free and labor scarce; in England land scarce and labor plenty" (*William and Mary Quarterly,* XIV, 162–163). The device was evidently issued to attract settlers.

present, hopes of future, worlds of varietie in that diversified world; do quicken our minds to apprehend what our tongues do declare and fill both with arguments of divine praise."[1] Raleigh's picture of the fabled Manoa, written in the style of Francisco Lopez' description of the court and magnificence of the emperor of Guaynacapa in Peru, must have whetted the appetite for gold of many a reader of the *Discoverie*, which was published in 1596. "All the vessels of his home, table and kitchen were of gold and silver and the meanest of silver and copper . . . He had in his wardrobe hollow statues of golde . . . He had also ropes, budgets, chests and troughs of golde and silver, heaps of billets of golde . . . Besides all this, he had an infinite quantitie of silver and gold inwrought."[2] To the home dwellers following the weary round of daily toil, the scenes presented by that great press-agent of English discovery, Richard Hakluyt,[3] whose *Principall Navigations, Voiages and Discoveries of the English Nation* appeared in its final form in 1600, were a panorama of exciting novelties—pictures of new peoples and places, habits and ways of life, with boundless possibilities of wealth and creature comforts. Credulous and unenlightened as they were English readers believed the tales and rumors that were handed on from man to man and formed the gossip of the tavern and the market place. The London theatregoer, though generally of the upper class only, must have gazed agape at Seagull, Spendall, and Scapethrift, whose lines in *Eastward Hoe* rivalled the accounts of the gold of Manoa that lured Raleigh to his ruin, as they told of the land where gold was more

1. Hakluyt, VIII, 319; Purchas, *His Pilgrims*, XIX, 231. It must be remembered that language of this sort was due in part to the inflated style of the day and in part to a desire to make an impression for propagandist purposes. There can be little doubt, however, that the tales of the English voyagers were eagerly read in many quarters, quickening the imagination and widening the mental horizon of many a young Englishman, such as the one of whom his father said, "In tender years he always lov'd to read, Reports of travailes and of voyages . . . he would whole dayes and nights (sometimes by stealth) be on such bookes, As might convey his fancy round the World" (Brome, *The Antipodes*, 1640).

2. Raleigh's *Discoverie*, p. 18; also pp. 24, 71–72.

3. An excellent epitome of Hakluyt's character and purpose may be found in Parks, *Richard Hakluyt and the English Voyages* (1929). Still better is Taylor, *Late Tudor and Early Stuart Geography, 1583–1650* (1933), which appeared too late for use in this volume. It emphasizes especially the widespread influence of Hakluyt's great work. Of no little importance was the influence of Hakluyt's predecessor, Richard Eden, who in 1555 published *The Decades of the Newe World*. The Hakluyt Society was founded for the publication of works of this sort and the latest volume (*Documents concerning English Voyages to the Spanish Main, 1569–1580*. Edited by Irene A. Wright. 1932) contains seventy-three Spanish documents and sundry addi-

plentiful than copper in England and where rubies and diamonds could be picked up on the seashore "to hang on their children's coats and stick in their caps, as our children wear saffron guilt brooches and groats with hobles on 'em." And there in Virginia, continues the play, "wilde boare is as common as our tamest Bacon is here," and you can "live freely there, without sergeants or courtiers or lawyers or intelligencers. You may be an alderman there and never be a scavinger; you may be a nobleman and never be a slave, you may come to preferment enough and never be a pander. To riches and fortune enough and have never the more villanie nor the lesse wit."[1] These were rousing words, and to the hearers at Blackfriars in 1605 and to those that read any one of the five editions of the play issued in the same year, they must have made an appeal similar to that of *Westward Hoe,* on the stage only a few months before, creating amazing fancies and stimulating endless curiosity.

Alluring indeed must these tales have been to overcome the natural repugnance of an insular and inexperienced people to make the voyage to this distant unfamiliar land, for the narratives of travel and adventure were filled no less with tales of shipwrecks, storms, and suffering than of gold and a bounteous nature, and with accounts of weird monsters, strange beings,[2] and terrifying natural phenomena intermingled with the descriptions of riches and the

tional English accounts, some of them reprinted, with an enlightening introduction by the editor, which with the documents themselves admirably maintains the Hakluyt tradition.

1. *Eastward Hoe,* ed. Harris, pp. 45–46. There are many similarly extravagant descriptions in the dramatic literature of that day: For example:

"Say all this is true, That I spent millions, what's that to you, I'd melt both Indies, but I'd feast 'em all." Dekker, *The Wonder of a Kingdom,* 1635.

"When each ship of ours, Was able to spread sayles of silke: the tacklings of twisted gold: when every marryner At his arrivale here had his deepe pockets Crammed full of Pistolettes: when the poorest ship-boy Might on the Thames make ducks and drakes with pieces of eight fetched out of Spayne." Anonymous, *Dick of Devonshire,* undated, but early seventeenth century.

"Now shall your lordship see a Spaniard's skill, Who from the plains of new America Can find out sacred simples of esteem To bind and unbind nature's strongest powers, This herb, which mortal man have seldom found, Can I with ease procure me when I list." Anonymous, *Grim, the Collier of Croyden,* 1606.

"This devil, whose priest I am and by him made, A deep magician (for I can do wonders) Appeared to me in Virginia." Massinger, *The City Madam,* 1632.

2. Raleigh reported Amazons, though he doubted their mutilation, and also men with eyes in their shoulders and their mouths in the middle of their breasts. Harcourt's men repeated the same tale in 1604—"men whose shoulders are higher than their heads" (*Discoverie,* p. 56). The editor of the *Discoverie,* Dr. Harlow, thinks that these were the origin of Shakespeare's "Anthropophagi," men whose heads do

comforts of life. The yarns of sailors contained rich ingredients for nightmares and the frightening of timid souls. One may wonder the more that in the early days, when such tales were more fantastic than at a later time, there could have been found not only men of the hardy, adventurous type who were willing to cross the water, but women also, two with children yet unborn that went to Roanoke, and boys and girls of tender age, such as took part in that same Raleigh expedition of 1587. Of the forty women and children who embarked for the Amazon in 1616 none ever returned or were heard of again.[1] Later when the sailors' narratives had lost some of their fiction and their exaggerations had been curbed, the voyage to America became a fairly common matter, and the shiploads of maids sent to Virginia in 1619 and following years, "for the making of the men feel at home," the women of the *Mayflower* and later vessels to Plymouth colony, and those that spent distressingly uncomfortable days and weeks in the one hundred and ninety-eight ships that went to Massachusetts Bay between 1630 and 1643, endured nothing worse

grow beneath their shoulders, *The Tempest,* 1609 (*ibid.,* xcix). But the source may be traced to Sir John Mandeville, with his similar tale of fabulous monsters. In Brome, *The Antipodes,* appears the following:

"Doctor.   Drake was a Dy' dapper to Mandeville, he then
              Had left a passage ope for Travailers;
              That now is kept and guarded by wild beasts,
              Dragons and serpents, Elephants white and blue
              Unicorns, and Lyons of many colours,
              And monsters more, as numberlesse as namelesse.

Peregrine.   What people sir (I pray proceed) what people
              Are they of the Antipodes? Are not such
              As Mandeville writes of, without heads or necks
              Having their eyes placed on their shoulders, and
              Their mouths amids their breasts?

Doctor.   In brief Sir, all
              Degrees of people both in sex, and quality
              Deport themselves in life and conversation
              Quite contrary to us."

Richard Brome wrote fifteen comedies. See *Momus Triumphans or the Plagiaries of the English Stage expos'd in a Catalogue,* Gerard Langbaine, 1688, p. 2. This work is a "Catalogue of Plays."

1. John Scott's "Narrative," Rawlinson, A. 175 ff., 356 ff. It may be noted that only four years after this voyage to the Amazon, the Pilgrim maids and mothers faced the possibility of a voyage to the Wild Coast, that is, to Guiana, or to "some of those fertile places in those hott climates" that were "rich, fruitful, and blessed with a perpetual spring," but wiser heads prevailed and the plan was never seriously entertained (Bradford, *History,* I, 61–62). But had it been entertained and carried out, the women would undoubtedly have gone—to their death.

than did the pioneer women of the westward movement in American history. But very real were these dangers and discomforts. The tossing of a small vessel in rough and stormy seas, the fearful winds and drenching waves, and the constant dangers from contagious diseases, such as scurvy and smallpox, in a ship crowded with passengers, furniture, provisions, and livestock, and providing at best unwholesome and unappetising rations and often inadequate clothing, must have made the voyage of from six to ten weeks a dreaded event. As the Rev. Francis Higginson said in his journal of the voyage of the Puritan company in 1629, "those that love their owne chimney corner and dare not go farre beyond their owne townes end shall never have the honour to see the wonderfull workes of Almighty God."

Not all who went to America did so willingly or with the desire to see the wonderful works of Almighty God. In the eyes of the home authorities colonization performed one of its most important functions in enabling the country to get rid of undesirable members of its population and so to improve its social condition. England in Elizabeth's day was distressed by "a monstrous swarm of beggars" and a no less monstrous brood of criminals, born in huge numbers in the wretched slums of the dirty, dilapidated towns or created by the class distinctions, joyless child life, pitiless laws, and filthy prisons that hedged about the youth of the lower classes. There was no excess of population in England, but there was unequal distribution,[1] as men from the decaying rural districts, forced into a sort of perpetual "moving on" by the vagrancy laws, infested the highways and wandered into the urban rookeries. There was great scarcity of

1. Beer, *Origins of the British Colonial System*, ch. III; Cheyney, "Some Conditions surrounding the Settlement of Virginia," *American Historical Review*, XII, 521–526. Robert Powell, *Depopulation arraigned, convicted and condemned* (London, 1636), refers to this unequal distribution of population and attributes it to the enclosures, the razing of houses and mansions, and the decay of agriculture (p. 7). The dangers arising from overpopulation in the towns and the attendant evils of beggary, vagabondage, and crime are among the subjects treated by William Simonds, in a sermon preached before the Virginia Company, April 25, 1609, entitled "Virginia Britannia" (Brown, *Genesis*, I, 288–289), and by Robert Gray in "Good Speed to Virginia," 1609 (*ibid.*, 298). John Donne, in more figurative language, expresses the same hope when he says that the settlement of Virginia "shall redeem many a wretch from the jaws of death [and] the hands of the executioner . . . shall sweep your streets, and wash your doors from idle persons and the children of idle persons, and employ them. [Colonization] is not only a spleen to drain ill humours of the body, but a liver to breed good blood" (*Works of John Donne*, Alfred ed. VI, 225–244). Brown has a brief notice of Donne, *Genesis*, II, 880.

food, which made men and women desperate and drove them to commit a great variety of petty crimes, whereby to secure money and subsistence. Thus there existed, particularly in the towns and suburban districts, an excess of population of the worst sort—beggars, vagrants, thieves, and the wretched poor, who had to be dealt with in one way or another. The press-gang and the crimp took their quota, the plague and the gallows had a larger share, and the workhouses and the prisons (horrible places of confinement) received their thousands. But still the problem remained unsolved. Of the few Englishmen of this type engaged in the early voyages for exploration and settlement, some were criminals by preference and nature, others from necessity and circumstance. Lack of money, food, and employment drove many of them to accept any opportunity that offered.

Transportation to the colonies appears very early as an official remedy for dire conditions at home, and from the first was adopted by judges in the criminal courts, town councils, and others in authority. Poor children, likely to become a charge upon the parishes, were sent over from many a provincial town, while London and Middlesex furnished a large number.[1] Maids were shipped to become wives and mothers, and notorious offenders were ordered by parliament to be banished to Virginia;[2] the poor were encouraged

1. This subject will be considered again in the chapter on Virginia. That vagrants were sent from other parts of England than London is evident from the Coffer Books of Winchester, "30 December 1625, 60s for the apparelling of six poor boys that went to Virginia" (*Hampshire Notes and Queries,* IV, 82–83); from the Account Books of a Devonshire town, "10s 4d. Paid for shoes for three boys sent to Virginia" (*Barnstaple Records,* II, 136); and from the records of a justice of the peace of Dorchester in which is the deposition of a poor laborer "that he came to this Towne to meet with his aunt and to entreate her to gett him a place to go to New England" (*Dorchester Records,* p. 666).

2. This plan of sending to the colonies "notorious and wicked offenders that will not be reformed but by severity of punishment, in order that they may no more infect the places where they abide within our Realme" was made the subject of a royal proclamation, dated December 23, 1617. Both Winthrop and Gorges give reasons similar to those in the text. Gorges wrote in 1611, "This peaceable tyme affords no meanies of ymployments, to the Multitude of people that daylie doe increase and manie ar inforced (by necessitie) to seek some wayes to sustaine themselves, and although this (of all other her the worst), yet in the multitude there is no feeling of honestie or Religion (as in the multitude there is litle) even this Course is aplauded and therefore their number is liklier daylie to increase" (Baxter, *Gorges,* III, 172). In its petition to parliament of 1624 the Virginia Company gave as one of its objects, "The removinge of the Surcharge of necessitous people, the matter or fewell of daungerous insurrections, and thereby leavinge the greater plentie to susteyne those remayninge within the Land" (*Virginia Company Records,* II, 526).

to go as servants and though kidnapping and spiriting were strictly forbidden,[1] the government lent its aid by giving legal sanction to a system of indenture and later established a registry office for "such servants as should voluntarily go or be sent to any of the plantations in America or elsewhere." This office had a chequered history, but seems to have functioned intermittently during the colonial period, though none of its records are known to be in existence. Local ports such as Bristol had each its own system, and under this arrangement thousands of indentured servants went to the American colonies.

Equally significant, though much less frequent, was the transportation of undesirable soldiers, political offenders, and those convicted of crime. On account of the peace with Spain many soldiers of fortune, disbanded or broken privates, sailors, and others, bred for war or themselves the product of war, were looking for active employment and, unable to settle down to the humdrum pursuits of peace, were in danger of becoming a public nuisance, if not a menace. The government was only too glad to get rid of men of this stamp and hustled many of them, who would in all probability have become burdens at home, off to America, where they succeeded, under the strenuous conditions of a sea-faring and pioneer life, in attaining a certain measure of respectability and even distinction in the New World. In later years transportation became a frequent form of punishment in a great variety of minor offenses, and was even suggested as a penalty in cases of smuggling, resisting officers, and importing "alamodes or lustrings" contrary to law.[2] Prisoners taken in war were despatched chiefly to Barbados and Virginia—Irish after Dro-

1. A large number of kidnappings are recorded and the subject is treated in the preface to the *Calendar of State Papers, Colonial,* 1661–1668, xxvii–xxix. In 1618 a man was executed because, among other crimes, he had counterfeited the royal seal and had taken up "rich yeoman's daughters . . . to serve his Majesty for breeders in Virginia" (*Court and Times of James I,* I, 108).

2. Resolution of a committee of the House of Commons, 1697–1698, "That such persons, their aiders and abettors, as shall be convicted of importing Alamodes or Lustrings contrary to law, and shall not within one month's time after such conviction pay the forfeiture imposed already by law shall be banished into some island of his Maj. plantations in America." *Report of the Committee to whom the Petition of the Royal Lustring Company of England was referred,* etc. (London, 1698), p. 53. The smuggling of goods and the obstruction of customs officers in Scotland went on until, in 1754, the High Court of Justiciary in Edinburgh ordered the banishment of three of the worst offenders and their transportation "to one or other of his Majesty's plantations," never to return to Scotland (Mackenzie, *Book of Arran,* p. 131). For transportation as a penalty for theft and rapine upon the northern borders of England, see Stock, *Debates,* I, 336–338, 423, II, 142, note 42, 411, 412, 417–418.

gheda, Scots after Preston, Dunbar, Worcester, and Penruddock, and English after the Monmouth rebellion of 1685.[1] Offenders against the Conventicle Act of 1664, chiefly Quakers convicted of attending field conventicles, were ordered to be handed over to the masters of ships sailing to America and delivered to the governors of the several plantations whither they were bound.

The transportation of those arrested for crime or condemned to death stands in another category. The laws of England were distinguished above those of all other countries by the large number of petty offenses for which the death penalty might be inflicted, and it was the lenient judge who substituted transportation for execution. Transportation of criminals was due also in part to the feeling that it was a waste to destroy so much good brawn and muscle, which might "yield a profitable service to the Commonwealth in parts abroad," when a new country might reclaim the criminal and make him or her (for women in large numbers were transported as well as men) a worthy subject of the king. But behind all else was the wish of the state to be quit of such undesirable people.[2] The practice

1. The transportation of political prisoners continued to a very late date. Stock, *Debates*, I, 247, 248–250, 252, 291 gives the debates in parliament after the insurrection of 1659. Harlow, *Barbados*, pp. 294–301, has an excellent account of transportation and the condition of labor in that colony before 1685. The political prisoners were far from willing to go and sometimes resisted very strenuously. In an unpublished newsletter, of date October 17, 1685, we are told that of the 800 deported to the West Indies after Monmouth's rebellion, 100 at Bristol, "aboard a ship to be transported to Nevis for Sir Wm Stapleton . . . threatened to knock the captain and his men on the head and go whither they pleased; but being forewarned he [the captain] hath taken occasion to prevent them" (Information furnished the *Times Literary Supplement*, February 24, 1921). On the same subject see 39 Eliz. c. 4; 18 Chas. II, c. 3; 31 Chas. II, c. 2; 4 Geo. III, c. 11, 1; *Calendar State Papers, Colonial, 1661–1668*, §§ 24, 32, 331, 769, 770, 772, 790, 791, 798; *Acts Privy Council, Colonial*, I, §631; *Calendar State Papers, Domestic, 1664–1665*, p. 4; Harding, *Bristol and America*, p. 4.

2. *Acts Privy Council, Colonial*, I, §§ 12, 13, 14, 50, etc. See also *ibid.*, 517. "This day several Lists of the Names of Prisoners remayning in the Prisons of Newgate, White-Lyon in Southwarke, Gate house at Westminster, New Bridewell (otherwise called the House of Correction) at St. James Clerkenwell, Bridewell in London, House of Correction at Westminster in Tottlefields, and the Prison of the Marshalsey were presented," etc. These prisoners were to be sent to Jamaica "for the advance of that plantation." Others also "of loose and idle conversation who remain in the said Prisons" were to go, thus "acquitting this Nation of them." In 1616 Gondomar wrote to Philip III, in order to impress upon him the undesirability of Virginia and its uselessness to Spain, saying that the colony was in such bad repute "that not a human being can be found to go there" and that "two Moorish thieves," who were granted the privilege of going to Virginia instead of being hanged, "replied at once, decidedly and with one accord, that they would much rather die on the gallows here, and

dates from the very beginning of settlement and continued to the end of the colonial period, when Botany Bay in eastern Australia took the place of the American colonies.[1]

Two other powerful and impelling motives appear, essentially different from those which have already been presented. The first was that curious mingling of the religious with the pecuniary spirit, which had characterized the crusading movement and had accompanied the early activities of every colonizing nation, except perhaps the Dutch, who never seem to have possessed the desire to convert anybody. This revival of the old crusading fervor in the guise of missionary enterprise finds expression in the pages of Hakluyt and in every statement of plan and purpose drawn up by the early companies and in every charter that was issued out of chancery at this period and for many years thereafter. In the preamble to the first letters patent erecting the Virginia companies of London and Plymouth, the hope was expressed that so noble a work would "hereafter tend to the glory of his divine Majesty, in propagating of Christian religion to such people as yet live in darkness and miserable ignorance of the true knowledge and worship of God," and might in time bring the infidels and savages "to human civilitie"[2] and "to a settled and quiet government." "To carry the benefits of Christian faith," "to enlarge the bounds of the Christian religion" or, as the *True and Sincere Declaration* puts it, "to preach and baptize into *Christian Religion,* and by propagation of the *Gospell* to recover out of the armes of the Divell a number of poore and miserable souls, wrapt

quickly, than to die slowly so many deaths as was the case in Virginia" (Brown, *Genesis,* II, 739–740). Local English court records are filled with entries of reprieves, as, "15 James I Stephen Rogers: for killing George Watkins . . . He puts himself guilty, to be hung, reprieved after judgement at the instance of Sir Thomas Smith, Knt. for Virginia, because he is of the carpenter's art." "6 August, 16 James I, Ralph Brookes was reprieved, at Sherif Johnson's order, so that he should be sent to Virginia." *Middlesex Session Rolls,* II, 224, 225. See also article by A. E. Smith, "Transportation of Convicts," *American Historical Review,* xxxix, pp. 232–249.

Though transportation was a more welcome penalty than hanging it was considered a severe punishment to be avoided if possible. Among the Domestic Papers are many entries such as these: William Bird of St. Andrew's, Holborn, tailor, prayed for free pardon for his wife, whom he "maliciously indicted for stealing a silver watch," without the clause for transportation; and "Warrant for inserting in the next general pardon William Fellowes . . . without any condition of transportation." *Calendar of State Papers, Domestic,* 1682, p. 207; 1683, pp. 340, 385.

1. Flanagan, *History of New South Wales,* 2 vols., 1878.

2. "Civilitie" was a word frequently used in this connection, meaning "civil government" or "civilization," preferably that of the English type.

up in death, in almost invincible ignorance." This was one of the main objects, officially at least, in the minds of all who promoted voyages of exploration and settlement in the years from 1580 to 1640. "Lastly, and above all the rest," says a Bristol document of 1622, "by this opportunitye, there is no country within this realme, but by this course hath a speciall occasion and meanes presented unto them to dedicate their best service to the God of Heaven and Earth, by endeavoring to advance his glory in seeking how to settle the Christian ffaith in those hethenishe and desert places of the World; which whoe shall refuse to further, lett him undergoe the blame thereof himselfe."[1]

Of similar purpose, with less of the spirit of the crusader and more of the humility of the monk and the zeal of the inquisitor, was the religious impulse which drove thousands of men and women to the New World for the sake of conscience and conviction, in their desire to worship God in their own way, which they believed was the only true way. Pilgrims, Puritans, Roman Catholics, Quakers, Huguenots, Moravians, Mennonites, Mystics, and Pietists all took part in the settlement of America, each group primarily to escape from a land—England, France, Germany, and Austria—where they were unable, either because of opposition or actual persecution, to live their lives as they wished. In these lands they were unable to gather in meetings or churches of their own convictions, to order their social and family relations according to what they believed to be the purpose of God, or to control the opinions and practices of others, who were everywhere in the majority, in matters of ecclesiastical polity, religious creeds, and political government. No one of these religious groups formed a completely homogeneous body of men and women, of entirely like minds, influenced by a common religious purpose, for the Reformation had thrown the European world into a state of religious confusion and disorder. Even the Pilgrims

1. Brown, *Genesis*, I, 53, 339; Hazard, *State Papers*, I, 184; *American Historical Review*, IV, 699. In its petition to the House of Commons in 1624, the Virginia Company placed first among its objects, "The Conversion of Salvages to Christianytie and establishing the first Plantation of the reformed Religion" (*Virginia Company Records*, II, 526). The clergy of the day were very zealous for the propagation of the Gospel among the heathen Indians, sometimes alluded to as "rude warriors," and sometimes as "noble savages, Virginian princes" (Chapman, *Mask at Whitehall*, 1613). Crashaw, Crackenthorpe, Donne, and Price all refer to the need of planting the church in America and the conversion of the heathen "from the divil to God" (Brown, *Genesis*, I, 255–256, 312–315, 362; Donne, *Sermons*, clvi).

were accompanied to America by a large number of those who were influenced by other motives than soul conviction; while the covenanted Puritans, formally admitted to church membership, constituted but a small part of that great body of colonists who laid the foundations of the Massachusetts Bay colony. The remainder, though undoubtedly in sympathy with the main Puritan ideals, were far from always seeing eye to eye with their leaders and were always possessed of as strong a desire for land and homes as for freedom of religious thought and opportunity for religious worship. No single impulse was at work driving these men and women to cross the sea and no single group of motives was common to all who for religious reasons undertook the task of settlement. Could we penetrate the minds of the humbler folk among them, whose thoughts have remained unrecorded—the followers not the leaders in the great migration—we should doubtless find that the burdens and necessities of life determined their decisions quite as often as did high ideals in government and religion. That the great majority of them were religious in spirit and submissive to what they believed to be the will of God cannot be doubted, but discontent with the material conditions surrounding their lives was always a potent influence leading these men and women to change their environment and to hope for better things in other climes than their own.

The whole idea of colonization, as worked out by the English in America, was new. Neither Portugal, Spain, Holland, nor France had been interested to transport men, women, and children overseas for other ends than trade and profit. There were no precedents for plantations, properly so called, in which homes were erected, tillage begun, domestic life cultivated, and the means wherewith to continue a separate social and economic life brought into being. English merchants had settled on the Continent in 1407 and again in 1505 and had been granted by the crown certain privileges for the purpose of maintaining good government among themselves,[1] but such partnerships did not constitute a plantation. Roberval had in his company the makings of a plantation, but its members were of too mongrel a sort to succeed. Gilbert had planned a colony in Newfoundland, but his associates were men only, rough, undisciplined and restless, not of the sort from which thrifty law-abiding settlers are made, and his experiment came to a fatal end. Raleigh went a

1. Lucas, *The Beginnings of English Overseas Enterprise,* pp. 61–62, 86, 92.

long way farther, when in 1587 he attempted to found on American soil a colony that had within itself all the rudiments of self-perpetuation and the promise of a continuous existence. He provided families, thus assuring to the settlement, as he hoped, children and grand-children to carry on the work, and he issued instructions for political government in order to give efficiency to the management of plantation affairs. His colony had within it the seeds of permanence and had it been located in a better place, it might in time have grown into something akin to a settled, self-governing community. It contained husbands and wives, mothers and nursing children; in it births took place, baptisms were performed, letters written and tokens sent, and within its borders peaceful industry prevailed and order reigned. This early experiment was planned in the spirit of wisdom and represented a new departure in colonizing methods. Its failure was the failure of circumstance. Just how much it contributed to the later successful efforts at colonization it is impossible to say. It embodied a new idea, the idea of a plantation designed for permanent not temporary residence, the energies of which were to be devoted not merely to the finding of gold, although that hope was always present, or to the carrying on of trade, although that too was a major object in all the seventeenth century settlements, but also to the raising of crops, the breeding of stock, and the accumulation of a surplus, within a definite area of land, hitherto unoccupied, fertile, and capable of profitable tillage. In this sense Plymouth and Massachusetts Bay, although very unsatisfactory colonies from the British point of view, were farther advanced as plantations than was Virginia during the first twelve years of its existence.

A notable experiment along these lines was made in Ireland, at about the same time with the settlement of America.[1] Ireland was a fertile land, undeveloped, and near at hand. It was Roman Catholic in faith and tribal in its social structure, and in consequence invited colonization, partly as a phase of English policy, in order to introduce a Protestant element into the land, and partly as an agrarian

1. Bonn, *Die englische Kolonisation in Irland;* Cheyney, "Some English Conditions surrounding the Settlement of Virginia," *American Historical Review,* XII, 514 ff.; *History of England,* II, ch. XLIII; Bagwell, *England under the Stuarts and during the Interregnum,* 3 vols.; Maxwell, "Colonization of Ulster," *History,* July, October, 1916, pp. 86–96, 147–156; Dunlop, "Sixteenth Century Schemes for the Plantation of Ulster," *Scottish Historical Review,* January, 1925; Hill, *Plantation of Ulster;* Kernohan, *Planting of County Derry; Londonderry and the London Companies, 1609–1629* (1928); Carr, *Select Charters of Trading Companies,* pp. lxxi–lxxxiii.

necessity, in order to utilize the wide areas of land—then but sparsely occupied and tilled and commercially undeveloped under the pastoral and tribal systems—that were wanted to meet the land deficiency in England.

In the sixteenth century Queen Elizabeth and Sir Henry Sidney had been exceeding zealous for the "plantation" of Ireland, a term which meant to them the rooting out of the natives from the soil, and among the early promoters was the same Sir Humphrey Gilbert, who had been interested in the Northwest Passage and in Newfoundland. But this early effort came to nothing, and though a number of similar plans were inaugurated during the later years of Elizabeth's reign,[1] no results of importance were accomplished until after the accession of James I. The early schemes had related chiefly to Munster, though three attempts had been made to gain a footing in Ulster,[2] where a few individual grantees had tried to establish themselves and their tenants in the face of bitter opposition on the part of the tribal chiefs. But with the flight in 1607 of O'Neill and O'Donnel, earls of Tyrone and Tyrconnel,[3] and the escheating of the greater part of Ulster to the English king (an incident in Irish history that has led to prolonged controversy as to its justice), that province of the north became the center of interest. Definite plans were laid for planting English colonists there, "to the great increase of his Majesty's revenue and to settle the countries perpetually in the crown." Many of the arguments that were advanced for Irish colonization were exactly the same as those that were used in pro-

1. Dunlop, in the *Scottish Historical Review*.
2. Ulster was the strongest, richest, and most Irish of the provinces. Since the end of the sixteenth century many Scottish highlanders had settled there, led by the Macdonalds. Efforts had been made by the English to drive them out, because of the alliance which had existed at the time between Scotland and Ireland, but after the personal union of the crowns of England and Scotland in 1603, the situation changed and from that time forward Scottish migration to Ulster was encouraged. John Chamberlain wrote to Sir Dudley Carleton, January 23, 1609, "The [Privy] Council have been very busy of late how to plant Ireland with English and Scots" (Huntington Library, HM, 2904).
In the Huntington Library are many papers (Ellesmere, 1711–1741, notably no. 1736, "A Demonstration," 1602) relating to these early attempts to colonize Ireland, chiefly toward the end of Elizabeth's reign. They concern the attainted lands of Munster, the repeopling of those lands, their division into seignories, and the conditions to be imposed upon those who shared in their distribution. These papers deserve study, as the tenures introduced into Ireland were the model for those of a seignorial sort that were set up by the English in America.
3. Wilson, "Flight of the Earls," *Nineteenth Century*, 55, p. 479; Kernohan, *The Planting of the County Derry*.

moting settlement in America.[1] It was argued that once the island
was properly "planted" it would provide an outpost against Spain,
which country had several times used Ireland as a convenient point
of attack upon England; that such plantations would be a means of
relieving England of her own excess urban population and social
congestion and would offer an opportunity to reward those who had
claims upon the English king, which could not be satisfied out of
the meagre exchequer; that a new settlement in Ireland would open
a market for English goods, should tribal ways be followed by
"civilitie"; and, lastly, that the new Ireland would be a source of
wealth for England and English merchants. King James urged on
the undertaking and appointed three commissions (1608, 1609, 1610)
to advance it, considering Ireland as his special care and eager to
complete the unifying process of the three kingdoms. His interest,
however, was not so much the furthering of English expansion as
the enhancing of his own personal dignity.

Under the direction of Sir Arthur Chichester, lord deputy of Ireland, the work of "plantation" went steadily forward. Chichester
was an able man, loyal to his duty, and honestly desirous of suppressing disorder and of bringing the country as quickly as possible out
of its tribal state into one that was "regular," that is, Anglicized,
settled, and peaceful. He had the inevitable mental limitations of all
Englishmen of his day, in deeming English institutions capable of
being transferred to any part of the world and of being successfully
implanted in any land from which the native stock had been
removed. But he was gifted also with a considerable amount of intelligence and, though without sympathy for the "barbarous" Irish,
as he called them, he did believe in recognizing their ancient rights.
But in this laudable belief he was overruled by the commissioners,
whose plans took little account of native land claims. The Ulster
territory was systematically partitioned, and the process of breaking
up the Irish tribal institutions was hastened by sending out of the
country to serve in foreign wars the warrior class, the "swordsmen,"
who formed the retinue of the chieftains and managed to live largely
on their neighbors.

In promoting emigration to Ireland the Privy Council made every

1. Doubtless many of those who took part in the settlement of Virginia had had
experience in Ireland. In 1620 one Captain William Newce was encouraged by the
Virginia Company in a project to send colonists to Virginia, because he had been
successful in doing the same for Ireland. *Virginia Company Records*, I, 446–447.

effort to enlist the support of the powerful livery companies of the City of London[1]—just as the Virginia Company was doing at the same time—and in 1609 entrusted to them the settlement of Derry, henceforth to be called Londonderry. They caused to be drawn up a statement, known as the "Motives and Reasons to induce the City of London to undertake the Plantation in the North of Ireland," that contains inducements not unlike those offered the same year by the men who were engaged in colonizing Virginia. In 1613, James I granted a charter to the Londoners, under the name of the Society of the Governor and Assistants of London of the New Plantation in Ulster, which was, however, quite different from that granted to the Virginia Company in 1612, though the position of the superintendent in Ireland, Sir Thomas Philips, was in some respects similar to that of a colonial governor and the attitude of the company to the king not unlike that of a private colony in America resisting the encroachment of the royal authority.[2]

The mainstay of the Irish colonizing movement was not, however, the London companies, but the fifty-nine Scottish "undertakers," as they were called, selected by King James, who not unnaturally had a partiality for his own countrymen, from a list submitted at his request by the Scottish Privy Council. To each of these "undertakers" a grant was made of from 1000 to 3000 acres, totaling 81,000 in all. During the years from 1609 to 1625, they planted Ulster province with thousands of tenants, the ancestors of the Scots Irish or Ulster Scots of our colonial history, and they did this at a more rapid rate than the Virginia Company was able to stock Virginia. Many of those

1. Huntington Library, Ellesmere, 1740. Articles agreed upon, January 18, 1609, between the Privy Council on behalf of the king and the committee appointed by vote of the Common Council of the City of London on behalf of the Mayor and Commonalty, concerning a plantation in a part of the province of Ulster. The City was to spend £20,000, to build 200 houses in Derry, and to be ready to provide 300 more. *Londonderry and the London Companies*, pp. 13–18. Chichester Philips, the grandson of Thomas, the first superintendent, said in 1682, that his grandfather charged the society with having broken its covenants with the king and that the latter on being prosecuted was fined £60,000. Thomas Philips, his father, who conducted the prosecution, spent all his personal estate in so doing. *Calendar State Papers, Domestic*, 1682, p. 309.

2. The parallel need not be pressed too far. It was, however, noticed at the time. "A motion was made," says an entry in the record book of the Virginia Company, "that for soe much as the Companies of London . . . had adventured good sums of monny toward the Plantation in Virginia some course might be thought uppon to excite them to make some proffits of the Lands due unto them, they having alredie done the like in Ireland with verie good successe." *Virginia Company Records*, I, 489.

interested in Virginia were interested in Ireland also—Sir Thomas
Smith, Sir John Popham, and Sir Francis Bacon, the last named of
whom, though not concerned with Virginia except as a subscriber
to the stock in 1609, had been influential in securing the patent for
the London and Bristol Company for the planting of Newfoundland
in 1610.[1] Chichester remarked that he would rather labor with his
hands in Ireland than "dance and sing in Virginia," and Bacon
thought that Ireland was the more promising land of the two. It
was many years before the American colonies—distant, but little
known, and unprotected both by sea and land—were able to make
a sufficiently strong popular appeal to attract settlers in large numbers. Cromwell tried to persuade the New Englanders to migrate
to Ireland in 1650; and even as late as 1680, Sir William Petty, who
had received lands in Ireland under the Cromwellian settlement,
queried "whether it be better to transplant out of England into Ireland or America?"[2]

This attitude is not surprising, for men of the day, until well on
toward the end of the seventeenth century, had very little knowledge
of America. Of its geography, its flora and fauna, and the conditions
of life in either New England, the South, or the West Indies, they
knew vaguely if at all, for such of them as possessed information—
and the number must have been very small—acquired what they
had from sources that were never very reliable and frequently wholly
erroneous. Some may have had a measure of familiarity with the
leading topographical features, knowing of the existence of a great
western land barrier, with large rivers flowing from it into the ocean,

1. Sir Francis Bacon in his essay on plantations says that Popham labored greatly
in behalf of the Irish scheme and wisely too, since that plantation or any plantation
was valuable that made it possible for many families to receive sustentation and fortunes and for England to discharge from her own bounds and from Scotland so many
people that were they to remain they might be the cause of future trouble. "Soe," he
says addressing the king, "shall your Majesty in this work have a double commoditye
in the avoydance of people here and in the making use of them there." He lays stress
on the fact that Ireland was a weak spot in England's defense and was needed for
England's safety and that under English control it would be sure to become a source
of profit to the realm. He urges that the "undertakers" be encouraged and wishes
"a closer correspondency between the commission [in Ireland] and the Counsell of
Plantations [in England], wherein," he adds, "I warrant myself by the president
[precedent] of a like Counsell of Plantations for Virginia, an enterprise differing as
much from this [of Ireland] as Amadis de Gawle differs from Caesar's Commen-
taries." There is a manuscript copy of this essay in the Huntington Library, El. 1747,
with several variant readings.

2. Petty Papers, II, 109–110.

but even these had no comprehension of its length and its breadth. For many years even the best of them believed that through the barrier was a passage leading to the South Sea and to China, and during the entire colonial period even well-informed men were very ignorant regarding the details of physical features and boundary lines. Many, aroused by the reports of gold and silver obtained by Spain after the discovery of the mines of Potosí in 1545, dreamed of similar mines in the northern continent, and for a century their descendants sought to find them. Of the products of the soil they continued to think in terms oriental and tropical, and of animal life in terms of strange creatures both on the land and in the sea. Many of them had a more certain knowledge of the West Indies, because English seamen had been preying on Spanish towns and fleets there for thirty years before the settlement of America, and from narratives and descriptions they had doubtless acquired a fairly accurate acquaintance with Caribbean routes and waters. As time went on and new routes were discovered, charts and maps drawn, and the arts of navigation improved, knowledge increased. With the widening of the scope of commercial enterprise, capital was diverted from privateering and illegitimate trade into the channels of a sounder and more substantial business activity, and, in consequence, pictures of America became more exact and the former unreal and fantastic world, inhabited by strange beings and alive with dangers and terrifying phenomena, gradually vanished.

Men prominent in official and mercantile life began to seek, early in the seventeenth century, new opportunities for the employment of capital and saw in the West a field of commercial profit, rivaling and supplementing the advantages of the East. Through the influence of such important personages as Sir John Popham, lord chief justice of the king's bench, Sir Thomas Smith, head of the East India Company, and Sir Ferdinando Gorges, governor of the fort at Plymouth —all leaders in many public and private enterprises—attention was called for the first time to the possibility of utilizing capital for the promotion of plantations in America as well as in Ireland. Whatever had been done thus far in that direction had been the work of private individuals, depending on unassisted and unprotected private resources. Men of the Popham-Smith type, with the example of the great trading companies before them, saw the value of employing a similar form of organization—the legal chartered company—for the purpose of advancing settlement as well as trade. To them private purses were "cowld comfortes to adventures" and had been "fownde fatall to all interprices hitherto undertaken, by reason of delaies, jeloces, and unwillingnes to backe that project which succeeded not in the first attempt." They believed it "honorable for a state rather to backe an exploite by a public consent then by a private monopoly." "Where Collonies are fownded for a public-we[a]ll," these advocates continued, "ma[n]ye continewe in better obedience, and become more industrious, then where private men are absolute signors of a vioage, for-as-much as better men of haviour and qualitie will engage themselves at a publique service, which carrieth more reputacon with it, then a private, which is for the most parte ignominious in the end."[1]

This statement, by whomsoever written, was an appeal for funds, in the form of a joint-stock, and for the enlistment of organized capital and the organized company in a colonizing enterprise under the control of the state. There had been an approximation to such a plan earlier, when Gilbert, twenty years before, had invited a group of associates, chiefly of Southampton, organized on a voluntary joint-stock basis, to coöperate in a voyage of trade and colonization.[2] Raleigh, too, a few years later, apparently realizing after the failure of his last expedition that his career as a colonizer was at an end, made over (March 7, 1589) some of the privileges of his patent to nineteen merchants and others of London, among whom were Sir Thomas Smith and Richard Hakluyt.[3] These men came together and formed a voluntary joint-stock association for the purpose of accepting Raleigh's offer and furnishing merchandise, munitions, victuals, and other necessaries in exchange for rights of trade and other perquisites. Hoping to gain their support in carrying on what he had begun, Raleigh gave them £100, admitted them to the freedom of the "City of Raleigh," granted them "free trade and traffique for all manner of merchandize or commodities whatsoever" in his "seignory of Virginia"; and promised to obtain for them, if he could, legal incorporation as a trading company under royal letters patent. Though the time for a trading company to take the lead in colonizing America had not yet come, it is nevertheless significant that Raleigh or

1. Brown, *Genesis*, I, 37–38.
2. *Calendar State Papers, Colonial*, 1675–1676, §§ 18, 19.
3. Hazard, *State Papers*, I, 42–45 (taken from Hakluyt).

someone else should have conceived the idea of a company as early
as 1589 and that some of those who offered to become coöperators
in his enterprise should have been influential in bringing about the
incorporation of the Virginia Company seventeen years later. It is
quite possible that did we know the names of all the associates we
would find that more of them had a part in promoting the actual
settlement of America in 1606.

Thus the early seventeenth century presents a shifting scene and
a new outlook. Men who had turned their eyes to the East were turning them to the West as well, interested not only in the expansion of
trade but in the expansion of England also. It was a period when
much that was medieval was running concurrently with the beginnings of modern things. While clinging to the past men were also
engaging in undertakings that were opening a new and unknown
world. The times though confused resounded with activities preg-
nant with purpose and brilliant results. Political and social conditions were in a state of flux, marking a conflict between the old and
the new. Feudal tenures, adapting themselves to a new agriculture,
were altering the status of class and caste. The constitutional government of the Stuarts was entering upon its unsuccessful struggle
of eighty-five years to maintain the divinity of kingship. Medieval
methods and the medieval conception of the social order were threatened at their foundations by the forces of a new individualism; in
fact, medieval habits and standards were breaking, though they were
not yet broken and were not to be broken for many a long year.

The period was one of definite constructive effort in many directions. Capitalism and commerce, the roots and sources of the mercantilist policy, were beginning their long careers as increasingly
dominant factors in the world's affairs. Capital, to which Englishmen owed their success in the field of foreign trade, was also to be
of first importance in the field of colonization. But English capitalists
were not confining their attention merely to that narrow fringe of
territory along the Atlantic seaboard which later became the seat of
the original thirteen colonies. Breaking through the barriers that
hedged in their medieval life and with the boldness of a people released from the limitations of their insular existence, they were on
the alert to take advantage of whatever new worlds and new waters
had to offer. During the very years when Jamestown, Plymouth,
and Massachusetts Bay were being settled, venturesome men were

sailing north, south, and west across the ocean, seeking opportunities for the employment of the wealth of the day wherever they could find an opening. From the Straits of Gibraltar and the Wine islands along the African coast to the Gulf of Guinea, and from Hudson Bay to the Caribbean isles and the Orinoco and Amazon rivers they were coursing in their small craft, searching vainly for gold and profitably for trade, and enduring untold hardships in the effort to exploit the resources they believed available in these distant lands.

These unities of origin and wide-spread seagoing activities are not apparent when the colonization of America is viewed solely from the American end and their significance is lost when the subject is treated only in the American field. Those who read American colonial history in the seventeenth century merely because of their interest in the history of the United States will miss much of the charm and fascination of the story and will never be able to grasp its meaning or the place of our colonies in the general history of the time.

The following pages will show that while those who engaged in the great adventure as promoters or participants were sometimes antagonistic and competitive, they were more often coöperative, with their efforts and interests frequently interlocking at critical points. Motives were strangely different but methods were much the same, and the Englishmen who came to America did not forget that England was their native land and that they, though transplanted, were Englishmen still.

But whatever the motor power that impelled them to cross the seas, neither precursor nor pioneer, profiteer nor promoter, Pilgrim nor Puritan could have accomplished his purpose without the aid of the funds that had accumulated during this period in the hands of the capitalistic classes of southern and southwestern England. It is true that the mercantilist groups were scattered and formed but a small part of the total population of the kingdom, but they were a power in the rising towns of the south—London and the outports of the West Country—and were working together toward common ends—the increase of wealth, the financial solvency of the state, and the glory of the kingdom. Despite the diversities of origin and the divergencies of purpose among those who at this early time took part in the settlement of America—actuated as they were by commercial, religious, and proprietary aims—the colonizing movement had unity and a oneness of being largely due to the coöperative activity of the mercantile and capitalist classes. Enthusiasm, religious zeal, and stoutness of heart might stir men's souls to action, but they could not meet the material needs that overseas colonies demanded. Loftiness of purpose might override men's fears of the dimly known western lands and conquer their reluctance to embark on dangerous voyages, but they could not provide ships and equipment, employ captains and seamen, and sustain communities of settlers until these had established themselves firmly in the new soil. The Virginia Company failed because of financial difficulties; the Pilgrims might never have made their famous journey had not London merchants financed their undertaking; the settlement of Massachusetts Bay is said to have cost its promoters £200,000, largely supplied by the merchant-capitalists of the company. English-America would hardly have been settled at this time had not the period of occupation coincided with the era of capitalism in the first full flush of its power, an era, the origin of which dates from the years of Elizabeth's reign and of which we of the twentieth century may be witnessing the transformation or the end.

CHAPTER IV

PRELIMINARIES OF SETTLEMENT: SAGADAHOC

I N the year 1606 the prospects for colonization were vastly more favorable than they had been in Raleigh's day. Peace had been made with Spain; prosperity was in the air; and capital was rapidly accumulating. The joint-stock system had been given a wide test and found capable of successful application in a great variety of undertakings and was leading to a vigorous trading activity, which reached its culminating point in the period from 1613 to 1615.[1] Foreign commerce in particular was flourishing and most of the companies were doing a profitable business. Other countries, too, were forging ahead. The French had set up their Canada Company in 1602 and four years later Champlain started on the first of his famous voyages. In 1602 the Dutch combined their various independent companies engaged in the East India trade into one large and influential body, the Dutch East India Company, the complement of which was the Dutch West India Company founded twenty years later. For purposes of discovery and colonization the incorporated company, with its greater strength and resources, was contesting the place, elsewhere than in England, which up to this time had been taken by the private adventurer. Though many believed that the company was much more likely to succeed than the individual, even when the latter was aided by associates from among the merchants themselves, yet in point of fact the company as a promoter of colonization had but a short life, while private initiative was responsible for by far the greater number of the English colonies in America. Thus at the very outset of our history appear, in contrast and almost in rivalry, two forms and methods of colonization both of which were destined to play the leading parts in effecting permanent settlement in America during the ensuing seventy-five years—the private adventurer or proprietor and the incorporated company. In origin one was aristocratic and feudal and in a sense representative of the past; the other was corporate and coöperative and in a similar sense

1. Scott, *Joint-Stock Companies to 1720*, I, 141.

contributory to the future. Yet in the long run both were to succumb to the greater authority and centralizing influence of the state.

It would seem that in 1605, the year of the Gunpowder Plot, certain prominent Roman Catholics had the idea of seeking a refuge overseas, in case further penal legislation should render continued residence in England undesirable for certain of their co-religionists. This plan, carried out, would have anticipated by more than a quarter of a century the settlement of Maryland and, as it happened, by one who was closely connected with this same group of leaders. The way of it was this. In 1605, the Earl of Southampton, a Protestant, and his son-in-law, Sir Thomas Arundell,[1] a Roman Catholic, had conceived the idea of preparing a way for Roman Catholic emigration to America and sent on a voyage to "Virginia" a well known sea-captain, George Waymouth by name, who had already participated in an exploring expedition to the northwest and was a skilful and experienced mariner, engineer, and draughtsman. Waymouth sailed from the Thames on March 5, 1605, and making his way to the Azores crossed the ocean to Nantucket, where because of contrary winds he went north instead of south, finally reaching the coast of Maine in May. There he spent a month, studying the region and consorting with the Indians, and on June 16 started for England, where he arrived at Dartmouth, July 18, bringing with him five Abnakis, whom he had enticed on board his vessel. The narrator of the voyage, James Rosier, is thought by some to have been a Roman Catholic priest,[2] and the *Relation* accords well with this view. Its language has a godly ring throughout; the promoters are declared to have had as their "sole interest" the promulgating of "God's Holy Church by planting Christianity"; and the company carried crosses, which they set up, "a thing never omitted by any

1. On Arundel see Brown, *Genesis*, I, 198, 244, 245, 311, 324. Many years before, in Elizabeth's reign, a plan was set on foot to transport English Roman Catholics to America and to establish them there as a colony. This plan seems to have originated with Walsingham, a leading promoter of colonization in the New World, and was to have been carried through with the aid of Sir Humphrey Gilbert and Sir George Peckham (for documents in the case see *Calendar State Papers, Colonial, 1675–1676*, §§ 1–15, 17, 21, 22, 27–29). Peckham was a Roman Catholic sympathizer, but not an avowed convert. He was intimate with Sir Thomas Gerrard, "a notorious papist." On this attempt see Merriman, "Some Notes on the Treatment of the English Catholics in the Reign of Elizabeth," *American Historical Review*, XIII, 492–500; Conyers Read, *Sir Francis Walsingham*, III, 400. The subject has also been discussed by the Roman Catholic historians, for whom see Merriman, p. 499, note 52.

2. Baxter, *Gorges*, I, 65 ff.

Christian travelers," just as did Champlain, July, 1608, on the Isle aux Coudres in the St. Lawrence and the Maryland leaders on the island of St. Clements on March 25, 1634. The Rosier narrative has many resemblances to the *Relation* of Father White, who accompanied the Maryland settlers.[1]

This famous voyage aroused great interest in southern and southwestern England and the Indians, the first ever seen there, became veritable prodigies to those who came into contact with them. Within a few months Sir John Zouche, probably a Roman Catholic and, it may be, acting on behalf of those who had promoted Waymouth's voyage, entered into an agreement with him, according to which the latter as "chief commander" was to accompany Zouche on a voyage to "Virginia," where Sir John and "his followers" were to found a settlement in the form of a seignory, of whom, as "lord paramount," Waymouth was to hold such lands as he should select. Here was a proposal for a proprietorship of the feudal type.[2] But the plan was never carried out. Among those who were aroused by Waymouth's discoveries and Rosier's *Relation* were Gorges and Popham, who received from Waymouth the Indian captives and busied themselves "teaching and training [the Indians] to say how good that country [was] for people to go there and inhabit it."[3] They were determined to forestall the Zouche scheme, if possible, and as Popham was a declared enemy of Edward, Lord Zouche, who had married Sir John's daughter, there may have been a personal as well as a business rivalry involved.

To this end, in the year 1605, Popham and Gorges, one representing the City of London, and the other the outports, Bristol, Plymouth, and Exeter, caused to be drawn up a petition in the names of Sir Thomas Gates, Sir George Somers, Richard Hakluyt, Edward-Maria Wingfield, Thomas Hanham, Raleigh Gilbert, William Parker, George Popham, and divers others, for a charter incorporating two companies, one of London and the other of Plymouth. The first four petitioners were from the London group, the last four came from Plymouth and its neighborhood. All were iden-

1. Rosier's narrative of the Waymouth voyage has been many times printed: by Winship, *Sailors' Narratives;* Levermore, *Forerunners of the Pilgrims;* Burrage, *Gorges' Province of Maine;* and Jameson, Original Narratives Series, *Early English and French Voyages.*
2. Historical Manuscripts Commission, *Eighth Report,* II, no. 203.
3. Brown, *Genesis,* I, 46, II, 969.

tified, in one way or another, with the adventurous life of the day, and all stood together in a measure of friendship or relationship. Gates was a tried soldier and seaman, who had seen service in the Netherlands and was later to be a governor of Virginia. Somers had shared with credit in many of the raids against the Spanish possessions and, as a member of parliament for Lyme Regis, was taking a prominent part in opposing monopolies. Hakluyt was a friend of Sir Walter Raleigh and the editor of *The Principall Navigations*. Wingfield had been a comrade-at-arms with Gorges both in the Netherlands and in Ireland. Gilbert, who was thirty-three years old at this time, was the sixth and youngest son of Sir Humphrey and a nephew of Raleigh, and through his grandmother was related to the Gorges family.[1] Parker was a sea-captain and merchant of Plymouth, who had taken part in many West Indian voyages and was later to become vice-admiral of the East India fleet. He was among the merchants who had covenanted to accompany Waymouth on his proposed second voyage to "Virginia" under Sir John Zouche. George Popham was Sir John Popham's nephew and he too had made many voyages to the West Indies, on one of which, in 1594, he had captured letters from the Spaniards, which seemed to confirm the stories of the riches of Guiana and thus provided Raleigh with valuable information.[2] Hanham was Sir John Popham's grandson (probably, some have thought him his son-in-law) and was the nominal commander of one of the vessels sent in 1606 by Gorges and Popham to spy out the land of northern "Virginia," in the search for a suitable site for a colony. Thus all were more or less tied together by bonds of blood, neighborhood, or interest. As the passage of the charter through the seals was a matter of months, unless the process was especially expedited, the petition must have been presented at some time during the late summer or autumn of 1605, probably after Waymouth's return on July 18 and before Gunpowder Day, November 5. Contemporaneously a statement of "Reasons for raising a Fund" was drafted, to be offered either to the king or to parliament, which was probably directed against the Zouche project,[3] because its main object was to show the weakness of a private undertaking. This statement asked for "priviliges and lysense to trans-

1. Baxter, *Gorges*, I, 11, note.
2. "Letters taken at Sea by Captaine George Popham, 1594," printed in Harlow, *The Discoverie of Guiana by Sir Walter Raleigh*, pp. 79–80.
3. Brown, *Genesis*, I, 36–42 and notes.

porte a collonie or colonies to America," but there is nothing to show that it was ever formally presented anywhere. Unhappily the Privy Council register for the years from 1603 to 1613 was destroyed by fire in 1619 and whatever evidence it might have contained is wanting.

The petitioners were successful in their plea. The influence and persuasiveness of Popham, Gorges, Gates, and Somers were more effective than was the opposition of Zuñiga, the Spanish ambassador, who was watching proceedings and would have been only too glad to kill the project if he could. The Roman Catholics in England, whether English or Spanish, had become officially enemies of the state, because of the discovery of the Gunpowder Plot, an event which may have delayed for the moment the progress of the petition but in the end undoubtedly aided the cause of the petitioners. Way-mouth, whose sympathies in the case are not easy to understand, attempted to take himself off to Spain, "with intent as is thought," so wrote Sir Dudley Carleton to John Chamberlain, in August, 1607, "to have betrayed his friends and showed the Spaniards a means how to defeat this Virginia attempt," but he was taken before he sailed and, perhaps to win his support, the government granted him a pension of 3s 4d a day "until such time as he shall receive from his Majesty some other advancement."[1] He died probably in 1612, leaving his character a puzzle to later generations. He was a friend of Gorges and also of Sir Walter Cope,[2] a promoter of commerce and a member of most of the leading chartered companies of the day. Waymouth may have resented the success of the London and Plymouth petitioners and have made an effort to thwart their plans.

The territory named in the patent,[3] which was issued April 10,

1. He was afterward employed in the shipyard at Woolwich. Brown, *Genesis*, II, 1049.

2. In 1611 Cope and Sir Arthur Gorges were patented by the king to set up a public register office for general commerce for twenty-five years, paying a yearly rent of £40. This office was to be known as The Public Register for General [Inland] Commerce. Cope was also the Master of the Wards, the court in which later the elder John Winthrop was an attorney.

3. The charters issued to the Virginia Company were first printed by Stith in his *History of Virginia* (appendices) and then reprinted in Hening's *Statutes*, probably from the copies among the Board of Trade papers. Since that time they have been copied from Stith or Hening by Hazard, Poore, Brown, and Thorpe. They are all enrolled on the Patent Rolls in the Public Record Office, as follows: 1606, Jac. I, 4th year, 9th pars, under Gates, Somers et al; 1609, Jac. I, 7th year, 8th pars, no. 5, under Salesbury, May 23; 1612, Jac. I, 9th year, 14th pars, under Virginia, March 12. The originals are not known to exist.

1606, incorporating two Virginia Companies, one for London and one for Plymouth,[1] was that part of America, "commonly called Virginia," which either appertained to England or was deemed at the time outside the actual possession of any Christian prince or people. It lay north of the 34° of northern latitude, that is, the Cape Fear River, and extended to the 45°, which cuts the present state of Maine a little above Bangor. King James seems to have been careful to recognize the right of Spain to all land actually occupied, but he followed Elizabeth's policy of denying the validity of the bull of 1493. According to this policy Guiana, the Leeward and Windward islands in the Caribbean, and "Virginia" lay outside both the Spanish and the Portuguese spheres and were open to English colonization.[2]

The region that lay about Chesapeake Bay was known to Raleigh, who in 1587 charged John White, the leader of his colony, to find a better place for a settlement than Roanoke had proved itself to be. He instructed White to follow the coast northward to the Chesapeake and there to select a satisfactory site for the city and fort that he intended should become the nucleus of his seignory. Thus southern "Virginia" was not an unknown land. As to northern "Virginia," Waymouth had brought back glowing tales of Maine, and his Indian captives had added their quota of information, such as it was, regarding the desirability of the region. So the petitioners knew exactly what to ask for. The boundaries were drawn so as to include both ends of the territory, and in order that neither company should encroach upon the other the further provision was made that while the London or South Virginia company might settle as far north as the 41°, the latitude of New York, and the Plymouth or North Virginia company as far south as the 38°, the latitude of the Potomac, neither was to settle within a hundred miles of the other. In actual operation this arrangement created a neutral zone between the two settlements a hundred miles in width, the exact location of which would be determined by the site selected by the first company to send out a colony. As the petitioners in making out the first draft

1. The creation of two companies instead of one was undoubtedly due to the intense rivalry which prevailed at this time between London and the outports, and to the jealousy that existed among the West Country ports because of the commercial supremacy of London.

2. Williamson, *The English in Guiana*, p. 77; Brown, *First Republic*, p. 82. Hakluyt in his tract, *Virginia Richly Valued*, concedes the land south of 34° to Spain, and in another tract, *New France*, that north of 45° to France.

of the patent must have considered this question very carefully and had in all probability agreed on the places where their respective colonies were to be, it is quite likely that they intended this zone to be just where the patent placed it, between the 38th and 41st parallels, that is, roughly between New York and Washington. King James, of course, had nothing to do with the matter. Each area, thus defined, formed a section of land, which according to the wording of the patent was to extend fifty miles north along the sea coast above the first settlement and fifty miles south, one hundred miles into the interior, and one hundred miles out to sea. It was a goodly possession and the promoters expected eventually to establish a number of plantations within its borders.[1] No enterprise of just this kind had ever been started before and we may not be surprised that some experimenting was necessary before the methods most suitable for governing these distant plantations could be contrived.

Eventual success was bound to depend on the way the settlements were managed. By the charter a resident council was provided for each colony, to consist of thirteen members, empowered to have charge of all local matters and, with a president elected by themselves, to serve as the sole governing board of the colony. Superior to these local bodies was a royal council in England of a like number of members (fourteen, as it happened, at first, and twenty-six later) entrusted with a general oversight of the entire region from the Cape Fear to the Ste. Croix. The members of this superior council were appointed by the king, those of the lesser councils by the companies. Thus general political and administrative control was retained in the king's hand, a plan which accorded well with James's idea of absolute power,[2] only the actual business of settlement, trade, and maintenance being left to the companies. As the charter did not go into details, instructions were issued the following November by the king, drafted doubtless by the Privy Council or by a committee appointed for the purpose, naming the members of the royal council and laying down in very elaborate fashion the rules and regulations by means of which good order and efficient administration might be obtained.[3]

Who was responsible for the idea of the royal council is far from

1. This is expressly so stated in the commission to De la Warr, Brown, *Genesis*, I, 378.
2. McIlwain, *Political Works of James I*, Introduction.
3. Brown, *Genesis*, I, 64–75, November 20, 1606.

clear. As Sir Thomas Smith, Sir Walter Cope, Sir Francis Popham (eldest son of the lord chief justice), Sir Ferdinando Gorges, and sundry merchants of London, Plymouth, and Bristol were among the first members of that council, it might be thought that the instructions as well as the first draft of the charter itself were the work of the original group of promoters. But as far as the West Country petitioners and the merchants generally are concerned this does not appear to be true. The deputy mayor of Plymouth wrote to the Earl of Salisbury, May 10, 1606, saying that the appointment of a royal council was distasteful to the merchants of that town, because "strangers to us and our proceedings," and this letter was followed up by another from Gorges to Robert Cecil, confirming the deputy mayor's statement, including among the protestants merchants of Exeter, Bristol, and London, and saying that because of the addition of a royal council they were unwilling to proceed any further. From these letters it is evident that neither Gorges nor the merchants were in favor of a council in England, and that therefore the suggestion must have come from Popham (as indeed is implied in Gorges' letter) or from some of the king's advisers.[1] Now we know that before the first charter passed the seals the text was undoubtedly scrutinized by Attorney General Coke and Solicitor General Dodderidge and had the great seal affixed by Lord Chancellor Ellesmere, the three men who, with Popham, were the greatest lawyers of the day. Coke, though a common law lawyer, a House of Commons man, and a champion of the outports as against London, was in sympathy, as was Sir Francis Bacon, with a measure of royal control and must have acquiesced in the provisions of the charter which gave the king full right to change the membership of the royal council when he pleased and to pardon offenders, grant land, and issue such further instructions as suited the royal will. It would have been little short of amazing if, in making provision for the government of this great area of royal territory, the first *terra regis* in the New World, the king should have been willing to divest himself of all right to intervene in its affairs.

On the other hand Popham and Coke, representatives of the common law, saw to it that the privileges of the colonists were well guarded. The latter, Englishmen going into a strange land, might well have been deemed, as were the colonists of Spain and France,

1. Baxter, *Gorges,* III, 122–126.

beyond the law as they were beyond the bounds of the kingdom. Instead of that, they and their children were expressly guaranteed all "liberties, franchises, and immunities" under the law that Englishmen were at the same time enjoying at home. These included trial by jury, benefit of clergy, and all the rights of possession and inheritance of land as in England. The new lands in America were legally a part of the king's demesne and were held as of a royal manor in England—in this case the manor of East Greenwich in Kent—in free and common socage, thus making it clear that though the new colonies might be outside the realm—as far as the payment of customs dues went and representation in parliament was concerned—they were within the realm in all that pertained to their legal and tenurial rights. Englishmen passing beyond the sea were Englishmen still, with an Englishman's safeguards and restrictions.[1]

1. Older writers, particularly in New England and Virginia, found in the words "liberties, franchises, and immunities" something akin to universal human rights. No such interpretation is possible. The words are to be taken literally, as meaning just what they were understood to mean in England at that time. They have nothing to do with civil liberty, self-government, or democracy; they were strictly legal, tenurial, and financial in their application.

A similar error of understanding is to be seen in the interpretation of the phrase, "as of the manor of East Greenwich," found in our early charters. Despite the belief of some of the New England colonists themselves and of later writers on New England history, the phrase had nothing to do with gavelkind or any other form of land tenure than that of "free and common socage." It had nothing to do with the tenure of East Greenwich or of Kent, as such. Lands granted in America were to be held of the king, as if they were parts of the manor of East Greenwich, or of Windsor, or of Hampton Court, or, it might be, of any other of the king's manors on ancient demesne. In Ireland lands were as held as of Carregrotion, or of Trim, or of Limerick, or of the castle of Dublin (*Calendar Patent Rolls, Ireland, Henry VIII*, p. 7; *Elizabeth*, pp. 275, 327; *Calendar State Papers, Carew, 1603–1624*, p. 2, etc.). The phrase was merely used descriptively, in the sense that no part of the *terra regis*, wherever found, could legally be conceived except as constructively belonging to a royal manor in England. It is interesting to note that when Charles II made over Bombay to the East India Company, he granted the island in free and common socage, as of the manor of East Greenwich. In granting Maine to Gorges, the king reserved "a tenure in socage as of his Majesties Mannor of East Greenwich" (Libby, *Maine Provincial and Court Records*, I, xviii), which comes to the same thing. The Bermuda Company made similar grants in Bermuda, to be held of the king as of the manor of East Greenwich in free and common socage (Lefroy, *Memorials of the Bermudas*, I, 551), and Dongan was following the same rule in New York, when he granted land in 1685 to Wyntie Allardts in Esopus to be held of the king by the same tenure (Huntington Library, Unaccessioned). East Greenwich was a favorite manor of the crown; lands were granted in England itself (Northumberland) as of that manor (*Calendar Treasury Books, 1672–1675*, IV, 399); and many royal proclamations were "Given at our Mannour of Greenwich."

Had the intention been to reproduce the precedents and practices of a particular

Despite the many pious phrases that the charter contains regarding the preaching of Christianity to the savages, the new undertaking was strictly a commercial enterprise and the early instructions concern themselves largely with the way the enterprise was to be carried on. The companies were authorized to invite and carry over adventurers, search for mines, and coin money. For the first five years all goods and merchandise sent from England were to be stored in a company warehouse or magazine in the colony, under the charge of a manager or cape-merchant, aided by two clerks to keep record of all articles taken in or given out, and these articles were to be retailed to the colonists according to need. The latter were to take an oath of allegiance to the king[1] and to promise to obey all laws set down regarding trade, in which others than the colonists might have a share, after paying a license fee of two and a half per cent in the case of Englishmen and of five per cent in the case of foreigners, but no direct trade was to be allowed with any foreign country. This arrangement was to last for twenty-one years. That the scope of the enterprise was wider than the territories allotted for the settlements appears from the emphasis laid on the discovery of a passage to the South or "East Indian" Sea, for in the second set of instructions from the royal council the adventurers were advised to choose for their settlement the river running farthest into the interior and in case this river had two branches to select the one which

manor, the phrase would have been "according to the tennour of" or "according to the customs of" and would not have been used in the case of a grant of land but only of the erection of a manor, as of Tisbury and St. George on Long Island, for example (Eberlein, *Manors and Homes of Long Island,* where the texts are printed). When Gorges granted lands (not erected manors) in Maine, the phrase was "as of his Honour, Mannour, Lordship, or House" in free and common socage (*York Deeds,* I).

The suggestion has been made, and with excellent reason, that the term *ut de manore* (as of the manor) stands in contrast with the phrase *ut de corona* (as of the crown), meaning that the territory was held of the manor and not of the crown, and so was liable to the minimum of exactions, lighter than those to which the chief tenants of the crown were subject. In this sense such granted territories were, so to speak, in the favored class of feudal tenancies, held by the easiest tenure (Barnes, "Tenure in English Charters," *Essays in Colonial History,* pp. 4–10).

1. "The first Virginia charter and the instructions accompanying it illustrate admirably the prevailing legal ideas regarding colonization, based on the old feudal principle that allegiance is inalienable. According to this principle a colony could not be an independent community but must be in the king's hand" (Wallace, *Transactions,* Royal Historical Society, 2d ser. X, 59–64). On the commercial side, the instructions are merely a composite of practices familiar to the trading companies, adapted to a situation that was in part old and in part new.

"bendeth most toward the northwest, for that way you shall soonest find the other sea." "You must observe if you can," so runs the instruction, "whether the river on which you plant doth spring out of the mountains or out of lakes; if it be out of any lake, the passage to the other sea will be the more easy, and is like enough that out of the same lake you shall find some spring which runs the contrary way toward the East Indian Sea; for the great and famous rivers of Volga, Tanis and Dwina have three heads near joyned and yet the one falleth into the Caspian Sea, the other into the Euxine Sea, and the third into the Polonian Sea." So much for the geographical knowledge obtained from the trading experiences of the Muscovy Company. If certain conditions prevailed in Russia, why might they not equally well prevail in America?

The companies were to provide money for the equipping and furnishing of ships and were to secure such men as the council approved, willing to make the venture. Just how the money was to be raised or how far the companies were to control the trade of the colonies are points not made clear, either in the charter or the instructions. Probably each company assumed a corporate character in order to provide a common stock from the contributions of its own members. There is nothing to show that the public was invited to purchase shares. For that reason, the organization was rather of the semi-joint-stock variety than the joint-stock, as each voyage was expected to pay for itself. Should the first voyage fail either a second stock would have to be raised or the attempt given up, and men venturing as colonists might find themselves stranded in a new and strange world without certainty of support from home. As the royal council had superior authority but no financial responsibility and as the companies had no administrative control and were responsible only to a limited extent for maintenance, it is evident that the securing of suitable colonists and the building up of a self-supporting and profitable colony was likely, at best, to be a difficult matter. In fact it seems probable, as eventually proved to be the case, that only men of the familiar rough, venturesome type would be found willing to take part, and they were not of the sort, as Gilbert and others had found to their sorrow, from which good and reliable settlers are made. Thus at the very outset the form of control provided by the charter was not well adapted to promote a successful colonizing movement, and it is not to be wondered at that the first attempt should have been a failure.

As Popham and Gorges were the leaders of the undertaking, they were naturally the first to take advantage of the opportunity which the charter afforded. Popham at this time was seventy-five years old, but Gorges was in the prime of life, about forty. Popham, a far abler man intellectually than Gorges, was largely, if not entirely, responsible for the idea of a public plantation as against a private venture and had lent the weight of his great influence at Whitehall to the securing of the patent, of which he was, doubtless, the chief author. But Gorges at forty was more virile and active than Popham at seventy-five and naturally was the one who took the initiative in sending out the first expedition and in selecting northern Virginia as the place for the experiment. He was a West Country man, had lived for years in the heart of the Devonshire district, which was the center of England's seafaring life, and was not only filled with zeal for the cause of colonization but had been deeply impressed both with the results of Waymouth's voyage and with the Indians whom Waymouth brought over. "The longer I conversed with them," he said later, "the better hope they gave me of those parts where they did inhabit as proper for our uses, especially when I found what goodly rivers, stately islands, and safe harbors those parts abounded with, being the special marks I leveled at as the only ones our nation met with in all their navigation along that coast, and having kept them full three years I made them able to set me down what great rivers ran up into the land, what men of note were seated on them, what power they were of, how allied, what enemies they had."[1]

Gorges was a royalist and a prerogative man of the Raleigh type and he never progressed in political thought beyond the traditions and customs of the central and local governments under which he lived or conceived of a colony in any proper sense of the term. When later he was dissociated from the influence of Popham and the London merchants he gave expression more freely to his sympathies as a believer in the feudal seignory as the best form of tenurial and social structure that a plantation should take. He cannot justly be called, as has sometimes been done, the father of American colonization, for he accomplished nothing of first importance that was destined to be permanent. On the other hand, in courage and persistence, he was better than the men of the Raleigh type, and in character and honorableness far above the average mercenary adventurer of Elizabeth's reign. He never sought his "owne profit," he

1. "A Description of New England," Baxter, *Gorges*, II, 9.

says in his *Description of New England,* "my ends being to make perfect the thorough discovery of the Country (wherein I waded so far with the helpe of those that joyned with me) as I opened the way for others to make their gaine, which hath been the meanes to encourage their followers to prosecute it to their advantage."[1] He can well be called the grand old man of our period of early settlement.[2]

The patent of 1606 was issued on April 10, and in August of the same year Popham and Gorges, in conjunction with others of the Plymouth company, victualed, outfitted, and despatched the *Richard of Plimouth,* Henry Challons, commander, Nicholas Hine, master, and John Stoneman, who had been with Waymouth and was to write a narrative of the voyage,[3] as pilot. They were ordered to make a "farther discovery of the coasts" and, if good occasion offered, to leave as many men as could be spared to occupy the ground. Taking a southerly course, contrary to instructions, they were driven by adverse winds farther than they intended, found themselves among the Windward Islands, and, in endeavoring to return, were captured by a Spanish fleet in the neighborhood of Porto Rico.[4] At Seville, to which city they were taken, they were examined as to the "manner and situation of the Countrie of Virginia" and strenuous but unsuccessful efforts were made to persuade Stoneman to furnish descriptions and maps of the coast and other parts of the region. They remained in prison for some three months or more, when Stoneman and a few others, the remainder apparently being sent to the galleys, succeeded in obtaining their liberty and made their way back to Plymouth. There Stoneman "shewed unto Sir Ferdinando Gorges and divers others the Adventurers the whole discourse of their unhappy Voyage, together with the miseries that we had and did endure under the Spaniards hands."[5]

Thus the first voyage set on foot for the spying out of the land

1. "A Description of New England," Baxter, *Gorges,* II, 69–70.
2. For a few new facts about Gorges, see *Maine Provincial and Court Records,* I, xlviii–lii.
3. There are two accounts of the voyage, one, the longer, by Stoneman (Brown, *Genesis,* I, 127–139), the other, sent by Cecil to Gorges, by Daniel Tucker, the factor or cape-merchant (Baxter, *Gorges,* III, 129–132). The first is commonly considered the more authoritative. Tucker's experiences were cited in parliament in 1607 (Stock, *Debates,* I, 11). Tucker himself was prominently connected with both Virginia and Bermuda and died in the latter island in 1625 (Brown, *Genesis,* II, 1033).
4. Gorges' "Description," Baxter, *Gorges,* II, 10.
5. Brown, *Genesis,* I, 137–139.

preparatory to an attempt at settlement, came to an untimely end. Happily, however, a second vessel, in which Popham particularly was interested,[1] proved more successful. Sent in October, under Thomas Hanham, commander, and Martin Pring, an experienced seaman of Bristol, it went directly across the ocean and reached safely the coast of Maine. Thence it brought back glowing accounts of the country and, what was more to the point, "the most exact discovery of that coast [so Gorges wrote] that ever came into my hands." This "wrought such an impression upon the Lord Chiefe Justice [Popham] and us all that were his associates, that (notwithstanding our first disaster) we set up our resolution to follow it with effect, and that upon better grounds, for as yet our authority was but in motion." The London company had already started its vessels for southern Virginia, the December before the return of Hanham and Pring, and it was high time for the Plymouth company to show its hand. Consequently, at the end of May, 1607, two ships were got ready, the *Gift of God* and the *Mary and John,* one commanded by George Popham, a near kinsman of the chief justice, and the other by Raleigh Gilbert (whose captain was John Havercombe), the two men who, with the elder Gorges, were the actual promoters of the expedition, both members of the Plymouth company and supposed to be experienced navigators.

These vessels set sail, one from Plymouth on May 1 and the other from the Lizard on June 1, carrying one hundred and twenty men, among whom were two of the Indians to act as guides and interpreters. Following the customary route by way of the Azores, with favoring winds, under pleasant skies and without serious mishaps, they reached the coast of Maine, where they came together on August 7 and anchored near Georges Island, seven miles north of Monhegan, at the mouth of the Kennebec. On the island they found the cross that Waymouth had set up, and there their minister, the Rev. Richard Seymour, a cousin of Gilbert and Sir Ferdinando, delivered a sermon, the first preached in New England. Seven days later, the *Gift of God* entered the Sagadahoc, while the *Mary and John,* having overshot the entrance, arrived two days afterward. A short distance up the river, they made choice of a fit place for a plantation— later called Sabino or Popham Beach—heard another sermon, listened to the reading of the patent, and then for the first time learned the names of those who had been placed in authority over them. For

1. Gorges' "Description," Baxter, *Gorges,* II, 11.

the next two months all the colonists labored at the building of a fort, upon which they mounted twelve pieces of cannon and within which they constructed, one after the other, a storehouse, a church, and some fifteen dwellings.[1] In addition, the carpenters framed "a pretty pinnace of about thirty tons, which they called the Virginia," the first vessel built by the English in America. This pinnace was to see service later in the southern colony.[2]

But the settlement did not prosper. As Gorges wrote to the Earl of Salisbury, the chief causes were the insufficiency of the food supply to carry the colonists through the winter and the "childish factions, ignorant timerous and ambitious persons" who "bread an unstable resolution and a general confusion in all theyre affairs . . . for first [he adds], the President [of the council, George Popham] himselfe is an honest man but auld [he was fifty-three] and of an unwieldly body, and timerously fearful to offende or contest with others that will or do oppose him, but otherwise a discreete careful man. Captayne Gilbert [aged twenty-four] is described to me from thence to bee desirous of supremacy and rule, a loose life, prompt to sensuality, little zeal in religion, humerouse, head stronge, and of small judgment and experience, otherwayes valient inough."[3] Furthermore, Gilbert may have had ulterior motives looking to the control of the colony, because of a claim based on his father's charter of 1578, and he may have been planning to obtain "divers of his friends [from England] to com[e] for him, for the strengthening of his party." But circumstances thwarted his designs, whatever they may have been.

On October 6, 1607, the *Mary and John,* having discharged her "vyttuals" was sent back to England to report and obtain more supplies, and the intention was to send back the *Gift of God* also, as soon as she had done the same and taken on a shipment of masts, thus showing that the original plan of those who fathered the expedition was to make the settlement a permanent one. But because of a threatened attack by the French, the latter vessel, required to watch

1. A plan of this fort and the other buildings may be found in Brown, *Genesis,* I, 190–191. It was sent by Zuñiga to Philip II, in a letter of September 10, 1608.

2. "Relation of a Voyage to Sagadahoc," *Early English and French Voyages* (Original Narratives Series); Burrage, *Gorges' Province of Maine.* The pinnace must have been unusually well built and the shipwrights competent men, for it made the voyage back to England before going into the service of the Virginia Company of London.

3. Baxter, *Gorges,* III, 158.

and ward, did not get away until two months later, December 16. After a disastrous voyage, full of trouble and excitement, it reached England and brought discouraging reports of the progress of the settlement.[1] The winter had proved, as is not uncommon in Maine, "extreme unseasonable and frosty" and supplies had been scarce, though the general health conditions appear to have been on the whole good. But the main trouble lay with the character of the settlers and the petty factional quarreling that went so far as to be observed even by the Indians. Popham wrote of the idleness of the men, their disregard for the public good, their divisions into parties, and their disgraceful personal conduct.[2] In consequence, he said, they had lost the respect even of the natives, who concealed their furs and other commodities and refused to do business. It was the same old story of beginning a settlement the wrong way—sending men only, of poor character and low ambitions, lawless and impatient of discipline. Not of such was a successful colony eventually to be made, and the Sagadahoc experiment was practically doomed to failure at the start. The miracle is that the Virginia settlement, begun in the same manner, ever survived. Happily it was resuscitated at the last moment, as we shall see later.

Calamity followed calamity. Ten days after the *Mary and John* left the Lizard, Sir John Popham died and in February of the next year his relative in the colony, George Popham, died also. Half of the original settlers had returned in the *Gift of God,* so that but forty-five were left to keep the settlement going, a number that apparently was never increased by additions from home. Sometime during the winter the storehouse and a number of the dwellings were burned, with loss of provisions and equipment that could ill be spared, and although new supplies—"victualles, armes, instruments and tools"—were sent in the *Mary and John,* when she returned the next year, and the associates in England showed no intention of deserting the enterprise, the colonists in Sagadahoc were in no mood

1. Much light has been thrown on the history of the *Gift of God* by Dr. Banks' discovery of documents among the papers of the High Court of Admiralty, "Popham c. Havercombe," Libel File, 73, nos. 274, 279, and accompanying papers among the interrogatories and examinations. See "New Documents relating to the Popham Expedition, 1607," *Proceedings,* American Antiquarian Society, October, 1929.

2. Baxter, *Gorges,* III, 161. Dr. Banks has recovered the names of only nineteen of those who took part in the expedition, many of whom were of the crews and so returned to England with their vessels.

to remain. When, therefore, Gilbert heard of the death in England of his elder brother, Sir John, and of his own accession to the Gilbert inheritance there, and received letters requiring his presence as the heir-at-law, he determined to return. There was no one to take his place and as the others had no attachment to the country or desire to continue in it, the decision was reached to abandon the undertaking entirely. "And this was the end of that northern collony upon the river Sachadehoc." It had never been a true colony. Though houses were built, gardens planted, and vegetables raised, the settlement was never more than a trading post, defended by incompetent and restless men, located in an uncongenial climate, and surrounded by Indians, whose friendship was never gained. Unable to secure adequate returns on their investment, for no mines were discovered and the native commodities available for barter proved very meagre, the associates in England, already aggrieved by the erection of the royal council in London under the charter of 1606, and discouraged by the death of Sir John Popham, were quite unwilling to throw away more money on a profitless venture that bore so unpromising an outlook. Had there been a few John Smiths among the settlers and had a hopeful staple like tobacco been discovered or had the Plymouth company had the strength and resources of the London company, then the first colony in New England might have turned out differently. But even that eventuality is doubtful, unless the personnel of the colony had been radically changed, and family life, private property, and a self-sufficing agriculture had become an integral part of its organization.

The Sagadahoc experiment had failed. For many years to come no Englishman, other than the fishermen already there, remained on the coast of Maine or became permanent planters. But the region was not an empty world. Even if there were no tobacco or other similar staple indigenous to the soil, there were inexhaustible "staples" in the woods and in the sea. From this time on men sought the coast and waters of Maine for furs and fish, and of the two the latter was at the beginning far the more important and profitable, because the European demand for fish was insistent and continuous. Hardy fishermen from England's West Country, and from Holland, Brittany, and the Basque provinces of France and Spain[1] had been

1. The French Basques, with their seaport at St. Jean de Luz, and the Spanish Basques or Guipuzcoans, with their seaport at San Sebastian, were undoubtedly among the earliest to frequent these waters, and were records extant could probably be traced

frequenting these waters, as well as those of Nova Scotia and New-foundland, for nearly a century at least, and still continued to do so in greater and greater numbers. Now that plantation-making had proved unsuccessful, the Plymouth Company, or such part of it as had the heart to persist, turned its attention to the fisheries. After 1608 Sir Francis Popham "having the ships and provisions which re-mained of the company and supplying whatever else was necessary for the purpose, sent several times to the coasts for trade and fish-ing,"[1] and John Smith says, as of the year 1608, that Popham "sent divers times one Captaine Williams to Monahegan only to trade and make corefish,[2] but for any plantation there was no more speeches." His ships were still frequenting these waters in 1614.[3]

There were also many other ships off the Maine coasts from London and the West Country and vessels were sent there even from Jamestown, Plymouth, and Massachusetts Bay to share in this profit-able business.[4] The Maine waters must have presented a busy scene during these years, filled as they were with vessels of at least four nationalities, whose fishermen set their stages and dried their catch on the nearby shores of Monhegan, Damariscove, and Pemaquid, and made, according to Smith's account, fourteen pounds a voyage to the common man, while the Dutch and French ships "made won-derful returns in furs."[5] Phinehas Pratt, at Damariscove in 1622, saw men belonging to a ship fishing there, who had "newly set up a maypole and were very merry,"[6] thus anticipating the famous maypole at Merrymount by six years.

The life of these fishermen was hard and rough and there is no doubt that many of these trading and fishing posts were centers of

back for two or three centuries earlier. Brereton, *Briefe and True Relation*, mentions a "Baske-shallop" in 1602; Champlain met Basques up the St. Lawrence as far as Tadoussac in 1610 (Original Narratives Series, *Champlain*, p. 178); the Pilgrims saw "Biskay shalops, fitted with both sails and ores," in 1623 (*American Historical Review*, VIII, 295); and the son of Sir William Alexander found at Cape Breton a Basque bark of 60 tons in 1629 (Insh, *Scottish Colonial Schemes*, p. 221). Later references to Basques in the *Calendar of State Papers, Colonial* are quite frequent. Prowse in his *History of Newfoundland* has an excellent appendix on the Basques, pp. 47–49. Also below, pp. 300–303.

1. Baxter, *Gorges*, I, 207.
2. Wet fish in bulk, undried and unsalted. See p. 302.
3. Smith, *Travels and Works* (Bradley-Arber ed.) I, 188; II, 697.
4. *American Historical Review*, VIII, 295–301; *Virginia Company Records*, I, 504.
5. Smith, *Travels and Works*, I, 265. At this time Smith had left Virginia and was an ardent "booster" for New England.
6. Pratt's Narrative, printed in Levermore, *Forerunners of the Pilgrims*, II, 809.

drinking, gambling, immorality, roguery, and other habits and practices characteristic of the business. Up the rivers were trading stations, where men exchanged trinkets, knives, hatchets, cloths, and
liquor for skins and where they made profits won either honestly
or dishonestly as the case might be. Some of the Maine fishing stages
were fairly permanent—as on the islands of Damariscove and Monhegan, and at Pemaquid point—where men lived during the winter,
either the fishermen themselves or servants employed to hold the
places. Vessels from all countries stopped at these settlements to
obtain water, salt, and fuel or to refit and repair, and those from
France and Spain frequently brought the fishermen wine, wherewith
to enliven their hearts or to drown their troubles. We know that in
1616–1617 Richard Vines, an early captain, explorer, and settler in
Maine,[1] spent one whole winter at Winter Harbor, the mouth of the
Saco, in order to show that life there was quite possible, and it is
evident that from this time on the region become a busy center of
trade. Vines had been in the country off and on since 1609, acting
as Gorges' agent, and he and others must have made many trips
back and forth between England and the Maine coast.

During the lean years in the history of the Plymouth settlement
the Maine waters were a veritable godsend to the Pilgrims. So profitable was the fishing and so characteristically generous were the fishermen that when in the year 1622, the colony, in need of food, for
want of which, says Winslow, "I have seen men stagger by reason
of faintness," sent the latter to the northward for aid, he found "only
entertainment and good respect with a willingness to supply all
wants." They would not, he adds, "take any bills for the same, but
did what they could freely, wishing their store had been such as they
might in greater measure have expressed their own love and supplied our necessities, for which they sorrowed; provoking one another to the utmost of their abilities."[2] Indeed these northern fishermen played a not unimportant part in the history of New England
in coöperating with the colonies to the southward and in emergencies aiding with supplies. At this time and for long afterwards, the
activities of the people of New England centered more largely on
fish than on furs and there can be but little doubt that the reputation

1. On Vines, Pope, *Pioneers of Maine and New Hampshire*, pp. 214–215; Banks,
History of York, I, index.
2. "Good Newes from New England," in Young's *Chronicles of the Plymouth
Colony*, pp. 11, 51.

in London and Western England of the richness of the cod-fishery in these waters played its part in drawing the Pilgrims thither. Fishing led to temporary occupation of the land and from that beginning a permanent occupation was likely to follow. The work of the Virginia Company of Plymouth, unproductive as it seemed to be, was not without its influence in the history of the settlement of America.

CHAPTER V

THE SETTLEMENT OF VIRGINIA

IN the meantime the Virginia Company of London had been forwarding its own plans for establishing a settlement in the southern part of the great "Virginia" tract. Raising its funds in a manner probably similar to that employed by the Plymouth Company, it despatched three vessels, the *Sarah Constant,* the *Goodspeed,* and the *Discovery,* on December 20, 1606, under Captain Christopher Newport, in sole charge and command "until such time as they shall fortune to land upon the said coast of Virginia."[1] These vessels are believed to have been hired of the Muscovy Company, and, as was the case with many another sea captain of the day, Newport was a sort of sailor of fortune, ready to enter the service of any group of men that wanted him. During the years from 1606 to 1611, first in the employ of the Virginia Company and later in that of the East India Company, he made five voyages to Virginia, thus laying the foundation of a distinguished career.

The vessels took the southern route by way of the Azores and Canary Islands, cruised for some time among the West Indies from Martinique to Porto Rico, and then bore northward, as many a later vessel was accustomed to do, through the Mona Channel to the Capes. On the 26th of April, the voyagers "descried the land of Virginia,"[2] and the same day entered the Chesapeake. Shortly afterward they set up a cross at a point which they named Cape Henry, in honor of the king's eldest son, whose lamentable death five years later deprived the throne of its ablest successor. After many strange experiences with the natives, they entered the James River, at the head of which they set up another cross and proclaimed King James of England "to have the most right unto it"; and then on May 24, having after some discussion decided on a site—that of the future Jamestown—they disembarked, only one hundred and five out of the one hundred and forty-four who started on the voyage.[3] Immediately these men began the erection of a fort, within which eventually they built dwellings and a church, just as the other company

1. Brown, *Genesis,* I, 76.
2. Percy, "Observations," *Virginia* (Original Narratives Series), p. 9.
3. Smith, *Travels and Works,* I, cxxix.

was to do at Sagadahoc.[1] Then too, as was done at Sagadahoc, following the custom established by the East India Company, they opened the sealed box containing their instructions and learned for the first time the names of their council—Captain Newport, Captain Gosnold, Edward-Maria Wingfield, John Smith, John Ratcliffe, John Martin, and George Kendall. Later, Wingfield was chosen president and Gabriel Archer, secretary or recorder. Fortunately, the instructions for the Virginia colonists have been preserved,[2] though those for Sagadahoc have been lost, but there can be little doubt that *mutatis mutandis* the two documents were the same, and that the plans for the two settlements were in all respects identical. Under these instructions the colony was governed for the first two years. They provided for a local council with a president, who had no other prerogatives than to preside and cast a double vote in case of a tie. The council could depose the president and expel any member by majority vote, and at the very beginning it exercised this privilege by excluding John Smith, because he was charged with having been mutinous on the voyage. Thus even before the settlement was fairly under way trouble began to brew, and it was only by the intercession of the preacher, the Rev. Mr. Hunt, that Smith, on June 20, was finally restored to his place.[3]

The circumstances attending the settlement of Virginia differed in no essential particular from those attending the attempts at settlement on the Amazon, in Guiana, in Newfoundland, and at Sagadahoc. The contemporary idea of colonization had advanced no further than to conceive of settlement in terms of ships, reasonably well equipped and captained, of hardy men sufficient in number but of any class or quality, drawn together in part by the prospect of gold or plunder and in part by the need of employment, and of supplies adequate for the purpose in hand. The early desire to obtain wealth from mythical mines or Spanish plate fleets, though far from spent, was yielding place to the wiser design of promoting trade in the commodities of the country, fish and furs chiefly, and of creating a legitimate barter. The first Virginia settlers had hardly progressed

1. As at Sagadahoc, they were instructed not to settle near the coast, lest the Spaniards attack them (Brown, *Genesis*, I, 81–82). For the topographical history of Jamestown, see S. H. Yonge, "The site of Old 'James Towne,' 1607–1698," *Virginia Magazine*, XI, XII, later issued as a separate volume, 2d edition, 1907, and Tyler, *Cradle of the Republic*, 2d edition, 1906, and their maps. Also *Virginia Magazine*, XI, 322–327.

2. Brown, *Genesis*, I, 76–77.   3. Smith, *Travels and Works*, I, 92–93.

beyond this point. They were not above gold and plunder and were interested in barter with the Indians, but neither they nor the company in England had yet learned in the hard school of experience the fundamental lesson that a colony to be successful and permanent must be self-supporting, that it must raise its own food, and render itself independent of supplies furnished by the promoters at home.[1] The men who settled Jamestown were not of the kind to plough and cultivate the soil, and before the first supply had come from England in January, 1608, they had exhausted their provisions, already heavily depleted by the five months' voyage, and were obliged to live on what the natives provided and the woods furnished. Captain Newport went back to England five weeks after his arrival, and from that time until his return with additional men and provisions, the settlement was the scene of endless quarrels, bickerings, and plots, which culminated finally in the execution of Captain Kendall for hatching a mutiny. Sickness and death prevailed and before the end of the year there were only thirty-eight men alive in the colony. The tale of these seven months is a ghastly epic of misfortune.

After the arrival of the first "supply" on January 4, 1608,[2] conditions improved, owing in part to Smith's presidency of the council, from September, 1608, to July, 1609,[3] and in part to a second "supply" which came in October, 1608, with more immigrants, among whom were artisans and laborers, and one gentlewoman and her maid. Buildings which had been burned down the previous year—the storehouse, church, and probably some of the dwellings—were rebuilt and attempts were made to manufacture glass, pitch, tar, and potash, to split lumber for clapboards, and to dig and plant some forty acres of ground. The colonists also began to raise chickens and livestock;[4] but it was only by threatening to drive the slackers out

1. The Puritan explanation of the failure of these early efforts at colonization rests on the belief that the former promoters committed three "great and fundamentall errors": the main end was carnal not religious; the first promoters employed unfit instruments—a multitude of rude and misgoverned persons, the very scum of the land; and the failure to establish a right form of government. *Winthrop Papers*, II, 143. Except that successful colonization need not necessarily be religious in purpose, the Puritans were right in their estimate.

2. Brown, *Genesis*, I, 172-177.   3. Smith, *Travels and Works*, I, 121.

4. *Ibid.*, 154. The following letter, never before printed to my knowledge, is of interest here, as showing one aspect of the colony's activities at this time.

"Capt. Peter Wyn to Most Noble Knight [Sir John Egerton] from James Towne in Virginia, Nov. 26, [1609].

I was not so desirous to come into this country as I am now willing here to end my days for I finde it a farr more pleasant and plentifull country than any report made

of the fort to starve in the wilderness that Smith compelled the drones among them to bear their share of the burden.[1]

However at best the experiment was not succeeding and the company in England became convinced from the reports of Newport, who was back from this third voyage,[2] and also from the accounts of the returned councillors, Wingfield, Archer, and Ratcliffe, that if the colony were to prosper its government would have to be radically changed. It saw that placing the control of the colony in the hands of a group of councillors, liable to faction and dispute, was leading to continued mismanagement, and it did not want a repetition of the failure at Sagadahoc. In the winter of 1608 and 1609 the company carefully considered the whole situation and reached the conclusion that there were two causes of the trouble: first, the length and danger of the voyage by way of the West Indies; and secondly, the form of government both at home and in the colony. To meet the first difficulty, the company determined to find a shorter way to Virginia, and to meet the second, decided to renew the charter and to obtain "such ample and large priviledges and powers" as to make it possible "to reforme and correct those [inconveniences] already discovered and to prevent such as in the future might threaten [the

mencon of. Upon the River wch we are seated I have gon six or seven score miles and so far is navigable. Afterwards I travailed between 50 or 60 myles by land into a country called Monacon who owe no submission to Powatan. This land is very high ground and fertill, being very full of very delicate springs of sweet water. The ayre more helthful than the place where we are seated, by reason it is not subject to such foggs and mists as we continually have. The people of Monacon speak a fair differing language from the subjects of Powatan, theyr pronunciation Being very like Welch so that the gentlemen in our Company desired me to be theyr Interpreter. The comodities as yet known in this country, whereof ther will be great store, in Pitch, Tarr, Sope-Ashes, and some dyes, whereof we have sent examples. As for things more precious I omit till tyme (which I hope will be shortly) shall make manifest work of it. As concerning yor request of Bland hounds I cannot Learne that ther is any such in this Country; only the doggs wch are here are a certayne kind of Currs like o^r mariners hey doggs in England; and they keep them to hunt theyr land foxes and Turkeys and such like, for they keep nothing tame about them." (Huntington Library, El., 1683. For a reference to this first journey into the interior of Virginia see Brown, *Republic*, p. 69). I am indebted to the authorities of the Huntington Library for permission to print a number of documents from their collections.

1. Smith, *Travels and Works*, I, 156–157; Brown, *Genesis*, I, 201–203, 205.

2. An entry in one of John Chamberlain's letters, February 14, 1609, probably refers to Newport's return to England. "There is likewise a ship newly come from Virginia with some pretty commodities and hope of more, as divers sorts of wood for wainscot and other uses, soap-ashes, some pitch and tar, certain unknown kind of herbs for dying, not without suspicion as they term it of cochineal." Birch Manuscripts, Huntington Library, HM. 2904; Brown, *Genesis*, I, 205.

settlers]." Once vested with the necessary authority, it would be able to "set and furnish out, under the conduct of one able and absolute governor, a large supply of five hundred men, with some number of families, of wife, children and servants, to take fast holde and roote in that land."[1] Here for almost the first time appears the idea of a true colony, at least so far as the personnel, though not the government, is concerned, marking a noteworthy advance over the older notion of a settlement made up of adventurers, standing in constant need of relief from home, and profitable only as far as it could return to the company sufficient shiploads of marketable products.

But to change the personnel was not enough, the company concluded, the form and character of the government at home too must be changed. The new charter, it is supposed,[2] was written by Sir Edwin Sandys, and, if so, then to him more than to anyone else must be credited the inception of an idea that marks a distinct (though not, as events were to show, a sufficient) improvement in the method of governing a distant plantation. Sandys—the name is pronounced Sands—was at this time forty-eight years old and had already been employed by the king in affairs of great trust and importance.[3] He was a member of parliament, having entered at the early age of twenty-five as the member first for Andover in Hampshire, then for Plymouth, Devon, and finally for Stockbridge in Hampshire, and as leader of the opposition had taken a vigorous stand in 1601 against monopolies. In 1607 he had spoken with great determination against the reincorporation of the Spanish Company, because of the outrages committed by Spain against English shipping, in which the offenses against Challons and his men played a conspicuous part. He had travelled widely on the Continent and was well known for his tolerant attitude in religious matters and for his progressive views on some of the leading issues of the day.[4] He had advocated the abolition of feudal tenures and the granting to

1. "A True and Sincere Declaration," Brown, Genesis, I, 341–342. It is perhaps worth while to remind the reader that at about this time the Privy Council was busy "plotting how to plant Ireland with English and Scots."

2. Brown, Genesis, I, 47.

3. Brief lives of Sandys may be found in Brown, Genesis, II, 992–994; Virginia Magazine, X, 415, XXIX, 234–242; and the Dictionary of National Biography.

4. He had written a pamphlet, Europae Speculum, Or a View or Survey of the State of Religion in the Westerne parts of the World, which exhibits a remarkable attitude of tolerance toward Roman Catholics.

all prisoners the right to employ counsel in their own defense. He was a member of the royal council under the charter of 1606 and of the council of the company under that of 1609 and was destined to remain one of its leaders to the end of its career. He had a house in Aldergate, London, not far from that of the Ferrars, who were also closely identified with the company's affairs, and there at times (certainly after 1619) the company held its quarter courts. The petition for the charter was probably written in February, 1609, and the charter itself, after passing through the various offices and being delayed for the insertion of the names of subscribers to the joint-stock, finally received the great seal on May 23, of that year.

The new corporation, established by the charter of 1609, was known as the Treasurer and Company of Adventurers and Planters of the City of London for the first colony of Virginia, and is commonly known as the Virginia Company. Its head was called a treasurer instead of a governor, for what reason is not clear, unless it be to avoid the use of the same term for both company and colony. This official was first nominated by the crown, but afterward was elected by a majority vote of the members. Eventually the corporation consisted of fifty-six companies of London[1] and six hundred and fifty-nine individuals—many of whom were of the Plymouth Company resident in London and elsewhere—and the number and distribution of those who subscribed are a witness to the widespread interest which the affairs of the company aroused in England. The charter created a joint-stock company, which that of 1606 had not, with one notable difference from the type of organization perfected three years later by the charter of 1612, in that powers of government were lodged with the treasurer and council and not with the company as a whole, meeting in a general court.[2] Thus the system of 1609 stands midway between royal control on one side and generality control on the other. The royal council of 1606 had been eliminated, but the body of the company was not yet entrusted with governing powers.

1. Including Trinity House. In March, 1611, Sir Thomas Smith wrote the brethren asking for their second payment on their subscription. Historical Manuscripts Commission, *Eighth Report*, I, 237.

2. This progressive development from the charter of 1606 to that of 1612, in the transfer of governing power from an outside royal council to the general body of the company itself, is a very significant matter, for it has a direct relation to the adoption of a popular form of government for Virginia and so eventually for all the royal colonies in America. Such adoption marks the beginning of the idea of generality control in America and so has a bearing on the growth of an American ideal.

The latter was not expected to meet except at the call of the treasurer and then only for the purpose of choosing its head or of electing members to fill vacancies in the council. The treasurer and council were empowered to establish "all manner of orders, laws, directions, instructions, forms and ceremonies of government and magistracy, fit and necessary, for and concerning the government of the said colony and plantation, also they were to have full and absolute power and authority to correct, pardon, govern and rule" all inhabiting in the colony, according to such ordinances as they should lay down, or, in default of such, then according to the "good discretions" of those whom they shall appoint to govern in the colony, only provided that such ordinances be not contrary to the "laws, statutes, government and policy of England."[1] The territory provided for was enlarged to extend north and south two hundred miles instead of fifty, and thus the company not only came into possession of an area six times as large as that granted by the previous charter, but now for the first time had direct and complete control of it.

At the head of the company as treasurer was placed Sir Thomas Smith, a man fifty-one years of age, who was among the most active commercial promoters of his day. He had been one of Raleigh's assignees in 1589; governor of the East India Company for more than twenty years, and of other companies, either actually or nominally, for shorter periods; an ambassador to Russia; one of the four principal officers of the navy; and a member of parliament for fourteen years. At the time he was made treasurer of the company he was a working member of many of the important trading companies of London and no one of greater prominence could have been selected to fill this important post. Now that the reorganized company was facing its first great opportunity, he threw himself into the enterprise with enthusiasm and unbounded energy, giving heavily of his time and money, in order that the new venture should be an unqualified success. For the next fourteen years he was indefatigable in his work for commerce and colonization, carrying for many years weighty responsibilities and burdens and furthering expeditions into many other parts of the world than Virginia. He was the leading business man of his time and his house in Philpot Lane, London, was the office of the Virginia Company, the place of meeting of many a general and special court of both the Virginia and the Ber-

1. Brown, *Genesis*, I, 208–237; II, 624–625.

muda companies, and the headquarters at which every prospective colonist was expected to present himself for inspection. Smith himself was the accepted and recognized head and forefront of all important commercial operations in London for a quarter of a century.[1]

The promoters of the company now made a wide appeal for financial support, fixing each share of stock or bill of adventure at £12 10s, with special inducements for those willing to contribute £25 and £50.[2] Letters were sent to the members of the Plymouth Company, many of whom entered their names, probably on the £25 basis, and to the London gilds and liveries, fifty-six of which responded favorably. Broadsides and prospectuses were issued and scattered widely and even the clergy were called upon to spread the

1. *Ibid.*, II, 1012–1018; *Virginia Magazine*, XXVI, 267–271; *Dictionary of National Biography*. A pleasing picture of Smith as governor of the East India Company is given by John Chamberlain in a letter of December 30, 1609, on the occasion of an event almost contemporary with his appointment as treasurer of the Virginia Company—the launching of a great ship belonging to the East India Company. "Sir Thomas Smith was graced with a great chain of gold and a medal put about his neck by the king's own hand" (Huntington Library, HM, 2904; Brown, *Genesis*, II, 1013). Lord Sackville in 1623 spoke of him as the one "who once and for long had bin the Primus moter in [the Virginia] companie" (*Virginia Company Records*, II, 259; and on p. 260 are Smith's remarks about himself at the age of sixty-five "already far stricken in years"). His house in Philpot Lane lay beyond Gracechurch Street, just off Fenchurch, east of Lombard. He had also a house at Deptford, which was burned down in 1619, and it is not impossible that many of the records of the company were burned up with it (Brown, *Republic*, p. 297).

Oddly enough, after Smith's death in 1625, the house in Philpot Lane was occupied by Increase Nowell, a merchant and member of the Massachusetts Bay Company, who in 1630 went to New England. *Winthrop Papers*, II, 172.

2. The following certificate contains the terms. It is all in printed form, except the words here italicized.

"*Mr. Richard Widdows Share.*

Whereas Mr *Richard Widdows of London goldsmythe* hath paid in readie monie to Sir Thomas Smith knight Treasurer of *Virginia*, the summe of *twenty and five poundes* for his adventure toward the said voyage, It is agreed, that for the same, he the said *Richard Widdows,* his heirs, executors, administrators or assignes, shall have ratably according to his adventure, his full part of all such lands, tenements and hereditaments, as shall from time to time be there recovered, planted and inhabited. And of such Mines and Mineralles of Golde, Silver and other mettals or treasure, Pearles, Precious Stones or any kind of wares or Merchandizes, commodities or profits whatsoever, which shall be obtayned or gotten in the said voyage, according to the porcion of money by him imployed to that use, in as ample maner as any other Adventurer therein shall receive for the like summe, Written this *22^d* of *March,* Anno Domini, 1608."

This document is to be found in the Huntington Library, where are also three other original certificates that were issued to the Earl of Huntingdon. The text of a fourth is printed in Brown, *Genesis*, I, 391–392. Widdows' name may be found in the list of subscribers.

news. The plan was for a single voyage,[1] on a large scale and with ample resources; and the enthusiasm and energy of the company was centered on the one great effort, for which alone the money was raised. In the same month of February Alderman Johnson, later sheriff of London, a man actively interested in mercantile affairs and a member of the Virginia, Bermuda, and other companies,[2] issued, on his own responsibility and unofficially, the *Nova Britannia,* a pamphlet designed to arouse the interest of "all such as be well affected to further the [enterprise]."[3] On March 10, 1610, Sir Walter Cope (probably) drew up a circular letter in the name of the company, which contains the following pious appeal. "The eyes of all Europe are looking upon our endeavours to spread the Gospell among the Heathen people of Virginia, to plant an English nation there, and to settle a trade in those parts, which may be peculiar to our nation, to the end we may thereby be secured from being eaten out of all profits of trade by our more industrious neighbors."[4] Though the interest was great and the hopes high, the drive for funds did not bring in the desired amount, and in December a new appeal was made.[5] The results were still unsatisfactory. As many of

1. The fact that this subscription and all the other extant subscriptions were issued to meet the expenses of but a single voyage—amounting to £10,000, payable in three instalments—shows that under the charter of 1609, the form of organization was rather that of the semi-joint-stock than of the joint-stock. The same conclusion can be deduced from the appeal sent out, probably in January or February, 1609, for skilled workmen and laborers (Brown, *Genesis,* I, 248–249), and from the necessity which arose of calling for more funds in December, 1610, to cover the costs of the one voyage, since the £10,000 had not been even fully subscribed, much less paid in. The leaders of the company do not seem to have contemplated a general joint-stock at this time, except in so far as they may have expected to use some of the money subscribed to support the plantations during the ensuing seven years. Brown, *Republic,* p. 79.

2. Brown, *Genesis,* II, 932.

3. *Ibid.,* I, 241. "This book was noe act of the Court [of the company], but a private man's work." *Virginia Company Records,* II, 181.

4. Huntington Library, HU. 495.

5. "The Council and Companye of Virginia, having for the advancement of Religion, honor, and happinesse of this kingdom employed the Lord Delaware, Sir Thomas Gates, and Sir George Somers, with many sufficient Gentlemen Citizens in the Plantations. At a Court holden the 5th of December 1610 have thus resolved,

That whereas divers Lords Knights Gentlemen and worthie citizens of London have at this time subscribed unto an adventure of £10,000, to be issued in three years at the rate of 5000 marks a yeare, ffinding the proportion far too short to set forth the 600 men appointed to be sent unto his Ldᶦᵖ by Sir Thomas Gates and Sir Thomas Dale the next ffebruarye, Have entreated you . . . to solicite the well affected gentlemen of that part" [to subscribe and to send their subscription to Sir Thomas Smith to so]"religious honᵇᵉ and hopefull an account." [They were to rethe subscribers defaulted on their second or third payments or on both, the sums paid in were never adequate for so elaborate an undertaking. It would look as if those with money to invest were none too sanguine as to the future of the Virginia colony, and it may be that a reason may lie in the plan of government which the council had drawn up for the settlement and the long period of time (seven years) that was to elapse before any subscriber could receive a return on his money.[1]

As by the charter of 1609 the royal council resident in England was abolished and the right of control vested in the council of the company, so the decision was reached, probably toward the end of 1609, to alter fundamentally the manner of governing the colony in Virginia, and instead of a local president and council, which had been the form of organization until this time, to appoint a single head entrusted with exceptionally large powers. The company made up its mind to try a new experiment by sending to America a single and absolute governor, with authority so extensive as to make him almost a dictator for life. It was a dangerous experiment. On February 28, 1610, the treasurer and council revoked "the power and

turn the names of such as refused] "that we may be thankful to the one and forbeare to importune the rest any further. And we do hope in the end to have such a returne as wyll answere all our expectations . . . And if there be in your country any honest labouring man or citizen that are willing to go in person, we further entreate you to let them know that if they repair to Sir Thomas Smyth's house in London any time before the shippes going away, which is appointed to be the 20th of February next, they shall be entertayned.

The Name   The Sum
                                        Jo. Wentworth."

1. The proposed plan of government under a single autocratic head may or may not have deterred prospective colonists from registering their names at Sir Thomas' house in Philpot Lane, but there can be little doubt that Alderman Johnson's unofficial pamphlet, *Nova Britannia,* had an unfortunate effect. Its various statements regarding the use of the fund, though afterward repudiated by the company, were discouraging. It said that all charges of settling and maintaining the plantation would be borne by the joint-stock for seven years, before any dividends would be paid or lands granted and that during these years the settlers were to work for the company and to receive their compensation in meat, drink, lodging, and apparel (Force, *Tracts,* I, 23–25; Brown, *Republic,* p. 104). This must have seemed a long time to wait both for dividends and for the private enjoyment of one's own labor.

Of course a large proportion of the amounts subscribed were eventually paid in. For example, in response to Cope's appeal of March 10, the Earl of Huntingdon subscribed £120, paying £40 on April 4, £40 on January 16, 1611, and £40 on December 2, 1613. For these payments he received a right to 1000 acres of land in Virginia, "whenever he shall please to send any one to plant on them" (HU, 499). Under the charter of 1612 Huntingdon was admitted one of the "brethren and free members" of the company.

authority of the president and council," and "vested for life all authority in one principal governor, commander, admiral and captain general over all colonies to be planted within the limits of the patent. He was to be called lord governor and captain general of Virginia and to govern according to such instructions as should be sent him by the council in London or any two of them." He might, if he wished, "take unto him" as many persons of the colony as he should think "fit and meete" to aid him in the making of laws and ordinances, or he might govern "by his own discretion," with as full and absolute power, authority, and command as the company possessed itself. He could appoint and control all officers in the colony, except such as might be named by the council in England, and he could name his own deputy, should he be obliged to leave the colony at any time.[1]

Fears of misrule were stilled for the moment by the selection as lord governor and captain general of Lord De la Warr, a high-minded gentleman and one of the council. Unfortunately he was unable to sail for his post at once, and as it was necessary for the expedition to start at the earliest possible moment, Gates, Newport, and Somers were sent on ahead. On May 15, 1609 (as is stated in Sir Stephen Powle's diary), "Oure 6 shippes lying at Blackwell [Thames dock, quite far down the river, at the east end of Poplar] wayed anker and fell downe to beginne their Viage toward Virginia, Sr Thomas Gates being the deputye governour,[2] until the L^d De la Warre doth comme thiather, which is supposed shall be about 2 months hence. Captayne Newport [vice-admiral], Sr George Sommers [admiral] and 800 people of all sorts went in these six shippes, besides 2 moare that attend the fleet at Plymmouth, and ther be inhabitauntes already at Virginia about 160. God blesse them and guide them to his glory and our good."[3] It was a great expedition,

1. For the commission to De la Warr, Brown, *Genesis*, I, 376–384; Rolfe's "Relation," *Virginia Historical Register*, I, 104–105.

2. Sir Thomas Gates was *ad interim* governor, until the issue of the commission to De la Warr the following February (*Virginia Company Records*, II, 47). The writer of the diary from which the above quotation is taken, Sir Stephen Powle, a member of the company and one of the six clerks in Chancery, was probably doing no more than repeat the common report that De la Warr was head and Gates his deputy (Brown, *Genesis*, I, 345). Gates had no commission, but his instructions are to be found in the Bodleian, Ashmolean, 1147, ff. 175–191.

3. Bodleian, Tanner, 168, f. 2. Gabriel Archer has an account of the voyage (Brown, *Genesis*, I, 328–332). See also "A Discovery of the Barmudas," Force, *Tracts*, III, 9–15.

the greatest that was to go to America until the sailing of the Massachusetts Bay Company in 1630, and many who watched it depart may well have echoed Sir Stephen Powle's pious wish.

But the nine ships, six from London and three from Plymouth, though taking the shorter way according to instructions—to leave the Canaries [100 leagues] to the East and from thence to run in a straight western course [for Virginia]—fell on evil times. "A most terrible and vehement storme, which was the taile of the West Indian Horacano," drove the vessels apart and that particular ship which carried Gates, Newport, and Somers, the leaders of the expedition, foundered on one of the Bermuda islands. Though all lives were saved, supplies and equipment were lost, and the three most important men, in whom alone authority was vested, were compelled to remain in Bermuda until May 10, 1610, not arriving in Virginia until the 23d.[1] In the meantime the others reached the colony safely and there found John Smith, president of the council, obdurate in his refusal to resign his post, on the ground that the newcomers had no sufficient credentials. He was morally and technically right, but weakened at the moment by an accident, in which he was seriously injured,[2] he gave up the contest, after considerable wrangling, and returned to England in the same vessel that brought the new colonists. Captain George Percy, eighth son of the Earl of Northumberland, was chosen president in his stead, and the old method of government continued, disastrously, for another year. Not until March 5, 1610, was Lord De la Warr able to leave England. Then "The Lᵈ De la Warr took his leave of all the company on Monday at Sʳ Thomas Smiths in Fillpot Lane, Treasurer of the Virginia Co., and on Satterday following, 10 Martii departed toward his house in Hampsheere and from thence he went to meet his shippes at Southampton ready furnished with plantes, seedes, and all other provisions and grayne as well to sowe and to victule 1000 men for one year. He had 3 shippes, one of 200T, one a fly boate of 400 tunnes and a pinnace of 120t. His style was Lord Governor and Captaine of Virginia."[3] He sailed from Cowes on April 1 and, after a fairly good voyage by way of the Azores, reached the colony on June 16, 1610.[4] There he found conditions reduced to the last extremity and the

1. Brown, *Genesis*, I, 328–329, 343; Smith, *Travels and Works*, II, 478.
2. *Ibid.*, 484–485, 613; Brown, *Republic*, p. 109.
3. Bodleian, Tanner, 168, f. 2b; Brown, *Genesis*, I, 413.
4. Brown, *Genesis*, I, 402–404.

colonists on the eve of deserting the settlement.[1] Jamestown had been strongly palisadoed and contained some fifty or sixty houses, a fort, and a church, but it was a failure as the site of a permanent colony. It was located on low and marshy ground, liable to fogs and mists, possessing but a scant supply of water, and that bad, and subjecting its inhabitants to all the evils and miseries of malaria and dysentery —agues and fluxes, as they were called—cramps, gout, and death from famine, the starvation disease, scurvy, and Indian attacks.[2] When Gates finally reached the colony from Bermuda, May 23, 1610, seven weeks before the arrival of De la Warr, he found a town "which appeared rather as the ruins of some antient fortification, than that any people living might now inhabit it. The pallisadoes he found tourne downe, the portes open, the gates from the hinges, the church ruined and unfrequented, empty houses (whose owners untimely death had taken newly from them) rent up and burnt, the living not hable, as they pretended, to step into the woodes to gather other fire-wood; and it is true the Indian as fast killing without as the famine and pestilence within. Only the blockhouse was the safe-tie of the remainder that lived; which yet could not have preserved them now many days longer from the watching subtle and offended Indians."[3] This was the "Starving Time" for Virginia, just as there were to be starving times for Bermuda, Plymouth, and Barbados, when men suffered and died, because they had not yet learned the art of colonization, and had come to America inadequately supplied and equipped and unfamiliar with the method of wresting a living

1. George Percy (1580–1632) has given us an account of these conditions in a writing which has survived but has been only in part printed, "A Trewe Relatyon of the Proceedings and Occurrentes of Momente which have happened in Virginia from the Tyme Sr Thomas Gates was Shippwracke upon the Bermudes ano. 1609, untill my departure outt of the Country which was in Ano. Dmi 1612." Extracts from this manuscript are printed in Neill, Virginia Vetusta, and in a Sotheby Cata-logue, April 23, 1925, on which date it was offered for sale. It is in this "Relatyon" that the sufferings of the colonists are pictured in such ghastly detail, and an account is given of the torture and execution of one of them for cannibalism. A less realistic description is that of Gates and others in Brown, Genesis, 404–415.

2. These were the same diseases that took heavy toll from all who in the nine-teenth century explored the regions of the Niger and the Congo. The writers of "The Brief Declaration" (Journals, House of Burgesses of Virginia, I, 34) said that the "bloody flux" was brought over in 1618, "which infected almost the whole colony. That disease, notwithstanding all our former afflictions, was never known before amongst us." This is a very difficult statement to believe.

3. Brown, Genesis, I, 405.

from the wilderness. In that one year the colony lost more than half its number and the rest were in a state of decrepitude and despair.

Gates could do little to relieve the situation, for having expected to find the colony flourishing and contented he had brought no more supplies than were enough for the voyage. With food remaining for only sixteen days, with all their hogs killed by the Indians, with not a hen or a chick in the fort, and with all the horses and mares killed for meat, with no seines or a sufficient number of boats for fishing, and with no assurance of aid from the hostile Indians they decided to abandon the settlement, and make for Newfoundland, where they hoped to meet with fishing vessels that would either give them employment or take them back to England.[1]

But events turned out otherwise than they had feared and Jamestown was not to prove another Sagadahoc. As Gates with his company of dejected colonists fell down the river, they met the advance guard of the incoming De la Warr fleet and were ordered to return. It was a memorable event in our history when Gates "bore up the helm again and that night (the wind favorable) re-landed all his men at the Forte," and when De la Warr, following, anchored his ship before the town, listened to a sermon by the preacher, who may well have dwelt on the miraculous intervention of God, and, causing his commission to be read, took charge of the settlement.[2] He first made a speech, "laying some blame on [the colonists] for many vanities and their idleness," and threatening if necessary "to draw

1. *Ibid.*, 406–407.
2. The following is the account of this notable event in Percy's "A Trewe Relatyon": "These miseries considered it was resolved upon by Sir Thomas Gates and the whole colony with all speed to return for England, whereupon most of our men were set to work, some to make pitch and tar for trimming of our ships, others to bake bread, and few or none not employed in one occasion or another; so that in a small space of time four pinnaces were fitted and made ready, all preparing to go aboard. And if Sir Thomas Gates had not laboured with our men they had set the town on fire, using this or the like words unto them: 'My masters let the town stand, we know not but that as homeless men as ourselves may come and inhabit here.' Then all of us embarking ourselves, Sir Thomas Gates in the 'Deliverance' with his company, Sir George Somers in the 'Patience,' myself in the 'Discovery,' and Captain Davis in the 'Virginia'; all of us sailing down the river with a full intent to have proceeded on our voyage for England, when suddenly we espied a boat make toward us, wherein we found to be Captain Brewster sent from my Lord La Warre, who was come unto us with many gentlemen of quality and 300 men besides great store of victualls, munition and other provision; whereupon we all returned to James Towne again, where my Lord shortly after landed and set all things in good order, selecting a council and making captains over 15 men a piece."

the sword of Justice," and then began to organize the government, selecting a council, and dividing the men into bands of fifteen, each under a captain. New energies, new supplies, and new leadership brought new courage and hope. Sir George Somers and Captain Samuel Argall went off to Bermuda for hogs and fish, and others, in order to save their scanty stores of peas and oatmeal, turned again to fishing in the river and adjacent waters and began to consider once more the neglected cornfields, the kitchen gardens, and the wild grapes of the hedges and woods. De la Warr realized, as he wrote to the company, that no permanent success could be attained unless colonists of a better quality were sent out, worthy to be "the carpenters and workers in this so glorious a building."[1]

But the crisis was not yet passed. Though De la Warr brought order and outward improvement to the town, restoring the church, renewing the palisades, and introducing a measure of dignity and display into all his official actions, he could not stem the tide of sickness and death. During the ensuing few months one hundred and fifty colonists, not yet inured to the conditions of Virginia climate and life, died of disease or at the hands of the Indians. De la Warr himself became dangerously ill and to save his life was obliged to quit the colony, March 28, 1611, leaving less than one hundred and fifty settlers behind under the charge of Captain Percy as deputy governor. He reached England in June and immediately sent a report to the company extolling the fertility of the country and endeavoring so to present conditions in the colony as to check the "coldnesse and irresolution" felt by the subscribers to the funds of the company.[2]

But the promoters in England had no intention of deserting the colony. They had already decided that success depended on the right ordering of affairs there "by some industrious person" and planned to send aid in two instalments, one under Sir Thomas Gates, who had returned from Virginia in September, 1610, and the other under Sir Thomas Dale, both of them soldiers of experience and for some years comrades-in-arms in the service of the States General of Holland.[3] They also called for further contributions, and in order to stimulate payments issued "A True Declaration of the Colony of

---

1. Brown, *Genesis*, I, 407, 410, 415.
2. "The Relation of Lord De-la-Ware," *Virginia* (Original Narratives Series), pp. 209–214.
3. Brown, *Genesis*, II, 870; *Republic*, p. 125.

Virginia," designed to encourage the faltering souls, who must have watched with dismay the tragic failure of the great fleets that had started out so hopefully in 1609 and 1610. The money was raised, either by new subscriptions or the meeting of unpaid instalments[1] and at the beginning of March, 1611, Dale sailed from London, reaching Jamestown May 23, two weeks before the arrival of De la Warr in England. He had three ships, carrying three hundred people and ample stores of provisions and livestock, increasing thereby the population to four hundred and fifty and materially adding to the number of horses, cows, and goats in the plantation.[2]

Little sowing and harvesting had thus far been done, but the outlook was promising, for Dale had taken hold with a firm hand and for the first time was bringing the lives and activities of the settlers into a state of order and regularity. He made peace with the Indians, repaired and restored the buildings, and, most important of all, founded Dale's Town (Henricus, Henrico, Henricopolis, named after Prince Henry) fifty miles up the river, where he built a fort, a watch house, a church, a storehouse, and dwellings for himself and his men.[3] The site was higher and more healthful than that of Jamestown and Dale had been impressed, as had all the earlier settlers who have left records of their experiences, with the fertility and attractiveness of the up country. When finally Sir Thomas Gates arrived in August with two hundred men, nearly all artisans, "fewer gallants to escape evil destinies," and twenty women, including his own wife and daughters, he found things in a fairly prosperous condition. The quality of the settlers, however, was still far from satisfactory, for as the company said those who went during the first years were far too often "lascivious sonnes, masters of bad servants, and wives of ill husbands," an idle crew who clogged the business and would rather starve than lay their hands to labor.[4] Dale himself wrote home in 1613, "I protest unto you before the Livinge

1. The Earl of Huntingdon paid his second instalment, January 11, 1611.
2. Deposition of John Clarke, *American Historical Review*, XXV, 467–473; Brown, *Genesis*, I, 501–508.
3. Smith, *Travels and Works*, II, 509–510.
4. Brown, *Genesis*, I, 355. Among the Manchester Papers is "A true relation of the state of Virginia," at the time when Sir Thomas Dale left it in April, 1616, in the form of a letter from John Rolfe to Sir Robert Rich, afterward the Earl of Warwick. Despite the efforts since 1610 of the treasurer and council to improve the quality of the settlers (Brown, *Genesis*, I, 354–356) Rolfe could still complain that the greatest want was "good and sufficient men as well of birth and quality to command, soldiers to march, discover and defend the country from invasion [and] artificers,

God, put them altogether, this country wilbe equivalent to [the best countries in Europe], if it be inhabited with good people."[1]

To the council in England two courses seemed open and necessary to follow: first, to accept in the future only such applicants as were "sufficient, honest, and good artificers"; and, secondly, in order to check insubordination and factional rivalry, to instruct Gates and Dale to enforce a rigid discipline and to invest them with the requisite authority to do so. Therefore, from 1611 to 1618 the settlement was ruled with an iron hand. Gates, as sole and absolute governor of the colony[2] and Dale, as his successor in office, were determined to rid the place of lawlessness and to improve its reputation at home as a well managed colony. To that end and to meet sundry emergencies they drew up at different times a number of laws, which were gathered into a code by William Strachey, the first historian of Virginia,[3] one of those who had been wrecked on the coast of Bermuda in 1609. He had reached the colony safely in May, 1610, and as secretary remained there a year. These laws, to which he gave the title *Laws Divine, Morall and Martiall*[4] and published as a whole in London in 1612, were not drawn up in England by Sir Thomas Smith, as was afterward alleged against him,[5] but by Strachey, Gates, and Dale in the colony. Though Smith in 1621 denied that he had had anything to do with them, saying that they were the work of "those worthye governours" themselves, he did defend them as justifiable under the laws of England. The worst of them were designed not for enforcement but only to terrorize evil doers. Strachey and Gates

labourers and husbandmen" (Historical Manuscripts Commission, *Eighth Report*, II, no. 208).

1. *Virginia Company Records*, II, 400.

2. Gates was acting governor from May, 1609, to February 28, 1610; De la Warr was governor from February 28, 1610, to June, 1611; Gates was governor from June, 1611, to March, 1614; Dale from March, 1614, to April, 1616; Yeardley, acting governor, April, 1616, to May 15, 1617; Argall deputy governor until the appointment of Yeardley as governor, November 18, 1618.

3. *Historie of Travaile into Virginia Britania*, Hakluyt Society, 1849. The manuscript from which this edition was printed is in the British Museum. There is another copy among the Ashmolean Manuscripts in the Bodleian.

4. Force, *Tracts*, III, no. 2.

5. This charge was brought by Alderman Johnson in 1623 (*Virginia Company Records*, II, 393–394). It must be remembered that under the charter of 1609 the council or any two of them could make laws for the colony, provided such laws were not contrary to the laws of England. This law making power was delegated to the governor in the colony, as may be seen in the commission to De la Warr (Brown, *Genesis*, I, 379). Smith's defense before the House of Commons is in Stock, *Debates*, I, 45–46.

probably drafted those of a more general or fundamental nature, based on the English common law, and Dale such as were needed to meet special occasions as they arose. There is no reason to believe that any of the laws, even those of strictly military character, were modeled after Dutch law or were translated from the martial law of the Netherlands, as Alderman Johnson charged, for there were no such laws or any like them in force in Holland at that time.[1] Many of the laws were, in their wording, severe and inhuman, but there is nothing to show that De la Warr, Percy, or even Gates, who was called a lenient man, ever attempted to go to such extremes as these laws implied. Dale succeeded Gates, who returned to England in the spring of 1614, holding office for two years. In April, 1616, he was succeeded by Yeardley as acting governor for a year and then Argall served as deputy governor until November, 1618.[2]

Upon Dale and Argall rests the chief obloquy of having enforced these laws with harshness. The charge is in a measure justified,

1. Prince in *Report*, American Historical Association, 1899, I, 320–324; Brown, *Republic*, p. 154. The court records, on the other hand, contain the statement, made in 1620, which may be taken for what it is worth, that the condemnation of one Captain Brewster, by a court martial under Argall's direction, was not "by vertue of the Lawes of England but upon the 32 Article of the Marshall Lawes of the Low Countries, by wch Disobedience to any principall Officer was made death" (*Virginia Company Records*, I, 366; the arguments in the case begin on p. 360). This "32 Article" cannot be identified. Wilkinson, in *The Adventurers of Bermuda*, says that the military part of the laws was written by Dale from a Dutch army book of ordinances which he brought with him, but gives no authority for the statement (p. 65 note). We know that Tucker carried the code to Bermuda.

Sandys' report in 1619 extols the work of Dale in language very different from that of Johnson in 1623, a time when men said many things that were either exaggerated or not true. It is also worthy of note that the first legislative assembly, that of 1619, thought the government set up in that year "too mild for many in the colony, whom unwonted liberty hath made insolent and not to know themselves" (*Journal*, I, 12). Even the honest Percy during the "Starving Time" inflicted torture by hanging a man up by the thumbs, with weights on his feet, for a quarter of an hour, in order to extract a confession. These were hard times, when punishments were severe and bodily suffering the end sought. Later in the history of the colony men were sentenced to have their ears nailed to the pillory and afterward cut off, while flogging was a common penalty for misdemeanors. Wyatt in 1623, advised the setting up of a "Marshall Court, at least *ad terrorem*, it may do much good." *Calendar State Papers, Colonial*, 1574–1660, p. 43.

2. See page 114, note 2. There was contemporary difference of opinion as to whether or not Argall was a deputy governor. He refused to accept the title himself, because he thought it demeaning, and demanded that he be called governor. But the facts are against him. He received only a commission and instructions as deputy governor, never as governor, though he is often called "governor" in the records. *Virginia Company Records*, I, 226, 360, 361; II, 52, 54; Brown, *Genesis*, II, 798; *Virginia Magazine*, X, 164.

though it is not so clear that Dale would have been condemned by unbiased men of his own day, unless they had other reasons for doing so.[1] Rolfe in his letter to Rich speaks of him as an excellent governor, and in 1621 Deputy Treasurer Ferrar of the company, who was not inclined to favor anything that happened before 1619, during the Smith administration, called him "that worthy knight and greate advancer of the Virginia action."[2] Dale's rule was disciplinary and severe, but it was not malevolent, and it must be remembered that the shedding of blood commonly attended discipline at the time. Even before Dale left the colony he had moderated the enforcement of the laws and the laws themselves were withdrawn gradually during the ensuing three years. Yeardley's rule was lax and probably inefficient, while that of Argall, which gave rise to prolonged debate in the councils of the company after 1619, was criticized because of its generally arbitrary character. That severe laws were needed to restrain the habits and practices of the particular brand of settlers that had come to the colony from the jails, bawdy-houses, and slums of London—and there were many such—can hardly be denied, but that such laws aided in any way to increase the prosperity of the settlement or to make the people more contented may well be doubted.

Meanwhile there were taking place in the organization of the company at home important changes which probably brought into sharper relief the situation in the colony. Compelling reasons were demanding that the company apply for a new charter to take the place of that of 1609, which was no longer adequate to meet the needs of a going concern. The colony had ceased to be an experiment; it had reached a point where it had a fair chance of permanency. Consequently, the charter needed broadening in four important particulars. In the first place, the discovery of the Bermuda islands and their probable value to the company was making neces-

1. On Gates see *Virginia Company Records*, I, 267; on Dale, *New York Colonial Documents*, I, 16–21; *Cambridge Modern History*, IV, 735. McCabe's defense of Dale in his account of the "first university in America" (*Virginia Magazine*, XXX, 133–156) is highly rhetorical and contains many errors. Bruce's opinion (*Economic History*, I, 220, note 2) is distinctly favorable.

2. *Virginia Company Records*, I, 483. Rolfe, who reached the colony in 1617 after a year's absence in England, would hardly have written so favorably had conditions been wholly bad (*Virginia Magazine*, X, 136–137). Argall's own account (*ibid.*, XV, 403–404) does not give as pleasant a picture, yet even he bears witness to the "good order and prosperity" that he observed.

sary an extension of boundaries, for the grant of 1609 did not include Bermuda. Secondly, dissatisfaction was prevalent because of the unequal distribution of powers, whereby the generality, with infrequent meetings and meagre privileges, were deprived of influence in the councils of the company. Thirdly, experience had shown that the company possessed insufficient authority to apprehend and punish such troublesome offenders as defaulting employes, mutinous seamen, and slanderous colonists. And, lastly, the unsatisfactory state of the finances demanded that other expedients than voluntary subscriptions be employed for the raising of money. The new charter, which was issued on March 12, 1612, met all these needs. It extended the distance at sea from one hundred miles to three hundred leagues, thus including within the boundaries of Virginia the Bermuda islands, lying well out in the Atlantic. It authorized the holding each year of four great courts composed of the generality or members of the company, in January (Hilary), May (Easter), June (Trinity), and November (Michaelmas), "for the handling, ordering and disposing of matters and affairs of greater weight and importance" than such as could be dealt with at the lesser courts, themselves made up of only five members of the council, always including the treasurer or his deputy, and fifteen members of the generality, constituting a quorum. These lesser courts might meet as often as they pleased for the transaction of ordinary business. The new charter greatly increased the power of these courts, granting them full authority to apprehend, examine, commit, or bind over for their good behavior any notorious offenders. And, lastly, it allowed the company to erect one or more lotteries each year for the raising of funds, and the king reinforced the same by a formal proclamation.[1]

These supplemental powers and privileges greatly strengthened the company and increased its prestige, for they extended its territory, buttressed its judicial authority, aroused anew the interests of its members, and gave it a new source of revenue, which was after-

1. In the library of the Massachusetts Historical Society is a broadside containing "A Declaration for the certaine time of drawing the Great Standing Lottery," to aid in the planting of Virginia, the money to be paid to Sir Thomas Smith, at his home in Philpot Lane, 1615. In the same year the Privy Council wrote to the seven deputy lieutenants of Northamptonshire, forwarding "A True Declaration of the Present State of the English Colony in Virginia," together with the project for a lottery, and commending the undertaking to them. Historical Manuscript Commission, *Buccleuch*, III, 183. On the same subject see Sharp, *London and the Kingdom*, II, 49–52.

ward spoken of as "the real and substantial food by which Virginia hath been nourished."[1] Furthermore, the broadening of the activities of the members—of those, that is, who by the payment of £12 10s or more were admitted as brethren or free brothers into the fellowship of the company—and the establishment of a common fund, designed for the promotion of the general welfare of the colony, placed the company on a regular joint-stock basis. Henceforth, to an extent unknown before, it was able to expand and enlarge its enterprises. Over and against these advantages must be set certain evils inherent in the joint-stock system—manipulation of voting in the great courts, sale and transfer of stock,[2] and a tendency to stock-jobbing, probably infrequent owing to the uncertainty as to profits. For every single subscription members received one hundred acres of land in the colony and those who had no desire to cross the water were allowed either to sell their rights or to send over men—servants and others— to occupy the land. Membership in the company was also given for meritorious services, such as were rendered by captains of ships, promoters of settlement, and skilled artificers and the like,[3] and even "strangers" could be enfranchised.[4] In 1623 there were said to be "neer one Thousand personns [in the company] whereof many times two hundred assemble at once."[5] As a general statement the latter estimate is probably exaggerated, though doubtless there were times when two hundred and even more might be present.[6] The numbers subscribing were the greater because of the fact that no oath of allegiance to the company was required as was the case with other companies.

The change in the character of the company, because of the great increase in the powers vested in the generality, was to have in the course of a few years momentous consequences, for it led eventually

1. *Virginia Company Records*, I, 51.

2. Such transfers had always to be ratified by the company. Sometimes they were questioned and once in a great while rejected. Compare "List of Shareholders," *Virginia Magazine*, IV, 299–310.

3. *Virginia Company Records*, I, 264, 273–274, 348, 446, 459, 467, 619; II, 20, 73–74, 275, 415. A distinction was made between "Adventurers" and "Planters." The former were those who subscribed and did not go to the colony; the latter those who both subscribed and went.

4. *Ibid.*, II, 14.

5. *Ibid.*, II, 300, 358. Miss Kingsbury in her Introduction to the *Records of the Virginia Company*, I, 71–78, gives an excellent account of the organization, business, and procedure of the company.

6. *Ibid.*, II, 275.

to a shift in leadership and control. Up to this time Sir Thomas
Smith had been treasurer and the leading spirit in the enterprise. He
and Sir Edwin Sandys had both been members of the council under
the charter of 1609 and continued to work together amicably enough
after 1612. Both had concurred in the situation in Virginia under
Gates and Dale, and there is nothing to show, as the records for
those years have been lost or perhaps were destroyed, that though
their ideas regarding the centering of authority and the distribution
of powers may not always have been in accord, they differed sufficiently to affect the operations of the company. Circumstances were
however soon to arise that brought into the open a series of personal
rivalries and factional disputes, in which Smith, Sandys, Warwick,
and others were involved, that in the end were to disrupt the company and lead to its dissolution. The starting point in the trouble
was not at first the affairs of the Virginia Company, but those of another and subordinate body, the Sommers Islands or Bermuda Company, in which Warwick was particularly interested.

Bermuda had been brought into prominence by the shipwreck
there of Sir George Somers and others in 1609. They had managed
to live on the islands for nearly ten months and a half, and Somers
in his letter to the company recounting his experiences had extolled
the fertility of the place and described it as "the most beautifull that
ever [he] came to, for fishe, Hogges, and fowle."[1] As a result the
company believed that the islands might become an important source
of supply for Virginia at this critical period of her history and an
advantageous strategic point of defense for the colony against Spain.
But as the company's resources were insufficient at this juncture to
carry two colonies, it planned early in 1612 to organize a smaller or
junior company within the larger body—a form of business enterprise that had been tried in the case of the supply store or magazine
and was to be tried later in a number of separate ventures that the
company was too poor to finance. Having secured a legal title to
Bermuda by the charter of 1612,[2] it sold its rights for £2000, November 25, 1612, to a subsidiary joint-stock group of its own members,
called the Undertakers for the Plantation of the Sommers Islands.

1. Brown, *Genesis*, I, 400–402. Somers died in Bermuda, November 9, 1610, as
Smith says "overtailing himself [he] on a surfeit died," that is, he overate and died
of acute indigestion. Smith gives full accounts of Somers' various connections with
Bermuda (*Travels and Works*, I, 172; II, 635–638, and elsewhere).
2. *Virginia Company Records*, II, 47–48.

The affair prospered and the business soon outgrew the limitations of a voluntary association, so in order to strengthen their position by obtaining royal protection and to enlarge their powers by a grant from the crown, the undertakers in 1614 surrendered the islands to the king as a preliminary step to their own formal incorporation as a joint-stock company. The leader in the movement was Sir Robert Rich, later Earl of Warwick, who had become a member of the Virginia Company in 1612 and was entering on his notable career as a promoter of colonies as well as an adventurer in the field of privateering and legitimate commerce. The Bermuda charter was issued June 29, 1615, incorporating the company under the title, The Governor and Company of the City of London for the Plantation of the Somer Islands, and granting it "all those islands formerly called the Bermudas or Bermuda Islands and now called Somer Islands" as their territory.[1]

Though legally the equal of and distinct from the parent company, the Bermuda corporation was in practice closely interjoined with the other. Its membership was only one hundred and twenty, with an average attendance of seventy or eighty, but it occupied the same quarters and with few exceptions all its members were members also of the other body. The head of the one was called "treasurer," of the other "governor," but at first the two offices were filled by the same person, Sir Thomas Smith, and the conditions of tenure in both cases were the same. Each company had four general courts with similar powers and forms of procedure. These courts met at the same time and in the same place for the transaction of business, the distinction between the two being indicated simply by a change in the person of the chairman, by the numbers voting, and by the nature of the business done. After 1619, when Sir Thomas Smith ceased to be "treasurer" but continued to be "governor" and the two companies had different heads, the Bermuda Company was looked upon as the lesser and inferior corporation, and in all that concerned the common welfare did little more than follow the lead of the elder body and adopt for itself the latter's decisions.[2]

Sir Thomas Smith, the treasurer of the Virginia Company since

1. Lefroy, *Memorials*, I, 83–98; Wilkinson, *The Adventurers of Bermuda*, pp. 90–92.

2. "Which Comp^a of the Somer Islands are all members of the Virginia Company and for the mutuall strength of both parties are soe to continue" (*Virginia Company Records*, I, 282). In 1623, when the tobacco contract was under debate at a quarter

1609, became in 1615, by authority of the charter, governor of the Bermuda Company also. As Warwick more than any one else had been the prime mover in the Bermuda business it is, perhaps, not strange that trouble should have arisen between them. The bone of contention was one Tucker, a protégé of Smith's, who had been commissioned governor of Bermuda in February, 1616, but who soon after gave offense to Warwick by arresting and imprisoning (with others) "one Mr. Riche, a kinsman of the Earl of Warwick,"[1] who in a certain quarrel had spoken arrogantly of the governor and charged him with "vainglory and presumption." This "usage had been taken in very ill part by their friends and families," and Warwick demanded of the company at home that it dismiss Tucker from its employ. Smith, "expressing much heat and passion," refused to do this, and the warmth thus engendered was increased when, upon Tucker's withdrawal, Smith supported as his successor a Captain Southwell and Warwick a Captain Butler, the latter a man "favoured by divers of the Lords of the company and in especiall long known to the Earle of Warwicke."[2] Sandys put forward his brother, George Sandys, but later withdrew him in favor of Butler, at the same time bringing pressure to bear upon Smith, by raising the question of Smith's competence as treasurer. By this reflection on Smith's integrity "such a heart-burninge and separation of affections (not to say spleen and malice) ensued ther upon betwixt them, as for ever after, that to such a height of heat these distempers became inflamed within a short time, that all their meetings and consultations seemed rather cockpits than courts."[3] Warwick and Sandys now drew together, for the former was angry because of a letter sent by Smith and others in the name of the company to Captain Argall,[4]

court of the Bermuda Company, the chairman moved that the Virginia Company might be called in, "whereof a large number had very longe attended in the Parlours," and "these points propounded and debated together with them." He deemed this course "so much the more reasonable because all the Summer Islands Companie save one or two were free of the Virginia Company." *Ibid.*, II, 264. Compare Lefroy, *Memorials*, I, 99-100; *Virginia Company Records*, II, 98, 160, 238.

1. For the trouble between Tucker and Rich, see Lefroy, *Memorials*, I, 128; Wilkinson, *The Adventurers of Bermuda*, pp. 120-123. John Smith has his version of the quarrel (*Travels and Works*, II, 661), calling it "small and ridiculous."

2. Butler, *The Historye of the Bermudaes*, pp. 99-101, 114-117. The narrative from which this extract and succeeding extracts are taken was written by Nathaniel Butler of the Warwick party, and the language used must be received with caution.

3. Smith, *Travels and Works*, II, 666; Butler, *Historye*, pp. 120-129.

4. *Virginia Company Records*, II, 51-53, 401-405.

chiding him for his government in Virginia.[1] The rift between Warwick and Smith was widened because of Warwick's freebooting activities which had brought him into trouble with the East India
Company, of which Smith was governor,[2] by his close association
with Argall as seen in the voyage of the ship *Treasurer,* and by the
marriage of Smith's son and Warwick's youngest daughter, Isabella,
apparently against Smith's wishes and certainly without his consent.[3]

A deal between Warwick and Sandys was the next step, Sandys
agreeing to aid in the election of Butler and Warwick promising to
aid Sandys in ousting Smith from the headship of both companies.
The deal was only partly successful. Butler was chosen resident governor of Bermuda and on Smith's refusal to stand for reëlection
Sandys was named in his place as treasurer. But the latter failed to
obtain the governorship of the Bermuda Company, for Smith got
the requisite number of votes for the office.[4] It is impossible to say
how far the exclusion of Smith was due to his own declared unwillingness to serve or to the combined attack of his opponents, which
was aided by secret voting and the new device of a ballot box, borrowed from the practice of the East India Company. He had clearly
expressed his desire to relinquish the office, being (as he said) advanced in years and burdened with many cares;[5] but on the other
hand Robert Cushman, writing to the Leyden church in May of
that year and commenting on the "dissensions and factions among
the Counsell and Company of Virginia" as one of the reasons why
he was not getting business done, says that Smith, "when he saw
some parte of his honour lost, was very angrie and raised a faction
to cavill and contend about the election. In which contentions [he
adds] they yet stick and are not readie to intermeddle in any busi-
nes; and what issue things will come to we are not yet certaine."[6] It
is more than likely that Smith, carrying many responsibilities, was
accustomed to leave details, both of administration and accounts, to
subordinates and that the results were not always satisfactory to
members of the company. It is doubtful, however, whether this sufficiently explains the situation. It is equally doubtful whether the real

1. *Virginia Company Records,* II, 51–53, 401–405.
2. The story of this case and the bitter quarreling that accompanied its various
phases can be followed in *Calendar of State Papers, East India, China, Japan and
Persia,* 1617–1621.
3. Brown, *Genesis,* II, 1014.   4. Butler, *Historye,* pp. 116, 127–132.
5. *Virginia Company Records,* I, 212.   6. Bradford, *History,* I, 85–86.

reason is to be found in the maladministration of the colony, which as early as 1616 was beginning to show signs of improvement. The hostility of Warwick for Smith was partly personal and partly a matter of class antipathy—the gentry against the merchants—intensified by Warwick's great ambition. Sandys, who had been Smith's assistant since 1617, was influenced by different motives. He disliked the methods by which the colony was governed and wanted the opportunity to perform certain experiments, of a kind not unlike those which had been tried out in the charter of 1612, looking to an increase, in the colony as well as in the company, of the powers of the generality.

For a decade Sir Thomas Smith had been the treasurer of the company and in that time had accomplished a colossal task, promoting the settlement of Virginia and nursing it along, under most discouraging circumstances, to a successful rooting in the soil of the New World. When we realize how much else he was doing at the same time, we can but wonder how he was able to find energy and opportunity to devote himself to such a multiplicity of interests. To him more than to any one else in England is due the success attained in the face of heart-breaking disasters that threatened the existence of the colony in those embryo years. By 1616 things were looking more hopeful in many ways, and despite what to many was an undesirable form of government, under a sole and absolute governor, real accomplishment was full of promise and encouragement. The end of the joint management of land and stock, begun in 1609 and lasting seven years, had now come, and the opportunity was at hand for establishing private ownership and of making it possible for the colonists themselves to obtain a profit from the work of their own hands. Joint ownership, which in no sense of the word resembles communal ownership, may have been necessary as a device for promoting colonization at the beginning, but the time of its usefulness had passed. John Smith in Virginia and William Bradford in Plymouth both condemned it. Said the former, "When our people were fed out of the common store and laboured jointly together, glad was he could slip from his labour, or slumber over his taske, he cared not how, nay the most honest among them would hardly take so much true paines in a weeke, as now for themselves they will doe in a day; neither cared they for the increase, presuming that howsoever the harvest prospered, the general store must maintaine them, so that wee reaped not so much corne from the labours of thirtie, as now three or four doe provide for themselves." Bradford is equally explicit.[1]

In 1613–1614 Dale had allotted to every man in the old settlement three acres of "cleare ground," in the nature of a farm,[2] exempt from all payments, except one month's service to the colony (at other times than the sowing and harvesting seasons) and two barrels and a half of ears of corn,[3] paid in to the magazine—obligations similar to those of a tenant paying "gafol" on an English estate. In fact, the holders of these farms were tenants of the company. This arrangement worked well, for in 1616 the company could say that the colony was in a very good and prosperous condition. "They sow and reape their Corne in sufficient proportion, without want or impeachment; their Kine multiply already to some hundreds, their Swine to many thousands, their Goates and Poultry in great numbers; every man hath house and ground to his own use, and now being able to maintain themselves with food, they are also prepared and ready, once having the meanes, to set upon the Minerals, whereof there are many sorts; as also to plant and how [hoe] such severall kindes of Seeds and Fruits, as may best befit the Soyle and Climate, to make the Land profitable to themselves and th' Adventurers."[4] Therefore the company proposed to offer to everyone who had subscribed or would subscribe £12 10s fifty acres of land to be confirmed as an estate of inheritance to him and his heirs forever and to be held as of the manor of East Greenwich in free and common socage, that is, by fealty and fixed rent. In 1618, as a part of Sandys' elaborate scheme for the advancement of the colony, which, as we shall see later, touched nearly every phase of its organization and was designed to transform it from a struggling settlement into a thriving, populous, and self-sustaining community, the company apportioned unoccupied lands for public purposes—so much for the ministry, so much for the college which it hoped to found, and so much for the company itself.[5] Upon these lands additional tenants

---

1. Smith, *Travels and Works*, II, 516; Bradford, *History*, I, 301–302.
2. So says Smith, but in *The Brief Declaration* of the ancient planters the distribution is credited to Gates.
3. A barrel of corn equalled five bushels, Winchester measure. Hening, *Statutes*, I, 170.
4. Brown, *Genesis*, II, 775–779.
5. *Virginia Company Records*, I, 266–271, 389–399, for the later land distribution. Also, *ibid.*, I, 220, 234, 256, 391, 426, and index under "Land"; Brown, *Republic*,

and servants were to be located at the expense of the company, that the lands might yield a profit to those for whose benefit they had been laid out. Grants were now made to others than subscribers, either to those who had done some special service to the company[1] or to private persons—at the rate of fifty acres for every one transported—who would go to the colony with family and servants. This, the famous "adventure of the person" or "headright" system,[2] became a characteristic form of land distribution not only in Virginia, but in many of the other colonies as well. In Virginia, after the fall of the company, it became a right inherent in the colony, as far as distribution was concerned, and continued to be used until its frequent abuse led to its modification and practical abolition toward the end of the century.

This introduction of private ownership in land and the profits of

pp. 333–334, 346, 377–378, 492–493, 691. For the general situation in 1623, *ibid.,* 617–623. For the East India school at Charles City (a preparatory school, the idea of which was originated by the Rev. Patrick Copland, below, page 231, note 2); and the college at Henrico (for the support of which many benefactors had made contributions in England) see *Virginia Company Records,* I, 152, 220–221, 540; Neill, *Virginia Vetusta* and *Macalister College Contributions,* 2d series, no. 2, *passim;* Bruce, *Institutional History of Virginia,* I, ch. VI; *William and Mary Quarterly,* new series, IX, 301–302.

The same system of tenancy-lands for ministry, school, public officials, and company was adopted by the subordinate company for Bermuda, originating, of course, with the same group of men in both companies. The best description of the system in Virginia in the year 1616, is that of John Rolfe, in his letter to Rich (Warwick). According to him, the main body of planters was divided into officers, laborers, and farmers, the first named having charge and care of the others, seeing to it "that both the one and the other business may be duly followed to the performance of those employments which from the one are required [the hired laborers], and the other [the farmers or tenants] by covenant are bound to. The laborers are of two sorts. Some are employed only in the general work, who are fed and clothed out of the store. Others, especially artificers, as smiths, carpenters, shoemakers, tailors, tanners, etc., do work in their professions for the colony, and maintain themselves with food and apparel, having time limited them to till and manure their ground. The farmers [tenants] . . . are bound by covenants both for themselves and servants to defend the colony against its enemies, to do watch and ward in the towns, to serve thirty one days for the colony when called upon, to maintain themselves and their families with food and raiment, and, finally, to pay yearly into the store or magazine, each for himself and every man-servant, two barrels and a half a piece of their best Indian wheat." The total number of colonists at this time was 351—205 officers and laborers and 81 farmers, and the rest women and children. Rolfe's letter is in Historical Manuscripts Commission, *Eighth Report,* II, no. 208.

1. *Virginia Company Records,* I, 427, 431, 459, 464–465, 469–470.

2. *Ibid.,* I, 75, 425; *Virginia Magazine,* XXV, 338–339; *Journal,* 1619–1659, p. 7; Force, *Tracts,* III, pp. 20–23, "Orders and Constitutions." A copy of these orders is among the Smith of Nibley papers in the New York Public Library.

cultivation was accompanied with a change in the activities of the people of the colony. They no longer spent their time in searching for mines or in trafficking with the Indians, but became farmers and planters and, under the encouragement of the company, made strenuous efforts to produce a variety of staples—grain, grapes, licorice, silk-grass—and to promote industry by setting up saw-mills and by producing naval stores, potash, glass, and iron. From the beginning the company had tried to bring about such results as these, but had made so little impression upon the London mercantile world that in 1615 a writer could say, "I cannot find [for commercial enterprise] any worthy place of forraine anchorage; for the Bermudas we know not yet what they will do; and for Virginia we know not well what to do with it, the present profit of those not employing any store of shipping."[1] In truth neither Virginia nor any other colony at so early a date was ready, even on a small scale, to enter a manufacturing stage, which above all things required what the colonists lacked, capital, labor, and skill. Later the company endeavored to meet the difficulty and did so, in part, by sending over not only English artisans but also skilled workmen from other countries— Poles, Germans, Swedes, French,[2] and Italians. But it was impossible to suppress the lure of tobacco raising which required little capital, any man's labor, and no great amount of skill. Practically anybody could raise tobacco, but not anybody could make glass, iron, potash, and naval stores.

John Rolfe in 1612 seems to have been the first to experiment with tobacco raising,[3] and with sufficient success to send a consignment to England in March, 1614, by the ship *Elizabeth*,[4] thus beginning the first export of what was destined to become the great staple of Virginia in colonial times. We may well believe that it was the discovery of this new and profitable commodity that had something to do with the company's decision to make a general division of the colony's lands, for the formation of a subordinate company at this time, to deal in certain Virginia commodities (chief among which were tobacco and sassafras) and known as the Society of Particular Adventurers for Traffique with Virginia in a joint-stock, shows that the

1. *The Trades Increase* (London, 1615), p. 21.
2. *Virginia Company Records*, I, 258, 351, 493, 494, 499, 504. The French were "divers skilfull men out of Languedock" transported for the making of silk.
3. Neill, *The Virginia Company of London*, p. 94.
4. Brown, *Genesis*, II, 639; *Republic*, pp. 173–174, 231.

members were interested once more in profits from the colony.[1] This new company, located of course in England, was under the direction of Alderman Johnson and was called the "magazine," a name formerly given to the store-house established in the colony under the seven year plan. The new "magazine" was, however, quite a different institution from the old. It had its court and its separate accounts, an arrangement which caused a great deal of pother during the years of its existence and was not settled for some time after it had ceased to function. It must have been badly mismanaged for eventually it showed a serious loss to the adventurers and went bankrupt.[2] The first magazine ships arrived in Virginia in 1616, bringing provisions, clothing, utensils, and the like, and similar consignments continued to be sent for a number of years, but the goods do not appear to have been always chosen wisely. On one occasion the store-keeper in the colony complained that the magazine in England sent needles when it ought to have sent ploughs![3] But the business began well and in 1617 20,000 pounds of tobacco were despatched to England.[4] The colonists, however, complained that the adventurers charged too much for their goods, and the adventurers, in their turn, complained that the farmers of the customs levied too high a duty on the tobacco imported. Then the society inevitably suffered from the quarrels in the company, for its members were in the main supporters of the Smith party.[5] An attempt at reorganization took place in 1620 and a new magazine was formed, but in 1621 that was already spoken of as having suffered heavily from the high price and poor quality of tobacco and from other causes.[6] Of its later history we know almost nothing.[7] In 1625 it was spoken of as "the late Magazine."[8]

The colony was growing very slowly. The resources of the company, even with the aid of the lotteries, were inadequate to meet the cost of development and expansion.[9] It was realized, as early as

1. *Virginia Company Records*, I, 227–228, 282; II, 54, 396; *Virginia Magazine*, XV, 401–402.

2. *Ibid.*, II, 218–219.

3. *Ibid.*, I, 241. In 1620 it was reported that there was but one plough in the colony, 350.

4. Brown, *Republic*, pp. 238–239, 272, 278–279, 290–291, 343, 563.

5. Scott, *Joint-Stock Companies*, II, 269–270.

6. *Virginia Company Records*, I, 519.

7. *Virginia Magazine*, I, 303; *Virginia Company Records*, I, 147 (no. 245), 480, 505, 632, 634; II, 297, 305; *Minutes of Council*, I, 93.

8. *Minutes of Council*, I, 118; compare 121.

9. There had been few new subscriptions and many cases of defaulted payments. Cham-

1617–1619, that a variety of ways would have to be contrived to enlarge the population and to increase the agricultural output. Among these aids were the subsidiary joint-stocks or private ventures of one kind or another that were set up under the auspices of the company; the free admission to the company of those who would promise to take up land in the colony and seat it with families and servants; and, most important of all, the encouraging of small groups or associations of men, organized on a joint-stock basis, to settle particular plantations or private colonies within the boundaries of the company's patent. These associates were to provide tenants, servants, and equipment from their own resources, and to engage in agriculture, Indian trade, or fishing,[1] as they preferred, in order that they might increase the staple output of the colony as a whole. The practice, a common one at the time and one frequently indulged in, was adopted by all the colonizing corporations—the Council for New England, which was the reorganized Plymouth Company,[2] the Bermuda Company, and the Massachusetts Bay Company.[3]

According to this arrangement private or voluntary associations were to be formed—sometimes called "societies of adventurers"—to whom would be assigned, under patent from the company, estates, manors, or plantations of considerable size. The patentees were to be vested with limited governmental powers, with specified privileges, over all tenants or servants brought over. The larger of these estates

berlain wrote to Carleton, August 1, 1613, "When the Virginia business was at its height, in that heat many gentlemen and others were drawn by persuasion and importunity to underwrite their names for adventurers. But when it came to the payment, specially the second and third time, their hands were not so ready to go to their purses as they were to the paper, and in the end flatly refused. Whereupon they are sued by the Company in Chancery, where this action finds such favor that they have ready dispatch and the underwriters are forced to make payment, which amounts to a round sum, between three and four thousand pounds. Among the rest your cousin Will Lytton was drawn on by Sir Walter Cope with persuasion that he should not need to adventure anything, unless he list; but only to give his name for encouragement to others and for a continuance to the cause. But now it comes to the reckoning he is fair to disburse £40 and his friend Sir Walter cannot protect him. Et sic solet beare amicos." Birch MSS., Huntington Library, HM. 2904.

1. In 1619 Smith's Hundred was given license "to go a fishing," *Virginia Company Records*, I, 285.

2. In the proposals of Sir Ferdinando Gorges, 1621, *American Historical Review*, IV, 690 (§30).

3. The Adventurers in the Whale Fishing Design, organized by the Bermuda Company, and the private joint-stock of Cradock, set up by the Massachusetts Bay Company in 1629, are of this character. In *Massachusetts Colonial Records*, I, 394, mention is made of "Mr. Cradock our governor and his associates interested in a private stock."

were of the nature of private jurisdictions or immunities, and the powers granted, according to the form of patent drawn up in 1620, were almost those of an independent colony. The company agreed that the captains or leaders of these associations, who should go to Virginia to inhabit "by vertue of their Graunts" and should "plant themselves their Tenants and servants," might have liberty, "till a form of government is here settled over them," to make orders, ordinances and constitutions, "associatinge unto them divers of the greatest and discretes of their companies," for the better ordering and directing of their servants and business, provided these ordinances were not contrary to the laws of England.[1]

Though at first the company promised to aid these private adventurers by loaning them corn and cattle in order to give them a start, it expected each of the groups to furnish its own supplies as soon as possible, to provide its own ships, and to send over at its own expense a governor, gentlemen, tenants, and servants, including a minister and a physician.[2] It gave the associations liberty to carry their commodities to whatever market they pleased—as the company

1. *Virginia Company Records,* I, 303, also 232, 560; II, 326. It was the claim to greater exemptions than those stated in the text that caused the representatives of Martin's Brandon to be excluded from the legislative body of 1619. How these privileges were interpreted by the associates themselves can be seen from the instructions given to Captain John Woodleafe, governor of Berkeley Hundred and Towne, by Throckmorton and Associates and now preserved among the Smith of Nibley papers in the New York Public Library, printed in *Bulletin,* III, 208–210. The patent (*ibid.,* 161–164) does not differ materially from the wording of the rule in the records of the Virginia Company (I, 303). Regarding the patent to Argall and his partners or associates see *ibid.,* II, 401–402, "whereby hee and his Company their heires and assignes (save only in time of necessary defence by Warr) were exempted from all power and authoritie and jurisdiction to be from hence derived or there established, that soe hee might raigne there as a great and absolute Master w^{th}out Lawe or controlment, and w^{th}out the fear of ever beinge called to any future reckoninge" (also *Virginia Magazine,* IV, 300). It is quite possible that in the patents of the year 1617 privileges and exemptions were granted, as in the cases of Argall and Martin, that are not found in the later documents. The special clause in the Martin patent may be found in *Original Narratives, Virginia,* p. 253. The original patent, which was issued in 1617, is (we are told) still preserved at Lower Brandon (*William and Mary Quarterly,* XX, 148). The patents granted to the Pilgrims in 1619 and 1620 are of this character (Bradford, *History,* I, 88 note, 189 note).

2. *Virginia Company Records,* I, 267, 315; II, 459. A full account of the activities of one of these groups may be found in the Smith of Nibley papers in the New York Public Library. In that collection one will see a copy of an early charter-party, the names of vessels, with itemized statements of supplies and lists of passengers, mention of governor, chaplain, preacher, surgeon, and physician, financial charges and accounts, extracts from letters, etc. Of the forty-seven papers in the manuscript volume some thirty have been printed in the *Bulletin,* I, III, either in full or in abstract.

had no intention of controlling their tobacco or other output—and it allowed them to reap what reward they could from their own efforts.[1] The idea of these "colonies" or "hundreds," as they were frequently called, was not so much to help the company on the commercial side as to replenish the colonial population in as short a time as possible "wth good multitudes of people."[2] The "societies" themselves remained in England, directing each particular "colony" from a distance, just as the company itself was doing.[3]

Though particular patents for private plantations had been issued by the company as early as 1617, notably that to Captain John Martin, which was afterward condemned as irregularly obtained, the rapid extension of the practice was undoubtedly due to the plans which Sir Edwin Sandys set on foot for the building up of the colony. In spite of the company's best efforts, its treasury was empty and it itself was in debt for the expenses, £75,000, already incurred in attempting to settle the "company or public lands." The magazine and other similar side lines were making little money for themselves, much less aiding the public welfare. The most promising outlook, therefore, for the increase of population and the promotion of industry and agriculture, seemed to lie in the proposals of "divers Lords Knights, gentlemen and citizens (grieved to see this great Action fall to nothinge)," who offered "to take the matter a new in hand and at their pryvate charges (joyning themselves into Societies) to sett upp divers particular plantations."[4]

There appear to have been some forty-four patents issued for such plantations between 1619 and 1623, inclusive, in return for which the patentees bound themselves to transport settlers and equipment to Virginia. Many of these grants were never taken up at all; others fell into the class of allotments to individual planters and were eventually absorbed into the common system; while a few attained the dignity of "colonies," of the type already described. The earliest of these was the Society of Smith's Hundred (1617), later called Southampton Hundred after the Earl of Southampton, of which Sir George Yeardley was the governor and captain.[5] It con-

1. *Journal of the House of Burgesses*, 1619–1659, p. 11; *Virginia Company Records*, II, 82, 315, 323.

2. *Ibid.*, I, 439.

3. *Minutes of Council*, I, 74; *Virginia Magazine*, X, 289.

4. *Virginia Company Records*, I, 350.

5. *Ibid.*, I, 347, 588; *Virginia Magazine*, VIII, 401; *Calendar State Papers, Colonial*, 1574–1660, pp. 213–214.

tained 80,000 acres and was situated on the north side of the James river, running from "Tanks Weyanoke" to the Chickahominy. Upon this "colony," the associates said in 1635, they had spent £6000. Sandys was its treasurer, and in 1619 wrote to the Earl of Huntingdon, sending him a "printed declaration of the business now in hand," and urging him to take up his allowance of 1000 acres (£120=960 acres) at a place "commonly called with us Nansimahum," wherever that was.[1] For this allotment, he said, a confirmation should be obtained of the king. The management of the earl's property in Virginia was placed in the hands of Nicolas Martiau, a Huguenot, and Benjamin Blewett, the former of whom in 1625 was living at Elizabeth City (Kickotan or Kecoughtan) with his wife and children and the latter was connected with the iron works up the river at Falling Creek.[2] When in 1619 the company granted the Pilgrims a patent for a similar plantation and expected them to go to Virginia, it considered the possibility of assigning to them an anonymous gift of £500 for the education of the children of the colony, but when the Pilgrims went to New England the money was handed over to Southampton Hundred.[3] The place of the Pilgrims in Virginia's history offers a number of interesting subjects for speculation.

The most important of all the private plantations and the first to take an organized form was (Richard) Martin's Hundred (1618), not to be confused with (John) Martin's Brandon (1617), further up the river and later called Brandon, a tract of 7000 acres located seven miles from Jamestown, down the river on the same side.[4] It was

1. Huntington Library, HU, 500, 504. The distribution of these lands, of which the money accounts were not settled till 1643, caused some legal complications later. There is a copy of Sandys' letter and other documents relating to Smith's Hundred in Historical Manuscripts Commission, *Hastings Manuscripts*, II, 57–58, 66, 68. The chief associates named are Yeardley, captain, Sandys, treasurer, "earls of Southampton, of Pembroke, of Warwick, the Lord Paget, the Lord Cavendish, the Master of the Wards [Cranfield], Sir Thomas Smith, Sir John Danvers, Sir Nicholas Tufton, to the number of 30 knights, gentlemen and merchants of the best account in London, whereof the least Adventurer must have 500 acres. They have already there 120 persons and are now [1620] sending 100 persons more and 40 cattle. The charges they have already spent will amount to the sum of 62l upon every five shares," p. 58.

2. Brown, *Republic*, pp. 441, 465; Historical Manuscripts Commission, *Hastings Manuscripts*, II, 66, 68. Martiau—sometimes written Martin, Marlier, and Martian— was a man of importance in the colony and the earliest ancestor of George Washington. *Nicolas Martiau*, by J. B. Stoudt (1932), with some fanciful deductions, contains the facts of Martiau's life, as far as they are known.

3. *Virginia Company Records*, I, 310–311, 313–314, 319, 350, 587.

4. *Virginia Magazine*, VII, 269–270. For a lugubrious letter written by one Richard

established in 1618 by the Society of Martin's Hundred,[1] the patent having been obtained the year before, and this society sent over two hundred and fifty people in the *Gift of God,* perhaps the same vessel that went to Sagadahoc. After the Indian massacre of 1622 its rehabilitation was considered necessary "for the security and plenty of the plantation."[2] It was entitled, as were all the others, to send its products, not through the magazine but directly to its own society in England, though it might deal with the magazine if it wished. Its governor and captain was Thomas Horewood.

One of the best known of these "colonies," because of the wealth of information which we have regarding it, is Berkeley Town or Hundred, the work of John Smith of Nibley near Bristol, William Throckmorton, who later married the sister of Sir Thomas Dale, and Richard and Maurice Berkeley of Berkeley. These associates sent out their first vessel, the *Margaret,* from Bristol, September 20, 1619, which arrived on December 14 with thirty-five men "all in safety and perfect health." Fifty-six more, men and women, sailed the next year in the *Supply,* and others in the *Furtherance* in 1622 and the *Bonny Bess* in 1623. The associates, organized in England as a company, with governor and council, raised money, gathered settlers, employed a minister and a surgeon, made contracts with servants, despatched provisions, utensils, and livestock,[3] and in general conducted themselves as a miniature of the larger company from which they received their patent. Nearly all of these "colonies" were engaged in raising tobacco, but one of them, never actually organized, that of John Zouche, son of the Sir John Zouche already mentioned and said, without much warrant, to be a Puritan, was planned for the triple purpose of raising tobacco, trading with the Indians for furs, and fishing in New England waters, the fish when salted to be exchanged in Virginia for commodities. One third of the commodities were to be sent to England for the use of Lord Zouche. Of many of these "colonies" the metes and bounds were never well determined during the lifetime of the Virginia Company, though in 1621 William Claiborne was appointed surveyor for that purpose.[4]

Frethorne from Martin's Hundred, describing his unhappy condition in 1623, see Historical Manuscripts Commission, *Eighth Report,* II, no. 325.

1. *Virginia Magazine,* II, 52.   2. *Virginia Company Records,* II, 482.

3. See also Historical Manuscripts Commission, *Fifth Report,* I, 340–341.

4. Among the particular plantations, in addition to those already mentioned, that were actually set up in the colony, were Archer's Hope on the York River, named after Gabriel Archer, the first secretary, Bargrave's Settlement (Brown, *Republic,* p. 250),

It is an interesting question, not easily answered, whether these patents for particular plantations permitted settlement in any part of "Virginia" other than that lying immediately about the James River. The only copies of patents that are extant are of those issued to Throckmorton and his Associates and to Peirce and Associates (the Pilgrims), and from the wording of these documents there is no reason for doubting that a particular plantation might be located in any part of the territory. The patentees were "to erect and build a town and settle and plant dyvers inhabitants there for the advancement of the general plantation of that country." They were to take up their land in any place or places not already or heretofore inhabited by Englishmen nor within ten miles of any other particular plantation, unless the same be on the opposite side of some great and navigable river. Although the manifest intent of the patent was that the plantations should be separate, economically self-contained units in themselves, and possessing each its own local government, yet the fact that they were to be subject to taxation, answerable for all impositions, burdens, and restraints imposed by consent of the whole, and liable to be called into public service at any time shows that even though they might be scattered they were to be near enough together to form a single and fairly compact settlement under a common authority. The latter requirement makes it impossible to believe that the company ever expected the grantees, Pilgrims or other, to take up their location as far away as the Delaware or Hudson rivers.[1]

While the company was thus encouraging private settlements for the purpose of increasing the population and economic strength of the colony, it was also doing as much as it could to promote immi-

Bennett's Welcome (*Virginia Company Records*, I, 562), Lawne's Hundred, dissolved in 1620 and afterwards known as Isle of Wight Plantation (*ibid.*, I, 414; *William and Mary Quarterly*, XII, 205–206), and Society of Truelove's Plantation (*Minutes of Council*, I, 43).

Among those that were projected but never located were the plantations of Diggs and Associates (*Virginia Company Records*, I, 483, 492), Bourchier and Associates (*ibid.*, I, 483), Hamor and Associates (*ibid.*, I, 492), Wainman and Associates (*ibid.*, I, 252), Woodleafe and Associates (*ibid.*, I, 232), Delbridge and Associates (*ibid.*, I, 259), Brook and Associates (*ibid.*, II, 15), Harwell, Sheldon, and others (*ibid.*), Blackwell and Associates (Bradford, *History*, I, 88, note), Wyncop and Associates, the Pilgrims (*Virginia Company Records*, I, 221, 228), and others, *ibid.*, I, 299, 303, 325, 345, 347, 354, 375, 380, 381, 398, 404, 407, etc. Even the town of Ipswich asked for a patent for a particular plantation, *ibid.*, I, 418.

1. *Bulletin*, New York Public Library, III, 161–164; Bradford, *History*, I, 246–251.

gration on its own account. Despite the accumulation of men and women, who had been sent over before 1616, the number of the inhabitants did not increase. In that year there were fewer men, women, and children, taken all together, in Virginia, than there had been in 1611, three hundred and twenty-four as against four hundred and fifty. In 1618 there were only six hundred.[1] Efforts were now made to increase this number and to enlarge the occupied area by sending three hundred tenants for the company's land and gardens, the governor's land, and the college land at Henrico, all of which were under the company's direct control. These tenants were to hold their tenements at a yearly rental and thus benefit the company, the governor, and the college, whenever that should be set up.[2] The company shipped also one hundred apprentices and servants and a hundred "young and uncorrupt maids to make wives to the inhabitants and by that means to make the men more settled and less moveable." In all cases where the maids married "public farmers," that is, tenants on the company's lands, the company promised to pay all charges of transportation; otherwise the husbands were to recompense the company for its outlay, at one hundred and fifty pounds of tobacco each, an amount which certainly would net a profit to the company.[3] It persuaded the City of London to furnish one hundred children in 1618 and another hundred in 1619 for the better supply of the colony, which the mayor and aldermen did "fearing lest the overflowing multitude of inhabitants should, like too much blood, infect the whole city with plague and poverty." In the next two years the company received from the city an appropriation of £500 for the same purpose.[4] In 1621 it tried to obtain the introduction of a bill into parliament requiring the "cities and towns corporate" in England to send the poor "with whom they were pestered" into Virginia, but the attempt failed, though a number of the corporate towns took advantage of the opportunity to get rid of their indigent population.[5] The usefulness of Virginia in this blood letting process was widely appreciated, as, except for Ireland and

1. Brown, *Genesis*, II, 782. Three hundred had gone back to England before 1616.
2. *American Historical Review*, XXVII, 498; *Virginia Magazine*, V, 383–384; VI, 231; XVI, 9; *William and Mary Quarterly*, IX, 83–85; XIV, 288; *Virginia Company Records*, I, 268, 349, 455, 456, 466. On the college, *ibid.*, I, 421, 521, 538.
3. *Virginia Company Records*, I, 255–256, 269, 566. Maidens were kidnapped to be sold in Virginia as early as 1618, *Virginia Magazine*, VI, 228.
4. *Analytical Index to the Remembrancia* (Guildhall), I, 361–362.
5. Stock, *Debates*, I, 37; *Virginia Company Records*, I, 489, 555.

Bermuda, it was the only available place for undesirables outside of England. We read of the "citty boys and citty maids" carried over in the ship *City* in 1618 and of the "Duty boys," carried over in the ship *Duty* in 1619. The latter, fifty in number, were despatched at the command of King James, constituting the "divers young people" of whom the king wrote to Sir Thomas Smith, January 13, 1619, "who wanting imployment doe live idle and followe the Court," which at the time was at the Newmarket races.[1] These boys and girls were generally put to service in the colony, either as apprentices or domestic servants of the tenants on the company's lands. Some of the later arrivals were spoken of as "weak and unserviceable people, ragged, and with not above a fortnight's provision," who frequently died and occasionally ran away to the Indians. But doubtless many grew up to be useful members of the colony, justifying England's efforts to rid herself, by just so much, of her vagrant population.[2]

Convicts from the jails of Middlesex and other counties joined the procession to America, the first being transported as early as 1617, thus inaugurating a long line of these unfortunates, saved from the gallows in England, in order to "yeilde a protifable service to the Commonwealth in parts abroad."[3] But they were unwelcome addi-

1. Historical Manuscripts Commission, *Eighth Report*, II, no. 253; *Virginia Company Records*, I, 250, 270–271, 304–306, 424, 477, 520; *Minutes of Council*, I, 117. "Whereas our Court hath of late been troubled with divers idle yonge people, who although they have been twise punished still continue to followe the same havving noe imployment; we havving noe other course to cleer our Court from them have thought fitt to send them unto you disiringe you att the next opportunitie to send them away to Virginia and to take sure order that they may be sett to worke there," otherwise "they will never be reclaymed from the idle life of vagabonds." Guildhall Records, Remembrancia, V, fol. 8. Smith's letter to the lord mayor, commenting on this letter from the king, is given in fol. 9, and shows that some of the boys and maids had been brought already from Newmarket to London, with others to follow, and as the company had no ship in which to send them or means to employ them, Smith begged the lord mayor that they might be detained in Bridewell and set to work there until the next ship should depart for Virginia. For the ship *City*, *Virginia Company Records*, I, 130 (83); *William and Mary Quarterly*, II, 61–62.

2. Historical Manuscripts Commission, *Eighth Report*, II, no. 318. The Council for New England in 1622 proposed to do exactly the same thing that the Virginia Company was doing, when it voted to persuade the City of London to send over poor children to New England and in 1623 to secure from the king a letter to the lieutenant of every shire "for the setting forth of their poorer sort of people to New England." *Proceedings*, American Antiquarian Society, 1867, pp. 61, 79, 85. This attempt was repeated in 1632, p. 111.

3. *Acts Privy Council, Colonial*, I, §§ 12, 13; *Calendar State Papers, Colonial*, 1574–1660, *passim*; Butler in the *American Historical Review*, II, 16–17.

tions to the population in Virginia and by 1663 had become so numerous as to engage in a desperate conspiracy in September of that year, which fortunately, however, was discovered and circumvented. On April 12, 1670, the Virginia counties of York, Gloster, and Middlesex petitioned the council of Virginia regarding the great number of "fellons and other desperate villanes sent hither from the prisons of England," begging that body to prevent the barbarous designs and felonious practices of these wicked men and to forbid any one engaged in trade with the mother country from bringing in "jailbirds." The matter was referred to England, where the Privy Council issued an order prohibiting the practice.[1]

But still the population did not increase. Death took its toll as remorselessly as it had done in the early years of the colony. From Easter, 1619, to March, 1620, the numbers decreased from 1000 to 867, and in March, 1621, though ten ships had gone across the ocean in the meantime with 1051 emigrants, only 843 remained. In one year 1095 had died, either on the way over or in the colony.[2] No wonder "some of the children designed by the City [of London]" refused to go.[3] To die from epidemics or in the process of getting acclimated or "seasoned" was not a pleasant prospect even for the vagrant and the criminal, and transportation acquired some of the horrors of prison life and the gallows.[4]

But the company was not to be daunted. Sandys had become the treasurer in 1619 and was determined to carry forward the elaborate

1. *General Court Records*, 1670–1676, I, 5; *Minutes of Council*, I, 514; *Acts Privy Council, Colonial*, I, §903. In 1729 the dwelling house of Thomas Lee, justice of the peace, and later acting governor of the colony, was burned down by a crew of transported felons, with the loss of outhouses and goods. *Calendar of Treasury Papers*, 1729–1730, pp. 80, 85, 93.

2. Brown, *Republic*, p. 415.

3. *Ibid.*, p. 353; *Genesis*, II, 740.

4. There seems to have been considerable difficulty at this time in persuading people to go to America. Sir Edwin Sandys said in parliament, April 10, 1621, that heretofore men were as unwilling to be planted in the West Indies "as nowe they are in Virginia" ("Pym's Diary of the Parliament of 1621," among the manuscripts of the Earl of Winchelsea, an item furnished by Professor Notestein).

It is commonly said that negroes were first brought to the colony in the *Treasurer*, the ship commanded by Captain Daniel Elfrith, in which Robert Rich (Warwick) was the principal shareholder. But the evidence is far from conclusive on this point. Statements made in 1623 indicate clearly that the negroes on the *Treasurer*, fourteen in number, were taken to Bermuda and set at work on Warwick's lands there (*Virginia Company Records*, II, 395, 402, 407; Wilkinson, *The Adventurers of Bermuda*, pp. 129–130). These negroes may have been taken from the Spaniards, but as War-plans for the advancement of the colony that had been formulated and in great part executed while Sir Thomas Smith was in office. These plans, to be discussed in a later chapter, covered almost every phase of the colony's organization and life. Already in 1618 and 1619 a beginning had been made, but in the summer of 1620 reinforcements were considered on a larger scale than before. The company proposed to send 800 "choyce persons"—500 tenants, 100 young maids, 100 boys for apprentices, and 100 indentured servants—to be procured partly by advertising and partly through the coöperation of "noble friends." The sending of these "apprentizes, servants and wives" was estimated in the summer of 1621 to have cost £2000, and it must have discouraged the promoters, at that time facing bankruptcy, to be informed by Robert Bennett, of "Bennett's Welcome," that "vittles being scarce in the country noe man will tacke servants."[1]

The severest blow that the company suffered at this juncture, was the loss of the lottery. The attempts made since 1612 to raise money by this means had stirred up a good deal of opposition. The first great lottery, held at the west end of St. Paul's in the summer of 1612, lasted for a month, and a London tailor won the first prize of "four thousand crownes in fayre plate, which was sent to his house in a very stately manner." The records of the London gilds show that these companies as well as private individuals speculated in tickets, the Grocers Company, for example, paying £62 10s for five lots and other companies doing the same.[2] The virtues of the lotteries were spread broadcast throughout southern England by various forms of propaganda, including, among other methods of publicity, the issuing of ballads, extolling the benefits sure to accrue to all sorts of people—"maydes that have but portions small," "knights and gallant gentlemen," "merchants of the western partes," "farmers and coun-

wick was the promoter of the Guinea Company (1618), it is quite possible that they were obtained in the usual way from Africa. John Smith says that a Dutch ship brought the negroes to Virginia and his statement may be quite true, for the Dutch came frequently to the colony and one of their ships may well have brought negroes in 1619 (*Travels and Works*, II, 541–542; Historical Manuscripts Commission, *Eighth Report*, II, nos. 261, 270, 275, 278). As the Dutch ship and the *Treasurer* had "consorted," the confusion is not surprising. Neill says that there were only twenty-four negroes in Virginia in 1624 (*English Colonization*, p. 121).

1. *Virginia Company Records*, I, 481; *American Historical Review*, XXVII, 508; Historical Manuscripts Commission, *Eighth Report*, II, no. 291.

2. Brown, *Genesis*, II, 248–249, 561, 570–572.

trymen"—all of whom would find prizes awaiting them, if they would but subscribe.[1] In 1619 Gabriel Barbour was appointed manager and for his efficiency in raising money, he was thanked on account of his "true and honest carriage of that buissinesse."[2]

But Barbour's way of conducting the lottery wrought its evils, for the people of the towns in which his agents were at work complained of the demoralizing effects upon trade and industry that were caused by the popular excitement which the lottery aroused. The complaints were brought to the attention of parliament, where the master of the wards and later lord treasurer, Lionel Cranfield, reported from the king[3] that the latter had never liked the idea of the lottery and had only agreed to it because he was informed that the colony could not subsist without it. He was prepared to suspend the privilege if its exercise was found to be a grievance. Therefore, in March, 1621, at the request of the House of Commons, the Privy Council ordered "that the further execution of these Lottaries bee suspended." This was done by proclamation four days later, March 8, on the ground that "the sayd Lotteries doe dayly decline to more and more inconvenience, to the hinderance of multitudes of our Subjects," and that their suspension was necessary "for the general good."[4] How far the suppression of the lottery was a political measure it is hard to decide, but the fact that the king and council acted on the recommendation of the House of Commons would seem to preclude such an assertion.

The overthrow of the lottery was little short of a crushing blow to the company, and as further expenditure from the common stock

1. The losers were consoled in the following lines:

> "Let no man think that he shall lose,
>   though he no prize possesse.
> His substance to Virginia goes,
>   Which God no doubt will blesse,
> And in short time send from that land
>   much riche commoditie,
> So shall we think all well bestowed
>   upon this Lotterie."

>   "London's Lotteries."
>   Rollins, Collection of Ballads, I.

2. *Virginia Company Records*, I, 556, 592.
3. Stock, *Debates*, I, 26–27.
4. *Acts Privy Council, Colonial*, I, §63; *Virginia Company Records*, I, 458, 492; *Royal Proclamations* (ed. Brigham), p. 31. The editor of this collection has annotated his text in the belief that the proclamation was for the purpose of suppressing lotteries in Virginia! On this subject see Scott, *Joint-Stock Companies*, II, 252–255, 272.

was impossible, because the treasury was empty, the device of the subordinate and voluntary joint-stock was resorted to on a scale larger than ever before. Companies or associations were created for "the sole making of Glasse and Beades," for "Apparrell and other necessary provisions such as the Colony stood in great need of," for "sending of 100 mayds to be made wives," for "the setting out of a Voyage to trade with the Indians in Virginia for furrs," and for "sending Shipwrights and other principall workmen for making Ships, Boats and other Vessells."[1] The new magazine, formed in 1620 was to provide not only cows, mares, goats, asses from France, and a large quantity of staple commodities, but also maids and apprentices. Continuing the work of earlier years, plans were set on foot for making salt, silk, oil, wines, hemp, and flax, for engaging "Dutch carpenters from Hamborough, skilful for the erectinge of Sawinge Mills," pushing forward the "Iron worke so long and earnestly desired," and furnishing fishing tackle and other necessaries and a grist mill.[2] This courageous programme, largely the work of Sandys and Southampton, was carried out in part at least during the years 1620 and 1621 in the face of increasing financial difficulties, with the result that in 1622, when the great massacre by the Indians took place, there were 1240 people in the colony, and the outlook for the iron works, salt works, the breeding of silkworms and the making of silk, the manufacture of glass beads for trading with the Indians, and the increase of English and Irish cattle seemed reasonably bright.

While it is very unlikely that any of these industrial enterprises could have been made successful, even under the most favorable circumstances—partly because of the seductive influence of the tobacco culture and partly because of the want of capital and the right kind of labor—yet more might have been accomplished had it not been for the attack of the Indians on the colony in 1622. This hideous tragedy cost the settlement about 400 lives, mostly of "seasoned" men, the mainstays of the colony, and brought great discouragement

1. *Virginia Company Records*, I, 258, 368, 504, 513, 514, 522, 538, 623, 627–628; II, 497; Hening, *Statutes*, I, 160; *Virginia Magazine*, XVII, 4. Compare also *Virginia Company Records*, II, 348–349, 384. For the "magazine of the maids" see *Minutes of Council*, I, 57, 59, and Dr. McIlwaine's article in *The Reviewer*, I, no. 4 (1921), to which reference is made on p. 57 of the *Minutes*, "The Maids who came to Virginia in 1620 and 1621 for Husbands." Shipwrights were sent over, and at least one shallop and possibly other vessels were built for the English adventurers, *ibid.*, 57, 76.

2. *Virginia Company Records*, I, 368, 523, 623, 629; II, 115.

in England, strengthening the opposition which had already been aroused against the policy of the company. But this set back did not cause immediately any cessation of effort. Patents of land continued to be issued[1] and colonists to be sent over, even while the company's troubles were increasing and the members were warring among themselves. A year after the annulment of the charter, the population had risen to nearly 1100.[2] The colony already possessed all the essentials of a permanent settlement—family and agricultural life, men, women, and children, artisans, hired laborers, and indentured servants, and a few negroes. Its numbers were increasing from within and without; its stock in oxen, cows, swine, and goats was growing rapidly; forty-two sail of ships were reported in 1623 as plying back and forth between England and Virginia; and in the main the people were peaceful and contented. It looked as if the Virginia colony had actually taken root.

1. "The Declaration of the State of Virginia," 1623, says that between 1619 and 1623 forty-four patents of land were granted to persons "who have undertaken to transport [each] one hundred men at the least." This "Declaration" and the "Relation" that accompanied it were written for a purpose and must be so interpreted. *Virginia Company Records*, II, 349–362, 373–377.

2. Brown, *Republic*, p. 612; *Virginia Magazine*, XIX, 121, says 1232. In 1628 there were 3000 (*ibid.*, VII, 259); in 1630, "upwards of 2500" (*ibid.*, VII, 381); in 1634, nearly 5000 (*ibid.*, VIII, 302).

CHAPTER VI

VIRGINIA'S RELATIONS WITH INDIANS, SPANIARDS, AND FRENCH

WHILE the colony of Virginia was thus gradually settling down as a successful, self-perpetuating plantation, in striking contrast to the earlier failures at
Roanoke, Newfoundland, and Sagadahoc, it was
attaining stability in its external relations also, for before the fall of
the company, to whose energetic efforts it owed its very existence, it
had been freed from the menace of attack from outside enemies.

The only serious danger at any time came from the Indians and
the Spaniards. Toward the former, the company had always endeavored to be honorable in its dealings; and though it never acknowledged the validity of Indian titles to the soil, it always
instructed the governors, whom it sent over, to buy lands of the Indians and to enter into friendly relations with them. But aggressions
on both sides led to reprisals, and during the earlier period Indian
attacks cost the colony dear in men and subsistence. The very feeble-
ness of the settlement emboldened the natives, who in Virginia as
elsewhere resented the coming of the white man and viewed with
sullen wrath his attempts to explore and occupy the country where
they lived. Several times they assaulted the fort, and were always on
the alert to cut off groups of men, whether at work in the fields or
on the march, and to kill stragglers who wandered too far from the
protection of the palisades. The English in their turn took their
revenge upon the "bloodye infidelles" and made many excursions
into Indian territory, destroying Indian towns and crops and overaw-
ing the redmen by the superiority of their weapons—guns in hand
or cannon from the ships. Their methods were often atrocious in
the use of poison and treachery.

In 1613 Sir Samuel Argall captured Pocahontas, daughter of Powhatan, the leading chief hostile to the English, and brought her to
Jamestown. This Indian girl had already played a romantic rôle in
the life of the colony, when at the early age of thirteen (according
to the familiar story) she had saved the life of Captain John Smith
and had later shown her friendship for the colonists by warning

them at various times of attacks planned by the men of her tribe.[1] On April 14, 1614, she married John Rolfe, who wrote of her to Sir Thomas Dale as "an unbelieving creature, to whom my heartie and best thoughts and have for a long time bin soe intangled and inthralled in soe intricate a Labarinth that I was ever aweared to unwind myself thereat."[2] This happy event brought peace for eight years, except for one brief uprising in 1617, and would possibly have prolonged the friendly relationship had not Powhatan died in 1618.[3] Under his brother, Opechancanough, chief of the Powhatan confederacy, Indian enmity smoldered, bursting into flame in 1622 in the terrible massacre of that year.[4] So fearful was the disaster that the company made application to the king for "certain old cast Armes remaynning in the Tower and the Mynorites; which though they were altogether unfitt and of no use for modern service, might nevertheless be serviceable against that people, whereunto his Majestie for the better strengthening of that Plantation graciously condescended."[5] Consequently a collection of old armor and firearms

1. Smith, *Travels and Works*, I, cxv–cxviii. Some authorities have rejected this tale as invented to embellish the *General History*, at the suggestion of the publishers, sixteen years after the supposed incident occurred (Brown, *Genesis*, II, 785, notes 1–5; 786, notes 1, 3; 787, notes 1–2), but the arguments are not convincing. Keble Chatterton, in his popular and uncritical life of John Smith, returns to the attitude of acceptance characteristic of the period before Deane, Neill, Henry Adams, and Brown wrote (Winsor, *Narrative and Critical History*, III, 160, note 4, 162, 211–212; Adams in *North American Review*, January, 1867, his maiden effort). The matter is not important, though some writers would impugn the reliability of all Smith's writings on the basis of the known inaccuracy of his narrative of his life before he came to Virginia, which Lewis L. Kropf calls "a worthless pseudo-historical romance" (London, *Notes and Queries*, 7 series, IX). Conclusive as Kropf's verdict is, it does not invalidate the Pocahontas story, which can be shown to be true in all probability. Too much stress, however, has been laid upon Smith's brief career in Virginia, which lasted but two years and closed when Smith was but twenty-nine years old, and far too little on his later career as writer, explorer, and map-maker of the New England coast. Smith was as much a "founder" of New England as he was of Virginia. He died in 1631, at the age of fifty-two.

2. *Virginia* (Original Narratives Series), p. 240; *Virginia Magazine*, XXII, 153; Bodleian, Ashmolean, 830, fos. 118–122.

3. In 1620 the company could speak of "a perpetual league lately made between the governor there and the Indian Kings," *Virginia Company Records*, I, 447, 504.

4. There is a good account of the massacre in Wertenbaker, *Virginia under the Stuarts*, pp. 48–54. It is not true to say, as does Scott (*Joint-Stock Companies*, II, 132) that the company ignored this disaster and minimized its significance in the history of the colony. The company fully recognized its seriousness.

5. *Acts Privy Council, Colonial*, I, §87 for the petition; British Museum, Cottonian, Otho, E. 8, f. 121, for the arms. Also *American Historical Review*, XXVII, 503–505; *Virginia Company Records*, II, 96, 99–100, 342; Smith, *Travels and Works*, II, 579. Lord St. John gave sixty coats of mail, *Virginia Company Records*, II, 135.

was sent to the colony, where we know that it was used, efficaciously, and probably with very picturesque effect, in the warfare that followed. In the end so complete was the victory of the English,[1] that except for a rumor of attack in 1627,[2] which never came off, and one serious uprising in April, 1644, which cost the lives of three hundred settlers, Virginia was destined to have no warlike troubles with the Indians during the remainder of her history.

The fear of the Spaniard was more unsubstantial and remote, but it was by no means imaginary. During the entire period to 1622, the Spanish ambassadors—Zuñiga to 1610, Velasco from 1610 to 1613, and Sarmiento de Acuna, better known by his later title of Count de Gondomar, from 1613 to 1618 and again from 1620 to 1622—kept a watchful eye on the settlements in Sagadahoc, Virginia, and Bermuda and inaugurated a system of espionage that penetrated even the royal council for Virginia from 1606—the date of its inception—until its abrogation in 1609.[3] This spy system included, possibly, some who held important offices of trust under government, and certainly, individuals in the colony, for there were those in Virginia, who supplied information, among whom was the Spanish prisoner, Molina, of whom more anon, who wrote, as he himself tells us, "with a root from the fields" and smuggled his letters hidden between the soles of shoes and in coils of rope.[4] These ambassadors

1. *Journals, House of Burgesses,* 1619–1659, p. 38 (§2).
2. *Minutes of Council,* I, 147.
3. Lefroy, *Memorials,* II, 21–22; Wilkinson, *The Adventurers of Bermuda,* pp. 62–63, 73–79. The contemporary feeling in England against the influence of the three Spanish ambassadors can be gathered from *Sir Walter Rawleigh's Ghost or England's Forewarner* (Utrecht, 1626), an attack on Gondomar, and from *The Second Part of Vox Populi or Gondomar appearing in the likeness of Matchiavelli in a Spanish Parliament,* with illustrations picturing Gondomar and the Spanish Parliament. This pamphlet, which is undated but after 1620, contains a general indictment of Spain. It was written by Thomas Scott, at one time chaplain to James I and later rector of St. Saviour's, Norwich. Scott was the author of many tracts, such as *Vox Populi or News from Spain* (1620), *Digitus Dei* (1623), *The Belgick Soldier* (1623 or 1624), *A Tongue-Combat* (1623), *An Experimental Discoverie of Spanish Practice* (1623). These pamphlets, to be found in the Yale, John Carter Brown, and Huntington libraries, are valuable for our history as expressing contemporary opinion not only of Spain but of Holland also. The *Vox Populi,* which is the best known, is printed in *Somers Tracts,* II, 508. For other of Scott's writings see *Dictionary of National Biography.*
4. Brown, *Genesis,* I, 117, 418, 455, 476, II, 554, 560, 738, 745, 951. Zuñiga suggested using Arundel, *ibid.,* I, 245, 311, 324. Note the information from an Irishman, eight months in Virginia, *ibid.,* I, 393, 399.
Of the eighty-four documents obtained from the General Archives at Simancas by Alexander Brown, and translated, not always accurately, by Professor M. Schele de Vere, all but four—the last of the series—are printed in the *Genesis.* The entire col-

and their spies kept the Spanish government informed of all that was taking place in England and in the colonies, from the sailing of Waymouth in 1605 to the return of Dale in 1616. The intelligence they obtained was not always accurate, for the leaders of the colonizing movement in England were as secret as possible in their proceedings and not infrequently gave out reports about the colonies that were manifestly intended to deceive;[1] while King James, who was interested in colonization only as far as it heightened his own importance, often dallied with the ambassadors or put them off with ambiguous phrases. Though at peace with Spain and anxious "to strengthen the bonds of friendship,"[2] he refused to interfere with the colonizing movement at its source, because he was unwilling to recognize the claim of Spain to territory north of the thirty-fourth parallel of latitude. If, however, "his subjects went where they ought not to go and were punished for it, neither he nor they would complain."[3] Thus Zuñiga got very little satisfaction out of the king, but he and his successors went on reporting regularly to Spain, sending maps, broadsides, charts, descriptions, relations, and copies of letters, and receiving letters and instructions in return. From the beginning to the end they urged Philip III to drive the English from Virginia and to destroy the colony, to uproot it when it was small and weak or to intercept the fleets from England and so by preventing an increase of the population to cause it to die for want of support.[4]

The council of state in Spain urged the same plan upon the king,[5] and even Molina at Jamestown wondered why this "Hydra" had not been strangled in its infancy.[6] All of these advisers seemed to fear that the colony would become a center of attack upon Spanish fleets or Spanish colonies in the West Indies or be turned into a resort of pirates and buccaneers, for they had got the impression that

lection is now in the New York Public Library. Other similar documents, from the British Foreign Office Papers in the Public Record Office, may be found there also, among the Bancroft Transcripts. There are many papers of this character in the Archivo General de Indias at the Exchange in Seville, some of which, secured by Miss Irene A. Wright, are printed in the *American Historical Review*, April, 1920, pp. 448–479, and in the *Proceedings*, Massachusetts Historical Society, 54, pp. 61–66. There are other documents in the Spanish archives relating to Virginia that have not been printed.

1. Brown, *Genesis*, II, 661, 680–681.
2. *Ibid.*, I, 119.   3. *Ibid.*, I, 120–121, 124.
4. *Ibid.*, I, 117, 124, 140, 147, 244, 259, 392 (Velasco's letter of June 14, 1610), 573.
5. *Ibid.*, I, 126, 143–144.   6. *Ibid.*, II, 646, 649.

"a soil so sterile" could never become the seat of a permanent settlement.[1] They called attention to the nearness of Virginia to Havana and to the fact that should a rupture take place between England and Spain, then Bermuda would offer a strategic opportunity for hostile operations.[2] They had reason for their fears. The time was one when corsairs were still swarming in western seas and when for more than a century, from the first seizure of a Spanish ship by an English crew in 1540, to the exploits of William Jackson in 1641 and 1642, privateers from England or English privateers sailing under foreign protection took heavy toll of Spanish fleets and bullion.[3]

Why Philip refused to heed the warnings of his councillors is far from clear. He was not indifferent, for he urged them to gather information and promised to give such orders as were necessary.[4] He made suggestions regarding sending spies to Virginia and even himself went so far as to institute inquiries of the governor of Havana. In 1609 and 1611 he authorized the despatch of two expeditions to investigate the situation: one from Florida, under the direction of Pedro de Ybarra, governor of Florida; the other, under the command of Molina and Perez, sailing from Lisbon. Ybarra on June 26, 1609, sent Captain Fernandez de Ecija to the northward "to reconnoiter all that relates to Virginia and the ports, bays, and reefs along its coast in the places that can be fortified and see whether the English or other nations have gone to those regions and whether they have set foot and fortified themselves in any, and where and how and with what peoples and forces, or whether they have settled in any place and by what route they have gone and of what quality the land is, and what these nations can obtain from it, and with what Indians they communicate and what is the distance from Florida to Virginia or to that place where they have settled, and with what measures and forces they can be driven from there and frustrated of their designs and punished." Burdened with the responsibility of carrying out this involved and comprehensive instruction, Ecija set sail in a pinnace, reached the Chesapeake, and obtained a body of information that was first brought before the council of war in Spain and eventually placed before the king (May 5, 1611).[5]

1. *Ibid.*, I, 121.   2. *Ibid.*, I, 443; II, 639.
3. Haring, *Trade and Navigation between Spain and the Indies*, ch. X; Newton, *Colonizing Activities of the English Puritans*, pp. 314–330; "Voyage of William Jackson" (Harlow ed.) in *Camden Miscellany*, 3d series, XIII, no. 4.
4. Brown, *Genesis*, I, 125, 181, 311.
5. *American Historical Review*, XXV, 463. Ecija's "Relation," which Brown could

The recommendation of the council, based on Ecija's report, was that the English settlement should be broken up at once and the colonists driven from Virginia "before they take more root and possess themselves of more land and fortify themselves, have greater forces and extend through other regions."[1] But on second thought, yielding to the customary Spanish habit of procrastination, the council finally decided that more information was needed and ordered Don Diego de Molina and Marco Antonio Perez, skilled navigators, to sail from Lisbon "in a caravel which had been equipped for them to reconnoiter the port and land called Virginia, which is on the coast of Florida."[2] With them as pilot went one Francis Lymbry, an Englishman, who had lived in Spain and is said to have been a pilot for the Spanish Armada.[3] Pretending that they were on their way to recover cannon from a sunken Spanish ship, these three men in their caravel visited the Chesapeake in the summer of 1611 and entered the James River. But incautiously going ashore they were seized by the colonists and detained as prisoners.[4] In revenge, the caravel carried off one of the settlers, John Clark, a pilot, who later, after his release by Spain, was employed as the mate of the *May-flower* in 1620.[5] During the next few years negotiations between the two countries concerned largely the exchange of these prisoners.[6] Perez died in Virginia; Molina and Lymbry were finally sent back to Spain by way of England in 1616, having lived at Jamestown for nearly five years, during which time Molina continued to com-

not find in Spain or obtain from the New York Historical Society (*Genesis*, I, 326) is quite accessible in the Archivo General de Indias at Seville. The transcript covers more than forty-seven type-written pages, too long for even an abstract to be presented here. Ecija intended to go along the coast as far north as the forty-fourth parallel, but reaching the Capes of Virginia became fearful and turned back. The place names can readily be identified and some of the incidents of the voyage are interesting and informing. I am indebted to my friend Mr. Victor Morris Tyler of New Haven for translating the document for me and for working out very skilfully the itinerary followed. The reference is Patronato, Legajo, 261.

1. *Genesis*, I, 466.   2. *Ibid.*, 454.
3. Neill, "Virginia Governors," *Macalester College Contributions*, I, 29.
4. Brown, *Genesis*, I, 507–510; "Clark's Narrative," *American Historical Review*, XXV, 454–455, 470–479; *Virginia Company Records*, I, 599.
5. Bradford, *History*, I, 116, note, 167, note, 174, note 1. Clark was the first to land on the island in Plymouth harbor, where the Pilgrims passed their first Sabbath in America. This island received the name "Clark's Island" and is so called today.
6. Chamberlain to Carleton, December 4, 1611, "The Spanish ambassador was sent for lately before the [Privy] Council, where it was roundly told him what continual wrongs and injustices our nation was still offered in Spain," Huntington Library, HM, 2904.

municate with his country, urging the king to send forces to suppress the colony.[1] Lymbry was hanged by Dale on the voyage, because he had been guilty, probably for the second time, of an attempt
to betray the colony to Spain.

In the end Philip did nothing whatever. Either he thought that
the colony would die of itself if left alone or he believed that the
English would abandon the settlement as a failure and carry the
people, as Gondomar said in 1614 was to be done, to Bermuda,[2]
which had a much better reputation for healthfulness than had Virginia. He may have reached the conclusion—if he reached any at all,
which is not likely as he had few independent opinions of his own—
that Virginia was a waste land without silver mines, and so not
worth to Spain the cost of a war with England. Such a war might
follow if he broke the peace, and he was doubtless satisfied to see
England spending men and money on a forlorn hope. The line of
demarcation, even in Spain, was not as sacrosanct in 1616 as it had
been in 1493, and though Philip may have been desirous of maintaining his political and territorial claims, he would hardly have
felt justified in doing so on behalf of so poor an acquisition.

With France the case was somewhat different. Though England
had refused to recognize the right of France to occupy land below
the forty-fifth parallel of latitude, the French had paid no attention
to this refusal and were already settling at points along the Maine
coast. No boundary lines had been drawn there as they had not been
drawn in the south, and the conflicting claims in both regions were
to be a subject of negotiation and war for a century and a half.
Three years before King James issued his charter of 1606 to the Virginia companies of London and Plymouth, King Henry of France
had granted, in 1603, to Sieur de Monts, a distinguished Huguenot
nobleman, a charter which conveyed seignorial and trading rights to
territory between the fortieth and the forty-sixth parallels and the
title of lieutenant general in Acadia.[3] De Monts associated with
himself, as the navigator of the expedition, Samuel de Champlain,
the greatest of French explorers. When the latter, starting on his
voyage in 1604, passed Sable Island, and went on to investigate the
Maine coast, de Monts established himself and his followers on an
island in the Ste. Croix river. But the rigors of the climate led to
the abandonment of that settlement and a withdrawal in 1605 to

1. Brown, *Genesis*, II, 653, 702, note.   2. *Ibid.*, II, 680.
3. *Farnham Papers*, I, 1–6 (Documentary History of the State of Maine, VII).

Port Royal in Nova Scotia. As was to be the case with the Popham colony at Sagadahoc three years later, an inadequate preparation, the wrong kind of colonists, and a woeful lack of courage brought the French attempt to an untimely end.

No sooner was the Sagadahoc settlement shown to be a failure than the French tried again, determined to seize "the opportunitie [as Gorges wrote] to settle themselves within our limits";[1] and for the first time introduced a religious and spiritual factor into the enterprise. Madame de Guercheville, a lady of the court, "ardently zealous for the glory of God and the conversion of souls," obtained from de Monts and the king, Louis XIII, a title to the territory and crossed the ocean, carrying with her two Jesuit priests, Fathers Biard and Massé, to work as missionaries among the Indians. The presence of the priests at Port Royal led to acrimonious discussions, which finally became so bitter that Madame de Guercheville and her friends removed to a point farther southwest, Fernald's Point on the western side of Soames Sound in Mt. Desert. There in the month of May, 1613, on a beautiful meadow site, well protected from wind and storm, this peaceful community found a refuge. But its period of happiness was short-lived. This idyllic company, the leader of which, La Saussaye, spent his time planting vines and fruit trees instead of building forts, had trespassed, unwittingly perhaps, on the soil of the North Virginia Company, which by the charter of 1606 was authorized to repel intruders.[2]

Information regarding the settling of the French in this quarter was brought to Virginia probably by returning fishing vessels, which were accustomed every year to go to the Maine coast to lay in a supply of codfish for the winter; and at once Sir Samuel Argall, ostensibly on a fishing voyage but with a commission to drive out the transgressors, was despatched northward. About the middle of July, 1613, he attacked the settlement, which after some resistance was compelled to submit, and he carried fifteen of the thirty Frenchmen, including the two Jesuit priests, naval officers, and others, back to Jamestown where they joined the two Spaniards and the Indian girl Pocahontas, who were already dwelling as prisoners in the colony.[3] Argall was again sent north to destroy what was left of the

1. Baxter, *Gorges,* I, 207.
2. Biard's "Relation," *The Jesuit Relations,* III, IV.
3. Brown, *Genesis,* II, 700–720, where is printed Biard's account and letter. For Argall's authority, *ibid.,* 733.

Ste. Croix settlement, in the course of which mission he plundered and burnt Port Royal. His was not a piratical expedition, as has sometimes been said, but one authorized by the Virginia Company, such as the Spaniards might well have sent against Jamestown itself, and was justified according to the ethics of the time and the accepted practices among colonizing nations. Argall was distinctly an improvement upon many a sailor of fortune of his day, and he was able to make a dignified and well-reasoned defense of his conduct in the Saint Sauveur investigation that followed, as the result of which he was acquitted. That the French settlement was in part a philanthropic and peaceful center of good works has heightened the harsh judgment which has been passed upon Argall, but even Father Biard could say that though he was "a very clever and cunning captain" he was "still a gentleman, with truly noble courage; his men were neither inhuman nor cruel in their treatment of any of us."[1] Argall's business was to check the advance of the French into territory granted to the Virginia companies, and he did what he was instructed to do without unnecessary brutality.[2] As the result of his activities the English settlements in America were relieved of danger from the French for more than half a century. After 1616 Virginia was safe from aggression on the part of both Spain and France.

1. *Ibid.*, II, 714.
2. *Virginia Company Records*, I, 230, 284–285, 324. For the charges against Argall, *ibid.*, I, 360–361, 374; II, 401–403. We know of Argall's Virginia career chiefly from his enemies. There is ample evidence to show that he was a man of humane sympathies, more so indeed than Dale himself (*American Historical Review*, XXVII, 499–502). Those who have condemned him so severely have made no sufficient study of the man in the light of his own times. He has been called unprincipled and rapacious and his government in Virginia has been severely treated by Virginia historians. Even Baxter, who is on the whole favorable to him, speaks of him as "a bold and unscrupulous man, intolerant of opposition and persistent in enforcing obedience to his authority." It is important to note that the charges against him were presented by Sir Thomas Smith and Alderman Johnson, the enemies of Warwick, who was Argall's supporter. (*Virginia Company Records,* I, 285; Neill, *Virginia Company,* pp. 114–116.) At the same time it is not necessary to accept, without considerable qualification, Mr. Sawtelle's attempt to justify his conduct unreservedly, in *Sir Samuel Argall, the First Englishman at Mt. Desert* (1923).

CHAPTER VII

THE TOBACCO CONTRACT[1]

BUT security without the means to enjoy it is of little worth and it is a striking fact that almost coincident with the elimination of Spain and France as dangerous claimants to the territory of southern and northern Virginia, came the discovery of tobacco as a marketable staple, capable of making the settlement self-supporting and financially independent. This discovery and the certainty of tobacco's profit-making value, which was demonstrated during the next few years, came at a time when the leaders of the company—among whom Smith, Johnson, Sandys, and the Ferrars stand out conspicuously—were taking the first steps in the carrying out of an elaborate scheme for the strengthening of the company and the betterment of the colony. This scheme was formulated in the years 1617 and 1618 and brought to maturity during the years 1620 and 1621. The minds of these men—notably of Sandys and the Ferrars—ranged over the whole of the company's interests and in four important particulars they saw the need of vigorous and comprehensive action. They would issue first of all a grand charter of grants and liberties, reorganizing the government of the colony somewhat after the model of their own system under the charter of 1612, and do away with the harsh and rigorous rule which had been enforced since 1609. This they did in 1618.[2]

In the second place, they would apply for a new patent for themselves, in which the name "governor" would be substituted for "treasurer" and "Virginia" for "southern Virginia," and by securing larger privileges and immunities be enabled to attract a more stable and enthusiastic body of subscribers and, by obtaining a confirmation at the hands of parliament, be in a better position to "strengthen

1. These chapters on the later history of the Virginia Company were written before the publication of Dr. Craven's admirable work, *Dissolution of the Virginia Company* (1932) and before the appearance of the remaining volumes (III, issued 1933, and IV, not yet published) of Miss Kingsbury's *Records of the Virginia Company*. As my conclusions do not differ materially from those of Dr. Craven I have not attempted to revise what I have written. Some of the documents printed and to be printed in Miss Kingsbury's new volumes I have seen in manuscript.

2. See chapter IX.

the Plantation in general by engaging of the whole state in the interest and support of the action."[1] This plan was first proposed in 1620, at about the same time that the Plymouth Company was obtaining its new charter, which transformed it into the Council for New England, but the action was never consummated.

In the third place, they would set on foot a more regular and systematic way of meeting the needs of the colony: by sending over a continuous series of ships, with men, provisions, utensils, and money; by making arrangements in the colony for churches, inns, guest-houses or hospitals, a free school, and a college; and by enlarging the list of colonial staples and the sending of skilled artisans, artificers, and gardeners, wherewith to widen the economic foundations upon which rested the prosperity of the colony.

And, lastly, they would add to their financial resources—already at a low ebb—by entering into an advantageous contract with the crown to handle in England for the benefit of the company and (as they hoped) for the profit of the planters in Virginia, the whole of the tobacco that England needed. To this subject we must give immediate attention, for in the successful execution of this project lay the future destinies of the company.

The use of tobacco was well known to the colonists before they went to Virginia. It had been brought to England from America by Hawkins, Lane, and others, and had advanced in favor among the better classes so rapidly as to draw from King James his famous "Counter-blast." The weed was valued not only for smoking, but for its supposed medicinal qualities as well, and for many years its use gave rise to a great variety of opinions as to its merits and demerits.[2] Despite strong opposition, both within and without the company, the production of tobacco, once begun, advanced with

1. *Virginia Company Records*, I, 102, 429, 437, 438, 441–442, 445–446, 450–451. There can be no doubt that Sandys and Southampton, in seeking a new charter, were aroused by the success of the Plymouth Company in obtaining its new charter in 1620, and by the grant to it of certain special privileges, such as the fishing monopoly (*ibid.*, 428). The name "Virginia" was chosen because the other company took that of "New England"—its corporate title was the Council for New England—which John Smith had fastened upon that region in his map of 1614 (Smith, *Travels and Works*, II, 694).

In the *Minutes of Council*, I, 22, there is a reference to the "Companies charter bearing date the 4th of May 1620." From the context it seems clear that this refers to an instruction from the company to the colony, as no charter to the company of that date was ever issued.

2. This controversy is so well known as to need no elaboration here. The greatest collection of tobacco literature anywhere to be found is that of Mr. George Arents of

giant strides. The colonists in Virginia had early noticed the Indian use of tobacco. George Percy, in 1607, mentions a savage who had a "garden of tobacco," part of which he gathered and "distributed to every one of us"; and, he says further, "they gave us of their tobacco, which they took in a pipe made artificially of earth as ours are, but far bigger, with the bowls fashioned together with a piece of fine copper."[1] In 1612, five years later, John Rolfe began to cultivate the plant as an experiment,[2] on some plot of ground, possibly at "Varina" in Henrico, where it is said, he lived after his marriage with Pocahontas.[3] He sent a small amount to England, in March, 1614, which reached there the following May.[4] From that time forward the tobacco-raising habit dominated Virginia and the output continued steadily to increase. It was raised partly by the company on the public lands and in the "company's garden"; partly by the private associations, which could do as they pleased with their own, provided they brought it to England; and partly by private planters, who probably were "restrained," as regards their crops, to the magazine. Over the eventual disposal of the second and third lots the company had no control.

During its entire career, the company opposed this growth of a single staple as detrimental to the welfare both of itself and of the colony, and particularly after 1619 it tried in every way possible to encourage a more diversified agricultural and industrial activity. At that time and afterward, Sir Edwin Sandys and John Ferrar planned, as we have already seen, to promote an ambitious programme, including the planting of new staples and the setting up of such industries as glass-making, brick-making, iron works, salt-making, and shipbuilding; but the effort failed, for not only did the massacre of 1622 put an end to many a likely enterprise but the

New York, containing 5000 books and pamphlets in English and foreign languages. The custodian, Mr. Jerome E. Brooks, is preparing a catalogue of the collection, and a history of the subject based on this material.

1. Brown, *Genesis*, I, 158. Also 160, 163, 166, 169.

2. Hamor, *True Discourse*, p. 24.

3. *Virginia Magazine*, II, 183. "Varina" or "Varinas" was the name given to the best Spanish tobacco from South America. There is mention of "Barinas" [Varinas] in western Venezuela (*American Historical Review*, XXVII, 742, note 1, 744). Virginia tobacco was sent in bundles, tied at the end, or in bulk until the latter was forbidden by statute. Spanish tobacco was sent in large rolls of fixed weight called "puddings" or "rolls".

4. *American Historical Review*, XXVII, 496, 520, note 90; Brown, *Genesis*, II, 659. Rolfe was still sending tobacco in 1621 (*Virginia Company Records*, I, 459). In 1617 he reported "a great plenty in the ground" (*Virginia Magazine*, X, 136).

artisans either proved incompetent or were drawn far too easily along the shorter road to prosperity—the cultivation of tobacco.[1]

In 1619 Sandys said with disgust, at a general court of the company, that "three years before there were returned from Virginia twelve several commodities sold openly in court to the great honour of the action and encouragement of the [Magazine] Adventurers; since that time there had been but little returned worth speaking of save Tobacco and Sassafras, which the people there wholy applying, had by this misgovernment reduced themselves into an extremity of being ready to starve (unless the Magazine this last year had supplied them with Corne and Cattle from hence) to the stopping and great discouragement of many hundreds of people, who were providing to remove themselves to plant in Virginia." The council, he added, had recently sent letters to Governor Yeardley, urging him to restrain "that immoderate following of Tobacco and to cause the people to apply themselves to other and better commodities," and declared that they would issue no more patents of land except on condition that a wider selection of staples be raised thereon.[2] In 1620 an order was sent over to be read in the hundreds and boroughs of the colony, forbidding the planters to cultivate any tobacco; and as late as June, 1622, Sandys could still talk about "this deceavable weede Tobacco, which served neither for necessity nor for ornament to the life of man, but was founded only on humor, which might soon vanish into smoake and come to nothing."[3] The

1. In 1621 Sandys said in parliament that he hoped in time the colonists would be able "to subsist by more sollid commodityes, silke and iron" and that "the silke of persia would not excell that which is made ther[e], for wee have the best mulburie trees in the world" (from the "P" and "Bel" diaries of parliament, items furnished by Professor Notestein). But his hopes, thus extravagantly voiced, were to have no fulfilment.

"The shipwrights' project had failed, chiefly through the loss of Capt. Barwick and six or seven of his principal workmen. The glass-works had succeeded no better, chiefly by reason of the conduct of the Italians employed there, 'for a more damned crew Hell never vomited.' Vincenzio had cracked the furnace with a crow of iron, Capt. Norton was dead, and the Italians were purposely making little progress, in order that they might be sent back to England." Historical Manuscripts Commission, *Eighth Report*, II, no. 318. The iron works were destroyed in the massacre.

2. As early as 1616, an order was issued that no one was to grow tobacco unless he had two acres of land for himself and each man servant sown with corn (Historical Manuscripts Commission, *Eighth Report*, II, no. 208). But this order concerned food for the colony only. In later patents all persons transported under the indenture were to apply themselves to the production of corn, wine, oil, silkgrass, hemp, flax, pitch, tar, soap, ashes, potashes, iron, clapboards, and the like and not wholly or chiefly to tobacco. *Bulletin*, New York Public Library, III, 164.

3. *Virginia Company Records*, I, 266–267, 329; II, 36. See also, 315, 413, 420,

company persisted in this opinion, officially at least, as late as January, 1624, when it said that "they did not doubt butt Virginia would shortlie subsist upon far better commodities than Tobacco."

But despite the company's dislike of "the scurvy weed" ("sot weed," as tobacco was frequently called)[1] and despite its doubts regarding the permanent value of the plant as a staple commodity for the colony, its members were obliged to recognize the fact that their only security and the only hope of prosperity for the plantation lay in the cultivation of tobacco. They began to see also that a profitable staple was a very good thing, as tending to make the system of labor more steadfast and productive. Consequently, while still deploring the neglect of other forms of agriculture, they accepted tobacco as

422, 423, 432–433, 449, 464, 503, 519, and *Virginia Magazine*, X, 418. This opposition to the use of tobacco was not confined to England; it seems to have been world wide in its scope (Beer, *Origins of the British Colonial System, 1578–1660*, pp. 82–85). Sir William Vaughan remarks that in using tobacco "Some lost their wits and the use of their senses in the taking of it." *The Golden Fleece*, pt. III, p. 3. In Dekker's play, "The Wonder of a Kingdome" (*Works*, p. 222), Nicoletto says:

"Now for that chopping herbe of hell, Tobacco,
The idle-man's Devill, and the Drunkard's whore,
I never meddled with her; my smoke goes
Out at my kitchen window, not my nose."

We find the same opposition to the planting of tobacco in Massachusetts Bay, where no man was to smoke publicly (*Massachusetts Colonial Records*, I, 101, 398, 403). Connecticut seems to have had no objection to planting but placed restrictions upon use, requiring that no one should "take it" unless he had a physician's certificate (*Connecticut Colonial Records*, I, 153–154, 558). Yet the elder Winthrop smoked tobacco freely, so much so indeed that he fell into the "immoderate use and love of it." In 1628 he instructed his son to purchase "half a pound of Verina and half a pound of Virginia" in London, to be sent to him at Groton. Later he broke himself of the habit (*Winthrop Papers*, I, 339, 366, 382, 413). Just what is to be inferred from Margaret Winthrop's message to her husband, "mother commend hir love to you all and thankes you for hir toobackco" (*ibid.*, 401), I do not know. The same question is raised in II, 68, "your unckle Tindale and Aunt . . . thank you for their [tobacco]." The editor makes no comment, but probably the herb was to be used for "outward application" only.

There are almost as many contemporary commendations of tobacco as there are expressions of disapproval. For example, in the anonymous *Masque of Flowers* (1613), the Indian Kawasha, contending that the merits of tobacco are superior to those of wine, says:

"Silenus toppes [taps] the barrel, but
Tobacco toppes the brain,
And makes the vapours fine and soote [sweet]
That man revives again."

Evans, *English Masques*, p. 108.

1. Cook's poem, "The Sotweed Factor," is well known. In 1698 Ned Ward wrote, "When we had each of us stuck in our mouths a Pipe of *Sotweed*, we began to look about us." *The London Spy* (ed. 1927), p. 10.

something they could not avoid and set about making the best of a situation which to all outward seeming they heartily condemned. Since 1617 the quality of the staple had been considerably improved, for in that year one Lambert had discovered that tobacco could be cured more satisfactorily when hung up on "lines" or racks than when thrown into heaps on the ground;[1] and the colonists, evidently taught by the Indians, were preparing it for shipment in the three forms of leaf, roll, and "pudding".[2] In 1620 the company itself turned its attention to this problem and granted to one Sumerscall a patent for improved methods of curing the plant, "whereby itt may be made more profitable then itt is."[3]

Having acquiesced in the cultivation of tobacco as an inevitable and unavoidable necessity, the two companies—Virginia and Bermuda—faced the difficult question of how to get the commodity from the planter to the consumer on the best possible terms. Their colonies lay outside England's fiscal barriers and under normal circumstances the importers would have to pay customs duties on all articles exported or imported. But as promoters of colonization they were, by their charters, given preferential treatment and were allowed for the time being at least to export necessities and to import colonial products for seven years free of all duty. This period for the Virginia Company would expire in 1619 and for the Bermuda Company in 1622, after which dates another charter provision would come into operation, that is, exemption from all duties, except the five per cent subsidy (five pounds per hundred).[4] As the current duty on foreign tobaccos was two shillings a pound and as the highest selling value of Virginia and Bermuda tobacco in England at this time was (according to the claim of the companies) but five shillings a pound, the operation of this provision meant that the companies would have to pay on their tobaccos but three pence a pound or, if the farmers in England made an average rate with

1. Winthrop in 1629 wrote to his son Henry in Barbados that the tobacco the latter sent was "very ill conditioned, fowle, full of stalkes and evill coloured." *Winthrop Papers*, II, 67.
2. *Virginia Magazine*, XV, 404.
3. *Virginia Company Records*, I, 364, 398.
4. The only studies that have been made of the tobacco contract, a matter of great consequence in the history of these companies, are by Beer (*Origins*, chs. IV–VI), Scott (*Joint-Stock Companies*, II, 272–283), and Craven (*Dissolution of the Virginia Company*, pp. 221–250). Beer and Scott wrote before the selections from the Sackville Papers, edited by Professor A. P. Newton, had been printed in the *American Historical Review*, but Craven has made excellent use of this material.

Spanish tobacco at two shillings, but sixpence a pound, a very distinct financial advantage.[1] But the companies were always at the mercy of the king's dislike of tobacco, and as it was unquestionably "within the true limitts of his Majesties prerogative utterlie to prohibite the importation of any newe uselesse or forraigne comodities, that in any way is hurtfull to the common wealth in general or wastfull to his subjects in particuler,"[2] the king might at any time place restraints upon its importation. Furthermore, a government in need of money might also at any time demand an increase of revenue and levy an additional duty despite charters. This contingency had been in part responsible for a compromise which was made in 1619, whereby the lord high treasurer, Lionel Cranfield, offered to prohibit all planting of tobacco in England, if, in return, the companies would pay a customs duty of a shilling a pound, which was nine pence more than they were bound to do by their charter, with tobacco at five shillings, and sixpence more, if the flat rate of ten shillings was imposed by the farmers. As this prohibition of tobacco planting in England promised to improve the companies' home market, though at the expense of the English planter, the companies agreed; and a proclamation was issued, December 30, 1619, forbidding all planting in England and Wales, on the somewhat specious ground that to do otherwise would "abuse and misemploy the soile of this fruitfull kingdome" as well as "choak and overthrow the trade of the colony."[3] Probably the real reason for the

1. Beer places the duty at sixpence, as do both Scott (II, 275) and the farmer, "J.S.", who made the offer for the farm of Spanish tobacco (*American Historical Review*, XXVII, 751–752). But "five pounds per centum," with tobacco at five shillings would make the rate three pence. It would be sixpence only if a general rate of ten shillings were made by the farmers. That this is what actually happened and that the companies protested against it as an unjust valuation is evident from the Virginia Company's petition in December, 1619 (*Virginia Company Records*, I, 282).

2. *American Historical Review*, XXVII, 748.

3. *Virginia Company Records*, I, 290–292; *Proclamations*, pp. 18–21, 27–31. It is well known that tobacco planting in England continued despite orders in council, proclamations, and acts of parliament. Officers sent to repress it were "well beaten for their labour" (*Virginia Magazine*, IX, 35). In 1635 this proclamation was taken as a sufficient warrant for the assertion by William Pearse (Peirce), one of the mutineers who drove Governor Harvey out of Virginia, that "his Majestie could not restrain them in Virginia from planting upon their own Land what they pleased" (*ibid.*, 34. See also *ibid.*, XVII, 352–358). The act of 22–23 Charles II, c. 26 (1670) was revived by 1 James II, c. 17, xiii (1685). On a bill of 1669 (not mentioned in *Commons Journal*) see Historical Manuscripts Commission, *Eighth Report*, I, 138–139. Planting was still going on in 1688, when Giles Dowles reported to the Treas-

proclamation was the fact that home-grown tobacco paid no customs duty.

The matter of the customs was not the only difficulty that the companies had to face. The English government at this time was accustomed to grant exclusive rights to certain individuals—farmers and patentees of the imposts, customs, and garbling—to import and inspect (garble) imported commodities, a practice which was extended to include tobacco, because it was necessary, as a proclamation of June 29, 1620, said, to restrain "the disordered traffique in that commoditie and [reduce] it into the hands of able persons that may manage the same without inconvenience."[1] The Virginia Company had already suffered much at the hands of the farmers. In 1619 Abraham Jacob had detained 20,000 pounds of its tobacco, because it would not pay an additional sixpence a pound, and refused to release it, even when ordered to do so by the Privy Council. A similar complaint against Jacob was raised by the Bermuda Company.[2] Furthermore, the patentees for garbling were demanding an extra four pence a pound for their work, thus increasing the cost of importation.[3] Members of the Virginia Company protested against these monopolies and carried the case into parliament, but without result.[4] In addition to these troubles, the companies had to meet the competition in the English market of Spanish tobacco, which though entering at a higher duty and selling at a higher price was a serious rival because of its superior qualities. The English smoker would have it even if he had to pay more for it.[5]

ury that he had suppressed tobacco planting in 200 townships (Treasury 4:5, p. 57). The whole subject is well treated in MacInnes, *The Early English Tobacco Trade*, chs. IV, V, the only helpful chapters in an otherwise disappointing volume.

The opinion expressed in the proclamation was upheld by the College of Physicians, which on September 28, 1628, rendered a report at the request of the Privy Council to the effect that English tobacco was "hurtful to men's bodies, falling short of other tobacco brought from more southern parts." Historical Manuscripts Commission, *Eighth Report*, I, 229.

1. *Proclamations*, pp. 27–31.
2. *Virginia Company Records*, I, 245, 272, 281–284; II, 175.
3. *Proclamations*, pp. 15–18; *Virginia Company Records*, I, 442–443.
4. Stock, *Debates*, I, 28, 30–34.
5. We have already noticed the case of John Winthrop who bought Spanish tobacco as well as Virginia. A pamphlet written by "C.T." and printed in 1615, entitled *An Advice how to plant tobacco in England and how to bring it to colour and perfection, The Vertues of the Hearbe in generall as well as in the outward application as taken in Fume. With the Danger of the Spanish Tobacco* (London, 1615), has this description of Varina. "It is noynted and flubbered over with a kind of juyce or syrope made of salt water, of the dregges or filth of Sugar called

Among the "crosses,"[1] of which the Virginia Company complained, was one of great significance for England's future colonial policy. This was the requirement that all tobaccos should be brought to England only. The official pronouncement came about in this way. The companies protested against the exclusive right of the farmers or customs patentees to control importation, on the ground that such a monopoly prevented the companies from making any direct importation on their own account. In reply the king and Privy Council agreed to break the farming monopoly, which they had granted to Sir Thomas Roe and his associates (with the reservation that they might alter it later),[2] so far as to allow the companies to import directly 55,000 pounds of tobacco themselves. As this amount did not equal the yearly output of the two colonies, Sandys suggested that the privilege be turned over to the Bermuda Company and that the Virginia Company be allowed to send its supply for the year to Middleburg in Holland.[3] The suggestion was not disinterested, as the Middleburg duty was only a half penny,[4] while that imposed at English ports promised to be sixpence or more, and one cannot avoid the conclusion that the proposal was advanced by Sandys to punish the lesser company for its election of Smith instead of himself as governor the year before.[5] That some of the Virginia planters had been accustomed to send tobacco to Middleburg, Flushing, or Amsterdam and were continuing to do so appears from other evidence and from the presence of a "companies factor" at Middleburg.[6] But this freedom of trade was vehe-

Molosses, of blacke honey, Guiana pepper, and leeze of wine, to which in some places they add a red berry called Anoto and other tawni Berries, with which the Indians paint their bodies and their beds. This tobacco is considered very unwholesome and dangerous." The writer urges people to buy the natural not the black or dyed tobacco. He mentions imports from Trinidad, Orinoco, Santo Domingo, and Bermuda, but none from Virginia, which is not surprising as the first instalment reached Bristol only in 1614.

1. *Virginia Company Records,* II, 176.
2. *Acts Privy Council, Colonial,* I, §§ 48, 49.
3. *Virginia Company Records,* I, 405–406.
4. *Ibid.,* 422.
5. Scott, *Joint-Stock Companies,* II, 274–275; Butler, *Historye of the Bermudaes,* p. 131.
6. *Virginia Company Records,* I, 526, 606; II, 108, 305; *Acts Privy Council, Colonial,* I, §77, speaks of the factors of the merchants now abroad (cf. *ibid.,* §96); *Calendar State Papers, Colonial,* 1574–1660, pp. 63, 84. Middleburg was one of the most important of the Dutch commercial centers and the first to be chartered as a city. It was in close touch with the trade of the Scottish boroughs, and in 1611 the question came up of transferring the Scottish staple from Campvere (Veere) to Mid-

mently opposed by the Privy Council, which declared in a memorable order of October 24, 1621, that "neither in policie nor for the honor of the state ([Virginia] being but a colonie derived from hence)" was any tobacco or other commodities to "be carried into any forraine partes untill the same [had] been first landed [in England] and his Majesties Customs paid therefore."[1] The companies, aroused by this order—the third shift of the governmental mind within a year and a half[2]—sent word to the Privy Council that they would bring in none at all that year.[3] But when informed that this was "an unduetifull answere," they replied, dejectedly, that only by "the rigor of the former contractor" had they been "driven to seeke forraigne parts" and that were the monopoly restored and they be forced to bring all their tobacco to England their plantation would be ruined."[4]

Then the suggestion was made that the companies assume the monopoly themselves. Who first made the suggestion is not clear. Sandys said that it had come from the governor and the deputy governor of the Bermuda Company, Sir Thomas Smith and Alderman Johnson, and this statement he repeated later when he said that the scheme "had its beginninge from an offer made by some

dleburg (Davidson and Grey, *The Staple at Veere*). Probably the Courteens, Peter and William, were the members of the firm in Middleburg that handled the Virginia tobacco (Brown, *Republic,* pp. 599–600). There is ample reason for believing, not only that the colonists continued to trade with the Dutch in tobacco for years to come but also that the Dutch came to Virginia and Bermuda, as later to Barbados, and took on cargoes in their ports and rivers. This persistent disregard of England's commercial policy was one of the causes that led to the capture of New Netherland in America in 1664. On the subject see *Virginia Magazine,* IX, 35, 41, 177; X, 424; XVII, 117; Wertenbaker, *The Planters of Colonial Virginia,* pp. 68–69.

1. *Acts Privy Council, Colonial,* I, §77; *Virginia Company Records,* I, 527–529, 530, 537. On November 2, 1622, the Council for New England declared that "to restrayne trade to this island [England] is hard." *Proceedings,* American Antiquarian Society, 1867, p. 68.

2. First, exclusion by monopoly; then an allowance of 55,000 pounds; and, finally, all to be brought to England (*Virginia Company Records,* II, 175). In regard to these frequent changes of the "royal mind," so much criticized by Virginia historians, it must be remembered that the planting of colonies and the importing of colonial products was a new experience and brought the king and his lord high treasurer face to face with a new situation. The Sackville documents, printed in the *American Historical Review,* show how much Treasurer Cranfield was concerned with the necessity of increasing the royal revenue and with finding out which was the best way to do it—whether by monopoly, free trade, or the farm of a part. In the matter of policy Cranfield and the Privy Council were feeling their way. One can hardly blame them for failing to reach a final decision at once.

3. *Virginia Company Records,* I, 526–530, 537, 564, 568.

4. *Ibid.,* II, 315, 322–323.

principall Members of the Companies."[1] Apparently he intended to imply that Smith and Johnson first put the idea into the head of the lord high treasurer, Cranfield (now Earl of Middlesex), for on still another occasion[2] he hinted that the offer had come from the lord high treasurer himself, "out of his noble affection and well wishinge to the Plantation." However that may be, the proposal was made in June, 1622, and immediately taken into consideration by the companies, as giving them "the sole managinge of all that commodity with reservation of a valuable rent to his Majestie, which he thought might redound to the great benefitt of the Plantations."[3]

The terms finally agreed on were as follows. In the first place, all importations of tobacco were to be completely controlled by the companies, including an amount of Varinas Spanish tobacco, not to be less than 40,000 pounds' weight during the first two years of the contract. Because excessive planting in Venezuela, Guiana, Brazil, and the Spanish West Indies was threatening to create a glut in the English market, Cranfield refused to consent to the bringing in of 60,000 pounds' weight, as the companies at first desired. The contract also allowed that all importations should be consigned only to the companies' officers and stored only in the companies' warehouses along the Thames in London. Had the contract been carried out, the companies would have erected two subsidiary joint-stocks for the management of the business.[4]

In the second place, the companies were to pay only the "ancient custom" of sixpence a pound for roll tobacco and fourpence a pound for leaf, and to hand over to the royal exchequer the amount received from the sale of one-third of all tobacco imported. The king, in his turn, bound himself to carry a full third part of the charges that were incurred after the tobacco, Spanish and other, had reached England. He was to pay no part of the freight, but was to meet his share of the customs and subsidy, and his proportion of the cost of landing, carrying, housing, keeping, tending, curing, and sorting the tobacco and of transporting it into different parts

1. *Virginia Company Records*, II, 67–68, 176.
2. *Ibid.*, II, 66. This statement is repeated in the "Discourse of the Old Company," *Virginia Magazine*, I, 240–241.
3. *Ibid.*
4. *American Historical Review*, XXVII, 757–762. According to the contract the king was to issue a proclamation prohibiting tobacco planting in Ireland as well as in England and Wales, but he never did so.

of the realm. He was to pay a third part also of all salaries of officials employed and of the costs of all possible suits at law.[1]

In the debate that took place in the courts of the Virginia Company,[2] criticism centered on three points: the bringing of all tobacco
to England; the amount of Spanish tobacco to be imported; and the
king's share of a third of the profits. The critics wanted the complete exclusion of all foreign tobacco, unless controlled by the companies, but they finally compromised on 40,000 pounds' weight,
though they considered this limitation "the hardest part and article
in the whole contract." They also wished to reduce the king's third
to a fourth, but finally gave in on that point also. The matter was
under consideration for the greater part of the year 1622, but was
not brought to a final vote until November 27. On that day, in "an
extraordinary court held for Virginia, being the Summer Islande
Quarter Court," the contract was approved by a majority of both
companies.[3] The bargain was ratified by the Privy Council the
February following.[4]

How far the contract was forced upon the companies it is difficult
to say. In reading the evidence one gets the impression that the
members did not want it,[5] but rather than break with the king and
the lord treasurer accepted it as "a bitter pill," because "prejudicial
unto them in matter of profitt."[6] The opponents of the Sandys
party, who left the meeting of November 27 before the vote was
taken,[7] claimed that the members were "overawed" by the chair-
men of the companies—the Earl of Southampton, who succeeded
Sandys in 1620, and Lord Cavendish, who succeeded Smith in 1623
—but both men denied the charge.[8] It is clear, however, that Sandys

1. The completed contract is printed in *American Historical Review*, XXVII, 742–
745; *Virginia Company Records*, II, 147, 148, 157.
2. For the debates, *Virginia Company Records*, II, 62–63, 66, 70–71, 85–87, 120–
122, 139–143, 302–311, 335–340; Beer, *Origins*, pp. 122–128.
3. *Virginia Company Records*, II, 146–157.
4. *Acts Privy Council, Colonial*, I, §95.
5. *American Historical Review*, XXVII, 755.
6. *Virginia Company Records*, II, 143–144. "This guilded pill," *Virginia Magazine*, I, 291. In judging the case, it must not be forgotten that the lord treasurer
was seeking revenue and the companies profit. With the lord treasurer in the ascendant it was not easy to reconcile these two objectives. We need not bring in the
political motive, as there is no evidence that politics had anything to do with the
case.
7. *Virginia Company Records*, II, 311.
8. *Ibid.*, 298, 302, 306. The charge was brought by one Byng of the opposition,
who was antagonistic to the Earl of Southampton. He explained later that the fear

favored the contract and in the voting had his followers well in hand. The review of the case, presented by his party in 1625, in the "Discourse of the Old Company," is disingenuous and not in accord with the evidence of the proceedings themselves. It reflects the bitterness engendered by the factional quarreling in the companies and must be read in the light of a defeated ambition.

The antagonism already aroused was greatly intensified when the method of managing the monopoly conferred by the contract was brought up for consideration. The committee in charge presented an elaborate list of "faithfull Officers to manage the business with Salaries proportionable in some measure for their paines,"[1] embracing an official personnel which ran from a director and his deputies to a number of lesser employees, at a total cost of £2500. The report was heard with "a general silence in the court,"[2] and when the names were read out—Sandys for director, John Ferrar for deputy and treasurer, and so on—the opposition became vocal. Many, even of Sandys' own party, disapproved of the salaries as much too large, while those of the opposition were enraged, not only at such an expenditure in the face of the financial bankruptcy of the companies,[3] but even more at the manifest intent of the scheme to strengthen Sandys' control over the affairs of both plantations. A long and heated series of debates followed, led by one of the council, Samuel Wrote, a first cousin of Cranfield, Earl of Middlesex, which lasted off and on for two months, during which little or no business was done. In February, 1623, Wrote was put off the council (though restored in July)[4] and temporarily suspended from the company.[5] But even this rather highhanded action did not bring the wrangling to a close or improve the reputation of the company.

mentioned was not *metus potentiae* but *metus reverentiae*. For Southampton's manner, on which Byng based his charge, see 302–303. The earl "sett him downe in his chaire, pulling his hatt over his eyes and foldinge his Armes acrosse and leninge backeward in his Chaire, as if all were lost," etc. Southampton was reported also to have told the members that unless they approved the contract they would lose the plantations. In the hearing before the Privy Council, Cavendish explained that the loss of the plantations would be inevitable because of the lowering of the price of tobacco, not because of any action on the part of the king.

1. *Virginia Company Records*, II, 148.　2. *Ibid.*, 152.

3. Historical Manuscripts Commission, *Eighth Report*, II, nos. 300–304, 307, 309. For the financial situation in 1622–1623, Brown, *Republic*, pp. 492, 493; *Virginia Company Records*, II, 258.

4. *Calendar State Papers, Colonial*, 1574–1660, p. 50.

5. *Virginia Company Records*, II, 258–259.

The Earl of Warwick, Sir Nathaniel Rich, his cousin, and Alderman Johnson, son-in-law of Sir Thomas Smith and in many ways the chief mover of the opposition, appealed at this juncture to the lord treasurer, who suspended temporarily the operation of the contract and ordered a hearing at which representatives of both parties were to be present.[1] The meeting was held, but at what place and on what date we do not know. On one side were Warwick, Rich, Johnson, Wrote, Byng, Caning, Argall, and Woodall, with Sir John Wolstenholme (also a member of the company) and other farmers of the customs, who opposed the contract; on the other, Southampton, Cavendish, Sandys, the Ferrars, Sir John Danvers, and "some more," supporting the companies and defending the contract.[2] Cranfield heard both sides "with a great deal of patience, interruptinge no man." But no decision was reached, and Cranfield finally ordered the companies to go on with the contract, "notwithstanding these differences and oppositions."[3] Then the Warwick party carried the matter to the Privy Council and another hearing was arranged, early in March, 1623, at which, though Warwick himself was absent, a larger group than before, representative of both sides, was present. There the matter was debated at length, morning and afternoon, and at the end the lord president of the council, Henry Viscount Mandeville, after laying down once more and with great firmness the rule that all tobacco must be brought to England first, asked the members of the opposition if they had any better plan to suggest, which would uphold his Majesty's profit and redound to the benefit of the plantations.[4] In reply, Sir John Wolstenholme, "seconded againe and againe by another gentleman one of the Customers," made a threefold proposal: freedom for every man to bring in what tobacco he pleased and after he had brought it in to dispose

1. *Ibid.*, 294–295. See also "Argument against the Contract," March 20, 1623, presented at some time before the hearing was held, *American Historical Review*, XXVII, 754–756.

2. Eighty-three names are given in the Manchester Papers, but it is not to be supposed that all were present, Historical Manuscripts Commission, *Eighth Report*, II, no. 327.

3. *Virginia Company Records*, II, 297.

4. *Ibid.*, 305, 311. Another hearing was held April 17, 1623, *ibid.*, 364–366; *Acts Privy Council, Colonial*, I, §98, and in the meantime, March 23, 1623, a powerful argument against the contract, with other papers later, was sent to the lord treasurer, *American Historical Review*, XXVII, 748–762, especially, 754–756. Mandeville, afterward the first earl of Manchester, had himself served as lord treasurer for a short time in 1620–1621, before Cranfield took office.

of it without restraint, thus getting rid of one of the worst features
of the monopoly; a uniform duty of twelve pence a pound, thus
rendering unnecessary the elaborate system of officers and salaries,
proposed by the Sandys party; and, lastly, complete obedience to
the rule laid down by the Privy Council that all tobacco should first
be brought to England. There can be no doubt that this simple and
effective plan, though bitterly opposed by Sandys, both then and
afterward, as tending to the ruin of the plantations, was favored by
the king's advisers, who were responsible for the royal revenues as
well as for the plantations. On April 14, 1623, they issued an order
for a special commission to make inquiry "of the true estate of the
plantation both of Virginia and the Sommer Islands, with all inci-
dentes thereunto belonging from the beginning until the present
time," and on the 28th ordered that the contract be dissolved as
tending "to the utter overthrow and subversion of the said Plantation."[1] The tobacco contract was dead.

1. *Acts Privy Council, Colonial*, I, §§ 98, 100; "Discourse of the Old Company,"
Virginia Magazine, I, 293–294. On March 30, 1623, the council in Virginia wrote to
Lord Mandeville, expressing its satisfaction at the annulment of the contract and
saying that the company's arrangements and contracts had been made "wholly without their consent and privity" (*Calendar State Papers, Colonial*, 1574–1660, p. 111).
The planters in Virginia frequently said afterward that the contract was projected by
men, whose ends were their private gains and lucre and not the profit of the crown
or the welfare of the colony. As late as 1628 they could speak of "these pernicious
contracts, which so often for these six years have been continually intruded and
made on their tobacco without their knowledge or privity." *Virginia Magazine*, VII,
264.

CHAPTER VIII

THE DOWNFALL OF THE VIRGINIA
COMPANY

THE opposition party had won the day and the outlook was
ominous for Sandys and his followers, who, having become by one means or another the preponderant party in
the Virginia Company, was controlling its destinies, just as
the Warwick group was controlling the destinies of Bermuda. That
the defeat of Sandys in the matter of the contract was due to any
direct interference by King James cannot be shown by any evidence
at our disposal. The issue was strictly one that concerned the relations between the companies and the plantations. The king and the
Privy Council were interested in the companies and their plantations, and their attitude toward each was determined, not by politics, but by the way each was conducting its affairs and advancing
or retarding the plantation under its charge. The king personally
expressed his concern for the progress of the plantations and his desire to favor the companies and to increase their rights and privileges, and even at the height of the controversy in 1623, reaffirmed
his promise to preserve the freedom of the Virginia Company, declaring that no man should be abridged of his right to speak freely,
so it be "with fitting report unto the government and the plantations."[1] In the election of May, 1620, when it became evident that
Sandys could not be reëlected treasurer, the king threw what influence he had in favor of Smith or Johnson and was undoubtedly ill-
pleased when Southampton was chosen and the right of free election was maintained by the company. At the same time he said, in
answer to the company's protest, that he had no intention of inter-
fering with its liberty of choice.[2] But he cannot have been satisfied,
as no one could have been satisfied, with the strife and dissension
which characterized the company's activities and scandalized the
London world during these later years. Sandys frequently insisted
that misleading and malicious information was carried to the king

1. *Virginia Company Records,* I, 429, 438; II, 216.
2. *Ibid.,* I, 384. For a similar statement in 1623, II, 28.

and the Privy Council by the company's enemies and that many aspersions and false rumors were spread about concerning himself.[1] He and others of his party charged Warwick and his supporters with being the instigators of these reports, but their unsupported charges at this crisis of affairs must be taken very cautiously. In any case the tenor of the remarks could hardly have been worse than the facts warranted, for the discord is plainly evident in the company's records.

After the break in 1619 between Sir Thomas Smith on one side and Sandys and Warwick on the other, which manifested itself first in the ousting of Smith from the treasureship and later in the attack on the Smith-Johnson management of the magazine, of which Johnson was the director,[2] the two leaders continued in friendly relations enough for about two years. The status quo was maintained with some difficulty during the long-drawn-out controversy over the conduct of Argall, who had been governor of Virginia at the time when the *Treasurer* had gone a-cruising among the West Indies against the Spaniards. Sandys, in order to relieve the company of blame, accused Argall of connivance if not actual participation and Warwick with complicity, and followed up his indictment with an appeal to the Privy Council.[3] His conduct placed Warwick in an embarrassing position, for the charge had been sprung suddenly, and it is probably from this time that we are to date the real rift in their friendly relations. Matters were made worse by the dispute over the case of Captain Martin in Virginia, who had claimed extraordinary privileges there by virtue of an old patent (irregularly obtained, the company said), and in consequence had been barred from taking his seat in the Virginia assembly of 1619.[4] Sandys suspected that Warwick and his allies were "Chiefe Abettors of Capt. Martin in this business," even though he must have known that the

1. *Virginia Company Records*, I, 329, 357, 359.
2. *Ibid.*, I, 241–242. Johnson was censured and resigned, *ibid.*, 243, 244.
3. *Acts Privy Council, Colonial*, I, §45; *Virginia Company Records*, II, 404–405.
4. *Ibid.*, II, 18, 26, 27, 43, 78, 119, 126–127, 140, 145, 161–162, 181, 216, 344; *Acts Privy Council Colonial* I, §120; Neill in *Macalester College Contributions*, 1st series, no. 5; Brown, "The Case of Captain Martin," *Virginia Magazine*, VII, 268–275; Craven, *Dissolution of the Virginia Company*, pp. 117–120. Brown says that James I was instrumental in having the extra privileges inserted in Martin's patent, but gives no authority for his statement. His article contains a good deal of speculation in his best manner, much of which is based on no evidence whatever, and must not be taken seriously. He was a good collector but a poor interpreter, as may be seen in his volume *English Politics in Early Virginia History*.

Privy Council, rightly or wrongly, was behind Martin and that when the latter returned to Virginia at the end of the year 1623 he bore orders to the governor and council there to receive him and his servants with respect and to allow them to enjoy peaceably "such lands and goods as belonge unto them."

But the alliance between the two men, even under favorable circumstances, could hardly have been permanent. Warwick was of the gentry-merchant class, a frequent participator in many commercial enterprises and an adventurer in the world of affairs. He was the largest stockholder in the Bermuda Company, one of the largest in the Virginia Company, and a heavy investor in the shares of other companies and in many private undertakings. He was by instinct dominant, cool, and aggressive. It is impossible to think of him as the tool of any man, least of all of King James, with whose absolutist ideas and divine right doctrines he had no sympathy, as his later career shows. He was hardheaded, a shrewd business man, practical and scheming, possessed of generous impulses, and always ready to help when in so doing he might serve some end of his own. At this time he was but thirty-six years of age. Sandys, on the other hand, was sixty-two years old, high spirited, something of a visionary, a tolerationist, and a liberal by temperament. When convinced of the rightness of his course, he could become intolerant and obstinate and persistent in seeking his ends. He was not a good business man; nor were Nicholas and John Ferrar, his chief allies, as wise as they should have been; and while Warwick was often ruthless and a believer in strong measures, Sandys for the purpose of maintaining his control was willing to resort to devices that savor of political practices. Both he and Southampton seem at times to have manipulated votes in order to gain their point.[1] He was charged by his opponents with suppressing information and concealing the truth about the condition of the companies and the plantations, though the charge is not well sustained. But there is reason to think that the records of the companies, as we have them today, do not contain all that might have been taken down by the secretary and that the omissions favor the Sandys party.[2] There is also reason to think

1. For example, *Virginia Company Records*, II, 437.
2. Scott, *Joint-Stock Companies*, II, 278–283. Dr. Scott is unfriendly to Sandys, largely because he is interested in the business aspects of the company, which offer ample opportunities for unfavorable comment. But he is not always exact in his statements, and once in his desire to show how the Sandys party managed the voting he makes a curious blunder. On page 281 he says, "It was alleged that on one

that the charges brought against Sandys and others of misusing the funds of the Virginia Company, or at least of spending them unwisely, are justified, for Sandys was a poor manager and seems to have had no natural business sense. That he endeavored to control appointments in the colony is not so clear,[1] but there is no doubt whatever that he could play politics as well as his opponents.[2]

The elaborate programmes of 1620 and 1621, splendidly conceived and in part carried out, were not followed up in 1622 and 1623. This relaxation of effort was in part due, without doubt, to the massacre of 1622 which checked further attempts at expansion in the colony; but it was also due to the bankruptcy of the company and the refusal of many of its members who had lost confidence and interest in it to complete their subscriptions and even to attend its meetings. After 1622 the carefully prepared plans for churches, inns, a hospital, a free school, and a college were all given up and very little was done for the colony during these last two years of the company's career. The bustling activities of 1620 and 1621 were yielding to the acrimonious debates of 1622 to 1624, years that mark the company's "extreme poverty," "the necessitous time," when having lost the privilege of the lottery, without stock and in debt,[3] and with all

occasion ladies and even serving-men possessed themselves of balls and placed them in the urn or box and that they were counted as votes." The record reads, "Divers lackies and Serving men at the Lower end of the Hall held up their hands against him" (*Virginia Company Records*, II, 198). For the charges of suppressing information and manipulating the record, *ibid.*, I, 329; II, 274, 499–500.

1. In the cases of George Sandys, his brother; Sir Francis Wyatt, his nephew by marriage; and Christopher Davison, the secretary (*ibid.*, I, 450, 489). It is an interesting fact that neither Sir Edwin nor his brother George were popular either in Virginia or in Bermuda. If the statements of the Virginia governor and council are to be taken as true of the colony as a whole, the planters there welcomed the change from the control of the company to that of the king, though they strongly opposed the admission of Sandys' enemies to membership on the committees that controlled the colony after the fall of the company. A letter from Virginia, written early in 1623 by one John Baldwin contains this statement, "Mr [George] Sandys hath dealt unkindlie with us, he maketh us serve him whether we will or noe and how to help it we do not know for he bareth all the sway" (Lefroy, *Memorials of the Bermudas*, I, 264). William Capps wrote the same year, "Mr. [George] Sandys he griped all for the company, for all your order of Court . . . the right worthy statesman for his own profit" (Historical Manuscripts Commission, *Eighth Report*, II, no. 322).

2. That Sandys could play the political game appears from his relations with Cranfield, against whom he and John Ferrar drew up a charge of bribery. This charge Sir Edward Coke presented in the House of Commons in April, 1624. The move was a piece of sheer politics, for the charge of bribery was never proved and Cranfield, then Earl of Middlesex, was later restored to his seat in the House of Lords.

3. *Virginia Company Records*, II, 109, 110, 164, 169, 222, 388; *Virginia Maga-*

sorts of complaints and petitions coming in, its governing board seemed wholly incompetent to meet the situation. It had kept no registry of people going to the plantations, had provided no way in which families and friends could get in touch with those who had gone overseas, was seemingly impotent in such matters as keeping a check upon passengers' goods and enforcing covenants between masters and servants, and, in some respects most neglectful of all, had set up no probate system in the colonies. Those who died in Virginia had relatives in England and many of them doubtless had property there, but the total lack of information regarding their fate, except as returning colonists brought the news, must have caused not only personal sorrow but also much business confusion. When we add to these manifestations of inefficiency, the demands of all sorts that were made on the company for recompense and wages and the suits at law that were threatened, we can understand the widespread belief at the time that both companies had wasted their substance through bad management and that the so-called "democraticall" way of carrying on business, which had been established by the charter of 1612, was proving a lamentable failure.

There can be no doubt that in the eyes of king, Privy Council, and others connected with government and also of many a contemporary watching the course of affairs, the organization of the company, its "popularness," and its "democraticall" character were in large part responsible for the factional quarreling and the savage personal dislikes which had arisen in the quarterly courts since 1619. That such antipathies had not, as far as we know, appeared in the years before 1619 would seem to indicate that the fault lay less with the organization than with the men who composed it, but there can be little question that the meetings of the generality offered a favorable *milieu* for the public exhibition of group and individual rivalries. These meetings were often attended by "disorderly and unworthy personns," who had no right to be present and take any part

zine, XVI, 5, "We are 2000lbs sterling behind which is a great discouragement," August 6, 1623. For unpaid subscriptions, *Virginia Company Records,* I, 390, 412, 484, 495, 551, 560, 580; II, 14; exhaustion of company's stock, *ibid.,* II, 13, 19, 260, 459; petitions, II, 111, 112, 113, 115, 117; charges and answers, II, 346–347, 348–351, 352–362. Sandys insisted that the exhaustion of the company's stock was due to the debts Smith left behind, a very unfair and untrue statement, for without the aid of Smith and Warwick, both good business men, Sandys would have been helpless in the matter of raising funds. He also accused the opposition of envy, of being behind in their accounts, and of fear lest they be called to book for ruining the plantations. In none of these accusations are his statements convincing.

in the proceedings; by footmen and servants, who had been admitted to the lower end of the hall and had apparently interrupted the voting; and by others whose arguments were carried on with "violence and unorderlynes." With Wrote's long-winded oratory the court became "overwearied," and Wrote himself was charged with transgressing the rules by speaking so often to one subject.[1] Wrote, in his turn, declared that "the business was carried fowly and disorderly and with much arte surreptitiously and to private ends," "hastily shuffled over," with "no due course taken for preparing of matters."[2] The king and the Privy Council, who had never openly expressed any objection to a popular form of government for the colony, could hardly fail to be unfavorably impressed by the unsatisfactory results of the experiment of 1612 and to have been only too ready, should the opportunity offer, to return to the system of 1606. The incorporation of "a multitude of persons of severall dispositions, amongst whom the affairs of greatest moment were and must be ruled by the greater number of votes and voyces" had been tried and had ended only in confusion and the neglect of the colony, and we may not wonder that king and council deemed it the better part of wisdom to alter the framework of the company and, while preserving and securing all private interests, to take the colony into their own hands. Just what would be done eventually with the form of government in the colony was a matter of later concern.[3]

The final break between Sandys and Warwick came in 1622 over the salary question, and from that time on the meetings lost whatever deliberative and harmonious characteristics they ever possessed.[4] Warwick and Nathaniel Rich now went over to the side of

1. *Virginia Company Records*, II, 167, 168, 198, 424. A writer in 1631 said, "The Plantation of Virginia was heretofore for many yeares governed by a corporation, during which government the Plantation had small and slow success as well in respect of the ignorance of those who governed the corporation in England commanding thinges unfitt and improper for that place, as also in respect of the severall factions in that Corporation who out of passion and particular interest did usually cross and hinder all thinges that were propounded by contrary parties, so that most of their assemblyes here [in England], instead of consulting for the general good of that Colony the time was spent in invectives one against another, with great sharpness and bitterness to the great prejudice of the Plantation." *Virginia Magazine*, VIII, 40.

2. *Virginia Company Records*, II, 165, 170.

3. *Proclamations*, p. 52; *Acts Privy Council, Colonial*, I, §§109, 112.

4. The line of cleavage ran through the membership of the Virginia Company and between the two companies, one of which was controlled by Sandys, Southampton, Sackville, and Cavendish and the other by Warwick, Smith, and Johnson.

Smith and Johnson and frequently absented themselves from the meetings of both council and court of the elder company.[1] But of their followers who remained, many were always ready to filibuster and obstruct and to oppose the Sandys group within and without. One William Canning had a fight with Thomas Keightley in the Royal Exchange and was fined.[2] W. Byng, "a mere good fellow, a man of no estate," for insolent remarks to the Earl of Southampton at the Privy Council board was sent to the Marshalsea prison.[3] Hard words were bandied back and forth at the meetings, lies passed, and threats made. In July, 1623, Warwick and Cavendish "fell so foul" of each other that a duel was avoided with difficulty.[4] At the hearing of April 23 before the king, Sackville carried himself so insolently that James "was fain to take him down soundly and roundly."[5] In the same year at a Virginia court a paper was read by Captain Nathaniel Butler, quondam governor of Bermuda and a Warwick appointee, entitled, "The Unmasked Face of our Colony in Virginia, as it was in the Winter of the year 1622," which presented a melancholy picture of the colony.[6] This paper, which Sandys and the Ferrars endeavored to answer clause by clause,[7] made them infinite trouble. They accused Warwick with being the chief instigator of it, because, as they said, he and the other merchants wished to get rid of the company altogether and to obtain control of the colonies for their own advantage. They even hinted that Warwick was willing to go over to Virginia as its governor.[8] The truth is that as re-

1. *Virginia Company Records*, II, 405–406.

2. *Calendar State Papers, Colonial*, 1574–1660, pp. 55, 56; Brown, *Republic*, pp. 589–591.

3. *Calendar State Papers, Colonial*, 1574–1660, p. 65; *Virginia Company Records*, II, 329.

4. *Calendar State Papers, Colonial*, 1574–1660, p. 51, Neill, *Virginia Company*, p. 413; Craven, *Dissolution of the Virginia Company*, pp. 308–310.

5. *Calendar State Papers, Colonial*, 1574–1660, p. 44. On November 20, 1622, John Donne, doctor of divinity and dean of St. Paul's, who had joined the company the May before, preached a sermon to the members, taking as his text, Acts, I, 8, "But ye shall receive power, after that the Holy Ghost is come unto you, and ye shall be witnesses unto me both in Jerusalem, and in all Judea, and in Samaria, and unto the uttermost parts of the earth." In the prayer that followed he calls on God to bless the government of the company "with dispositions to unity and concord."

6. *Virginia Company Records*, II, 374–376; Brown, *Republic*, pp. 506, 518; Prince in *Report*, American Historical Association, 1899, p. 362. The last named calls the "Unmasking" "a blundering if not a lying" paper. This is far too sweeping an opinion. Blundering it may have been, but it told some unpalatable truths. See the references, given on page 172, note 1, below, to letters from the colony.

7. *Virginia Company Records*, II, 381–387.   8. *Ibid.*, 401–404.

gards Warwick's attitude toward the colony we know only what his opponents tell us, and the evidence upon which conclusions have hitherto been based is mainly that furnished by Sandys and the Ferrars. Manifestly such conclusions cannot be accepted *in toto* or as final.

By the end of 1623, the prestige of the Virginia Company had seriously diminished and its usefulness as a colonizing agency had become greatly impaired. Affairs had reached such a pass that the colony, still bearing the scars of the massacre and in a pitiable condition from bad and insufficient food,[1] was stumbling along without guidance and without support. No money could be raised at home, all undertakings had stopped, the stream of settlers and supplies had either dwindled to very slender proportions or had ceased altogether. The members of the company were so entangled in a labyrinth of charges and counter charges that there seemed no way out of the maze. Extrication from their predicament had become, as John Chamberlain wrote to Sir Dudley Carleton, "a thornie business,"[2] and to many a man of the day there must have been no other solution than to get rid of the company altogether.

The royal government gave the leaders of the factions on both sides every opportunity to present their respective cases. Hearings were held at one time or another before the king, the lord treasurer, and the Privy Council, and no one has a right to say that the judges had already made up their minds before the hearings began. The Sandys party carried the matter into parliament, though the issue was one belonging only to the executive branch of the government, and they did so because they thought that there the chances of success would be the greater, in that the dispute could be made a political rather than an administrative issue and a decision could be reached on political grounds rather than upon the merits of the case. But the king took the matter out of the hands of parliament, partly because it did not belong there and partly because it was likely to breed "much faction and distraction" among the members, "being followed on both sides with much eagerness and animositie."[3]

1. *Virginia Magazine*, VI, 374–377; *Virginia Company Records*, II, 459; Historical Manuscripts Commission, *Eighth Report*, II, nos. 318–326.
2. Lefroy, *Memorials*, I, 337.
3. Stock, *Debates*, I, 66–68. As the Warwick-Rich side of the story has never had an adequate hearing, owing in part to the absence of anything but *ex parte* evidence, it is worth while to consider carefully Sir Nathaniel Rich's speech in parliament on this occasion (p. 66). It contains a fair statement of the Warwick party's

What the result would have been had parliament attempted to review the facts in dispute cannot even be conjectured, though we know that King James's parliaments were not fond of monopolies and that Sandys had already laid himself open to the charge of having tried to establish a monopoly in tobacco.[1] It is possible that the occasion might have been used for another quarrel with the king, as many of the members of the company were also members of the House of Commons. A contemporary writer says that the king's letter withdrawing the case "was assented unto by a general silence, but not without some soft muttering that by this means and example" other business also might be taken out of the hands of parliament.[2] Another contemporary may be describing the effect with equal accuracy, when he says that for the king to settle the business himself was the best course to pursue and was "no doubt pleasing to the major part."[3]

King James, guided by his advisers, acted with a strict regard for the rights of the company. In reply to a petition from Alderman Johnson, presented early in April, 1623,[4] he ordered the Privy Council to appoint a commission of inquiry, the patent for which passed the great seal on May 9.[5] By this patent Sir William Jones and six others were instructed to make a searching inquiry into the affairs of both companies, in order to discover whether the letter of the charters had been adhered to, "according to the true intent and meaning thereof," or had been "violated, infringed or broken."[6] At the same time the king ordered the Privy Council to consider the business of Virginia and to manage the colony until it was once more on its feet. In response to this order, the Privy Council had a meeting on April 17, at which the members of both companies were

point of view and rings as true as do the speeches of Sandys and his followers and much more so than do the statements made later in the "Discourse of the Old Company."

1. Only the next year, 1624, parliament passed an act (21 and 22 James I, c. 3) containing this clause, "That all monopolies . . . to any person, bodies politic or corporate whatsoever, for the sole buying [or] selling . . . of anything within this realm . . . are altogether contrary to the laws of this realm."

2. *Virginia Magazine*, VI, 394.   3. Lefroy, *Memorials*, I, 337.

4. *Virginia Company Records*, II, 373–374; Neill, *Virginia Company*, pp. 387–389; Historical Manuscripts Commission, *Eighth Report*, II, nos. 328, 329.

5. *Acts Privy Council, Colonial*, I, §98; *Virginia Magazine*, XVI, 113–119; Lefroy, *Memorials*, I, 290–291, 323–324.

6. The members of the commission were evidently gathering material for their report during May and June, 1623. Historical Manuscripts Commission, *Eighth Report*, II, nos. 330–335, 340–363.

present and were enjoined "to agree of one general letter to goe from them all, upon the heads wee [the Privy Council] have appointed them," and to allow "no pryvate letters" to go from any man "differing in anie point from the generall." They were instructed further that when the wording of this general letter had been agreed upon by the companies, the Privy Council would send it to the colony.

The companies met in April and discussed the entire situation.[1] They prepared the text of the general letter, but as the Privy Council did not like what they had written and ordered them to prepare another, they met again on May 2 and revised the draft to accord with the council's idea of the form such a letter should take.[2] Two copies of this draft were sent off, one to Virginia and one to Bermuda,[3] containing instructions to the colonists—the first that had been despatched of any importance for more than a year—regarding their relations with the Indians, staples, tobacco, guest-houses, and sickness. The Privy Council, convinced by letters it received from the colonists (which it had ordered the companies to send, unopened, directly to the council board), that the colonists were in misery and want and that immediate measures should be taken for their relief, commanded the Virginia Company to send over men and supplies at once. This the company promised to do,[4] provided those indebted to the joint-stock would pay the instalments due on their subscriptions. These efforts on the part of the Privy Council to compel the company to come to the aid of the colony which it had shamefully neglected, show the wide-spread dissatisfaction which existed with the way affairs in Virginia had been managed by the company during the preceding two years.

The simple truth is that the Virginia Company had reached a point where it was unable to meet its obligations and, to use a modern phrase, was obliged to go into the hands of a receiver. In con-

1. Lefroy, *Memorials*, I, 290–291 (Middlesex's account of the meeting), 293–295, 297–298 (letter to Bermuda).

2. *Acts Privy Council, Colonial*, I, §100; *Virginia Company Records*, II, 365, 367–369. Outlines of the proposed letter are given in *American Historical Review*, XXVII, 763–765. The model of the letter, drawn up by the Privy Council, is in *Calendar State Papers, Colonial*, 1574–1660, p. 48. Note also Nathaniel Rich's proposed insertions, Historical Manuscripts Commission, *Eighth Report*, II, no. 335.

3. Neill, *Virginia Company*, pp. 391–394.

4. *Virginia Company Records*, II, 460, 461, 463; *Acts Privy Council, Colonial*, I, §109.

temporary language, it had been, in July, 1623, taken over by the crown and put under the management of the Privy Council. Had this not been done, probably no attempt would or could have been made at this time to relieve the colony. As it was, the council and the Jones commission brought pressure to bear to force the company to act, the former more than once urging the factions "to live together in that concorde, unitie, and joinct care of the common good of that Plantation, which becometh the undertakers of such an action."[1] It ordered the company to raise money in any way that it could for the purchase of food and the sending of ships and people and the erection of guest-houses in each city and borough.[2] As no one wanted the colony to fail, it ordered that wages be paid out of the royal exchequer, and that the company might continue to be managed as a going concern,[3] it exercised the powers conferred upon it by its commission and called for books, papers, and accounts, as would any receiver or legal assignee today. And because Cavendish, Sandys, and the Ferrars had "contrived and sett down in writing, and caused publiquely to be read, a longe and impertinent declaration, consisting for the most parte of bitter and unnecessarie invectives and aspersions, upon the person of the Earle of Warwicke and others whom they stiled his instrumentes and agentes" (which the council perused, "it contayning five or six sheetes of paper"), it ordered these men "to be restrayned of theire libertie and confyned to theire severall lodgings or homes (as persons guilty of a contempt against the directions and Commaundes of this Table) where they are to remayne untill his majestie or this board shall give further order."[4] Cavendish was released in five days and the others three days later—a not very serious penalty.[5]

During the months that followed the Privy Council held stead-

1. *Acts Privy Council, Colonial*, I, §101.
2. *Ibid.*, I, §§104, 106, 112, 125; *Virginia Company Records*, II, 495-496; *Virginia Magazine*, XVI, 4-6; *Calendar State Papers, Colonial*, 1574-1660, p. 48 (35, i); Neill, *Virginia Company*, p. 392. For the ships, men, and provisions sent over between May and November, 1623, *Virginia Company Records*, II, 496.
3. *Acts Privy Council, Colonial*, I, §§98, 107, 113, 124.
4. *Ibid.*, §102.
5. The older Virginia historians, whose mission it was to defend Sandys and his administration, were wont to interpret these acts of the Privy Council as "interference," an unwarranted and unjust encroachment upon the "liberties of the company," and they did so because they were convinced that the king and his councillors were playing politics. The only contemporary justification for this view is contained in an anonymous letter of 1631, where the charge is made that the meet-

fastly to its purpose. While instructing the Jones commission to continue its inquiries, it appointed, on July 22, 1623, a special committee of its own members—Lords Grandison, Carew, and Chichester, all of whom had served in Ireland and had been concerned with the plantation of Ulster—to frame such orders as they thought fit for regulating the government of Virginia.[1] About the same time the Jones commission made a report[2] recommending a new charter, which would take the government of the colony out of the hands of the company and place it once more in the hands of the crown, as had been the case under the charter of 1606.[3] No change was to be

ings of the Virginia Company were construed by the crown as furnishing an opportunity to criticise the government (*Virginia Magazine*, VIII, 40–43). Unless such criticisms were deliberately left out of the minutes by the secretary or by the Ferrars when they had the minutes copied, the records themselves are a sufficient refutation of this charge. One need not be anxious to defend Warwick and his followers, in order to reach the conclusion that the Privy Council had ample reason for its course. The attempt of Sandys and the Ferrars later to vindicate themselves, as in the "Discourse of the Old Company," on the ground of "our Integrity and their Guilt," seems at times almost hysterical. This is not surprising. These men faced the complete failure of an enterprise on which they had set their hearts, and in their disappointment they lost their heads and their tempers. Such a want of self-control appears in the court meetings, in the hearings before the commissioners (*Calendar of State Papers, Colonial*, 1574–1660, p. 40) and the Privy Council (*Acts Privy Council, Colonial*, I, §102), and in the writings penned in their own defense.

That Virginia historians should have taken these writings at their face value is amazing. They are full of inaccuracies, invectives, and aspersions, and are clearly *ex parte* in character. The demoralization of the company in 1623 and 1624 was a matter of common knowledge and contemporary opinion was unfavorable to the continuance of the situation. The planters in the colony knew of it, and approved, in the main, the course which the Privy Council followed.

1. This committee functioned for less than a year and probably accomplished nothing of importance. Grandison and Carew were appointed on a council of war by the king, May 1, 1624, and their places were taken by the lord president, Mandeville, and Lord Paget, *Calendar State Papers, Colonial*, 1574–1660, pp. 50, 62.

2. Historical Manuscripts Commission, *Eighth Report*, II, no. 382.

3. Captain John Bargrave, whose brother George (so Brown tells us) married the daughter of Captain John Martin of Martin's Brandon, in various treatises written before 1624, frequently recommended, by indirection perhaps rather than by positive statement, that the king take the government of Virginia into his own hands (*Virginia Magazine*, VI, 228). Bargrave became engaged in a long controversy with Sir Thomas Smith and Alderman Johnson over the magazine's monopoly of trade and sent petitions both to the Privy Council and to parliament (*Acts Privy Council, Colonial*, I, §§86, 93–94; Stock, *Debates*, I, pp. 41–49; *Virginia Magazine*, VI, 225–228, 378–381; VII, 187–188; Craven, *Dissolution of the Virginia Company*, pp. 276–283). The case eventually went into Chancery. Bargrave was a persistent constitution-monger, and wrote not less than five treatises on the government of Virginia before the summer of 1622 (*Calendar State Papers, Colonial*, 1574–1660, p. 30; *American Historical Review*, XIX, 559–578; XXVII, 508, note 61, 511–514; Brown, *Republic*, p. 529). He may have written others afterward (*Calendar State Papers, Colonial*

made in the government in the colony, the company would be left free to manage all matters of trade and settlement, and property owners would be fully protected in all that concerned their vested rights.

On July 31, Attorney General Coventry and Solicitor General Heath, who had been instructed three days before to examine the Virginia Company's charters and the report of the Jones commission and out of these to prepare the legal draft of a new charter, declared that the king might justly resume the government of the colony and that if the company refused to surrender its charter voluntarily and accept a new and amended patent, then legal proceedings might be begun to bring its existence to an end. On October 8, 1623, the draft of the new patent was finished, providing for a royal council in England and a governor and council in America, and the matter was then put before the company for decision. The latter tried to secure a respite, but when the Privy Council showed itself ill-pleased with this procrastinating policy, it called an extraordinary court on October 20, at which the surrender was voted down by all but nine voices, those of Argall, Thomas Wroth,[1] John Martin, William Caning, Woodall, Pallavicene, Mease, and two others, whose votes were of doubtful legality.[2] Warwick, Rich, and others among the leaders were conspicuously absent. On hearing of this refusal, the attorney general immediately made application for a writ of *quo warranto,* which was issued out of the court of king's bench on November 4. The suit was opened on November 28, but was postponed first until January 20, 1624, and a second time to April 11. It was then tried, Attorney General Coventry making the plea. Decision was rendered on May 24 by Chief Justice Ley against

1574–1660, p. 70; Historical Manuscripts Commission, *Eighth Report,* II, no. 402). There is a Bargrave manuscript in the Huntington Library (HM, 962) which deals in part with the state of the company and the tobacco contract. It was probably written at some time between June and November, 1622. Its opening paragraph, which must have been added the next year, is taken bodily from "The New Plan," printed in the *American Historical Review,* XIX, but the remainder of the treatise is entirely different from that document. In the main part of the work Bargrave speaks of the "crooked and soure course we are now in" and of the king's third under the tobacco contract as having overthrown the whole business. The paper shows Bargrave to have been an ardent believer in the divine right of kings.

1. Sir Thomas Wroth had married the sister of Sir Nathaniel Rich. Historical Manuscripts Commission, *Eighth Report,* II, no. 448.

2. *Virginia Company Records,* II, 473–474. This decision was confirmed at a regular quarterly court on November 19, with only seven dissenting votes, evidently those mentioned above, *ibid.,* 494.

the company. The charter was declared vacated and the Virginia Company, after a life of eighteen years, came to an end. The colony was taken into the king's hands as a royal colony, the first in England's history, and by proclamation the next year, after the death of James, was formally incorporated into the royal demesne, under the scheme of government laid down in the order of October 8, 1623.[1] The steps in the process had been in due conformity to the rules of English law.

The fall of the company was due to its lack of success as a colonizing and profit-making agency. Unlike its models, the older joint-stock companies, which found their markets and sources in the eastern world already prepared and immediately available for profit, the Virginia Company had first to create its colony in America before any adequate profit from it could be expected. It fell in the effort to accomplish this result and lost its charter before it could bring into existence a working agricultural and industrial community such as it needed in order to return to its subscribers any earnings on their investment. It attempted to achieve too much on an insufficient and precarious capital, with the result that the colony suffered from a population that was always in excess of its means of subsistence. Also the company was torn asunder by internal dissensions, arising partly out of its mismanagement of the funds and partly out of its failure to remedy the deplorable condition of the colony during the later years of the company's control. Personal enmities intensified the dissension and it is not impossible that the executive branch of the government in its conflict with parliament—where Sandys and many of his party were among the members—may have relished the opportunity to strike a blow at their legislative opponents. But the political issue was inconspicuous as compared with the business issue, which finally drove Sandys and Warwick apart. The Warwick party was in the minority but was possessed of greater business sagacity, whereas the Sandys party, though a majority in the voting, lacked administrative shrewdness and wisdom. The Sandys policy threatened to wreck both company and colony, though one may not say that Warwick in command would have done any better. England was trying her first experiment in colo-

---

1. For the order in council, *Acts Privy Council, Colonial,* I, §119; *Virginia Company Records,* II, 503–504. For the course of the suit, *ibid.,* I, 103. A copy of the records of the suit, as entered in the *coram rege* roll of the king's bench, is in the Library of Congress and will be printed in Miss Kingsbury's last volume.

nization by means of an incorporated company, which since 1612 had been organized on a popular plan. As an instrument for the management and control of a distant plantation, in a new and untried country, where self-support was difficult and sickness and disease were a daily occurrence, a body of this kind, with its many discordant voices, was too hydra-headed to be effective. In the end the colony was left to work out its own salvation.

CHAPTER IX

THE FIRST LEGISLATIVE ASSEMBLY
AND AFTER

THE Virginia Company of Plymouth or, as it was called after 1620, the Council for New England, and the Bermuda Company had still to run their respective courses, but the Virginia Company of London, now known simply as the Virginia Company, had ceased to exist. For eighteen years it had endeavored to establish a permanent English colony in America, but in spite of the fact that much enthusiasm had attended its birth and that large sums of money had been spent, from which unhappily its subscribers received little if any return on their investment, the company had displayed more zeal than business acumen and the colony had never met the expectations of the promoters. Inevitably the task was one of great difficulty and the efforts of the company had been baffled by the financial embarrassments at home, and by sickness, deaths, and Indian massacres in the colony, which had depleted the stock, sapped the vitality, and discouraged the hopes of the settlers in America. One rich legacy, however, remained, namely, the form of popular government introduced by the company and maintained for five years.

The introduction of a popular assembly in Virginia was, in all probability, the work of Sir Edwin Sandys, though there is nothing to show that others in high authority in the company at the time offered any opposition to the plan. It was a first step in the carrying out of a great programme for the strengthening of the company and the building up of the colony that was destined in the long run to prove too ambitious for the company's resources and to involve the promoters in so many financial difficulties and factional rivalries as nearly to wreck the colony and to bring about in the end the company's downfall. On the part of those who conceived it—Sandys and the Ferrars—the scheme showed courage and imagination, but it was too pretentious and the company broke under the strain of too great an effort. These men tried to do too much all at once and, like many other progressive and optimistic leaders in the world's history, they did not sufficiently reckon with the obstacles that lay in their path. Of the four parts of this programme, which we have already described, two—the obtaining of a new charter and the negotiating of a tobacco contract—had fallen by the wayside; a third—the plans for supplying the colony, admirably conceived and for a time energetically prosecuted—had foundered on the rocks of the Indian massacre and the company's bankruptcy; only the fourth—the charter of grants and liberties—was to leave behind it any permanent traces.

This famous document, no copy of which is known to exist as a whole, was drawn up sometime before November, 1618, at a time when Sir Thomas Smith was still treasurer and Alderman Johnson was deputy and a member of the council, and when Warwick and Sandys, the latter assistant treasurer, were in close accord. Without the approval of these men the charter could never have been adopted.[1] Though, as time went on, strong objections were raised to the "popularness" and "democraticall" character of the company itself, no objection is anywhere recorded on the part of anyone, from the king down, to a popular form of government for the colony. Probably, if we may judge from the refusal of the commissioners for Virginia to recommend its continuance in 1623, there were many who believed such a form of government in a distant plantation to be both premature and unwise. There was no established precedent for such an experiment, for this was England's first colony to reach a stage where such an experiment was possible, and there was no sufficient reason, legal or other, why a popular assembly should be set up in Virginia, at least until that colony should make such advances in stability, security, and numbers as to warrant some measure of popular control. Certainly the right to vote was not included at this time among the "liberties" of Englishmen—as was, for example, the right to a writ of habeas corpus under the common law. In 1619 popular government in a colony was a doubtful novelty and there were those in Virginia as well as in England who predicted that it would lead to quarreling and confusion.

1. The suggestion has been made that Smith and Johnson agreed to the Sandys programme, because they wished to control the trade of the colony through the magazine (called by the writer "the Smyth syndicate") and were willing to let Sandys run the colony on the governmental side, if they could run it on the commercial side. The suggestion is interesting but somewhat fanciful. Stephenson, "Some Inner History of the Virginia Company," *William and Mary Quarterly*, XXII, 91–92.

It is more than probable that the experiment would not have been tried at this time had not Sandys been an influential member of the company and on good terms with all the others. He had moral courage, foresight, and confidence enough to realize that what was needed in Virginia was not a change of governors but a change of government, and that peace and contentment would not come to the colony as long as the executive system of a governor and council was retained as the sole form of legal and administrative control. If we may judge from his own plans, he was aware that popular government would not be feasible as long as the conditions existing up to this time continued to prevail and that do what he might the success of the experiment was problematical; that even though popular government were provided and instructions sent "for the better establishment of a Commonwealth,"[1] success could be obtained only in case the colony were encouraged and enriched, materially and morally, by more and better colonists, a wider range of industry and agriculture, and the introduction of such civilizing agencies as churches, schools, a college, inns, hospitals, and more comfortable homes. Were these things assured—and they were not assured in 1619—he felt that the experiment might help the colony, otherwise a failure might do much to hinder progress. There were those who saw in rule "by the greater number of votes and voices" a system that favored only inefficiency and disorder. There were others than King James—men open-minded and experienced—who disliked and feared this way of carrying on a government. Such a method may be a matter of course today; but it was not a matter of course in 1619.

The drafting of the charter of grants and liberties was the company's reply to the complaints that had been accumulating of Argall's way of managing affairs in Virginia. It was a long document, a veritable code of privileges, orders, and laws, that dealt with the affairs of the colony in all their bearings and was designed to bind the members of the colony and their heirs forever. It put an end to the rule inaugurated by Gates and Dale and introduced a system of popular control that was undoubtedly copied from the practice of the company itself in its quarterly gatherings of the generality. It outlined at great length the revised method of making land grants, according to which the company was to retain such grants in its own hands instead of delegating them to the resident gover-

1. *Journals of the House of Burgesses*, 1619–1659, p. 36.

nor.[1] It provided for the continuation of the system of "incorpora-tions," originally introduced by Argall in 1617, when he located the bounds of the four great "incorporations and parishes of James Citty, Charles Citty, the citty of Henrico and Kiccowtan."[2] It gave rules for the location of new plantations and said something about quit-rents and taxes—regarding the last of which we would gladly know more. It provided for proper relations with the Indians and contained instructions for an efficient management of trade and the best method of running the magazine. It probably included also a statement of the plans of the company, formulated in 1618, for the setting up of particular plantations, and it may have outlined, in whole or in part, the form of indenture to be used in the issue of patents to associates. It presented also a body of laws for the colony, embodying some statements of underlying political principles, such as Bargrave charged Sandys with uttering, regarding "a free state in Virginia," "a free popular state," and no government to be put on the colonists but by their own consent.[3] There is some reason for believing that it contained as well a résumé of what the company proposed to do for the colony in the ensuing few years. And, finally, it instructed the governor, Sir George Yeardley, to whom the docu-ment was addressed and into whose hands it was placed for trans-mission to Virginia, to call at an early date after his arrival in the colony a general assembly of the planters.[4] How long it was under consideration by the leaders of the company we do not know, but it was read and ratified at a quarter court held on November 28, 1618, and Yeardley sailed with it for Virginia the January follow-ing.

By his commission, which may have been a part of the charter or, more probably, was a separate document by itself, Yeardley was authorized to summon a general assembly once every year and no oftener—unless it might be for extraordinary and exigent necessity—to consist of two members from each "corporation"—hundred, bor-ough, and particular plantation—for the purpose of finding out and

1. *Virginia Company Records*, II, 94–95; *Virginia Magazine*, II, 154–165.
2. Brown, *Republic*, p. 254.
3. Historical Manuscripts Commission, *Eighth Report*, II, no. 368.
4. Of this charter only the section relating to grants of land has been preserved (*Virginia Magazine*, II, 154–165), but the remaining portions can be inferred from the proceedings of the first assembly, from later commissions to the governors, and from occasional references elsewhere. *Minutes of Council*, I, 25, 34, 72; Brown, *Republic*, p. 530; *Bulletin*, New York Public Library, III, 162–163.

executing "those things as might best tend to their good."[1] Acting under this authorization, as soon as possible after his arrival in April and after he had carried out sundry other orders, he issued a proclamation[2] stating "that all those that were resident here before the departure of Sir Thomas Dale [April, 1616] should be freed and acquitted from such publique service and labours which formerly they suffered, and that those cruell lawes by which we had soe longe been governed were now abrogated, and we are now governed by those free lawes which his Ma^tys subjects live under in England. And further that free libertie was given to all men to make choice of their dividents of land and, as their abilities and means w^d permitt, to possesse and plant upon them. And now that they might have a hande in the governinge of themselves, it was granted that a generall assemblie should be helde yearly once, whereat were to be present the Govr and Counsell with two Burgesses freely to be elected by the inhabitants thereof: this assembly to have power to make and ordaine whatsoever lawes and orders should by them be thought good and proffittable for our subsistence."

Just how the terms of this proclamation were enforced or what methods of election were employed we do not know certainly, but there is reason to believe that the word "inhabitants" was construed very liberally. From the language used in a later act of 1646 the inference may be drawn that not only were freeholders, householders, and servants who had served their time allowed to vote, but that servants still under indenture were included also.[3] As there were no negroes in the colony at this time, the question of a negro vote did not arise. Presumably, therefore, all the inhabitants in the colony, except women, children, and apprentices under age, took part in the election. No age limit is mentioned, but there is evidence to show that the voting age was placed at seventeen and above, because everyone over sixteen had to pay his pound of tobacco

1. *Virginia Magazine,* I, 160.   2. *Journal,* 1619–1659, p. 36.
3. Hening, *Statutes,* I, 334. Under this act indentured or covenanted servants were accounted "freemen" and were qualified to vote. Of course it does not follow that what was done in 1646 was also done in 1619. Servants under indenture were disfranchised by an act of 1655, which limited the franchise to "freeholders, leaseholders, or otherwise tenants," one person in a family (Hening, *Statutes,* I, 412). A further limitation took place in 1670 when the franchise was confined to "freeholders and housekeepers, who only are answerable to the public for the levies" (*ibid.,* II, 280). The few convicts in the colony must have been barred, for they were neither freemen nor indentured servants.

levied for the purpose of meeting the expenses of the assembly. Officially, at least, the suffrage privilege in Virginia for the first half century of its history was extraordinarily liberal, much more so in fact than in England itself at the same time, a state of affairs almost as remarkable as the establishment of the assembly itself, and the more surprising in view of the fact that the general assembly, according to Governor Wyatt's instructions of 1621, was strictly enjoined to "imitate and follow the policy of the form of government, laws, customs and manner of tryal" used in the mother country,[1] whereas the act of 1670 makes it perfectly clear that up to that time English practice had not been followed. Voting in the "towns, boroughs and hundreds" was undoubtedly viva voce or by show of hands, for we are told that in 1624 the burgesses were chosen "by the major part of voices."[2] It is more than likely that influential "governors or chiefs of [particular] plantations" had something to say as to the selection of their own representatives and perhaps controlled the voting within their plantation area. We know that a few of them attended in person, probably chosen by acclamation. The elections were held in the summer of 1619, soon after June 19, and the elected delegates, twenty-two in number, two from each of the eleven districts, met in the church at Jamestown[3] on the 30th of July, the first legislative body to meet in America.

The most convenient place that could be found for the preliminary meeting was the choir of the church. John Pory, the speaker—how selected we do not know—sat right in front of the governor, who was in the seat he was accustomed[4] to occupy when attending church service, while the councillors were arranged on either side. John Twine, the clerk, was next and Thomas Pierse, the sergeant, was at the choir rail ready for any emergency that might arise. The gathering was opened with a prayer by the Rev. Mr. Buck, the minister, whereupon the elected members, instructed by the speaker,

1. Hening, *Statutes*, I, 113; Hazard, *State Papers*, I, 133. The act of 1670 was expressly designed to bring the law of the colony into accord with the law of England: "And whereas the lawes of England grant a voyce in such elections only to such as by their estates real and personal have interest enough to tye them to the endeavour of the publique good."

2. Brown, *Republic*, p. 570.

3. *Virginia Magazine*, XII, 38. This was the third church building, the one constructed of wood by Argall.

4. "In his accustomed place" undoubtedly refers to the governor's seat in church and not to his place in council meetings. There was a separate council chamber in 1625, *Minutes of Council*, I, 57.

withdrew into the body of the church, each taking the oath of supremacy before being admitted to his seat. Exception was taken to the presence of Captain Warde of Warde's plantation, because he had settled in Virginia without a patent from the company in England, but after considerable debate, in view of his services and the right of each plantation to have representation, he and his fellow burgess, Lieutenant Gibbes, were admitted, on promising to rectify the omission. Warde fulfilled his promise the following year.[1] More important still was the refusal of the assembly to admit the burgesses from Martin's Brandon, on the ground that Martin's patent, obtained in 1617, freed him "from any commaunde of the Colony, excepte it be in ayding and assisting the same agst any forren or domestical Enemy."[2] The assembly claimed that this clause relieved him of the obligation to obey any laws that the assembly might pass and that therefore his burgesses ought to have no part in making them. Martin, who had been in Virginia since 1607, returning off and on to England and out of sympathy with the authorities either in England or in the colony, had evidently been outspoken in his opposition to Yeardley, Rolfe, and others. He appealed his case to the company, but was eventually required to take out a new patent in 1623, containing terms similar to those imposed on the promoters of other particular plantations.[3]

In the meantime speaker Pory, who beforehand had arranged carefully the order of business and reduced all matters to be dealt

---

1. *Virginia Magazine*, I, 347.   2. *Journals*, 1619–1659, p. 4.

3. *Virginia Company Records*, II, 344. For the progress of the case, *ibid.*, II, 18, 26, 27, 43, 78, 119, 126–127, 140, 145, 161–162, 181, 216; *Virginia Magazine*, VII, 131–132, 134–146; *Minutes of Council*, I, 29, 61, 62, 63. Brown's article and Craven's work have already been referred to.

Martin was certainly not in sympathy with the company organization in England or with the government in the colony, and he voted to surrender the charter at the extraordinary court of the company, held October 20, 1623. Just what his political opinions were can only be inferred. He was probably in accord with the political ideas of James I, as was Captain Bargrave. Though he quarreled with Bargrave over cattle in Virginia, he was seemingly in agreement with him in matters of governmental policy, and we know that Bargrave was an ardent believer in the divine right of kings. The following quotation from one of Bargrave's essays shows the trend of his thoughts on government. "For the King's right noe man will doubt, but it immediately cometh from God; and being the Soule, the Center and the Sunshine of our Government from it we derive all the happiness and unity of a Commonwealth. To derogate from it or to usurp upon the said soveraigne power is death. All good subjects by how much they reverence it by soe much they hould themselves abused if any subordinate minister . . . make himself their Lord by encroaching upon this sacred right."

with "into a ready method," presented to the burgesses the charter of privileges, the main parts of which he had methodized in
the form of four books, for the easier consideration of committees. Each part was taken up in turn; certain petitions were drawn
up for submission to the company asking for various modifications
and extensions of the laws sent over; sundry instructions to previous governors were converted into laws—particularly such as concerned trade, morals, agriculture, apparel, and the general welfare
of the colony—and a number of new laws were framed based on
the experience of the burgesses with the needs of the people at large.
Some matters of a quasi-judicial nature were either acted on directly or referred to the council, and then after levying one pound
of tobacco upon every man and man-servant above the age of sixteen, to be collected the February following, for the compensation
of the speaker, clerk, sergeant, and provost marshal of Jamestown,
the assembly was prorogued to meet March 1 of the next year. Before ending the session, the burgesses framed two requests of considerable importance, which they asked should be presented to the
company. The first was that the laws passed might become opera-
tive at once, even though the company should eventually disallow
them; and the second that they might be permitted, in their turn,
to express disapproval of any laws that the company should send
over for their guidance, in case they thought such laws not suited
to the best interests of the colony. These were noteworthy requests
and it is equally noteworthy that in the "Ordinances and Constitutions" sent over with Governor Wyatt in 1621, the company granted
the second, saying that "no orders shall bind the colony unless they
be ratified in the general assembly."[1]

The assembly of 1619 lasted but six days. The weather was hot,
the speaker indisposed, and many of the members, one of whom
died during the session, were ill. They felt called upon to apologize
to the company for breaking-up so suddenly, due, as they said, to
sickness and the "intemperature of the weather," and to ask pardon
for not having brought their work to a greater perfection, hoping
that the company's courtesy would accept their "poore indevour"
and its wisdom be ready "to supporte the weakness of this little
flocke." The climate of Jamestown in July and August was not
favorable to clearness of thought or rapidity of action and we may

1. Hening, *Statutes*, I, 114; Hazard, *State Papers*, I, 133.

wonder that under the circumstances the burgesses should have accomplished as much as they did.

Whether or not the members came together the following March we do not know, as there is no evidence of such a meeting, but in all likelihood they did do so, for the time was favorable and conditions, though worse later, were no more adverse in 1620 than they had been in 1619. The next assembly of which we have knowledge, and for which elections must have been held soon after the arrival of Wyatt in October, 1621, met in November and December of that year, but lasted only a few days.[1] Whether others were called in 1622 and 1623 is uncertain, as the massacre of March 22, 1622, that "deadly stroake," which brought "great amazement and ruine" to the state, must have thrown everything into confusion and have made it necessary, at least in 1622, for the governor and council to act alone, "recollecting the stragglinge and woefull inhabitants, soe dismembered, into stronger bodies and more secure places."[2] Conditions were almost as bad the following year, when the company was neglecting the colony, food was scarce and insufficient, and sickness and death increased at a terrifying rate. No mention is made of such assemblies in the "Brief Declaration" which was drawn up in 1624, reviewing the history of the colony, and the emergency would seem to call only for executive action. The last assembly under the company came together in February and March, 1624, the membership of which was almost entirely different from that of 1619. A new governor, council, and secretary were in office, and a new situation, the impending overthrow of the company, confronted the colony. The air must have been full of rumors as to what was likely to happen and news from England must have been awaited with grave concern. The assembly spent much of its time composing answers to Alderman Johnson's petition, which had been presented to the king in April, 1623, and to Butler's "Unmasking," both of which the members thought reflected upon themselves. It also drew up sundry petitions to the king and the Privy Council against the restoration of the former autocratic rule before 1619, and took into consideration "A Brief Declaration," which was prepared by such of the "ancient planters"[3] as were still living, in order to show king and Privy Council how bad those conditions had been.

1. *Journals*, 1619–1659, p. 17.   2. *Ibid.*, p. 37.
3. According to the statement in Hening, *Statutes*, I, 124, the "old planters," to whom certain privileges were accorded, were those "that were here or came in at

Already the authorities in England had begun their inquiry into the state of the colony, and a considerable part of the time of the assembly was spent in answering questions asked by the commissioners whom the Privy Council had appointed the October before and who had arrived sometime during the winter of 1623 and 1624.[1] This commission was composed of five men, of whom four—John Harvey, John Pory, Abraham Peirsey (Peirce), the cape-merchant in 1619, and Samuel Matthews—had lived in the colony and had interests there. The identity of the fifth, John Jefferson, is doubtful. Pory, who had been the speaker of the assembly in 1619, was especially instructed to present to the new assembly various orders of the Privy Council, particularly that of October 8, 1623, regarding the proposed new government for the colony. The commissioners travelled from plantation to plantation and were treated with respect, though not greeted with enthusiasm.

The assembly answered willingly enough the questions that the commissioners put before it, but refused to attach the signatures of its members to any documents attacking the company, denying the right of the commissioners to ask it to do so.[2] It refused to furnish them with copies of the various papers that it had drafted, preferring to send these papers to England on its own account and by its own messenger, John Pountis, treasurer of Southampton Hundred.[3] But Pory bribed Edward Sharpless, clerk and acting secretary, to give him copies of the papers, for which offense Sharpless was sentenced in May by the governor and council to stand in the pillory and to have his ears nailed thereto and then cut off.[4] This sentence was reduced to the cutting off of a piece of one ear only and Sharpless's return to his former position as the indentured servant of one Dilke, to whom formerly he had been bound.[5] This treatment of Sharpless was construed by the local opposition, with some justice,

the last coming of Sir Thomas Gates [June, 1611]"; according to the *Journals* (p. 4) the "antient planters" were "such as before Sir Thomas Dales departure [April, 1616] were come hither upon their owne charges, and such also as were brought hither upon the Companies costs." The second date is the one to be accepted, and the "old planters," to whom Bargrave wanted to give "some noate of honour to distinguish them from the others" (*American Historical Review*, XIX, 576), were those who came to the colony before April, 1616.

1. *Acts Privy Council, Colonial*, I, §113; *Virginia Magazine*, XV, 134.
2. *Journals*, 1619–1659, pp. 37–42.
3. *Minutes of Council*, I, 77; *Acts Privy Council, Colonial*, I, §175; Hening, *Statutes*, I, 128.
4. *Minutes of Council*, I, 14.   5. *Ibid.*, I, 52.

as an affront to the king[1] and is difficult to condone, no matter how great the provocation may have been. Though at the time sentiment in the assembly and probably in the colony at large ran officially in favor of the company, it is evident from the lists of signatures and recorded incidents that there were not a few among the planters who disapproved of the content and language of the documents and of the treatment of Sharpless. Captain Martin, seeing the latter in the pillory and being told that Wyatt and the council had ordered him to be put there, said he hoped "to see some of them sitt there them selves shortly and doupted not but some of them would wish his eares one againe shortly."[2] How large a following Martin had in the colony cannot even be conjectured, but from what we know of the dissatisfaction with the company's management prevailing there in 1623[3] and can infer from later events the conclusion is not unwarranted that the number was considerable. Martin was a thorn in the flesh to the governing authorities in Virginia and one can but wish that for the sake of posterity he had written a commentary on affairs similar to *The New England Canaan* by Thomas Morton.

The assembly fully realized that the end of the company's rule was at hand and sought to save what it could for the colony by making two important requests—one contained in the letter to the Privy Council and the other included in the laws which were passed toward the close of the session. In the first it begged the council not to entrust the governors who were to be sent over (under the new plan of administration, embodied in the recommendations of October 8, 1623) with too much authority but to restrain them as formerly by recognizing the right of the local council to act in an advisory capacity and by allowing the colony to retain the liberty of a

1. *Calendar State Papers, Colonial,* 1574–1660, p. 74.

2. *Minutes of Council,* I, 61. In October, 1624, "Cap[t] Marten demandinge of this Examinate why Edward Sharpless was sett one the Pillory and lost his Eares, this Examinate answered that it was for disclosinge of the Secretts and Councell of the Governor and Counceill. Cap[t] Marten answered it had been better it had nott been doune. And further said that Cap[t] Marten said that for the wrongs he had received from S[r] George Yardley he wold be rited when he cam upp, or otherwyse the Governor and Counsell should shew Themselves Rebells and that Cap[t] Marten said that there was a new Gov[r]nor and Counsell to come over and that non of these that now are of the Counsell should contynew ther place." (*Ibid.,* p. 21, also 22.) Wyatt, the next year, wrote the Privy Council that he had been forced to suspend Martin from the commission for Virginia to which he had lately been appointed by the king (*Calendar State Papers, Colonial,* 1574–1660, p. 74).

3. Historical Manuscripts Commission, *Eighth Report,* II, nos. 318–326.

general assembly, "then wch nothing can more conduce to our satisfaction or the publique utilitie."[1] In the second, it touched on one of the few powers that the House of Commons in England was indubitably exercising at this time—the control of taxation. "The governor [said the assembly] shall not lay any taxes or ympositions upon the colony, their lands or commodities other way than by the authority of the General Assembly, to be levyed and ymployed as the said Assembly shall appoint."[2] In these two utterances are contained all the law and the gospel as far as self-government in a colony is concerned.

But for the moment the outlook for representative government in Virginia was not encouraging. So strongly was the tide of conviction in official circles in England setting against the continuance of the former popular privileges of both company and colony that it seemed unlikely either would receive much consideration at the hands of the English government. Pory went back to England in May, 1624, taking with him the report of the commissioners, which he was able to hand in to the Privy Council about the middle of June, a month after the dissolution of the Virginia Company. There can be little doubt that this report, the content of which is not known, had some influence in arousing the council to take action regarding Virginia, now under the king's immediate control. A month later, on July 15, it appointed a commission headed by Viscount Mandeville, lord president of the council, for the purpose of examining into the state of the colony and of exercising all the powers that had formerly been granted to the defunct company. Thus the commission took the place of the company and became under the king the administrator of the colony for the time being. It was a very large and unsuitable body of more than fifty-five members, among whom were Lord Paget, Sir Richard Weston, Sir Humphrey May, and Sir Robert Killigrew, and others, some of whom were added later, bearing familiar names, Sir Thomas Smith (died September 4, 1625), Mildmay, Heath, Calvert, Gorges, Coventry, Thomas Wroth, Wolstenholme, Nathaniel Rich, Argall, Johnson, Nathaniel Butler, Samuel Wrote, William Byng, and more of the same sort, opponents of the Sandys party in the company.[3] Six

1. *Journals*, 1619–1659, p. 27.   2. Hening, *Statutes*, I, 124.
3. Hazard, *State Papers*, I, 183–188; *Virginia Magazine*, VII, 40–43; *Acts Privy Council, Colonial*, I, §§123, 124; *Calendar State Papers, Colonial*, 1574–1660, p. 69 (25).

made a quorum and could do business, thus effecting a complete overturn in the governing body, by making it possible for the Warwick party to control the colony.[1]

The Mandeville board was expected to report eventually on the desirability or otherwise of issuing a new charter to the company, but its first duty was to administer the affairs of the colony. To that end it obtained a patent from the king, August 24, 1624, entrusting the government in Virginia to Sir Francis Wyatt, who had been governor under the company from 1621 to 1624, and "other discreet persons residing in the parts of Virginia." Among these "discreet persons" were Abraham Peirsey (Peirce) and Samuel Matthews, the former commissioners, who after Pory's departure remained in the colony to perform and execute the powers incident to a governor and council there, "until some other constant and setled course be resolved upon and established by us."[2] No mention is made in Wyatt's commission of a general assembly, and it is fairly evident that the Mandeville board had no intention of recommending the calling of any such popular body. During the winter of 1624 and 1625 the colony continued to be governed by Wyatt and the council only, while John Harvey, who had been one of the five appointed in 1623 to look into the affairs of the colony, stayed in Virginia to gather material upon which the Mandeville board might base its recommendation to the king. Harvey went back to England in February, 1625, and delivered his report sometime before April 16[3] of that year. What would have been the final issue it is impossible to say, for all proceedings were stopped by the death of King James on March 27; and whatever were the intentions of the Mandeville board, its plans thus far made were brought, by the death of the king, to an unexpected and, in the eyes of its members, to an untimely end.

1. In the "Discourse of the Old Company" the protestants complained that this was exactly what happened—the control of the colony was thrown into the hands of the "enemy" (*Virginia Magazine,* I, 28). Though the Privy Council asserted that the commission accomplished a great deal that was useful, the writers of the "Discourse" denied it, insisting that the commission had done more harm than good, evidently having in mind the suspension of the general assembly. For their opinion of the commission, see *ibid.,* pp. 298–300.

2. Hazard, *State Papers,* I, 189–192; *Virginia Magazine,* XVI, 121–123.

3. On that day he is mentioned as "being lately returned out of Virginia." His report is entitled, "Declaration of the State of Virginia at my comminge from thence in February last." Brown, *Republic,* pp. 610–612, 640.

Though Charles I, who now succeeded to the throne, was much less prejudiced against the company than his father had been, and apparently was willing to give careful consideration to the company's presentation of its own case, the outlook was still far from certain. As the Mandeville board had lapsed with the death of the king,[1] leaving the colony standing immediately under the king's control, the Privy Council, early in April, 1625, appointed two committees of its own members to consider the importation of tobacco from Virginia and presumably the best course to follow for the government of the plantation.[2] Hearings were held in the presence of these committees and both the Sandys party and those "for the other parte" were invited to appear and present their suggestions in writing. Sometime after April 16 and before May 15,[3] Sandys and the Ferrars drew up what is known as the "Discourse of the Old Company," in which they reviewed at great length and with noticcable bitterness the situation from the beginning. They disparaged their opponents both individually and as a whole and condemned the Smith administration, exactly as had the assembly of Virginia in its "Brief Declaration," with an injustice that at times borders on malice. The authors of the "Discourse" asked that the old company be restored, with all its powers and privileges, as an incorporated body of adventurers and planters, and that its patent be confirmed by act of parliament,[4] or, if that were not possible and the king wished to keep the colony in his own hands, that then a select council be chosen of honorable men, who were not enemies of the company, to administer affairs. They protested vigorously against a new tobacco contract which had been entered into the previous year with one Edward Ditchfield—treasurer of the Bermuda Company and a former member of the Virginia Company— as certain to lead to the ruin of the colony.[5]

Whether the "Discourse" was too long and wearied the commit-

1. It is spoken of as "the late commission" in the "Discourse."

2. *Acts Privy Council, Colonial*, I, §142.

3. "Nyne moneths" after the appointment of the Mandeville commission, July 16, 1624. *Virginia Magazine*, I, 299.

4. This was, in part at least, the scheme which Sandys brought forward in 1620–1621, when he planned to obtain a new charter for the company.

5. On the recommendation of the old board of commissioners for Virginia, October 18, 1624, a warrant was issued the next month appointing Edward Ditchfield and five others officers at the port of London for searching and sealing tobacco. Hazard, *State Papers*, I, 198–202; British Museum, Additional Manuscripts, 12,496,

tee—as the writers feared that it would—or the language was too extravagant and alienated the committee's sympathies—as is not at all unlikely—can only be conjectured, but it seems clear that in some way or other the Sandys party overreached itself. On May 13, 1625, the king declared his policy in an important proclamation refusing absolutely to revive the company. "Our full resolution is [so reads the text], to the end that there may be one uniforme course of Government in and through our whole Monarchie, that the Government of the Colonie of Virginia shall immediately depend upon Our Selfe, and not be committed to any Company or Corporation, to whom it may be proper to trust matters of Trade and Commerce, but cannot bee fit or safe to communicate the ordering of State-affaires, be they of never so meane consequence."[1] This was definitely a continuance of the policy of James I and a return to the plan provided for in the charter of 1606, and raises the question in one's mind why, four years later, a charter should have been granted to the Massachusetts Bay Company, largely for the purpose of developing the Salem plantation already in existence in New England. The decision must have brought great disappointment to the Sandys group, for it showed that within a month after the hearings of April 11 and succeeding days and very soon after the receipt of the "Discourse," the Privy Council, little impressed by the Sandys argument, was willing to draft a proclamation for the king to issue containing a statement of purpose entirely antagonistic to the wishes of the old company. Evidently the "Discourse," upon which Sandys and the Ferrars had worked so hard, had failed of its effect.

In the meantime Wyatt continued as governor of the colony, though his commission had not been formally renewed after the death of the king. He had no authority to call an assembly, but in order to obtain an expression of the will of the planters, in view of the situation created by the fall of the company—for he had not yet heard of the death of James I—he summoned a "convention" to meet on May 10, 1625, for the special purpose of drafting an appeal to King James. This "convention," composed of twenty-three delegates, elected by the "freemen"[2] of the plantations, sat for three or four days under the title of the "Govr Counsell and Collony of Vir-

ff. 400 ff. On the whole subject of the Ditchfield patent, Beer, *Origins*, pp. 137 ff.; *Virginia Magazine*, I, 307–309; *Calendar State Papers, Colonial*, 1574–1660, p. 71. For the tobacco contract of 1628, *Virginia Magazine*, VII, 258–264.

1. *Proclamations*, p. 53.   2. Probably including indentured servants.

ginia assembled together."[1] The gathering had no legal standing, as its summons had not been authorized by the crown, and Captain Martin, as might have been expected, raised objections saying that the governor and council had no right to call it and he knew that the king and Privy Council "did not allow of it."[2] Fearing that the petitions and the "Brief Declaration," sent over by the assembly of 1624, had not reached the king's hands, because the messenger, John Pountis, had died at sea, it made fresh copies of these papers and added a special statement of its own concerning the new plan of government and the Ditchfield contract, to both of which it was opposed. It also asked, in case the company was not restored and a select council was to be appointed for the oversight of the colony, that the latter be composed of four men in whom the "convention" expressed confidence—Paget, Weston, May, and Killigrew—all of whom had been members of the former Mandeville board and three of them adherents of the Sandys administration.[3] The planters in the colony as well as the writers of the "Discourse" wanted no government by the opposition party. The documents were entrusted to Sir George Yeardley, who was going to England; and the convention begged the king "to affoarde a gratious hearinge to their messenger."[4]

Yeardley arrived in England shortly before October 4 and immediately sent in a petition to the king asking that he be commanded to attend the Privy Council.[5] It is possible that both he and Harvey, who had gone to England with his report the February before, were summoned to present their respective cases to king and council, for in the letter which the Privy Council sent to the colony,[6] we are told that "the present miserie and wants" of Virginia had been "related at large both to his Majestie and this Board." Yeardley had been especially instructed to ask for aid in the form of men, munitions, apparel, tools, and other necessaries, to protest against the admission of the company's opponents to any share in the government, to beg that no contract be forced upon the planters—who ought to have the right to make the best of their own labor—and to request that the "liberty of General Assemblies" be continued and confirmed.

1. *Journals*, 1619–1659, pp. xxx, 43; *Minutes of Council*, I, 55–56; *Virginia Magazine*, XXIII, 14.
2. *Minutes of Council*, I, 62.
3. *Journals*, 1619–1659, p. 43; *Virginia Magazine*, XV, 360–363.
4. *Journals*, 1619–1659, p. 43.   5. *Virginia Magazine*, XV, 364.
6. *Acts Privy Council, Colonial*, I, §154.

The Privy Council replied favorably to the first three of these requests, but as to the fourth, went no further than to say that the planters should "holde all such reasonable privileges as they have formerly enjoyed," and that Wyatt would be continued in the government and the existing councillors in their respective places. These were all important and encouraging concessions and one cannot but feel that Yeardley must have presented the case of the colony with much more tact and judgment than Sandys and the Ferrars that of the company. The Privy Council spoke of Yeardley with approval, and when he asked for the special protection of the council while in England for a year, granted his request, as to one whose service had been "usefull for the good of the state."[1] The "joyfull and welcome"[2] news was carried to the colony and from the reply[3] that was returned at the beginning of the next year, 1626, we may infer that the colonists were rejoicing in the king's promises, quite content to be in the king's hand, and were already reconciled to the fall of the company and the death of King James.[4]

But still the king took no step looking to the reëstablishment of the assembly in the colony, and since the gathering of the delegates in "convention" in May, 1625, no popular meetings had been held.[5] Wyatt, who for some time had been anxious to return to England and had obtained the king's permission to do so, was now superseded by Yeardley. In the latter's commission, which was issued March 14, 1626, the king said that "being forced by many other urgent occasions in respect to his late access to the crown," he would continue the existing form of government until he "should find some more convenient means upon mature advice to give more ample directions for the same";[6] and in the instructions which were

1. Acts Privy Council, Colonial, I, §155.
2. Virginia Magazine, XV, 366.
3. Calendar State Papers, Colonial, 1574–1660, p. 77 (1); printed in full, Virginia Magazine, XV, 365–368.
4. In July, 1642, the Virginia House of Burgesses issued a "Remonstrance" or representation to the colony, in which it speaks of "the late company's oppression" (Journals, 1619–1659, p. 69). Further on in the same document it comments on the "liberties and privileges and settling our estates" as "often heretofore assaulted and threatened and lately invaded by the late corporation" (p. 70).
5. The statement is made by the editor of the Virginia Magazine, XIX, 121, and by Wertenbaker in Virginia under the Stuarts, p. 63, that other "conventions" than that of May, 1625, were called later in that year and in 1626. The two letters upon which the editor and Professor Wertenbaker rely were written by the governor and council (Virginia Magazine, XV, 365, 370) and refer to meetings of that body only.
6. Hazard, State Papers, I, 230–234; Virginia Magazine, XIII, 298–302. This was

drawn up on April 19,[1] he made no mention of anything more than the selection of councillors. It is evident that nothing thus far had been done toward settling the question of an assembly. But Wyatt, before he left Virginia, had in combination with his council, written a long letter to the Privy Council suggesting that an assembly should be allowed to convene "in spetial cases,"[2] as it was considered desirable to obtain occasionally the advice of the planters in matters that conduced to the settling of the plantation, and it may be that he had in mind some need similar to that which led to the calling of the "convention" of 1625. But if so, he was unsuccessful in his appeal, for neither the king nor the council made reply. When in 1627 Yeardley died and Harvey was sent out as governor, no change was made in the wording of the patent issued on March 26 of that year.[3] No legislative assembly legally so called or exercising law-making functions had been held or could have been held since 1624, for the "convention" of 1625 was not a legislative assembly, having been summoned for but one purpose, the drafting of an appeal to the king.

This appeal as presented by Yeardley had made (as we have already seen) a favorable impression upon the Privy Council, which seems to have approved of Wyatt's suggestion that an assembly be allowed to convene in special cases. This meant that should an emergency arise the governor would be warranted in calling the planters together, as a whole or through their delegates, to discuss the matter. It did not mean that such a body was to come together regularly for law-making purposes, and indeed it may be doubted whether law-making in the modern sense of the term was uppermost in the minds of those who were asking for the privilege of general assemblies. They were more interested in administration than in law-making, as was the case with all similar bodies of that day. When, therefore, in the year 1627 the tobacco question once more became exigent, the anticipated emergency arose and in this wise. On August 9 the king issued a proclamation[4] forbidding any one, merchant or other, to import tobacco into England without the king's license, requiring that this be done only through commis-

a renewal of the patent of September 18, 1624, issued by King James, *ibid.*, XVI, 121–123.

1. *Acts Privy Council, Colonial,* I, §162; *Virginia Magazine,* II, 393–396.
2. *Virginia Magazine,* XV, 372.   3. *Ibid.,* XVI, 125–131.
4. *Proclamations,* pp. 62–65.

sioners appointed for the purpose. Acting on orders from the Privy Council, the king despatched a letter and the attorney general an instruction in the king's name to the new governor, Captain Francis West—who had been chosen to his office by "the opinions and voices of the council," according to the instructions laid down in the royal commission of November 14, 1627[1]—authorizing him to call a general assembly to debate this one special issue.[2] The object of the attorney general's instruction was to assure the planters that in this instance at least their wishes, as indicated in Wyatt's letter, were to be consulted and that they were to be allowed to say what they wanted to say regarding any new tobacco contract that might be made. The assembly, which sat for only three or four days toward the end of March, 1628, differed in two important particulars from the "convention" of 1625: its summons was authorized by the crown and it imposed a levy upon the colony for the meeting of its expenses. But even with these differences it was essentially similar to the gathering of 1625 and in no way a revival of the assembly of 1624, for it exercised no administrative or legislative functions and, as far as we know, followed no form of parliamentary procedure. It was called to discuss the king's letter regarding tobacco and other commodities, and when that business was disposed of and an answer written it broke up.[3] The laws in force in the colony from 1624 to 1629 were those sent over with the Charter of Grants and Liberties in 1619 and such others as had been passed by the assemblies of 1619, 1621, and 1624. There was nothing in the royal letter

1. *Minutes of Council,* I, 157.

2. *Ibid.,* I, 168; *Virginia Magazine,* VII, 258. The entry in the *Minutes* is as follows. "The Letter from his most Excellent Matie being read at this Court . . . and divers other Instructions from Sr Robert Heath his Maties Atturney Generall . . . it was thought fitt that their should be a letter written unto the Atturney Generall to advertise him that the letter from the King came not to our sight untill it was to late to observe those Instructions wch concerne Tob[acco] and Particularly: But that [according] unto his Maties Commaund are resolved that there shall be a Generall Assembly called and summoned to be here at James Citty upon the tenth of March to consult and advise concerning the several Parts and points of his Maties letter, soe that . . . we intend touching every Particular to answer the same." Further mention of the assembly is made on page 175 of the *Minutes;* and on page 185, where Captain Marshart's mission is referred to, is the statement that the assembly levied three pounds of tobacco a poll, for every person paying tithes to the minister, to meet the various charges.

3. The assembly drew up two petitions also and prepared a commission for two of its members, Bennett and Marshart, to go to England and there join with Wyatt in an effort to obtain a modification of the royal proclamation and to procure a bark of fifty tons with guns and provisions.

to lead the colony to suppose that the king would consent to the calling of another assembly the following year or at any other time, and legally no assembly could meet without the king's consent. The situation in 1628 after the *ad hoc* gathering had adjourned was similar to that of 1624 after the assembly of that year had come to an end.

It is even uncertain how soon after 1628 we can begin to speak of a regular assembly in the colony, pursuing a normal legislative and parliamentary course and duly authorized by the crown. There is mention in the instructions to Governor Harvey, August 6, 1628, of a "Grand Assembly" that was to be called for the purpose of providing a palisade to run from Martin's Hundred to the York river, to guard the colony against the Indians, but with no other business on its docket, as far as the text of the instructions is concerned.[1] This assembly, if we are justified in calling it such, duly met, on October 16, 1629, and confined its activities almost entirely to the object named, but its routine of work and procedure was more elaborate than in the case of either of the previous "conventions" and, as far as the records show, it exhibited many of the characteristics of a regular body. The calling of such "conventions" in 1628 and 1629 may well have seemed to the governor and the planters a sufficient precedent for a continuation of the practice every year and for the reassumption of law-making powers, because from this time on, with the possible exception of the year 1636— for which no record can be found—annual assemblies were held and laws passed.[2] There is no reason to doubt that these assemblies assumed all the rights and privileges of regular representative bodies and followed each its own variety of parliamentary practice. But nevertheless the fact remains that during the years from 1624 to 1639, the king gave no sign that he approved of assemblies doing

1. *Acts Privy Council, Colonial*, I, §211; *Virginia Magazine*, VII, 267–268.

2. For 1630, Hening, *Statutes*, I, 147; 1631, *Journals*, 1619–1659, p. 55; 1632, February 21 and September 4, Hening, I, 153, *Virginia Magazine*, III, 22, 25, IX, 56; 1633, February 1 and August 21, Hening, I, 203, *Virginia Magazine*, III, 22, IX, 57; 1634, *Virginia Magazine*, IX, 57, XIII, 391; 1635, *Calendar State Papers, Colonial*, 1574–1660, p. 195 (44); 1637, *Journals*, 1619–1659, p. 126, *Virginia Magazine*, IX, 57, "Patents," State Land Office, I, no. 2, pp. 689–690, where mention is made of an act of assembly held February, 1636/7; 1638, *Journals*, 1619–1659, p. xxxvi, *Virginia Magazine*, IX, 58; 1639, Hening I, 229 (act xxix), *Virginia Magazine*, IX, 58. As the assemblies were frequently held in February and March, account has to be taken of old and new style in determining the year in which an assembly was held.

business on their own initiative or was willing to authorize the
governor to call them annually. These houses of burgesses in Virginia passed many laws which had force in the colony, but, as far as
we know, only a very few of these laws were ever sent to England
for confirmation and not one of these few was ever acted upon by
the Privy Council.[1]

The first instruction since 1628 to a governor to call an assembly
of any kind was that issued to Harvey on his return to the colony
in January, 1637, when he "published his Maties pleasure for an assembly"[2] to meet on the 20th of February following. But there is
nothing to show for what purpose this assembly was called or
whether Harvey was authorized to call such a body every year. All
of the governors since 1624, when the colony was taken over by the
king, must have had commissions and probably all had instructions.
The king had frequently promised to renew the "privileges" of the
colony,[3] but until we come to the instructions to Wyatt of January,
1639, no document exists that contains a fulfilment of that promise,
as far as concerns a revival of the assemblies under the company. In
those instructions Wyatt was told to call a general assembly once
every year in which the governor was to have a negative voice.[4] It
is of course quite possible that similar orders had been sent to earlier
governors and that the calling of annual assemblies with parliamentary powers was understood at Whitehall to be already allowed
with the full consent of the crown, but there is no evidence at hand
to prove that this was so.

On the contrary, there is reason to think, as we shall see later,
that until 1638 no certain decision had been reached in England as
to the final form that the government in Virginia should take. That
the king and the Privy Council had tacitly and in a measure openly
recognized the legality of the assemblies already held is clear,[5] but
that during these years since 1624 they had not decided on the definitive course to be followed seems certain also. Until 1631 the
king had governed his colony through the Privy Council and its
committees. But by that year so many petitions had come in, on one
side from the Sandys party asking for the restoration of the old
company, and on the other from the colony asking for the legal

1. *Virginia Magazine*, VII, 369–370; *Journals*, 1619–1659, p. 55.
2. *Virginia Magazine*, IX, 175; X, 265.
3. *Ibid.*, VII, 267.   4. *Ibid.*, XI, 54–57.
5. *Acts Privy Council, Colonial*, I, §211 (17, 18)

recognition of its general assembly,[1] that on May 24 of that year the king appointed Lord Dorset and some twenty others, among whom were representatives of both the old factions, to consider the situation and make recommendations as to what was best to be done.[2] This commission in its report suggested that a president and council be named in England to have general oversight of the colony; that a governor and council in the colony be continued to have a general oversight of local affairs; and that the governor, council, and planters meeting in their general assemblies—which significantly enough the committee seemed to assume were already in existence—should be authorized to make laws, "correspondent to the lawes of England and but probationary onely until confirmed here." Furthermore, the commissioners recommended that a new Virginia company be created to take the place of the old, with all the latter's rights, goods, liberties, and privileges, saving to the king, however, "the supreme and royal power of the government."[3]

This attempt to reëstablish the old company under a new patent was unsuccessful. So many and so vigorous were the protests against the recommendations of the commission,[4] which had already instructed Attorney General Heath to proceed with the drafting of the patent,[5] that the suggestion went no further and no new Virginia company was ever formed. The proposal was rejected at this time, as it had been before, because "altogether inconvenient for his Majesties service both here and there."[6] In 1633 petitions were sent in from the old company for a renewal of "their antient charter" but without results.[7] Again in 1640 another attempt was made by George Sandys, Sir Edwin's brother in Virginia, who had been sent to England the year before as agent for the colony and who presented a request purporting to come from the planters for a renewal of the charter. This he did either in violation of his instructions or through a misunderstanding of them. The request was read in the House of Commons and later, after the Virginia assembly had sent in a strong protest, was rejected as "contrary to the king's intent."[8]

1. *Virginia Magazine*, VII, 369; VIII, 40.
2. *Ibid.*, VIII, 29, 33. The patent was issued June 27.
3. *Ibid.*, 36–39; *Acts Privy Council, Colonial*, I, §403. The report is wrongly entered in the *Acts* under the year 1638 instead of 1631.
4. *Virginia Magazine*, VIII, 36–39.   5. *Ibid.*, 39–40.
6. *Ibid.*, 41.   7. *Ibid.*, VIII, 153.
8. *Journals*, 1619–1659, p. 66; *Calendar State Papers, Colonial*, 1574–1660, p. 324; Stock, *Debates*, I, 101, note 4. Dr. Stock seems to think that Sandys' petition was

Thus ended the long struggle for the revival of the Virginia Company, which had gone on intermittently since the annulment of 1624 and had failed largely because of the bad impression which the factional quarreling among its members had made on those in authority and because of the manifest preference of the colony for an immediate dependence on the crown. Even as late as 1662 a writer was merely repeating the current opinion of the day when he referred to the "fraud and deceit" which characterized "the conduct of the East India Company, the Virginia Company and other companies," though he could not say that they "deserved the imputation of fraud which is cast upon them."[1] Thus the famous company passed from the scene of its labors, never to return. Its work was accomplished, for the colony was now firmly established, and its own greatest contribution to the world, the grant of representative government to a colony, was at last after many vicissitudes safe beyond peradventure.

It is apparent, however, that in the years from 1628 to 1638, despite the fact that they were holding representative and law-making assemblies each year, the planters in Virginia did not feel quite certain of their right to do so. The king had not given his formal consent to their taking this matter into their own hands and until he had done so their proceedings and laws would, legally speaking, have no validity.[2] Therefore, they continued their petitions to England. In 1629 Harvey appealed to the king begging him to authorize

authorized by the assembly, but the facts are otherwise. While no doubt there were differences of opinion among the members, the majority was opposed to the revival of the company and in its "Declaration" says distinctly that Sandys had mistaken his orders. The sentiment in the colony, since the fall of the company, had been in favor of the royal control and against the revival of the company, though there were undoubtedly many varieties of view as to the form the royal control should take. Probably the planters were unanimous in rejecting government by a commission, a majority of the members of which were enemies of the company, preferring royal control and government through the regular executive channels. They had felt in the past that the tobacco contracts had been in the interest of the company and not of the colony and believed that they would get better treatment directly from the king himself. In this belief they were justified. Under the administration of the crown, not only had Spanish and English tobacco been prohibited—at least officially—but the duty on English colonial tobacco had been reduced one-half, the charge for garbling had been removed, and an allowance had been made, as a drawback, in case of reëxportation. *Virginia Magazine,* IX, 176–178; Wertenbaker, *Planters of Colonial Virginia,* pp. 65–70.

1. *The Royal Trade in Fishing* (London, 1662).

2. A century and a half afterward William Paca of Maryland, in commenting on a Maryland act of 1702, passed by an assembly which had met after the death of

the Privy Council "to consider what is fitt to be done for the ratefy-
ing of the priviledges formally granted, and holding of a general
assembly to be called by the Governor upon necessary occasions,
therein to propound laws and orders for the good government of
the people, and for that it is most reasonable that his Maties subjects
should be governed only by such laws as shall have their originall
from his Maties royal approbacon, it be therefore so ordered that
those lawes, so there made, only stand as propositions until his
Matie shalbe pleased, under his great or privy seale, or by the Lords
of his noble privy council to ratify the same."[1] In 1632, the assembly
in transmitting its laws and proceedings to the Dorset commission,[2]
said, "Wee beseech your Lorpps that you in yor grave judgm^te will
be pleased to interprett our intentions in all those Acts, to be wholly
for the welfare of the Colony, and such as wee, by large experience
in the place are assured to be most proper for the advancement
thereof: And wee become humble suitors, that now when these af-
fayres shall agayne be established all former liberties and priviledges
may be confirmed unto us accordinge to his Majesties gracious letters patents since the dissolution of the late Company."[3] Again on
February 8, 1634, Governor John West and the council wrote, "Wee
are continually solicited by the Inhabitants to be humble petitioners
to your Honnors for the confirmation of theire lands and priviledges, which although promised by his Majesties letters of Privie
Seal, yet hitherto not effected";[4] and they were the more concerned
about the matter because of the grant of Maryland to Lord Baltimore in 1632 and the appointment of the Laud commission in England, April 28, 1634, to examine and rectify all complaints from the
plantations.

These citations clearly show that the authorities in England had
not yet definitely determined the form that the government of the
colony should take and that the king was still in a position to deprive the Virginians at any time of the privilege of an assembly if
he so wished, for no such body could legally come together without

the king, William III, without authorization from the crown, said "The assembly
. . . called without a fresh writ of summons was illegally and unconstitutionally
convened." Maryland Gazette, September 10, 1772.

1. Virginia Magazine, VII, 369.
2. Not "to the Privy Council," as says the editor of the Journals, 1619–1659,
p. 55.
3. Journals, 1619–1659, p. 55.
4. Public Record Office, Colonial Office, 1:8, no. 3 (inadequately calendared).

his consent. But though he was trying to govern without parliament in England, he probably had no intention of denying to Virginia the liberty of a representative gathering of the freemen, if we are to accept his own statements and those of his ministers. He was involved in many perplexing financial problems at home, but Virginia was his own dominion and for her he had sympathy and a measure of affection. It would look very much as if the planters in the colony were engaged, unconsciously no doubt, in leading the king to a decision, by acting first and explaining afterward, endeavoring by means of petitions and requests couched in carefully guarded language to hold the king to his promises. They kept the assembly alive during these years, though they knew they had no legal right to do so, as they were without any direct authorization of the crown.

Thus the Virginians themselves were largely responsible for the establishment of self-government in a royal colony in America. The work of the company might well have been undone by the king after 1624 and indeed for fifteen years the issue was in doubt. But with the instructions to Wyatt in 1639 and those to Berkeley in 1641 the doubt was removed and from that time on the house of burgesses in Virginia stood on the impregnable rock of the royal consent. When, by the instructions of January, 1639, Wyatt and his councillors were ordered "as formerly once a year or oftener, if urgent occasion shall require, to summon the burgesses of all and singular plantations there, which together with the governor and council shall have power to make acts and laws for the government of that plantation, correspondent as near as may be to the laws of England, in which assembly the governor was to have a negative voice as formerly," then full recognition was finally given to the previous proceedings of the planters and a popular assembly was permanently settled as an essential part of this the first colony in the king's hand. Not only was the Virginia settlement assured of its future, but what was even of greater importance for the later history of the royal colonies in America, a precedent was set according to which the people of any royal colony was assured of their right to share in the making of laws, the levying of taxes, and the taking into consideration those many other things, chiefly of a local and prudential nature, that meant most to men two and three hundred years ago. As the result of fifteen years indecision on the part of the crown and of action on the part of the colony, the principle was finally laid down that a royal colony should be, in part at least, a self-administering community, with a governor and council appointed in England and a representative assembly chosen by the freemen or freeholders in the colony. Though self-government was in no sense of the word democratic government and though popular interest in law-making was never very keen during colonial times, nevertheless the very presence of such a gathering in a royal British colony in America was a factor of vast consequence in the development of American political practices.

CHAPTER X

VIRGINIA IN 1641

WITH the coming of Sir William Berkeley as governor of the colony in 1641 the settlement of Virginia reached the end of an important period of its history. The time of experimentation was over and there began an era of adaptation to English needs and influences which was to continue to the end of the century. But no plantation in America could attain its full status as a colony until the government in England had worked out its own colonial policy and had given shape to that system of administration and control which was to define, for the remainder of our colonial period, the relationship between the mother country and her colonies. That policy was not fully worked out until after 1696.

In the year 1641 Virginia occupied the tidewater region from the Chesapeake to the Falls of the James, an area that ascended gradually not more than two hundred feet for the entire distance. Through this flat country flowed the James river very slowly past the plantations and farms on either side, offering for more than half its length, a broad and safe waterway for ocean-going vessels of moderate tonnage. The settlements extended from Accomac to the Falls. Though by 1641 the inhabitants had not settled very far to the south, they had begun to spread northward to the Chiskiack or York river and their lands were laid out and their homes built on both sides of King's creek and down the south side of the river to its mouth. In 1632 there were two plantations there and a few years later the entire lower part of the neck between the James and the York was occupied. Before 1650 the best lands along the James had been "seated" and the frontier to the northward was gradually advancing toward the Rappahannock and the Potomac. Under Harvey the movement was rapid. New palisades were built between the two rivers, with houses adjoining, thus giving to the lower part of the peninsula a range for cattle safe from Indian attacks. By 1634 the colony was well enough peopled and extended over a sufficiently wide area to be divided into eight shires or counties. The effect of tobacco planting and cattle ranging was to scatter the population and to prevent the colonists, however much the authorities in England might desire them to do so, from gathering at any point into towns or compact communities. At this time the inhabitants numbered upward of seventy-five hundred, with perhaps two hundred and fifty negroes.

The city of Jamestown itself made little progress, though in 1638 it was considerably enlarged and new houses were built, among which was one of brick for Richard Kemp, the secretary, with gardens along the river front, and later additional brick houses were put up and plans for a state house were started. But the attempts to boom the town were never very successful and Jamestown never was to the colony, as Williamsburg became afterward, a place of residence for the planters and the center of their social and political life. Williamsburg was originally called "the Middle Plantation," where as early as 1630 Governor Pott had a farm, which became a palisaded post against the Indians in 1632. Later Governor Berkeley, the Ludwells, and the Lees, lived there and it became the capital in 1699, because though but seven miles away, it was more conveniently and salubriously located. There some of the wealthier planters had their houses as well as their country mansions—buildings that for long were very modest structures, because money was scarce and labor expensive; and there during portions of the year the government was carried on, business was done, fairs were held, and life was gay and festive. Jamestown, on the other hand, was the sole port of entry on the river from 1607 to 1624 and in the latter year was legally set apart as such by the assembly, which, in order to prevent forestalling and regrating,[1] forbade any ship to break bulk until it arrived there and required that all contracts for tobacco be made there.[2] Though merchants protested against this rule and the Dorset commission disobeyed it in at least one instance,[3] the king in his instructions to Harvey in 1637 expressed his approval[4] and the rule was confirmed by statute in 1642.[5]

The people of the colony consisted of freemen, indentured servants, apprentices, and negroes, of which upward of seventy-five per cent had come over under some form of indenture, either as servants or apprentices or as boys and girls from the cities and towns of

1. Hening, *Statutes*, I, 150–151; *Minutes of Council*, I, 106, 107, 114, 116, 121.
2. Hening, *Statutes*, I, 126, 163, 191, 206, 214–215.
3. *Calendar State Papers, Colonial*, 1574–1660, p. 158.
4. *Virginia Magazine*, III, 29.   5. Hening, *Statutes*, I, 245.

England, London in particular. Many of these, perhaps half, eventually became freemen, acquired small farms, cultivated tobacco, and became useful and sometimes influential members of the colony. As the early seventeenth century wore on and the settlement expanded, the larger areas required for cultivation demanded more laborers and the number of the indentured servants tended to increase, until the time came when the value of the negro as a plantation servant and finally as a slave by law led to the substitution of black labor for white and the consequent diminution of the number of servants imported.[1] Among the freeholders were undoubtedly a considerable number of men of excellent and even high-born family connections, such as George Percy, son of the Earl of Northumberland, Francis, John, and Nathaniel West, sons of Lord De la Warr, Thomas Paulett or Pawlet, brother of Baron Paulett of Hinton St. George and grandson of the Marquis of Winchester, and others, often younger sons seeking adventure or maintenance. Many had been matriculates of Oxford or Cambridge, such as Dr. John Pott, Gabriel Archer, Hugh Bullock, John Pountis, John Pory, Richard Kemp, and Christopher Davison, while there are many persons named in the lists of the time or in such as have been compiled since[2] who bear the designation "gentleman," a title of rank below that of the noble but above that of the yeoman, the particular social rating of whom cannot be exactly discovered. On the whole, however, there was no considerable number of "scions of great English houses" and not many men of the better class in proportion to those of humble birth.

But one thing seems quite clear that during the period under consideration the control of government was in the hands, almost entirely, of men of rank and influence and good social standing. Scarcely a single indentured servant had risen as yet to a position of political importance or had obtained any share in the administration of the colony, though some of them, and perhaps many, seem to have been in origin above the level of menials, to have had good family connections in England, and in a few instances to have been even of gentle birth.[3] There were at this time, of course, no "cava-

1. In 1671 there were 40,000 people, of whom 6,000 only were servants.
2. "The List of the Livinge and Dead in Virginia," February 16, 1623, *Colonial Records of Virginia*, Senate Document, 1874; "Census of People in 1624 and 1625," *William and Mary Quarterly*, VII; Hotten, *Emigrants, 1600–1700* (London, 1874).
3. Bruce, *Social Life in Colonial Virginia* (2d ed. enlarged, 1927). This work deals almost entirely with the better classes and has little to say regarding the small

liers" in the colony, for the term has a political not a social significance, and in a proper sense is identical with "royalist" and belongs
to the period after 1650. There were many merchants and the sons of
merchants, who both at this time and afterward, they and their descendants, became men of wealth and the founders of some of the
best known of Virginia's colonial families.

The Virginia of this period was a colony of small landowners and
not of large plantations and wealthy planters. The largest of the
early grants by the company to its subscribers rarely went over a
thousand acres and many of these holdings were either not taken
up at all or else were divided among small farmers, men of slender
means and probably often of still more slender skill in agriculture,
who though numerically large were socially and politically of relatively little importance. They formed, however, the backbone of the
community, constituting in the total the largest group of tobacco
raisers and, economically speaking, were the basis of the colony's
wealth. In origin they were either freemen, who had come over at
their own expense and entered at once into the social and civil life
of the colony as planters and farmers and holders of public office, or
else they were indentured servants, who had bound themselves to
serve four or five years before they were free to enter upon a career
of their own. By no means all indentured servants became farmers
on their own account. Many doubtless dropped into the class of the
ne'er-do-wells or died in bondage. Others became hired laborers,
working for a daily wage, others rented small properties, while perhaps a still smaller number obtained in one way or another a small
acreage whereon to produce, with the aid of wife and children, a
crop of tobacco.[1] Though socially inferior and with little desire or
opportunity for political preferment, they were important because
of the crops they raised and the right to vote which they possessed.

farmer, who formed the largest part of the population. An excellent supplement to
it is the study by Professor Wertenbaker, *The Planters of Colonial Virginia* (1922),
which is an elaboration of the same writer's *Patrician and Plebeian in Virginia,* a
preliminary and less satisfactory essay. Despite Professor Wertenbaker's results, as
embodied in the later volume, I believe that he has exaggerated the political importance of the indentured servant, who emerged from his bondage and became a
freeman, and has not made it sufficiently clear that no final conclusion can ever be
reached as to the numbers of people of various classes who came to Virginia before
1650.

1. Apprentices, on emerging from their apprenticeship, received fifty acres according to the custom of the country, but no servant was entitled by law to land on
completing his service.

With the increase in the number of negroes the position of the servant tended to improve, partly because of the presence of an inferior
class and partly because they could themselves become employers of
labor, for many a servant-farmer was able in time to have a negro or
two of his own.

Lands were either leased or held in fee simple, with the payment
of a quit-rent to the king. By 1641 probably all the private "colonies" or "particular plantations" had lost their identity and with the
"public lands" of the defunct company had become merged into the
lands held by tenure under the crown. The planters were building
better houses, were setting out orchards and planting gardens,[1] and
were raising stocks of cattle and swine. But all the earlier industrial
enterprises had failed, and except for a small amount of shipbuilding[2] and the necessary construction of houses and other buildings,
all artisan activities had ceased. The attempts to make glass, iron,
potash, wine, and the like had all come to an end and Virginia entered upon its career as an agricultural colony, with its future dependent on a single staple—tobacco.[3]

During this period corn and tobacco were the two leading staples,
but corn was raised almost entirely for home consumption, and tobacco alone was shipped to England, where it sold sufficiently well
to bring a profit to the planters. As soon as the importance of tobacco was realized many attempts were made to improve its quality. Originally it seems to have been thrown into heaps on the
ground, a procedure which must have resulted in the production of
a great deal that was discolored and rotten; but after Lambert dis-

---

1. Gardens and cornfields had to be impaled to protect them from the hogs, which
ran more or less at large. To indicate ownership hogs had their ears slit or cropt
and cows had their horns marked or were given names. *Minutes of Council*, I, 29.

2. *Virginia Magazine*, VIII, 150. The only vessels named are shallops, which were
of sufficient size to enable the colonists to "vend such staple commodities" as might
be available as a surplus. Probably the voyages mentioned to New England (Cape
Ann, Damariscove, etc., generally designated as "Canada") and to the Cape Fear
were made in English-built vessels, for the shallop was small and hardly suitable for
open sea navigation. In the one case where details are given, the shallop was but
18½ feet by 6½ feet, with sails and oars. *Minutes of Council*, I, 39.

3. The company to 1624 and the royal government afterward continued to be
hopeful regarding other staples and industries, but the chief obstacles in the way of
success were, as we have already seen, want of skill, capital, and time, and the high
price of labor (*Virginia Magazine*, VII, 259). Tobacco could be raised by anyone,
even the humblest, with a minimum of capital and labor, and the returns came
quickly. Even the planting of corn, which at one time was compulsory and had
gone so far as to furnish a supply for New England, was neglected for tobacco. In
1630 corn had to be sought for outside the colony. *Virginia Magazine*, VII, 380.

covered that it could be cured more satisfactorily on racks or lines, the leaves became better conditioned and less rank and sour. But during colonial times the proper preparation of tobacco was always a matter of much concern, the curing processes were never perfect, and in the days before the inspection system was introduced large quantities of wet tobacco were shipped, which, mixed as it was, the good with the poor and the very bad, often proved unsalable or of but little value in the English market. So dependent were the colonists on this staple for their maintenance that it became at this early period the one most important subject of controversy with the mother country. The very idea of a contract was a "terror and a discouragement" to those who, as the assembly wrote the king, had "laboured in the confused pathes of those labyrinths."[1] Probably in the year 1628 the easing of the tobacco situation was quite as important to the planters as was the reëstablishment of the popular assembly, and the fixing of a satisfactory price, the prohibition of English and foreign tobacco, and the abolition of the contract as far as the colonists were concerned were the conditions deemed most likely to bring relief to the colony. The planters were strongly opposed to the requirement that all tobacco be sent to England only and frequently asked that the privilege of sending to the best markets, that is, to Holland, be restored. But this request was always emphatically refused, notably by order in council of July 2, 1634, and by letter to the governor and council two weeks later, and it was in part Governor Harvey's insistence on obedience to these instructions that led to his deposition the following year.[2]

Life in the colony was hard and only those of strong constitutions, immune to local ills, were able to endure. Sickness and death

1. *Virginia Magazine*, VII, 259–264; *Journals, 1619–1659*, p. 45. As early as 1619 the House of Burgesses passed an act providing for the inspection of tobacco intended for exportation and for the destruction of that which was of mean quality. During the years from 1624 on, many attempts were made both to reduce the quantity and to improve the quality of the staple, all of which may be found in Hening's *Statutes* and need not be recapitulated here. The matter was of very serious consequence, because of the rapid increase of the output. Brock estimates that from 1619 with 20,000 pounds, the supply had risen in 1639 to 1,500,000 pounds and the price had gone down from 3s. to 3d a pound. "A Succinct Account of Tobacco in Virginia, 1607–1790," Tenth Census, *Report of the Productions of Agriculture*, p. 224.

2. *Acts Privy Council, Colonial*, I, §§ 332, 334; *Virginia Magazine*, VIII, 302. There was, of course, no custom house at this time in the colony. The "magazine" ships were instructed to sail from England in June and to be in the colony in September, evidently with the idea of remaining there until such time as would bring them home by Candlemas (*Virginia Magazine*, XV, 401–402). Later, after the fall

must have been of such frequent occurrence as to become matters of daily experience, though news spread slowly, for the country was wide and knowledge of what was happening in one part came infrequently to another. There was always a great demand for ministers, physicians, and medicines, and at this early period clothing cannot have been any too plentiful. The large number of men and women of the servant class and of boys and girls from the English towns must have imported a coarseness of speech and demeanor in an age when vulgarity, indecency, and uncleanliness were widely prevalent anyway, and when men's attitude toward each other was little softened by feelings of humanity or sympathy. There was a great deal of quarreling, abusive language, and fist-fighting, and charges were hurled about freely without regard to rank or station. At least one case is recorded during this period of a charge of witchcraft against a "goodwife" at Kickotan, but apparently it came to nothing.[1] Heavy drinking was inevitable and there was no doubt frequent imbibing of "sack strong waters and other drinks of like kynde," of "Canary and Malligo and Allicant Tent Bastard Muskadell," and of aquavitae, beer, cider, and "Tamarindos," whatever that was, possibly one of the many varieties of arrack.[2] Punishments were characteristic of the time. Men were hanged (whipped from the fort to the gallows), towed at a boat's stern (a substitute for ducking), stood in the stocks or the pillory, laid in bolts, degraded from rank, tied neck and heels, whipped at the whipping post, sometimes with a lash to which fishhooks were attached but more often with a cat of small lines or whipcord—a punishment called "kissing the post."[3] Fornication, which was common enough everywhere—in England, New England, and Virginia—was dealt with

of the company, the ships as a rule arrived early in winter and "lay" from forty to eighty days, a period usually provided for in the charter party, with a discount of £3 a day for every day the ship lay under forty, which was the period commonly agreed on. The clause generally read, "and there shall stay and abide for the space of forty working days next after her first arrival there" (Justice, "An Additional Collection of Instruments," in *A General Treatise of Money and Exchanges*, part V). In Virginia there was always much disagreement between planters and the London merchants as to when the "lay days" began and how long they were to last. In File 4, Virginia Historical Society, there is a charter party of 1770, which provides that the "lay days" should begin with the time of reporting at the custom house and should run eighty days from that date. Examples could be given, however, of "lay days" beginning when the ship was ready to take in tobacco and continuing on for the more usual time of forty days.

1. *Minutes of Council*, I, 111, 112, 113.   2. *Ibid.*, 5, 8, 72.
3. *Ibid.*, 3, 5, 12, 14, 15, 18, 22, 23, 85, 93.

as an ecclesiastical offense and the incontinents were required to wear white sheets and make confession in the presence of the congregation.[1] Sexual immorality among the lower classes was frequent enough.

A large majority of the cases involving discipline and punishment must have concerned the servant class, if we may draw conclusions from the few instances of dereliction preserved in the court orders and in the meagre body of county court records that has escaped the ravages of time, fire, and vandalism.[2] The tale of life everywhere in the colonies at this time, from Maine to Virginia, is pretty much the same, for the conditions that prevailed in these early settlements were those of the frontier, rough and unconventional. But it must always be remembered that the accounts which have been handed down to us of colonial habits and practices are such as came before the courts for judgment and so represent the worst aspects of colonial life. Though it is easy to idealize our ancestors, both as to their characters and as to their conduct, it is still easier and equally unnecessary to go to the other extreme and make them worse than they really were. About all that can be said certainly is that the recorded instances of deviation from rectitude and of deeds without a name by no means represent the normal conditions prevailing among a majority of the people.

1. In one case, a woman charging another with bastardy was commanded by the court to stand before the congregation and make an apology for the slander. *Ibid.*, I, 31, 33.

2. *Ibid.*, I, 465–469. Dr. Bruce has analyzed with great thoroughness and skill the few remaining records of the early county courts in his *Institutional History*.

CHAPTER XI

EARLY YEARS IN BERMUDA, 1612–1652

CLOSELY bound up with the fortunes of Virginia, during its early years under the company, and the seat of a noteworthy experiment in colonization, in many ways not dissimilar to that of Virginia, was a group of small islands, lying five hundred and eighty miles out from the Atlantic coast, in about the same latitude as the present city of Charleston. These were the Somers or Bermuda islands, shaped in the form of a fishhook with the eye at the eastern end, one of which so far outstripped the others in size and habitability as to give the whole the character of a single island. This coral reef possesses a salubrious climate and a romantic history, which is somewhat lost in a debatable if not a mythical past. The islands were first discovered by the Spanish and the Portuguese and were known to English voyagers as early as 1593, and acquired the reputation that Raleigh gave them two years later of "a hellish sea for thunder, lightning, and stormes."[1] They did not enter the domain of English colonial history until 1609, when Sir George Somers was wrecked there in his voyage to Virginia. Brought thus to the attention of the Virginia Company they became an object of so much importance, as a possible source of supply for the older settlement and a valuable strategic post in the struggle with Spain, that the company obtained an enlargement of its own boundaries in 1612 and planned to use the islands in furthering its colonial designs. Argall is reported to have gone there in 1610 to secure provisions if possible, but the trip if ever made came to nought.[2] The islands were first called Virginiola, then the Somers Islands, the Bermudas (from the Portuguese navigator Bermudez), and Bermuda. In 1611, the Virginians proposed to build a fort there and maintain a garrison, but the expense promised to be too great and the enterprise was abandoned. In 1613 and

1. *Discoverie*, p. 73. Wilkinson, *The Adventurers of Bermuda* (1933), the only history, properly so called, of the islands in the seventeenth century, devotes considerable space to the pre-English period. My chapters were written before this work appeared.

2. Smith, *Travels and Works*, II, 503.

1614 the settlers thought of moving out there themselves—if we are to believe the statements made by the Spanish minister—but nothing came of the plan, if it ever was formed, which is doubtful.[1]

With the granting of the islands to the Virginia Company in 1612, attempts were made to develop them, but as the company had all it could do to support its own plantation on the James, it turned the business over to a subordinate association of its own members with authority to control the government and manage the trade. This voluntary group of partners and subscribers was known as the Undertakers for the Plantation of the Sommers Islands and in April of that year it sent out their "welbeloved friend" Richard Moore in the ship, the *Plough,* with "men, women and mariners" to occupy the islands. These settlers built a fort and a storehouse, after the fashion of all the early pioneers, and expected to receive, according to promises already made, for each family transported a portion of ground for house, garden, and "backside." But this promise was not fulfilled. They expected also to find pearls, ambergris, silkgrass, tobacco, and oil from whale-fishing and had hopes of a "yellow wood" that was hard and heavy, "the vertue and propertie whereof are yet unknown to us." Of this the undertakers wanted a ton of the biggest sort as well as another ton of any "coullored wood," that they might make trial of them. They in their turn sent nets for fishing, and promised to despatch, every now and then, as occasion and need might arise, goods and provisions for the relief of the island. Moore and his companions promised to worship God, to keep the Sabbath, to exclude "all Atheists, Papists, Anabaptists, Brownist, and all other Heretiques and Sectaries whatsoever," to serve the king, to obey the undertakers, and against all undertakers "manfully to fight as true Englishmen" for commonwealth and gospel.[2]

Moore wrote back enthusiastically of the islands, mentioning "Turkles" of huge size, fish and fowls of many kinds, all sorts of fruit, but saying nothing of pearls and silkgrass. He found there also three men who had remained on the island after the shipwreck of 1610 and had established themselves on high ground, built a house, planted corn and other vegetables, and were guarding a great piece of ambergris and a few seed pearls, which they had discov-

1. Brown, *Genesis,* I, 495; II, 560, 680.
2. Lefroy, *Memorials of the Bermudas,* I, 58–64; Force, *Tracts,* III, no. 3.

ered shortly before.[1] These men had prospered during their years on the island, were healthy and hearty, and said that they had not been sick a day in all that time. Moore was delighted with the wholesomeness of the climate and wrote that the "aires of England are far more subject to diseases than these islands are."[2] He noted many sperm whales, palm trees, cedar trees, and tobacco plants and declared that the islands were enchanted, wronging neither friend nor foe, but yielding all men their expectations.

But this happy land, fruitful and peaceful by nature, soon became a scene of jealousy, greed, and mutiny, all because of the ambergris —a highly prized and valuable waxy substance from the sperm whale, used at the time in medicine, confectionery, and perfumery[3] —which the three "old planters" had discovered. The serpent entered into Eden and the harmony was broken. Controversy and complaint followed, the precious substance was fought over and wasted and only with difficulty was enough secured to net the undertakers some £6000, sufficient, however, to enable them to

1. Smith, *Travels and Works*, II, 640–641.
2. Lefroy, *Memorials*, I, 71.
3. The origin of ambergris, which was a perquisite of the Admiralty, was unknown as late as the middle of the eighteenth century. "Some assert [says Postlethwayt's *Universal Dictionary*] that this precious gum is formed only of honey-combs and wax, which tumbles down from the rocks. Others say it is nothing but the excrements of some birds. Others again that it is the spawn or sperm of a certain kind of whales, or of some amphibious sea-animal, but this is mere conjecture; for there have been sometimes such large heaps or collections of this ambergrease found, that it is not natural to have recourse to this explication. There are some who maintain that it is nothing but the skum of the sea. However all agree that these several matters become solid and acquire their scent by the agitation of the waves, by the saltness of the sea, and by the heat of the sun, which purifies and bakes them" (I, 52–53, 1751). In 1761, Rolt (*A New Dictionary of Trade and Commerce*, 2d ed.) could say that the origin of ambergris was the subject of a great variety of opinions among naturalists, but that the most probable account of its formation was held to be the honey-combs falling into the sea from the rocks or trees where the wild bees built their apiaries. These honey-combs were sometimes swallowed by animals, and afterward were cast up into the sea or found in their bowels (under "Ambergrease"). But by 1766 the origin had been discovered through chemical methods, and it was proved that ambergris was a "true animal concrete, formed in balls in the body of the male spermaceti whale," but even then it was believed that the whale swallowed the substance and did not create it (Mortimer's *Dictionary of Trade and Commerce*, 1766, under "Ambergris"). The science of chemistry was still in its infancy. In 1718 Woodes Rogers wrote that ambergris was found in large quantities among the Bahamas (*Calendar State Papers, Colonial*, 1717–1718, p. 375). There is an excellent description of ambergris in Melville's *Moby Dick*, and Wilkinson (pp. 67–72) has a good account of the ambergris quarrel in Bermuda.

underwrite their adventure.¹ Because of this windfall, the beginning of colonization in Bermuda was much more successful than it had been in Virginia and for a number of years the islands had preference in England over the older settlement and subscribers were more easily obtained. By the end of 1613 the enterprise was fairly launched and surveys of the land were begun, though as yet no private grants of arable had been made. New supplies and new settlers were sent out, and though famine at times threatened to distress the inhabitants, there was no such prolonged period of sickness and starvation as in Virginia. By the end of 1614 there were in the colony at least six hundred people.² The undertakers, aroused by the success of their venture, now applied for a regular charter of incorporation. This they secured on June 29, 1615, and the Bermuda Company entered on its career as an independent colonizing agency, destined to last for nearly seventy years.

Moore returned before his time had expired, having proved that he was a good carpenter but a poor governor. He had "grown as jealous of the company as they sone after of him," charging its members with sharp and bitter speaking against him in their quarter courts for what they called in their letters "his peevishness and presumption." "With teares tricklinge downe his cheekes," he said that they vexed him to the very soul and he would stay in the island no longer. At his departure he placed the government in the hands of six men, each to serve as governor for a month, an act which, as Nathaniel Butler said afterward, was the very worst that he committed during the whole time of his abode.³ Then began the rule, or rather the misrule of the six, 1615-1616, when liberty and license reigned and a perpetual Christmas ensued. "He was considered the bravest and tallest fellow who could drink deepest, bowl best with saken shot in the governor's garden . . . and winne most loblolly."⁴ The settlers felt but a small burden of responsibility.

1. Scott, *Joint-Stock Companies*, II, 261.
2. Brown, *Genesis*, II, 755.
3. Butler, *Historye of the Bermudaes*, pp. 39–45; Smith, *Travels and Works*, II, 649–652.
4. Loblolly was water gruel, or "spoon meat" as it was sometimes called. It is frequently mentioned in the documents of the period and was known in all the colonies from New England to Barbados. "Loblolly pot" is found in Morton's *New England Canaan* (Prince Society), p. 128, and one Richard Frethorne, writing home of his unhappy state in Virginia in 1623, says that since he landed he had eaten nothing "but pease and loblolly" (Historical Manuscripts Commission, *Eighth Report*,

They had as yet received no holdings of land in permanence, all stock and land were possessed in common, as were those in Virginia during the earlier years, when the settlers were tenants at will of the company. They neglected agriculture, allowed rats, which had been brought to the islands in one of Captain Elfrith's ships, so to multiply as to become a menace to health and despoilers of such food as they had,[1] created factions among themselves, and bred deep discontents against the company. Having nothing to lose, with little foresight and less honesty, they upbraided those in authority and declared, as one of them said, that they would rather be hanged than live any longer slaves to the gripping and covetous merchants.[2]

The Bermuda Company, with Sir Thomas Smith as its governor, determined to put an end to this state of affairs, and convinced that "the originall of those gamboleinge times proceeded from the miserable insufficiencye of the commanders there"[3] selected as the new governor Captain Daniel Tucker, brother of the head customs searcher at Gravesend and a resident for five years as cape-merchant in Virginia. Tucker reached the island in 1616, instructed by his commission to take over the government for the ensuing three years and to carry out strictly the orders drawn up for his guidance.[4] Special directions were given him as to the character of the government he was to set up and, most important of all, provision was made for a distribution of land among the members of the company. The islands had already been divided into eight "tribes" or districts, as later Virginia was divided into eight shires, each of which containing 1250 acres was afterward named for one of the original posses-

II, no. 325). Ligon's description is as follows, "Pounding [Indian corn] in a large Morter and boyling it in water, to the thickness of Frumenti; and so put in a Tray such a quantity as wil serve a messe of seven or eight people; give it them cold, and scarce afford them salt with it. This we call *Lob-lollie*. But the Negres, when they come to be fed with this, are much discontented and crie out, O! O! *no more Loblob*" (*Barbados*, p. 31). See also Lefroy, *Memorials*, I, 583 note, 616. There was a "Loblolly Cove" in New England, mentioned in a vice-admiralty court trial over the ownership of a whale which was stranded there. Court of Admiralty Records, Massachusetts, III, fo. 11.

1. The same scourge of rats overtook Virginia in 1609. Smith, *Travels and Works*, I, 155; Historical Manuscripts Commission, *Eighth Report*, II, no. 210.

2. Butler, *Historye*, p. 52.

3. *Ibid.*, p. 69. The Spanish authorities, stirred by the reports which were spread abroad after the discovery of the ambergris, made an effort to investigate, perhaps to seize the islands, but were driven off by a shot from the fort.

4. Lefroy, *Memorials*, I, 105–119.

sors of as many as ten shares of stock, the distribution being determined by lot. In the new arrangement each adventurer or stockholder was given twenty-five acres for each share of stock that he held, not necessarily all in one tribe but scattered among many tribes. Lands were also set apart for public use, a policy decided on for Bermuda at about the same time as it was for Virginia and in much the same form, because originated by the same group of men. Eventually plans were made for a free school. These public lands were the property of the company and were not to be alienated or subdivided in any way. Their total area was about one seventh of the whole and included, as in Virginia, a reserve of four glebes or two full shares for the support of the minister, at this time the Rev. Lewis Hughes. Other portions were set apart for the maintenance of the government, the sheriff, the secretary, and the captain of the forts, equalling in all twenty-six shares, of which the government reserved for itself twelve shares or three hundred acres. The remaining portions of the public lands were let to persons, who in a collective sense were called "the colony." They cultivated their allotments and paid to the company quit-rents at the rate of two pounds of tobacco per acre or fifty pounds per share. The company possessed these lands at the time of its dissolution in 1684, when they became crown lands, the rents of which went to pay in part the governor's salary,[1] until sometime after 1768 the last of them were finally sold.[2]

Upon these lands Tucker placed the colonists, setting them at various sorts of labor, such as felling timber, hauling trees, squaring and sawing the logs, clearing ground, and planting corn. Over them he placed overseers, who were to see that they worked from sunrise to nine in the morning and from three in the afternoon until sunset. These men, some of whom were tenants of the company in its corporate capacity and others of the members individually considered, had at first no other allowance than meat, drink, and clothes, and pay in the form of a base money brought over by the governor that had a hog stamped upon one side of it and was consequently called by the people "hog money."[3] But as the settle-

---

1. Butler, *Historye*, pp. 105–106; Smith, *Travels and Works*, II, 661–665; Lefroy, *Memorials*, I, 200–202. For the public lands, *ibid.*, 201, §107, and for the corresponding system tried out in Virginia by the Virginia Company, *Virginia Company Records*, I, 350; II, 535, 542; Historical Manuscripts Commission, *Eighth Report*, II, no. 208.

2. *Acts Privy Council, Colonial*, III, §553.

3. Lefroy, *Memorials*, I, 100–101; Butler, *Historye*, p. 76. Very few specimens of

ment took on better form and new tenants were sent out, an arrangement was made whereby tenants worked the shares on half profits, thus changing their status into something like that of a copyholder, ensuring for them a measure of private gain. In 1620 this arrangement was made compulsory for all tenants.

In all probability, though the information on the subject is not entirely conclusive, the methods in vogue in Bermuda of this period were not unlike those employed by Gates and Dale in Virginia. Such similarity is not surprising as both systems represent a common plan and originated with the same group of leaders of both companies in England. The accounts given by Tucker and Butler correspond very closely with John Rolfe's description of conditions in Virginia at the time when Sir Thomas Dale left the colony in April, 1616.[1] As a result, says Smith in his history, every man being settled where he might constantly abide, the settlers "knew their business and fitted their households accordingly: then they built no more cabbins, but substantial houses; they cleared their grounds,

---

these rare Bermudian coins are known to exist. They were of brass, of the denominations of twelve-, six-, three-, and twopence. General Lefroy in 1877 had specimens of the first and second and in 1881 acquired one of the last variety. This money must have disappeared early, for in 1621 Butler reported that the only money in the islands was tobacco (Historical Manuscripts Commission, *Eighth Report*, II, no. 288).

The finding of hogs on the islands—an experience met with by the discoverers of all the smaller Caribbee islands—caught the popular fancy in England and is frequently mentioned in the literature of the time. Middleton in *Anything for a quiet Life* (1623, Dyce edition, 1840) speaks of

"This fine peacable island
. . . . . a land of peace,
Where hogs and tobacco yield fair increase."

Another play mentions the "fisherman," who "sayling by the Barmoothes saw a fire asingeing of a hog" (*Two Wise Men and All the Rest Fools,* anonymous, 1619, ed. 1913). John Taylor, the Water-poet, wrote several garbled lines, which he called *Epitaph in the Barmooda Tongue,* (*Poems,* 1630 ed. p. 61), the words of which were to be pronounced with the grunting of a hog.

1. Tucker harried the unprivileged, undisciplined and poorer classes in Bermuda in much the same manner as Dale and Argall were doing in Virginia at about the same time. Butler says that Tucker's policy of vigorous punishment was "fastened upon and squared after the Virginia rule" and that Tucker had in his hands a copy of Strachey's *Laws, Morall and Martiall* and often consulted it (*Historye*, p. 77). The six hundred inhabitants came largely from London and the eastern counties, with very few from the west or southwest, and were of about the same kind as those that went to Virginia—independent settlers, who went on their own, indentured servants, apprentices, vagrants, criminals and, after 1619, negroes. There were "gentlemen" as well as servants, but probably by far the largest number was of the middle class. See Butler, *Historye*, pp. 111, 114; Lefroy, *Memorials*, I, 127-140; Smith, *Travels and Works*, II, 666.

and planted not onely such things as would yield their fruits in a few months, but also such as would afford them profit within a few years, so that in a short time the Countrey began to aspire and neerely approach unto that happinesse and prosperitie, wherein now it flourisheth" (1624). A magazine was set up, similar to that in Virginia, which though it aroused complaint was on the whole well administered, and every encouragement was given to those interested in the raising of tobacco. In 1618 thirty thousand pounds were sent to England, which proving good and coming to a rising market gave great contentment and assurance to the company "to proceed lustily in their plantation."[1]

But Tucker's methods of government were not conducive to a long continuance of peaceful conditions. Tucker was an able and experienced man but he had a violent temper and made short shrift of those who were obstinate and lazy. His course of action aroused so much discontent and led to so many jealousies that he finally determined to return to England. There he was charged before the company with vainglory and presumption, with oppression and cruelty, and with using his position and the company's property to his own profit. The charges gave rise to the first quarrel among those who had been influential in organizing the Virginia and Bermuda companies, particularly Smith, Johnson, Warwick, Sandys, Cavendish, Southampton, and Pembroke, and ended in the ejection of Smith from the headship of the Virginia group, which he had held for ten years. This victory began the quarrel between the two companies and, in combination with other causes, eventually brought about the downfall of the older organization. In Tucker's place as governor of Bermuda, Smith and Warwick succeeded in securing the election of Nathaniel Butler, and in retaining their hold on the Bermuda Company, which remained under the control of Smith and Johnson, with Warwick the largest investor in its stock and promoter of its various enterprises.

Butler went out as governor in 1619 carrying with him instructions that were much the same as were those which Yeardley carried to Virginia earlier in the same year. "We require you [so the instructions read] that as sone as you maye after your arrivall in the Islands, you doe assemble your counsell and as many of the ablest and best understandinge men in the Islands, both of the clergy and

1. Butler, *Historye,* p. 110.

the laitie, as you and your counsell shall thinck fitt, wherein we wish you rather to take too many than too fewe, both because every man will more willingly obey laws to which he hath yeilded his consent; as likewise because you shall the better discover such things as have need of redrease by many than by fewe: and that in this assembly you deliberately consult and advice of such lawes and constitutions as shalbe thought fit to be made for the good of the plantations, and for the maintenance of religion, justice, order, peace and unitie among them. As also upon what penalties you thinck fitt, the performance of each lawe to be enjoyned: wherein we advise you to be very moderate, allways so proportioninge the penaltye to the offence, that the greatnesse of the punishment doe not encourage the delinquents to offend out of hope of pardon, as it falleth out wher this rule of moderation is not observed. And what in assembly shall, by the major or better part, be agreed upon, we would have you distinctly to advertize us by the return of the next shyp, that they may be ratefied and confirmed by the authoritie of the Court here, [in] such manner as by his Majesties Letters Patents is limited and appointed, with such alterations, explanations, or amendments as to sayd Court shalbe thought meet and convenient. And this course of assemblinge of the gravest and discreetest men in thoes Islands, to consult and advise with you and your counsell of such things as may conduce to the general good of that plantation, and to the well governinge of the people ther, we advise you to hold at least once a year,[1] and of your resolutions and determinations from time to time to advertize us, that they may be established and confirmed by order of our Courts here as aforesayd: and in the meane time you shall not need to doubt to putt in execution any such wholesome Orders or Constitutions as shall by the major part in the sayd assemblies be agreed upon. Provided that the same be not repugnant to the lawes of England nor contrary to this your present instructions, or to the standing lawes by us established."[2]

Who drafted this remarkable document we do not know, but it was issued in the name of the Governor and Company for the

1. A later order changed this to once in two years, Lefroy, *Memorials*, I, 209.

2. Butler, *Historye*, pp. 190–191. Though the privilege of popular election is not mentioned in the instructions, Butler undoubtedly understood that the "burgesses" were to be elected by the inhabitants of the colony and there is no reason to believe that this was done otherwise than in Virginia.

Plantation of the Somers Islands and must have received the approval of Smith and Johnson, even if they did not have a part in its actual composition. From the point of view of the political principles enunciated, it is quite as noteworthy as is the similar instruction issued to Yeardley, which Sandys is supposed to have drawn as one part of his great scheme for the renovation of Virginia in 1618–1619. Though it does not recognize in so many words the right of popular election, it does show that Sandys had no monopoly of the idea of popular self-government for an English colony in America. As Butler was a Warwick adherent and from his own account of his stewardship was in sympathy with the instructions given him, it would seem as if Warwick may have had some hand in drawing up the paper. The fact that the instructions to Yeardley were issued while Smith was still treasurer of the Virginia Company and the further fact that the instructions to Butler were issued while Smith was the governor of the Bermuda Company would seem to demand some readjustment in our views regarding the origin of these important concessions. The conclusion is unavoidable that Smith, Johnson, Warwick, and others of the Bermuda Company were as friendly as was Sandys to the idea of a self-governing colony, and we know that Warwick in later years was a stanch upholder of the principle of self-government in Massachusetts, Plymouth, and Rhode Island.

Governor Butler called the assembly to meet at Georgetown (the town of St. George) on August 1, 1620, just a year after the dissolution of the similar body which met at Jamestown and inaugurated the first legislative assembly in America. The Bermudian body came together "in the newe framed church, fitted for that purpose," and it stands a close second as to the date of its meeting and an unchallenged first when viewed from the standpoint of the unbroken continuity of its meetings for fifty years, 1620–1669. In that church were gathered the governor and his council, the bailiffs of the tribes, and two burgesses from each tribe, elected by plurality of voice by the chief inhabitants of the tribes.[1] In issuing writs of election rather than of summons Butler undoubtedly went beyond his instructions, probably following the Virginia model in doing so. In numbers the Bermudian assembly was slightly smaller than that of Virginia, but it appears to have been organized on a well-ordered parliamentary

1. Lefroy, *Memorials*, I, 267.

basis.[1] Butler's account of the proceedings at Georgetown shows us a parliamentary body which on the whole followed more closely parliamentary procedure in England than had the assembly at Jamestown, the year before, and that, too, despite the fact that John Pory, the Virginia speaker, had himself been a member of the English parliament and knew its manner of conducting business. In two respects, however, the Bermuda assembly fell short of both the English and the Virginia practices: it had no speaker, leaving that rôle to be played by the secretary; and all the members sat together as a single house, instead of separately as two houses, holding sessions only in the morning, the afternoons being given up either to consultations with the governor at his house or to meetings of committees for the framing of the next day's business.

The work of the assembly was strictly legislative, for, as the proceedings go to show, it performed no judicial functions. The secretary read the bills on three successive days and the members spoke, with heads uncovered, only once to a bill each day and were enjoined to speak briefly and to the point, addressing other members impersonally and using no reviling or "nippinge" speeches whatever. Bills passed by weight of voices, but if the secretary could not tell where the decision lay he could call for a standing vote—ayes up, noes in their seats—a form of procedure not unlike a division. When all was finished the governor "dismissed and broke up the assembly with a short speech, according as the former passage of businesse had given him occasion."[2] Fifteen laws were passed: relating to servants and apprentices; aged and impotent persons sent to the colony by the adventurers in England; fortifying kings-castle; making "rotten and unmerchantable tobacco"; bridges; supply of corn in the forts; the general assize; highways; preservation of the breed of tortoises; vagabonds; public store of corn in every tribe; guarding cornfields against poultry; fences; levy of a thousand pounds of tobacco toward the expense of public works; and, lastly, the tenure and position of governors, a law in the form of advice to the adventurers in England to avoid faction and dispute. These laws were all sent to England to be confirmed by the company.

One cannot but be impressed by the account[3] which Governor

1. Lefroy, *Memorials*, I, 267. On this assembly and on Bermuda's constitutional history in the colonial period, see Lefroy's article in *Archaeologia*, XLVII, 65–82 (1883).
2. Butler, *Historye*, pp. 197–203; Lefroy, *Memorials*, I, 165–179.
3. Lefroy, *Memorials*, I, 230–233, 272–275.

Butler gives of the orderliness and businesslike efficiency of this body of inexperienced legislators and by his own parliamentary skill in carrying through the proceedings to a successful consummation. Yet this is the same man who two years later wrote the "Unmasking of Virginia," a work termed by many writers a malicious libel. That Butler was a Warwick partisan and an opponent of Sandys and the Ferrars is well known, and it is not unlikely that he was interested to show how much better Bermuda was managed under the leadership of Smith, Warwick, and Johnson than was Virginia under Southampton and Sandys. Factions arose in Bermuda during his administration and there were plenty of charges and counter-charges. Butler had his grievances and the people theirs, but the complaints were directed rather against the company in England than against each other in the colony and concerned matters of minor but not unimportant detail rather than issues of large moment. There was one complaint brought against Butler by the Spanish ambassador in connection with the goods of a Spanish vessel wrecked on the islands, a matter that was taken very seriously by the company and by it carried up to the Privy Council, but the governor's conduct does not appear to have involved any very serious misfeasance of duty.[1] More serious were the charges brought against him by the company itself of high-handed and even illegal conduct, but as the charges must have been based upon *ex parte* information it is hard to know how much credence is to be given to them.

In 1622 the planters in the islands appealed to the king against the members of the company—not the members of the superior sort, earls, lords, and gentlemen, but "only such adventurers of inferior rank as by their multiplicitie of voyces doe beare down all good propositions and motions and thereby carrie the greatest sway at the present in managing the affaires of the Islands"—a curious commentary on the benefits of "democraticall government" and the wisdom of majority rule. Probably their complaint was ill-founded, if we are to judge from the good work which the company accomplished during the same year in drafting a code of laws, which taken as a whole was almost equivalent to a constitution for the colony. This code was drawn up by the company and must have

1. *Ibid.*, I, 239–255, 266; *Acts Privy Council, Colonial,* I, §85; *Virginia Company Records,* II, 407–408.

been adopted by majority vote at one of the great quarter courts, since nothing of importance touching the state of the islands could be ordered otherwise.[1] Its provisions concerned nearly every detail of the government: lands, officials, inhabitants, trade, and defense, standing to the colony of Bermuda in somewhat the same relation as did the charter of privileges to the colony of Virginia. These laws became the working constitution for the colony as long as the company lasted. According to them an assembly was to be called every second year, as a single house, the governor acting as president, vested with authority to cast a negative vote in legislation. The council, if unanimous, could also negative laws. The delegates from each tribe were increased from two to four, and eight were to come from the public lands. Plurality of voices was to carry a bill, which before it became a law had to be confirmed by the company. No taxes or impositions were to be laid otherwise than by the authority of the general assembly and were to be collected and appropriated only as the assembly directed.[2] These were important concessions to popular rule in Bermuda and would seem to show that whatever the planters might think to the contrary, the quarter courts of the company in England, in which a "multiplicity of voices" prevailed, were interested in "good propositions and motions" and were competent to legislate for the welfare of the colony.

Butler was dismissed in the autumn of 1622 and went to Virginia, later finding employment as governor of Old Providence Island. He was of the rough and ready sort, a pirate under the skin, as were many of those who served crown, country, and company in those days. But he was neither a brute nor a liar, and one cannot read his history of the islands without having respect for his intelligence, his literary skill, and his possession of at least a modicum of scholarship, for he had learning enough to translate a liturgy from French into English.[3] Had he not embroiled the country with Spain at an inopportune moment, it is possible but not probable that he would have been retained longer in the company's service, for he had

1. *Virginia Company Records*, I, 406.   2. Lefroy, *Memorials*, I, 200-228.
3. *Ibid.*, I, appendix ii; Butler, *Historye*, pp. 171-173; Smith, *Travels and Works*, II, 671-672. Of Butler's literary sagacity the following is an illustration: "And nowe being to fall upon somewhat more serious and fashionable times, it is exacted that our stile also prove more sober and grave, for it is a decorum requirable and becominge all historians to fit their phrase to their matter, for otherwise it shewes as unseemely and mishapen as to apparell a dwarfe in one of the garde's coates." *Historye*, p. 75.

many enemies in England, who seized upon the complaints and charges against him, exaggerated though they were, and were prepared to demand an investigation into his conduct of affairs. Butler himself was not on good terms with the company, whose policy he deemed meddling and injurious, and he went to Virginia where Warwick wished him to undertake an investigation of conditions following the massacre. After three years of administration in Bermuda he left the colony in a fairly prosperous state, although the people there were complaining almost as vociferously as were those in Virginia because of the low price of tobacco and because of the obligation imposed by the company that they send to England their entire crop, undivided, by the magazine ship, which came every year and bought the tobacco at cut-throat rates.[1] They wanted, as did the Virginians, to use their tobacco for trading with the Dutch, a traffic made impossible if all the tobacco had to be reserved for the magazine ship before each planter's share was allotted to him. The islands were small and none too productive and there was no staple except tobacco that offered a supply for the English market. At first the raising of sugar had been encouraged by the company, but finally that was forbidden because the need of wood for boiling would cause the destruction of the fuel supply of the islands.[2]

In the early years when the Virginia and Bermuda companies existed side by side, the colony was well managed on the whole and the inhabitants were contented. The fact that the report of the Jones commission, which had been appointed in 1623 to inquire into the affairs of both companies, was favorable to the Bermuda Company,[3] and that in 1624 no attempt was made to take away the company's charter, as was the case with the charter of the Virginia Company, shows that the Privy Council and the commissioners felt that Bermuda was being looked after satisfactorily. Also the further fact that the company weathered the storm which wrecked the older organization, speaks well for the enterprise and good sense of Smith, Johnson, and Warwick, each of whom was in turn a governor of the Bermuda Company.

In its origin and in many of the incidents of its early history Ber-

1. Historical Manuscripts Commission, *Eighth Report*, II, nos. 284, 295; Smith, *Travels and Works*, II, 684–685.

2. Lefroy, *Memorials*, II, 330, 362, 420.

3. For the favorable report of the commission, Historical Manuscripts Commission, *Eighth Report*, II, nos. 384, 385.

muda resembled Virginia, both in the policies adopted and in the staples produced. Both settlements were the outcome of the same movement in England and had behind them the same group of men, actuated by the same motives and using almost identical colonizing methods. But in its later history Bermuda had little in common with Virginia. That the Bermuda Company was unmolested while the Virginia Company was disciplined is in some ways the more remarkable when we realize that during this period and for long afterward, there existed in the colony a strong Puritan-minded group which was responsible for many a conflict between the civil and the ecclesiastical authorities. In fact Bermuda came into closer touch with the Puritan settlement of Massachusetts Bay and Old Providence Island than with Virginia, because of the presence in the islands of many men—ministers and others—who were possessed of strong Calvinistic theological leanings and of Calvinistic ideas regarding the relations between church and state. The Puritan movement in general embraced all sorts and conditions of religious and moral discontent, from the Brownists or Separatists to the non-conforming clergyman and low churchman of the Anglican church, and representatives of these various gradations of opinion—political, ecclesiastical, and social—took part in the colonizing movement and scattered widely over the colonizing area. Wherever they went, they were watched and their careers followed by those who were engaged in the same movement at home, and many of them were called back to take their place in the home ranks and to work in England for the success of the Puritan cause. There is no certain evidence of strict Puritans in Virginia much before 1642—for Virginia as the seat of a strongly established Anglican church had no room for either Puritans or Roman Catholics—and there were no Separatists, properly so called in Bermuda, for it, too, was officially Anglican. But even so in the latter colony there were a great many men possessed of strong Puritan principles and convictions, whose careers were not at all unlike those of Samuel Skelton, Francis Higginson, John Cotton, Thomas Hooker, and John Davenport of Massachusetts Bay, Connecticut, and New Haven. Until the Restoration, and in a lesser degree even afterward, Bermuda was in close touch with New England in sympathy and doctrines.

As early as 1617, Lewis Hughes, one of the two ministers who were members of Governor Tucker's council, wrote to Nathaniel

Rich, "The ceremonies are in no request, nor the book of Common Prayer, I use not at all. I have by the help of God begun a Church Government by Ministers and Elders. I made bold to chose four Elders for the town publicly by lifting up of hands and calling upon God when the governor was out of the town in the Main."[1] Tucker did not like this proceeding, but allowed it because, as he said, the minister was of "so peevish a disposition" that to thwart him would have left the colonists without any religious service at all.[2] Between the two there was constant wrangling and "endless uncivil broiles," and the many "bad discontents" in church matters did not come to an end until Tucker left the islands in 1618. Hughes followed in 1620 and peace reigned for a time, but the company, outraged at Hughes' exhibition of ecclesiastical laxity, sent out with Butler's successor, Captain John Bernard, November, 1622, four clergymen of the Church of England—George Stirk,[3] Nathaniel Bernard, Joseph Wright, and Robert Staples—evidently with the idea of putting an end to the non-conformist demonstrations. Wright died early, but the others had hardly got themselves established on the islands before they too began to show Puritan proclivities and in conjunction with Stirk's father-in-law, Stephen Painter, himself a Puritan and destined later to become a troublesome opponent of the government, began to quarrel with Bernard's successor, Woodhouse. As a result the men were heavily disciplined: Stirk and Painter were banished and Nathaniel Bernard was expelled from the council, fined, and imprisoned.[4] Again new ministers were sent out—Copland and Morgan—but they too, though Anglican in name, proved to be non-conformist in sympathy; and the situation was hardly improved by the return of Stirk, in the same ship with a new governor, Captain Philip Bell, the decree of banishment having been reversed.

The peace was soon broken. Bell quarreled with Painter over the question of vestries in the parishes, some of which, established in 1627, had been suspended by Bell soon after his arrival, because he believed that under the influence of local leaders they were "desyr-

1. Historical Manuscripts Commission, *Eighth Report*, II, no. 209.

2. *Ibid.*, no. 229.

3. Kittredge, "George Stirk, Minister," *Transactions*, Colonial Society of Massachusetts, XIII, 16–59. Another excellent article, bearing on the same subject but of a later period, is by Worthington C. Ford, "Sampson Bond in Bermuda," *Proceedings*, Massachusetts Historical Society, 55, pp. 295–318.

4. Lefroy, *Memorials*, I, 463, 466.

ing and goeing about to advance [themselves] above all authoritie or governm^t." Apparently Bell, who was a man of excellent family in England, an adherent of the Warwick party, and at this time about thirty-eight years of age,[1] was afraid that the local vestries, under the influence of "Independency," might become centers of political opposition to himself. With the ardor of comparative youth dealing with discontent and wilful contrariness, he charged Painter with being the "head and ringleader," a man "of such Luciferiane pride and such a headstrong perverse nature and disposition that without pleasing or submittinge to him no man cann live in piece or quiettness where he is or hath to do." He wrote of Painter's "fiery and factious spirit," so enkindled "that he hath underhand wrought a faction and partye to himselfe against me." Bell was evidently warring with what he believed to be a puritanic and "democraticall" party in the colony, with Painter at its head and the ministers among his followers, and viewed the situation as one of local and clerical autonomy against centralized authority.

Bell left the colony in 1629 and under his successors, Wood, Forster, and Sayle,[2] all men of marked personal characters and Puritan convictions—though Sayle was not a church member—the non-conformist group suffered little molestation. Under Sayle it became the controlling element in the islands, setting up a "government of ministers or an assembly of ministers, esteeming the government to be

1. Bell was an experienced man and one of the most interesting characters in early West Indian history. He was later governor of Old Providence Island, 1631–1637, and then of Barbados, 1641(5)–1649. Newton, *Colonizing Activities of the English Puritans, passim,* and Harlow, *Barbados,* ch. II.

2. Wood was possessed of common sense and considerable humor and made a good governor. When Stirk went to England about his salary, Wood wrote, "take this from mee that I never knew a Skotsman to this day to loose the least pretence hee had to a Title of or a thing due unto him and I am of opinion that you shall find Mr. Stirke, meeke as he hath been reputed, more vyolent in his courses than Mr. Ward [a nephew of Nathaniel Ward of Agawam, who went to England with Stirk] who is professedly oppositious," (Lefroy, *Memorials,* I, 532, 570. For Stirk's petition of 1634 regarding his "wages," Historical Manuscripts Commission, *Eighth Report,* II, nos. 418, 419, 422). A proclamation by Forster, in true Matheresque style and with characteristic Puritan wordiness, is printed by Lefroy (*Memorials,* II, 70–72). Colonel William Sayle was closely identified with the Bahamas and the Carolinas as well as with Bermuda. Sir John Yeamans said of him in 1670, "a man of no great sufficiency yet the best that I could get, experienced in several places, but old and weak, a zealot, an independent these 24 years." He was lieutenant or deputy governor of Bermuda, 1641–1642, 1643–1645, 1658–1662. He died in Carolina in 1671 (*Shaftesbury Papers, passim*).

theirs who have the sway of it," as Richard Norwood, surveyor, schoolmaster, and oldest inhabitant, wrote the company in 1641. "The ministers have gone to such lengths," he added, "as to make a man quite out of love with the government of the clergy, as they are called."[1] Notwithstanding the opposition of the royalists and of those possessed of high church principles, the low church, non-conformist preaching and teaching steadily prevailed under the driving power and personal proselyting methods of Patrick Copland,[2] John Oxenbridge, William Goulding, and Nathaniel White, all of whom had been sent over as clergymen of the Church of England to minister to the company's flock in Bermuda. They held, says Norwood, private meetings weekly, "which they call Loblolly Feasts," and practiced "Universal Catechising [of] all men and women weekly begun here almost two years past, and pressed upon us with great vehemency and that all shall be tied to answer according to that Catechism of Mr. Oxenbridge's called Baby Milk or some other." In other words, these men tried to introduce into Bermuda New England polity and discipline and so far succeeded in establishing their influence in the islands as to plan a *coup d'état* in 1644, for the purpose of setting up an independent church, under the pastorate of Nathaniel White, with Goulding and Copland serving as elders, which should be free of all control by the state. They declared then and there that they renounced and relinquished their offices as ministers in the Church of England and entered into a covenant to be a church by themselves, into which they would receive any such as would submit thereunto. Their leading lay member was Stephen Painter, who "publicly acknowledged Mr. White as supreme head

1. *Calendar State Papers, Colonial,* 1574–1660, pp. 323 (94), 326 (6, 7), 328 (10); Lefroy, *Memorials,* I, 653–655; II, 9, 10–12, 20, 118.

2. Patrick Copland, as chaplain in the service of the East India Company and chaplain of the Virginia Company, had already been concerned with Virginia affairs, particularly with the raising of funds for the school which the Virginia Company planned to erect at Charles City, preparatory to the college at Henrico. He preached an eloquent sermon on the subject, April 18, 1622, in the church of St. Mary-le-Bow, but the massacre of 1622 brought all these plans to an end. There is a memoir of Copland by Edward Neill (New York, 1871), in which this sermon is printed (ch. III), and an account of his early efforts in the same writer's *English Colonization of America,* pp. 106–180. Neill does not, however, mention the fact that Copland was a native of Aberdeen, had been educated there, and later endowed his alma mater bountifully by founding a chair of divinity in Marischal College, Rait, *The Universities of Aberdeen,* p. 147. Two new Copland letters are printed in *William and Mary Quarterly,* n.s. IX, pp. 301–302.

of their church next unto Christ and none above him." This issue was the culmination of many years of effort to convert Bermuda into a Puritan sanctuary.[1]

But the colonial government and the people generally in the islands were not in sympathy with this act of secession, for in Bermuda as in England at the same time the Puritans were in the minority. White and Painter were indicted for high treason and the attempt to establish Independency in the islands received a severe set-back, which brought gloom to the Puritan cause, notably in Massachusetts Bay. There Winthrop and the elders were watching with grave concern the course of events in Bermuda, and at this juncture, which coincided with a crisis in their own relations with the Long Parliament and the Warwick commission, they could think of nothing better to do than to "call the churches to a solemn seeking of the Lord" in behalf of their suffering brethren in those distant islands.[2]

Painter and White carried their case on appeal to the company in England and were acquitted of the charge against them, for neither the Long Parliament nor the Warwick commission, in which the Independent party, supported by the army, was daily gaining strength, were in any mood to coerce the Puritans overseas, either

1. Lefroy, *Memorials*, I, 570–571, 573, 575, 580, 584–585, 594, 615–619, 621–622.

2. Winthrop, *Journal* (Original Narratives Series), II, 295; *Massachusetts Colonial Records*, II, 167. In November, 1646, the general court of Massachusetts appointed a day of humiliation in behalf (*inter alia*) of "the sad estate of the church of Bermuda."

There was at this time a very close connection between Bermuda and New England. Stirk's son entered Harvard College; Nathaniel Ward, who went back to England with Stirk in 1630, was a nephew of Nathaniel Ward of Agawam; Michael Wigglesworth, author of the *Day of Doom*, was in correspondence with Nathaniel White and himself visited Bermuda in 1663; the Rev. Patrick Copland was a friend of Winthrop's and wrote him occasional letters and was called by Winthrop in 1648 "a godly man of near eighty years of age" (*Journal*, II, 352). The Remonstrance and Petition presented by Dr. Robert Child in 1646 was circulated in Bermuda as well as in New England and Virginia and among the Dutch, and on the ship *Supply*, which bore another similar petition addressed to parliament, there were present as passengers Captain William Sayle and the Rev. William Goulding, the latter of whom preached a sermon on shipboard (Winslow, *New England's Salamander*, pp. 116, 130, 133; *Collections*, Massachusetts Historical Society, 3d series, II). The Bermuda ministers frequently stopped at Boston on their way to England and talked matters over with their Puritan brethren ("Bermuda Colonial Clergy in New England," *Publications*, Colonial Society of Massachusetts, XII, 166–174), and during these years there was a considerable commercial connection and exchange of commodities between the two colonies, particularly of potatoes and corn.

in Massachusetts Bay or in Bermuda. The Independents were tolerant in religious matters, as the Presbyterians were not, and took a
much more lenient view of religious vagaries than did even their
fellows in New England. Already in the year 1645 the parliament
had promised Bermuda that all there should enjoy liberty of conscience, free from the cognizance of the civil magistrates, a promise
that the elders in Massachusetts found very difficult to understand.[1]
When, therefore, the cases of Painter and White came before the
Bermuda Company, the latter refused to act contrary to the dictum
of parliament and upheld the appeal.[2] Then the royalists in the islands took the matter into their own hands. In July, 1649, the so-
called "country party" rose against the Dissenters, proclaimed their
loyalty to the king and crown of England—a bold thing to do as
Charles I had lost his head only a few months before—and compelled the governor and council to take action.[3] White, Painter,
Copland, and others were banished from Bermuda and went with
their former governor, William Sayle, to his new plantation in
Eleuthera in the Bahamas. There they set up another independent
church in order to "enjoye Christ in the puritye of his ordinances,
without this Bermudian imbitterment."[4] But the place, which Johnson in his *Wonder-Working Providence* calls "a most barren rock,
shallow earth, not helpful to produce food for the inhabitants,"[5]
proved a very unhappy refuge even for those who were "flying the
avengers of non-conformity," and most of the courageous but over-
credulous band eventually broke away and returned either to Virginia, Bermuda, New England, or old England.[6]

By 1652, when the Commonwealth finally won its victory over its

1. Winthrop, *Journal*, II, 351–352; Stock, *Debates*, I, 169–170; Lefroy, *Memorials*,
I, 600.

2. Lefroy, *Memorials*, I, 586–590, 591, 600–601, 635–636, 638, 642, 643.

3. *Ibid.*, I, 650–651; II, 23.

4. The story of Sayle's experiment with Eleuthera concerns a curious episode among
the many curious episodes of this period, connected with the wanderings of the
Puritans in their effort to find a resting place overseas suitable for a church and
community organized after the divine plan. Sayle secured his patent to the rocky
island in 1646 and, though not a covenanted Christian himself, was a godly instrument in the hands of the ministers in Bermuda. In 1649 he took Copland and seventy others, constituting a covenanted church, to Eleuthera. The entire expedition
was a dismal failure and brought only suffering and distress upon those who took
part. Stock, *Debates*, I, 210, note 358.

5. *Wonder-Working Providence* (Original Narratives Series), p. 267; Lefroy,
Memorials, II, 9.

6. Lefroy, *Memorials*, II, 20, 86, 89.

enemies, all danger of retaliation on the part of the royalists and Anglicans was over. In that year the Bermuda Company, officially royalist up to this time, submitted to the "Commonwealth of England as it is now established" and from then to the Restoration in Bermuda, as in Maryland, Virginia, and Barbados, the Puritan party was in the ascendant. White was recalled, Painter returning from Eleuthera by way of Boston and England was welcomed back and made a councillor for life, and Puritan polity in church and state became the vogue. Even after the Restoration the religious life of the colony continued "loose and lax, irregular and phanatique," the offices of the Anglican Church were entirely neglected, and the Dissenting order almost entirely crowded out the Anglican worship and discipline.[1] One of the charges brought against the company was its neglect of the Church of England in the colony.[2]

Thus the two colonies of Virginia and Bermuda, begun under similar auspices, followed wholly different courses in their later careers. Virginia remained rigidly Anglican and royalist in sympathy;[3] while Bermuda became the home of a large number of nonconformist ministers—Presbyterians, as they gradually came to be— who with their followers divided the island into contentious factions, with the Dissenters a determined and often an acrimonious fighting group, either in opposition or in control.

Why this should have been so it is far from easy to say. Virginia,

1. After the Restoration one William Righton, an insurgent leader, engaged in various sporadic efforts to transform Bermuda into an independent and self-governing colony, similar to the colonies of Massachusetts Bay and Connecticut. Righton is said to have taken part in the Puritan activities of the Interregnum, to have been a servant of Hugh Peter (*Calendar State Papers, Colonial*, 1681–1685, §602), and to have imbibed some of the doctrines of the Levellers and Fifth Monarchy men, but the evidence substantiating these statements is not very satisfactory. Something will be said about him later.

2. Lefroy, *Memorials*, II, 433, 454, 487, 488, 508, 515 note; *Calendar State Papers, Colonial*, 1681–1685, §1097.

3. In 1643 the Virginia House of Burgesses passed an act (Hening, *Statutes*, I, 277) requiring all ministers to conform to the orders and constitutions of the Church of England and instructed Governor Berkeley to compel all non-conformists "to depart the collony with all convenience." Johnson, in his *Wonder-Working Providence* (p. 265) remarks on this law, "Oh poor Virginia, dost thou send away the Ministers of Christ with threatening speeches?" and he firmly believed that the Indian attack of April, 1644, was God's vengeance on the colony for so doing. At almost the same time Massachusetts Bay was driving out Anabaptists, apprehending Jesuits, forbidding the Indians to pow-wow to their gods, and banishing Dr. Child and others. She was also putting down gaming, dancing, playing shuffleboard, bowling, etc., especially in ordinaries (*Massachusetts Colonial Records*, III, 68, 102, 114, 201, 224).

of course, very early fell into the hands of the crown, while Bermuda remained for seventy years under the control of the company and, despite all that the latter said to the contrary,[1] its members were either neglectful of the Anglican church in the islands or else were actively in sympathy with the non-conformist group there. Why so many ministers should have been sent out, from Lewis Hughes to Nathaniel White, professedly Anglican in faith but non-conformist in their innermost sympathies, who set up in time a "government of ministers" and eventually brought about schism and separation, is an interesting problem, not easy to solve. For thirty years Warwick was the guiding spirit of the company[2] and he must have been responsible beyond anyone else in authority, for in his hands, in largest part, until his death in 1658, lay the appointment to benefices in the islands. No such series of puritan-minded ministers was ever sent to Virginia and none of those sent over lapsed into non-conformity and separatism, as did Samuel Skelton and Francis Higginson in Massachusetts, and as did the clergymen in Bermuda very soon after their arrival.[3] Are we to conclude that Warwick, graduate of Emmanuel College, contemporary of Preston, Cotton, and Downing, friend of Winthrop, and, in general, aider and abettor of the Puritan cause at home as well as in the colonies, was intentionally furthering in Bermuda as later in New England, the destinies of the Puritan party? A study of the Bermuda Company and its plantation during these years goes far to dispel the notion, once held, that Warwick in opposing Sandys and the Ferrars in the Virginia Company, was acting in behalf of King James and the political ideas that he represented. There is nothing in Warwick's relations with Bermuda—a colony in which he was much more interested than he ever was in Virginia—to support such an opinion or to make him out an enemy of popular government. On the contrary in many of his political and religious views he was probably more radical than were those whom he opposed.

1. Lefroy, *Memorials,* I, 558–561.
2. Warwick's successor as governor of the company was the second earl of Manchester, a man of strong Presbyterian tendencies.
3. See below, pages 378–380.

CHAPTER XII

THE FALL OF THE BERMUDA COMPANY

THE history of Bermuda is of importance to the student of English colonization because it is the only English colony which for seventy years remained under the proprietary control of a corporate company, with its seat in England and its colonists hundreds of miles away. The Bermuda Company was created a joint-stock organization in 1615 and though quite early—in 1626—at the request of and for the convenience of the members it took a regulated form, it continued to exist as the legal proprietor of the colony until 1684. In 1626 the joint-stock arrangement was given up and each member or adventurer was allowed to trade with his own private stock, provided he did so with the company's magazine ship or ships, which were sent to Bermuda at least once a year.

The first magazine ship, the *Diana,* went out in 1618 and, except for the years of the first Dutch war, vessels continued to go regularly throughout the period of the company's control. Sometimes two ships were sent out, carrying commodities of all sorts, as well as letters, instructions, news intelligence from England, and passengers, and thus became the official medium of communication between the company and the colony. When it reached the colony, the ship usually anchored in Castle Harbour or St. George's Harbour or Nonsuch Bay for the customary period of forty days, during which the planters and the tenants were expected to bring their tobacco and whatever else the company or the crown required them to send back to England for entrance at the port of London. No one, either in England or in the colony, was allowed to make use of any other vessel, whether his own or that of a foreigner, on the ground that private trade and foreign trade entailed a great loss to the company and was a prejudice to the country.[1] This requirement, in the early years, called forth many protests from the Delbridges of Barnstaple,[2] who wanted the outports of the West Coun-

1. Lefroy, *Memorials,* II, 505 (1a), 510.
2. John Delbridge was at this time probably the most important and influential of all the West Country merchants. He seems to have obtained in some way certain

try to have a share in the business and resented the monopoly which London secured by reason of this limitation. Later the protestant was Perient Trott, a merchant of London and a member of the company, who after acquiring in 1659 the twenty-three shares owned by the Earl of Warwick became a persistent opponent of the company's policy.

By 1660 Bermuda had developed agriculturally about as far as it could. The area was small and the population increased very slowly, reaching 2000 in 1628, 3000 in 1656, and 8000 in 1679, when the islands attained their saturation point. In these same years Virginia had respectively 7500, 20,000, and 50,000. People were drifting away from Bermuda, going to Antigua, Trinidad, Barbados, Tobago, St. Lucia, Jamaica, the Bahamas, the Carolinas, and New England,[1] a form of inter-colonial migration that was characteristic of the seventeenth century, but which in the case of Bermuda undoubtedly depleted heavily the working strength of the colony. Nevertheless in point of numbers the Bermuda islands in the years after 1660 were always overpopulated,[2] tobacco raising was growing less profitable, and the planters were turning their tobacco fields into grazing pastures for cattle.[3] Strict orders were issued by the company against the waste of timber, chiefly cedar, and palmetto, which were used for the building of boats, the thatching of houses, and the making of hats. The population included planters, tenants on half shares, indentured servants, apprentices, negroes, Indian slaves, and Scottish and Irish political prisoners—men, women, and children. The

definite privileges from the Council for New England in regard to fishing, for in 1622 the council made inquiry into "what course Mr. Delbridge of Barnstaple taketh against any touching abuses done in New England," and discovered that he had taken action against five Barnstaple men and attempted, but without success, to deal with five more. *Transactions*, American Antiquarian Society, 1867, November 8, 1622.

1. Lefroy, *Memorials*, I, 557; II, 290, 298, 300.

2. "Though Barmoodoes be wonderful healthy and fruitful, yet it is but a Prison to the Inhabitants, who are much streightened for want of room" (Robert Horne's "Description," 1666, *Carolina*, Original Narratives Series, pp. 66–67). "Our Island of Barmudoes being overpeopled and the natives thereof much straitnd for want of land," etc. (Letter to Lord Ashley, February 17, 1670, *Shaftesbury Papers*, pp. 160–161). "Many others have sent me word from Bermudas that the inhabitants are too numerous" (Governor Woodes Rogers of the Bahamas to the Board of Trade, October 31, 1718, *Board of Trade Journal*, 1717–1718, p. 375).

3. Tobacco continued to be sent to England, certainly as late as 1690 (*Calendar Treasury Books*, IX, 894), but in 1708 it was no longer planted by the inhabitants (*Calendar State Papers, Colonial*, 1708–1709, p. 176). In 1710 it is not mentioned at all among Bermuda's staples (*ibid.*, 1710–1711, p. 327).

two most important classes were the planters and the tenants. The first were freeholders, members of the company, who had by right of purchase acquired stock, which entitled them to freehold land in the tribes held of the crown as of the manor of East Greenwich in free and common socage.[1] Of these there were about four hundred in 1679, with properties valued at an average of one hundred pounds each.[2] The tenants or tenants at will,[3] who were located partly on the estates of the planters but in larger numbers on the twelve shares or public lands of the company,[4] were of the nature of copyholders, in that they held their tenancies on the half profit system, allowing their landlords, whether planters or company, half the produce of the tobacco or provisions raised and sold. The tenants of the Virginia Company, who were located on the public lands, were of the same status, as were those for a time of the Old Providence Company, until the system was abolished there in 1636.[5] Tenancy by halves was never popular in the colonies and soon disappeared as a form of land tenure. Freehold and the payment of quit-rent became the prevailing practice later in Bermuda as elsewhere.

Each of these classes had its grievances. The tenants felt that their lands and leases were at the mercy of the company, that they were liable at any time to be rack-rented, and that the company was profiting at their expense. The landowners objected, and at times defiantly, to the persistent determination of the company to restrict their freedom of action and trade and to exploit them in the interest of its own profit. They did not like the regulations which confined their exports and imports to the magazine ships and they evaded it as often as they could.[6] Later they protested vigorously against the order which required all boat owners in the islands to give bond that their boats should not carry any cedar, tobacco, or whale oil to any other than the company's vessel. They objected to the penny a pound duty on tobacco shipped to England, which was imposed by the company to meet the expenses of the government in the islands, alleging that such expenses should be met out of the re-

---

1. Lefroy, *Memorials*, II, 536.   2. *Ibid.*, II, 431–432.
3. *Ibid.*, I, 417; II, 189 (5, 6), 593.   4. *Ibid.*, I, 200–201; II, 543.
5. Bruce, *Economic History of Virginia*, I, 230–231; *Calendar State Papers, Colonial*, 1574–1660, p. 228.
6. Lefroy, *Memorials*, I, 472; II, 58, 194, 195, 209, 309, 322, 347, 371, 402, 513, 548, 555. See also *Calendar of State Papers, Colonial*, 1681–1685, §840, for a later case in point, and for a general statement, *ibid.*, 1704–1705, p. 598.

turns from the public lands, which they deemed more than ample for the purpose.[1] They refused to agree that all planters worth £20 sterling should provide arms for the defense of the islands, unless such provision was confirmed by act of their own assembly. In a remarkable series of protests of the year 1671 they declared that they were free subjects of the king of England and as such had a right to the fruits of their own labor and the products of their own acres to their own advantage. To be deprived of either was to be defeated of their birthright.[2] Both in words and actions they demonstrated the truth of the company's charge that they were disregarding and openly deriding its authority, slighting and disobeying its orders, and rejecting its advice and counsels.[3] This sweeping and condemnatory answer to their protest bore unmistakable witness to the truth that the company itself was steadily waning in influence and in its ability to control the activities of the islanders.

Another Bermudian grievance was the attempt of the company to obtain a monopoly control of the whale-fishery, which the islanders claimed as a natural perquisite of their own, the planters in particular deeming it a privilege especially allowed them in their land grants. In 1662 the company, following the familiar practice of organizing an inner group of adventurers, when funds were lacking for the promotion of some hopeful enterprise, started a subsidiary association for the advancement of the whale-fishery in the mid-Atlantic. This association was called The Adventurers in the Whale-fishing Design. Though the parent body had no interest in the scheme as such, having promoted it in part to show the world that the company was still a going concern, many of its members, both in England and in the islands, were subscribers to its stock, at the rate of fifty shillings a share, according to the number of shares owned. No one else was to engage in the fishery, except such as were authorized to do so by consent of this subsidiary body in leases formally granted,[4] and all oil was to be sent to England in the company's ships and in those only. Needless to say these orders were not obeyed. A majority of the planters refused to join the subsidiary association at all, claiming that they had a right, if they wished, to fish for whales on their own account, a claim that the company

1. Lefroy, *Memorials,* II, 534; for other forms of taxation, 535 note.
2. *Ibid.,* II, 351–357, 537, 549.   3. *Ibid.,* II, 360–362, 370.
4. *Ibid.,* II, 510.

vigorously opposed, on the ground that the fishing clause in the grants did not cover the open sea.[1] Despite this contention, many of the planters openly flouted the company's orders and in collusion with irresponsible tenants and servants seized whales at sea and on the shore and disposed of their products to unlicensed and foreign vessels, in which the oil and whale fins were carried to Barbados, New England, and elsewhere, and there sold. Even the government in the islands was very lax in enforcing the commands from England, either neglecting to carry them out at all or else doing so only to the company's disadvantage, sending to England only the poorer grades of oil or but a part of that which the company declared was its due. In the end the whale-fishing partnership proved a failure and the various persons concerned reaped but a meagre profit. More important still, the partnership did little or nothing to strengthen the reputation or authority of the parent body, which was one of the objects for which it was formed. The monopoly was retained by the crown after the fall of the company, and the lieutenant governors of Bermuda received the whale licenses as a part of their salary, until in 1730 the monopoly was broken and the fishing thrown open to all the king's subjects.[2]

More serious from the standpoint of colonial administration was the changing character of the company itself, due in part to the inevitable displacement of old members by new, consequent upon the passing years, and in part to the influence of the Puritan Revolution, which led to the forfeiture of some shares and the sale of others. The company had weathered, with considerable difficulty the crisis of the Commonwealth and the Protectorate, losing its charter for a time and falling under the control of the Council of State.[3] Restored to its former position after the return of the monarchy, it gradually lost its original corporate character and became more and more a mere rump group of proprietors, imposing its will on the colony. As membership in the company was confined to those who held shares of land in Bermuda and as the greater number of the shareholders after 1679—variously estimated at different times as three-quarters, seven-eights, and nineteen-twentieths—were resident

1. Lefroy, *Memorials*, II, 181, 203, 223, 245, 246, 254, 261–262, 275, 282, 302, 305, 332. For a copy of such a land grant, I, 551; II, 443–444, 510–511, note, 549.

2. *Acts Privy Council, Colonial*, III, §197.

3. Lefroy, *Memorials*, II, 480, 487, 512; *Calendar State Papers, Colonial*, 1677–1680, §§1052, 1184.

in the islands, it came about that a minority, in the form rather of a board than a company,[1] was administering the islands to its own advantage. Such a situation was anomalous and probably illegal and shows what might have happened to Virginia had the Virginia Company been restored in 1640. This almost grotesque situation, together with the restraints placed upon the trade of the islands and the monopoly conferred upon the magazine ships of the company and upon the adventurers in the fishery, led to many outbreaks of discontent in the colony particularly after 1670.[2]

Another and equally significant grievance concerned the exercise of that right of self-government which the inhabitants had enjoyed since the calling of the first assembly in 1620. Though the Ber-

---

1. "The Bermudas Company originally consisted of 150 of the Chiefe of the nobility Gentry and merchants who had and were Proprietors of the whole Island and the Inhabitants were only their Servants and Tenants at half profit, and so continued the state of the company for some time, till at last those persons selling their Interests to the Inhabitants then and there Planters, and by divers of such sales the Company fell into the hands of those who had little or no interest in the Plantation, and as it has been this last age all the members of the Company have not an eighth part of the Land of the Country. The Government thus falling on the shoulders of men of little interest there, occasioned the miscarriages which have since happened." "The present company consists of Broakers, Tobacconists, non conforming Ministers, net makers and Retailers of small wares, fit persons for the management of a Plantation," Lefroy, Memorials, II, 487, 488. See also pp. 512–513, 540, where the same subject is discussed and the personnel of the company in 1684 is given.

2. The leader of the discontent on the commercial side was Perient Trott, who secured lands in Bermuda as early as 1652 from one Henry Gardiner, whose brother George had first obtained them in 1631. In 1659 Trott purchased the whole of the Earl of Warwick's shares and so became a large shareholder in the company and a freeholder in the colony. During the years that followed, Trott (according to the company's statement made in 1670), "regarding not the good and welfare of the Company while he was a member thereof (as he ought to have done) but seeking his own ends and private gain, though to the ruin of the Company and great damage of the said Sommer Islands, hath used indirect ways and means for several years past by privately sending ships to the said Islands without the privity or knowledge of the said Company and contrary to the said laws" (Lefroy, Memorials, II, 325–327). To bring about Trott's bankruptcy the company instituted an inquiry into his title to the Warwick lands, and finding that the lands were entailed persuaded Charles, fourth earl of Warwick, to demand their return, which he did successfully. After the earl's death in 1673 Trott regained possession by agreement with Thomas Barrington, Henry St. John (father of Viscount Bolingbroke), and Daniel Finch (later Earl of Nottingham and a governor of the company), who had married the co-heiresses of the house, the daughters of Robert the third earl and elder brother of Charles. Trott died in 1680 and the lands were sold in 1680, 1682, and 1692 by his heir Samuel and his second son Nicholas (later governor of the Bahamas and the cousin of Nicholas, Jr., afterward chief justice and judge of the vice-admiralty court of South Carolina). In the course of the quarrel, Perient Trott issued a pamphlet at-

mudian assembly had never possessed the full privilege of initiating legislation, which was retained by the company,[1] and though all laws that were passed had to be sent to England for the company's approval before they could take effect in the colony, nevertheless the possession of the right to elect members to an assembly and to coöperate in the making of laws for the colony was highly prized in the islands. This right had been exercised for half a century, but with the coming of Sir John Heydon, lieutenant governor from 1669 to 1681 and almost the first person to hold that office who was not a native, this privilege ceased to be enjoyed, and with the concurrence of the company no assembly was summoned (with the single exception of the year 1673, when an assembly was called for the sole purpose of presenting grievances)[2] for fourteen years. The result was that the colony passed through a period of executive control by the governor and council, during which taxes were imposed without the consent of the inhabitants and, as certain complainants in the islands alleged, "divers crimes and offenses" were committed by Heydon that savored of autocratic and arbitrary rule. The charges against the governor were dismissed by the Privy Council,[3] after a full hearing of the case; but the loss of an assembly could not be so easily met, for it concerned not a few aggrieved malcontents but all the people of the colony, and touched a self-governing principle that had become so well established in the colonies generally as to constitute a precedent impossible to ignore without rousing a protest. This fact was perfectly understood both in England and in Bermuda.

With the failure of the experiment of 1673, when an assembly was summoned and employed its time in drawing up an elaborate statement of grievances and demands, no additional body was convened for ten years. During that time, in letters and petitions to the company, the inhabitants seized every opportunity to signalize

tacking the company, entitled *A True Relation of the Just and Unjust Proceedings of the Somers Islands Company in relation to Twenty Shares of Land* (1676), many copies of which he sent to Bermuda, where sixteen or seventeen of them, all that could be seized, were publicly burned by order of the governor, Sir John Heydon (*Calendar State Papers, Colonial*, 1677–1680, §211).

1. "We have given you laws, do you but execute them," Lefroy, *Memorials*, II, 509.

2. *Ibid.*, II, 382–384.

3. *Ibid.*, II, 495, 505, 507; *Calendar State Papers, Colonial*, 1681–1685, §§ 222, 261, 273, 283.

the fact that an assembly ought to be called.[1] In 1678 they said in a petition to the king that the company had ordered no more assemblies to be held, so that the inhabitants, for want of such an intermediary through which to voice their troubles, were "about ruined with the Company's ordering and imposing unjust taxes upon their commodities and making of your Majesty's poor subjects in a manner slaves."[2] Similar complaints followed in succeeding years. That the situation was in largest part due to Heydon's wilful methods—for he minded neither the inhabitants nor the company—is clear from the fact that after his recall in 1681 the company yielded to the demand of the colony, and in its instructions to Heydon's successor, Cony, in 1683, authorized the summons of an assembly. This gathering of deputies took the form of a single chambered body, sitting under the presidency of the governor, called not for the purpose of legislation but for the drafting of the needs and distresses of the colony. The assembly met on November 24, 1684, only three days before the issue of the final judgment dissolving the company, and drew up a vigorous petition to the king, setting forth the injustice and illegality of company rule.

Before passing on to consider the circumstances under which this final judgment was issued, it may not be without interest to reflect upon one important phase of the situation confronting us. In popular estimation, prejudiced by the long-dominant Whig tradition, the government of the Stuarts generally and that of James II in particular has always been charged with hostility to popular government in the colonies. This estimate has been to a large extent based on the refusal of the English authorities after 1684 to sanction the right of the people of New England to a popular assembly and their setting up there a form of executive administration similar to that of Bermuda after 1669 and of New York after 1664. Yet the significant fact remains that in the first royal commission for Bermuda, the one issued in 1684 to Cony, who was reappointed as the royal governor after the downfall of the company, the king authorized the calling of an assembly of the freeholders and planters, "according to the usage of our other Plantations in America," in the customary form of governor, council, and assembly, with the same

1. Lefroy, Memorials, I, 463, 466–467, 474, 500; Calendar State Papers, Colonial, 1677–1680, §§990, 990, i, ii, 1052; 1681–1685, 1087.
2. Lefroy, Memorials, II, 518, 522, 537–538.

powers as elsewhere exercised. During the more than half a century preceding this event popular assemblies had been regularly functioning in Virginia, Barbados, Jamaica, and the Leeward Islands—all royal colonies—without molestation or demur. It is not easy for anyone to say with confidence that the Stuarts and their advisers were opposed in principle to popular government in the colonies, in view of the evidence against that view, and it may be that there was something peculiar in the New England situation, arising out of the Puritan practice of playing fast and loose with the Lords of Trade, that brought down upon the Massachusetts Bay people the distrust of those in authority over them. The Puritans were fighting at every turn and by every expedient under their hand to prevent incorporation into the English system of colonial organization and government. This fact must be taken into account in any attempt made to explain the relations of Massachusetts in the seventeenth century with the authorities at home who were concerned with the shaping of a colonial policy. England's attitude toward Massachusetts was not typical of the position she had taken or was to take toward the colonies that came under the royal control.

The continued efforts of Trott and others to break the company's monopolistic rule finally had the desired effect. The petition of 1679 was referred to the Lords of Trade, who called representatives of both sides before them at various times and, while deciding that many of the grievances were on the whole "of little weight," found enough in the complaints to convince them that in certain matters of a judicial character the company had acted illegally and should be either remodeled or discontinued.[1] With this report of its committee the Privy Council concurred and it ordered that the company either consent to a redefinition of its powers along the lines recommended by the Lords of Trade or expect to receive a writ of *quo warranto* and face a suit before the court of king's bench on behalf of the crown for the annulment of its charter.

Probably a majority of the islanders welcomed this proposal to

1. Trott had obtained, under special license from the king ("by misrepresentation and surprise," as the company claimed) a right to trade privately with Bermuda. On protest from the company this privilege was withdrawn and the license cancelled (*Calendar State Papers, Colonial,* 1675–1676, §444; 1699, §1117). Angered by this withdrawal Trott petitioned the king against the company, but without success (*ibid.,* 1677–1680, §9, i, ii; *Acts Privy Council, Colonial,* I, §§1110, 1113; Lefroy, *Memorials,* II, 449). Continued petitioning had better results. The petition of

get rid of the company and to bring the colony under the control of the crown, but there were two factional groups that took every occasion to cry down royal rule. One of these was composed of the planters and merchants who had prospered in one way or another under company management and looked upon the members in London as "our nursing Fathers" caring tenderly for an infant colony.[1] The other, made up of a much more radically-minded set of men, desired the overthrow of the company, but only with the hope that in such event the colony would be granted the right to govern itself, determining its own form of government and electing its own officials, after the fashion of the New England colonies. These men represented the influence of the levelling movement in England of twenty years before, when the Baptists and the Fifth Monarchy extremists worked together for the overthrow of the Protectorate in order to set up a self-governing commonwealth. Sectarian in temper, intolerant in attitude, verbose and intemperate in speech, and logical only in that they carried their convictions to the utmost limits of application, they battled unsuccessfully for thirty years in Bermuda to establish Puritan rule, which they believed to be the only guaranty of a perfect state. Much of the language used at this time by the leaders of the movement, to the effect that "the Pope was the whore of Babylon and drunk with the blood of the Saints," has a very contemporary protestant and non-conformist ring, and recalls the speech of many in the continental colonies at the same time, particularly in Maryland. The insurgent movements in North Carolina, Maryland, and Virginia found their counterpart in Bermuda and the hysteria of the period found its expression wherever English colonists went. Rumors unsubstantiated and magnified in Bermuda, as elsewhere, kept the people, credulous and ill-informed, in a constant state of uncertainty and suspense. The situation in

1679 was referred to the Lords of Trade, who made report as above. The lords were impressed chiefly by two of the sixteen items presented in the petition. These were, first, that the subject's right of petition to the king had been obstructed either by the governor or by the company or had been prevented altogether; and, secondly, that the exercise of justice in the islands had not been in the hands of the properly constituted judicial authorities there, but had been usurped by the company in London in excess of its corporate powers. (Lefroy, *Memorials*, II, 476–478, 490; *Calendar State Papers, Colonial*, 1677–1680, §§1061, 1062, 1081, 1154, 1159, 1184; *Acts Privy Council, Colonial*, I, §1333).

1. Lefroy, *Memorials*, I, 493, 514–515, 581.

Bermuda and the other colonies was but an overseas phase of the contemporary agitation in England.[1]

In its reply to the order of the Privy Council the company uttered a *non possumus*. It declared that it would make no change in its policy or attempt to meet in any way the wishes of the islanders in the matter of their trade grievances, and would not agree to any alterations in its charter privileges. Its obstinacy is amazing. No orders or instructions that it had ever issued to its governors were more arrogant than those sent to Bermuda on the very eve of its own downfall. The members seem to have been overconfident of their influence at court and of their ability to weather this crisis as they had weathered others. But the end was approaching. In 1679 the attorney general was ordered to proceed against the company

1. While Perient Trott was the opponent of the company on the commercial side, standing for free trade and the overthrow of the monopoly, William Righton, the elder, was one of its principal opponents on the religious and constitutional sides. Tailor by trade, preacher and exhorter by preference, lawyer by necessity, insurgent and sectary by temperament, and a man illiterate and ungrammatical in speech and writing, Righton exercised the functions of a clergyman in the islands, doing more in the way of stirring up strife than of saving souls and edifying his hearers. In 1664 he was silenced by the company and ordered to return to England, but he soon went back to the colony. Again expelled in 1678, he returned to make trouble for Heydon and Cony, in common with others of his kind, Henry Byshe or Bish and William Milborne, the brother of Joseph, the Fifth Monarchy man, and of Jacob, the associate of Leisler in New York, and himself the one who a little later made trouble for the Puritans at Boston. For an understanding of the situation at the time in England, from which most of these "Fanatic Dissenters" came, one should study the entries in the *Calendar of State Papers, Domestic,* Charles II, to June 30, 1683, the date of the last volume issued in the series ending with 1689.

The activities of these men did not abate with the fall of the company. In 1685 Cony wrote the Privy Council of "the dayly designs of the old discontented party, as Wm Righton, Samuel Trott [son of Perient and the author of a book called *The Liberty of the Subjects of England*], Richd Stafford, Wm Penniston, Anthony White, etc., who are soe enraged that his Ma^{ty} hath not left the country to their Government that they not only slight his late Ma^{tys} Commission but disown any power I now have here" (Lefroy, *Memorials,* II, 554; *Calendar State Papers, Colonial,* 1685–1688, §396). The Cony charges were sent to England and an investigation was ordered. Cony took depositions (*ibid.,* §§840, 841, i–lx, 1553) and finally ordered the arrest of the leaders for mutinous conduct, sending them back to England. Righton died before July, 1687, and Milborne took himself off to Boston, where he was committed for scandalous writings. Samuel and Perient Trott submitted and were made councillors. Cony was undoubtedly a tough customer and Righton and Milborne in their charges spoke of him as one who "curses, swears and strikes men in his drunken debauches which are frequent" (*ibid.,* §1913). The two sets of charges should be compared for they disclose two entirely irreconcilable points of view, characteristic of the age. William Milborne, Jr., was a Quaker and a sea-captain and an equally irrepressible insurgent, but in the field of trade not of government. He was his father's son.

and in 1680 the writ of *quo warranto* was issued. The company fought every step of the way.[1] Delays ensued, owing partly to the inevitable slowness of legal procedure at all times, partly to the hope entertained by the authorities that the company would reform its ways and accept a modification of its charter, and partly to the efforts which the company itself made to block the process and the want of funds available for meeting all the legal expenses on the part of the prosecution. The cost of serving the *quo warranto* alone came to one hundred pounds, and those in London who were expediting the business had to appeal many times to the planters in the islands for money to carry on the work. Furthermore, there is evidence to show that the effort to overthrow the company was not in all respects a disinterested desire to serve the colony. One Francis Burghill or Broghill, who was ambitious to become the first royal governor of the islands, was acting in collusion with Righton and the Trotts, who wanted to bring the rule of the company to an end in order to erect a self-governing commonwealth, and he obtained from them masses of evidence in the form of charges and complaints against the company and its governors. He also secured petitions addressed to the king from other inhabitants also of the islands.[2] How far his efforts contributed to the final result it is impossible to say. That he was fishing in waters already troubled is clear and that he was able to muster a formidable array of charges for use in the trial appears from the evidence, but the company was condemned already. Burghill led the attack and aided in giving the final blow. The trial came on in 1683, when in November the attorney general began the examination of the company's books and papers "in order to the better prosecution of the *quo warranto*";[3] and the final judgment was rendered, vacating the charter "for many misdemeanors and misgovernments" of which the company

1. The process can be followed in the documents printed by Lefroy, *Memorials,* II, 479 to the end. The company was accustomed to hold its meetings in Sadlers Hall at the upper end of Cheapside, for the use of which it paid £16 a year rent.

2. *Calendar State Papers, Colonial,* 1681–1685, §§1075, 1098, 1695, 1763, 1783–1785, 1834, 1972. For Burghill's desire to be governor, §§1835, 1782. Among the Rawlinson Papers in the Bodleian is a volume, known to Scott and Wilkinson but not to Lefroy, containing material relating to Bermuda and to Burghill's activities (Rawlinson, D. 764; for a description see Andrews and Davenport, *Guide,* pp. 407–408). Scott (*Joint-Stock Companies,* II, 295–297) credits Burghill with more influence than the evidence seems to warrant; Wilkinson (*The Adventurers of Bermuda,* pp. 370–371), is more cautious and non-committal.

3. *Acts Privy Council, Colonial,* II, §136.

stood condemned, on November 27, 1684. From this time forward Bermuda was a royal colony.

The history of Bermuda in the seventeenth century is instructive and suggestive as illustrating many important phases of English colonization. Begun under the guidance of the same group of men who promoted the plantation of Virginia, it represents at the beginning the same ideas and methods of settlement that found application in the founding of that colony. Later it came under Puritan influence and was dominated by the same desires for religious independency that drove the non-conforming Puritans of eastern England to accept the separatistic ecclesiastical polity of New England, with the leaders of which the Bermudian ministers and others were in close accord and constant contact. After the Restoration it gave refuge to the extremists who had been rebellious in England during the Protectorate, and became the scene of action for a group of men who wished to try out levelling principles in government and to erect, after the model of Massachusetts Bay and Connecticut, a self-governing state free of proprietor or king. And during the entire period it illustrates on a small but sufficient scale the problem of monopoly versus free trade in commercial affairs that was agitating the whole English world during the century. At the same time it was growing up as a colony, testing out important forms of popular government, extending as far as the limited natural conditions would allow its trade, agriculture, and fishery, and laying a secure foundation for its career as a normal British colony. After 1684 Bermuda entered the royal group, conforming in its plan of government and in its relations with the mother country to the other royal colonies in America.

CHAPTER XIII

THE COMING OF THE PILGRIMS

DURING all these years of intense and almost feverish activity in England, when the colonizing movement was getting under way and two permanent settlements, in Virginia and Bermuda, were rooting themselves deeply in the soil of the New World, a small group of English people, without other interest than that of finding a place where they could live and worship in the way most fitting in the eyes of God, were residing in Holland, the most enterprising and progressive of all the states of Europe at that time. Having fled from England in 1608, they went first to Amsterdam and then to Leyden, manfully endeavoring to support themselves and their families by such labor as offered itself and to preserve their identity as a body of covenanting Christians, "enjoying much sweete and delightful societie and spiritual comforte together in the wayes of God." There they sojourned, as weavers and bakers, printers, carders, and dealers in merchandise, marrying and giving in marriage, baptizing and burying, and in other ways also playing a part in the life of the community. A small number, not more than seven, were admitted as citizens of the city, but the great majority sojourned there merely as residents, far more interested in problems of religious faith than they were in matters of worldly concern. They themselves were more troubled about their obligations toward God than about the problems of earthly existence, and fortunately the Dutch, never religious propagandists, let them pretty much alone. In the very year, 1611, when Virginia was passing through the greatest crisis in the history of her settlement, her future hanging in the balance, they, the Pilgrims, were rejoicing in the purchase of a house and grounds, adjoining the cathedral in the heart of Leyden, where they might foregather for worship in peace and contentment. In 1612, when the Virginia Company was acquiring a new charter and was about to launch its enterprise in Bermuda, William Bradford, who had come of age the year before, was admitted a citizen of Leyden, Robert Cushman bought a house for himself and his family, and the members of the little community thanked God for his mercies, because for the first time after considerable delay they were able to come together in their own meetinghouse—the newly bought dwelling in the Klogsteeg or Bell Alley.

These people were separatists from the Church of England. They believed that a true church was a company or body of holy and faithful souls under the guidance of pastors and teachers, freely elected by "the Lord's godly and free people." Never a large number at best, even in London where were the most important of the Brownist conventicles, the Separatists had suffered heavily at the hands of the English bishops; and this particular group had been compelled to leave their homes in Nottinghamshire, Lincolnshire, and Yorkshire, to give up their worship in the manor house at Scrooby, where William Brewster was the government post despatcher and the leading man among them, and to find refuge in Holland. There in the comfortable environment of the city of Leyden they steadily improved their worldly estate, finding contentment in their new home and a measure of material prosperity, and enjoying what was to them of the utmost importance, almost entire religious freedom.

How far the Leyden Separatists knew of the events taking place in England during these years it is impossible to say. At the beginning their own problems were insistent and must have absorbed their entire attention, but as the colonizing movement took form and such incidents of major importance as the sailing of Gates and De la Warr in 1609 and 1610 attracted wide notice, particularly in London and the sea-faring world, they must have obtained some knowledge, however imperfect, of what was happening in connection with the activities of the Virginia Company. After 1612 and 1613 the leaders among them probably kept themselves fairly well informed of affairs in England. Though Leyden was not a mercantile and commercial city, on a par with Amsterdam, Middleburg, and Flushing, it was a great seat of learning, and the Pilgrims could have obtained there, from Dutch sources, news of what was going on in the outside world. The Dutch were middlemen in gossip as well as in trade, and with their ships on every sea looking for business wherever they could find it, they must have brought back to the homeland tales of adventure and enterprise in colonization from every part of the world into which their mariners penetrated. Then, too, correspondence between England and Holland was frequent and regular; traffic between London and the Zuyder Zee was an intimate concern of the London merchants; English soldiers had been serving for years in regiments employed by the States General of Holland; and Separatist clergy were beginning to go back and forth between the two countries. When the Virginia Company found itself in need of funds, it extended its financial activities widely, partly by the use of lotteries, partly by appeals for subscriptions to its religious and educational enterprises—the school, the college, and the conversion of the Indians, and partly by assessments on its members and calls for unpaid subscriptions on its common stock. Thus the company was making itself known to the public of southern England and the quarrels and dissensions among its members came to the ears of all who had any concern therein and to many who had not. That the leaders of the Leyden community knew of the affairs of the Virginia Company and of the expeditions going to the Amazon, Guiana, and Newfoundland cannot be doubted, and this desire for information would increase as their own dissatisfaction with conditions in Holland made such information doubly welcome. In all likelihood, the knowledge of English affairs possessed by the Pilgrim group was often misleading and fragmentary and based on what was little better than rumor, but it was probably very considerable in amount.

Colonization was widening its sphere, and more and more parts of the Atlantic coast line were becoming familiar to navigators and merchants. Hakluyt and Purchas were spreading knowledge and arousing interest. Captain John Smith, who had returned from Virginia in 1609 and was continuing his explorations, first under the Virginia Company and then the Plymouth Company, was opening up the whole region from Cape Cod to the Penobscot River. He had explored the coast in an open boat, made surveys, drawn maps, written books, and travelled about, doing all that he could to call attention to New England and to stimulate migration to this northern region. He helped New England to live down the bad name acquired from the failure of 1607 and 1608 and he counteracted the opinion held by Sir Ferdinando Gorges that the country was "cold and in respect of that not habitable by our nation."[1] His first publication on New England was issued in 1616, and with it the map of the country, the names on which were inserted, we are told, by Prince Charles, afterwards Charles I. As fishermen and traders were

1. Baxter, *Gorges*, II, 17.

frequenting the region in larger and larger numbers, one feels fairly sure that the Leyden community and certainly the Separatist groups in London and elsewhere in England must have learned something of the general situation in America, even before their fears for the future of themselves and their children made them feel the necessity of seeking a refuge in some part of it.

Life in Leyden was not in all ways satisfactory. Members of the community were becoming restless, work was hard, and the burdens were so many that some were sinking under the strain and others were discouraged because of the troubles that distressed them. They saw their children losing touch with old England, not only forgetting their native speech but hardly remembering even that they were of English origin. They saw no opportunity to give these children a proper education, such as they themselves had had (meagre though in fact that education must have been), and they were afraid lest these same children should be corrupted by contact with Dutch ways, such as the neglect of the Sabbath, of which they did not approve, and which they tried but unsuccessfully to remedy. "They could not," says Cotton Mather, "with ten years endeavour bring their neighbors particularly to any suitable observation of the Lord's Day, without which they knew that all practical religion must wither miserably."[1] Rebellious themselves, they doubted whether among the Dutch they would ever enjoy the ordinances of God in their purity or retain unspoiled the simple truths of the Gospel. They feared lest their children should fail in attaining their full stature as Christians, when they were in constant danger of being drawn away by evil example into extravagant and dangerous courses, getting, as Bradford says, "the raines off their necks and departing from their parents. Some became soldiers," he adds, "others took upon them far viages by sea; and others some worse courses, tending to dissoluteness and the danger of their soules, to the great grief of their parents and dishonour of God. So that they saw their posteritie would be in danger to degenerate and be corrupted."[2] The leaders took these matters into very serious consideration among

1. *Magnalia Christi*, Bk. I, ch. II, 5. The Massachusetts Bay Company particularly enjoined upon its colony at Salem under Endecott that the people observe the Sabbath from three o'clock on Saturday afternoon, spending the rest of the day in catechising and making ready for the next day's proper observance. *Massachusetts Colonial Records*, I, 395.

2. Bradford, *History*, I, 55.

themselves and discussed them with prayer and fasting, seeking the mind of God and his blessing.

Furthermore, they saw no opportunity in Holland of accomplishing anything for the propagating and advancing of the gospel of the kingdom of Christ and believed that such would be possible only in some remote part of the world, where they might serve as God's agents, even though in doing so they should be no more than stepping stones aiding others to the performing of so great a work. They were not proselyters, but only wished, as they said forty years later, "to serve our God with a pure conscience, according to His will revealed,"[1] and to undergo any hardship to the attainment of that end. They feared lest the Spanish rule would return to Holland when the twelve years' truce which had been arranged with Spain, March 30, 1609, should come to an end, and they believed that the Spaniards would prove as cruel as the American savages. They had heard of the inhumanities of the Spanish inquisition, from men who had been imprisoned in Spanish dungeons and had worn Spanish shackles, as had Stoneman of the Challons expedition of 1606; or from Englishmen who had suffered in the torture rooms of the inquisition in Spain and in the Canaries,[2] all of whom returned with tales of treatment which must have whetted England's hatred against Spain and have brought much disquietude to shrinking hearts as the end of the truce drew near.

But there was another side to the story. Even more terrifying than the horrors of the Spanish inquisition were those vast and unpeopled countries of America, to which men and women were going and which could be reached only after a long and hazardous journey, subject to inconceivable perils and casualties of the sea. Some of them may well have recalled the horrors of that "fearfull storme" which drove them for nearly two weeks across the North Sea in 1608 and remembered with terror their prayers for safety and their final deliverance. Then they were going to kind people and a civilized land; now they would be confronted with a voyage many times as long, with countries where savage and brutish men ranged up and down, and with conditions of want and privation which were sure to bring sickness and death. Yet on the other hand they

1. *Calendar State Papers, Colonial*, 1661–1668, §102.
2. "English Merchants and the Spanish Inquisition in the Canaries," *Publications*, Camden Society, XXIII.

must have been familiar with the fact that before 1619 many men, women, and children had made the voyage and had survived to tell the tale, for in Virginia in that year there were at least a hundred women, and in Bermuda perhaps half as many, safe and well contented. The voyage to America was not an unknown experience, even for tender maids and expectant mothers, yet when the decision was finally reached to go to America, many in Leyden shrank from the venture and only a small part of the total number finally agreed to the plan.

No enterprise in overseas settlement thus far undertaken can compare with this desperate project of the Leyden Separatists. Without adequate resources, either of supplies or of transportation, without supporters, patrons, or friends at court, without royal permit or patent, this band of wanderers, believing their calling lawful and urgent, their ends good and honorable, and their guide God himself, looked toward the New World and debated long and earnestly the best course to follow. Some, and those not the least among them, knowing perhaps of the Harcourt and North expeditions, particularly the latter's second venture of 1619, thought of settling in Guiana, regarding which glowing accounts had been brought back, perhaps by Dutch captains trading in the region of the Amazon, of the fruitfulness and fertility of the country—a land favored with a perpetual spring, where vigorous nature brought forth all things in abundance without any great labor on the part of man. But others disliked hot countries with their probable grievous diseases and feared that the jealous Spaniard would resent their presence there. Raleigh's expedition of 1617 and his execution the next year may have been fresh in their minds.

At this juncture the Virginia Company offered a possible solution of their problem. Endeavoring to meet the deficiencies of its common stock and to stave off financial bankruptcy by creating subordinate and voluntary joint-stocks for particular ends, it was offering special privileges and patents to groups of undertakers, who either would go to Virginia themselves or would send over tenants and servants for the purpose of setting up private plantations. As we have seen already these undertakers, through their captains or governors in the colony, were empowered to make regulations and ordinances for the purpose of controlling their servants and directing their trade, provided these regulations were not contrary to the laws of England. When the suggestion was first made to the people at Leyden, apparently by the Virginia Company itself, that they take advantage of this opportunity, many of them feared lest in Virginia as in England they might suffer persecution for religion's sake. But on learning that they could live in Virginia as a distinct body by themselves, under their own governor and ordinances, subject only to the government of the colony as a whole, and that probably some of their friends in England could obtain from the king a grant of religious toleration, which they would need because Virginia was an Anglican colony, they decided after long and prayerful communing with themselves, to begin negotiations. They did not want to live outside their own king's dominions under any other sovereign than their own lawful prince, for, unlike the later Puritans, they always acknowledged themselves the loyal subjects of their own "dread soveraigne," James or Charles as the case might be.[1] For this reason they rejected several proposals that were afterward made by the Dutch merchants to settle elsewhere in Holland, as at Middleburg, or to cross overseas to New Netherland, where they might have been the first settlers on the Hudson River and have planted "a new Commonwealth," under the auspices of the States General of Holland.[2]

The decision was far from easy to make and the Leyden people were not the only company that was called upon to make it. A group of Walloons or French-speaking Belgians also sought to take up a particular plantation in Virginia, in a manner similar to that proposed at Leyden; but the project was not enthusiastically received by the Virginia Company, and in 1624 the Walloons went instead to the Hudson and became the first settlers of New Netherland, that is, of the province of New York that was to be.[3] In the years 1617 and 1618 Guiana or the Wild Coast,[4] Virginia, and the region about the mouth of the Hudson River seemed to offer more attractions for permanent settlement than any other parts of the

1. Clearly so stated in the "Seven Articles," §3; in the Mayflower Compact; and in the Plymouth records, *passim*.

2. Winslow, *Hypocrisie Unmasked*, p. 91; *New York Colonial Documents*, I, 22–23. According to Winslow the offer included transportation and the furnishing of every family with cattle, a tender not unlike that of the Virginia Company, which promised to lend each particular plantation plenty of corn and cattle for its ease and benefit upon the first arrival of its settlers, *Virginia Company Records*, I, 267.

3. *New York Colonial Documents*, III, 8–12; American Historical Association *Report*, 1909, I, 206–207; *Narratives of New Netherland* (Original Narratives Series), p. 75, note 2; *Calendar State Papers, Colonial*, 1574–1660, pp. 498–499.

4. On the "Wild Coast," *English Historical Review*, 1901, p. 669.

Atlantic seaboard. New England, as the northern region was beginning to be called, was still something of an unknown quantity. No compact body of people, as yet had succeeded in establishing itself on those primeval shores.

The leaders of the Leyden company, particularly John Robinson, the pastor, and William Brewster, Jr., the elder of the church and the only "gentleman" among them, were not without friends and connections in England, who proved to be of service in the prosecution of their enterprise during the next three years, 1617 to 1620. Chief among these friends was Sir Edwin Sandys himself, whose elder brother, Samuel, was the lessor of the manor house and mill, where for many years the father of William Brewster, Jr., had been receiver and bailiff, ordinary keeper and government despatch agent. Not unnaturally Sir Edwin would look with favor upon any request from the son of his brother's highly esteemed tenant at Scrooby, so that when in the summer or autumn of 1617 the Leyden church sent to England two of its members, Robert Cushman and Deacon John Carver, Robinson's brother-in-law, they must have carried a letter from Robinson and Brewster to Sandys asking for his coöperation. We are told by Sandys' opponent Bargrave that Sandys moved the Archbishop of Canterbury "to give leave to the Brownists and Separatists to goe thither," but that the archbishop refused his consent because the Brownists by their doctrines claimed a liberty of worship and a disregard of monarchy that were highly reprehensible.[1]

Cushman and Carver got into touch with "diverse selecte gentlemen of his Majesties Counsell for Virginia" and in order to relieve the company of any charge of disloyalty or unorthodoxy they laid their cards openly on the table, and in a body of seven articles,[2] drawn up by Robinson and Brewster, presented to the council the opinions held by the Leyden church. Sandys was of this council and we may infer from his known ideas on government that he was not opposed to the fundamental principles involved, either in government or religion. Whether his own attitude toward the government of the Virginia colony, as expressed in the charter of privileges, was

1. Historical Manuscripts Commission, *Eighth Report*, II, no. 368.
2. The "Seven Articles" are printed in *Collections*, New York Historical Society, 2d series, III, 301-302; Bradford, *History*, I, 73-75; Lord, *Plymouth and the Pilgrims*, pp. 96-98; Walker, *Creeds and Platforms of Congregationalism*, pp. 89-90.

affected by the Separatist ideas in general of course cannot be said, but Bargrave's picture of Sandys, saying "that if our God from heaven did constitute and direct a form of Government it was that of Geneva," certainly points in that direction, unless Bargrave was distinctly falsifying the evidence. Though the archbishop would have nothing to do with the articles, the Virginia Company accepted them, possibly through Sandys' influence. Winslow writing twenty years later, says that the company approved the plan of the Pilgrims, declared that the thing was of God, and loaned them £300, which was afterward repaid, and we know that the company in 1619 proposed to place in their hands the "trayninge and bringinge upp" of the infidel children for which purpose an unknown person had made a gift of £500. Evidently the company was fully prepared to accept the Pilgrims as settlers whatever their credenda might be. But when the matter was called to the attention of the king, by Sir Robert Naunton, the secretary of state, and James was asked to allow the Leyden people liberty of conscience under his gracious protection, he refused to give official consent but promised not to molest them.

For the moment this answer disconcerted the men in Leyden, but the more they thought about it the more hopeful the situation appeared. They reasoned rightly that the royal intention was a better warranty than a royal seal, for if at any time there should arise a desire to wrong them, a seal as broad as a house floor would not help them, because reasons could easily be found for recalling or reversing it. Therefore they again sent messengers to England, in the winter of 1617–1618, to renew the negotiations, and gave them letters to Sandys and Sir John Wolstenholme, also a member of the council, who with Sir Robert Naunton had been their chief advocates in the company. These letters contained expressions of thankfulness for the singular love shown by Sandys and the singular pains taken by Wolstenholme in aid of the petitioners, and the writers endeavored in them to state even more clearly than before the Leyden position on sundry points, partly doctrinal and partly political, that had been raised by the Privy Council in regard to the seven articles.

Owing to the fact that the progress of affairs was delayed by the dissensions within the company in 1619, and for the moment the business of obtaining a patent for a private plantation could not be

perfected, the negotiations dragged on and many messengers passed
to and fro between Leyden and London.[1] Cushman, in London in
the spring of that year, must have watched with dismay the dis-
lodgment of Smith and the elevation of Sandys and have wondered
when the turmoil would sufficiently abate for favorable action to be
taken. The affair had consumed too much time already and the delays brought great discouragement to the expectant people at Leyden. The apprehensions of those who had agreed to take the voyage
were in no way allayed by the experience of one Blackwell, an elder
of the Separatist church in Amsterdam, who having obtained a
patent from the company for a particular plantation in Virginia,
had sailed "toward winter" in 1618 with one hundred and eighty
passengers. He and one hundred and thirty of his company had
died on the overcrowded and ill-fated vessel. News of the terrible
disaster reached Leyden in the summer of 1619 and must have cast
a mantle of gloom over the already nervous community.[2] The election of Sandys to the treasurership brought, temporarily at least,
peace to the Virginia Company, and, as the time seemed at last
propitious, the petition for a patent was renewed. By the advice of
friends the request was made, not by any member of the Leyden
church, for that would have made public a purpose which they
desired to conceal, but by one John Wyncop, a clergyman who was
or had been a tutor in the family of Thomas, third earl of Lincoln
at Sempringham in Lincolnshire, and who at this juncture wished
to go to America. Preliminaries must have been begun early in
May, but not until June 19 was the company's seal finally attached
to the patent for a particular plantation such as the Separatists hoped
to establish in Virginia.[3]

The contents of this patent, like those of the forty or more
patents which no longer survive, will never be known; but it is
reasonable to suppose that all these documents were drawn after a
common model, corresponding to the extant patents of the South-

1. The center of Separatist life in London seems to have been Heneage House in
Duke's Place, that section of the City to the east in Aldgate Ward, just inside the
wall. It was bounded by Heneage Street, Shoemaker's Row, and High Street, a
locality inhabited by foreign Protestants and English Separatists, where non-conformity reigned. Banks, *Proceedings*, Massachusetts Historical Society, 1897, pp. 61–
62; *English Ancestors*, pp. 11–16. Coleman Street, not far away, was a well known
resort of dissenters.
2. Bradford, *History*, I, 87–92.
3. *Virginia Company Records*, I, 221, 228.

ampton Associates and the Peirce Associates of a later date.[1] In all probability the Separatists were granted certain portions of land upon which they were to lay out a town-plantation, where under a leader—governor, captain, commander, or chief—they would be privileged to make such orders, ordinances, and constitutions as were necessary for their local well-being. There is no reason to doubt that they fully intended to go to Virginia, though no specific place is mentioned in either of the extant patents and probably none was mentioned in the Wyncop patent. According to the practice of the company, no assignments of land in Virginia were made until the actual arrival of the colonists. There was plenty of land at this time on or near the James River and none of those who received patents and acted on them went elsewhere. Had the Pilgrims gone to Virginia they would have been allowed a very considerable measure of local independence, but they would have been subject to the higher authority of the governor and council. They would have been obliged to pay all taxes and impositions levied by the assembly for the general support of the whole, and in order to meet these obligations, they would have had to receive lands near the seat of government at Jamestown. They could not have borne their share of the public burdens had they settled as far away as the mouth of the Hudson, and after the Virginia Company's prolonged controversy with Captain Martin over "exorbitant privileges and transendent liberties," they would hardly have been allowed by the company to occupy land so far away as to make their plantation an independent, petty government by itself. There was nothing unusual about the Wyncop patent, even though Winslow calls it "a large patent."[2] It was required to agree with the "originall," as the record says,[3] "wch if it doth not they have promised to bring it into court and cancell it."[4]

But the Wyncop patent was never used and all the labor expended

<hr/>

1. The Southampton patent is to be found among the Smith of Nibley papers in the New York Public Library and is printed in the *Bulletin* of the library, III, 161–164; the Peirce patent is printed in Bradford, *History*, I, 246–251. The wording of the two documents is essentially the same.

2. *Hypocrisie Unmasked*, p. 90.   3. *Virginia Company Records*, I, 228.

4. Bradford's statement, "At length the conclusion was to live as a distincte body by themselves under the general Government of Virginia" is in entire accord with this view. But Bradford must have known that Virginia was an Anglican colony and that the Pilgrims could hardly have continued to live there without conforming. Probably the leaders realized this as time went on and their convictions on this point may have led to the giving up of the plan to go to Virginia. From a further state-

on it went for nothing. The document was, without doubt, sent over to Holland and inspected there, but meanwhile important events had taken place that seriously affected the situation. Brewster, the church elder, and Brewer, a member of a leading Kent family, who had matriculated as a student at Leyden university, had set up a printing press in the attic of Brewer's house in Leyden and begun to print books and pamphlets of a propagandist sort. Most of them were controversial but of a relatively harmless character, and it was not until 1619 and the issue of Calderwood's *Perth Assembly* that trouble arose. This book contained a vigorous denunciation of King James's attempt to force episcopacy upon the Scottish church and Calderwood in writing it laid himself open to the charge of sedition.[1] In reprinting the book, Brewster came under the same charge and was obliged temporarily to go into hiding. The Wyncop patent was granted in June and during the summer Brewster was avoiding the authorities on both sides of the Channel and his friends were doing everything in their power to keep him out of sight. This was no time for the Separatists to appeal to the king or the company for support or even connivance. Where Brewster was from the summer of 1619 to June of the next year is not known, but the fact that the business of the patent was resumed during the winter of 1619–1620 and that preparations for departure were being made at that time leads one to believe that he was in London directing affairs and trying as rapidly as possible to complete the plans.[2] He might easily have done these things while in hiding, particularly after sufficient time had elapsed to soften the royal wrath and to

ment in one of Bradford's letters, written after they had gone to New England, "we are but one particular colony or plantation," we are able to infer that the Pilgrims in Plymouth believed themselves to stand in the same relation there to the New England Council that they would have stood in Virginia to the Virginia Company. The system of particular plantations was put into application in New England just as was being done in Virginia at the same time. *Collections,* Massachusetts Historical Society, 1st series, III, 52, "Bradford's Letter Book."

1. Thomson, "Life of Calderwood," in Wodrow's edition of his *History of the Church of Scotland.* New information regarding the Brewer-Brewster printing press is given in Harris, Jones, and Plooij, *The Pilgrim Press* (1922), and Plooij, *The Pilgrims from a Dutch Point of View* (1932). These works, together with Plooij and Harris, *Leyden Documents relating to the Pilgrim Fathers* (1920), furnish a few additional facts regarding the life of the Pilgrims in Holland, but of so detailed a character as to be unavailable for citation here.

2. Could he have been concealed in Duke's Place, which Dr. Banks says had become at this time a collection of tenements "like rabbit warrens for the teeming denizens of this locality"? As a hiding place the retreat was safe and as a headquarters it was ideal.

dim the memory of the unfortunate experiment in printing. It was during this interval, in February, 1620, when the Separatist plans seemed to be at a standstill, that the Dutch made their offer of a location under the auspices of the States General. As we have seen, this offer was considered by Robinson and finally rejected altogether.

One reason, at least, for the rejection of the Dutch offer was the appearance at this time of one Thomas Weston, a personage in our early colonial history who was possessed of more spirit than judgment, more optimism than sagacity, a man of the sanguine venturesome type, whose career is more or less intimately bound up with the history of three settlements, Plymouth, Virginia, and Maryland,[1] and with the fishing interests of Maine. Weston was a citizen and ironmonger of London and closely identified with the Ironmongers Company, whose hall was in Aldgate Ward, not far from Duke's Place. At this time he was the treasurer and leader of a group of merchant adventurers in London who were engaged in various trading activities, and he had as one of his associates John Peirce or Peirsey, a clothworker and citizen of London and a brother of Abraham Peirsey or Peirce, the Virginia cape-merchant.[2] Like many another promoter of his day, he wished to take advantage of the Virginia Company's offer of a particular plantation to those who would aid the settlement on the James; and, having been prevented by the Merchant Adventurers of London from continuing his traffic with the Continent, he hoped that he and his associates might engage in trade with the New World.[3] On February 20, 1620, under

1. *Maryland Archives*, IV, 376. See pages 330, note 1, 331, note 2.
2. Adams, *Three Episodes in Massachusetts History*, I, 46; Brown, *Republic*, p. 354; Bradford, *History*, I, 99 note.
3. The account of Weston in the *Dictionary of National Biography* is poor and inaccurate. He is held in rather higher esteem today than formerly, as appears from the fact that Dr. Banks dedicates his book, *The English Ancestry*, to his memory as one "whose courage and vision made possible the epochal voyages of the *Mayflower* and the *Fortune*." The group of merchant adventurers who aided the Pilgrims was not organized originally for that special purpose. This voluntary association of which Weston was the head had been in existence for a number of years, engaged in various enterprises of a business nature, and had run afoul of the Merchant Adventurers of London, who charged Weston with interloping, that is, shipping woolens and other cloths to the Low Countries without their license. This charge was brought in 1618 and as the practice was ordered to be stopped by the Privy Council, Weston and his associates, checked in their traffic with the Continent, turned their attention to the possibilities of trade with New England, using the Pilgrims as allies, in part, of that undertaking. Friis, *Alderman Cockayne*, pp. 366–370, 370 note 3.

the name of John Peirce and his Associates, he obtained a patent from the company for land in Virginia,[1] and with that in hand, doubtless after intercourse with the Separatists living in Heneage House, perhaps with Brewster himself, he went to Leyden for the purpose of interesting the Separatists there in his project. He was already well acquainted with some of them, whom he had met at Heneage House, and seems to have had some part in their earlier negotiations, perhaps in connection with the Wyncop patent.[2]

At Leyden Weston had conferences with John Robinson and others of the church there and urged them to have nothing to do with the Dutch offer and as little as possible to do with the Virginia Company.[3] He must have argued against the use of the Wyncop patent and endeavored to persuade the Separatists not to go over as an independent company under the Virginia Company, but to join with him and his associates in using the Peirce patent, strengthening his argument by saying that the merchants would look after the business end of the undertaking and supply the funds. This offer of financial assistance, of which the Pilgrims stood so sorely in need, from one whom they believed to be their friend and ally and actuated by religious as well as commercial motives, must have come as a veritable boon to them in their poverty and distress. Weston promised the support of what appeared to be a strong financial organization, which would contribute the money while the Pilgrims furnished the labor. In July, 1620, he came forward with a definite series of proposals,[4] which the Pilgrims accepted and, those of them who were intending to go, believing that their problems were by way of being solved, sold their property in Leyden and put the money into a common stock for the purchase of provisions and other necessaries for the voyage.

But the situation proved far less simple than it seemed to be. Grave doubts arose as to the best place to go and Weston himself wavered in his decision. He suggested giving up the Peirce patent and applying to the proposed Council for New England, about to be created as the reconstructed successor of the moribund Plymouth Company, for a grant in the northern part of the old "Virginia" territory, because he thought that the fishing there was likely to

1. *Virginia Company Records,* I, 249, 303.
2. Bradford, *History,* I, 99.   3. *Ibid.,* I, 99, 107.
4. *Ibid.,* I, 104–106.

prove more lucrative than anything Virginia had to offer.[1] Among the Leyden people, as among the merchants also, there were some who did not like the idea of going to Virginia because they believed that trouble was sure to result from Separatists going to an Anglican colony. Also they were disturbed by the disputes among the members of the Virginia Company and some of the merchants took such an aversion to the plan that they "fell into utter dislike" with Virginia and declared that they would have nothing to do with the undertaking if the Pilgrims persisted in going there. So the divisions of opinion spread and widened, until "they of Leyden, who had put off their estates and laid out their moneys, were brought into a great streight, fearing what issue these things would come to." But it was finally agreed by a majority of those who were willing to go that it would be better not to go to Virginia, because in so doing they would forfeit a considerable portion of their financial support and might become involved in the troubles of the Virginia Company, the outlook for which was none too promising on account of the bad condition of its treasury.[2] They too, as well as the merchants, were allured by the excellent prospects offered as a means of self-support,[3] by the fishery in the northern waters, which was gradually overcoming the bad repute into which New England had fallen in the earlier years, and by the fact, well bruited abroad, that the Council for New England was to be granted a monopoly of the fishing, a concession against which the Virginia Company protested with all its might.[4] The proposed monopoly made a very strong appeal to Weston and his associates, who considered a monopoly of trade necessary for existence.

But unfortunately the charter for the Council for New England,

1. Weston was probably influenced in his opinion not only by the reports of successful fishing in New England waters but also by the writings of John Smith who was doing all that he could to promote New England as a place of settlement for profit. The wide-spread reputation that the fishery acquired played an important part in inducing both the Pilgrims and later the Puritans to go to New England.

2. "The colony being thus weak and the treasury exhaust," May 17, 1620. *Virginia Company Records*, I, 350.

3. Later Bradford wrote to the merchants in London, "Fishing must be the cheife, if not the only means to doe us good" and "It is for certain that great profite is here raised by fishing." *American Historical Review*, VIII, 296, 297.

4. *Virginia Company Records*, I, 277 (December 1, 1619), 285, 321, 329, 339–340 (May 11, 1620), 410–411 (November 4, 1620). The Virginia Company carried the attack into parliament the next year, where Sir Edwin Sandys led the opposition to the monopoly. Stock, *Debates*, I, 35, 37, 39, 49, etc.

which was confidently expected to pass the seals in the summer of 1620, was held up before delivery, and in consequence neither Weston nor anyone else could obtain a patent legally issued.[1] Therefore the Pilgrims, unwilling to delay longer, resolved to adventure with the patent they had—that granted to Peirce and his Associates— which shows that at the outset they fully intended to go to Virginia and there to establish themselves as a distinct body under the government of that colony. That they did not expect to lose their identity among the Virginia planters would appear from Robinson's farewell words about their "intended course of civil communitie" and their becoming "a body politik," using amongst themselves civil governments and choosing their own lawful administrators.[2] It is not easy to imagine what would actually have happened if the Pilgrims had gone to Virginia with these ideas in mind, for Virginia was an Anglican colony that wanted neither Separatist, Puritan, nor Roman Catholic. Furthermore, the massacre of 1622 might have wiped out the Pilgrims altogether.

The arrangement entered into with Weston and his associates— seventy in number according to John Smith, gentlemen, merchants, and handicraftsmen, living in and about London, and all subscribing to a common fund[3]—is characteristic of the way these enterprises were underwritten by the undertakers of that day, though in this case certain peculiar conditions were present. Those going to America—from Leyden and elsewhere—were to be neither tenants nor servants, but were to stand on equal terms with the associates in England as partners in the enterprise. Three groups of interests were involved. First, the group of the adventurers in England, each of whom contributed one or more shares, at £10 a share, to the common stock; secondly, the group of the adventurer-planters, some of whom may have been Pilgrims, who intended to go to America but were able to put in £10, either in money or supplies, and so were reckoned as possessing two shares each, the equivalent of £20, one share representing an actual money payment, the other the subscriber's labor; and thirdly, the planters themselves, most of whom were the Pilgrims, who could contribute nothing except

1. The writ of privy seal, as recorded on the patent rolls, is dated November 3, 1620. The unexpected delay in issuing the charter was undoubtedly due to the fishery dispute.

2. Bradford, *History*, I, 132, 133.

3. Smith, *Travels and Works*, II, 782–783.

themselves and their capacity for hard and profitable work, but in making the final distribution were reckoned as possessing one share each, or £10. The company was not an incorporated body but only a voluntary joint-stock organization and all were to share, each according to his investment, in the allotment of profits. In accord with the accepted practice of the day, already tried out by the Virginia and Bermuda companies, followed later by the Old Providence Company, and upheld by promoters as obligatory in all colonizing enterprises, both capital and profits were to belong to the joint-stock for seven years, at the end of which time they were to be divided proportionately among the partners. The capital was construed as including lands, houses, goods, chattels, and all animals; the accumulated profits were what they might be.[1]

While thus we have in the case of the Plymouth settlers the common-fund-and-deferred-profit system familiar to all, we have also some conditions that prevailed nowhere else. The company, consisting of both adventurers and planters, instead of remaining in England and founding, supplying, and managing its colony from a distance, as the incorporated companies had done and were to do,[2] was divided into two parts, one remaining in England and the other going to America. It is doubtful if this could have happened legally had the company been an incorporated body, but as a voluntary association of partners it was able to do pretty much as it pleased, provided the partners were agreed. Each group had its own organization. The first, made up of the seventy adventurers, who as capitalists risked their money in fitting out the venture, had a president and treasurer, chosen annually, and held regular court meetings, at which all ordinary business was transacted. This form of organization—a familiar one—had probably existed for some years, how long we do not know, but it certainly was not created solely for

1. The money paid in to the capital stock has been estimated at £1200, which was £300 less than it should have been. By 1624 the expenditures had risen to £7000. *Ibid.*, II, 783; Bradford, *History*, I, 119; Scott, *Joint-Stock Companies*, II, 311.

2. The six incorporated companies—the Virginia Companies of London and Plymouth, the Bermuda Company, the London and Bristol Company, the Massachusetts Bay Company, and the Old Providence Company—each remained in England and founded a colony in America—Sagadahoc, Jamestown, Bermuda, Newfoundland, Salem, and Old Providence. The method was the same in each case, even though Sagadahoc, Newfoundland, and Old Providence did not long survive and the Massachusetts Bay Company was soon transformed.

the purpose of coöperating with the Pilgrims, for the association, with changing membership, had been active long before the Pilgrims began their negotiations. The second group, the colonists—Pilgrims and others—were risking their lives and their happiness in going to America and toiling there. As it was fundamentally important for them to hold together as a body politic, they chose a governor soon after sailing and became in time a self-governing plantation, for the adventurers in England had no right to exercise civil authority over them.[1] Thus we have a kind of double-headed arrangement, entered into by a business company and a religious group, which promised trouble. Each in a sense was quite independent of the other, for though the Pilgrims could receive counsel and advice from the merchants, they were free of all orders or commands. Even those who were sent by the merchants to America with the Pilgrims, skilled artisans serving for hire and the young men and boys who went over as servants and apprentices, were beyond the merchants' control, subject only to the government in the colony and receiving their meat, drink, and apparel out of the common stock there.

On the very eve of departure a misunderstanding arose regarding the agreement with Weston and the merchants, which for a moment proved exceedingly embarrassing. Cushman in his negotiations with the Londoners had accepted two conditions which the leaders in Leyden thought unfair to them. One of these was the insertion in the agreement of a clause that gave to the merchants a right of half ownership in the houses and lands of the colony when the seven-year period had expired; and the other, the omission of a clause which had previously been included, according to which each planter was to be allowed two days a week of free labor for himself. Each of these changes seemed likely to work a hardship upon the settlers after they had reached America, and the men of Leyden expressed their strong disapproval of Cushman's way of doing things, saying that they had never authorized him to add or omit any article that changed the intent of the contract. Robinson wrote to Carver complaining of "the prentishipe of 7 years and not a daies freedom from tasks," which promised to be the lot of the Pilgrim in his new life. But Weston refused to continue under any other terms, which from a business point of view were reasonable enough; and

1. Smith, *Travels and Works,* II, 782–783.

as there was neither time nor opportunity to make an issue of the matter Cushman, though restless under the criticism to which he had been subjected,[1] saved the day by disregarding the protests from Leyden and going ahead with the arrangements. The Pilgrims who had already bought a vessel with which to cross the North Sea could do nothing else than accept a situation which they could not avoid. Cushman may have been imposed upon by the merchants, but under the circumstances it is difficult to see what else he could have done. The merchants were bound to make the best terms they could, for they were taking financial risks and entering upon a very speculative enterprise; and among the assets upon which they counted were the labor and property of the Pilgrims in America. They could hardly be expected to view the arrangement from other than a business man's point of view.

The Leyden Pilgrims, out of a part of the money obtained from the sale of their possessions, had already purchased a vessel, the *Speedwell,* to carry them to Southampton, there to join another vessel, the *Mayflower,* which had been hired by Weston and the merchant adventurers to take up the larger number of those who were to accompany the Leyden contingent on their voyage across the ocean. The *Speedwell,* which was the smaller of the two vessels, was to act as a transport and to remain in the colony, attendant on fishing and such other affairs as might be for the good and profit of the settlers in their new home.[2] After many touching experiences at Delfshaven, the port of embarkation,[3] whence they departed on July 22, 1620, and during the voyage across the North Sea, the Ley-

1. Bradford, *History,* I, 127–129. Cushman wrote a pathetic letter, while the vessels lay at Dartmouth, August 17, 1620, explaining the situation, *ibid.,* I, 141–146.
2. Bradford, *History,* I, 121. Bradford does not give the name of the vessel which brought the Leyden Pilgrims to Southampton. It may be found in Morton's *New England Memorial.* Nor does he give the name of the *Mayflower,* which is first mentioned in the *Plymouth Colony Records,* XII, 4. His many omissions and disproportions of space and stress have led Dr. Banks, perhaps too emphatically, to say that as an historian he was "an excellent attorney for the Leyden church doctrines and defender of its personal adherents." Not unnaturally Bradford was interested in only one side of the Pilgrim story and could hardly have avoided dwelling at length upon that which intimately concerned him, to the exclusion of much that is to the modern writer equally important.
3. The accounts given by Bradford and Winslow of the pathetic circumstances attending the departure from Delfshaven differ in one material respect. Bradford says that the parting took place on shipboard, Winslow that it occurred on the dock or quay. Either event might have happened.

den group of something more than thirty, out of a total of two hundred and thirty-eight members of the Leyden church, arrived about the end of the month at Southampton. There they were joined by Carver and Cushman and others from London and vicinity, who had been waiting for seven days, having left London in the *Mayflower* about the middle of July. The number that went aboard at London cannot be certainly known, as some of them did not make the final voyage, but it cannot have been far from eighty.[1] Only one among them, Christopher Martin of Billericay in Essex, can be identified as a Separatist. The others were hired by Weston and the merchant adventurers as laborers in the colony and were Church of England men and women, if they professed any faith. The two vessels sailed from Southampton on August 5, but inasmuch as the *Speedwell,* a small boat of sixty tons, proved unseaworthy on the voyage down the Channel, they put in at Dartmouth on the 13th "to their [the Pilgrims] great charg and losse of time and a fair winde." After repairs were made, they started again ten days later and having got one hundred leagues beyond Lands End found the *Speedwell* leaking so badly as to make it unsafe to proceed. Back they went to Plymouth and there the transport, seemingly a decrepit craft, overmasted and cranky, was abandoned and the decision was reached, most unwillingly, that the *Mayflower* should go on alone, with as many as it could carry of those who were prepared to make the voyage, despite the unpromising beginning and the uncertain future. The remainder returned to London.

The memorable voyage of the Pilgrims began, therefore, with the departure of the *Mayflower* from Plymouth, September 16, 1620. After many days of kind and courteous entertainment in that seaport, with a fine, favoring gale blowing, this courageous company started on its adventurous journey across the Atlantic. There were on board, as usually estimated, one hundred and one persons, besides the officers and the crew. Thirty-five of these were from Leyden and sixty-six from London and Southampton. The number may be distributed as follows: fifty-six were adult passengers, twenty were

1. Figures for this preliminary period cannot certainly be given. At least one Separatist sailed from Delfshaven who did not go to America. Perhaps there were others. One or two of the artisans may have been hired in Southampton and not in London. Probably twenty of the Londoners returned after the *Speedwell* was abandoned, and at least one Separatist, Robert Cushman, with his family at that time gave up the voyage. There may have been others who did the same.

boys, and eleven were girls, some of whom were children sent from London by the merchant adventurers; and in addition there were nine servants and five adult men, not Separatists, who had been signed on in one capacity or another for the voyage. Some forty-eight others made up the officers and crew. Thus we have on board eighty-seven passengers of all ages, and fourteen others, indentured servants and hired artisans, which make a complement of one hundred and one, the entire body on board numbering one hundred and forty-nine.[1] Though the vessel, a ship of one hundred and eighty tons burden,[2] which had formerly been engaged in the wine trade between English and Mediterranean ports, carried no freight, it was heavily loaded with household furniture, domestic utensils, and other necessities for use in the settlement, and with provisions in the form of salted beef, vegetables, butter, bread, and the like packed in barrels, and hogsheads of beer, partly for drink and partly

1. Miles Standish, who was bred a soldier in Holland and was not a Separatist, was taken on as a military man. John Alden was probably not at first a Separatist, though he undoubtedly became one afterward. Of the children, Dr. Banks says, "Seven minors came on the *Mayflower,* who were not children of any of the passengers and only one was described as having any kinship to any of them." He conjectures that these children may have been of the same class as the boys and girls sent to Virginia by the City of London and by the king—waifs of the parishes and idlers following the court. They were probably none of them from Separatist homes. Only two of them survived adult years or remained in Plymouth and became heads of families. *Proceedings,* Massachusetts Historical Society, 60, pp. 147–148; *English Ancestry, passim.*

2. The *Mayflower* has been the object of more curiosity and conjecture than any other ship in history. It was a staunch, chunky, slow-sailing vessel, square-rigged, double-decked, broad abeam, with high upper structure at the stern, the passengers occupying cabins or quarters between decks, or, in the case of the women and children, in rough cabins forward below the poop. Regarding its history, which can be followed in the London Port Books from 1610 on, though no mention is made there of this particular voyage, probably because the vessel carried no cargo liable to customs duty, see R. G. Marsden in the *English Historical Review,* XIX, 169. Two articles, experiments in historical speculation, have been written by J. Rendel Harris, *The Last of the Mayflower* and *The Finding of the Mayflower* (Longmans, 1920), which need not be taken seriously. They were written by Dr. Harris at the age of seventy-five and doubtless were for him a stimulating mental exercise, with the idea of arousing controversy. But the suggestions made in them are too fantastic even for controversy. For an estimate of their historical value see an unsigned review in the *American Historical Review,* XXVI, 799–802. Banks, *English Ancestry,* ch. V, gives further information based on researches in the Public Record Office. The only book of value on the *Mayflower* and its landfall is Nickerson's, *Land Ho—1620* (1931), a very careful and accurate study. Items of detail in large numbers can be found in the volumes of *The Mayflower Descendant* and *The New England Genealogical and Historical Register,* particularly the latter, 70, pp. 337–342, "The Mayflower, her Identity and Tonnage."

as a preventative of scurvy. There were also dogs and possibly goats, swine, and chickens, but no cattle. A bull and two heifers came over with Winslow in 1624.[1]

The master or captain of the vessel was Christopher Jones, an experienced skipper and whaling captain, who had been master of the vessel for some ten years and was part owner with three others. He was a person of prominence in his town, Harwich, and a thoroughly kindly man and competent sailor, at this time about fifty years of age. In addition there were four mates, one of whom was John Clark, the pilot, with whom we are already acquainted from his connection with the early history of Virginia, four quartermasters, at least one carpenter, two or three cooks, one or more gunners —for the ship carried ordnance and ammunition and may have had a letter of marque—and a boatswain or two.[2] Five men, among whom was John Alden, were hired at Southampton. Alden was employed as a cooper to look after the beer hogsheads and remained in the colony instead of returning to England, probably because of the attractions of Priscilla Mullins, whom he may have known and courted before he joined the ship. The other hired employés were John Alderton, Thomas England (or English), signed on in Holland as master of the *Speedwell,* William Trevor, and one Ely, all of whom served as extra seamen and later, for a year, as assistants in carrying on the work of the colony. There was also Christopher Martin, the supercargo, who had already spent some time in Kent gathering provisions for the voyage. He was, according to Bradford, who had strong likes and dislikes and to whom Martin must have given offense, a stubborn, ill tempered man.[3] There was also a doctor among the Pilgrims, Samuel Fuller, and a ship's surgeon, Dr. Giles Heale, not mentioned by Bradford, who remained in the

1. Either in the *Charity* or the *Ann,* Bradford, *History,* I, 352, note 2. Bradford mentions "a great iron scrue the passengers brought out of Holland" (*ibid.,* I, 150), which Dr. Plooij suggests may have been the screw of the Brewer-Brewster printing press. Others have thought it of the nature of a jack-screw, likely to be useful on shipboard. Mourt in his "Relation" (Young, *Chronicles of the Pilgrims,* p. 175) speaks of a "spaniel" and a "great mastiff bitch."

2. For Jones see Banks, *English Ancestry,* pp. 18–21. That the Pilgrims thought well of both Jones and Clark appears from their naming a river after the one and an island after the other.

3. The reader of Bradford must be careful about accepting his opinion regarding those whom he criticizes. Martin's character is defended by Mason and Nightingale, in *New Light on the Pilgrim Story,* pp. 92–94.

colony during the winter, returning with some of the others the following April, when the *Mayflower* went back to England.[1]

The vessel was overcrowded[2] and insufficiently provisioned and the sufferings on the voyage must have been considerable, even though the actual mortality was low. Only three or four of the crew and but one of the passengers died. The subsequent mortality, however, was very high, for the members of the company paid the penalty of their sixty-five days at sea, in a general sickness that carried off half their number and half the ship's crew during that first terrible winter. They died of scurvy, that dreaded starvation disease, and general debility, the result of long confinement, unnutritious food, and a badly proportioned diet.[3] In all the transatlantic voyages of this period the want of proper food was as serious in its aftermath as it was during the actual voyage. One boy, Oceanus Hopkins, was born at sea and another, Peregrine White, on shipboard before landing. On the whole the ship must have been well handled by the crew, though Bradford has nothing favorable to say about them, considering them a godless, uncharitable, intemperate lot, and it is more than likely that the relations between them and the pas-

1. Banks, *English Ancestry, passim; Proceedings,* Massachusetts Historical Society, 60, pp. 146–148. Burgess, *John Robinson,* p. 262, and Dexter, *The England and Holland of the Pilgrims,* p. 589, note 4, both mention Heale, though Banks speaks of him as "hitherto unidentified."

2. Later the Massachusetts Bay Company reckoned 120 persons as the maximum for a 200 ton vessel, so that the *Mayflower,* according to that estimate, carried twenty-nine more than she ought (*Massachusetts Colonial Records,* I, 66). In sixty cases where Winthrop gives the number of passengers the average comes to a little over a hundred each. Diffenderfer, in his *German Immigration into Pennsylvania,* p. 51, says that on an average vessels of 200 tons bringing the Germans to America carried 300 passengers each. But this was a century later.

3. Richard Mather, writing fifteen years later, gave his experiences as follows. "And a speciall meanes of the healthfulnesse of the passengers by the blessing of God wee all conceyved to bee much walking in the open ayre, and the comfortable variety of our food; for seeing wee were not tyed to the ships diet, but did victuall ourselves, wee had no want of good and wholesome beere and bread; and as our land-stomaches grew weary of ship diet, of salt fish and salt beefe and the like, wee had liberty to change for other food which might sort better with our healthes and stomaches; and therefore wee used bacon and buttered pease, sometimes buttered bag pudding made with curraynes and raisins, and sometimes drink pottage of beere and oatmeale and sometimes water pottage [loblolly] well buttered." *Journal,* p. 30. Undoubtedly the voyages of fifteen years had taught the people of England many lessons about the needs of ocean travel, and the greater wealth of the Puritans made better provisioning possible. One notices the frequent use of butter in the account above and will remember that the Pilgrims had to sell "3 or 4 ferkins" (224 pounds) before starting on their voyage (Bradford, *History,* I, 127, note 1).

sengers were none too friendly. The sailor's contempt for the landsman would hardly be lessened by the religious habits and speech of the Pilgrims, which the average seaman would characterize as psalm singing and cant.

On November 9–19, the *Mayflower* sighted Cape Cod, after "longe beating at sea," and as Captain Jones must have recognized the region from the accounts of Smith and Dermer, who had already visited and described the coasts, it was at first thought best to put about and continue the vessel's original course to the southward. But becoming entangled in the shoals and rocks of Monomoy Point, with the wind failing them, the Pilgrim leaders changed their plan and two days afterward dropped anchor in Cape Cod bay.[1] There they remained, sending out various exploring parties to try out the land, until just a month later, December 11–21, one exploring party landed on the shore of Plymouth harbor. Within a week the *Mayflower* itself entered the bay, a site was selected, the first house for common use was begun on December 25, and gradually the families were transferred to the shore. The town was laid out on the site of an old Indian cornfield, probably near the site of an old Indian village, and houses, in two rows "for more safety," were built on each side of a roadway, running up the hill from the shore, which they called Leyden Street, with homesteads and garden plots.[2] Each man built his own house, as it was believed that by such a course men would make more haste than by working in common, and lots were cast for position.[3] Though hampered by the deaths of many in the "general visitation" that followed, the Pilgrims were spared the horrors of an intensely cold winter, for even though at best the frost must have seemed severe to those not accustomed to it, the temperature in 1620–1621 was probably higher

1. It used to be thought that the landing at Plymouth was either accidental or the result of treachery. The latter view has long since gone by the board. As to the former the late Mr. Kinnicut argues that the Pilgrim leaders knew the place well, through their connection with the Earl of Lincoln, whose sister had married John Gorges, and whose tutor had been Wyncop; that in this way Sir Ferdinando Gorges knew of the Pilgrim plans and tried to divert the company from Virginia to New England; and that as Weston and the Pilgrims had wanted to come under the authority of the Council for New England it required but a relatively trifling incident to bring about a change of plan. *Proceedings,* Massachusetts Historical Society, 48, pp. 103–118.

2. For the laying out of the town see Mourt's "Relation" in Young, *Chronicles of the Pilgrims,* pp. 124, 167, 206, 229; the same, *Chronicles of Massachusetts Bay,* p. 224.

3. For the distribution of lots, Hazard, *State Papers,* I, 100–103.

than usual. They were likewise relieved of serious danger from the Indians, for the latter, greatly reduced in numbers by an epidemic of the years 1617–1619, were on the whole friendly.[1]

Despite many handicaps and discouragements, the little community, once begun, grew slowly, even though painfully. Many settlers died but others came to take their places, crossing to America in the *Fortune,* the *Charity,* the *Ann,* the *Little James,* the *Mayflower,* and the *Handmaid* during the ensuing decade. John Smith estimated the population in 1624 at 124.[2] In 1630 it was nearly 300; in 1637, 549.[3] In 1628 the Dutchman, Rasier, described the town as lying on the slope of a hill, stretching east toward the seacoast, with a broad street leading down the hill and another crossing it in the middle north and south. The houses were well constructed of hewn planks, with gardens behind, also enclosed, so that the houses and court yards were arranged in very good order, with a stockade against a sudden attack. At the ends of the street were three wooden gates. In the center on the cross street stood the governor's house, before which was a square stockade with four mortars mounted upon it, so as to enfilade the streets. Upon the hill was a large square house with a flat roof of thick sawn plank, stayed with oak beams, upon the top of which were six cannon, capable of shooting iron balls of four and five pounds' weight and commanding the country. The lower part of this building was used as a meeting-house, where preaching took place on Sundays and the usual holidays.[4]

1. Bradford, *History,* I, 221–222; Adams, *Three Episodes,* I, ch. I. This epidemic was a matter of common knowledge in England. Gorges and Winthrop both speak of it, the former in his "Description of New England" as "a great and general plague which so violently rained for three years together" (Baxter, *Gorges,* II, 77), and the latter in his "Diverse Objections" of 1629, "God hath consumed the Natives with a great Plauge in those partes, soe as there be few Inhabitantes lefte" (*Winthrop Papers,* II, 141). In his letter of 1619 to Samuel Purchas, Dermer wrote, "I passed along the coast where I found some antient plantations, not long since populous, now utterly void; in other places a remnant remains but not free of sickness. Their disease the Plague, for wee might perceive the spots of those that usually die" (printed in Burrage, *Gorges and the Grant of the Province of Maine,* p. 129). The plague is mentioned in White, *The Planters Plea,* p. 14, and in the charter for the Council for New England (Thorpe, *Charters,* 3, p. 1828).

2. Smith, *Travels and Works,* II, 782.

3. Hazard, *State Papers,* I, 300; Dexter, "Estimates of Population," *Historical Papers,* p. 155, note; Green and Harrington, *American Population before the Federal Census of 1790,* p. 11.

4. "Letter of Isaac de Rasieres to Samuel Blommaert." *New Netherland* (Original Narratives Series), p. 112.

The people who lived in this unpretentious settlement were simple country and city folk, in origin farmers and peasants from the English counties and workers from the lanes, alleys, and tenements of London and adjoining parishes. They were nearly all from the middle and lower classes of England and were without social or political distinction. Those from Leyden were from the midland counties in largest part, but as only thirty-five of the Leyden church went to America, it is evident that the remainder of the company were of London and Middlesex origin, constituting a majority of the passengers on board. Probably nearly all of these were strangers to the Leyden people, not Separatists at all, but persons sent over by Weston and the merchant adventurers to work and not to pray.[1] Those constituting the Separatist Church in Plymouth were men and women whose life had been of the soil, but who finding themselves within the walled city of Leyden had been compelled to turn to craftsmanship and artisan work in order to earn a living. Even the few who became teachers and students worked at their trade. A small number only were entitled to be called "mister" and "mistress"; all the rest of adult age were "goodman" and "goodwife" or "goody." Brewster was the only one of the Scrooby group who had been in contact with a university and even he failed to graduate. He and Bradford alone of the Leyden group had any administrative or financial ability or in America showed any capacity for leadership. Those who became the conspicuous men of the colony, with the exception of Winslow, Carver, and possibly Allerton, who though from Leyden was not much in sympathy with the Separatists, were largely of London origin. Miles Standish was from London and joined the party at Southampton.

Most of the Separatists who came to America in the *Mayflower* had had little or no education and those who followed during the next nine years added nothing to raise the standard of literary or educational culture. In thirty years less than a score of university

1. Bradford (*History*, I, 189–190) speaks of "the strangers amongst them," and Lyford (of whom more later) in his letter to the merchants, August 22, 1624, says that the Pilgrims were "the smallest number in the colony" (*ibid.*, 399). Dr. Banks has established beyond a reasonable doubt that a majority of those at Plymouth had been brought up in the forms of worship of the Established Church; that of the seventy-two heads in 1624 at least fifty were from London, and its suburbs, and that none of these had any discoverable connection with the Separatist group from Leyden. *Proceedings*, Massachusetts Historical Society, 62, p. 35.

men came to Plymouth[1] and of these only three remained and pursued their ministerial calling. In seven out of eleven towns of the colony as a whole, the pastorate during these years was vacant or unestablished, while Plymouth itself was without a minister from 1624 to 1628 and from 1654 to 1669.[2] For fifty years the colony was without a public school and during that time furnished no student to the higher education, even of the standard that Harvard then required. How far this intellectual apathy was due to inferior mentality, to lack of opportunity, or to poverty and how far to disinclination it is hard to say. The Venetian ambassador in England wrote in 1637, "The Brownists abhor letters, study, learned men, and think that ignorance is the only key to Heaven. For this reason their followers have ceased to associate with others and have withdrawn to New England, which is further north than Virginia, calling it New Canaan, which to the Hebrews was the land of Promise."[3] Yet there were books in the colony. At his death in 1643 Brewster left a library of nearly four hundred volumes; Bradford had in his library eighty volumes; and even Miles Standish, doughty warrior that he was, whose hand was better fitted for the sword than the pen and whose eye was trained to see Indians rather than letters, left about fifty. Many of these books were acquired after their owners had reached the colony, showing that books were not infrequently sent for, to be brought over by the ships that went back and forth across the ocean. Probably a majority of the Pilgrims had some books, for of seventy inventories examined, belonging to the earlier period, only a dozen fail to mention books among the items—chiefly bibles, catechisms, and the like. Taking the contents of the Plymouth libraries, as far as they are known, we find fewer theological works than in the libraries of the Massachusetts Bay colony later.[4] The Separatists were not theologically minded.

Though a minority as to numbers, the Pilgrims were in the main a homogeneous group, both in social rating and in religious views and purpose. They formed a covenanted church, fashioned after

1. Dexter, "Influence of Universities," *Historical Papers*, p. 102; Bradford, *History*, I, 134, editor's note; Wright, *Literary Culture in Early New England*, pp. 15, 24–29.
2. "Plymouth Colony Records," *Publications*, Colonial Society of Massachusetts, XXII, xxiii–xxiv.
3. *Calendar Venetian Papers*, 1636–1639, "Relation of England." The ambassador, Carrer, had recently been reading Morton's *New England Canaan*, printed in Amsterdam in 1637, and had got his ideas from that muddy source.
4. Wright, *Literary Culture*, pp. 26–29.

primitive models, which according to their own ideas of ecclesiastical polity was separatist and independent and a law unto itself. They were seekers after religious opportunity and permanent homes in an uncontaminated environment. The maintenance of their religious faith was their first thought, all else was secondary, and during the early years of their life in America they stood apart from the majority of the inhabitants of the colony, a church by themselves that admitted of no ordained ministry and made no provision for the religious welfare of those who were not of their own membership. As they were very unwilling to allow anyone not of their own choosing to exercise religious functions, it was inevitable that many of the settlers were deprived of the religious comforts and ministrations to which they had been accustomed at home and were destitute, from their point of view, of the means of salvation. When, therefore, in 1624, at a time when there was no pastor among them, even of the Separatist Church itself, there arrived the Rev. John Lyford, a clergyman of the Church of England sent over by the merchant adventurers, to whom complaints may have come from those in the colony religiously disfranchised, a peculiar situation developed. As Elder Brewster was not permitted to administer the sacraments, marriages had been performed by the civil authorities and baptisms had been omitted entirely. Such deficiencies were felt to be a great hardship by those to whom the sacraments of marriage and baptism were an essential part of their religious life and Lyford braved the wrath of Bradford and others by administering the communion, baptizing at least one child, and conducting service according to the Book of Common Prayer. For this he was driven from the colony and afterward maligned by Bradford in his *History* as "a vile man and an enemy to the plantation." Lyford may not have been a commendable character and probably was not, but there is nothing in his later career at Nantasket, Cape Ann, and Virginia to bear out Bradford's charges, which were manifestly based on hearsay.[1] The treatment the Pilgrim authorities accorded

---

1. Bradford, *History*, I, 380–405, 414–419; Banks, "Bradford on a Religious Rival," *Proceedings*, Massachusetts Historical Society, 62, pp. 34–53. Dr. Banks says "Of [Bradford's] right [to expel Lyford] there may be serious doubts . . . Lyford had a competent legal status in a plantation owned by the Merchant Adventurers as principal stockholders," p. 48. Both the Pilgrims and the Puritans were inclined to be credulous when it was their interest to be so, as in the charge of murder brought against Thomas Morton, a charge now disproved.

It must be remembered that Oldham, Hilton, Conant, and other early settlers,

this man, their covert opening of his letters, their defaming of his character, and their expelling him from Plymouth after his trial and conviction constitute an unpleasant episode in their history. They feared, since he would not join them, that he was planning to set up an Anglican church in their midst and was sending letters to the merchant adventurers containing accounts to the disadvantage of the colony.

The Pilgrims were concerned for the preservation of their peculiar form of ecclesiastical polity and the maintenance of their own way of life, both of which they believed to be sanctioned by the Bible and good in the sight of God. For this they had crossed the ocean, had endured hardships, and suffered sickness and death. They believed it a sin to allow their effort to be frustrated and brought to nought by those who did not think as they did. Their task was not an easy one. There were among those who came over in the *Mayflower* many—manifestly from London—who had begun to show a mutinous spirit even on shipboard and who afterward became a troublesome group for the Pilgrims to deal with. They were "lusty young men and many of them wild enough, who little considered whither or about what they went," whom the Pilgrims had to accept but wished they were "of beter condition." Some of those who came later, in 1623, "were so bad, as they were faine to be at charge to send them home again the next year."[1] Some refused to work on Christmas Day at the call of the governor and spent their time in the street, "pitching the bar, playing stool ball and such like sports."[2] Others committed thefts and "smarted well for it," and one at least, Billington, was "found guilty of willful murder, by plaine and notorious evidence," and was accordingly hanged, raising

who play a more or less conspicuous part in this period of New England history, were all Church of England men, though it is extremely likely that their religious convictions and religious duties rested but lightly upon them. Yet they were men of the type that would easily resent the narrow sectarian attitude of the Separatists and the rigid if not arbitrary rule of Bradford as the governor of the colony. Neither the Pilgrims at this time nor the Puritans afterward were the only people living along the New England coast, but their strength lay in their unity and compactness as religious communities and in their uncompromising attitude toward all other forms of religious belief. The others—and they were numerous—were isolated, individualistic, and nomadic, to whom religion was not the chief end of existence. Hence the eventual victory lay with the less tolerant and more highly organized religious groups.

1. Bradford, *History,* I, 231, 233, 316–317.
2. *Ibid.,* 245–246; Seymour, *The Oldtime Game of Wicket.*

thereby the interesting question of the right of the colony to pass a sentence of death.[1] There were others too—"untowarde persons mixed among them from the first"—of whom some left for Virginia, others went back to England, and a few stayed on in the colony. Even at Plymouth it proved impossible for the Pilgrims to remain "undefiled from the world," for they had been obliged to bring with them to America a very troublesome part of the world which they wished to avoid. But more embarrassing even than the presence in the colony of these backsliders and malcontents were the merchant adventurers in England, to whom the Pilgrims were bound by legal and financial ties. These London merchants, part owners of the land and stock of the settlement, had done a great deal to succour the undertaking in its earlier years, and had supplied equipment and funds without which Plymouth, in all probability, would never have been founded. Naturally these men had an interest in the colony and a legitimate claim to a right of interference in its affairs. Such interference was opposed by the Pilgrims as a deliberate attempt—which it certainly was not—to break down the religious exclusiveness of the Pilgrim organization. Some of the merchants individually may have had sympathy with the religious aspects of the undertaking but to the adventurers as a whole the experiment was purely a business affair. The objectives sought by the two groups of partners to the scheme were irreconcilable, and in the end the only solution of the difficulty lay in the withdrawal of the discouraged London associates from all part in the enterprise.

1. Bradford, *History*, I, 110–111; Hutchinson, *History of Massachusetts Bay*, I, 464–465. For an execution in 1648 for child murder, *Plymouth Colony Records*, II, 134.

CHAPTER XIV

THE NEW PLYMOUTH COLONY

FROM the beginning Plymouth colony was agricultural, but the settlers early turned their attention to fishing and to trading with the Indians in order to make such profit as they could to meet their share of the bargain with the adventurers. They also experimented with salt-making, and tried their hand at boat-building, but with only moderate success. One of their first obligations was to secure, if possible, a title to the soil which they tilled. As they had settled in New England and not in Virginia, their Peirce patent of 1620, granted by the Virginia Company, was of no value to them; but, through the aid of John Peirce and James Sherley,[1] the treasurer of the merchant adventurers, who made the application to the Council for New England (of which Gorges was the prime mover and directing head), the merchants obtained a second Peirce patent, June 1, 1621. This patent was issued to Peirce and Associates, that is, to the merchants and Pilgrims together as a voluntary joint-stock company for the promotion of a plantation in New England, and it vested the title to the lands in the two groups jointly.[2]

A few words must be said at this point about the second Peirce patent, technical and somewhat arid though the subject may be, for by this patent the legal status of the Pilgrim community was determined for nearly nine years. This patent was simply an indenture, identical in form and language with the patents granted by the Vir-

1. James Sherley was a London goldsmith, who carried on his business at the sign of the "Golden Horseshoe" on London Bridge. His house was nearby in Crooked Lane. He was sympathetic with the Pilgrims in religious matters and was of service to them in helping many of the Leyden people, who had not gone to New England in the *Mayflower*, to cross the ocean in later vessels.

2. Bradford's editor, Mr. Ford, says (I, 360, note) that the "Associates" were the "Pilgrims then at Plymouth," and he quotes from the Plymouth records the statement that Peirce was only a name "whose associates we were." It is impossible to believe that the Pilgrims would or could legally act independently of their London partners and the "we" of the quotation must be inclusive of all in the partnership. This view is confirmed by the attitude of the merchants toward the Peirce patent of 1622 and by Peirce's mention in his chancery bill of the merchants as "his associates." *New England Genealogical and Historical Register*, 67, p. 149.

ginia Company to the many groups of associates planning to found particular plantations in its colony on the James. It must, therefore, have been the same as the first Peirce patent and the Wyncop patent in all essential details.¹ It is not a grant properly so called, for it contains no mention of boundaries and defines no territory. It is rather an order for the allotment of certain amounts of land—one hundred acres for each person transported and fifteen hundred for public use—to be taken in any place not already inhabited; and the fact that it was issued shows that the Council for New England planned to establish within its own grant particular plantations exactly as the Virginia Company was doing at the same time in Virginia. In one important respect, however, the situation differed from that in Virginia. In the latter colony the company, acting under the authority vested in it by its charters, had set up its general government before issuing its patents for particular plantations; in New England, on the other hand, the council of 1620 issued its first patent before setting up its general government. In point of fact it never did establish a general government for New England at all, and for three good and sufficient reasons: the weakness and ineffectiveness of the Council for New England as compared with the courage and enthusiasm of the Virginia Company; the widely scattered location of the particular plantations in New England as compared with the compact group of settlements on the James; and the complete dislocation of Gorges' plans by the intrusion of the Puritans into New England. But more of this anon.

The merchant adventurers in London and their associates at Plymouth were to hold the lands thus allotted of the Council for

1. The text is printed in Bradford's *History*, I, 246–251, and in the *Farnham Papers*, I, 45–53. Bradford wrote in 1627, "we are but one particular colony or plantation in this land, there being diverse others besides, unto whom it hath pleased those Hon. Lords of his Majesty's Council for New England to grant the like commission and [the same] ample privileges" ("Letter Book," *Collections*, Massachusetts Historical Society, 1st series, III, 52). Just what Weston meant when he speaks of this second Peirce patent as "better than your former and with less limitation" (Bradford, *History*, I, 234) it is difficult to say, as the second patent cannot have differed essentially in language and content from the first. The only feature not in the extant Virginia indenture and consequently not in the first Peirce patent is the liberty to fish in the waters and upon the coast of New England. As this privilege was a monopoly of council and as the possession of this monopoly was one of the reasons why Weston wished to turn from the Virginia Company to the Council for New England even before the Pilgrims sailed for America, it may be that this is what he had in mind. Fishing had an important place in the minds of all concerned.

New England at a yearly quit-rent of two shillings a hundred acres and were to enjoy the same privileges as were possessed by those who took out patents for Virginia. But while the patent itself was drawn to a common form, it did not meet the New England conditions. First, the Plymouth settlement was so remote from any other settled colony or place that the Pilgrims were able to establish their own independent government without regard to any higher authority that might eventually be decided on for all New England; and, secondly, their colony was occupied not by tenants and servants of the English promoters, as was the case in Virginia, but by partners in the enterprise, who took no orders from their fellow partners in London. In reality, as far as the lands they held in America were concerned, both were tenants of the Council for New England. Then, too, it must be remembered that by 1622 the organization of the merchants had begun to disintegrate. Its members had broken with Weston and bought out his share of the stock. They were beginning to split into factions. Many, who took a business man's view of the whole affair and wanted some return on their money, had withdrawn from the partnership and others were threatening to do the same. In consequence those actually in charge were becoming fewer and fewer in number—Sherley, Pocock, Coulson, Collier, Thornell, and Keene—and even they were "much disheartened among themselves through many cross occurrents, especially in respect of a great loss sustained by a ship then lately taken and pillaged by the French,"[1] etc., and by the poor success of the Pilgrim plantation as a commercial venture. Thus the people of Plymouth were being thrown more and more on their own resources.

At this juncture John Peirce, thinking perhaps that both the time and the occasion were favorable, took the opportunity to perfect the conditions under which the patent had been issued and to obtain the conversion of the indenture into a more formal grant, an arrangement the terms of the indenture entitled him to make at any time within seven years.[2] First, he caused "letters of association" to be made out, legalizing the status of those who had been accepted as his "Associates," and sent one copy to the Pilgrims who were the

1. This ship was the *Fortune*, taken by the French, January 12, 1622, in the English Channel on its way back from the plantation. *Calendar State Papers, Colonial,* 1574–1660, p. 124 (112); Bradford, *History,* I, 268–269, and notes; Smith, *Travels and Works,* II, 260.

2. Bradford, *History,* I, 249, lines 27–36.

associates in New England. Then, on the same day, April 20, 1622, he surrendered his patent, and received back the counterfoil, which rendered the indenture null and void. He then obtained from the president and council for New England a new instrument in the form not of an indenture but of a deed poll,[1] which transformed what had hitherto been a tenancy into what was a sort of lordship or seignory. The new document was, as Bradford says, "of much larger extent" and, because it represented a perfectly proper legal process, was secured without difficulty from the council. No copy of the text is known to exist, but its terms (though not its form) were no doubt similar to those of the indenture between the council and Mason and Gorges which was perfected the August following,[2] and which created a seignory held directly of the crown instead of a tenancy held of the council as were many of the council's grants. Had the new patent been allowed to remain, the Pilgrims would have stood to Peirce as formerly they stood to the council, he holding the lands in free and common socage of the king as of the manor of East Greenwich. Bradford, shocked at the situation in which the Pilgrims found themselves placed, says that under this patent Peirce would have been able to treat the Pilgrims as his tenants and to compel them "to sue to his courts as the cheefe Lord,"[3] a legal truth perhaps but in fact rather a remote possibility. But the merchant adventurers brought pressure to bear on Peirce and compelled him to assign the patent to James Sherley, their treasurer, promising him "a valuable consideration" in return. This consideration, whatever it may have been, was never paid and Peirce carried the case into chancery, with what result is not known.[4] Probably he

1. "A *deed poll* is said to be a deed testifying that only one of the parties to the agreement hath put his seal to the same, where such party is the principal or only person, whose consent or act is necessary to the *deed*. And it is therefore a plain deed, without indenting and is used when the vendor only seals and there is no need of the vendee's sealing a counterpart, because the nature of the contract is such, as it requires no covenant from the vendee." Jacob, *Law Dictionary* (10th ed.) under "Deed."

2. *Farnham Papers*, I, 66–68. The same privilege was accorded the Pilgrims in their Cape Ann patent from Lord Sheffield.

3. Bradford, *History*, I, 306–307 and notes; *Proceedings*, American Antiquarian Society, 1867, pp. 91–93; Scott, *Joint-Stock Companies*, II, 309.

4. In the case of John Peirce, as in that of the Rev. John Lyford, the accounts given by Bradford are open to suspicion. In each the Plymouth historian has presented what are clearly garbled stories, demonstrably unfair to the two men. Peirce's account of the transaction, as contained in his Chancery Bill, need not necessarily be accepted as an unbiased statement in order to charge Bradford with

died without having received any compensation. The former patent of 1621 was restored to full validity and until 1630 this patent furnished the only title that the Pilgrims had to their lands and the only right which they had in law to exist as a self-governing community.

The business side of the undertaking was certainly not encouraging and it would have been little short of a miracle if, under the circumstances, it had been so. Many of the merchants were estranged by the extreme religious opinions held by the Pilgrims—condemned as pernicious by the ecclesiastical authorities in England—and they were confirmed in their dislikes by the complaints of returning settlers, who inveighed against both the country itself and the practices of the Separatists.[1] They lost confidence in the Pilgrims as business partners, because the latter spent too much

pretty deliberate misrepresentation. In the bill Peirce says nothing of the reasons why he secured the patent of 1622 or of the 500*li* demanded as compensation, upon which Bradford lays so much stress, but he does tell a straightforward story and gives a great deal of new information. The facts as he states them are as follows. In 1621 conditions in the colony were very bad and the merchants, discouraged, divided among themselves and without funds, turned to Peirce for help. Peirce says that James Sherley and four or five others sent Robert Cushman to persuade him to provide a ship and to undertake a voyage to New England, in order to help the plantation in its distress, and they promised to recompense him for his outlay. With considerable difficulty he got a ship, stocked it with passengers, provisions, and goods, part of which the merchants provided, and twice, once in October, 1621, and again in January, 1622, tried to cross the ocean, but each time was forced to return. The merchants blaming him for these failures, which involved them in further loss, sued a writ out of the court of admiralty and placed him and the ship under arrest. They charged him not only with the losses of the voyage but also with "some supposed unjust dealing touching the said plantation and untruely pretended that your Orator had not fulfilled his bargain but had broken some covenants and donne great wrong unto them." At Portsmouth, where he was arrested, Peirce could not get bail, so his brother Richard gave bond for 600*li*, which secured his release and he returned to London. From this time forward, the merchants, through his brother Richard, tried to persuade him to give up the patent, promising to deal "bountifully" with him. But he refused. Then they brought pressure to bear on Richard (just what hold the merchants had on the latter does not appear) and finally, because his ship and goods were "under arrest," he yielded and under compulsion assigned the patent to Sherley, on pretence of a valuable consideration (perhaps the 500*li*), which was never paid. After a year's delay, he struck back, first offering to submit the case to arbitration, then appealing to the king, and finally, these attempts coming to nothing, carrying the case into chancery. What Peirce sued for was recompense for his losses in money and reputation, and payment of the full value of his patent, "according as it was then worth when it was taken from your Orator." Regarding the outcome we know nothing. *New England Historical and Genealogical Register*, 67, pp. 147–153.

1. Bradford, *History*, I, 362–367.

time "in discoursing, arguing, and consulting" and not enough in working and performing the conditions agreed on.[1] They were disheartened not only by their own losses and the unfortunate outcome of Peirce's voyages, but also by the complete failure of two Pilgrim ventures, involving the loss of the *Little James*[2] and the collapse of the fishing experiment at Cape Ann, about which something will be said later. Consequently, finding themselves out of pocket, with money going out and nothing coming in, they refused to make any further advances, stopped sending supplies, and left the colonists to shift for themselves.

Fortunately for the people of Plymouth at this juncture, local conditions were improving. Garden plots had been assigned very early and now in 1624 permanent allotments were made of one acre each, in order that each man might raise enough corn to supply the needs of his own family.[3] This important change came about in this way. When it became evident that nothing more was to be expected from England, the planters, says Bradford, "made suite to the governor to have some portion of land given them for continuance, and not by yearly lotte, for by that means, that which the more industrious had brought into good culture (by much pains) one year came to leave it the nexte, and often another might injoye it; so as the dressing of their lands were the more sleighted over and to lese profite. Which being well considered, their request was granted."[4] Thus a noteworthy advance was made toward private ownership of land, a forward step which, however, was not completed until 1632, when lots farther from the town for meadow and pasture were distributed to meet the needs of the expanding settlement.

In the year 1625 came the final break with the London merchants,

1. Bradford, *History*, I, 233.
2. The *Little James* was a pinnace built for the adventurers and sent over in 1623 under Emmanuel Altham, captain, and John Bridge in immediate charge. Of the voyage over Bridge wrote to Sherley, "No man shall mak me venter to sea againe with men upon the sam conditions, for they car not whitch end went forwardes." The vessel was three months and two days on the voyage, and seven days in fog. After its arrival, it was sent to the Maine coast on a fishing voyage and at Damariscove went on the rocks. Bridge and two men were drowned, April 10, 1624. The loss fell not on the Pilgrims but on the merchant adventurers and only served to increase the factional discontent. *Proceedings*, American Antiquarian Society, 1867, p. 88; *Proceedings*, Massachusetts Historical Society, 44, pp. 178–182; 61, pp. 148–151.
3. *Plymouth Colony Records*, I, 5 b; Bradford, *History*, I, 346–349.
4. *Ibid.*, I, 372.

whose failure to receive any appreciable profit from their investment led not only to depression and discord but to such a decline in the value of the stocks as to render them of little or no value in the market. Hence the company could raise no more funds. When this became fully known to the leaders in the colony and they realized that nothing more could come to them out of London, they sent Miles Standish over the water to see if he could not get some help from the Council for New England. But the times were unpropitious. The war was on with France, Gorges was either at Dieppe or absorbed in his military duties at Plymouth, a plague was devastating the City, and the council had ceased for the time being to hold its meetings. Trade was dead and money so scarce that Standish had to pay fifty per cent for the £150 that he succeeded in borrowing. But he was able to talk matters over with some of the merchants and so to come to a preliminary understanding regarding their future relations.[1] Therefore, when the next year the Pilgrims, who had fully made up their minds to buy out their London partners, sent over Isaac Allerton to complete the transaction, he found the way in a measure prepared. But even so, Allerton accomplished his task "with much adoe and no small trouble" and only after negotiations which lasted from October 26 to November 15, 1626, was he able to sign an agreement on the latter date, whereby the Pilgrims bound themselves to buy the shares for £1800, to be paid at the rate of £200 a year for nine years, and, in addition, to take over the debt of the company, which had been reduced from £1400 to £600.

This was a very heavy sum for the poor colony to carry and the way the difficulty was met shows considerable business ingenuity. With the buying out of the merchants, the dual system of management was brought to an end and the entire control of the undertaking was centered in the colony in America. The joint-stock and the colony became one and Plymouth in form though not in law became a joint-stock corporation.[2] Assets and debts were now di-

1. *Ibid.*, I, 436–438; "Letter Book," p. 58.
2. The "generality" or stock holders of this de facto corporation consisted of all the adult males in the colony who wished to join and share in the stock. They were the "purchasers" making up the new partnership, now become quasi-corporate in character. Fifty-three of these were in Plymouth and five in England—Sherley, Beauchamp, Hatherly, Andrews, and Thomas. The fifty-three in the colony were known as the "Old Comers." *Plymouth Colony Records*, II, 4–5, 177; Bradford, "Letter Book," pp. 47–48, 70–73.

vided among the planters—the "purchasers," of whom fifty-three were in the colony and five in England—the former, the assets, consisting of the land and the stock, that is, cows, goats, swine, etc.; the latter, the debts, of £1800 to be paid to the merchants and £600 to the company's creditors. A share of the assets would come to twenty acres with a certain proportion of livestock. Single men were allowed one share each, heads of families were allowed as many shares as there were members in each family. Servants were given no shares unless the master so pleased. As the livestock was limited, one cow and two goats were assigned to every six persons. Thus a share in the new corporation consisted of twenty acres of land plus one sixth of a cow and one third of a goat—the land being in addition to what was granted in 1623–1624, and the animals, of course, being held in common. These—land and livestock—formed the collateral for the debt.[1]

But the Plymouth planters had no money with which to pay for their shares; therefore Governor Bradford and others from among the leading members of the colony took counsel together and decided to form a partnership or holding company for the purpose of managing the trade of the colony for a certain number of years, until the total indebtedness was paid off. During this time each shareholder was to pay three bushels of corn or six pounds of tobacco. Then when the whole was paid and the colony set free, the holding members would "returne the trade to the generalitie again at the end of the term." Thus eight men—Bradford, Standish, Allerton, Winslow, Brewster, Howland, Alden, and Prence—held themselves responsible for the debt of the colony, and with them were associated in England, Sherley, Beauchamp, Andrews, and Hatherly,[2] who had been of the London company and were in

1. *Plymouth Colony Records*, XII, 9–13. At the end of ten years the surviving cattle, together with half the increase, were to be redistributed—the other half of the increase remaining with the past owners. Altogether, there were divided among the family groups 11 cows, 2 steers, 1 bull, 22 "shee" goats, 1 calf, and 2 calves "earnestly expected." There is no record of any "hee" goats. It is difficult to say why no distribution was made of the pigs and chickens observed by John Smith in 1624 and frequently mentioned in the *Records* after 1630 (for example, XI, 15–16). The pigs may have died or been slaughtered and the chickens may have been recently imported. The holding of stock in common could not have lasted very long.

2. Hatherly spent some time in the colony and served as assistant, treasurer, etc. He was chosen as a commissioner of the United Colonies, and was one of the council of war. He lived in Scituate in 1623 and again in 1632–1666. It is evident from Bradford's "Letter Book" (pp. 29–34) that there was a party among the London merchant adventurers possessed of a strongly religious and perhaps Separatist feel-

sympathy with the aims of the Separatists. This arrangement was to last for six years.[1]

These eight men were to have a complete monopoly of the trade of the colony and the exclusive use of its boats—two pinnaces and a shallop—together with control of its stock of furs, skins, beads, corn, hatchets, and knives. Their source of profit would be trade with the Indians for beaver, otter, mink, and other furs, fishing for alewives, herring, halibut, bass, salmon, trout, shad, cod, and mackerel, and the raising and sale of corn. They entered into trading relations, by way of the Manomet portage, with the Indians of Buzzard's Bay, with the Dutch at New Amsterdam, and with the natives of the northern coast as far as the Kennebec and Penobscot[2] rivers. They sent Winslow in 1632 to investigate the possibilities of the Connecticut valley, and they may have attempted to open up a trade with Virginia, but that is very doubtful.[3] In order to prevent the settlers about the Piscataqua from monopolizing the Kennebec trade, they obtained from the Council for New England in 1627 a patent—the privileges of which are not known—and erected there a trading house, well up the river on the site of the present city of Augusta, and made it a post furnished with commodities for both summer and winter, suitable for trade with the Indians and with the fishermen off shore.[4] The Kennebec concession was afterward materially enlarged by the Bradford patent of 1630.[5] The Pilgrims had some

ing, and that this group, led by Sherley, was antagonistic to the purely business group. A number of the merchant adventurers are known by name, but of only a few can any further information be obtained.

1. Bradford, *History*, II, 8–9, 28–30. The best account, in popular form, of the business dealings of the Pilgrim colony may be found in Usher, *The Pilgrims and their History*. Osgood and Scott also treat of the subject.

2. The Indian trade on the Kennebec proved so profitable that by 1633 the undertakers were able to send a large invoice of beaver to England—"thirty-three hundred and sixty pounds weight and much of it coat beaver which yielded twenty shillings per pound and some of it above." This enabled them to go a long way toward paying their debts in England. In 1634 the amount was 3738 pounds; from 1631 to 1636, it rose to 12,530 pounds of beaver and 1136 pounds of otter. Bradford, *History*, II, 172–173, 229; Winthrop, *Journal* (Original Narratives Series), I, 131.

3. Mr. Ford's statement to that effect (Bradford, *History*, II, 43, note 3) is not borne out by the evidence cited (*Journal of the House of Burgesses of Virginia*, 1619–1659, p. 46). He may have had in mind the vessel that came from Virginia in 1631 (Winthrop, *Journal*, I, 64).

4. Bradford, *History*, II, 40–41; Burrage, *Beginnings of Colonial Maine*, pp. 185–188, and map, p. 186. This map is more clearly reproduced in Bradford, *History*, II, 176.

5. Note the Pilgrim interest also in Machias, Burrage, *Beginnings*, pp. 266–267.

interest also in a trading post on the Penobscot, now Castine, which they acquired through the activities of a roving, unscrupulous trader of the day, Edward Astley, who had been recommended by Allerton and outfitted by the London merchant adventurers. Astley had obtained from the Council for New England a license to trade in that region. Bradford calls him "a very profane young man," who had for years lived among the Indians and had acquired both their language and their primitive habits. Astley got into trouble for trading in firearms and ammunition among the Indians, was arrested, and shipped back to England. Thus the Pilgrims came into possession of the post.[1]

These various enterprises were conducted by the undertakers with commendable energy. Large stocks of beaver, corn, wampum, and lumber were accumulated, some of which was used for barter in New England but more for shipment overseas in order to liquidate the colony's indebtedness. Allerton was sent over in 1627 for the purpose of arranging a market and again in 1628 to buy supplies and trading goods.[2] He proved anything but a satisfactory agent. Whether he was deliberately dishonest is doubtful; he may have been no more than unbusinesslike and careless. He combined his agency for the Pilgrims with buying on his own account—a dual activity, in which Bradford thought he had more of an eye to his own advantage than to that of the colony. He borrowed money at what Bradford thought were ruinous rates of interest, as they were, and in his dealings with the English factors ran up accounts that put the Pilgrim undertakers heavily in debt. In fact when in 1631 a reckoning was called for, the latter found that they were more deeply in debt than ever and they became extremely suspicious that they had been dishonorably treated by Allerton acting in combina-

1. Bradford, *History*, II, 106–108; "Letter Book," pp. 72–73; *Proceedings*, American Antiquarian Society, 1867, p. 108; *Calendar State Papers, Colonial*, 1574–1660, p. 140 (40–41); *Acts Privy Council, Colonial*, I, §289; *Proceedings*, Massachusetts Historical Society, 41, p. 493. The Kennebec claims of the Plymouth colony extended from Casco Bay to Pemaquid and north from the ocean to Carratink Falls. The colony established there a court of law and for over twenty years had a "body of laws" for the protection of the region. In 1661 it sold out to a group of Boston merchants. For the early history of the territory see Sprague, *Journal of Maine History*, III, 15–18, 83–88, 98–100; British Museum, Additional Manuscripts, 15,488; New York Public Library, Kennebec Papers, 1754–1756, in which is a plan of the region, showing the "Late Colony of New Plymouth" and its claims on the Kennebec.

2. Bradford, *History*, II, 59–60.

tion with Sherley and Hatherly.[1] That which they bought seemed always to come to more than that which they sold, so that their former debt of £600 had risen to £5000. Bradford had a very poor opinion of Allerton who, both in England and in his various enterprises on the New England coast[2] appears to have dealt very shabbily with his fellow Pilgrims and to have gone ahead far too often without counting the cost. Bradford says, perhaps not quite fairly, that they were "hoodwincte," "abused in their simplicity, and no better than bought and sold." Finally, in 1631 the undertakers got rid of Allerton, whose accounts were so badly mixed up that they could not be disentangled, and some time after that date he left the colony.[3]

With the shaking off of Allerton as the agent dealing with the English factors, the business concerns of the colony became more prosperous. Its opportunities were increased greatly by the settlement of Massachusetts Bay, which occurred in 1630. The colony began to grow in outward estate, larger extents of arable were prepared for corn and larger pastures were provided for cattle. Cattle and maize and wheat[4] became the leading staples and as they tended to rise rapidly in selling value the returns were very advantageous. More people came in, men scattered along the shores about the bay, seeking new farms and wider fields of action. Contacts with the newcomers to the northward became more frequent and a general expansion took place. The old town of Plymouth was, as Brad-

1. *Ibid.*, 129–132.

2. For Allerton at Machias, Burrage, *Beginnings*, p. 267, and for additional comments on his character, *Proceedings*, Massachusetts Historical Society, 47, p. 343.

3. It is difficult to believe that Allerton was a Separatist, though he must have conformed, outwardly at least, or he would not have been entrusted by the Pilgrims with so many important missions. After he left the colony he went first to Marblehead, then to New Amsterdam, and finally to New Haven. He owned a trading vessel, which plied back and forth between the last two ports, as in 1643 and 1646 he is recorded as being, in different months, in both places. His loose business methods pursued him to the end for, in 1659, after his death his son Isaac refused to administer his estate, because he found it "so dissipated that it would be both troublesome and chargable to gather it in." Allerton was interred in the old burying ground on the Green in New Haven. He had united with the First Church there and was assigned a pew in the second seat in the "cross seats" at the end. Winthrop, *Journal*, I, 94; *Plymouth Colony Records*, II, 133; *New Haven Colony Records*, I, 302; *New Haven Town Records*, I, 410; *Dictionary of American Biography*, II, 216–217 (a much too flattering account).

4. "They have tried our English corn [wheat] at New Plymouth plantation, so that all our several grains will grow here very well and have a fitting soil for their nature." *New England Plantation* (1630), p. 7 (Humphrey's Tracts, no. 11).

ford says, "left very thin and in a short time almost desolate."[1] Though the six year period had elapsed, the undertakers, acting by order of the governor and assistants, continued in control of the trade from year to year until 1639, when Bradford and his partners gave warning that they would hold it no longer.[2] But the relations with the factors in England, to whom they still owed £1200, were not finally terminated until 1648 and then only through the intermediation of commissioners from Massachusetts Bay and at a heavy loss to the undertakers. To pay off the last £400 Winslow and Prence sold their homes, Alden and Standish three hundred acres of land, and Bradford a farm. The final settlement reflects little credit upon the factors in England, for they clearly made good, at the expense of the colony, the losses incurred in their various unfortunate ventures and speculations. "From the first agreement to pay £1800 to the final closing of the transaction," says Bradford's editor, "the record shows the Plymouth people passively submitting to a manifest fraud perpetrated on them." It certainly had been a "tedious and troublesome business, unprofitable to all," and the Pilgrims, deficient in business sagacity but strong in honesty and high moral purpose, were the sufferers.[3]

During these years the legal right of the Pilgrims to administer a civil government had rested on no certain foundation. In the beginning they had been literally alone in a region occupied by no other Englishmen than themselves, and had been without a friendly hand to aid them, except for the distant fishermen in northern waters, with whom they could come in touch only by a voyage of considerable length and danger. They had come to America, as Bradford says, with "no friends to wellcome them nor inns to entertaine or refresh their weather beaten bodys, no houses or much less townes to repaire too, to seek for succoure."[4] Though they were but a minority of the company on the *Mayflower* and in the colony, they were a homogeneous group bound together in covenant with God, a compact and united congregation for the management of prudential as well as ecclesiastical affairs. They had no charter of government, but there was little danger that they would be ousted from

1. "Likely to be dispeopled," *Plymouth Colony Records*, I, 17 (2). Bradford expressed his regret in a poem, *Proceedings*, Massachusetts Historical Society, 1869–1870, pp. 478–482.

2. *Plymouth Colony Records*, I, 31, 126.

3. Bradford, *History*, II, 332–333.   4. *Ibid.*, I, 155.

the lands upon which they were living. They were familiar with church government as ordained by all Separatist groups, in which ministers were chosen by their congregations and all authority was vested in the assembly of church members, and they naturally and readily applied the same polity to affairs of a civil order. As an expedient to meet a temporary emergency they entered at the very beginning into a compact with each other to covenant and combine together as a political as well as a religious community, for the better ordering and preserving of peace and justice and the furthering of the ends for which the movement was begun. This agreement was the famous Mayflower Compact.[1]

The Pilgrims were a small group—but the dominating group— within the larger body of passengers on board, and they realized the necessity, if their religious integrity were to be preserved, of keeping in their own hands the entire control of affairs. Opposition to their leadership had already begun to show itself on the voyage over, and they thought it only a matter of ordinary precaution to take such steps as would check discontent and mutiny and assure their ascendancy in the colony. Before going ashore, where the rebellious members of the company might become less manageable than on shipboard, they drafted a solemn agreement, which was signed in the cabin of the *Mayflower* by forty-one adults, of whom nineteen were from Leyden, sixteen were from London, four were servants, and two were sailors.[2] These men promised all due obedience and submission to whatever laws, ordinances, acts, constitutions, and offices should be thought most meet and convenient for the general good of the colony. It was a preliminary understanding, suitable for any particular plantation, necessary because some on

1. The text of the Mayflower Compact was first printed in Mourt's *Relation*, London, 1622. The names of the signers, which Bradford omits, are in Morton's *Memorial* (ed. 1855), p. 26, reprinted in Hutchinson, *History of Massachusetts Bay* (Mayo ed.), II, 349. The religious counterpart of the compact, that is, the ecclesiastical covenant, is given, probably in abstract, in Bradford, *History*, I, 20–21. "They shooke off this yoake of Anti-christian bondage, And as the Lords free people, joyned themselves (by a covenant of the Lord) into a church estate, in the felowship of the Gospell, to walke in all his wayes, made known, or to be made known unto them (according to their best endeavours) whatsoever it should cost them, the Lord assisting them." See Walker, *Creeds and Platforms of Congregationalism*, p. 83, note 1.

2. There were nine who did not sign at all—all servants except James Chilton (probably too ill, as he died soon after). Henry Samson did not sign, as he was probably under age, but his uncle Edward Tilley did. Probably the servants who did not sign were sick. All the responsible people appended their names to the agreement.

board had shown a disposition to break away from Pilgrim control, declaring that when they came ashore "they would use their owne libertie, for none had power to command them, the patente they had being for Virginia and not for New England, which belonged to an other government, with which the Virginia Company had nothing to doe."[1] In drawing up the compact the Pilgrims were taking advantage of the privilege accorded them in their patent of forming a government until the company at home should provide one for them. Legally speaking, they should not have taken this step until the Peirce patent of 1621 had been secured, but in 1620 the need was imperative and gave them ample warrant for their action. They were carrying out Robinson's injunction at parting that they become "a Body Politic using among [themselves] Civil Government, choosing those that would promote the common good and yielding unto them all due honour and obedience."[2]

This civil version of a church government—a voluntary agreement of no legal validity—was the basis of their political organization until the receipt of the Peirce patent in 1621, which granted the Pilgrims and their associates the right to adopt such by-laws and ordinances as were for their proper government, the same to be administered by such officers as by most voices they should elect and choose to put in execution. The Plymouth settlement was not a state but a plantation and is so called in the Peirce patent and in Bradford's *History*. The compact signed in the cabin of the *Mayflower* is a plantation covenant, providing for local government in all that concerned the prudential affairs of the community. It was based on the social compact idea, which Parson Wise defended, in his disquisition on the compact or covenant as the basis of a state, in saying that "all men naturally free and equal, going about voluntarily to bring themselves into a political body, must needs enter into divers covenants," and which the petitioners of 1637 had in mind when they said that "all bodies politic are composed of voluntary members" and that "no commonweale can be founded but by free consent."[3] The settlement, as recognized later by the Council for New England, was the first of many similar plantations designed by Gorges to be set up in New England under a common central government, with a governor general at its head. The erec-

1. Bradford, *History*, I, 189.   2. Burgess, *John Robinson*, p. 255.
3. Wise, *A Vindication of the Government of New England Churches* (Boston, 1717), pp. 44–45; *Hutchinson Papers*, I, 76, 80.

tion of such a government and the appointment of a governor over all was in the mind of Gorges from the beginning and was an ever-present reality to the people settled in the various plantations in New England, until the coming of Andros, an appointee not of the council but of the crown, marked the first attempt to carry out the plan. But by that time Massachusetts Bay had become too powerful and the attempt was a failure.[1]

Nothing could have been more simple than the form of political organization which the Pilgrims set up for the management of the plantation and the maintenance of peace and order. There was no need of anything more. These people were knit together in a sacred bond and covenant of the Lord and to violate this covenant was against their conscience because by virtue of it they held themselves "strictly tied to all care of each others good and of the whole by everyone and so mutually."[2] As they chose their ministers so they chose their governors, by vote of the whole body of properly quali-fied persons. There is some reason to believe that they had already selected Deacon Carver as their governor (they were authorized to do this under the Wyncop patent) on the *Speedwell* after they left Southampton, for before they sailed he had been entrusted with their preparations for departure, and Bradford speaks of his elec-tion, after the signing of the Mayflower Compact, as a "confirma-tion." Carver continued to serve as governor until his death in April, 1621, when Bradford was chosen to succeed him. During the years from 1621 to 1656, with the exception of five years when others were elected, Bradford was named governor thirty times, and when in office exercised a kindly though almost an autocratic authority. There was in practice nothing popular about the Plymouth system. The governors and their assistants, of which there was one at first, five after 1624, and seven after 1633, were all chosen by the freemen of the community—as the members came to be called after 1626—who may have thought they were exercising full freedom of choice. In point of fact, however, their choice was little more than a ratifi-cation of government by the best men. The dispensing of justice

1. Ample provision for the appointment of such a governor general is made in the charter of 1620 incorporating the Council for New England (Thorpe, *Charters,* 3, p. 1833). Such appointment is referred to in the Bradford patent of 1630, which authorized the colony to secure incorporation if it could and to pass laws provided they were not contrary to the laws of England or to "the frame of governmente by the [Council for New England] hereafter to be established," *ibid.,* pp. 1844–1845.

2. Bradford, *History,* I, 76.

and the general oversight of affairs lay entirely in the hands of the governor and council, for the freemen were called together only at the wish of the governor and with his consent and then but seldom and only for action on weighty matters. Bradford was the "government" and the arbiter of the destinies of the colony. It is doubtful if anything was ever done against his wishes or advice and one can well believe that the burden resting on him of service and responsibility was a heavy one. He was undoubtedly sincere in the desire which he several times expressed to be rid of the office. There was nothing arbitrary or selfish in his attitude toward the office, but he was the ruler of the colony and in important crises bent the people to his will.

After 1626 colony and corporation were one and the same and the whole organization took on more and more the form of a chartered government. This was true in fact but never in law. The Pilgrims were never able to obtain a charter of their own from the crown, though they ardently desired to do so and made many attempts and spent much money to that end, both at this time, perhaps in 1664, certainly in 1683, and again after the fall of Andros in 1689, when the application to the king was renewed but without success.[1] The colony's right to exist as a self-governing state rested always on the Mayflower Compact, buttressed by the Peirce patent of 1621, until that was supplemented, perhaps we should say confirmed, by the later patent obtained by Allerton for Bradford and his associates

1. *Plymouth Colony Records*, V, 62; VI, 36–37, 57, 99, 259, 260; *Calendar State Papers, Colonial*, 1685–1688, §1389; 1689–1692, §183. On the effort of 1629–1630 to obtain a charter from the king, when Bradford prepared a petition to be laid before the Privy Council, possibly containing the terms of the patent desired, see Sherley's letter (Bradford, *History*, II, 72). Sherley was sure that the patent could be secured, saying that when this was done the colony would be complete and "might bear schuch sway and government as were fit for your ranke and place that God hath called you unto.' Bradford was probably encouraged by the grant of a charter to the Massachusetts Bay Company the year before and knew that Warwick was helping the Puritans and was willing to help the Pilgrims. Warwick had obtained the Bradford land patent of 1630 and his failure to get a charter and so to complete his work is somewhat difficult to explain. Sherley says that Allerton bungled things as usual, attending the Privy Council day after day but never getting a hearing or a chance to present Bradford's petition and finally being obliged to come away leaving things in the hands of a solicitor. Sherley hints ("Letter Book," pp. 70–71) that money was at the bottom of the failure, the colony not being able to afford the fees, and the lord high treasurer, Weston, later Earl of Portland, being unwilling to waive them or to forego the payment of customs, as the colony desired, on account of the bad state of the royal finances.

In 1664 the "body of freemen of this corporation" voted that an address be sent from the Council for New England, with the aid of both Gorges and Warwick.[1] This patent, signed by Warwick as president of the council is commonly called the "Old Charter" and was issued January 13, 1630.[2] It granted no powers of government and added nothing to the legal strength of the colony on the governmental side, but it did define, and for the first time, the boundaries of the colony—which Winslow, who knew more about the back country than anyone else, must have carefully drawn up—and it confirmed the title to the lands about the Kennebec and conferred upon the colony free liberty of trade and fishing. At last the Pilgrims were proprietors of both soil and jurisdiction. The privileges of this patent Bradford shared with the original purchasers—the Old Comers—and he kept the document in his own possession until March, 1641, when with the consent of the other undertakers he surrendered it into the hands of the whole court—the freemen of the corporation of New Plymouth.[3] By the court it was returned to Bradford for safety and is today in the archives at Plymouth.

Interesting as the Old Charter is, it was of little value as a bulwark of defense or a palladium of liberty. Under it the Pilgrims gained no legal or civil powers that they had not exercised before, except in the one matter of a more exact definition of their bound-

the king for the further confirmation of the patent, but it is not clear that the address was to include a request for a charter. More likely it covered no more than a confirmation of the colony's title to its lands as defined by the patent of 1630 (*Plymouth Colony Records*, IV, 62).

In 1680 the colony received a letter from the king promising "to enlarge our patent liberties and privileges." The general court immediately resolved to send over agents "to waite his pleasure for the compleating of the said gracious tender to us" (*ibid.*, VI, 36–37). But the Lords of Trade, to whom the application was made, refused the request on the ground that whenever the king granted away his rights of government it was almost impossible to enforce the acts of trade (*Collections*, Massachusetts Historical Society, 4th series, V, 74, 91, 93; Toppan, *Edward Randolph*, I, 185, 209; III, 265–267, 317; Jacobsen, *William Blathwayt*, pp. 124–126).

There are no Plymouth records from October, 1686, to June, 1689, when the colony resumed its government and found itself in an "unsettled estate, destitute of government and exposed to the ill consequents thereof," as its title was based on prescription only. The first general court authorized Governor Thomas Hinckley to send congratulations to the new king and queen and to ask for a confirmation of their rights and privileges (*Plymouth Colony Records*, VI, 208–209). This Hinckley did, in the name and behalf of "the oldest colony in America" (*Calendar State Papers, Colonial*, 1689–1692, §183). Probably no answer was ever returned.

1. "Letter Book," p. 70.
2. Hazard, *State Papers*, I, 298–304; Thorpe, *Charters*, 3, pp. 1841–1846; *Farnham Papers*, I, 108–116; Bradford, *History*, II, 69–72.
3. *Plymouth Colony Records*, V, 4, 5, 10–11.

aries. Their title to govern themselves rested on no more secure foundation than the usage of sixty-six years, "according to the free liberties of a free people," as the code of 1685 expressed it,[1] for they had continued to exist and to govern themselves, year in and year out, without interruption or demur from England, "graciously owned and acknowledged therein" as a legal government by the king, particularly after the Restoration.[2] During this long period the colony had steadily enlarged its political functions and had taken on a more elaborate governmental form.[3] After 1626 the simplicity of the early system gave way to a greater complexity, both in the appearance of the colony and the nature of the central administration. Individuals and families scattered in search of ranging ground for their cattle and began to take up lots and build homes away from Plymouth. Thus new towns came into existence—Duxbury (1636–1637), Scituate (1636), Sandwich (1638), Yarmouth (1639), and Taunton (1640). In 1643 there were ten such towns and in consequence a system of representation took the place of the old meeting of the freemen, which had been held yearly at Plymouth. Plymouth the plantation had become New Plymouth the colony, the mother of plantations. The parent church had begot other churches, an event which Bradford greeted with grave apprehension, as involving the ruin of the churches of God in New England, because provoking the displeasure of the Lord against them.[4] The Pilgrim ideal of a single covenanted body of Christians, isolated from the dangers and depravities of the world about them, had proved impossible of realization.

1. Bradford, *History*, II, 238; *Calendar State Papers, Colonial*, 1689–1692, §183, "By prescription according to Coke, that oracle of the laws."
2. *Plymouth Colony Records*, VI, 36, 209.
3. Technically Plymouth was not a "colony" during these years, as it had no title from the crown. Yet it called itself a colony and was always recognized as such. In Bradford's letter of 1623 (*American Historical Review*, VIII, 298) it is so designated and the word is used over and over again in the Plymouth records (VI, 16, 20, 68, 70, 175, 179, etc.). But as a colony Plymouth was neither royal, proprietary, nor corporate, and the king had no control over its affairs, in no way defining by charter his relations with it. He occasionally sent letters to it, expressing his satisfaction, and promising to do something, and thus gave to it a qualified recognition. These letters were generally read at the general court and were looked upon as conveying a quasi-legal sanction. The colonial status of Plymouth is an interesting question in political science. Probably we had best call it a de facto corporate colony. As it had ceased to exist before England put the final touches on her colonial policy, it was never a colony in the eighteenth century meaning of the term.
4. Bradford, *History*, II, 153.

In 1636 the colony had advanced so far along the road to statehood as to require a revision and enlargement of its laws and ordinances, and a code, known as the Great Fundamentals, was drawn up,[1] which as printed in 1671 opened with the following words: "Wee the Associates of the Colony of New Plymouth, coming hither as free-born subjects of the Kingdome of England, endowed with all and singular the Priviledges belonging to such: Being assembled Do Enact, Ordain and Constitute" (the laws that follow in eight paragraphs). The code closes thus: "these foregoing Orders and Constitutions are so Fundamentally Essential to the just Rights, Liberties, Common Good and Special End of this Colony, as that they shall and ought to be inviolably preserved."

Thus the single plantation of 1620 had become a well developed and organized political community, with governor, deputy governor, and assistants, elected yearly by the freemen of the corporation, in their meeting at the mother town. Laws were enacted at the general court, made up of two representatives from each town, chosen by the freemen of the town, together with the governor and assistants sitting as a single house. There can be little doubt that the Plymouth colony was patterning itself after the Massachusetts model. The important position to which the colony had attained received ample confirmation, when in 1643 it was invited to become one of the four colonies that brought into existence the New England Confederation. It had gradually become, partly by natural adaptation and partly by the influence of example, an institution that in all essential particulars was identical with a regular corporate colony. Probably Bradford and his successors actually worked out the very same conditions of government that he and Winslow sought to obtain from the crown when they petitioned for a charter in 1629, and consequently the constitutional course of the colony after 1630 was pretty much the same as it would have been had the charter been obtained. This policy was successful as long as the skies were serene, but with the enforcement by the mother country of a new colonial and commercial programme after 1660 and 1675 and the rise to dominance of the colony's northern neighbor, Massachusetts, the want of a legal right to exist proved its ultimate undoing. Despite all its leaders could do to ward off the evil day, Plymouth

1. *Ibid.*, 238–240; Hazard, *State Papers*, I, 408–410.

was annexed to Massachusetts in 1691 and its identity became merged in that of the larger and more powerful province.

In the story of American colonization the Pilgrim plantation at Plymouth occupies a place apart from the normal colonizing process, in that its origin and purpose were entirely out of touch with the features of settlement characteristic of the time. Instead of a company of hardened and undisciplined adventurers, such as in every case thus far had accompanied the earlier efforts from Maine to the Amazon, we have a small group of simple, inexperienced folk, unaccustomed to the rough and tumble of sea life and perilous adventure and unfamiliar with the ways of the world and its manifold complications. Instead of pursuing booty or gold or profit for the sake of profit—for they wanted nothing more than comfortable maintenance and freedom from debt—they eschewed all worldliness, self-glory, and the predatory pursuit of wealth and made their main purpose in life the seeking the kingdom of heaven and its rewards. To such a people the things of this world were of no more than temporary account, and nothing held larger place in their thoughts than did their sense of responsibility to God, the community, and each other. In their simplicity and humble-mindedness they had no other aim than to live decently and righteously and in accord with what they believed to be God's purpose in directing their course. To this end they rejected all ecclesiastical traditions and accretions due to human experience and paid no attention to human desires and instincts as distinguished from those that were divine, or to the demands of human nature in other than the ordinary needs of human existence. They rejected some of the richest of human manifestations, in literature, art, music, and the drama, as in no way belonging to the world to come, and could find no congenial place for the higher diversions of the human soul in an atmosphere dominated by the doctrines of election, predestination, imputed righteousness, and freedom of the will.

Hence in all save his religious sincerity the Pilgrim never rose far above the ordinary round of daily toil and the meeting of the ends of material existence. His confidence in his own sanctification led to a certain self-righteousness and assertive faith in his calling that sometimes found expression in an attitude of partisanship and of disapproval of the world around him. But in his outlook on life and morals, the Pilgrim was freer than were his Massachusetts brethren, who took too little account of human frailties and ascribed to a corrupt and Satan-infested mind acts and thoughts that were either harmless in themselves or today would call for medical not theological attention. The Pilgrim sublimated pain and discomfort into a moral discipline and frowned on ease and pleasure as obstacles in the path to heaven. He made this world a thing of dust and ashes and believed it to be his bounden duty to suffer and endure. In the face of a grim eternity his was the task to master the sinful allurements of a world doomed to destruction and in the security of his retreat to prove himself the captain of his own soul. Though the Pilgrim community lay apart in something of a backwater, away from the moving stream of American civilization, and though Pilgrim contributions to the literature and culture of America are negative, the religious organization of the Pilgrims may have had some influence upon the Massachusetts church system and it is quite possible that their practice of choosing their governors by vote of the whole body of qualified persons may have aided Roger Williams of Rhode Island, and through him Thomas Hooker of Connecticut, to develop their ideas regarding government by consent of the people and so to have played a part in the fashioning of an American institution. Two other aspects also of Pilgrim history will always hold conspicuous place in the minds of all. Never up to this time, in the great work of planting Englishmen on the shore of the New World, had there been such a group of motives at work among men as those which drove the Pilgrims to found a permanent home in the largely unoccupied lands of New England; and rarely has an example of moral righteousness been more often acclaimed as a positive influence for good upon the lives of later generations. The Pilgrim Fathers have always held and will always hold a unique place among the venerated saints of mankind.

CHAPTER XV

THE LURE OF NEWFOUNDLAND AND NOVA SCOTIA

TO the Pilgrims New England was something more than a religious refuge, it was a home also, within which would have to be met the material needs of their physical being. Its lands were expected to furnish them with the means of subsistence and its woods and waters with furs and fish for use and, as they profoundly hoped, for profit also. They needed a surplus not only to pay their just debts but to improve the condition of the community as well, and they planned to find it, in part at least, in the fishery. When King James was informed of their proposed venture and asked " 'What profit might arise from those parts,' 'twas answered 'Fishing.' To which his majesty replied, 'So God have my Soule, 'twas the Apostles owne calling.' "[1] But in their dependence on fishing as a livelihood or as furnishing a surplus commodity that might be a staple for exchange with England, the Pilgrims were without a sufficient knowledge of the run of the fish and the ways of the fishery. Plymouth, unfortunately, lay too far south for easy access to the best fishing waters and even Cape Ann, where they tried out their only important fishing experiment—for the Kennebec posts were chiefly designed for furs—was reached only after a voyage of considerable difficulty. They were never successful as fishermen and early seemed to have realized that agriculture and the fur trade were to be their more gainful forms of activity. After the break with the merchant adventurers they made but few attempts to fish for profit, either in the near-by waters or in those that lay to the northward.

The seamen and merchants of the maritime states of Europe had associated the coasts of Massachusetts, Maine, Nova Scotia, and Newfoundland with the fishery, long before these coasts had become serious objects of colonization. There, from times more remote than there are records to recount, the enterprising adventurers

1. Winslow, *Hypocrisie Unmasked*, p. 90.

of western Europe had found in these indented bays and harbors and off the islands and banks that fringed these shores a rich treasure which was as real, if less romantic, than the gold and tropical commodities that played so large a part in the imagination of the period. To these shores, from the days of Columbus and Cabot, if not earlier, had gone the fishing boats of the Portuguese, of the Basques of San Sebastian and St. Jean de Luz, of the Gascons from Bordeaux and Bayonne, of the Britons and Normans from northern France and of the English from the West Country of Devonshire and adjoining counties. In small boats, averaging about sixty tons burden, these bold fishermen had crossed the ocean and with their cargoes of cod, mackerel, and herring had found a ready sale in the maritime markets of France, Spain, Portugal, and the Mediterranean, where the lenten season and other periods of fasting created a demand far out of the ordinary for every kind of fish.[1] With hook, net, and seine, partly off shore and partly on the banks, they gathered in their treasure, using the land only for setting up their stages, flakes, and troughs, drying and salting their catch, and placing their huts, storehouses, and cook-rooms for temporary use. Only occasionally and then in small numbers did they remain in residence during the winter. For the most part they returned from year to year, a few perhaps with the idea of staying on for a considerable length of time, but even these with no thought of permanent colonization. Their interest lay in the wealth of the waters and not in the produce of the soil, and it may be doubted if even Sir Humphrey Gilbert in 1583, when on the shores of St. John's harbor he raised the English flag and took possession of Newfoundland, had any higher purpose than to establish a rendezvous for fishermen and a retreat for marauders in the conflict with Spain.[2]

Thus until the beginning of the seventeenth century, the region from Cape Cod to Labrador was but the southernmost part of that great area of the northern Atlantic—from Newfoundland through the Irish and North Seas to Iceland and beyond—in which fishing

1. Sabine, *Report on the Principal Fisheries of the American Seas* (1853), part II, pp. 35–132, is still the best account.

2. There must have been a well organized and continuous series of fishing stations along these coasts, particularly the coast of Maine, before 1620. These stations were used by hundreds of fishermen and traders, and some of them may have contained fortified buildings and warehouses that were designed more or less for permanence. Such buildings are mentioned by both Bradford and Winthrop.

was the leading industry. Fish dried and salted and packed in barrels, fish uncleaned, fresh, or green, called "corfish,"[1] carried in bulk and not in barrels, and train oil, at that time more often from the cod than the whale, to the number of 100,000 to 200,000 fish and from five to ten tons of oil to a vessel, constituted a staple commodity of an importance far outweighing as an item of food anything else in the market except grain. It was the more valuable, according to the economic ideas of the day, because it was gained solely by industry and the labor of men, without money in exchange, and at no more expense than the cost of victuals and outfit. It was a business that employed many artisans and maintained many families at home.[2] Just as at a later date explorers and traders led the westward movement in America, so in the sixteenth and seventeenth centuries explorers and fishermen were the forerunners of westward adventure in the northern waters of the Atlantic. The small decked vessel, the open rowboat, the fishing with hooks from the vessel's side, the soft fisherman's hat and his barvel or apron,[3] the hard but often rollicking life, with its proverbial good nature, genial hospitality, and generous impulse toward those in need—all these were familiar and characteristic aspects of life along the ocean frontier. Fishing more than trade with the Indians drew men on to attempt settlement, and not a navigator from Martin Pring to John Smith but mentions the fishery and lays stress upon the advantage to be derived therefrom.[4]

Bristol, in the seventeenth century, was the greatest seaport in

1. The making of dry fish was peculiar to Englishmen; the Hollanders and French took only "correfish." *Proceedings*, American Antiquarian Society, 1867, p. 67.

2. Whitbourne, "Discourse of Newfoundland," printed in part in Prowse, *Newfoundland*, and as a separate pamphlet. An abridged edition was issued in 1870 under the title *Westward Hoe for Avalon, In the New-found-land, As described by Captain Richard Whitbourne of Exmouth, Devon, 1622* (edited and illustrated by T. Whitburn).

3. Barvels are fishermen's large leather aprons. This word was in use as early as 1629 (*Massachusetts Colony Records*, I, 404) and probably very much earlier. It was known along the Maine coast in 1639 (*Documentary History of the State of Maine*, III, 171, 172, 297). It is still in local use in New England, particularly in Essex County, where fishing has been the chief source of the prosperity of the people.

4. John Smith, both in his "Description of New England" and in his "New England Trials [or Experiments]," laid great stress upon the value of the fishery. The latter work was written as early as 1618 and published in 1620. A second edition was issued in 1622. It was reprinted in Force, *Tracts*, II, in Smith, *Travels and Works*, II, 233–273, and in facsimile by John Carter Brown, 1867. The "Description" is in Smith, II, 186–229.

western England. Hakluyt was one of the prebendaries of Bristol cathedral; Popham had formerly been recorder of Bristol; and Gorges, who lived at Plymouth, had a house near Bristol and was in touch with all the southwestern maritime centers. All of these men naturally turned to Bristol and its active body of Merchant Venturers for aid and coöperation in their various undertakings. Hakluyt had been influential in persuading these Venturers to send out young Martin Pring in 1603 and Popham was able to raise among them enough subscriptions to equip a second ship, with Hanham as commander and Pring as navigator, which in 1606 reached the coast of New England. Gorges had persuaded Bristol merchants to invest in the Virginia Company of Plymouth, and at least one of these subscribed to the stock of the sister company in London, when in the year 1609, under its new charter, its books were thrown open to the public.

Bristol was alive with interest in the western voyages and was deeply concerned in all that had to do with the herring fishery.[1] Many of the merchants of the city were more or less familiar with Newfoundland, because of their early connection with Gilbert and Peckham, and considered it as lying particularly within their sphere. They felt, as said Sir William Vaughan later,[2] that "God had reserved Newfoundland for us Britains, as the next land beyond Ireland and not above nine or ten dayes saile from thence" and that "islanders should dwell in islands." With influence at court, where Walsingham, an enthusiastic friend of colonization, had been the patron of every important exploring enterprise for many years, and where Sir Francis Bacon, then solicitor general, was writing his "Discourse on the Plantation of Ireland," they determined to emulate London, their rival in trade. In 1610 they made application to the king for a charter establishing a Bristol company of their own, similar to those companies in London and Plymouth,

1. As early as 1582–1583, Thomas Aldworth and other Bristol merchants subscribed 1000 marks for a voyage of discovery, and Whiston, Aldworth, and others contributed to the Pring voyage of 1603. Aldworth's son was a great adventurer in trade and one who was successful in merchandise. He was master of the Merchant Venturers in 1609 and served in the same office later. He and Giles Elbridge (not to be confused with the Delbridges of Barnstaple), who married his niece and was his partner and executor and a warden of the Merchant Venturers, received the grant of Pemaquid, February 29, 1632, from the Council for New England, containing 12,000 acres "near the river commonly called or known by the name of Pemaquid." *Farnham Papers*, I, 165–172.

2. *The Golden Fleece*, pp. 5–6.

which the king had chartered only four years before. Their leader was Sheriff John Guy, a young and ambitious member of the Merchant Venturers, afterward alderman of Bristol and a member of parliament. With the support of Henry, Earl of Northampton, Sir Lawrence Tanfield, and Sir Francis Bacon—all in high office under government—he obtained a charter, May 2, 1610, incorporating forty-eight men as the Treasurer and the Company of the Adventurers and Planters of the City of London and Bristol for the Colony of Plantation in Newfoundland.[1] About twelve of the forty-eight patentees were of Bristol, members of the Merchant Venturers there.

This charter erected a joint-stock company of the usual type, with a treasurer, council, and generality, holding its lands as of the manor of East Greenwich, with a right of coinage and a monopoly of trade but not of fishing. The lands thus granted comprised the whole of the island of Newfoundland. The treasurer, John Slany, and the council—all London men—had their seat in that city and were vested with full powers to establish and govern such colonies as they might promote. In many important particulars the charter was similar to that of 1609 issued to the Virginia Company of London and was designed to accomplish for Newfoundland exactly what the charters of 1609 and 1615 were designed to accomplish for Virginia and Bermuda.

John Guy, who was the master mind in the whole undertaking and had already written a treatise "to animate the English to plant there," went out as governor of the new colony and led the adventure in three ships, July, 1610, with a company of thirty-nine persons of both sexes, including his brother William and members of his own family, together with all necessary utensils and stock— seeds, domestic animals, fowls, and the like.[2] This promising expedition started for Newfoundland only a month or two later than that which bore Gates, Newport, and Somers on the ill-fated voyage that terminated in their shipwreck on the Bermuda reefs. The vessels had a fine crossing of only twenty-three days and finally

1. Carr, *Select Charters of Trading Companies*, pp. 51–62; Prowse, *Newfoundland*, pp. 122–125.

2. Guy's instructions, from British Museum, Cottonian, Otho, E. viii, f. 5, are printed in Prowse, pp. 94–96. In the Lambeth Palace library is a "Jornall of a voiadge in the Indeavour" by John Guy, which concerns the second voyage of 1612. This narrative is not printed by Prowse. The latter does, however, present many of the letters from Cupers Cove, either in full or in part (pp. 125–128).

made a landing in Conception Bay, at a place variously called Cupers, Cuperts, or Cupid's Cove. There the colonists spent the winter, which was more moderate than usual, with snow never more than eighteen inches in depth and ice never thick enough to bear a dog, as Guy reported. They did not want for food, the fishermen were "most joyful and comfortable" to them, and they lost by death but four of the entire company. They built a storehouse for provisions and a dwelling house for habitation within an enclosure 120 by 90 feet. They mounted their cannon to command the harbor and with a workshop, a saw pit, and a smith's forge—using good fir charcoal—they built a twelve-ton decked boat and six fishing boats and pinnaces. The second winter was not as successful. The colony was threatened by pirates, the weather was much colder, the beer froze, cattle died, and scurvy invaded the settlement. Guy returned twice to England, leaving his brother and William Colston in charge. In 1615, for no other reason than his excellent reputation as a ship-captain and adventurer, the company sent out as governor, Captain John Mason, then about thirty years old, and he remained at the head of the colony for the ensuing six years.[1] He explored the island, made a map, and wrote a "Brief Discourse," which he dedicated to his friend Sir John Scott of Edinburgh and sent it to him to read. The tract was printed at Edinburgh in 1620. Guy's colony was the first to weather a winter in Newfoundland and to demonstrate that the island was capable of permanent habitation.

Aroused by the success of Guy's settlement, divers citizens of Bristol purchased of the London and Bristol Company a tract of land to the northward of Cupers Cove—a part of the peninsula between Conception Bay and Trinity Bay—and in 1617 started there a colony known as Bristol's Hope, with Harbour Grace as its chief center. There they built many fair houses and lived very pleasantly, growing rye and raising swine and goats. But of the colony's later history little is known. There is reason to believe that the plantation gradually became a fishing settlement and was still in existence as late as 1639 and 1640, when the promoters planned to send over 180 persons to serve as a shore contingent, supplying the fishing boats with victuals.[2] These Bristol merchants, as well as the London and

1. Insh, *Scottish Colonial Schemes*, pp. 33–39; Tuttle, *Life of Captain John Mason*, pp. 11–13, 220–221; map facing p. 131; "Brief Discourse," pp. 143–158.
2. *Acts Privy Council, Colonial*, I, §413. The passage is obscure, but it can relate to no other settlement than Bristol's Hope. The petitioners say that their enterprise

Bristol Company, had fishing boats in those waters and were actuated by the same motives as those which sent Guy's colony to Cupers Cove. In their petition of 1639 they announced their intention "to keepe and imploy in a fishing Trade upon that coast all the yeare, for which workes it [was accustomed] to export Provisions from hence" and to that end had built two ships to be used for the perfecting this fishing plantation in the interest of "a good employment for ships and an increase of seamen." How much longer the settlement lasted it is impossible to say.

Similarly influenced by the London and Bristol enterprise was a fantastic Welshman, Sir William Vaughan, one of the most picturesque of early colonial characters, who living at Tarracod (Torcoed) in Carmarthenshire watched the Devonshire and Bristol people sending out their fleets to Newfoundland and saw in that distant island "our Colchas where the golden fleece flourishes on the backes of Neptune's sheep, continually to be shorne."[1] He pictured Newfoundland as "Great Britain's Indies never to be exhausted dry"; and that he might have a part in its development he purchased of the London and Bristol patentees the part of their grant which extended southward from Guy's colony to Trepassy. Thither in 1618 he sent two colonies of men and women with full intent, as he says in *The Golden Fleece,* to follow himself and to spend the remainder of his life in this arcadian abode.[2] He called his settlements "Cambrioe Colches" and "Golden Grove," the latter after his birthplace in Wales. As a factor in colonization the venture amounted to nothing, but it is famous for two things: its literary output; and the connection with it of Captain Richard Whitbourne.

Vaughan was of a strongly literary turn of mind, colorful and imaginative. Carrying out his promise to share with his settlers the fortunes of the new land, he went over in 1622 and while there composed two works, *Cambrensium Cariola* and *The Golden Fleece,* written in 1623, two years before he returned to England. Thus the earliest work composed in northern America and perhaps

began long before the great migration into New England; that their plantation was apart from all others and had no relation to them; and that their settlers were all "regular people" (that is, not Puritans), neither factious nor various in religion, "but conformable to his Majestie and the Lawes of the Church of England." The petitioners were Bristol merchants and the date of the petition is January 4, 1639.

1. *The Golden Fleece,* p. 9.   2. *Ibid.,* pp. 6–7.

the first strictly original literary effort put forth in the English speaking part of the New World took form in southern Newfoundland.[1] In *The Golden Fleece* he praises fishing, saying that Christ in making fishermen "fishers of men" showed that he preferred Peter, Andrew, and the other apostles—plain persons and simple—before the great ones of the earth, and valued fishing over silver and gold. He argues in behalf of his plantation in Newfoundland as an aid to the fishery and believes that the "golden fleece" is destined to repair the decay of trade, which he thought to be losing ground in the northwestern parts of Europe. In his final chapter, he pictures Apollo calling before him the leaders of the colonizing movement —Guy, Slaney, Mason, and others—bidding them say whether or not the "golden fleece" of Newfoundland were destined to become the stabilizer of the world's trade.[2] A conversation carried on among his characters discloses the fact that the differences which had already arisen between the settlers and the fishermen and which were to affect materially the fortunes of Newfoundland during the colonial period of its history, were well understood even at that early date. In closing, he expresses the hope that Apollo will order both parties to reconcile their disagreements and work together for the common welfare of all.

Vaughan's enterprise is also noteworthy because it enlisted the support of Captain Richard Whitbourne, sometimes called the John Smith of the north, whose writings are on a par with Vaughan's own. Whitbourne had had an exciting and adventurous career, since the day forty years before, when on his first seafaring expedition he had set sail from Southampton to go to Newfoundland for the purpose of trading, killing whales, and making train oil. He was with Gilbert in Newfoundland, when the latter took possession of the island in the name of the queen, served against the Spanish armada, was with Easton the pirate, for whom he obtained a pardon in England, and in 1617 was entrusted by Vaughan with the

1. George Sandys' translation of Ovid's *Metamorphoses* was made in Virginia in 1621–1622. Vaughan's religious attitude, as contrasted with that of the non-conformists, can be inferred from certain lines in his *The Church Militant* (1640), a curious history in verse. "Accounting Capes, Bells, Organ, Surplices, Or shaven crowns, as Rites, not Substances, To barre the Faith or Conscience of a Saint . . . I will accept what Outward Garbes they please, Ile Kneele, sit, stand, or else in Sackcloth Fast, So that I may win Soules; no Flesh Ile taste . . . Such shapes I take for harmelesse Policie," p. 309. The preface is dated, December 30, 1639.

2. *The Golden Fleece*, chap. 3, and pp. 22–37.

charge of one of his colonies and the oversight of its activities. In his "Discourse"—the best known of his writings—he gives an account of Newfoundland, its climate, inhabitants, bays, rivers, and harbors, and dilates at length upon the fishery, describing its character, the methods employed, the ships in service, and the extent of the catch. The work is not only valuable for the information it furnishes but is interesting also for its literary form.

Vaughan bankrupted himself by his venture and was obliged to sell one part of his tract to Henry, Lord Cary, Viscount of Falkland, and another part to Sir George Calvert, each of whom had been a friend and fellow student of his at Oxford. Falkland's section was only six miles wide and lay next north of Vaughan's remaining part, which was at the extreme south; that of Calvert, which was five times as large, covered the entire area between Falkland's and Guy's. Though Falkland, who was greatly interested in colonization, both in Ireland and in America, opened an agency at the lower end of St. Martin's Lane-in-the-Fields within the liberties of Westminster and invited all who might wish to go to America to register their names and enter into negotiations, nothing came of the venture. He issued a book of "Proposals," authorized the gathering of colonists of all sorts and conditions, without much regard for character or competency, and sent them over to settle his grant; but the whole undertaking ended without leaving any trace behind.

Calvert's essay began more auspiciously. Indeed it was the only successful attempt made at this early date to plant shore settlements in Newfoundland in the face of the powerful West Country fishing interests, which opposed in every way possible the founding of permanent plantations. Aroused by Whitbourne's "Discourse," Calvert purchased the northern portion of Vaughan's property in 1620 and by 1622 had sent over a great number of men and women, equipped with all necessary provisions for a colony. There, at Ferryland on the east coast, these settlers lived quietly and peaceably, building houses, cleaning up the land for arable and meadow, and preparing kitchen gardens for cabbages, carrots, turnips, and the like, even providing a place for the planting of tobacco. Calvert set up an office, perhaps in Bloomsbury, and prepared to entertain and encourage all who would accept his terms for transportation to Ferryland. His agent was able to offer, as already in being, dwellings with stone chimneys, a storehouse, a brewhouse, a wharf, a forge, and salt works, all within a palisade made of sub-

stantial stakes, seven feet high and sharpened at the top, enclosing
four acres of ground; also fields of barley, oats, peas, and beans already planted, gardens filled with lettuce, radishes, carrots, cole-
worts, and turnips, and a climate less cold than was frequently
found in England.[1] In the accounts sent over by the first governor,
Edward Wynne, there was intentional exaggeration for the purpose
of inducing immigration, for Calvert, who went over later was not
impressed with the climate and said so in unmistakable terms.

But for the moment the outlook was hopeful, sufficiently so indeed to encourage Calvert to enlarge the scope of his undertaking.
In 1622, unwilling to continue longer as a tenant of the London and
Bristol Company, he applied to the king for a royal charter, and
after some delay secured his patent. The charter was issued on
April 7, 1623,[2] and not only confirmed him in possession of the
land he had bought of the company, but so considerably extended it
that it stretched from one side of the Trepassy peninsula to the
other and north and south from Falkland's to Guy's with an opening on Conception Bay. This concession gave Calvert a frontage on
three waterfronts—at Ferryland on the east, at Placentia on the
west, and at Conception Bay on the north—and included all islands
within ten leagues of the eastern shore. By the terms of the charter
this region was erected into a province, the province of Avalon, to
be held in capite by knight service, constituting a county palatine
over which Calvert had full authority as absolute lord and proprietor, with the right to make laws in an emergency without the
consent of the freeholders. Liberty of fishing was reserved to all the
king's subjects, together with the privilege of salting and drying fish
on the shores of the grant.

Except for the small community at St. John's, which seems to
have begun as an adjunct of the fishery, Calvert's plantation at
Ferryland was the only one that gave promise of permanence.

1. Prowse, *Newfoundland,* pp. 132–133 (extracts from Purchas); Steiner, *Report,*
American Historical Association, 1905, I, 114–120.

2. The original of this charter is entered on the Patent Rolls. Copies may be
found in full in Scharf's *History of Maryland,* I, 39–40, and in part in Prowse,
Newfoundland, pp. 131–132. It will be noticed that in this case, as in that of Massachusetts six years later, the king gave away land which he had already granted to
another petitioner, the London and Bristol Company. As far as we know this was
done without the consent of the previous grantee and the legality of the act is open
to question. In neither case was the previous grantee called upon to release the territory regranted, as was done in the case of Sir William Alexander, noted later in this
chapter.

"Both for buildings and making trial of the ground," wrote Sir William Alexander in his *Encouragement to Colonies,* "Calvert hath done more than was ever performed by any in so short a time, having on hand a brood of horses, cows, and other bestials, and, by the industry of his people, he is beginning to draw back yearly some benefits from thence." Suspecting that his governors, Wynne and Powell, were not serving him well, as in fact they were not, he went himself to the colony in 1627, remaining there but a few months. He came back again in 1628, but the climate did not suit him and he expressed a strong desire "to shift to some other warmer climate of this new world, where the wynters be shorter and lesse vigorous," as he wrote King Charles from Ferryland, August 19, 1629.[1] "For here your Majesty may please to understand that I have fowned by too deare bought experience which other men for their private interests always concealed from me, that from the middle of October to the middst of May there is a sadd face of wynter upon all this land, both sea and land so frozen for the greatest part of the tyme as they are not penetrable, no plant or vegetable thing appearing out of the earth untill it bee about the beginning of May, nor fish in the sea, besides the air so intolerable cold as it is hardly to be endured. By meanes whereof, and of much salt water, my house hath beene an hospitall all this wynter, of 100 persons 50 sick at a time, myself being one and nyne or ten of them died. Hereupon I have had strong temptation to leave all proceedings in plantations and being much decayed in my strength to retire myself to my former quiett; but my inclination carrying me naturally to these kynde of workes, and not knowing how better to employ the poore remainder of my days[2] than, with other good subjects, to further the best I may the enlarging of your Majesty's empire in this part of the world. I am determined to committ this place to fishermen that are able to encounter storms and hard weather and to remove myself with some 40 persons to your Majesty's dominion of Virginia, where if your Majesty will please to grant me a precinct of land with such privileges as the King your father my gracious master was pleased to grant me here, I shal endevor to the utmost of my power to deserve it." Calvert, now Lord Baltimore, arrived in Virginia the following October, but unable to take the oaths of supremacy and

1. *Maryland Archives,* III, 15–16.
2. Calvert was not yet 50 years old; he died at 52.

allegiance because he made "profession of the Romishe Religion," he withdrew to England, where three years later he died, before his own patent for the "precinct" he asked for in a more southern and favorable part of America had passed the seals.

Calvert's community in Newfoundland lasted longer as an independent settlement than did any of the others, because it was buttressed by the authority of a royal charter and was managed with unusual intelligence and care. But in the end it became little more than a claim in the Baltimore family, which was maintained until 1754. In 1637 Charles I, assuming that all the patentees had deserted their grants—though in law Baltimore's title from the king was still good—bestowed the whole island upon Sir David Kirke and others. Kirke went out in 1638 with a hundred men, as governor of the island—a position to which he had been appointed after the restoration of Canada to the French in 1632—and took possession of Baltimore's house in Ferryland for himself. But he was never able to make good his proprietary claims and was later brought into court by Cecilius Calvert, Lord Baltimore, on the ground that he had surreptitiously obtained his patent and dispossessed the petitioner illegally of his rights in Newfoundland.[1] Baltimore petitioned the crown in 1662 and was successful in his effort to oust the usurpers, and Lewis and John Kirke, heirs of David who had died sometime before 1654, were ordered to deliver up all houses and lands within the province of Avalon.[2] Baltimore resumed control and appointed a governor, who tried to reëstablish the colony, but the attempt failed and with the final departure of his governor soon after 1674 proprietary lordship in Newfoundland came to an end. The claim remained in abeyance until its revival in 1753 by Frederick, Lord Baltimore, who wished to restore the settlement under a resident governor. His petition was referred to the Board of Trade, which reported adversely and the matter was closed and never reopened.[3] Ferryland remained in the hands of the fishermen, and in

1. *Calendar State Papers, Colonial,* 1574–1660, pp. 404, 412, 415, 481; Berkley, "Lord Baltimore's Contest with Sir David Kirke over Avalon," *Maryland Magazine,* XII, 107–114.

2. *Calendar State Papers, Colonial,* 1661–1668, §§62, 452; British Museum, Egerton, 2395, ff. 308–310. For further details, Scisco, "Calvert's Proceedings against Kirke," *Canadian Historical Review,* VII, 133–136.

3. The report of the Board of Trade is of considerable interest. It reads as follows: "Pursuant to your Lordships Order dated the 26th of July last [1753], We have had under Consideration the humble Petition of the Right Honble Frederick

this case as elsewhere in Newfoundland the interests of the soil were completely submerged by the all-powerful demands of the sea. Doubtless many of those who had been Baltimore's tenants and servants, as well as many of those who had gone overseas to people the other settlements, continued—they and their descendants—to live in Newfoundland for generations to come—the progenitors of many a Newfoundland family of today.

All of these attempts to found plantations on the soil of Newfoundland, though begun with energy and supported by considerable resources and two royal charters, and though representative, equally with the efforts of the Virginia companies of London and Plymouth, of the contemporary zeal for colonization, gradually languished and withered away, leaving almost no traces behind. Of Guy's settlement we hear nothing after 1628. The Vaughan and Falkland projects, ill-conceived and ill-manned, never took deep root, and early came to untimely ends. The Bristol's Hope venture survived until after 1640 at least and its settlers lingered on, as did

Calvert Lord Baltimore in the kingdom of Ireland, setting forth his Claim to a large tract of Land in the Island of Newfoundland, by the Name of the Province of Avalon, and to all royal Jurisdiction and Prerogatives within the same; and praying that his Majesty will be pleased to allow and approve of John Bradstreet, Esqr to be Governor of the said Province of Avalon on the Nomination and Appointment of the Petitioner, as Lord Proprietary of the said Province.

As the Claim appeared to us to be a matter of great Importance, We thought it our Duty to refer the said Petition, together with all such Books and Papers of this office as might give any Light or Information in the matter in question, to his Majesty's Attorney and Solicitor General, and to desire their Opinion upon it. And having lately received their Report, We beg leave to lay the same before your Lordships.

His Majesty's Attorney and Solicitor General have reported to Us, 'That they have taken the said Petition, Books and Papers into their Consideration, and have been attended by the Lord Baltimore and his Agents, and/ heard what they had to offer in support of the said Petition. That as, notwithstanding the Determination in 1660 in favor of the Grant in 1623, there is no evidence of any actual Possession of the Province claimed, or Exercise of any Powers of Government there by the Baltimore Family. As on the contrary, it is most probable, that at least from the year 1638 they had been out of possession; As from the year 1669 there have been many Proceedings which appear from the same Books and Papers, and even an Act of Parliament passed in the Reign of King William the third, inconsistent with the Right now set up, without taking the least Notice thereof, and without any Claim or Interposition on the Part of the Baltimore Family; And as his Majesty's Approbation of a Governor ought to be in Consequence of a clear title of Proprietorship, They are humbly of Opinion that it is not adviseable for his Majesty to comply with the said Petition.'" C.O., 195: 8, pp. 329–332. "The Case of the Hon. Frederick, Lord Baltimore, relating to the Province of Avalon in America," 1753, is among the Calvert Papers in the Maryland Historical Society.

many another group here and there, because land occupation of a
sort was necessary for the prosecution of the English fishery. The
same was true of the St. John's colony, which served the fishermen
and in time became the leading fishing center of that part of the
island, catering to the activities of both the fishermen and the
traders. The failure of the plantations to gain at this time a permanent footing on the island was due in part to the inexperience of
those employed to manage them and in part to the inclemency of
the climate and the unsuitability of the soil for cultivation on a large
scale; but in much larger part to the opposition of those in England
—the western adventurers from the counties of Somerset and Devon
—who wanted no colonies in those regions of the world where the
best fishing grounds were situated. They wished no local settlements or local governments to interfere with their control of the
fishery and for many years tried to retain their monopoly and have
it confirmed by royal patent and act of parliament. They finally
gained their ends, as far as the king was concerned, in the Western
Charter of 1634,[1] which gave royal recognition to their ancient
rights and privileges and put a stop to the interference of the inhabitants in the operations of the fishery. Sixty-five years later, in
1699, the essential features of that charter, modified and expanded
to suit the experiences of more than half a century, were given
statutory form in the Act to Encourage the Trade of Newfoundland, a strongly mercantilist measure favorable to the fishery.[2] These
two acts, one royal and the other parliamentary, explain better than
anything else why it was that Newfoundland never became a colony
in colonial times. Its history ran a different course from that of
Virginia or Barbados, for example, because its wealth lay not in the
soil but in the ocean. The cod, not tobacco or sugar, was Newfoundland's staple.

The activities of Gorges in colonizing New England and of Guy
and Mason in their efforts to found and maintain a settlement at
Cupers Cove brought upon the scene another personage, a man less

1. *Acts Privy Council, Colonial*, I, §323; Prowse, *Newfoundland*, pp. 154–158,
where the Privy Council orders are called, with a complete misunderstanding of the
situation, "Star Chamber Rules."
2. 10–11 William III, c. 25. Prowse in his denunciation of the patent of 1634 and
the act of 1699, the issue and passage of which he quite erroneously attributes to
bribery, misses the point entirely. He seems to think that the fishery should have
been sacrificed for the colony, but on that question no mercantilist of the time
would have agreed with him.

practical than either Gorges or Guy, but far less visionary than Vaughan, the temperamental and imaginative Sir William Alexander, laird of Menstrie in Scotland, poet, dreamer, and "man of contemplation who by misadventure, as it were, became a man of action."[1] Alexander was a friend of Vaughan's and their conversations are recorded in *The Golden Fleece,* showing that both were ardent and sanguine followers of the fortunes of colonization in America and sensitive to their own lack of success. Alexander was aroused to a high pitch of enthusiasm and hopefulness by the tales of settlement and attempted settlement that came to his notice and was quickened in zeal by reading Captain Mason's richly colored and flattering "Discourse." As he saw a New France, a New Spain, and a New England arising in the West, so he dreamed of a New Scotland, just as later adventurers were to plan for a New Albion, a New Hampshire, and a New Somersetshire in the New World. Meeting Mason in 1621, he was fired with a desire to found a colony of his own and selected for his purpose the region between Newfoundland and New England, which up to this time, except for the series of unsuccessful attempts to settle at Port Royal on the part of the French, was largely untouched by either planters or fishermen. When his wishes were made known to the king, James, always a Scot at heart, notified the Scottish Privy Council, August 5, that Sir William had "a purpose to procure a forraine plantation, having made choice of landes lying between our colonies of New England and Newfoundland, both the governors whereof have encouraged him thereto." Gorges, as president of the Council for New England, was called upon by the king to release this part of the council's territory, either by patent under the corporate seal or by a verbal understanding; and this having been done, the Scots Council dutifully replied to the royal request by granting in the king's name and under the great seal of Scotland, September 10, 1621, a tract to be known as New Scotland or Nova Scotia, to be held of King James, as king of Scotland.

This charter, designed as the title deed to a great proprietorship in the new world, conveyed to Alexander all the territory coterminous today with Nova Scotia, New Brunswick, and the land lying between New Brunswick and the river St. Lawrence, a truly princely domain, justifying Sir Thomas Urquhart's comment that

1. Insh, *Scottish Colonial Schemes,* p. 91.

Alexander was born a poet and aimed to be a king. The document is unlike any other charter issued to a proprietor in America. Proceeding as it did from the Scottish and not the English chancery, it bears the marks of a medieval feudal and tenurial law that was older than anything prevailing at that time in England and was representative of a land where personal loyalty was still conspicuous and where feudal relationships were still a living reality. In medieval Latin, the charter conferred upon the proprietor powers that in their range and archaic peculiarities are a witness to the entire disregard by the contemporary legal mind in Scotland of the element of time and to its solemn ignorance of the conditions in America under which the terms of the charter were to be enforced. Nova Scotia might well have been a propriety located in Scotland itself and held under a patent dating from the twelfth century. The clerks followed precedent in their legal phraseology and the result is a masterpiece of legal pedantry.[1]

Under the authority of this incredible document, Alexander made his first effort to give reality to his dreams. In June, 1622—a few months after the massacre in Virginia and only a short time after John Peirce obtained his patent from the Council for New England—he procured a ship in London, brought it to Kirkcudbright, equipped it with stores and a small group of emigrants from Galloway and its neighborhood—whom with difficulty his agents persuaded to embark—and started it off on its voyage to America. Hindered by unavoidable delays and unfavorable winds, the vessel did not reach Newfoundland until the middle of September, too late to attempt a settlement, and after a winter at St. John's among the fishermen, the members of the company, such as were left of them, limited their efforts to voyages of exploration. No attempt was made to found a colony, and this first venture proved a failure, involving its promoter in a heavy financial loss.

Still sanguine of success but convinced of the necessity of a change of plan, Alexander issued in 1624 his *Encouragement to Colonies,* a learned but impracticable prospectus, rich and colorful in style but academic and ineffective in its power of appeal, encouraging, as has been well said, no one but its author. The *Encourage-*

1. The Latin text of the charter may be found in Hazard, *State Papers,* I, 134–145, and the English text in Slafter's *Sir William Alexander,* pp. 127–148. It may also be found in *Nova Scotia Papers,* pp. 2–15, and in Rogers, *Memorials of the Earl of Stirling,* II, 179–195.

ment failed as completely as had the voyage. Then Alexander turned to the king for help. James responded and tried to galvanize the scheme into life by offering to create a series of Nova Scotia baronetcies, applying the same artificial stimulus that had been successfully tried in Ireland in order to promote the plantation of Ulster, when 205 English landowners bought their titles at a total cost of £225,000. But the canny Scot was not to be taken in by the similar offer for Nova Scotia. He was by nature cautious and thrifty and on this occasion was suspicious of even the existence of Sir William's transatlantic lordship. Those to whom the appeal was made refused to be lured by the royal offer and saw no advantage in becoming Nova Scotia baronets on the terms laid down. Each new baronet was expected to furnish "sex sufficient men, artificers or labourers sufficientlie armeit, apparrelit, and victuallit for two years," with "one thousand merkis Scottis money" to be paid to Sir William to meet "his past charges and endeavouris."[1] These terms were modified later to the payment of three thousand marks only, two thousand of which were to be devoted to the furthering of a colony.

But still the Scottish gentry refused to respond, even though the conditions were made increasingly attractive and precedence was accorded the new baronets over the lesser barons in Scotland. The Nova Scotia dignities did not prove popular and the amount of money they produced must have proved exceedingly disappointing. The precedence given these upstart lordlings roused the indignation of the Scottish lairds and a parliamentary convention of estates, held at Edinburgh in 1625, went so far as to petition Charles I "to suspend the precedencie grantit to their barronettis untill the tyme that the plantatioun for the whilk this dignitie is conferred be first performed by the undertakeris."[2] The lairds promised, if the plan of settlement proved really feasible, to bear the cost themselves without "any retribution of honour to be given therefor." Though a few accepted the king's offer and took seisin of their lands on the Castle-hill of Edinburgh, there was no enthusiasm for the new titles, and that part of the programme, designed to appeal to the vanity of men, was wrecked because of the Scots' unwillingness to be parted from their money with no prospect of an adequate return.[3] The

1. Rogers, *Memorials*, I, 69–74; Insh, *Scottish Colonial Schemes*, p. 63.
2. Stock, *Debates*, I, 434–435.
3. Insh, *Scottish Colonial Schemes*, pp. 62–65; *Baronia Anglica Concentrata*, two

value of the proposed order was still further impaired by the decision of the English House of Commons that the new baronetcies
should have no place among the degrees of honor in England, thus
depriving them of an important part of their distinction.[1]

Even though the king failed in his effort to aid Alexander in the
latter's laudable but mistaken purpose and the English parliament
showed itself manifestly antagonistic to the whole scheme, the Scottish proprietor and lord of a spacious domain, "with a joyful countenance and alacrity of mind," set about the equipping of another
little fleet, which he brought together in the spring of 1627. But the
vessels designed for the voyage never left England on their way
across the Atlantic, for miscarriages, misunderstandings, and mis-
adventures seemed to dog every step of the way. Still undisturbed
and still hopeful of his colonial plans, Sir William tried once more
and with the coöperation of his eldest son, William, Lord Alexander,
whom he sent across in the spring of 1629,[2] he succeeded in landing
some seventy men and two women at Port Royal on the Bay of
Fundy, on the same spot where de Monts had planted his French
settlement twenty years before. The place was practically unoccupied, save by a few habitants who were living in the neighborhood,
survivors of the French colonizers, the greater number of whom
had abandoned the locality and set up a new station farther to the
southeast. Alexander's success in this instance was due not to any
improvement in his colonizing methods, which were as scatter-
brained as before, but to an agreement which he reached with the
company of merchant adventurers, created in 1628 for trade with
Canada and led by Jervas Kirke, William Berkeley, and Robert

volumes (1843–1848). The second volume of this work contains an historical account of the settlement of Nova Scotia and of the founding of the baronetcies (pp.
210–300). Winthrop in his *Journal* (II, 181) says that the father of La Tour had a
grant of a Scottish baronetcy in Nova Scotia under the great seal of Scotland, and
we know that the grandfather of Sir James Hay received the barony of Smithfield,
six miles long and three miles broad, for which Hay petitioned in 1683 (*Calendar
State Papers, Domestic,* January–June, 1683, p. 170). It is also interesting to note that
Queen Anne at one time thought of reviving the "Ancient Order of Baronets in
Nova Scotia" in order to encourage the planting of that place ("Proposal [from
Arthur Moore] for the enlarging the Trade of Great Britain," in Papers relating to
African Affairs, vol. I, 87, Stowe Collection, Huntington Library). It is said that the
approach to the castle of Edinburgh where seisin was given is still legally Nova
Scotia territory, but I have been unable to verify this statement.

1. Stock, *Debates,* I, 102, 105.

2. Dr. Insh argues successfully for the year 1629 as the date of settlement, instead of 1628, the year previously accepted. *Scottish Colonial Schemes,* appendix B.

Charleton. These men, finding that Alexander's claim to a sole right of trade and plantation in Canada stood in the way of their plans, agreed to allow him undisturbed possession of Acadia in exchange for trading rights on the river St. Lawrence and to admit him to membership in the company. Under this arrangement and in vessels belonging to the company—a part of the fleet of six privateers that the company was sending to Canada—Alexander was able to get his colonists across the Atlantic and to start a settlement at Port Royal on the soil of Acadia. This settlement was made at about the same time that Captain David Kirke was capturing Quebec and that Lord Baltimore was expressing his desire to leave Ferryland and go to a warmer climate. Less than four months before, a group of Puritans in England had succeeded in obtaining from the crown a charter incorporating the Massachusetts Bay Company, and during the same period Allerton from Plymouth was completing his negotiations with the English factors and involving his Separatist brethren in financial obligations disastrous to their colony.

The Scottish success was short lived. Though Alexander was able to reach an understanding with the merchant adventurers and to overcome the obstacles that had hitherto barred his way to America, he was now confronted with a situation that was beyond his control. No compromise was possible with Richelieu and France. The great cardinal's interest in colonial and commercial affairs culminated in the formation of two companies, the United Companies and the Company of New France, for the purpose of opening up trade with Canada and of extending the influence of France in the New World. England and France were at war, and for the moment the opportunity was not favorable for Richelieu to despatch to Canada the warships and transports that were waiting in readiness in the harbor of Dieppe. But with the year 1629 peace was made, and though Charles I continued to befriend Alexander's colony for another two years, the end was inevitable. The exigencies of the royal policy and the emptiness of the royal treasury, which needed badly the 400,000 crowns still due on the queen's dowry, demanded the restoration of Canada to France, which in turn involved the return of Acadia and Quebec and the sacrifice of the plantation at Port Royal. All that the Kirkes had accomplished in the conquest of Canada and all that Alexander, after many painful efforts, had managed to achieve in Nova Scotia were undone by the provisions of the treaty of Susa, April 24, 1629, and by the treaty of St. Germain-en-Laye of March 29, 1632.[1] In 1631, Alexander, created earl of Stirling as a sort of compensation for his losses, was ordered by the king, at the request of the French ambassador, to demolish the fort, remove the colonists, and abandon Port Royal, "leaveing the boundis altogether waist and unpeopled as it was at the tyme when your said sone landed first to plant ther."[2] The next year the treaty was signed which ended all the hopes that the laird of Menstrie may ever have had of founding a New Scotland in the world overseas.

But Charles I had done more than sacrifice Port Royal and Quebec. By his bargain with Richelieu, which met with bitter opposition in England, he lost the good will of his people, who resented his disregard of what they conceived to be England's best interests, and by just so much estranged the men who were to be the leaders of the parliamentary party in the struggle that was to come. The treaty of St. Germain-en-Laye, which brought to an end Alexander's ambitious plans, strengthened the hold of France upon the soil of America that was not to be broken for one hundred and thirty years. The signing of this treaty was more than an act of disloyalty to his Scottish subjects, of whom he was their Scottish king. It was a witness to the failure of Charles as king of England to understand the colonial strivings of the English people, to whom the founding of colonies in the New World was already becoming one of the major interests of their expanding national life.

1. Davenport, *European Treaties*, I, 300–304, 315–323. Papers relating to this subject, 1629–1633, may be found in *Canadian Archives*, Report for 1912, appendix D. By the treaty of Susa Charles and Louis made peace; by that of St. Germain-en-Laye they agreed to the restoration to France of all places occupied by the English in "New France, Acadia, and Canada." In 1633 Quebec and Port Royal were formally handed over to the companies which had received them by grant from the French king.

2. Insh, *Scottish Colonial Schemes*, p. 85.

CHAPTER XVI

GORGES AND HIS PROJECTS FOR
NEW ENGLAND

AMONG all these men—Vaughan, Falkland, Calvert, Gorges, Mason, and Alexander, friends and acquaintances and representative of the group that was interested in a proprietary form of colonization—Gorges was by far the most important. Yet during these early years from 1608 to 1620 he was inactive, watching the accomplishments of others. All his own efforts to found a permanent colony had failed. Though he had fathered voyages of exploration and had invested large sums of money in ships despatched to New England waters for fishing—notably the expedition of Captain Thomas Dermer in 1619, the last enterprise of the old Virginia Company of Plymouth[1]—by 1620 he had nothing to show for all his trouble. The settlement at Jamestown was growing in strength and numbers; Bermuda was entering on a new period of its history under Tucker and Butler; Guy's colony at Cupers Cove was flourishing for the moment under Captain John Mason; and the Bristol merchants were displaying unusual energy and enthusiasm for the cause of their plantations in Newfoundland. It was high time for Gorges to bestir himself if he were not to lose the charter by disuse and to see his rival, the Virginia Company of London, carry off all the honors in the race for settlement. For thirteen years his company had been inert, except as far as occasional members had sent over vessels to engage in the fishery and Gorges himself had despatched certain agents to explore the coast of Maine and report on conditions there.[2] In the face of the growing interest which the merchants and others of southwestern England, London, and even Scotland were showing in Newfoundland, Nova Scotia, and the Maine coast, where fishing was the great allurement,

1. On Dermer, Levermore, *Forerunners*, II, 576–584.
2. Smith, *Travels and Works*, I, 240–242. Smith says that the Plymouth Company sent over "opiniated and unskilfull men, that had not experienced diligence, to save what they took, nor take what there was." He adds that the fault was in the company and not in New England.

it was eminently desirable that the business of the Virginia Company of Plymouth be placed on a more efficient and profitable basis.

Gorges had large plans and was tireless in his efforts to put them into execution, for it was incumbent upon him, as the leading member of the company, to see that Plymouth was not outfooted by either London or Bristol. To the attainment of that end he now set his hand. The original Virginia Company of Plymouth had been in largest part fashioned not in Plymouth but in London and in conformity with the ideas, not of Gorges and his associates, but of the London promoters. Since the issue of the charter of 1606, creating both companies, the Virginia Company of London had twice undergone revision, once in 1609 and again in 1612, while the Plymouth Company had remained unchanged. Freed thus from all connection with the London group, Gorges, in a manner thoroughly characteristic of his class, decided to obtain a charter according to his ideas of what such a charter should be. He wanted no perpetuation of the London plan of a generality, quarter courts, and "democraticall" procedure; he wanted no commercial organization, no mere elaboration of a trading company, no stockholders, and no system of votes by a majority of voices. The reorganization he desired was of an entirely different character from that which had been brought about in the other company, in 1609 and 1612, by the merchants of London.

Gorges was an aristocrat, a representative of the lesser feudal class of landed proprietors, a prerogative man of the type of Gilbert, Raleigh, Vaughan, Falkland, Calvert, and Alexander, who though seeing in the New World opportunities for profit from trade and fishing, viewed those opportunities less from the vantage point of the merchant than from that of the owner of landed estates. He was of the gentry, and in common with many others of his kind wished to reproduce in America the proprietary customs and local manorial institutions with which he was familiar in England, and to set up there estates and tenancies and other features of the existing agricultural and seignorial system at home. He therefore planned to reorganize the Plymouth company along proprietary not commercial lines, and to invite as participators not the merchants or the gild brethren, whose interests lay in trade and industry, but members of the nobility and of the landed propertied class. On March 3, 1620, he petitioned the king, in the name of the "counsell for the second colonie and other the adventurers in the Western Part of England for the plantation of the North Parts of Virginia in America," asking for an enlargement of their patent, "that they maye with more boldnes goe on as they have begun . . . with the alteration onely of some few things and the addition" of others, which was a modest way of requesting an almost complete change in the fundamental character of the patent.[1] As usual the king referred the matter to the Privy Council, which instructed the solicitor general[2] to prepare the draft of a charter—the first plan of which was undoubtedly the work of Gorges himself, aided, it may be, by others—and on November 3, 1620, the patent was issued. The eight months' delay was caused by the inclusion among the privileges of the exclusive right of fishing in the northern waters, which, as we have already seen and shall see again, was bitterly but unsuccessfully opposed by the Virginia Company of London. The patent passed the seals with the objectionable clause intact, though further protests and a debate upon the subject in parliament delayed delivery until the following June.[3]

The new patent incorporated a group of forty men, of whom at first none were merchants, as one body corporate and politic, by the name of the Council established at Plymouth in the county of Devon, for the planting, ruling, and governing of New England in America. This body corporate is commonly known as the Council for New England or the New England Council. It was not a company but a board of proprietors, composed of some of the most distinguished of the king's officials and courtiers, the list reading, as has been said, "like an abstract from the Peerage."[4] It included a duke, two marquises, six earls, a viscount, three barons, nineteen knights, the dean of Exeter, and seven esquires—a notable company enough, even though most of the members were either sleeping partners or inactive associates. Later, when funds ran low, some merchants were admitted on the payment of a large "fine" of £110 each. Among these were William Erves, Christopher Levett, afterward appointed the first governor general of New England, and

1. *New York Colonial Documents*, III, 2–3; *Farnham Papers*, I, 16–18; *Virginia Company Records*, I, 321, 329; Baxter, *Gorges*, II, 30–31.

2. *Acts Privy Council, Colonial*, I, §59.

3. The charter was held up in the Crown Office until after June 18, 1621, when by order of the Privy Council it was delivered to the patentees. This point is discussed more fully farther on.

4. Adams, *Three Episodes*, I, 122.

Abraham Jennings of Plymouth.[1] This body was authorized to select its own president and other officials and to fill all vacancies in
its own membership, keeping the number always at forty. It was
made the sole proprietor of a huge, undivided domain, extending
from the fortieth to the forty-eighth parallel of latitude and from
sea to sea. No one concerned with the drafting or issue of the patent, in those days of conflicting and overlapping grants, seems to
have realized that this patent disregarded the London and Bristol
Company's right to the region north of the forty-fifth parallel, just
as the London and Bristol grant had disregarded the title of the old
Plymouth Company. One wonders if any of the crown lawyers or
chancery officials ever consulted the old patents in making out a
new one, or ever studied the geography of the regions they so easily
gave away.

This enormous area was to be held of the crown in free and common socage, as of the manor of East Greenwich, and the council
was fully empowered to divide up the territory as it pleased. It
could make sub-grants whenever it desired, giving to such subordinate colonies or plantations any name that was fitting, appointing
their officials and ordaining and establishing for them all necessary
laws. In its own good time it could erect a central government with
a principal governor or governor general, endowed with martial
powers, as complete as were those exercised by the lieutenants of
the English counties, and with civil and criminal power "to correct,
punish, pardon, governe, and rule" all such of the king's subjects "as
shall from time to time adventure themselves in any Voyage thither
or that shall att any time heer after inhabit" in New England.[2] The
council was also privileged to set up particular plantations within its
territory, as the Virginia Company was doing, or to found, if it preferred, colonies on its own account. As was the case with all incorporated colonizing agencies, it was to enjoy freedom from all "sub-
sidies and customs for the space of seven years" and from all "taxes
and impositions upon all goods and merchandizes as shall be brot
and imported into our Realm of England" for the space of twenty-
one years, except only the customary five per cent "according to the
ancient trade of merchants." These clauses are merely extracts from
the Virginia Company's charter of 1609. Likewise copied is the

1. *Calendar State Papers, Colonial*, 1574–1660, p. 47 (32); Burrage, *Early History
of Colonial Maine*, pp. 164–165, 169.
2. Thorpe, *Charters*, 3, p. 1827.

clause granting to all colonists overseas such liberties, franchises, and immunities as they would have enjoyed had they remained within the realm of England.[1]

More important to the council than even these indulgencies, which were the contemporary stock phrases of the charter-mongers, was the grant, either directly or by implication, of a monopoly of trade and fishing within the land and waters of the territory assigned. This monopoly took the form of an injunction to all the king's subjects not "to visit, frequent, trade or adventure to traffick into or from the said territories, lands, rivers, and places aforesaid," unless the consent of the council were obtained beforehand in writing under the common seal. As fishing could not be carried on successfully without access to the land, this meant that no one was to fish in the waters lying between the fortieth and forty-eighth parallels without the permission of the council, that is, of Gorges himself. As hitherto the Virginia Company had enjoyed free approach to the northern waters for fishing purposes, it resented the action of the crown and Privy Council in conferring this monopoly upon the Council for New England and both in its own general courts and in parliament made its resentment felt. It based its objection upon the ground that under the charter of 1606 each company was free of the other and entitled each to fish in the other's waters, the sea being to all as free as the air. It declared that "now the lotteries were almost spent" fishing was about the only source of profit and it petitioned the king against the monopoly as something surreptitiously

1. Some peculiarities may be noticed in the legal status of the Council for New England. The patentees, unlike all later groups of proprietors, such as those of the Carolinas and the Bahamas, were incorporated as a body politic and so had the standing and powers of a trading company. But unlike a trading company they had no governor, deputy governor, quarter courts, or generality, no joint-stock subscribed by any one who wished to put money into the venture. Furthermore, they formed a closed, self-perpetuating body, standing halfway between a trading company and a chartered (but not incorporated) feudal proprietary. They were thus a hybrid group, partly incorporated and partly feudal, which accounts in large part for their lack of strength and efficiency.

The territory granted these patentees was more than an area of land; it was a feudal propriety or principality, such as Gorges himself wanted; and in character it was even more feudal than was the palatinate of Durham at the time. Gorges wanted a feudal state, containing lesser feudal states such as were granted to Mason and Gorges, John Peirce, Robert Gorges, and others. The statute of Quia Emptores was not waived, as was the case in colonial grants generally, so that all subinfeudated lands were held not of the council but of the king. Something will be said on this point later.

obtained.[1] The king replied that if anything prejudicial to the southern colony were to be found in the new patent such had been inserted without his knowledge and should be removed. But eventually, after many hearings and much debate on both sides the Privy Council "saw no cause wherefore [the Council for New England] should not enjoy what the king had granted."[2] Action was then transferred to the House of Commons, where in committee with Coke in the chair, Gorges was charged with securing a monopoly contrary to the law and privileges of the king's subjects, and a battle parliamentary began between free fishing and monopoly which lasted until 1628, when Charles I temporarily dispensed with his parliaments.[3] Each year a bill for free fishing was introduced, but each year, for one reason or another, it failed of passage. The struggle between the Virginia Company and the New England Council merged into the larger conflict between the fishery and the proprietary interests in Newfoundland, which was not ended until the Western Adventurers obtained from Charles I the charter of 1634. Gorges never profited from his monopoly and in his charter of 1639, confirming his title to the soil and government of the "Province of Maine," a clause was especially inserted saving to all the king's subjects "liberty of fishing as well in the sea as in the creeks of the said province and the priviledge of salting and drying of their fish and drying of their nets upon the shore."[4]

While the Council for New England may have valued fishing as the most profitable of its resources, it was not, properly speaking, organized for the business of either fishing, plantation, or trade. It was a land company, the proprietor of a great territorial demesne, to be divided and distributed among the feofees and tenants, who were themselves to undertake the work of actual colonization. Though it undoubtedly had as one of its objects the planting of

1. *Virginia Company Records*, I, 277, 285, 321, 329, 339–340, 397, 410–414, 416, 428; Stock, *Debates*, I, 49–54, 56–61, 66, 67–72, 74, 75, 77, 78, 79–80, 82, 88; Baxter, *Gorges*, II, 32–46. Gorges refers to this quarrel in the Act for the resignation of the Great Charter of New England, when he says, "whilst ourselves at home were assaulted with sharp litigious questions before the Lords of his Maties most hon^{ble} Privy Council by the Virginia Companies and that in the very infancy thereof." *Proceedings*, American Antiquarian Society, 1867, p. 128.

2. Baxter, *Gorges*, II, 34; *Acts Privy Council, Colonial*, I, §65.

3. Baxter, *Gorges*, II, 36–37; Stock, *Debates*, I, 50, note 111. The best account of this controversy is by Charles Deane in Winsor, *Narrative and Critical History*, III, ch. IX.

4. *Farnham Papers*, I, 233.

colonies on its own account, for which it would provide people, equipment, and government, it was less ready to man ships and furnish settlers than to encourage others to do so. The most important part of its business, as events were to show, was to organize, govern, and apportion this territory as one would a feudal principality and its main activity during the fifteen years of its history proved to be the making of land grants. Gorges, in his *Brief Discourse,* has disclosed his ideas regarding these various matters. He pictures a province, of which either he or some one else would be the governor general on the place, administering the territory somewhat after the fashion of the central and local governments in England, but with a marked feudal coloring. The governor general would be assisted by a council, composed of patentees in New England, with such other necessary officials as a bishop, chancellor, treasurer, marshal, admiral, master of the ordnance, and the like, and also a general assembly (a "court of parliament," as it is called in Robert Gorges' charter), made up of delegates from the local divisions and summoned at the will of the governor and council for the making of laws. The divisions would consist of counties, baronies, and hundreds, with local officials similar to those in England, and the heads of the counties and baronies would be allowed to subdivide their territories into lordships and manors and to provide for courts baron and leet as at home. There would be also cities, great and small, and towns incorporated for purposes of trade, each of which would govern itself; would be authorized to send a delegate to sit in the assembly with the delegates from the counties; and be allowed to have a voice equally with the rest.[1]

How far the Council for New England intended to go in the di-

1. Baxter, *Gorges,* I, 234–237; II, 65–70. In his *Description of New England,* Gorges outlines his plans for his own "Province of Maine." In a letter to the king, May 12, 1634, he reveals what he thinks a "plantation" in New England should be. The occasion of this letter was the appointment of the Laud Commission of April 28, when Charles I had in mind the taking over of the Massachusetts Bay colony into his own hands, as his father had done with Virginia, and in anticipation of that event Gorges offered him advice as to how to handle the situation. He urged the king to divide New England into several provinces, both for ease in dispensing justice and for convenience in matters of defense, and over these to place governors and other assistants and officers for administration. Over all he would have a lord governor or lord lieutenant, who was to be a person of honor, representing the king, and with him were to be a lord bishop, a chancellor, a treasurer, a marshal, an admiral, a master of ordnance, a secretary of state, and other necessary subordinates, no one of whom was to be "papistically nor seizmattically inclined." Baxter, *Gorges,* III, 260–263.

rection of raising capital for enterprises on its own account it is not easy to determine, though in its proceedings a clear distinction is made between "the publike and the private undertakers." The accumulation of a fund was bound to be onerous in any case, notwithstanding the support of the "gentlemen of honour and blood," who were its members, but it was rendered more difficult by the controversy that arose over the fishing monopoly and the exceptions taken in the House of Commons to the patent itself. Within a year after the issue of the charter, Gorges made his first appeal. He turned to his neighbors, the merchants of the cities of Bristol and Exeter and of the towns of Plymouth, Dartmouth, Weymouth, and Barnstaple, and urged them to organize for the purpose of furthering trade and fishing and of advancing settlement in New England. He made a personal attempt to obtain their coöperation, but the merchants were wary and shrewd enough to see that his proposals were ingenious rather than practicable, particularly such of his proposals as concerned the capital stock that he wished each town to raise and hand over to him for disbursement. Though Gorges offered the towns patents for private plantations, as the Virginia Company had done—for the town of Ipswich had taken out a patent for a plantation in Virginia—he received little encouragement in so doing. The merchants of Bristol considered the "articles" Gorges drafted so difficult of acceptance that they resolved to do nothing without "further deliberation and also advice of the Adventurers of other Ports with whom they mean to confer."[1] They did not like the idea of forming a joint-stock company throughout the western towns, which was to be subordinate to the New England Council, and they thought the cost of licenses (£13.6.8, each) on the New England coast far too high. Though Gorges persisted and even drew up a body of reasons showing the benefits that might accrue to the western parts of the kingdom by the founding of plantations in New England and though he made liberal offers of land to particular persons and to gentlemen of eminence, he was not successful. In January, 1623, the Council for New England ordered the preparation of a letter to be sent, in the king's name, to the lords lieutenants of the counties of Somerset, Devon, and Cornwall and to the corporations of the cities of Bristol and Exeter, urging them to encourage settlement in New England, and this letter was duly

1. *American Historical Review*, IV, 685–689.

sent on the 8th of December following. Of it several copies have been preserved,[1] and that to William, Earl of Pembroke, lord lieutenant of Somerset—himself a member of the council and one greatly interested in colonization in Virginia and Bermuda[2]—urged him not only to take a hand in the undertaking himself but also to move "other gentlemen and persons of qualitie and meanes in that countye to join [with him] in the advancement of that plantation." But with the single exception of the town of Dorchester, already inspired by the Rev. John White to undertake a settlement of its own —of which more later—these letters were without result. There was no enthusiasm among the merchants in general or the city corporations for Gorges' impractical and grandiose schemes, and Bristol was already deeply involved in her adventure at Cupers Cove in Newfoundland.

One cannot but be impressed by Gorges' energy, misdirected though it was and expended with great lack of judgment and ordinary common sense. Not only were his various propositions to the western cities and towns unworkable from a business point of view—as the Bristol merchants realized, for they would have nothing to do with them—but even more impossible of accomplishment were his plans for transferring to the wilds of America forms of tenure and local administration wholly out of their element in an undeveloped frontier. He could not rid himself of the idea that what was good in England was likely to be good in America also and that institutions which had become a part of England's life could be readily transferred to a new soil. He could not believe that baronies, lordships, courts baron and leet, and other familiar forms of manorial jurisdiction at home were hopelessly misplaced in an unsettled wilderness. The Scottish patent to Alexander, the English patents to Calvert and Gorges, and the Fundamental Constitutions written by John Locke for the Carolinas at a later time furnish am-

1. *Ibid.*, 700–702; Historical Manuscripts Commission, *Exeter*, pp. 169–170; *Calendar State Papers, Colonial*, 1574–1660, p. 54 (52), American Antiquarian Society, *Proceedings*, 1867, pp. 38, 39. A letter from Francis, Lord Russell, lord lieutenant of Devon, mentioning the king's letter and advocating the "adventuring and furthering the plantation in New England as the advancing of Religion and enlarging of Territorie," is in Historical Manuscripts Commission, *Exeter*, pp. 166–167. Lord Russell promised to contribute to the undertaking an amount "sized according to my affeccion, and not to the meannesse of my fortune."

2. He was the elder brother of Philip, Earl of Pembroke, who was a son-in-law of Sir John Naunton and a patentee of Barbados, and was interested also in the Northwest Passage, the East India Company, and the Guiana Company.

ple reasons why so many of these proprietary schemes either failed outright or came to untimely ends. Feudal relations and practices dominated at this time the minds of the English lawyer and local gentry just as they continued for long afterward to influence the laws in England governing tenure and the descent of real property. Even when confronting settlement in a new world, Englishmen could not dispossess themselves of the conviction that English law, English rights of real property, and English methods of administration would take root and flourish in any part of the colonial world.[1]

The land within which Gorges proposed to erect this stately principality in the year 1620 was unoccupied by white men, save the small group of Pilgrims at Plymouth and scattered fishermen here and there along the coast from Cape Ann to the Penobscot. The island of Monhegan was the center of the fishing industry, where as Bradford says "the boats may goe quickly in and out to sea at all times of the tide and well stoed with fish neer at hand and convenient places to make it and build stages in,"[2] conditions not true either of Plymouth or Cape Ann, as the Pilgrims were to find out later to their sorrow and loss. To the west were a few Dutch at Manhattan and beyond the Penobscot was French Acadia, soon to be the scene of Alexander's unfortunate expedition. Still farther to the north were the inconsiderable settlements in Newfoundland, where Captain John Mason was exploring the harbors and bays and preparing the first map of that island, reproduced a few years later in *The Golden Fleece* of Sir William Vaughan. Everywhere were tribes of Indians, decimated by the plague and by "many horrible Slaughters and Murthers . . . to the utter Destruction, Devastation and Depopulation of that whole Territorye, so that there is not left for many Leagues together in a manner, any that doe claime or challange any kind of Interests therein nor any other Superior Lord or Souveraigne to make claime thereunto"[3]—evidently the picture of the country that Gorges had in his mind.

After the arrival of the Pilgrims, the first to make a settlement on

1. It is very interesting to note how seemingly impossible it was for an Englishman of this period or even of later periods to conceive of an outlying English dependency—whether in Ireland, America, Tangier, Senegambia, or Van Diemen's Land—as governed in any other way than at home.

2. *American Historical Review*, VIII, 297; *Proceedings*, American Antiquarian Society, 1921, pp. 309–310. Bradford wrote in 1623 of the "Duch on one side and the French on the other side and the fishermen and other plantations between."

3. From the charter of 1620, *Farnham Papers*, I, 23–24.

these shores was a company of some fifty or sixty "rude and profane fellows," a lusty crew, sent over by Thomas Weston, the old
ally of the Pilgrims, who, having broken with them and later with
the merchant adventurers, was launching a private and possibly a
rival venture of his own. Having been successful in obtaining a patent for the Pilgrims only a little while before, he would not fail, if
he could, to secure such a grant for himself on a similar expedition
bent; but no copy of such a grant, if it ever was issued, is known to
exist and only a hint is found of his intention to obtain one. If he
applied for a patent, as is likely, the evidence seems to show that he
did not succeed in getting it, so, in all probability, his expedition
was without authorization of any kind.[1] However that may be, the
fact remains that in June of that year, 1622, his company, under the
leadership of Andrew Weston, landed at Plymouth, where they
were distinctly not wanted but where they were charitably entertained and their sick cared for until they could find a suitable site
for themselves. Eventually they removed to a point on the southern
shore of Massachusetts Bay, known as Wessagusset, the present
Weymouth, and there erected such buildings as were necessary for
the setting up of a plantation designed for trading and fishing.[2] The
venture was a disastrous failure. Christopher Levett gives the reasons.[3] "About two years since one Mr. Weston sent over about 50
persons to plant, with little provision; when they came there, they

1. Bradford (*History*, I, 258) inserts a letter from Weston in which the latter says
that he intends to take out a patent. Robert Cushman confirms this statement in a
letter to Bradford of 1623, when in speaking of Weston's going to New England he
says that the men Weston carried "are no men for us," adding that he "hath taken
out a patente for himselfe" (*ibid.*, I, 269). According to *Acts Privy Council, Colonial*
(I, §79), successful application was made to the king, February 17, 1622, either by
the Council for New England or by Weston himself, for permission to transport
ordnance in the *Charity* for the use of Weston's plantation. This would seem to
indicate that both the king and the Council for New England approved of Weston's
expedition. On the other hand the king in November, 1622, issued a proclamation
against interloping and disorderly trading in New England (*Proclamations*, pp. 32–
34) which is thought to have been directed against Weston and his men, who are
called "interlopers," a term that would hardly have been used had Weston been
authorized by king and council to make the settlement. Furthermore, in the minutes
of the council, May 31, 1622, Weston is mentioned as if he had gone to New England "in contempt of authority" (*Proceedings*, American Antiquarian Society, 1867,
pp. 59, 60).
2. The Weston episode is well told in Adams, *Three Episodes*, I, chap. IV, and in
Winslow, "Good Newes from New England" (Young, *Chronicles of the Pilgrims*,
chaps. XIX–XXII). Also Bradford, *History*, I, 271–272, 284–287; II, 46.
3. Levermore, *Forerunners*, II, 633.

neither applied themselves to planting of corne nor taking of fish, more than for their present use, but went about to build Castles in the Aire, and making of Forts, neglecting the plentifull time of fishing. When winter came their forts would not keep out hunger, and they having no provision before hand, and wanting both powder and shot to kill Deare and Fowle, many were starved to death and the rest hardly escaped. There are foure of his men which escaped now at my plantation [on Casco Bay], who have related unto me the whole businesse." After causing the Pilgrims a great deal of trouble the company, such men as were left of it, dispersed in 1623, and thus the first attempt to settle on the coast of Massachusetts Bay came to an ignominious end.[1] Nothing permanent remained, except a blockhouse or fort and a stockade.[2]

Similar in character to Weston's attempt at colonization was that of Captain Wollaston, "a man of pretie parts," as Bradford calls him, who with three or four men of quality, many servants, and a supply of provisions and implements of husbandry landed at a place a little to the northwest of Wessagusset, called Passonagessit, within the limits of the present town of Braintree, the northern precinct of which is today the city of Quincy. They called the place Mount Wollaston. "Having continued there some time," says Bradford, "and not finding things to answer their expectations, nor profit to arise as they looked for, Captain Wollaston takes a great part of the servantes and transports them to Virginia."[3] He was a bird of passage, touching here and there and leaving no important trace be-

1. Bradford (*American Historical Review*, VIII, 298) writing under date, September 8, 1623, says, "Mr. Weston's colony is dissolved."

2. Weston, who was never personally present at Wessagusset, after various adventures and not very honorable escapades, went to Virginia, where he received a grant of land and was elected a burgess to the convention-assembly of 1628. He engaged in fishing and trading expeditions to the Maine coast ("Canada"), was often involved in controversy, and was occasionally under arrest. Later he went to Maryland, where he also acquired property and was admitted a freeman in the colony. He died in England in 1646 and left many debts behind him. His was a strange career of alternate success and failure, touching the history of the colonies at many points yet of significance only in connection with the Pilgrims, whose history would probably have taken a very different turn had he not come to their aid at a critical time. He was typical of one class of men of his age, a roving, resourceful trader, unstable and hot tempered, and in more or less trouble wherever his lot was cast. *Journal of the Virginia House of Burgesses, 1619–1659*, I, 51; *Minutes of Council*, I, Index; *Maryland Archives*, I, 91, 170, 230; IV, 376, 377, 378, 482, 486; *New England Genealogical and Historical Register*, I, 201–206.

3. Bradford, *History*, II, 45–47.

hind. The only survival of his brief sojourn on the shores of Massachusetts Bay is the name of a hill in Quincy, Mount Wollaston,[1] a locality well known to the Puritans later under the same name.

Of more interest than the coming of Wollaston was the arrival in the same vessel of one Thomas Morton, who made his first appearance in New England at this date, bringing with him thirty servants and provisions of all sorts fit for a plantation. There is to the student of early New England history no more engaging or diverting character than this gentleman-lawyer of Clifford's Inn, whose whimsical career amid the encircling gloom of the Pilgrim and Puritan surroundings lends color and vivacity to the scene. According to his latest biographer,[2] he was a gentleman by birth, of the propertied class, with a lawful right to use a coat of arms. In England, during the years from 1618 to 1623, when perhaps forty years old or more, he became involved in a chancery suit with the eldest son of a widow, of about his own age, whom he married in 1621. He had met her first, when as an attorney he was engaged to protect the property of her first husband from the cupidity of the heir-at-law, during the settlement of the father's estate. By a judgment of June 8, 1623, the case went against Morton, who had disappeared the February before and had not been heard of again by

1. Practically nothing is known of Wollaston's career. He must have remained in Virginia but a short time, for in 1624 we find him in charge of the *Unity*, with Rastell, his companion at Mount Wollaston, as master, engaged in carrying Captain John Martin back from England to the colony. Rastell became involved in a suit before the governor and council there, because, as Martin alleged, he had failed to fulfil his contract. Though no other record remains, as far as is known, of Wollaston's activities, in all probability he spent his life as an itinerant sea-captain in the service of one owner or another. Such a life was common with scores of sea-captains of the period.

2. Banks, *Proceedings*, Massachusetts Historical Society, 58, pp. 147–193, a notable article, and *History of York*, I, 159–160. Dr. Banks makes it clear that Morton could not have come to New England in 1622, as is commonly stated, even though he is himself responsible for the date. Later, in 1636, Morton said that he first went to New England "about twelve years since," that is, in 1624 (*ibid.*, 59, pp. 92–93). See also *Historical Collections*, Essex Institute, 49, pp. 253–256, where his will is printed; Bradford, "Letter Book," p. 61. Shortly before his death in 1931, Dr. Banks wrote me, "You may be interested to know that I have acquired further documents about Morton—one from the Diocesan Registry at Wells, a suit in the ecclesiastical court (Bishop's consistory) based on an allegation of slander or blasphemy—the interesting point of which is Morton's remark on 'going to church' and his statement that he had a 'pectoral cross,' which he wore as a souvenir of a friend. This was in 1619 when he was living in Axbridge Co. Somerset. Morton was perhaps a Catholic." If Dr. Banks' conjecture is correct it would preclude the idea, frequently entertained, that Morton was a pagan.

his family. He was charged with having sold his wife's wearing apparel and with declining to obey the court's decree, "endeavouring to find out holes whereby to elude performance of these things."[1] Where he concealed himself until he shipped with Wollaston and where he obtained money to buy equipment and employ thirty servants are not known. There is some reason to believe that he had in a fashion acquired a patent to lands in New England, either at this time or afterward, for Samuel Maverick, writing about 1661, speaks of Morton's having a patent many years before, and Morton in his will disposes of a number of parcels of land lying along the Kennebec river.[2]

Morton was a bohemian, a humorist, a scoffer, and a libertine, with no moral standards of thought or conduct. After Wollaston had deserted his place of settlement, Morton "having more craft than honestie" watched his opportunity and with liquor and other "junkats" prepared a feast for his servants. Having got them "merry" he persuaded many to remain with him, promising on his part, inasmuch as he had a share in the plantation, to free them from their indenture and to make them partners and associates with him, all living together as equals, supporting and protecting one another. This plan having been agreed upon, they turned the settlement into a place of revels, after the manner of old England, and in so doing scandalized the Pilgrims who were living only twenty-five miles away. The crowd at Wollaston fell, says the shocked Bradford, "into great licentiousness, and into all profaneness. And Morton became lord of misrule, and maintained (as it were) a school of Athisme. And after they had got some goods into their hands, and got much by trading with the Indians, they spent it vainly, in quaffing and drinking both wine and strong waters in great excess, and as some reported 10*li* worth in a morning. They also set up a May-

1. *Proceedings,* Massachusetts Historical Society, 58, p. 188. The son, George Miller, charged Morton with marrying his mother "to shoe his owne cunninge and unlawful ends and to gaine the whole estate to himself," and the case resolved itself into a conflict between "a middle-aged veteran of many encounters" and "a young wild-cat," both of whom "soon threw off all symptoms of friendly intercourse" (pp. 151, 171). The article effectually disposes of Bradford's charge that Morton had committed murder in England, in consequence of which he had to flee to America (pp. 156–157).

2. Gardiner, *New England's Vindication* (Gorges Society, I, ed. Banks), written in 1660, says definitely that the Council for New England "granted sundry Pattents, as to Capt. Willeston, Mr. Tho. Morton . . . and others, to settle in the Bay of the Machechusetts," p. 23. This statement may include a grant to Weston.

pole, drinking and dancing about it many days togeather, inviting the Indean women, for their consorts, dancing and frisking togethir (like so many fairies or furies rather) and worse practices . . . Morton likewise (to shew his poetrie) composed sundry rimes and versies, some tending to lasciviousness and others to the detraction and scandall of some persons, which he affixed to this idle or idoll May-polle. They changed also the name of their place, and in stead of calling it Mount Wollaston, they called it Meriemounts, as if this jolitie would have lasted forever."[1] But as we shall see soon these things were not to last forever. The tug of war between Morton on one side and the Pilgrims and Puritans on the other was yet to come.

Meanwhile, Gorges and the Council for New England had not been idle. In 1622 and 1623 they issued five patents that are known and probably others that are not known, such as possible grants to Weston, Wollaston, and Morton. Those that are a matter of record are the patent of March 9, 1622, to Captain John Mason—the Marianna grant—covering Cape Ann and adjoining territories between the forty-second and forty-third parallels of latitude;[2] that of August 10 to Gorges and Mason of the province of Maine, lying along the seacoast between the Merrimac and the Kennebec, which in 1629 the two partners divided between themselves;[3] that of October 16 to David Thomson and his associates, a tract including six thousand acres and an island at the mouth of the Piscataqua, where Thomson attempted to settle in 1623, by arrangement with three merchants of Plymouth, but whence after living there for three years he moved to an island in Boston harbor;[4] that of December 30 to Robert Gorges, of whom more later; and that of May 5, 1623, of six thousand acres to Christopher Levett, who was appointed a councillor and afterward named governor general of New England, and who was proposing with the aid of a company of Yorkshiremen to erect a city which was to bear the name of his birthplace, York.[5] Thus at the very beginning of its career, the council initiated the special work for which it was chartered—the

1. Bradford, *History*, II, 47–49.   2. Tuttle, *Life of Mason*, pp. 170–177. 3. *Ibid.*, 177–183; *Farnham Papers*, I, 64–71.

4. *Proceedings*, Massachusetts Historical Society, 1876, p. 358; Bradford, *History*, I, 340; Tuttle, *Mason*, p. 15.

5. *Farnham Papers*, I, 72–73; Baxter, *Christopher Levett* (Gorges Society); *Collections*, Maine Historical Society, II; Levermore, *Forerunners*, II, 604–642; *Calendar State Papers, Colonial*, 1574–1660, p. 47. Levett was not the founder of York, as he

distribution of land. Many of these grants, both at this time and later, in the form and wording of the patents and the conditions of tenure, disclose the essentially feudal character of the council. Though it issued indentures for particular plantations, as the Virginia Company had done and was doing, it created also, and much more to its liking, petty fiefs, the grantees of which were possessed of extensive powers, holding directly of the king and not of the council.[1] That this enforcement of the statute of Quia Emptores was distasteful to Gorges and the others appears from the fact that when in 1623 they drafted a plan for a new charter they introduced a clause allowing them to grant lands in New England "to bee held of them by any tenure such as they shall think most fit, Notwithstanding the Statute of *quia emptores terrarum*," and investing them with power to create tenures, "either according to the lawes of England or the ffeodall lawes or any other law," notwithstanding the same statute.[2] Had the council ever obtained this charter, which it never did, its transformation into a feudal proprietary would have been complete.

But the distribution of land and the subletting of fiefs were not the only activities in which the council was authorized to engage by its charter, for it was vested also with the power to found colonies of its own. Founding colonies was, however, a very different matter from distributing land. The latter not only cost nothing, but probably brought in considerable revenue, inasmuch as the council did not issue patents to others than its own members without fees. On the other hand colonizing ventures cost money, and the council, not a joint-stock concern, had no other funds than the contributions of its members. In 1622 and 1623 Gorges had promoted sundry fishing expeditions, but the expense of these was small as compared with the high price of colonization. Yet colonization, in the form of a great proprietary domain in New England, of which he should some day be the head, was probably the one thing nearest to Gorges' heart, the goal of his ambition. How the necessary funds were to be

later occupied only a part of his patent and built his house on Casco Bay. Edward Godfrey was the first to reside, in a rough log cabin, on the site of the present town. Banks, *History of York*, I, chap. IV.

1. Because in such cases of subinfeudation the statute of Quia Emptores was enforced. These lands were "to be holden of his Ma^ty his heyres and successors as of his Manor of East Greenwich in the County of Kent in free and common socage and not in capite or by knights service." *Farnham Papers*, I, 66.

2. *Proceedings*, American Antiquarian Society, 1867, pp. 90–91.

raised was a serious problem, for he always had trouble in keeping the various members of the council sufficiently interested to extract money from them, and consequently at this juncture he had to call for additional help. He caused to be admitted a number of new members who were "gentlemen of honour and blood" and also six merchants of the West Country with money to invest, thus tapping a source of capital which at first he had completely ignored in making up his original list of "aristocrats." This enlargement of the council having been effected, he persuaded his associates to issue to his son Robert, recently returned from military service in the Venetian wars, a patent for a propriety in New England, that was defined in the text as a part of the mainland commonly called or known by the name of Massachustack, extending ten miles into the interior, to be held of the king by the sword, that is, the finding of four able men to attend upon the governor general for any service required. This was tenure by knight service.[1] The patent was issued December 30, 1622.

With this territory as his principal demesne, Robert Gorges was appointed governor general of all New England and given a council consisting of Captain Francis West, afterward governor of Virginia, who was created admiral; Captain Christopher Levett, who was planning to erect a settlement of his own farther north; the governor of Plymouth colony, who, of course at this date, was Bradford; and others to be named from time to time. Robert Gorges spent the winter of 1622–1623 in making preparations, gathering supplies, bringing together a hopeful company, and guarding by every means at his command against the failure of what was expected to be the beginning of orderly colonization in New England and the forerunner of other and larger expeditions that would place church and state there on a secure foundation and reproduce as nearly as possible the political, social, and ecclesiastical institutions of the old country. As Virginia of the same date was building on the ideas of Sandys and the Virginia Company, so the New England of Robert Gorges was to be built on the ideas of Sir Ferdinando and the Council for New England.

In order to win over the members of the council and to give them

1. Hazard, *State Papers*, I, 152–155; Bradford, *History*, I, 372. The same tenure was employed in the distribution of 1635. Such tenures were not abolished by law until 1661.

something in the way of a tangible return on their investment, Gorges provided, in somewhat dramatic fashion, for a distribution of territory among them. There had been an earlier division of 1622, when Lenox, Calvert, and Arundel had been given "devidents," extending from Saco river to Pemaquid and back into the interior thirty miles, to be held of the crown by the sword.[1] The country was to be called New Albion, titles of honor and precedency were to be allowed, and a public city was planned. Though the division was never consummated, it shows the ideas that influenced Gorges and the others in determining the form that New England colonization should take. The second division, that of June 29, 1623, was staged in the king's presence. Gorges felt that such a division was necessary in order to forestall parliamentary interference with the monopoly privileges of the council and to meet the criticism of those among the members who objected to contributing money without knowing what their shares were to be. John Smith's map was used and the region thereon depicted was divided into twenty parts, for which the members present drew lots. The king himself drew lots for the Duke of Buckingham, the lord keeper, John, Lord Bishop of Lincoln,[2] and Lord Gorges, who were absent. Nothing is said about the terms of the grants, but probably they were the same as those of 1622. This division, likewise, was never perfected, no patents were ever drawn, and no titles were ever created. These early proceedings were later forgotten and ignored and their only interest for us lies in their witness to the pretentious expectations of those who took seriously their own membership on the Council for New England. They show a growing eagerness on the part of the landed classes for wider estates in the new world to supplement their losses in income at home. The second division is of interest also in the use of Smith's map and in the copy of that map, with the shares marked upon it, which still sur-

1. *Proceedings,* American Antiquarian Society, 1867, pp. 62–64; *Farnham Papers,* I, 61–64.

2. The Bishop of Lincoln had been admitted to membership, on paying his subscription, only twelve days before (*Proceedings,* American Antiquarian Society, 1867, p. 96). Just what this subscription amounted to there is no way of knowing. The £110 demanded of the merchants was the fee customarily paid for a patent authorizing the erection of a particular plantation, such as that of Peirce and others. Though the Virginia Company issued many such patents, the Council for New England seems to have issued very few of them and so could hardly have counted on that side of its activity as bringing in much revenue.

vives, a silent deponent to a spectacular but futile proprietary gesture.[1]

With this distribution effected and at least half of the council satisfied for the moment (the other half seems to have paid little or no attention to the proceedings and made no pretence of coming to the meetings), Robert Gorges set forth on the great adventure, which was to create a new principality in America. He carried with him the most elaborate colonial outfit that thus far had been sent over, consisting as it did of men, women, and children—mechanics, farmers, traders, six "gentlemen," and two clergymen, Morrell and Blaxton or Blackstone.[2] It also included ample supplies and all necessary equipment for the voyage and the settlement. Robert Gorges had done his work well, even though he had had to rely on insufficient means, for Sir Ferdinando, having failed in his effort to obtain help from the adjoining towns of Gloucestershire, Devon, and Somerset, was compelled to fall back on the resources of his own family and on the contributions of such members of the council as were willing to put up money for the enterprise. These resources were taxed to the utmost in order to make an efficient and successful beginning of the great experiment. One wonders sometimes at the hopefulness and sheer courage of these men, who were willing to risk so much in what we now know was a fruitless and misguided endeavor. It was one thing to divide up territory on paper; it was quite another to utilize this territory as a source of profit from tenancies and trade. The failure of these men to realize anything whatever on their investments or to advance in any material way the cause of colonization constitutes one of the most amazing chapters in the story of early settlement in America, for in no other single instance were the results more tragically the reverse of expectations than in the effort which Robert Gorges made to fulfil the hopes of his father in the summer and autumn of 1623.

Mistakes were made at the very outset, for the company, instead

1. The map was first printed in Alexander's *Encouragement to Colonies*, 1625, and was inserted in Purchas' *Pilgrimes* (IV, 1872), issued the next year. It has since been reproduced in part in Thornton, *The Plantation at Cape Ann*, in the *Proceedings*, American Antiquarian Society, 1875, p. 30, in Winsor, *Narrative and Critical History*, III, 306, and in Bradford, *History*, I, 375. The facts regarding the division are in the original records of the council, *Proceedings*, American Antiquarian Society, 1867, pp. 96[8], 94[4]. See also *Farnham Papers*, I, 73-75; *Proceedings*, American Antiquarian Society, 1875, pp. 49-56; Smith, *Travels and Works*, II, 892.

2. Adams, *Three Episodes*, I, 322-328.

of going directly to Robert Gorges' own grant on the upper side of Massachusetts Bay, landed at Weston's old camping ground at Wessagusset, vacated but six months before. There during the last days of September, taking possession of the buildings which Weston's party had left behind, Robert Gorges made every effort to tide over the winter.[1] He spent some time in visiting Plymouth to the southward and the Piscataqua region farther north and in endeavoring to make his authority felt as governor general.[2] There is some reason also to think that he visited the scene of his own grant, taking formal possession of the territory, settling a plantation there, and placing it in the charge and under the custody of some of the tenants and servants, who had been sent over by members of the council.[3] But of the existence of such a plantation there is no other record than the unsupported assertion of the promoters in England. Gorges never occupied the grant himself, but settled down at Wessagusset to the monotonous and demoralizing life of a New England winter, with its hardships and weary routine. Trouble inevitably arose. Dislike of the country, discontent bred of adversity, suffering due to insufficient provisions and inadequate housing, and a fire in the settlement, all these disasters soon set the company by the ears and roused in many a longing for old England. To Robert Gorges, accustomed to a military life and deprived of the excitement of warfare, even against the Spanish ships that he had hoped to seize, and to the Rev. William Morrell, his chaplain, whose wish to establish episcopacy in the wilds of New England and to become superintendent—some have called him bishop—of the New England churches grew less roseate as the months wore on—to both of

1. Bradford, *History*, II, 327–328.

2. He was able to accomplish practically nothing in this direction. His one effort to establish his authority ended in an undignified controversy with Weston, while his attempt and that of his admiral, Francis West, to exercise the fishing privileges of the Council for New England foundered on the refusal of the fishermen to recognize his right to collect license fees from them.

3. How else are we to explain Gorges' statement that Robert Gorges "being made governor in those parts went in person and took absolute seizure and actual possession of that country by a settled plantation he made in Massachusetts Bay, which afterwards he left to the charge and custody of his servants and certain other undertakers and tenants belonging unto some of us, who were all thrust out by these intruders [the Puritans] that had exorbitantly bounded their grants from east to west"? The inference from this is that Robert Gorges did establish a plantation between the Charles and the Saugus rivers, visiting it in person, establishing servants upon it, and then obtaining possession by right of occupation. This point will come up again in considering the title of the Massachusetts Bay Company.

these men life at Wessagusset must soon have become intolerable. In the spring of 1624 Gorges deserted the plantation and returned to England. Morrell remained another year, going back in 1625. During his sojourn at Wessagusset he composed a metrical account of the country in English and Latin, which ends with the words, "To see here built I trust, An English kingdom from this Indian dust,"[1] a hope never to be fulfilled, for New England was destined to become anything but an English kingdom.

The others of the company soon dispersed. Some went to Virginia, a few remained at Wessagusset, while others, a noteworthy group, wandered along the coast and established homes where they could. The Rev. William Blaxton, B.A., M.A., Emmanuel College, Cambridge,[2] called by Cotton Mather, "a goodly Episcopalian," removed to the western slope of Shawmut peninsula (Beacon Hill), where near an excellent spring, he built a house, planted an orchard, raised apples, and cultivated a vegetable garden. In 1630 he became a freeman of the Massachusetts Bay Company. Leaving Boston in 1635, disillusioned because of the intolerance of the Puritan magistrates, he went southward to the eastern shore of Narragansett Bay, saying as he departed, "I came from England because I did not like the Lord Bishops, but I cannot join with you because I would not be under the Lord Brethren." He too wanted to worship God in his own way.[3]

Another of the Gorges group, Samuel Maverick, a young man of twenty-two and a notable character in later New England history, removed with his wife to Winnisimmet (Chelsea) and later to

1. On Morrell, *Proceedings*, Massachusetts Historical Society, 2d series, 4, pp. 73–76; 61, pp. 86–87; and for the poem, *ibid.*, 1st series, 1, pp. 124–139.

2. *Proceedings*, Massachusetts Historical Society, 61, pp. 86–87.

3. Blaxton was at this time about thirty years of age. He was of the Church of England, but was half a Puritan, as were so many others of the day, and detested prelacy. Yet while in New England he continued to wear his canonical coat (Johnson, *Wonder-Working Providence*, p. 46), which shows that he was still a low church Anglican. His house was on the slope of West Hill, southwest of Beacon Hill (western corner of Beacon and Spruce streets), where he lived for ten years with his apple trees, his vegetables, his flowers, his pig, his two servants, and his books. In 1635 he moved, with all his belongings, to what later became Rhode Island, but at the time was claimed as a part of Plymouth (the northwestern corner), in what is now the village of Lonsdale in the town of Cumberland, three miles north of Pawtucket and six miles from Providence. He called the place "Study Hill." He was a bachelor until he married at the age of sixty-three, the ceremony being performed, oddly enough, by John Endecott, at that time governor of the Massachusetts Bay Colony. (Bliss, *History of Rehoboth*, pp. 2–14; Banks, in *Pro-*

Noddles Island in the Bay, where he fished, traded, and farmed. Though the Massachusetts Bay people allowed him to remain they never approved of him, nor did he long continue on friendly terms with them while in the colony. Later he withdrew to New Amsterdam. After the Restoration he came into favor in England, wrote a *Briefe Description of New England,* corresponded with the lord chancellor, the Earl of Clarendon, and was appointed one of the royal commissioners in 1664 to investigate New England, thus turning the tables on the Puritan Commonwealth. He was a man of good family, education, and property, of a kindly and generous disposition, and having come to America without religious motives he was tolerant and sympathetic toward others. He must have been possessed of unusual tact to get on with the Puritans as long as he did. Later, after he had learned to know them better, he was not so restrained.[1]

Thomas Walford, a blacksmith, settled with his wife at Mishawum (Charlestown), but he was hounded out by the Puritans and finally went to Portsmouth, where he was welcomed by the Anglicans there, given a grant of land, elected a selectman, and chosen warden of the Anglican Church. John Balch in 1624 went to Cape Ann and later to Salem, and William Jeffrey, a gentleman as was Maverick, also went to Cape Ann, but afterward returned to Wessagusset. On the other hand, John Bursley and a saving remnant stayed at Wessagusset, thus giving to that settlement, later the town of Weymouth, a continuous history from the coming of Robert Gorges to the present day and assuring to it the distinction of being the second permanent place of residence in New England and the first on Massachusetts Bay. These men were all of them pioneers, deserving quite as much as do the Pilgrims and Puritans, the

ceedings, Massachusetts Historical Society, 61, pp. 86–87; *Collections,* the same, 2d series, X, 171–172; 3d series, III, Lechford's *Plaine Dealing*). Blaxton's remains were removed in 1886 (*Proceedings,* the same, 2d series, 2, pp. 480–481). Bolton, in *The Real Founders of New England,* pp. 62–64, furnishes some additional information about Blaxton, Maverick, Walford, and others of these early pioneers.

1. Winthrop, *Journal,* I, 115; *Proceedings,* Massachusetts Historical Society, 2d series, 1, pp. 367–373; Johnson, *Wonder-Working Providence,* pp. 63–64; Sumner, *History of East Boston;* Libby, *Maine Province and Court Records,* I, xxxviii, xlvii–xlviii; "Brief Description," in *New England Historical and Genealogical Register,* XXXIX, 33–48; and *Proceedings,* Massachusetts Historical Society, 2d series, 1, pp. 231–248. Maverick's correspondence with Clarendon is in *Collections,* New York Historical Society, 1869. For his later relations with Massachusetts Bay, *Publications, Colonial Society of Massachusetts,* XXI, 28, note 1.

gratitude of posterity. The treatment of some of them by the Puritans adds nothing to the lustre of Puritan fame.[1]

Thus Gorges' pretentious expedition ended in an overwhelming failure. It strikes one with astonishment that so impossible an undertaking should ever have been begun or that Englishmen, even of the landed classes, should have had so little understanding and imagination as to believe success possible. The collapse left New England pretty much as it was before. Outside the Plymouth colony and in addition to the shifting fisher folk, there may have been in 1625 half a hundred white settlers scattered here and there, from Natascot (Hull) and Wessagusset to the mouth of the Piscataqua,[2] engaged in agriculture, fishing, and trading, of whose lives and characters we know relatively very little. They were a restless people, who had come to America because they were dissatisfied with conditions in England and preferred the novelty and even the loneliness of an abode in the wilderness. Had this not been so more of them would have returned to England as opportunity arose. Except at Plymouth there was no unity among them. They were individualistic, inclined to adventure, lovers of isolation, and but slightly possessed of the group instinct. In time they either passed away in solitude, leaving few traces behind, or were absorbed, often against their wills, and died as members of larger and better organized social communities. Each contributed his share to the opening of the new country into which he came, and in his struggles, sufferings, and efforts to live a civilized life helped to prepare that country for those who came later and were more successful. The Pilgrim who came to Plymouth and the Puritan who came to Massachusetts Bay were not the first in the land, and owed much to others who had been there before them. Fishermen and traders were plying their craft up and down the coast of New England and into the interior; fishing vessels, bearing men of all sorts and conditions, were sailing back and forth and out into the ocean from points as far south as Cape Cod and north as far as the St. Lawrence, and restless wanderers were trying first one place and then another in their effort to live and make a profit and satisfy their migratory instincts. The strength of the Pilgrim and the Puritan lay in their religious unity

1. For an account of all these early pioneers and their settlements, see Bolton, *The Real Founders of New England*, appendix B.

2. It has been estimated that there may have been 500 people in New England before the coming of the Puritans.

and their desire for permanent homes in a land where they would be let alone. Though they were not colonizers in the strictest sense of the term, for they wished to sever as completely as possible their connections with the mother country, they were more so than the others, who without fixed religious purpose were but transients on New England soil, the forerunners not the founders of New England.

CHAPTER XVII

THE FORMATION OF THE MASSACHUSETTS BAY COMPANY

THE movement that eventually brought the Puritans to New England began as a fishing venture, not unlike other similar ventures made here and there during this early period. The way of it was this. In 1623 the Pilgrims, urged on by their associates, the London merchant adventurers, who wanted profit not prayers, looked about for an enlargement of their activities. Hearing, probably from Phinehas Pratt,[1] of the merits of Cape Ann and learning, too, that David Thomson, then of Piscataqua, and even Weston himself were planning to obtain rights in that region, they sent Edward Winslow to England, bearing a letter from Bradford, dated September 8, 1623, to secure a patent for Cape Ann.[2] On January 1, 1624, Winslow, with the aid of Robert Cushman, received from Lord Sheffield, one of the members of the Council for New England who had shared in the division of 1623, a patent for a tract of land at Cape Ann, in the forty-third degree of north latitude, together with the use of the adjoining waters and liberty to fish freely.

Unfortunately for the Pilgrims there were flaws in their title. Though the indenture says that the territory was within Sheffield's "devident," it was, according to the map, within that of the Earl of Warwick and therefore a Sheffield grant would be of no validity, unless Sheffield was acting under some other patent, of which no record exists.[3] Furthermore, the indenture granted land "not nowe being inhabited or hereafter to be inhabited by any English," whereas in 1623, before the deed was passed, there were already (as we shall see) fourteen Dorchester men on the place and about thirty-two more who came the following year, making some forty-

1. Pratt was one of Weston's colonists at Wessagusset and went to Plymouth in March, 1623. He was familiar with the fishing conditions northward as far as the Piscataqua. Levermore, *Forerunners*, II, 820.

2. *American Historical Review*, VIII, 296.

3. The Pilgrim patent is printed in Thornton, *The Plantation at Cape Ann*, and in Bradford, *History*, I, 407–410.

six in occupation before the Pilgrims arrived. Therefore, the document was, as Hubbard calls it,[1] "a useless patent" and of no value in the face of the resistance offered by those who were already in control of the territory. The Pilgrims built a fishing stage there and placed a man on watch, who proved of little service, engaging rather in trading for furs than in fishing. Then they sent another also, "an ignorante, foolish, self-willed fellow" (they were generally unsuccessful in the men they employed) to make salt there for curing the fish they hoped to catch, but nothing came of the experiment and in the end the claim, when put to the test, broke down completely. The money spent for the patent was an entire loss to the Pilgrims, and that too at a time when their relations with the merchant adventurers were approaching a crisis.

For a number of years the town of Dorchester had been actively considering an undertaking of its own. This undertaking was no isolated affair. In studying the various enterprises of these early years of the seventeenth century one cannot but be struck by their interlocking character. We have already seen the close connection that existed between the Virginia, Plymouth, and Bermuda companies and their influence upon the Merchant Venturers of Bristol in the attempts which the latter made to found a colony in Newfoundland. We have seen also the influence of the Bristol enterprise upon Vaughan, Falkland, Calvert, and Alexander, and the place of Captain John Mason in the Newfoundland scene. We have had it borne in upon us how closely the Pilgrims were bound up with the Virginia Company and the Council for New England as well as with the merchant adventurers of London, and are interested to learn that the counsellor John White, a member of the Dorchester company, who afterward aided the Massachusetts Bay Company to secure its charter, was in all probability the same John White who in 1625 was the lawyer for the Lyford faction in England in its controversy with the Pilgrims and who headed the committee of the adventurers in coming to that noteworthy settlement with Allerton and the Pilgrims which was made in 1626.[2] Others of the London adventurers, too, had a part in the founding and upbuilding of the Massachusetts Bay colony, while some of the Dorchester promoters of the Massachusetts enterprise had owned and probably continued

1. Hubbard, *History of New England*, p. 110.
2. Bradford, *History*, I, 416; II, 6.

to own shares in the Virginia Company. Gabriel Barbour, active member of the latter company and the authorized agent for its lottery, had opened a branch of the lottery in Dorchester in 1619 and had contributed to local charities there;[1] and we may be sure that it was but a simple and natural thing for the Rev. John White later (1627) to turn to London for help, just as the Bristol Venturers had done in forming their Newfoundland company in 1610. All these varied activities were but scattered manifestations of a common movement, characterized by two motives generally found working together—religious unrest and an interest in colonization, including profits from the fur trade and the fishery. The three great legal agencies in this colonizing movement were the Virginia Company of London, the Council for New England, and the London and Bristol Company, with charters from the crown, and upon one or other of these corporate bodies all concerned in colonial enterprise, whether individuals or groups of associates, whether looking to Virginia, New England, or Newfoundland as the scene of their activities, were dependent for their rights and privileges. No one could legally act except under the auspices of one or other of these companies, unless he was able himself to obtain a charter of incorporation from the crown.

With the erection of the Council for New England in 1620 Dorchester was ready to take advantage of the new opportunity. The town had already felt the spur of the prevailing religious dissatisfaction and was adopting stricter rules of conduct in such matters as church-going, preaching, and the observance of the Sabbath. Stimulated, it may be, by the colonizing ambitions of Bristol and the fishing successes of Weymouth—a flourishing seaport situated a few miles to the southward, which was already engaged in fishing off the coast of Maine—it early began to consider the possibility of taking part in the movement. In 1622 Richard Bushrod,[2] an influential Dorchester merchant and bailiff, in his own name and that of his associates, obtained from the Council for New England a fishing license, which entitled him to make a voyage to New England partly for fishing and partly for discovery; and the next year a patent for a particular plantation was granted by the council (Febru-

1. Rose Troup, *John White*, p. 57. Stirk's petition of 1634 was addressed to Lord Saye and Sele, Lord Brooke, Sir Nathaniel Rich, and Gabriel Barbour.
2. Richard Bushrod was an ancestor of Bushrod Washington, nephew of George Washington.

ary 18, 1623), on behalf of the western merchants, to Sir Walter Erle, a Dorsetshire member of the Virginia Company, who was named in the patent as the "governor" of the proposed plantation. Erle, having secured his patent, probably at the request of the Dorchester people, who had already entered upon their fishing adventure, brought the question of a formally organized company to the attention of those interested, and in March, 1624, a meeting was held at Dorchester, which is somewhat grandly described by a local diarist as "The New England Planters Parliament."[1] At this meeting the whole business was carefully considered and arguments presented for and against the undertaking. There, doubtless, were read three important documents: the royal letter to the lord lieutenant of the county, recommending coöperation; a paper of "Reasons shewinge the benefitt of Plantinge in Newe England," which may have been drawn up by the Rev. John White himself in 1623, for circulation in the county;[2] and the report of Richard Bushrod on his experiences and findings in New England. As a result of these deliberations upon the information presented, a company of associates was formed, reaching in time the number of 119 members, made up as follows: fifty of the Dorset gentry and a half-dozen of Devon; thirty merchants from Dorchester, Shrewsbury, and Exeter; twenty clergymen, four widows, a few Londoners, and the rest men in the lower walks of business life. A fund was raised that eventually came to more than £3000, at the rate of £25 a share, payable in five yearly instalments,[3] for the purpose of carrying out the plan.

The object of the company was to found a fishing plantation in New England. White, who may justly be called the originator and

1. Rose Troup, *John White, the Founder of Massachusetts*, p. 63. Mrs. Rose Troup has written more than a biography. Her life of John White, taken in conjunction with her earlier work, *The Massachusetts Bay Company and its Predecessors*, has placed the whole story of the preliminary stages in the founding of Massachusetts on a new level of accuracy and suggestive interpretation. My indebtedness to both volumes is evident throughout these pages.

2. Historical Manuscripts Commission, *Exeter*, pp. 167–168.

3. The names are given in Rose Troup, *John White*, appendix III, taken from lists among the Chancery records. Their presence there is in connection with a suit brought against the Dorchester company, because John Tilly—a *Mayflower* emigrant, a manager of the fishing at Cape Ann before the appointment of Roger Conant, and later a sufferer at the hands of the Indians—and others employed by the company seized, without the latter's knowledge, some barrels of salt left there on the shore by the captain of the *Zouch Phoenix*. This vessel, which is called the *South Phoenix* in the Virginia records, is mentioned in a complaint brought by Captain John Martin of Martin's Brandon against Rastell, Captain Wollaston's old partner at Mount Wol-

director of the movement, had a twofold object in mind. Watching, as doubtless he had often done, the fishing boats sailing, double-manned, out of Weymouth harbor, he conceived the idea of meeting what appeared to him the two greatest needs of promoters and fishermen alike. As more men were wanted for fishing than for navigating the slow-going craft of the day, it seemed to him foolish and a great waste of time to carry these extra hands all the way to New England and back, thus greatly increasing the overhead charges, because of the time lost while the men were idle and the ships lay in harbor. He saw, too, that frequently the vessels returned with their catch to English or Spanish markets too late to dispose of their fish to advantage. He thought if the promoters could have men on the spot, ready to begin fishing early in the season, they would not only be saved the cost of a double complement, but by taking advantage of the fishing months of February, March, and April would be able to make an early sale and increase their profits. Such a thought naturally led to the idea of a plantation, made up largely of these extra men, who in the off-season could, with others among them, cultivate the soil, hunt and trap, and in so doing supply vegetables and fruit and fresh meat not only for themselves but for the sailors also. Having visualized such a profitable plantation, White saw the profound necessity of ministering to the spiritual and religious needs of these far away people and of making the settlement a center of religious activity for all who might frequent those coasts. Thus he wished that the new Dorchester company, under the patent which the Council for New England had granted to Erle, should commit itself to a double task—the founding of a plantation

laston, who was in charge there after Wollaston went to Virginia but who followed him to the latter colony in 1626. Bradford calls him the "merchant," that is, the supercargo, a position that he was occupying at the time of Martin's complaint.

Rastell was the owner and supercargo of the *Unity,* with Wollaston as captain. Martin had chartered this vessel to bring him back to Virginia from England, sometime after February, 1624, when he told the Virginia Company that he was about to return to the colony with his servants and goods. Rastell, who was on board during this voyage, ordered Wollaston to go to Cape Ann, as he wished "to speak with" the captain of the *Zouch Phoenix,* before the latter got away, and consequently was charged by Martin with a breach of contract. It is interesting to find Rastell, Wollaston, and Martin, birds very much of a feather, consorting on the same vessel. To add to the scenic effect, Thomas Morton, too, comes into the picture in connection with the pilfering of the salt. *Somerset and Dorset Notes and Queries,* X, 107; *Proceedings,* Massachusetts Historical Society, 43, pp. 493–496; *Virginia Council Minutes,* I, 25–26; *Virginia Company Records,* II, 510; Rose Troup, *John White,* pp. 100–103. Mrs. Rose Troup does not know of the Virginia evidence.

which should concern itself on one hand with fishing, planting, and the fur trade and on the other with the propagation of religion in the New World.

White was the rector of the Church of the Holy Trinity in Dorchester,[1] and had as one of his allies and the treasurer of the new company, John Humfry, whose place in early New England history and in the history of Old Providence Island is one of interest and importance. The new company itself was an unincorporated body of associates, subscribers to a common fund, the most influential that had been formed in the southwest of England since the founding of the London and Bristol company in 1610, and it started on its career with the high hopes of all its supporters. Even before the meeting of "The New England Planters Parliament" in 1624, the promoters of the undertaking, in the summer of 1623,[2] had sent out, on a fishing voyage to New England, the *Fellowship,* a vessel of fifty tons, laden with men and provisions, but it arrived too late at Cape Ann to accomplish anything profitable and returned, after leaving behind fourteen men, with supplies for the winter, to occupy the place. The next year, 1624, they sent out a larger vessel, a fly-boat of one hundred and forty tons, accompanied by the smaller boat, the *Fellowship,* mentioned above, which knew the course; but owing to delays the vessels arrived too late, found little fish, and after leaving some thirty-two men behind returned, with heavy loss to the undertakers. Undeterred by these failures and courageously determined to carry on, the company borrowed a thousand pounds, and made a third

1. Hubbard, in his *History of New England,* p. 107, calls White "one of the chief founders of the Massachusetts Bay colony." The Rev. Hugh Peter joins to the name of White that of Dr. Arthur Lake, bishop of Bath and Wells, speaking of them as the two who "occasioned, yea, founded that work" of colonizing Massachusetts. We are told that Lake was so zealous in the great scheme that he declared to White "he would go himself [probably as the resident clergyman] but for his age," which was 55 (Thornton, *The First Records of Anglo-American Colonization,* p. 6). It is strange that Mrs. Rose Troup, in her *John White, the Founder of Massachusetts,* should say nothing about Lake; she mentions his name, but quite incidentally in a footnote (p. 399). A brief life of Lake is given in the *Dictionary of National Biography,* but it throws no light on Peter's remark. Professor Morison tells us that he was a fellow student of White's at Winchester and New College (*Builders of the Bay Colony,* p. 27).

2. That the year 1623 marks the beginning of the activities of the Dorchester merchants and their associates of the West Country is attested by White in a letter written in 1634: "Eleven Years sithence and upwards divers knights, gentlemen and others did agree to joyne together in purse as joynt adventurers for the settling of a plantation in New England."

trial, despatching in 1625 three vessels—the *Fellowship,* the fly-boat, and the *Amitie;* but this venture turned out no better than the others.[1]

The local conditions at Cape Ann served only to aggravate the situation. After a year's experimenting with two agents, Tilly and Gardner,[2] to look after the fishing and planting at Cape Ann, the company in 1625 appointed a single head, Roger Conant, a brother of John Conant, one of its own members. Roger had come to Plymouth in 1623, but not finding the Separatist rule congenial, as he was of the Church of England, went off the next year to Natascot (Hull), a fishing island about seven miles by sea from Shawmut (Boston), which offered a convenient place of refuge to such as did not like the Separatist way of doing things.[3] In 1625, invited by the company, Conant, Oldham, and Lyford, with Thomas Gray, John Gray, Walter Knight, and others, left Natascot for Cape Ann, Conant to be the manager of the place, Lyford to be its clergyman, and Oldham to take charge of the trade with the Indians. Oldham delayed his departure for a year, but eventually joined the settlement, where the Anglican element was dominant. Conant as manager found himself, almost at once on arrival, called upon to frustrate an attempt of the Pilgrims who under Miles Standish asserted their claim to the place in a dispute over the fishing stage or wharf they had built the year before. The defiant attitude of Standish in the conflict that ensued led the historian Hubbard to say, "A little chimney is soon fired; so was the Plymouth captain, a man of very little stature, yet of a very hot and angry temper. The fire of his passion soon kindled, and blown into a flame by hot words, might easily have consumed all, had it not been seasonably quenched."[4] Worsted in the encounter and aware of the weakness of their claim, the Plymouth people, under Conant's persuasive influence, having con-

1. The account of the voyages is to be found in *The Planters Plea,* written by White, which has been three times reprinted (by Force, Humphrey, and the Massachusetts Historical Society) and once reproduced in facsimile (Sandy Bay Historical Society and Museum, Rockport, Massachusetts, 1930).

2. Hubbard, *History of New England,* p. 106.

3. *Ibid.,* pp. 106–107. On Conant see Bradford, *History,* I, 418, note; Bolton, *The Real Founders,* p. 105; Rose Troup, *Roger Conant and the Early Settlements on the North Shore of Massachusetts,* and *John White,* pp. 82–83 and index.

4. Hubbard, *History of New England,* p. 111. Conant lived until 1680, dying at the ripe age of eighty-nine. In a deposition of July 1, 1671, he said that he had been in New England for forty-eight years and three months, which would place his arrival at Plymouth in April, 1623. Hubbard lived until 1704 and knew Conant and

sented to compromise on condition that a new stage be built, withdrew from Cape Ann, went to the Kennebec, and left the fifty or more Dorchester settlers in full possession of the territory.[1]

But possession did the Dorchester settlers little good. They struggled on, fighting a losing game. As White wrote in *The Planters Plea*, "No sure fishing place in the land is fit for planting nor any good place for planting found fit for fishing, at least neere the Shoare. And, secondly, rarely any Fisher-men will work at Land, neither are Husband-men fit for Fisher-men but with long use and experience."[2] New misfortunes completed the bankruptcy of the company, which, at last, "wearied of adventuring in that kinde by reason of their losses," brought the undertaking to an end in 1626, in which year "the plantation was dissolved and deserted." The merchants attributed their ill luck to the heavy charges of the vessels— the *Fellowship* requiring an entirely new set of sails and the fly-boat having to be made over at a cost of £800; to poor success at the markets; the fall in the price of shipping—when the vessels came to be sold after the collapse of the company; and to bad management at Cape Ann, which though possessing a good harbor furnished little available arable for planting, and was as Christopher Levett remarked, too far, by twenty miles, from the best fishing waters.

Truly Cape Ann was becoming a place of buried hopes. A majority of the planters—the "landsmen," as White calls them—being sent for by the company returned to England, but "a few of the most honest and industrious resolved to stay and take charge of the Cattell sent over [in the *Amitie*] the year before."[3] Conant with

talked with him. He must have had this story from Conant's own lips. Some of the information in his history has the value of first-hand evidence.

Thomas Morton, in *The New England Canaan*, also speaks of Standish as a small man, calling him "Captain Shrimp." According to those who exhumed what they believed to be the bodies of Miles Standish and his children, the skeleton of the captain measured but five feet and seven inches, the height of a distinctly undersized man. Huiginn, *The Graves of Miles Standish and other Pilgrims* (2d ed. 1914).

1. Mrs. Rose Troup, in *The Massachusetts Bay Company and its Predecessors*, pp. 11–14, and in *John White*, ch. IX, has amply demonstrated the falsity of the statement, based on John Smith (*Travels and Works*, II, 783), that the Dorchester Company held its lands as tenants of the Pilgrims and the London merchants. As she says, Bradford himself never made any such claim in his *History*. Improbable in itself and refuted by the facts of the trial mentioned above (page 347, note 3) the claim rests upon no evidence worthy of credence.

2. *The Planters Plea* (ed. Massachusetts Historical Society), p. 413.

3. *Ibid.*, p. 418; Adams, "The Fishing Plantation at Cape Ann," *Historical Collections*, Essex Institute, XIX, pp. 81–90.

exceptional patience and skill, held together this saving remnant, but realizing that to remain at the cape was futile, because the outlook for agriculture and farming was discouraging, marshaled his company, about thirty in number, including women and children, and in the autumn of the year, conducted them, by water along the coast southward, to Nahum-Keike (Naumkeag, later Salem), where as the "Old Planters" they became the greatly revered founders of the town of Salem. Though Lyford left them for Virginia, soon after their arrival, the others remained, among them men from Plymouth, Wessagusset, and Natascot, some of whom, following their bent as individuals, or "particulars," as the Plymouth people called them, had already moved two or three times, and in a few instances were destined to move still again, leaving Salem for other settlements and even other colonies.[1]

But not all of the Dorchester company in England were willing to give up the undertaking without further effort. White was fired with the desire, always present in his mind, to provide religious instruction for "the fishermen and others of our nation" upon the New England coast and to spread the Gospel among the heathen. He even hoped to make ready a place to which those might go who were out of sympathy with the high church tendencies of the Anglican communion, but who could not go to Plymouth, where the Pilgrims had set up an ecclesiastical polity and worship that renounced the Church of England and all its works.[2] He was himself an Anglican, neither Separatist nor rigidly non-conformist, belonging to that increasing number of those who, while lamenting the conditions into which the church had fallen, believed that it was possible to reform the church from within.[3] He had been reading Mourt's *Relation,* printed in England in 1622, and Winslow's *Good News from*

1. Phippen, "The Old Planters," *Historical Collections,* Essex Institute, I, 97–100, 145–153, 185–189; IV, 127; Lapham, *Old Planters of Beverley,* pp. 1–11; Thornton, *Landing at Cape Ann,* p. 63. Oldham did not go to Salem. He was an independent trader on his own account and can hardly be said to have had any abiding place. At one time or another he tried nearly all of the New England settlements—Plymouth, Natascot, Cape Ann, Watertown, and the river towns of Connecticut (see below, p. 376, n. 1). Lyford tried but unsuccessfully to persuade others to go with him to Virginia, where he became the minister at Martin's Hundred, and seems to have been well thought of in that colony. *Virginia Council Minutes,* I, 188, 196.

2. Hubbard, *History of New England,* p. 107.

3. "Non-conformity to the inventions of men in the worship of God" is the phrase usually associated with those who were convinced of the unlawfulness of conformity and refused to accept the ceremonies of the Church of England. As

New England, which had been written while the author was in England and published by Purchas in 1625, and it is not impossible that he may have had conversations with Winslow himself, during the latter's visit to London to secure the Cape Ann patent. More important still was the fact that he had heard from Roger Conant, who wrote that Naumkeag "might prove a receptacle for such as upon the account of religion would be willing to begin a foreign plantation" in that part of the world. As this idea fitted in with his own, he conceived the possibility of retaining the settlement for religious even more than for secular purposes, because he believed that the "principall scope whereat the Colonie aimes" was religion. He therefore wrote to Conant not to desert the business, promising to secure a patent and to provide men, provisions, and goods for trading with the Indians. Conant and the others stayed at Naumkeag, built a few thatched houses on a neck of land between two arms of the sea—later to be given the name of Beverly—and there at the hazard of their lives, through a cold and forbidding winter, awaited help from England.[1]

At about the same time in the year 1627, as Thomas Dudley wrote in his letter to the Countess of Lincoln, "some friends being together in Lincolnshire fell into some discourse about New England and the planting of the Gospel there; and after some deliberation we imparted our reasons by messages to some in London and the

---

Winslow put it, "Wee came from hence . . . to avoid . . . the hierarchy, the crosse in baptisme, the holy dayes, the Book of Common Prayer, etc." (*New England's Salamander,* p. 138). White was a puritan but not a non-conformist in this sense. He remained within the church and was never in danger of suspension, as always were the non-conformist clergymen, many of whom, in strict accordance with the rubrics of the church, were forbidden, not unreasonably, to preach publicly. William Lilly, the astrologer, in his autobiography, says of one Arthur Hildersham, who was silenced, "He was an excellent textman, of exemplary life, pleasant in discourse, a strong enemy to the Brownists, and dissented not from the Church of England in any article of faith, but only about wearing the surplice, baptizing with the cross, and kneeling at the sacrament." This admirably describes many a minister and layman among those who wished to remain within the fold of the church. Richard Mather, who was silenced in 1634, said that he had not worn a surplice for fifteen years (*Life and Death of Richard Mather,* p. 54). It is difficult to see how those who broke their ordination oaths could have been treated otherwise than by suspension. No serious persecution, though doubtless some hardship, accompanied such treatment, which cannot be compared in severity and brutality with the outrages perpetrated against the Quakers and Anabaptists—"Fanatical Dissenters," as they were called—during the last years of the reign of Charles II. For instances see *Calendar State Papers, Domestic,* 1682, 1683, *passim.*

1. Hubbard, *History,* pp. 107–108; Phillips, *Salem in the Seventeenth Century,* map.

West Country, where it was deliberately thought upon."[1] White puts the matter a little differently in saying that after the Dorchester people had decided to go on with the undertaking they conferred "casually with some *Gentlemen* of *London* [and] moved them to adde unto them as many more. By which occasion the businesse came to agitation a-fresh in *London* and being at first approved by some and disliked by others, by argument and disputation it grew to be more vulgar," that is, better known.[2] That all plans for the enlargement of the enterprise originated with White and the Western puritans goes without saying, but it is equally clear that circumstances were drawing together three groups of men to unite in a common undertaking, which in its larger aspects was approved by all. Ideas, not essentially dissimilar, were germinating at the same time in three different parts of England and the association of those who held them was far from a merely fortuitous happening. That in the final issue White, the Londoners, and the East Anglian puritans were to find many reasons for disagreement as to the exact ends to be sought, the events of a later time were to show, but for the moment a oneness of purpose animated all. The result of this combination of men of like minds was a series of meetings in London, at which the decision was reached to organize a New England Company to take over the moribund Dorchester enterprise and to plant a religious colony upon the place where Conant and the Old Planters were struggling, amid the hardships of a New England winter, to hold the group together.

The first business was to secure a patent of land, but success was long delayed and the troubled and isolated planters were compelled to undergo a second wintry season before success was finally attained. The Dorchester merchants were relatively inconspicuous men and in their case as in that of the Erle patent, the Council for New England required the sanction of gentlemen of honor and blood, in quality similar to its own members, before making a grant of its land. To meet this condition, White sought sponsors from among the men of influence, family, and wealth of the neighborhood, who could fulfil the council's requirements and were willing to aid the new undertaking. These were, first, Sir Henry Rosewell of Ford Abbey, Devonshire, high sheriff of that county and one of

1. Force, *Tracts*, II, no. 4, p. 7; Young, *Chronicles of Massachusetts Bay*, p. 309.
2. *The Planters Plea*, p. 195.

the characters used by Samuel Butler in making up his composite Hudibras. He was probably connected with the prominent puritan family of Rosewells, for he was puritan in sympathy and willing to do what he could for White, his friend and neighbor. Next was Sir John Young, the son of a former high sheriff of Devonshire and a resident of Colyton, just over the Dorset border, whose son Walter had been a member of the company. Last of the three was Thomas Southcote or Southcott, a wealthy Devonshire merchant living at Mohuns Ottery, near Honiton, who also had been one of the Dorchester company. They were the silent members, who never took any active part in the movement, but were solicited to coöperate, because of the weight of their names with Gorges and Warwick. The working members were also three: John Humfry, one of White's parishioners and a former treasurer of the company, whose father had been a "capital burgess" of Dorchester. Humfry was probably living there at the time, having only a few months before buried his second wife, Elizabeth Pelham. He was known to Theophilus, fourth earl of Lincoln, whose sister he afterward married, and he may have been brought into the list of patentees through the earl's influence.[1] Next was Simon Whetcome, a wealthy cloth-worker of London, related to the merchant family of Sherborne, Dorset, whose brother, Robert, had been a member of the company. Whetcome was afterward one of the assistants of the Massachusetts Bay Company and prominent in its affairs as long as it remained in England. He never went to America. Lastly, we have John Endecott, the reason for whose selection has never been satisfactorily given, as he was not a Dorset man nor, as far as is known, a friend of White's. He had recently married a niece[2] (or at least a near relative) of Mathew Cradock, an influential London merchant, who was soon to be chosen the first governor of the new company, and it is not impossible that he was recommended by Cradock as a desirable patentee and, later, as the one most willing and best fitted to lead the expedition that the company planned to send over should the patent be secured.

The exact character of the patent and the steps taken in obtaining

1. Rose Troup, "John Humfry," *Historical Collections,* Essex Institute, LXV, 294.

2. The marriage with Cradock's niece is mentioned in the company's letter to Endecott (*Massachusetts Colonial Records,* I, 383). There seems to be no evidence to warrant the statement frequently made that Endecott was White's parishioner at Dorchester.

it are both uncertain. In 1627 and 1628 the Council for New England was inanimate if not actually moribund and it is doubtful if any sessions were held or if any business was done. This point will be discussed in the next chapter, but for the moment it may be said that Gorges was in Plymouth, occupied with his war duties, and Warwick, the president of the council, was in London with the seal in his possession. It was he to whom the petitioners, named above, must have sent their formal application for a patent, as there was no one else to whom such an application could be made. Whether they approached him in his official capacity, as president of the council, or in his private capacity, as the recipient of a grant, May 31, 1622,[1] in common with Lord Gorges, Sir Robert Mansell, and Sir Ferdinando Gorges, of land "in the Massachusetts," it is difficult to say. In the absence of all records for the years 1627 and 1628, the statement that the grant was officially made by the council and in the usual way, must be looked upon with suspicion. Warwick as president could not legally pass a patent alone, though doubtless he could have done so were he able to obtain the written consent of as many as were customarily present when grants of land were made. Apparently, up to this time, little or no attention has been paid to that particular clause of the charter of 1620 to the Council for New England which requires that at least a majority of the members be present on such occasions. In fact so many difficulties accompany any attempt to show the issue of a grant by the council itself in 1628 that one is forced to seek a solution elsewhere. It is possible that the supposed grant by the council may turn out to be nothing more than a reassignment or transfer by Warwick, with the consent of his associates, of the grant noted above, which he and the others had received in 1622. That something of the kind took place may be inferred from a passage in the records of the Massachusetts Bay Company, "It is also thought fit and ordered that the Secretary shall wryte out a coppy of the former grant to the Erle of Warwick and others, which was by them resigned to this Company, to be presented to his Lordship, as he having desired the same."[2] If that is the case then the petitioners obtained nothing more by way of a patent than the resignation of this early grant.

But even this solution involves difficulties and contradictions. How

1. *Proceedings*, American Antiquarian Society, 1867, p. 59.
2. *Massachusetts Colonial Records*, I, 53.

are we to reconcile the statement in the charter, which says that the grant was in the form of a patent from the council, with the entry in the records, which implies that it was in the form of an assignment from Warwick of an earlier grant to himself and his associates? There is no reconciliation, unless we can assume that what Warwick transferred was not a regular patent but a confirmation under the common seal of the council of the earlier grant. Two other questions arise. First, was the original grant to Warwick and his associates of the nature of a freehold tenancy, held of the council, or of a petty fief, held of the crown? and, secondly, and much more important, did the original text contain the exact boundaries of land that are so carefully named in the Massachusetts Bay charter of 1629? To the first question no answer can be given beyond the general statement that in all probability men of such high standing as the original patentees—Warwick, Lord Gorges, Mansell, and Sir Ferdinando—would hardly have been content with a freehold tenancy, but would expect nothing less than a land grant commensurable in character with their own dignity and rank; and to the second that while such exact definitions of land were unknown to the inferior forms of tenure, as in the Peirce patent, for example, they were common enough in the grants of feudal proprieties. The grant of 1622 to Warwick and his associates could perfectly well have conferred on the patentees a petty fief to be held of the king in free and common socage as of the manor of East Greenwich, with its boundaries carefully defined.

In the absence of the originals of any of the possible documents—the original patent to Warwick and his associates, its transfer to the New England Company, or the supposed grant by the New England Council—any conclusions are bound to be more or less conjectural. It has always been assumed that the copy of the New England Company's patent, imbedded in the Massachusetts Bay Company's charter of 1629,[1] is to be taken at its face value, as accurately reproducing the original text. This is far from certain. The original document was carried to New England in 1630 and has since disappeared, though other documents of that day have been preserved. Was it destroyed as incriminating evidence? The Gorges' descendants made the charge in 1677 that the grant contained in the charter of 1629,

1. *Proceedings,* Massachusetts Historical Society, 62, pp. 252–254, the latest edition of the text of the charter.

which is in form a grant from the council, was a pretended grant and was never actually issued.[1] Even at the time Gorges himself claimed that the grant was an enlargement "by his Majesty," as if it differed from the earlier Warwick patent, containing additions which made it in fact a different document. When the Privy Council had the case before it in 1632, it too became suspicious and ordered the "patentes" to be brought before it, presumably that it might compare them, one with another, but there is nothing to show that this was actually done. Though the Council for New England had "patent books"[2] and kept copies of its patents, it apparently could furnish no copy of this document and the Privy Council was compelled to ask for the original text. But that was not accessible, as it had gone over the water. In view of the dangers threatening the Massachusetts Bay colony in the years from 1635 to 1637, it is not impossible that the colony leaders thought it wise to get rid of the original document.[3] No satisfactory conclusions can ever be reached on these points unless more evidence is found, but there is always bound to remain in the minds of many a suspicion that the Warwick transfer of 1628, if that is what the New England Company obtained, was not deemed sufficient by those who were aiming at a royal charter, and that in giving it the form of a grant from the council, they introduced some alterations and enlargements, particularly in the matter of land boundaries, to suit their needs. At best, the problem is a very puzzling one and no satisfactory solution has ever been offered.

But taking the grant as it stands in the charter, let us examine its terms. The text states that the patent was issued on March 19, 1628, not by assignment from Warwick and others but by the council directly, and that it gave to Rosewell and Associates, that is, to the

1. *Calendar State Papers, Colonial,* 1677–1680, §358.
2. *Ibid.,* 1574–1660, p. 193 (36).
3. That the destruction of inconvenient documents was not unknown to the nonconformists of the seventeenth century appears in the case of the records of the Court of High Commission, which have entirely disappeared and were probably deliberately destroyed by order of the Long Parliament shortly before 1645, the date of Laud's trial. Registry books, act books, immense files of pleadings and lawyers' briefs, and bales and sacks of miscellaneous papers do not, as a rule, vanish without leaving more than a bare remnant behind. Usher, *The Rise and Fall of the High Commission,* pp. 38–40, 323, 330 note. There is nothing inherently improbable or unduly condemnatory in thinking that the Massachusetts Puritans did something of the same kind. The years from 1635 to 1637 were a desperate time in the history of the colony.

New England Company, a definite, carefully bounded area of land, extending from three miles north of the Merrimac to three miles south of the Charles, "in any and every part thereof," and from the Atlantic Ocean to the South Sea. Measured by the coast line, from the Merrimac to the Charles, the dimensions were moderate, but they were sufficient to deprive the assigns of Robert Gorges of lands to which they were legally entitled. If these dimensions represent the Warwick grant of 1622, we are unable to account for the fact that the later patent of December 30, 1622, to Robert Gorges should have covered a territory already granted to Warwick and to Gorges himself as one of the associates. If they represent a direct grant by the council itself, then Warwick was deliberately and intentionally disregarding Robert Gorges' claims and flouting his father's request, perhaps because he was opposed to all of Sir Ferdinando's plans. As to the wider implications of the boundaries, we need not suppose that those who drafted the terms, whoever they were, had any knowledge of the upper courses of those meandering streams—the Merrimac and the Charles—or were designedly planning a general encroachment on the rights of others. Broadly construed, as Massachusetts tried to construe them later, the boundaries would have taken from the Plymouth colony, not yet fortified by the Bradford patent of 1630, half its territory and from Mason and Gorges all their lands in New Hampshire and Maine as far as Saco Bay.

The New England Company, thus organized by patent in the year 1628, was composed of nearly ninety members, six of whom had belonged to the original Dorchester group.[1] They constituted a voluntary, unincorporated joint-stock company with a fund amounting to £2915, approximately the sum usually estimated as sufficient to start a plantation. They sat as a court in a house in Cornhill,[2] where they transacted their business and prepared all the details for the coming expedition. Among those who gathered there were men whose names are familiar to every student of Puritan colonization. Mathew Cradock, wealthy merchant of the Skinners Company and promoter of many commercial enterprises; Sir Richard Saltonstall, nephew of the lord mayor of London, a justice of the peace, and

1. Rose Troup, *The Massachusetts Bay Company*, pp. 19–21; *John White*, pp. 110–117.

2. Not Governor Cradock's house, which was in St. Swithin's Lane, Candlewick Ward.

lord of the manor of Ledsham; Isaac Johnson, brother-in-law of the Earl of Lincoln; John Venn of the Merchant Taylors Company and later a regicide; Hugh Peter, the well known Puritan minister; Increase Nowell, John Humfry, John Endecott, Richard Bellingham, Richard Bushrod, and, of course, the Rev. John White. There were many others, too, the names of whom have been and have not been preserved. They were not all Puritans, but whether conformists or non-conformists, they all were possessed of strong religious sympathies and a determination to give their undertaking a distinctly religious character. As Cradock wrote to Endecott in 1629, "Wee trust you will not be unmindful of the mayne end of our plantation, by endevoringe to bring the Indians to a knowledge of the Gospel." Their immediate object was to raise enough money to send ships with men, provisions, and equipment to the aid of Conant and his fellow planters at Naumkeag and to build up there a prosperous settlement as a center of religious activity and an overseas home for those of like mind with themselves, who might desire to find a retreat in America from the disillusioning conditions, as they saw them, in their native land. They were not Separatists, and it may well be doubted whether there were any among them who did not look on the Pilgrims as undesirable schismatics.

Before going ahead with its plans the New England Company came to some understanding with the old Dorchester group, which had as about its only asset the stock, material, and services of the planters in its settlement at Naumkeag. Whether money passed or whether the old company turned over the settlement to the new without payment is not quite clear. Almost the last activity of the Dorchester remnant was to despatch, in two ships from Weymouth, March 20, 1628, supplies of various kinds for Naumkeag—welcome additions to the comfort of the worried settlers there—cattle, provisions, clothes, and salt, together with three passengers who must have brought the news of the change in the situation at home—the acquirement of a new company and a new patent.[1] With the despatch of these vessels the Dorchester Company brought to a close its four years of honorable but largely unsuccessful activity, during which as White says, in words often quoted, "the first stocks employed, though consumed, were to serve for a foundation to the

1. Rose Troup, *John White,* pp. 115–116, giving information gleaned from the Weymouth Port Books in the Public Record Office.

work, just as in the building of houses the first stones of the foundation lie buried underground."[1]

Then at last, the New England Company, having completed its preparations, despatched on June 20, 1628, John Endecott with perhaps forty others in the *Abigail,* sailing from Weymouth on the voyage to New England. This vessel of 120 tons, probably hired for the purpose by the Dorchester remnant, was loaded with a varied assortment of clothes, provisions, wines and liquors, ammunition, muskets, and "costlets."[2] The colonists reached Naumkeag on September 6, finding there the group of Old Planters, headed by Roger Conant, who had made shift, with difficulty, to live through two hard winters, with an insufficient supply of provisions and a none too adequate shelter from the elements. The New England Company had no authority to make Endecott governor, as it had no patent of incorporation, but it did appoint him "chief-in-command," as Bradford says, superseding Roger Conant, who though a man of tact and character had not succeeded in making the original venture at Cape Ann profitable from a business point of view. On the ground that the New England Company had acquired all the rights of the Dorchester Company, Endecott on arrival took control of the settlement and all within it, and in so doing got into trouble at the very beginning with some of the Old Planters, who resented his interference and denied his claims. But he had his orders and enforced them in none too gentle or tactful a manner. He knew that he was to provide a home for others that were to follow and to get ready "convenient howsinge" against their coming. He had been selected as "a fit instrument to begin the Wildernesse-worke," as one who was "of courage bold, undaunted yet sociable, and of a chearfull spirit, loving and austere, applying himselfe to either as occasion served."[3] For the task in hand he was a better man than Co-

1. *The Planters Plea,* p. 194.   2. Rose Troup, *John White,* p. 116.
3. Johnson, *Wonder-Working Providence* (Original Narratives Series), p. 44. Endecott had few lovable qualities. He was stern, unyielding, and on some subjects a zealot. Johnson apostrophizes him as "strong, valient John," whom Christ had called to be his soldier, but the Old Planters, most if not all of whom were Anglicans and demanded service according to the Book of Common Prayer, deemed themselves slaves (*Massachusetts Colonial Records,* I, 387) and took, in very bad part, his determination to suppress the Church of England in the colony. They preferred Roger Conant, who though a less forcible man was one much easier to get along with. Endecott's later career discloses his attitude toward those who differed with him— the heathen Indian, the Quaker, the prisoner before him for judgment, and the

nant, as he had fewer scruples or qualms of conscience when he was doing what he considered to be the Lord's work. For six months, from September, 1628, to May, 1629, he governed the little settlement as the sole executive head, without aid or advice, except from the company at home, and it was not until after the New England Company was merged into the Massachusetts Bay Company that his autocratic rule was limited by the appointment of an advisory council. He ruled this little group of less than a hundred souls with sternness and severity, strictly heeding the company's injunction that he have a diligent and watchful eye over the people, bringing them out of the "woeful state and condition they are now in" and inducing them to live lives that "are unblameable and without reproof." He was to "be of good courage, goe on, and due woorthilye," and the Lord would prosper his endeavor. He interpreted his orders literally and made no compromises with the frailties of human nature.

One of the first acts that he performed after his arrival was to pay his respects to Thomas Morton's old resort at Merrymount. The Pilgrims had already invaded the place, sending Miles Standish with a corporal's guard to break it up and scatter its occupants. Standish had seized Morton and sent him back to England three months before Endecott reached the colony, the ship bearing Morton across the water passing the *Abigail* in mid-ocean. The Pilgrims objected to Morton, not so much for his revelries as for his rivalries in dealing with the Indians, selling them arms and ammunition contrary to the royal proclamation of 1622, and competing with themselves successfully in the fur trade. Morton understood the Indian much better than did the Pilgrims or the Puritans and his

Brownes and other upholders of the Anglican service who were disaffected with the Puritan government. It also shows his dislike of forms and devices that offended him —the Book of Common Prayer, the cross of St. George, and the Maypole. He was hard, intolerant, and at times cruel. Even the Massachusetts government caused him "to be sadly admonished for his offense" in mutilating the flag at Salem in 1635, charging him with "rashness, uncharitableness, indiscretion, and exceeding the limits of his calling" (*ibid.*, 146); and again in the same year "committed" him for losing his temper (*ibid.*, 157). Endecott once apologized to Winthrop for striking "goodman Dexter," acknowledging that he was rash, but saying that Dexter's conduct "would have provoked a very patient man" (Hutchinson, *Collection of Original Papers*, 1769, p. 51). The best that can be said of him has been said by Chapple ("The Public Service of John Endecott," *Historical Collections*, Essex Institute, 70, pp. 403–407), an essay in the best Palfrey manner. It is odd that Endecott should have chosen for his seal a skull and cross-bones (*Collections*, Massachusetts Historical Society, 4th series, VI, appendix, ii).

method of handling them proved not only enjoyable but eminently profitable. No Pilgrim could compete with an Indian as a trapper and none could equal Morton in his ability to get on with the red-men and to obtain their confidence and their furs. How far Merry-mount was becoming a resort for a "wicked and debauched crew," made up of all the lawless elements up and down the New England coast, as Bradford says, is impossible to determine, but as there were only seven men there, besides Morton, when Standish attacked the place, and of these five were for the moment absent on a fur hunt, the Standish exploit cannot be rated as a very impressive feat of arms. While Morton was in England, where he was unmolested because no charge against him could be found that was sufficient to warrant punishment, Endecott, acting it may be on orders from the company, crossed the Bay, hewed down the offending maypole, and dispersed those of Morton's companions who still remained there. Merrymount was rechristened Mount Dagon, the place of Philistine idolatry.[1]

In the meantime in England preparations for aiding the planta-tion were hurried along. While drawing up new instructions for Endecott, May 30, 1628,[2] the New England Company was arrang-ing to send over more ships with supplies and passengers, among whom were to be ministers for the settlement, which for the two years of its existence had been without spiritual guidance. Cradock,

1. The only accounts of Morton and the Pilgrims that are in any way satisfactory are both by Adams in his *Three Episodes* and in his introduction to the *New England Canaan*. But the first of these is in parts highly imaginative and because based on Bradford is hostile to Morton. One does not need to be a writer "of Church of England proclivities" to treat Morton fairly. He deserves our approval for two rea-sons. His career lightens the mirthlessness of the Puritan story; and his *New England Canaan* is the only really humorous treatise on New England in the seventeenth century, unless we except Nathaniel Ward's *Simple Cobbler*, which is wit made to order. No man who wrote the *New England Canaan* could be as vile as Bradford and Adams make him out to be. Morton's career is the subject of Motley's novels, *Morton's Hope* (1839) and *Merrymount* (1849), and of Hawthorne's short story "The Maypole of Merry Mount."

The proclamation of 1622 was reissued in 1630, apparently at the request of the Massachusetts Bay Company (*Massachusetts Colonial Records*, I, 48). This second proclamation is a very rare item for collectors. Morton told the Pilgrims that he could not be arrested for violation of the proclamation, as it was not law and could not bind him in New England. He knew the judicial decisions better than did the Pilgrims, for the judges had already declared that the king could do no more than admonish his subjects to keep the law that was already in existence.

2. Hutchinson, *History of Massachusetts*, I, 9, note. These instructions are no longer extant.

Saltonstall, and Isaac Johnson, having already invested heavily in the company's stock, were considering ventures on their own account, in the form of private plantations independent of company management, and Cradock eventually sent over a body of servants, as Saltonstall did later to Connecticut, under an agent, one Patricson, who started a farm on lands along the Mystic river, near what is now Medford. This enterprise, which became a center of agriculture and trade, was, on the business side, quite independent of the government of the colony and lasted until 1650, when its affairs were wound up. There may have been other similar business ventures of "particular persons or companies of merchants or undertakers," not unlike the private "colonies" in Virginia, but if so they have left no record behind them. The Cradock experiment was not successful for it amounted to little in itself and only served to create friction between Cradock and the colony and in the end to lead to an open rupture, which is not often mentioned in Puritan annals. The treatment Cradock received is not pleasant to contemplate, but it was in keeping with the early policy of the Massachusetts magistrates in their determination to discriminate against all who retained any affection for the mother church. Cradock, who was one of the fathers of the whole movement and at the beginning had been spoken of as one of the "special instruments for the advancing and strengthening of our plantation . . . in the infancy of it" was deeply offended by what he considered the harsh and unsympathetic attitude of the colony toward him. He, of all men, hardly deserved the treatment he received at Winthrop's hands.[1]

At this juncture, with its plantation already under way at Naum-

1. There are frequent references to Cradock's plantation in the records, and in the company's letter to Endecott of April 17, 1629, the latter is expressly enjoined "to give all good accomodation to Mr. Mathew Cradock, who with some particular brethren of our company have deeply engaged themselves in their private adventures . . . without any charge to the Company's general stock" (*Massachusetts Colonial Records*, I, 391–392. Compare also, *ibid.*, I, 29, 37ª; III, 213; Rose Troup, *The Massachusetts Bay Company*, pp. 25–31). The servants on the plantation were probably Anglican in sympathy and were frequently in trouble. Two of them, William Cole and his wife, later went to Exeter and then to Hampton (Libby, *Maine Province and Court Records*, II, 385, note 289). When in 1630 one of them, Bratcher, was killed by a man named Palmer, who was acquitted of the murder, two others, Fox and Ratcliffe, charged that the acquittal was obtained by bribery and were disciplined by the government for casting out "malicious speeches" against the commonwealth. The significance of this in Ratcliffe's case will appear later.

Saltonstall's effort to set up a "particular plantation" centered in Connecticut, whither he sent Francis Stiles and a company of servants, rather in the interest of the

keag, the New England Company was confronted with a possible flaw in its title to the land allotted by its patent. As we know already, the Council for New England in 1623 had granted to Robert Gorges a section of land, lying to the northeast of Massachusetts Bay, ten miles along the coast from the Charles to the Saugus and thirty miles into the interior, and there is reason to think that some of his tenants and servants were at this time located there. Before his death Robert conveyed his title to his brother John, who in turn made sub-grants to John Oldham, John Dorrel, his brother-in-law, and William Brereton. Sir Ferdinando Gorges, in approving the original transfer of land to the New England Company, had made a special reservation that his son's rights were to be in no way impaired thereby, but whoever drew up the patent disregarded Gorges' request, seeming to take it for granted that Robert Gorges had forfeited all rights to the territory by non-user, apparently ignorant of the fact that Gorges' servants were there, holding by right of occupation. At any rate, here were Oldham, Dorrel, and Brereton with claims to the territory, and while the leaders of the company, acting on legal advice,[1] may have thought them "voyde in law," and said so, they were far from sure that such would prove to be the case. It seemed, therefore, but a matter of wisdom to obtain for the company a secure legal status, both as to its lands and its rights of government and, by going over the heads of Gorges and the Council for New England, to obtain a charter of incorporation from the king under the great seal. The move was a shrewd one, for thereby the company would no longer be subordinate to the council but would stand on an equality with the other incorporated companies created for trade and plantations. The attempt was successful and on March 4, 1629, a charter passed the seals which transformed the New England Company into the Massachusetts Bay Company, an

grantees under the Warwick deed than of the Massachusetts Bay Company. Their arrival on the Connecticut river led to a dispute with the Dorchester settlers of Windsor, and though Stiles and his party were allowed to reside at the upper end of the plantation, they could obtain no large allotment on the west side of the river and were obliged to be content, eventually, with a grant of 2000 acres on the east side, at Warehouse Point below Springfield. Neither Stiles nor Saltonstall's sons made any attempt to improve the property, the location of which got them into trouble with Massachusetts, and it was eventually sold. "Saltonstall park," as it was called, is frequently mentioned in Stiles, *Ancient Windsor*.

1. It must have been John White, the counsellor, who advised the company that the Robert Gorges patent was "voyde in law." *Massachusetts Colonial Records*, I, 389; Johnson, *Wonder-Working Providence*, p. 37.

incorporated body or body politic, with "ample power to govern and rule all his Majesty's subjects that reside within the limits of our plantation."[1]

The circumstances attending the grant of this famous charter are far from easy to understand. In fact the issue of all the patents of this period with which Warwick's name is associated is so shrouded in mystery as to arouse doubts regarding the regularity of the proceedings. The patent of 1628, the charter of 1629, and the Warwick Patent of 1632 to the lords and gentlemen have all been the subject of controversy, largely because of the difficulty of finding satisfactory evidence about them. Our knowledge fails at critical points, and we can but wonder whether any of the processes were intentionally concealed. The time was one of war with France, which did not come to an end until November, 1629. Mason, as treasurer of the navy, was busy with his official duties, and Gorges, having served as commander of one of the vessels of the war fleet, was deeply immersed, as governor of the fort of St. Nicholas at Plymouth, in preparations for defense. He was undoubtedly ignorant to a large extent of what was going on in London or at Whitehall, for he was dependent on slow-moving and infrequent letters for information. Had he been in a position to interfere, it is quite possible that as a prerogative man and a royalist he might in some manner have checked the efforts of those who were taking advantage of the situation. It is doubtful if any others of the active members of the council know or cared about what was happening. On the other hand, the petitioners for the charter had two powerful friends at court, Sir Dudley Carleton, created Viscount Dorchester in 1628 and at the time one of the principal secretaries of state,[2] and the Earl of Warwick, a busy man during these years as lord lieutenant of Essex and the promoter of many privateering expeditions, but an opponent of Gorges and a friend of the Puritans. John White, the counsellor, a former member of the Dorchester Company and of the merchant adventurers of London who aided the Pilgrims, was the solicitor and legal adviser, and Richard Bellingham of the New England Company, formerly recorder of the town of Boston in

1. *Massachusetts Colonial Records*, I, 386.
2. Chalmers, in his *Political Annals* (I, 147–149) and his *Introduction to the History of the Revolt* (p. 41) is responsible for the statement that Dorchester was influential in obtaining the charter. I have not been able to discover the source of his information.

Lincolnshire, called by Israel Stoughton "a great man and a Law-ier,"[1] who was later to become a judge, a magistrate, and a gover-nor in Massachusetts, may well have lent the aid of his legal skill. Lord Saye and Sele and Nathaniel Rich helped the cause to such an extent that Stoughton could say, "Wee are all much bound to my Lord Say for his cordial advice and true affection. As also to my Lord Warwicke. Sir Nathaniel Rich deserves much acknowledge-ment of his wise handling."[2] More important than all else was the wealth of the leading members of the New England Company. Cradock, Saltonstall, Whetcome, Venn, and Hewson were all rich merchants of London, Isaac Johnson was of the gentry with landed estates and property in the country, and they and others must have drawn heavily on their resources to meet what may charitably be called gratuities, fees, and legal expenses. Cradock said at the time that they obtained the charter "from his Majesty's especiall grace, with great cost, favor of personages of note and much labor."[3] We know nothing about the details, for the transaction was undoubt-edly carried on with the utmost caution. The enemies of the Massa-chusetts Bay colony always maintained that the charter was sur-reptitiously obtained, not illegally—unless the expenditure of a large amount of money constitutes an illegal act, as it would not have been so construed in that day—but covertly, without the knowledge of the New England Council and in entire disregard of the coun-cil's legal rights.

In the issue of this charter the king deliberately took from the Council for New England a large part of the territory which his father had granted in 1620 and annulled rights of government and possession which had already been conferred under the great seal of England, by another charter still of full validity. Such an act might easily be construed as arbitrary and in a sense unjust, were it not that such encroachments were more or less frequent in the case of seventeenth century land grants in the New World, because a knowledge of geography was not an acquirement of the court offi-cials of that day. The Massachusetts instance is, however, a particu-larly flagrant one, for the petitioners at any rate knew exactly what they were doing. They probably argued that the efforts of the Coun-cil for New England had come to naught and that because of the

1. *Proceedings,* Massachusetts Historical Society, 58, p. 453.
2. *Winthrop Papers* (*Collections,* Massachusetts Historical Society, 4th series), I, 3.
3. *Massachusetts Colonial Records,* I, 387.

failure of the Robert Gorges expedition its interest in the settlement of New England having lapsed, it had ceased to be a functioning body and so had forfeited its franchise, a claim that would not have stood for a moment in the eyes of the contemporary lawyer. The argument based on opportunist grounds was the stronger of the two. Here was a land in danger of reverting to what it had always been—a fishing coast, neglected and unclaimed by its lawful patentees. It was, therefore, for the Puritans a moral obligation—in their hearts, no doubt, a religious obligation—to substitute for a dying proprietary corporation, kept alive by the activities of a very few men—one of whom, its president was in sympathy with their cause—a group of active, wealthy, and religiously minded men with a beneficent mission in view. As it happened, however, in the sequel, the Council for New England was to show unmistakable signs of life and only accidental circumstances were to prevent its winning an eventual victory over its opponents.

The charter thus granted to the Massachusetts Bay Company was of the usual type of a trading company, its text embellished with pious forms and phrases characteristic of its origin. It erected a group of twenty-six men into a corporation possessing an extensive area of land, carefully bounded, which, according to the statement of those who wrote the first draft of the charter, had been granted to the New England Company by the Council for New England. If the land clauses of the charter are what they purport to be—an accurate rendering of the terms of an earlier patent—then the Massachusetts Bay Company received no more land than the New England Company already controlled. This was not, however, true of the government. The charter created something that had not existed before, the right of these men as a corporate body to rule and administer the territory under their authority and to exercise complete sway over any colonies or plantations that might be set up on its soil. Their corporate name was the Governor and Company of the Mattachusetts Bay in Newe-England and they composed "one body politique and corporate in Deede, Fact and Name." The Rev. John White and John Humfry, the sole survivors of the original Dorchester Company, had come a long way since that meeting in 1624, when, under the Erle patent, the "Planters Parliament" had decided to promote the plantation at Cape Ann. Now they were members of a powerful corporation, with territory and powers hardly dreamed of before. The governing body was to consist of a governor, a deputy governor, and eighteen assistants, the names of the first incumbents being inserted in the text; later these offices were to be filled by election out of the general body of the freemen, that is, of the generality, made up of those who had been admitted as members to enjoy the freedom of the company. The latter were to be called together four times a year, at Hilary, Easter, Trinity, and Michaelmas, in a general court or assembly, at which the members, or as many as could attend, were to be present for the election of officers, the admission of new members, and the making of laws and ordinances for the good and welfare both of the company in England and of any plantation that might be set up in America.

In its main features, the charter was manifestly modeled upon that of the Virginia Company of 1612, but with the greater redundancy of language and attention to details that were characteristic of the Puritan mind. Consequently, the text is much longer than is that of the charter of 1612, particularly in all that relates to the administration of affairs and the aims and purposes of the company. In these respects it is very explicit. Who among the petitioners was responsible for the original form in which the document was cast is nowhere disclosed, but probably the counsellor, John White, framed the petition. Some of the phrases may have surprised the crown lawyers, whose business it was to prepare the bill for the seals, but even they must have realized that they were dealing with men imbued with an intense religious purpose and that the language was harmless. Such sentences as these had probably never before been met with: "and for the directing ruling and disposeing of all matters and things whereby our said people, Inhabitantes there, maie be soe religiously, peaceablie and civilly governed, in their good life and orderlie conversacion, maie wynn and incite the Natives of the Country to the knowledg and obedience of the onlie true God and Savior of Mankinde, and the Christian fayth, which in our royall intencion and the Adventurers free profession is the principall ende of this Plantacion."[1] At the same time great stress is laid upon the power and authority of the company in all matters relating to the administering of the plantation, the enjoyment of all

1. Such pious utterances were not, of course, confined to the charter of the Massachusetts Bay Company, but no other charter contains as many of them or as elaborately worded as does that of 1629. *The Planters Plea* and the letters to Endecott are couched in the same vein. It is never difficult to detect a Puritan document of this period.

liberties and immunities of the free and natural subjects within any of the king's dominions, and the right of the occupants to resist invasion by force of arms. The design of the petitioners to establish a religious community in New England, their determination to ward off any attacks upon it by Gorges or others, who were interested in a proprietary form of settlement and whom the issue of the charter was certain to affront, and the desire to secure all the privileges accorded the most favored corporation in England in matters of trade are manifest in every part of the document.

The petitioners were of varying grades of Puritan sentiment. A large number of them, particularly from the West Country and some at least from London, were conforming members of the Church of England, whose desire was to purify the church from within, but they were in close accord with their non-conforming brethren from the East Anglian region in their zeal for the advancement of the cause of Christ, whether in England or America. Among these non-conformists were Saltonstall, Downing, Dudley, Johnson, Ward, Ludlow, Bradstreet, Bellingham, Eaton, Endecott, Nowell, and Pynchon, from London and the North and East counties, many of whom did not come into the movement until some time after the charter was obtained. They were all non-conformists, forming a close corporation of relatives and friends. A few, notably the Brownes, were attached to the Church of England and had no intention of departing from it, and they in common with many others greeted with disapproval the later trend toward separatism in the colony. The number of those who became members of the company, as far as they can be identified, was one hundred and ten,[1] and of these at least three—Pocock, Andrews,[2] and Revell—had been among the merchant adventurers who aided the Pilgrims. The mercantile members, to whom profit and the acquirement of wealth were still factors of importance, were much less conspicuous than in the New England Company and became less and less conspicuous as time went on and the religious motive gained ascendancy. This gradual transformation of a trading corporation, organized with a strong commercial as well as a religious end in view, into a colonizing company with religion as its leading purpose is easily

1. *Archaeologia Americana,* III, cxxxiv–cxxxvi.
2. Pocock, acting under instructions from New England, was in 1645 the colony's agent in London, and Andrews in the same year gave Harvard College £500. Winthrop, *Journal,* II, 222.

visible, but the steps in the process cannot be readily followed because of the want of detailed evidence.

The Massachusetts Bay Company was a trading company organized for the purpose of setting up a colony in America that should be both a religious refuge and a profit-making plantation. It was expected to remain in England, as were all such incorporated companies, and to found and govern its colony or colonies from thence as the Virginia and Bermuda companies had done and as the Providence Company was soon to do. To have planned otherwise would have been without precedent, and no one familiar with chancery procedure and the conservative nature of the English legal mind can but believe that had any other intention been revealed at the beginning the charter would never have passed the seals. The evidence of the dockets is sufficient to prove that those who aided the passage of the charter through the seals expected the company to remain in England and transact its business there[1] and that the omission of the place of residence from the charter was merely an inadvertence, in no way intentional.[2] That many of those who were members of the company expected to go to the colony at one time or another is more than likely, and there is reason to believe that some of them at least were anxious to know how far the principal company in England intended to exercise the right, conferred by the charter, to control their affairs there. The charter provided for an open corporation, the membership of which might in time cease

1. The docket reads, "Incorporating them by the name of the Governor and Company of the Mattachusetts Bay in Newe-England with such clauses for the electing of Governors and officers here in England for the said company and power to make lawes and ordinances for setling the Government and Magistracie for the Plantation there." Quoted by Charles Deane in his paper on "The Forms of Passing a Letters Patent" (*Proceedings*, Massachusetts Historical Society, 1869, p. 173). In the charges brought against the colony, at the hearing before the Lords of Trade in 1675, the complainants insisted that the company was "a corporation of England to reside in England," and that the docket was a witness to the fact that "the Governor and Company were created a corporation to have residence in England like other corporations of England" (*Calendar State Papers, Colonial*, 1677–1680, §356). The charter itself contains the phrase "according to the course of other Corporations in this our Realm of England."

2. The statement to the contrary is based solely on a passage in Winthrop's essay on "Arbitrary Government," written fifteen years later, at the time of the Hingham crisis, in defense of the authority of the magistrates (*Life and Letters of John Winthrop*, II, 440–459). Winthrop's words are, "With difficulty we got this abscinded," "this" meaning, supposedly, the place of residence. The fact that Winthrop was not in any way connected with the obtaining of the charter, as he was not a member of the New England Company, should be sufficient to show that he is not referring to

to be friendly to the religious aims of the colony and so far interfere in its government as to alter completely its original purpose.
Such a contingency must by all means be avoided and it is more
than probable that out of the doubts that arose on this point came
the idea that the only way to meet the emergency was to take company and charter to America, and so to protect the City of God in
the wilderness and the life and worship set up therein against all
interference from outside. In the minds of these men and of those
who joined the company later the ridding themselves of all outside
earthly authority was fundamental to the success of the Lord's mission, for they believed that final control should be in their own
hands and not be exercised "arbitrarily" from England, either by
company or king.

This point has not been stressed sufficiently by writers on Massachusetts history, though it is apparent enough to any one following
the course of Puritan action from 1630 to 1684. The Puritans in
America wished to establish a state of their own which should be
independent of all alien control, not only of the principal company
in England but also of king and the English parliament. In this
respect, as in other respects, they differed fundamentally from the
Pilgrims, the latter of whom, though they rejected the Church of
England, always recognized the higher authority of the king, parliament, and New England Council.[1] The Puritan made no such
acknowledgment. He recognized the existence of the king, but not
the latter's authority over him. Winthrop in 1635 thought that
Winslow's petition to the Privy Council for a commission authorizing the Pilgrims and others "to right and defend themselves against
all foraigne enemies" was a mistake and "undertaken by ill advice,
for such precedents might endanger our liberty, that we should do
nothing hereafter but by commission out of England." His paper
on "Arbitrary Government" is one long defense of this position.

---

the charter at all; or if that is not proof enough the further fact must be deemed
conclusive, that once a charter was on its way through the seals no changes could
possibly be made. It is beyond belief that any one could have persuaded the solicitor
general or the patent clerks in three offices to alter the instrument in any such particular as the deliberate elimination of the place of residence for the company.

That which was "abscinded" was not anything in the charter, but the continuance
of the company's government in England, and the "with difficulty" refers to the debate in the meetings of the company, of which Winthrop must have been fully
aware.

1. *New York Colonial Documents*, II, 410.

Emmanuel Downing avoided the main issue when he wrote to Sir John Coke that no colony could be "so foolishly besotted as to resist the protection of their natural prince." Protection, yes, but not obedience in return.[1] In the minds of Winthrop and the others, the Lord's intention in this work overrode all the claims that England might have to authority over them. Two points of view could hardly have been farther apart than those of the Puritans, obeying what they believed to be the commands of God, and those of the public officials in England, influenced by the laws, customs, and needs of the kingdom.

It is difficult to tell just when the New England Company merged into the Massachusetts Bay Company. Legally the date would be March 4, 1629, the day on which the royal letters became patent, but actually the New England Company remained in charge of affairs for perhaps three weeks longer. In fact the one company merged so imperceptibly into the other that it is not easy to say when one ends and the other begins.[2] But on March 23, the Massachusetts Bay Company was formally organized, with the officials named in the charter in their respective places, Mathew Cradock, governor, Thomas Goffe, deputy governor, eleven assistants, a secretary, a treasurer, and a beadle; and from this time forward, these officials, sitting in the deputy governor's house at the corner of Philpot Lane, with the aid of a general court now and then to consider weightier affairs, performed the necessary work of settling and equipping the first plantation and of other plantations to follow. They continued the business begun by their predecessors—hired vessels, gathered ordnance and ammunition, provided provisions, soap, candles, implements and utensils, beer, wine, and liquor, and purchased steel, iron, merchandise for trading with the Indians, clothing, shoes, house furnishings, sail cloth, hay for fodder, and cattle. They arranged suitable terms with men who were hired to go as artisans

1. Bradford, *History*, II, 196–198; Winthrop, *Journal*, I, 163–164; II, 24; Historical Manuscripts Commission, *Twelfth Report*, appendix II, 38–39. The question came up very pertinently in 1645 and 1646, in connection with Dr. Child's appeal to parliament, and is discussed by Winslow in his *New England's Salamander discovered*, pp. 123, 137–138. See also the reply of the general court to the petition of the Remonstrants, Winthrop, *Journal*, II, 307.

2. The letter sent to Endecott, dated April 17–21, is signed by "The governor and deputy of the New England Company for a Plantation in Massachusetts Bay," yet it is clearly written in the name of an incorporated company.

and craftsmen, and with a minister, a teacher, and a surgeon. They secured laborers of all sorts, contracted with indentured servants and made arrangements for women and maids. They discussed the best way of dividing lands and gathered books for transmission to the colony, among them the Book of Common Prayer. At last, in full control of the situation, the Massachusetts Bay Company was ready to carry forward its work in an efficient and constructive manner.

CHAPTER XVIII

THE GREAT PURITAN MIGRATION

THE ensuing six months saw the company pursuing its course as a normal trading corporation. Having made a beginning with the outfitting of the plantation, its officials summoned, on April 30, 1629, a "full and ample court," at which for the first time Endecott was duly "elected and established" as the governor, properly so called, of the Salem community.[1] In order to clear their title of all imperfections, they entered into negotiations with Oldham and Brereton, hoping that an accommodation might be reached at the earliest possible moment with those claimants to land within their territory. Brereton willingly enough gave up his pretensions and accepted in exchange a grant of land "within the company's privileges and plantation";[2] but Oldham, true to his contentious character and slippery methods of doing business, held up the proceedings for two months, by demanding the right to manage the company's fur trade, promising a profit of three hundred per cent for the company and, for himself, such returns as were received over and above that amount. But the leaders of the company declined the offer, suspecting that Oldham was altogether "a man unfitt for us to deale with."[3] Though they believed that the claim was "voyde in law," they were very eager to get rid of it, but finding him "soe affected to his owne opinion as not to be removed from it, neither by reason nor any persuasion," unless he were allowed to "beare sway and have all things carryed to his owne likinge," they let him go his own way. Later, after its removal to New England, Oldham made his peace with the company, became a resident of Watertown and an assistant, received five hundred acres of land, and finally ended his wandering and tempestuous career in 1636, when he was murdered by the Indians off Block Island, while on a trading expedition, an event which, coupled with a

1. *Massachusetts Colonial Records*, I, 399.
2. *Ibid.*, 68.
3. *Ibid.*, 388–389, 398; Adams, *Three Episodes*, I, 214–215.

similar murder of one Captain Stone, brought on the Pequot War.[1]

At last, late in April, 1629, the plantation fleet, which had been lying for some time in the Thames ready for departure, got under way for New England. Led by the *George,* which with the official instructions and a load of cattle was despatched first, it went in sections, the *Talbot* and the *Lyon's Whelp* following on April 25 and the *Four Sisters* and the *Mayflower* three weeks later. It constituted the largest and best equipped expedition that had ever left for New England and the second largest that had ever set sail for America. The Rev. Francis Higginson, who with his family was on the *Talbot,* has left a spirited account of his voyage, which lasted from April 25 to June 29, when the ship entered Naumkeag harbor, finding there the *George,* which had arrived seven days before. The passage was short and speedy, comfortable and easy for the most part, pleasurable and agreeable, and free from "the scurvy and other maledictions." The passengers had a "pious and Christian-like passage," with a ship's crew that, unlike the seamen of the *Mayflower* in 1620, proved as religiously inclined as one could wish. Though the vessel was crowded and there was some sickness, no one died except one "wicked fellow that scorned at fasting and prayer."[2] May and June proved better months in which to cross the Atlantic than October and November and in the ten years since the sailing of the Pilgrims much had been learned regarding the proper preparations for a voyage. More important than all else was the fact that behind the expedition was the strength and wealth of a powerful company.

Endecott met the vessels at Cape Ann and conducted them to Naumkeag, where Higginson found half a score of thatched cottages and a large house newly built for the governor, constructed, according to depositions taken fifty years afterward,[3] out of the

1. The founding of New England presents no more persistent or undisciplined character than "Mr." John Oldham. For nearly fifteen years he led a restless life, filled with varied experiences typical of a frontier existence. He was intimately bound up with the history of Plymouth, Cape Ann, Natascot, and Massachusetts Bay, and at the end of his career became one of the founders of Connecticut, visiting that valley in 1633, leading a party of men to the site of Wethersfield in 1634, where he spent the winter, and continuing his trading activities in that region until his death. Stiles, *Ancient Wethersfield,* I, 19, 22, 24–25, 55; Winthrop, *Journal,* I, 183–189; Young, *Chronicles of Massachusetts Bay,* pp. 169–170.

2. Young, *Chronicles of Massachusetts Bay,* pp. 235–238; *Proceedings,* Massachusetts Historical Society, 62, pp. 283–299.

3. *Historical Collections,* Essex Institute, 13, pp. 136–140.

"big house" at Cape Ann that had been built by the Dorchester people. This structure had been dismantled by Endecott, with doubtful legality, soon after his arrival in September, 1628. Some of the new arrivals, who numbered altogether two or three hundred, were instructed to find other places along the Bay in which to settle; but enough remained in Salem to render necessary the immediate erection of more houses and the immediate use of new tools and implements of agriculture to enlarge the activities of the people, who were engaged in tilling the soil, planting corn, cutting hay, and preparing boards and barrel staves.[1]

Neither the newcomers nor the Old Planters were Separatists. They were non-conformists who had no desire to separate from the Church of England, but who disliked many of the forms and practices of the church, which they characterized as accretions and corruptions. They were of the same mind as those who left England a year later, participants in a greater migration, who declared at the time of their departure that their intentions had been misunderstood and that both the leaders and the generality of the company counted it an honor to call the Church of England their "dear Mother," the ceremonies of which they spurned and the errors of which they abjured, but whose welfare they desired and would always pray for.[2] Just what form of church polity the newcomers would have adopted, had no influence been brought to bear upon

1. In its letter to Endecott, April 17, 1629, the company forbade the settlers to continue the planting of tobacco begun by the old planters, on the ground that the use of tobacco was generally disavowed and utterly disclaimed by some of the leading adventurers among them. *Massachusetts Colonial Records*, I, 388.

2. Young, *Chronicles of Massachusetts Bay*, p. 296; Hutchinson, *History of Massachusetts*, I, 487–489. Higginson's own remarks, as quoted by Cotton Mather (*Magnalia*, 1702, p. 74), are as follows. "When they came to Land's End, Mr. Higginson, calling up his Children and other Passengers unto the Stern of the Ship, to take their last Sight of England. He said, '*We will not say as the Separatists were wont to say at their leaving of* England, Farewel *Babylon!* Farewel *Rome!* But *we will say,* Farewel Dear *England!* Farewel the Church of God in *England,* and all the Christian Friends there! *We do not go to* New England *as Separatists from the Church of* England; *though we cannot but separate from the Corruptions in it: But we go to practice the positive Part of Church Reformation, and propagate the Gospel in* America.' " Doubts have been thrown upon the sincerity of those who issued at Yarmouth, April 6, 1630, *The Humble Request,* from which the sentiment in the text is taken, as if it were designed for publicity purposes only, drawn up by the Rev. John White and signed by Winthrop, Saltonstall, Johnson, Phillips, Dudley, Coddington, and Charles Fiennes to throw the authorities off the scent (Hubbard, *History of New England,* pp. 126–128; Morison, *Builders of the Bay Colony,* pp. 47–48, 76; Rose Troup, *John White,* pp. 204–211). Its language is certainly not in keeping with the

them after their arrival, is a matter of mere speculation, though we know that even among conforming Anglicans, as in New Hampshire and Maine, ritual and ceremonial had no place in their worship at this early period in New England. Without doubt the same would have been the case in Massachusetts.

But the matter was not put to the test. When the first expedition reached Salem on June 29, 1629, its pastor, Skelton, a minister of Lincolnshire silenced for his non-conformity, and its teacher, Higginson, a minister of Leicestershire, similarly silenced and threatened with arrest, found that the problem of church organization was already reaching a solution, and in this wise. Dr. Samuel Fuller, physician and deacon of the Plymouth church, had visited Salem early in the year on a mission of mercy and found in Endecott a willing and sympathetic listener to his discourses on church methods and the outward forms of divine worship. Feeling, as the latter said in his letter to Bradford, that God's people were "marked with one and the same mark and sealed with one and the same seal and have for the main one and the same heart and are guided by one and the same spirit of truth," he brought pressure to bear on Skelton and Higginson, and in conjunction with them erected at Salem, on July 20, three weeks after their arrival, a church shaped after the Separatist model. Thus the first Puritan church in New England took on an independent or congregational form, based on a mutual agreement or compact, whereby they bound themselves to the Lord in an indissoluble bond to break which was a "great sin." This covenant reads, "We covenant with the Lord and with one another and do bind ourselves in the presence of God to walk together in all his ways, according as he is pleased to reveal himself unto us in his blessed word of truth."[1] But in Salem as in Plymouth there were

sentiments, elsewhere expressed, of the Puritan leaders, and the fact that it was signed and made public at the last moment at Yarmouth and not earlier at Southampton rouses the suspicion that it did not originate with the signers, but was prepared and brought to their attention by White as a precautionary measure. The Rev. Henry Wilder Foote, however, does not agree with this view and accepts *The Humble Request* at its face value, as a spontaneous expression of loyalty toward the Church of England, arguing that it was probably written on board by George Phillips, afterward minister at Watertown (*Proceedings,* Massachusetts Historical Society, 63, pp. 196–207).

1. Walker, *Creeds and Platforms,* p. 116. Roger Williams' withdrawal from the Salem church was deemed by Cotton as a breach of the covenant and so a violation of the foundation principle upon which the church was founded. *Narragansett Club Publications,* II, note 42, at the end.

still many—such as the Old Planters—who remained outside the covenant, preferring the liturgy and polity of the Church of England. There were also others—"libertines," as they were called—whom Endecott was instructed to punish according to the law of England ("as neere as may be") and to compel them to live under one government and one law.[1] Salem was far from being a homogeneous religious community, and these early experiences go far to explain the attitude of the church there six years later under Roger Williams.

The step taken by Endecott, Skelton, and Higginson was the more natural because of the essential similarity of their religious thought with that of the Pilgrims. In social rank and experience Pilgrim and Puritan had little in common. In their formal expression of ideas regarding the Church of England and their relation to the king's authority over them they were diametrically opposed, for the Pilgrims, wishing to erect a church without a bishop, repudiated the English communion in all its parts, though they recognized the king as their royal master; whereas the Puritans, wishing to erect a state without a king, repudiated, as far as they dared, the authority of the English crown, though they recognized the Church of England as their dear mother in all things spiritual, and never forbade their people when going to England to attend service in the parish churches.[2] On the other hand, in doctrine and in their faith in the Bible as the inspired guide of their lives, they were both Calvinists, adhering to the dogma of foreordination and the total depravity of man. The Puritans' attitude toward the Church of England was rather traditional and sentimental than logical and consistent, for they were really at one with the Separatists in rejecting the Book of Common Prayer, the sacraments, and the validity of ordination according to the canons of the church, and in adopting a polity and form of worship such as they conceived to have

1. *Massachusetts Colonial Records,* I, 393.

2. "Cotton's Answer to Roger Williams" (1647), *Narragansett Club Publications,* II, 66, 121–142, 152, 162, note 55, 176, 234. Perry Miller, in *Orthodoxy in Massachusetts, 1630–1650* (1933), demonstrates convincingly that the emigrating Puritans "were already disposed to erect a Congregational regime" in Massachusetts before coming to New England, and that they did not "contract their church polity by a species of contagion from the Separatists at Plymouth" but "would have proceeded along essentially the same lines had there been no Plymouth at all" (pp. 127, 128, 131, 136). His analysis of the continuity of Congregational thought, of the "elaborate casuistry of non-separation," and of the origins and characteristics of the New England way of the churches is altogether admirable and conclusive.

been in use in primitive times.[1] They hoped to build in America a reformed church, that might be "of more use and comforte, to hir moother church in future tymes of calamitie," when the church at home was "ecclipsed in parte, darkened or persecuted" and it was "juste to seeke refuge for saftye, especially where safest hope maye be founde." Or as elsewhere put, perhaps by Winthrop himself, "The service of raysinge and upholdinge a partic[ular] Church is to be preferred before the betteringe some parte of a Churche all readye established."[2] While no Separatist could have written in just this way, the margin of difference is very slight and the non-conforming Puritans were moderate separatists without knowing it and their proposal to found a model church in America was bound to end in the setting up of a church of their own on the half-way separatist or independent plan.

Another important factor must be taken into account. As we have seen in studying the history of Bermuda, the clergymen (from Lewis Hughes to Nathaniel White), sent out by the Bermuda Company to administer the service according to the Church of England, almost without exception turned non-conformist and adopted an attitude that was at bottom separatist in its rejection of the Book of Common Prayer and its fondness for independency. This tendency in Bermuda culminated, as we have already seen, in the attempt of White in 1644, to renounce all connection with the Church of England. While we can hardly charge the Massachusetts Bay Company, as we can the Bermuda Company, with laxity in the selection of its first ministers, the fact remains that Skelton and Higginson did just what Hughes, Stirk, Copland, and White did in Bermuda, rejected the Church of England and its formalities. In both cases we are to see, to no small extent, the influence of distance and the frontier environment, for freedom from the restraints of a highly organized, ritualistic body was as welcome to those who were religiously

1. "Let the matter and forme of your churches be such as were in the Primitive Times (before Antichrists Kingdome prevailed) plainly poynted out by Christ and his Apostles in most of their Epistles, to be neither Nationall nor Provinciall, but gathered together in Covenant of such a number as might ordinarily meete together in one place, and built of such living stones as outwardly appear Saints by calling." Johnson, *Wonder-Working Providence*, pp. 26–27. On the general subject, Walker, *Congregationalists*, ch. IV; Burrage, *Church Covenant Idea*; Ellis, *The Puritan Age*; Shepard, *Subjection to Christ* (London, 1657).

2. *Winthrop Papers*, II, 128–129, 132.

minded as was to the tenantry freedom from the restraints of feudal law. The silenced clergy of England were already on the way to complete separation and it needed only the influence of Fuller and Endecott, the long distance from home and the bishops, and the wide spaces of soil and air of New England to convince Skelton and Higginson that they were after all separatists under the skin. It is not surprising, therefore, that they should have accepted, without serious demur, the fundamental ideas of the Congregational polity. Thus arose the First Church of Christ in Salem, an independent, self-governing body and a law to itself, the members of which—converted Christians only, according to the Puritan idea of conversion—were joined together for the worship of God. This church became the model, not for a reformed Church of England, but up to a certain point for all the later churches in Massachusetts and Connecticut, and the "New England Way," a compromise between extreme separatism and a national church, had an influence upon the ecclesiastical organization at home during the minority rule of the Puritans at the time of the interregnum.

But the company in London, as well as others interested in the New England plantation, did not look with approval upon this turn in the religious affairs of the colony. They had not spent the large sums needed for equipment and transportation in order to establish a second Pilgrim community in America, and they feared lest the reports of what had been done might influence public opinion in England and injure the cause that they had at heart.[1] The situation became acute when Endecott, finding that John and Samuel Browne, who held high place as freemen of the company and members of Endecott's council at Salem, were endeavoring to keep alive the Church of England service in the colony, unceremoniously shipped them back to England, because, as he said, "New England was no place for such as they." The debate that followed in the court of the company disclosed the unmistakable fact that two parties were in formation: the "merchants," Cradock, Goffe, Venn,

1. John Humfry wrote to Winthrop, December 30, 1630, hoping that some new and better satisfaction would "bee given to the good people here [in London] that wee go not away for Separatism, the apprehensions whereof (against the best assurance and protestation I can make) takes deepe impression in them." "I trust," he adds, "we shall againe redintegrate both ourselves and the undertaking in the former good opinion which hath been conceaved of us and it." *Winthrop Papers*, I, 8 (*Collections*, Massachusetts Historical Society).

and others, representative of the more moderate Puritan views, characteristic of the Rev. John White and the West Country leaders; and the religious extremists, hardly yet in command, but becoming more and more influential as the months passed. The decision reached on September 29 to open or detain letters which the Brownes had written to friends in England, in order to see if they contained anything prejudicial to the plantation would seem to indicate the growing preponderance of this more extreme group. But at this time the company went no further than to warn Endecott not to do it again, lest it get them into trouble with the authorities.[1] The incident was, however, a warning of crises to come.

Coincident with the Browne episode, and undoubtedly in part responsible for the lenient treatment which Endecott received, was the change that was gradually coming over the purposes and plans of the company, due in large part to contemporary conditions in England, which were making it an uncomfortable place for the Puritans to live in and were convincing many that residence would better be sought elsewhere. Events in parliament and out were stiffening Puritan resistance, notably in Middlesex and East Anglia, and were drawing together into cohesive groups inclined to vigorous action noble and common man, merchant and landholder, who possessed pro-puritan sympathies. All the king's foreign policies had come to disastrous ends; the Protestant churches in Europe, before the rising tide of the counter-reformation and the imperial successes of the early years of the Thirty Years' War, were threatened with destruction; parliament after two tempestuous sessions had been dissolved with no promise of continuance; and the king, who had been acclaimed with so much enthusiasm a few years before, was causing only disappointment and gloom. Non-employment was increasing, trade declining, poverty and distress, rioting and robbery were apparently more prevalent than ever and the government seemed incompetent to check the general disorder. The Star Chamber and the Court of High Commission were inflicting penalties on those who opposed the royal demands or broke the canons of the church, and while in both cases the hardships and injustices were less real than the Puritans thought and the powers of the courts

1. *Massachusetts Colonial Records*, I, 51–54; Young, *Chronicles of Massachusetts Bay*, pp. 123, 168, 288–291.

were exercised without undue severity, the effect on the minds of parliamentarians and non-conformists alike was as profound as if both courts had become instruments of tyranny. Puritan ministers were silenced or deprived of their benefices and some suffered severely; Puritan writings were banned and burnt; and there are a few instances, though not certainly authenticated, where the holders of lesser offices under government were feeling the weight of royal and ecclesiastical displeasure.[1]

During the five months following the issue of the Massachusetts Bay Company's charter conditions seemed to grow worse rather than better and among many of those interested in colonization a desire to leave England was already making itself felt. One group of these men formed a veritable clan, knit by ties of blood, marriage, propinquity, and personal friendship[2] and by a common loyalty to religious ideals. They lived in East Anglia and its neighborhood—in Norfolk, Suffolk, Essex, and southern Lincolnshire—a region extending from the Thames to the Wash and including the districts of Kesteven and Holland, where lies the municipal borough of Boston. Within this region, for reasons not readily understood, Puritan sympathies found expression more strongly than anywhere else, a fact which has given to these counties the name of the Cradle

1. Humfry wrote in 1630: "Dr. Laiton hath after an escape been taken and received half of his censure, viz, 12 lashes with a 3 corded whip, one eare cut off, one nostril slit, and stygmatized in the face." He adds, "Divers godly lecturers and ministers dayly are put by. Mr. Weld of Essex is now upon the stage and expects his doome." *Winthrop Papers,* I, 11 (*Collections,* Massachusetts Historical Society). On the other hand Professor Usher can write, after an exhaustive study of the Court of High Commission, "A Puritan minister, who had given much trouble by his persistent nonconformity and opposition to the bishop's orders and had in consequence been suspended and deprived by the Commission, was soon relieved from his suspension, and merely admonished to 'carry himself moderately and discreetly,' and not to preach in the cures of which he had lately been deprived nor in London without the bishop's licence. This order, of course, allowed him to preach elsewhere. Laymen imprisoned for attendance at conventicles were released on promise of future conformity, without any proceeding against them for their past breach of the law. A man who was unable to find the proper sureties for his bond was freed simply on his own bond and oath to perform the sentence of the Court. Such measures do not seem unduly harsh or severe." *The Rise and Fall of the High Commission,* p. 268.

2. Park, "Friendship as a Factor in the Settlement of Massachusetts," *Proceedings,* American Antiquarian Society, 1918, pp. 51–62. "The cement which held these men together was the cement of like-mindedness primarily." Friendship was a factor of secondary importance, but, as Mr. Park says, "this secondary motive force did come into a certain operation and did exert a certain influence in the settlement of Massachusetts."

of Puritanism.[1] Here at Groton in Suffolk lived the Puritan squire, John Winthrop, member of a family of substance and reputation, a matriculate of Trinity College, Cambridge, and a justice of the peace, having held his first court at the age of eighteen when he became lord of the manor on attaining his majority in 1604.[2] To the northward at Sempringham in Lincolnshire was Theophilus, fourth earl of Lincoln, chief among the Puritan peers, whose wife, Bridget, was a daughter of Lord Saye and Sele, and one of whose sisters, Susan, became in 1630 the third wife of John Humfry and another, the better known Arbella, at an earlier date had married Isaac Johnson. Associated with the Lincoln household as a manager of its properties was Thomas Dudley, whose daughter afterward became the wife of Governor Bradstreet. Winthrop's sister had married Emmanuel Downing, father of Sir George Downing of later fame, after whom Downing Street was named. All of these men were on terms of intimacy with each other and all were either engaged already in the colonizing movement, as was the case with John Humfry, or were watching its progress, some with doubting, others with hopeful and expectant eyes. Winthrop, an attorney by profession, at this time was holding an inferior magistracy in the court of wards and liveries,[3] as was also his brother-in-law, Downing, and was accustomed to be away from home for long periods of time. He seems early to have taken an interest in Barbados—recently occupied—whither he sent his son Henry, an adventurous and improvident youth, with men and equipment for the purpose

1. Essex at this time was belligerently puritan, for the condition of the established clergy there was little short of scandalous. It is a significant fact that the worst of all witch-worryings was limited to the counties where Puritanism was supreme and that the Earl of Warwick should have presided at the Essex summer assizes of 1645 when 32 women were indicted and 19 hanged. Ewen, *Witch Hunting* (1929), pp. 100, 231. It was in Essex that the Rich family held estates and there the Earl of Warwick lived when in residence out of London.

2. Mather, *Magnalia* (1702), Bk. II, p. 8. According to Adam Winthrop's diary this event took place October 25, 1609. *Winthrop Papers*, I, 103.

3. The court of wards and liveries had to do with the heirs or wards, as they were called, of the king's tenants who held *in capite*, during their nonage. It was located in the neighborhood of the Inns of Court and Winthrop had his chambers in the Inner Temple. Downing lived not far away, at the Bishop's Head in Fleet Street, Peterborough Court, near the Fleet Ditch or Conduit. Humfry has sometimes been included with Winthrop and Downing, but without evidence. For a very thorough account of the court of wards and liveries and of Winthrop's connection therewith see Mr. Robinson's exhaustive edition of "John Winthrop's Notebook of Cases, 1623–1629," in *Winthrop Papers*, II, 1–48.

of establishing a plantation, and he and his sons continued their connection with the island for many years.[1] That he ever contemplated going to the West Indies himself is extremely unlikely, as the way was better prepared elsewhere for the carrying out of what he conceived was the Lord's will regarding himself.

Winthrop from early years must have followed the progress of settlement in America, for his occasional remarks about the many failures there disclose familiarity with the conditions under which those settlements had been made. Living in London he must have known of the efforts leading to the incorporation of the Massachusetts Bay Company, though he did not identify himself with it by becoming a subscriber to its stock. His son John had thought of joining the expedition under Endecott in April, 1628, for what object is not known, but in the end, probably from a dislike of Endecott, had changed his mind and gone off on a sailing voyage, lasting fourteen months, which took him through the Mediterranean as far as Constantinople, and during which he visited Venice, Leghorn, and Padua. It was during his son's absence that John Winthrop, his father, came face to face with the most important decision of his life—whether to remain in England or to quit the country forever. Great things were hanging in the balance as the result of that decision.

Many reasons were at work urging Winthrop to a definite conclusion. In common with many another of the Puritan leaders, he was thoroughly disheartened at the condition of England, as he saw it from the Puritan point of view. He was among those who were saddened by what they considered England's intemperance and corruption, the evil state and example of her centers of learning, her treatment of the non-conforming clergy, and the influence in high places of Arminianism, which because of its defense of the free agency and moral responsibility of man and its disbelief in the absolute importance of God in human affairs, was the arch enemy of Calvinism. He, too, saw the land growing "weary of her inhabitants, soe as man, whoe is the most pretious of all creatures, is here more vile and base than the earth we treade on," and he, too, thought that the wrath of God was soon to descend upon England and that it was but a matter of wisdom to "avoid the Plauge when it is forescene than to tarry till it should overtake us." These im-

1. Harlow, *Barbados,* pp. 268–269.

pending calamities were very real to the Puritan alarmists and were probably among the causes that drove many of them—the rank and file as well as the leaders—to join the New England colony.[1]

Thoughts of this kind took shape slowly. In Winthrop's mind they were hastened by arguments worked out, either by himself or by the Rev. John White, and presented in an elaborate treatise which in manuscript was circulated among Puritan friends as a justification for immediate action. This treatise, "General Observations for the Plantation of New England," contains "reasons to be considered for justifieinge the undertakers of the intended plantation in New England and for incouraginge such whose hartes God shall move to join with them in it." "Whoe knows [says the treatise] but that God hath provided this place to be a refuge for many whome he meanes to save out of the generall callamity, and seeinge the Church hath noe place lefte to flie into but the wildernesse, what better worke can there be, then to goe and provide tabernacles and foode for her against she comes thether."[2] Thoughts such as these, considered, discussed, answered, and reconsidered, were a powerful influence in crystallizing opinion, and pondered as they were by the chief members of the London and East Anglian groups furnished material for debate and provoked ideas with which they wrestled during the months before final conclusions were reached. As a commentary upon the actual situation in England and elsewhere the statements of fact in the treatise are worthless, but as an expression of the Puritan outlook upon the world of that time they are enlightening.[3]

Not only was Winthrop disheartened regarding the calamitous

1. Richard Mather in 1635, "foreseeing also (*sapiens Divinat*) the approaching calamities of England, meditated a Removall into New England." *Life and Death,* p. 54, and Hooker in his sermon, *The Danger of Desertion* (preached in 1629 and printed in 1641), makes similar comments on the signs of the times.

2. *Winthrop Papers,* II, 138–139. The belief that God had selected New England as the chosen land was profoundly held by the Puritans who went there. Winthrop himself in 1640 wrote to Lord Saye and Sele of "this good land which God hath found and given to his people," adding that "God had chosen this country to plant his people in." *Journal,* I, 334. Cotton in his sermon, *God's Promise to his Plantations* (London, 1634), devotes much space to the same idea—"This place is appointed me of God" (p. 7).

3. The authorship of the "General Observations" is in dispute. Mr. Robinson in *Winthrop Papers,* II, 106–111, argues for Winthrop; Mrs. Rose Troup in *John White,* pp. 165–174, 423–432, for John White. The former believes that Winthrop drew up the paper and sent copies of the first draft to White and others; the latter that White

state of England, he was discouraged and depressed regarding his family affairs also. He was in debt, owing more than he was able to pay without selling his own land.[1] He had many children, some of whom were a heavy expense to him, and were he to divide his property among his three eldest sons he would not have enough wherewith to maintain his family and his remaining children. In June, 1629, he either gave up or was deprived of his position in the court of wards and liveries[2] and returned to Groton. Domestic and personal troubles weighed heavily upon him. In 1628 he lost a brother-in-law and a little later his mother; he suffered from two serious attacks of illness in London in the spring and autumn of the same year; and an infected hand not only caused him distress but so impaired his ability to write as to interfere with the proper performance of his duties and the proper conduct of his private business. His letters to his wife take on more and more of a religious, melancholy coloring. "My deare wife [he wrote, May 15, 1629] I am verly perswaded God will bringe some heavye Affliction upon this lande, and that speedylye . . . If the Lord seeth it wilbe good for us, he will provide a shelter and a hidinge place for us and ours as a Zoar for Lott, Sarepthah for his prophet etc: if not, yet he will not forsake us: though he correct us with the roddes of men, yet if he take not his mercye and lovinge kindnesse from us we shalbe safe." A month later he wrote that he was returning from London in as short a time as possible, "and after that, I hope, we shall never parte so longe againe, till we parte for a better meeting in heaven, but where we shall spende the rest of our short tyme I knowe not." This was in June, 1629.

wrote the original and that a copy of it fell into Winthrop's hands. Both deny that Higginson had any hand in its composition. The various forms of the document are printed in the *Winthrop Papers*, II, 111–127, where will be found also the comments upon it by Robert Ryece, as well as Sir John Eliot's copy of the New England tracts, pp. 127–149. See also Richard Mather's arguments, *Life and Death*, pp. 55–56.

1. He sold Groton for £4600 in 1630. The transaction was conducted by Emmanuel Downing, who did not go to New England until 1638. *Winthrop Papers*, I, 36 (*Collections*, Massachusetts Historical Society).

2. The statement is frequently made that Winthrop was deprived of his office because of his Puritan sympathies. There is no certain proof that this was the case and the weight of one's conviction is against it. Downing, equally a Puritan, did not lose his place. I believe that Mr. Robinson (*Winthrop Papers*, II, 100) is entirely right in thinking that Winthrop's withdrawal was voluntary, due to the fact that the office and living in London were an added expense. "I shalbe a saver in them both," he wrote his wife, June 29, 1629. The master of the court was Sir Robert Naunton, who was not unfavorable to the Puritans.

Events now moved forward rapidly. On July 28, Winthrop and his brother-in-law Emmanuel Downing, rode north, on horseback, to confer with the Earl of Lincoln at his estate near Sempringham, about eighteen miles from Boston, and to consult with the earl's brother-in-law, Isaac Johnson, regarding the great adventure. Whether they bore with them on this journey a draft of the "General Observations" is a point that need not be discussed, for it is wholly likely that there was a copy of the treatise in the earl's hands and that the issue of the document was itself an original cause of the journey. At the meeting the pros and cons of the arguments and objections therein advanced must have been argued at great length in typical Puritan fashion, and it may be—though we have no information on this point—that the conclusions reached were submitted for consideration to others of the Puritan group, White, Cradock, Saltonstall, and Humfry, in order to obtain from them an opinion as to the wisdom of the course approved. The idea of migration was in the air and must have been the subject of careful thought on the part of those—individually and collectively—who held official position in the Massachusetts Bay Company. On the very day when Winthrop and Downing rode to Sempringham, probably at the invitation of Isaac Johnson himself, who was an influential member of the company, Cradock, the governor, read in full court "certain propositions conceived by himselfe," the chief of which was "to transfer the government of the plantation to those that shall inhabite there, and not to continue the same in subordination to the company heer, as now is." In making this suggestion Cradock had no idea of recommending the transfer of the charter and company to New England, for the words will not bear any such interpretation. His notion was so to increase the governing powers of the plantation as to make it practically independent of the company in London and thus to make it the more difficult for the latter to interfere in plantation affairs. This situation may have been created by the company's reprimand of Endecott for his treatment of the Brownes, and seems to show that the members of the company were already beginning to divide on plantation policy, some standing by the original purpose for which the company was founded, others being more interested in the plantation as a religious refuge and not averse to its separatistic tendencies.

Cradock's suggestion was quite in line with the Puritan plan of an independent plantation, which was to serve as a divinely chosen retreat for those who were debating among themselves the necessity of leaving England forever. It may have entered his mind as a possible compromise between the two extremes, for with Winthrop and Downing both in London at the time and familiar with what was going on and with Saltonstall and Johnson members of the company, Cradock must have known the trend of their thoughts and have endeavored to meet it as far as he could. He was sufficiently aware of the irregular nature of his own suggestion as to caution the members "to carry the business secretly that the same be not divulged." His recommendation, as was to be expected, aroused debate and a good deal of opposition and was put over for further consideration. He enjoined his hearers to think about it "privately and seriously," to set down their reasons in writing for and against it, and to produce their conclusions at the next general court.

The debate which followed Cradock's suggestion of July 28, brought out the opinion of many that to make the plantation independent of the company was contrary to the true intent of the charter and so might be construed as illegal. So strong was the opposition, that the proponents of the plan, both within and without the company, realized the need of more concerted action, if a favorable final vote was to be obtained, and some among them began to talk of even a bolder project, that of transferring not merely increased governing powers but the company itself to America. Cradock, when he made his suggestion, had no intention of blotting out the company in England—he was too good a merchant for that —but this was exactly what the Puritans now proposed to do and it may be that they had already worked out the plan at the Sempringham conference. At any rate, on August 26 twelve of them—Saltonstall, Dudley, William Vassall, Nicholas West, Johnson, Humfry, Sharp, Nowell, Winthrop, Pynchon, Kellam Browne, and William Colbron—met at Cambridge and there entered into an agreement "to endevour the prosecucion of this worke, as by God's assistance," binding themselves to be "ready in our persons and with such of our severall familyes as are to go with us and such provision as we are able conveniently to furnish ourselves withall, to embark for the said plantacion by the first of march next [1630], at such port or ports of this land as shall be agreed upon by the Company, to the end to passe the Seas (under God's protection) to inhabite and con-

tinue in new England. Provided, always that before the last of September next the whole government together with the Patent for the
said plantacion bee first by an order of Court legally transferred and
established to remayne with us and others which shall inhabite upon
the said plantacion."[1]

The important part of the agreement lies in the proviso. The
earlier portion, in which the subscribers bind themselves to go to
New England, is in line with Cradock's suggestion, but the proviso
contains a new proposal, here presented for the first time, as far as
we know, to the effect that the subscribers go to New England only
in case the company and the charter go there also. Evidently the
Puritan leaders had no confidence in an increase of governing
powers for the plantation, as long as charter and company remained
in England. Winthrop and the others reasoned, and from the point
of view of their mission they reasoned rightly, that the Massachusetts Bay Company in England was an open corporation, that is,
anyone purchasing its stock became a member and could vote at its
meetings. In consequence it might happen that in time the personnel of the company would change so as to be entirely out of sympathy with the Puritan plans as carried out in America. To leave
the ultimate control over the colony in New England, with its Puritan aspirations, in the hands of a company in England that might
eventually become indifferent or even hostile, or might possibly
have its charter taken away, thus throwing the colony into the
hands of the crown, was to allow God's purpose to be thwarted by
the intervention of man. The only way to prevent such a result was
to get rid of the company in England, and to Winthrop's ingenious
mind (or to the ingenious mind of some one else) that could most
easily be done by taking company and charter along with them to
New England, thus swallowing up the company in the colony. In
this way the company would be under Puritan control and could
be manipulated to serve Puritan ends, which, Winthrop argued,
were the ends of God.

The proviso contained also a second condition—the transfer of
charter and company must be legal. Winthrop was an attorney and
though he had had no regular training as a lawyer, except possibly
for a short time at Gray's Inn, he must have had as much knowl-

1. The agreement has been frequently printed, most recently in the *Proceedings*
of the Massachusetts Historical Society, 62, pp. 279–280.

edge of the law as he needed for his manorial and magisterial duties. If Cradock's suggestion involved the question of legality, then much more certainly would the proposal made at Cambridge to take company and charter out of England raise an issue in high quarters should it become known. Such an act was not only without precedent but it was entirely foreign to the underlying purpose of this or any other trading company. It meant the complete obliteration of the company as a trading corporation in England, a step of such doubtful legality that the signers at Cambridge agreed to it only in case it could be taken legally and by order of the court of the company. The Puritans were much concerned about the matter, and in the course of their discussion proposed to secure the advice of a regular counsellor, as to whether or not the act was justified in law. But there is nothing to show that this was ever done. The order of the court of the company was duly obtained, but in the matter of legality it may be that they went no further than to accept the advice of the lawyers of their own group, on the ground that to go outside themselves for an opinion would break the secrecy, which they agreed, both at London and at Cambridge, was essential to success. It may even be that they decided to go ahead without legal advice, hoping that in the disturbed state of the times their departure with company and charter would pass unnoticed.

The Cambridge agreement was duly presented at a special meeting of the general court of the company on August 28, and two committees were appointed, one headed by Wright, Adams, Theophilus Eaton, and Spurstowe to draw up the arguments against the proposal, and the other by Saltonstall, Johnson, and Venn, two of whom were signers of the agreement and the third a captain and merchant tailor of London, to take the other side. Cradock was not present at the session, which was presided over by Deputy Governor Goffe, but Saltonstall, Johnson, Humfry, and Nowell were there, prepared to defend what the Cambridge signers had done.[1] On the next day, the 29th, the committees reported and the vote was taken, twenty-seven members being present out of a total generality of one hundred and twenty-five.[2] Seven of these were signers of the Cambridge agreement, nine afterward went to Massachusetts, and of

1. *Massachusetts Colonial Records*, I, 50.
2. An authoritative and admirably annotated list of the members is given in Rose Troup, *The Massachusetts Bay Company and its Predecessors*, pp. 131–161.

the remainder many were outstanding Puritans, such as John Davenport, and his parishioner George Foxcroft, John Pocock, who aided the Pilgrims, Samuel Aldersey, who left Davenport £20 in his will, Waller, S. Vassall, Harwood, Perry, Webb, and Simon Whetcome. Cradock was not there at that time either, and even Spurstowe stayed away. One may not say that the meeting was packed, but certain is it that those present were in the main favorable to the Cambridge plan, because they were prominently identified with one phase or other of the radical Puritan movement. The vote was probably a foregone conclusion, so that when the question was put, "As many of you as desire to have the pattent and the government of the plantation to bee transferred to New England, so as it may be done legally, hold up your hands," the result was already known. By no stretch of the imagination can the vote taken be said to represent "the general consent of the Company," as the record puts it. Again the question of legality was left unanswered. As the Cambridge agreement required that for the agreement to be binding on the signers, this question be decided before the last of September, it is very likely that it was settled in some way or other satisfactory to themselves during the four weeks that followed the meeting of August 29. But the fact that two of the Cambridge signers did not live up to the agreement raises an interesting question as to their reasons for not doing so.

The signers of the Cambridge agreement had won a notable victory, which not only assured for them the controlling place in the company, but made inevitable the admission to membership of such a man as Winthrop, who up to this time had taken no part in its affairs. His name appears now for the first time in the records of the company at the meeting held on September 19, when he was appointed one of a committee to arbitrate the case of the Brownes. Then at a general court held at Deputy Governor Goffe's house on October 20, 1629, a clean sweep was made of the company's official staff. Cradock and Goffe retired and Winthrop and Humfry were chosen in their places. The company had now a new leader and a working membership committed to the plan of erecting in New England a Puritan state, a separate, self-governing community that should be free of all dependence on a principal authority in England, possessing and exercising for itself all the powers vested in the company under the charter. Henceforth the seat of the Massachu-

setts Bay Company was to be in New England and under the guidance of Winthrop and his fellow Puritans a new experiment in
colony building was to be tried in a new land. As the charter was
in no way designed to be the constitution of a state, it is evident that
the Puritan plan could be successfully carried out only by a constant and persistent violation of its terms. There is no reason to
believe that the Puritan leaders anticipated the necessity of so doing,
but the exigencies of the situation rendered such a course inevitable.

After a winter of strenuous effort and the expenditure of large
sums of money, contributed by members of the company and others
interested in the Puritan cause,[1] a fleet of eleven ships was brought
together at Southampton. Of these, four—the *Arbella*,[2] *Talbot, Ambrose,* and *Jewel,* bearing Winthrop, the charter, and the bulk of
the company of seven hundred passengers, the remainder being carried in the *Mayflower, Whale,* and *Success*—started March 29, 1630,
and made their way down the Channel,[3] accompanied by two or
three Dutch vessels on their way to the East Indies. The *Mayflower,
Whale,* and *Success,* with the remaining vessels, the *Charles, William and Francis, Hopewell,* and *Trial,* left a month later, carrying
some of the passengers, forty cows, sixty horses, many goats, and

1. For the details of preparation, expense of travel and sailing, character of the
vessels, and incidents of the voyage, see the admirable work of Dr. Banks, *The
Winthrop Fleet of 1630,* chaps. III, IV, and V. This book has also a chapter on the
passengers and their origins and an appendix containing an alphabetical list of their
names, as far as known, and such information about them as can be recovered.

2. The *Arbella* was the *Eagle,* a vessel of about 400 tons burden, which was
bought by Cradock and others and chartered to the company for £750. Cradock
also owned the *Ambrose* and the *Jewel.* The *Eagle* had but recently returned, dock-
ing at Woolwich, February 3, 1629, from service as the flagship of Sir Kenelm
Digby's privateering fleet in the Mediterranean, which had been engaged in a private
enterprise undertaken in the interest of the king's war with France. It is possible that
the younger Winthrop's friendship for Digby—they corresponded for many years—
may have had something to do with the buying of the vessel. There must have been
some connection between Digby and the Puritans, for Winthrop, Sr. mentions his
name in one of his letters, and we know that afterward Digby, though certainly a
Roman Catholic, sent books, mainly theological, as a gift to Harvard College. These
books apparently perished in the disastrous Harvard library fire in the eighteenth
century (1764). In June, 1631, Digby was made one of the commissioners to consider
the state of the colony of Virginia and two years afterward became a member of the
Council for New England. *Collections,* Massachusetts Historical Society, 3d ser. II,
118; *Proceedings,* 59, p. 24: *Winthrop Papers,* I, 403; Wright, *Literary Culture,* pp.
41–42, notes 68, 69. A delightful essay on Digby by Professor Allardyce Nicoll may
be found in *The Johns Hopkins Alumni Magazine,* June, 1933, pp. 330–350.

3. The *Jewel* and the *Ambrose* and later the *Talbot* put back to Cowes, but
caught up with the *Arbella,* before that ship passed the Scillies.

such large quantities of freight that a few of the cows, goats, and horses had to be thrown overboard during the voyage.[1] On their way out they met a vessel from Virginia bringing tobacco to England, saw Mason's vessel, the *Warwick,* start for Piscataqua, bearing the governor appointed under the Laconia patent of November 17, 1629,[2] and on April 25 overhauled two ships outward bound, which proved to be under the command of one of the Kirkes, *en route* to Canada, where the brothers had taken Quebec from the French the year before. A month or two earlier, in February and March, the *Lyon* from Bristol, with eighty passengers from the West Country, had started for New England, and the *Mary and John,* a vessel of four hundred tons, from Plymouth, with the Rev. John Warham, the Rev. John Maverick, Roger Ludlow, Roger Clap, Edward Rossiter, and other West Country people on board to the number of one hundred and forty. The Rev. John White came to Plymouth to see them off and preached a sermon, just as John Cotton had done at Southampton.[3] It was not until a year later, February, 1631, that another Puritan colonizing body, the Providence Island Company, sent out the *Seaflower* on its way to the island of Old Providence in the Caribbean. The activities of this company were all a part of the same general movement.

The course of the *Arbella,* which is carefully recorded in Winthrop's journal and admirably mapped by Mr. Horace Ware in the *Transactions* of the Colonial Society of Massachusetts,[4] lay directly across the Atlantic from the Scilly Isles to the coast of Maine. The voyage proved favorable, despite an occasional storm and heavy seas, and the *Arbella* flagship (the *Talbot* having early been lost sight of and the *Ambrose* and *Jewel* lagging behind) rounded Cape Sable

1. Johnson, *Wonder-Working Providence,* p. 57; Winthrop, *Journal,* I, 51.
2. See next chapter, page 422, note 1.
3. Roger Clap, *Memoirs,* pp. 39–40. At Southampton on the eve of departure, the Rev. John Cotton, vicar of St. Botolph's, Boston, "who went along with them from Boston in Lincolnshire to Southampton," preached a farewell sermon, which was printed the same year as *God's Promise to his Plantations* and later reprinted at Boston in New England. Cotton himself did not go over until 1633, when he became teacher in the Boston church and so remained until his death in 1652. "Scottow's Narrative," *Collections,* Massachusetts Historical Society, 4th series, IV; *New England Historical and Genealogical Register,* II, 151, 318; Banks, *The Winthrop Fleet,* pp. 35–36; "John Cotton, Life and Times," Young, *Chronicles of Massachusetts Bay,* pp. 417–430.
4. *Transactions,* Colonial Society of Massachusetts, XII, 191–203. Dr. Banks, ch. V, gives a corrected chart, but it is that of Mr. Ware, with additions. For a further addition, *ibid.,* 27.

on June 6, sighted the Maine coast off Agamenticus (York) on the
10th, and entered Salem harbor on the 12th. The other three vessels
continued to arrive, one after the other, either at Salem or Charlestown, up to July 2, while the second section, bearing the stock, furniture, utensils, building materials, and some of the passengers,
reached New England at various dates up to July 6. Captain Squeb
of the *Mary and John* put off his passengers at Natascot, whence
they made their way with some difficulty, first to Charlestown and
then to Dorchester where they settled.[1] In all, as a result of a well-
organized propaganda campaign, seventeen vessels left England for
New England in the year 1630, bound for Salem, Charlestown, Dorchester, Natascot, and Plymouth, carrying considerably over a thousand passengers. These and the people who came after them went
to New England, but others in large numbers, during the decade
that followed, went to Bermuda and the islands of the Caribbean.
The men, women, and children of the *Arbella* were but the van-
guard of a great migration to England's possessions in the New
World.

These people, though by no means all Puritans or intent only on
setting up a City of God in the wilderness, represent the greatest
colonizing exodus that England has known in the entire history of
her colonizing activities. That which distinguishes the voyage of the
Arbella from all other voyages in which Puritans took part—
whether to Ireland, Bermuda, or the Caribbean—was that it saw
the transfer across the Atlantic of an organized, officered company,
possessed of power to command and to execute; an incorporated
body, free to govern itself practically as it pleased; a state in the
making, dominated by a powerful conviction as to its place in the
divine scheme. It was led by the largest and most important group
of men that ever at any time came overseas to New England; men
of wealth and education, of middle-class origin with a quantum of
political training, hardheaded and dogmatic, and more stubborn in
their adherence to a religious and political purpose than ever were
Bradford, Brewster, or Winslow. They looked upon themselves as
commissioned of God to create a purer church and a cleaner social
order than those which prevailed at home and were mastered by the
idea of "the saving remnant," whom God had elected to do his will
—an idea that has played a prominent part in the history of all reli-

1. Roger Clap, *Memoirs*, pp. 40–41; Winthrop, *Journal*, I, 50.

gious sectarianism. The strength of the Massachusetts Bay colony lay as much in the character of its leaders, the large number of its people, and the uniformity of its religious polity and teaching, as in the opportunity which the possession of the charter afforded. It is estimated that in the years from 1630 to 1643 nearly two hundred ships—Johnson says one hundred and ninety-eight[1]—left England for Massachusetts, at a cost for furnishing, equipment, and transportation of £200,000, bearing not less than 20,000 people, constituting perhaps a third of those who left England during these years.

The advanced guard did not tarry long at Salem. As a site for the chief town of the new commonwealth it "pleased them not," says Dudley in his letter to the Countess of Lincoln; so men were sent to investigate the coast to the southward, where the company had already instructed Endecott "to fortify and build a towne" for the use of the expected colonists and had sent over one Thomas Graves as a qualified engineer to assist him.[2] Endecott selected Mishawum (Charlestown) as the site of the town and built there at first a single great house, possibly in order to anticipate the claim of John Oldham by occupying a part of Robert Gorges' land, which John Gorges had granted to Oldham. There were settlers already there— Thomas Walford, the blacksmith, in his thatched and palisaded dwelling,[3] and it may be others from the old Robert Gorges' company—and there were some of the Old Planters, who were either sent by Endecott or forced to leave Salem because they did not find contentment there under his management. During the summer of 1630 many of the new arrivals went on to Charlestown to occupy the houses that Endecott and Graves had built for them, but a number of them, not satisfied with the place, crossed over to that strangely shaped peninsula known as Shawmut (Boston), pushed on to Mystic (Medford), and went up the Charles river to Watertown, with the idea of using that place as a site for the fort which they planned to erect against the Indians. Some crossed the neck to Roxbury or kept on down the coast to join the West Country people at Dorchester. This rapid dispersion during the first year of the settlement greatly troubled the leaders, but there was no help for it as the water supply at Charlestown was inadequate and the ac-

1. *Wonder-Working Providence*, pp. 58, note, 61. Cotton Mather gives the same number, *Magnalia*, Bk. I, p. 17. He also estimates the cost of the expeditions at £200,000 (£192,000 in Historical Manuscripts Commission, *Pepys*, p. 270).
2. *Massachusetts Colonial Records*, I, 391.   3. Adams, *Three Episodes*, I, 220–221.

commodations were insufficient for all. Some two hundred deaths took place, due largely to famine, with the resulting fever and scurvy, and Dr. Fuller, who had served the people so well at Salem the year before, was unable to save the sick, being without drugs and "things fitting to work with."[1] On the return of the ships to England about a hundred went back, partly out of dislike of the government, which restrained and punished their excesses, and partly through fear of famine, not "seeing other means than by their labor to feed themselves and glad we were to get rid of them."[2] The heavy mortality, which included Lady Arbella and her husband, Isaac Johnson, and men of such prominence as Edward Rossiter, led to a general expectation among the friends of the colony in England that it would not survive the winter, owing to the cold and the scarcity of provisions.[3]

In the midst of all these troubles and anxieties, the government of the colony was organized and set in motion. The last general court had been held in London at the house of Thomas Goffe, the former deputy governor, on February 10, 1630. A meeting of Governor Winthrop and the assistants was called at Southampton and another on the *Arbella* just before sailing, at the latter of which Thomas Dudley was chosen deputy governor in the place of John Humfry, who was staying behind. Probably no formal meetings were held on shipboard, but the company as a corporate unit was functioning right along and there was no break in the continuity of its existence. The next gathering of governor and assistants was on August 23 at Charlestown, in the midst of the general despondency, at which meeting provision was made for a minister and a surgeon and for a beadle to wait on the governor.

Before the company left England some uncertainty was felt as to how the business interests were to be managed, now that the company had gone off on its religious mission leaving the trading concerns very much in the air. It was finally decided to erect a subordinate body, technically within the company but actually remaining in England, made up of members of the company—some in England and some in America—who were to have the entire control of the trading stock, to pay all charges, and at the end of seven years to

1. Bradford, "Letter Book," p. 76.
2. Young, *Chronicles of Massachusetts Bay,* pp. 314–315.
3. *Winthrop Papers,* I, 38–39 (*Collections,* Massachusetts Historical Society).

return the amounts invested to those who had subscribed. Certain conditions were laid down defining the relations of this subordinate body to the company and certain agreements were entered into regarding the conduct of the business. The arrangement was similar to that of the Virginia Company with the magazine, with the first Bermuda company, and with the other subordinate undertakings which were promoted within the body of the company, when the common stock was insufficient to carry on the venture. It had points of resemblance also to the expedient adopted at Plymouth, when in 1628 eight men of the colony and four in England were entrusted with the management of the joint-stock of the colony in the interest of trade and profit. The adjustment in the Massachusetts case was effected December 15, 1629, and after the company had gone to America its joint-stock remained in England as a trading fund and was kept quite distinct from its common stock, which consisted of whatever the colony possessed in land, buildings, and livestock in New England, though for many years afterward subscribers to the original stock in England continued to demand as their right shares of land in the colony.

The men in charge of these dwindling trading interests were Cradock, Eaton, Wright, Goffe, and Humfry in England and Saltonstall, Winthrop, Dudley, Revell, and Johnson in America, with Aldersey living as treasurer in England. By 1634 Winthrop and Dudley were the only ones left in the colony, so that from that time forward the management centered its interest in London and the trading joint-stock was managed from that end.[1] The company as a corporate government in New England had nothing to do with it, just as it had nothing to do with the private undertakings of Mathew Cradock or Richard Saltonstall, and it held itself in no way responsible for the debts incurred in either case. This solution of the joint-stock problem marked a sharp differentiation between the original joint-stock which was for trade and the new common stock which was for the maintenance of the plantation and became in time the common fund of the colony in America.[2] Of the activities

1. "The whole trade of the plantation is maintained by such undertakers as remain in Old England," Downing to Sir John Coke, December 12, 1633. Historical Manuscripts Commission, *Twelfth Report*, appendix II, 38–39.

2. *Massachusetts Colonial Records*, I, 62, 65, 68, 238; Scott, *Joint-Stock Companies*, II, 314–315; Rose Troup, *The Massachusetts Bay Company*, chaps. X, XI. Mrs. Rose Troup devotes two chapters to this subject, in which she points out certain errors

of the undertakers very little is known. They were still doing business as late as 1638, when their acting-treasurer—Harwood, who took Aldersey's place—was called upon to render an accounting, but no records of their transactions have survived and it is not known certainly when their enterprise came to an end. They had to do with the traffic in furs and any other commodities that the colonists could furnish, and from the profits of sales were expected to pay dividends to the subscribers. Probably no dividends were ever paid and all that many of the subscribers ever received were certain portions of land in the colony at the end of the seven year period.[1]

With the placing of the joint-stock in the hands of a board of managers, thus conserving in some measure the financial interests of the original subscribers, and with the starting of the company itself on its religious mission to America, there to set up a Puritan state under the aegis of a trading company's charter, a remarkable transformation was effected, without parallel in the history of commercial and colonizing enterprise. A trading company was entering on its process of evolution into a commonwealth, which was to exercise all the powers contained in the charter and such others, implied or not, as were necessary for its successful operation. The charter gave corporate strength and unity and shaped the system of administration, but it was valued chiefly as a wall of defense against outside intervention, whether of private individual or king, and upon it the colony rested its legal right to exist. How far the Puritan leaders anticipated the troubles the future held in store for them no one can say, but that they confidently saw in the possession of the charter, in the distance from England, and in the divine protection a sufficient security against the world from which they had withdrawn cannot be doubted. They wished to control their own affairs and to maintain a religious community, in a country hitherto unoccupied, that should represent, not man's will and purpose, but that of God, as far as they could discover it, which in their profound convictions was very far indeed. Their faith in God's protecting care was illimitable.

in Scott's work. See also Young, *Chronicles of Massachusetts Bay,* pp. 315–316, 319, 321. For the refusal of the colony to carry any responsibility for the debts of the undertakers, Cradock and others, *Massachusetts Colonial Records,* II, 226; III, 213; IV, 297.

1. *Massachusetts Colonial Records,* I, 307; II, 132, 246; Hutchinson, *History of Massachusetts,* I, 13.

CHAPTER XIX

GORGES AND THE PURITANS

WHILE the Puritans were working out their destiny and becoming more intense and determined in their desire to find a refuge in America, a new danger was arising in a not unexpected quarter. The plans of that most persistent of colonial promoters, Sir Ferdinando Gorges, had received a crushing blow by the inrush of the Puritan settlers and the planting of an incorporated company within the very center of the territory which had been granted by royal patent to the Council for New England. This had been made possible because of the fact, already stated but needing restatement here, that between 1625 and 1629 the New England Council had almost ceased to function as an active organization and its members were either losing an interest in its welfare or, as in the case of Gorges himself, were being drawn off into the king's service to the neglect of their affairs in America. At the very time when the Puritan plans were gathering momentum and the Puritan leaders, with impressive earnestness, were preparing to sacrifice home and country in obedience to what they believed to be the divine command, the chief members of the New England Council—prerogative men, all of them—were becoming absorbed in matters of state and war. Probably not more than a quarter of the original patentees had ever taken any part in the council's business, and even of those only a few were able to give either time or thought to what they must have considered a minor enterprise. By 1629 Buckingham, Lenox, Holdernesse, Apsly, and Sutcliffe were dead; Middlesex, the former lord high treasurer, with whom the Virginia Company had been involved over the tobacco contract, was in retirement; Arundel was deep in public business; and the Bishop of Lincoln was taken up with the duties of his diocese. Carlisle was distracted by the demands of his West Indian proprietorship; Sheffield was vice-admiral of York; Spelman, sixty-six, though still destined to have some part as an adviser, was reported in 1630 as "very aged and very blind"; and Edward, Lord Gorges, and Mansell, though still active, were immersed in parlia-

mentary controversy. Warwick, Ferdinando Gorges, and possibly Dr. Barnaby Gooch were the only members available at the time of the Puritan migration for the prosecution of active business.

The man most anxious to stem the Puritan tide was, of course, Sir Ferdinando himself, but during these years he was captain of the castle and island of St. Nicholas in Plymouth harbor, was heavily burdened with the duties of defense against invasion, and for a brief period was personally in charge of one of the king's ships at Dieppe. With him was Captain Love, who had also shared in the division of 1623 and was closely associated with the protection of the coast. Captain John Mason, though not a member, had received in 1622, after his return from Newfoundland, the Mariana grant covering the territory from Naumkeag to the Merrimac, had gone to Cadiz in 1625, had been appointed treasurer and paymaster of the navy, and during the war with France had been occupied with the performance of his official duties. It was in front of his house in Portsmouth that Buckingham was murdered in 1628 by the disgruntled naval officer, Felton. During these years Warwick alone, unless we include Gooch, of whose coöperation we know nothing, was in a position to keep the council alive and his sympathies, as we know, were not with Gorges but with the Puritans. There is reason to think, from the absence of all records, that no meetings were held or minutes kept, and that Warwick was the whole council and did pretty much as he pleased.[1] There was little interest in northern colonization at this time, partly because of the failure of the Robert Gorges expedition and partly because of the distracted state of public affairs in England.[2] Not even Christopher Levett, who made a voyage to New England in 1624-1625 and wanted to found a colony there, was able to arouse any enthusiasm in England for colonizing ventures in America, and was obliged, soon after his return, to obtain employment as captain of a ship in the expedition against Spain. Plymouth, the legal seat of the council, was inconveniently located as a place of meeting and a journey thither was not to be taken lightly. To many a public man of the day, the council was

1. Dr. Deane in his prefatory remarks, Proceedings, American Antiquarian Society, 1867, pp. 58–59, inclines to this view, as does Mr. Brigham in his excellent comments on the subject, ibid., 1912, p. 242.

2. Some account must be taken of the plague that was raging in northern Europe at the time, though it did not reach England until 1630 and was not at its height until 1636, when 10,400 died in London.

largely if not entirely forgotten, and if to the legal mind there was any reason to consider that it still existed in all likelihood it was thought to have lapsed from disuse.

This condition of affairs gave to Warwick his opportunity. He was a member of the council and had shared in the distribution of 1623, and sometime before the spring of 1628 he had been chosen president, how and by whose votes we do not know.[1] It is quite possible to believe that at this juncture the petition of the New England Company for a grant of land galvanized the council into action and led Warwick to take matters into his own hands. With the seal in his possession[2] he might have called a meeting at his house in Holborn, not far from Gray's Inn, and have got together Lord Gorges, Spelman, Mansell, and Gooch, all of whom attended meetings after 1631. On the other hand, he may not have done this at all. In default of a regular council meeting, he may simply have "resigned"—the word used in the Massachusetts records—the grant which he and others had received from the council in 1622. It is at least significant that between May 5, 1623, and November 17, 1629, the council issued no grant, of which we have record, except this supposed patent to the New England Company; and it is equally significant that there is not a shred of evidence to show that any such grant could have been made legally.

With the drawing to a close of the war with France and Spain, Gorges was free to turn his attention once more to colonial matters and to take up the work of the New England Council. Between November 17, 1629, and June 26, 1632, the council issued no less than from seventeen to twenty patents of land, of which all but one

1. According to the charter a president could be elected only by a majority of the members. Such a majority could not have been brought together in 1628. Whether the requirement of the charter could be met by proxy voting or by any form of verbal or written consent is unlikely. In studying the proceedings of the New England Council one is forced to conclude that the terms of the charter were frequently violated and that many of the council's acts were, if strictly construed, illegal.

2. The council seems to have had more than one seal, as Gorges in 1634 speaks of the "seals of the company" (*Calendar State Papers, Colonial*, 1574–1660, p. 193 [36]). The charter authorized the council "to appoint whatever Seale or Seales they shall think most meete and necessary" and we find mention of a "common seal" and a "great seal." The latter was undoubtedly the one used in issuing patents and was that which Warwick had in his possession. It was plainly stated later that with Warwick out of the presidency patents could not be issued as long as that seal remained in Warwick's hands (*Proceedings*, American Antiquarian Society, 1867, p. 111). For an essay on the great seal itself, *Trelawny Papers,* appendix viii.

—the Bradford patent of January 13, 1630—were put out in the interest of Gorges and his friends, and concerned lands that lay north of the Merrimac river. Warwick was still president of the council and all of the meetings were held at his house. Though Gorges may have had some knowledge of the real situation as early as the spring of 1630, when the close of the war released him from his military duties, he cannot have known with certainty the true significance of the Massachusetts Bay Company's charter before the summer of 1632, when John Humfry let the cat out of the bag in telling the council that the requirement of a license from the president and council for passengers going to Massachusetts was a violation of their charter.[1]

Humfry's statement brought into the open for the first time the news of what Warwick had been doing and led to an immediate demand on the part of "some of the council" that the patent of 1628 be brought to the board for inspection. Humfry in reply said that it had gone to New England. At once an inquiry was instituted and Humfry, Cradock, and Saltonstall—the last named recently returned from New England—were called on for information. Furthermore, an order was issued, November 6, 1632, "that all Patents formerly granted should be called for and perused and afterwards confirmed if the Councell shall see fit." The situation became so strained that Warwick ceased to attend the meetings. He had accomplished his main purpose, even though he had failed to round out his work in two particulars. He had failed to secure for the Pilgrims a confirmation of their grant in the form of a royal charter that would erect their colony into a legal corporation, and he had just missed obtaining from the council, in the interest of a group of Puritan lords and

1. Sherley writing to the Plymouth colony, March 19, 1630, says "For I am persuaded Sir Ferdinando (how loving and friendly soever he seems to be) knows he can, nay purposeth to overthrow, at his pleasure, all the patents he grants, but this [charter] being obtained he will be frustrate of his intent." Bradford "Letter Book," p. 71. From this statement it would appear that Gorges was back at the council at that time and as early as this had obtained an inkling of what Warwick was doing. Emmanuel Downing wrote to Sir John Coke, Dec. 12, 1633, "Sir Ferdinand Gough [Gorges] with some others his co-partners have these many years past laboured to make a plantation in New England, where having spent their money and travail in vain, being ashamed of their own and envying their neighbours' prosperity, have of late made claim to the very ground where Mr. Winthrop, with a colony, hath built and planted, labouring either to overthrow this patent of incorporation, or to have other government established." Historical Manuscripts Commission, *Twelfth Report*, appendix II, 38.

gentlemen—some of whom were associated with himself in the formation of the Old Providence Company—a patent for a large extent
of territory in southern New England, extending westward from
Narragansett Bay. In the first instance he had been blocked by the
bungling methods of Allerton and the opposition of Lord High
Treasurer Weston; in the second by his own fall from power in the
Council for New England. The draft of the so-called "Warwick
Patent" of Connecticut was prepared on June 21, 1632, and a committee appointed to settle it. But Warwick never attended a meeting after that date and the patent was never perfected.[1] The meetings were removed from his house to that of Captain John Mason,[2]
the seal of the council was taken out of his hands and restored to
the control of the treasurer,[3] and he ceased to have any further part
in the council's affairs. All mention of the proposed patent disappeared from the council records. It failed of consummation because
henceforth Gorges was in control and would have none of it.

With the removal of Warwick from the presidency of the council
and his withdrawal from all participation in its concerns, Gorges
was free to go ahead with his own plans for a complete reorganization under his own leadership. He enlarged the membership by admitting men favorable to himself, especially Captain John Mason,
eventually chosen vice-president, and he made the further suggestion—never carried out—that the twenty-one admitted up to June
29, 1632, be increased to forty, among whom were to be merchants as well as gentlemen of quality. At the meeting of November, 1632, an elaborate agenda of business was drawn up, of which
the most important items were the completion of the number of

1. "My lord of Warw. will take a Pattent of that place you writ of for himselfe
and so we may be bold to do there as if it were our own." *Winthrop Papers*, I, 4
(*Collections*, Massachusetts Historical Society). This shows that Warwick was planning to obtain the patent as early as 1630. There is no doubt that the lords and
gentlemen and later the people of Connecticut thought he had obtained it and acted
accordingly. But while other patents of 1631 and 1632 are duly entered in the records (pp. 53, 57) there is no mention of a patent to Warwick.

2. The remaining meetings were held at various places—Captain Mason's house
in Fenchurch Street; the Earl of Lindsay's house in Channel (Canon) Row, Whitehall; Lord Gorges' house in St. Martin's Lane, Westminster; the Earl of Carlile's
chambers in Whitehall; and Lord Stirling's house. The later records of the council's
meetings are incomplete.

3. The seal does not appear to have been actually returned until after November
26, 1632, but as no patents were sealed between June, 1632, when Warwick retired,
and 1635, no definite statement can be made as to when it was returned.

councillors, the scrutiny of all patents hitherto granted, the sending of commissioners to New England to determine all differences and redress all grievances, and, most interesting of all, the obtaining from the king of a new charter with enlarged proprietary powers, modeled on that which had been granted to Lord Baltimore for Maryland about four months before. As Baltimore's charter was feudal and proprietary in character, though of a nature exceptionally favorable to the grantee, we have in this proposal a significant disclosure of Gorges' intentions from the beginning and of his desire to erect in New England an absolute proprietorship after a feudal plan. The New England Council, though proprietary in fact was corporate in law, but Gorges, in planning to petition for a new charter, intended, with the aid and advice of Sir Henry Spelman— the council's legal authority on patents from the beginning—to get rid of the corporate element entirely and to take his stand openly as a believer in a feudal and proprietary form of colonial settlement.[1]

The chief obstacle in the path of success was the Massachusetts Bay colony of the Puritans, which, based as it was upon a charter equally authoritative with that of the council, made impossible the proprietorship which Gorges desired to erect, unless it were removed or rendered subject to the authority of the council. If the intruders were allowed to remain as they were, all hope of carrying out his original plans was at an end. Gorges had no enmity toward the Puritans[2] and did not wish to remove them in a bodily sense from New England, but he did wish to effect the annulment of their charter, in order to bring them under the control of the coun-

1. There is no more remarkable phase of the history of New England patents than the progressive evolution from the charter of 1606, incorporating the Virginia Company of Plymouth, through the corporate-proprietary charter of the New England Council of 1620 and the proposed feudal charter based on the Maryland model of 1632, to the Gorges patent for Maine of 1639, one of the most strikingly seignorial and proprietary charters ever issued for land and government in America.

2. Richard Mather writes in his journal, May 29, 1635, "And soone after wee came aboard there [King's Road, Bristol] there came three or four more boates with more passengers, and one wherein came Sir Ferdinando Gorge, who came to see the ship and the people. When he was come hee enquired whether there were any people there that went to Massachusetts Bay, whereupon Mr. Maud and Barnabas Fower were sent for to come before him; who being come he asked Mr. Maud of his country, occupation or calling of life, etc, and professed his good will to the people there in the bay, and promised that if hee ever came there he would be a true friend unto them." *Journal*, pp. 7-8.

cil and of himself as the governor general of New England that he hoped to be.

At this crisis of affairs he received aid from an unexpected quarter, that is, from New England itself, for no sooner had the Massachusetts colonists reached their destination and held their first court of assistants at Charlestown in August, 1630, than they turned their attention to the further scourging of Thomas Morton. The Pilgrims had shipped him back to England in June, 1628, and Endecott had completed the work of purifying the land by cutting down the maypole at Merrymount the autumn after. But Morton had returned in the summer of 1629 and during the year that followed, before the arrival of Winthrop, had resumed his former life at the same spot and with the same gusto. This fact came to the knowledge of the Puritan leaders soon after they reached New England and at their first official meeting they decided to arrest Morton and try him for his misdeeds. No mercy was shown, the sentence had been decided on beforehand, and Morton was condemned to sit in the stocks in the presence of the gaping crowd as an example of a sinner and a warning to the loose-minded. He was compelled to see his house burnt down before his eyes and was sentenced to be shipped back to England in the first available vessel.[1] Needless to say he arrived in England in no very amiable frame of mind and his immediate alignment with Gorges and his allies was later to cost the Massachusetts people many anxious hours. Whatever his shortcomings may have been, Morton was a lawyer of no mean ability, and the ferreting of a lawyer of parts into the circumstances of the passing of the charter and its transfer to America was something that the Puritan leaders would have been quite willing to prevent.

The Puritans had already begun the elimination of the undesirables in the colony, according to their idea of what that term included. Even as early as the summer of 1629, before the company went overseas, Endecott at Salem had sent the Brownes back to England and in so doing had incurred the displeasure of Cradock and the council of the company in England, who wrote to him not to do anything that would injure the reputation of the company at home, or to act in any similar case without instructions from them. But the company now turned Puritan had no such scruples.[2] Faith

1. *Massachusetts Colonial Records*, I, 74, 75; Winthrop, *Journal*, I, 53; Adams, *Three Episodes*, chap. XV.

2. *Massachusetts Colonial Records*, I, 51–54. The company did not scruple to open

and practice must be uniform and though men who kept their preferences to themselves would be let alone, those who gave outward expression to undesirable religious convictions would not be tolerated. In Massachusetts Bay as in Plymouth there were many Church of England adherents, some of whom, no doubt, were unrestrained in their dislike of the Puritan attitude. It seems that the plantation of Mathew Cradock was a center of disaffection and his servants there were an unruly lot, given to speaking "wickedly and boldly against the government and the governor." For so doing Philip Ratcliffe, one of them, was ordered to be whipped, to have both ears cut off, and to be fined forty shillings in addition. Roger Clap in his *Memoirs* says that he saw the thing done and Winthrop tells us that the sentence was "presently executed." Not unnaturally Ratcliffe, when he recovered from his wounds and finally returned to England, was ready to do anything to obtain his revenge on his hated enemy.[1]

More noteworthy still was the experience of Sir Christopher Gardiner, a picturesque character, who claimed descent from Stephen Gardiner, Bishop of Winchester, and boasted of his adventures as a traveller and of his first honor of knighthood received at Jerusalem, when he was made a knight of the "Golden Melice." He was probably a Roman Catholic, as much as he was anything, who had turned Protestant before he came to the colony, about a month before the arrival of Winthrop, pretending that he had forsaken the world and wished to live a retired life. There is no reason to think that he had come over on any special mission from Gorges or any one else to watch the settlement or report on its policy and progress, but the Massachusetts people managed so to treat him as to bring about that very end. He was intelligent and well informed and quite competent to tell what he knew when the time came. It is probable that he had left England in part because of matrimonial tangles and of scandals that he needed to live down. The Massachusetts authorities, impressed by his pretensions and his title, did not dare treat him as they had treated Morton and Ratcliffe; but

the Brownes' letters sent to England, any more than did the Pilgrims hesitate to open those of Lyford or Winthrop those of Sir Christopher Gardiner, fearing lest the letters might contain matter prejudicial to their respective colonies. They saw no moral or ethical wrong in so doing.

1. *Massachusetts Colonial Records*, I, 77; Clap, *Memoirs*, p. 35; Winthrop, *Journal*, I, 64; Young, *Chronicles of Massachusetts*, pp. 361–362; Adams, *Three Episodes*, I, 259–262.

they arrested him and sentenced him to banishment as an immoral person, which he undoubtedly was, though they shrank from executing the sentence of banishment, even after Winthrop had opened his letters and decided that he was a Gorges emissary. Gardiner finally went back to England of his own accord, and in no very pleasant mood made a report to Gorges that was distinctly hostile to the colony.[1]

These were the allies that came to the assistance of Gorges when he was scheming how to get the Massachusetts Bay Company's charter out of the way in order to clear the ground for his own experiment in colonization. The five men—Gorges, Mason, Morton, Ratcliffe, and Gardiner—met at Gorges' house in Plymouth and there formulated plans for the execution of this project. Gardiner drafted a relation of conditions in New England—possibly the report itself or a statement based on the report which he had made to Gorges—and this paper, accompanied by petitions and other evidence, was sent to the Privy Council.[2] There it was taken into consideration, December 19, 1632. A committee of council was appointed, consisting of the Archbishop of York (Richard Neill), the Lord High Treasurer (Weston), the Lord Privy Seal (Coventry), the Earl of Manchester, the Earl of Pembroke, the Earl of Arundel, the Earl of Dorset, Viscount Falkland, the Bishop of London (Laud), Francis, Lord Coltingham, Sir Thomas Edmonds, and the principal secretaries of state, Sir John Coke and Sir Francis Windebanke. This committee, or any four of them, was authorized to investigate and make a report. Its members were to call "to their assistance such other persons as they shall think fit; shall examine how the patents for the said plantation have been granted, and how carried; and shall examine the truth of the aforesaid information or such other information as shall be presented to them. And shall make report thereof to this Board and of the true state of the said plantations, as they shall find them now to stand." They were also authorized to summon before them such of the patentees and such of the complainants and their witnesses as they thought fit.

The business of the committee was pushed forward rapidly, and on January 19, 1633, it made its report. Just how thorough had been

---

1. Bradford, *History*, II, 136–145 and notes; *Proceedings*, Massachusetts Historical Society, 1883, pp. 69–88.
2. *Acts Privy Council, Colonial*, I, §§302, 303.

its investigations, completed within a month, we cannot say. It had interviewed Saltonstall and Cradock and, presumably, Gorges, Gardiner, Morton, and Ratcliffe. Probably the letter of Captain Wiggin to Secretary Coke, containing an account of the plantation, in which Wiggin described Winthrop as "a discreet and sober man, assisting in any ordinary labor and ruling with mildness and justice" was read and had an effect favorable to the colony.[1] Wiggin reported as an eye witness against the "false rumors spread abroad" by Gardiner, Morton, and Ratcliffe, "all discontented and scandalous characters," as he called them. Edward Winslow also sent in a petition from the Fleet prison, where he had been confined for being a Separatist and for marrying people in the colony,[2] in which he spoke of Morton as a delinquent twice banished, of Gardiner as a Jesuit, and of Dixie Bull as a pirate,[3] and he hoped that so hopeful a colony might not be ruined. Downing also wrote to Coke from London, hoping that "those lewd and scandalous persons [Morton et al.] might receive condign punishment" and that the plantation be allowed to proceed with encouragement "as it deserves."[4] The result of this accumulated evidence favorable to the colony, strengthened by the defense of Secretary Coke who was well primed by Wiggin and Downing, was a report from the committee upholding the colony as beneficial to the kingdom and profitable to those who had adventured in the undertaking. The Privy Council approved the report and promised that the king would not only maintain the privileges of Massachusetts Bay but would also supply anything further that might tend to the good government of the place and the prosperity and comfort of the people. It expressed its belief that the colony might be actually beneficial to the realm in furnishing

1. Wiggin was governor at Piscataqua, representative there of the Puritan lords and gentlemen. Winthrop, *Journal*, I, 69, 99, 111, 131, 137, 147, 279, 295; Libby, *Maine Province and Court Records*, I, II, indexes.

2. Winslow had gone to England as the agent for the Plymouth undertakers, taking upward of 4000 lbs. of beaver and other skins. *Calendar State Papers, Colonial, 1574–1660*, p. 157; Winthrop, *Journal*, I, 163–164; Bradford, *History*, II, 189, 198–199, 202–203. "Mr. Winslow lies still in prison and is like so to continew, for I do not heare when the lords will meete again for plantation business." *Winthrop Papers*, I, 43 (*Collections*, Massachusetts Historical Society).

3. On Dixie Bull, *Trelawny Papers*, p. 23; Winthrop, *Journal*, I, 101–102; Bradford, *History*, II, 142, note 1.

4. *Calendar State Papers, Colonial, 1574–1660*, p. 158; Historical Manuscripts Commission, *Twelfth Report*, appendix, II, 38–39.

naval stores, should the Danish Sound ever be closed to English ships.[1]

This decision of the Privy Council was based rather upon the moral and commercial merits of the case than upon grounds that were either legal or ecclesiastical. Gorges had not, therefore, exhausted his resources. Just what influences were brought to bear upon the council during the ensuing three and a half months cannot be stated, but it is evident that a further investigation showed the necessity of considering anew the conditions attending the settlement not only of New England but also of the plantations as a whole.[2] On May 1, 1633, the same committee was continued with the Archbishop of Canterbury as its chairman.[3] This committee must have set on foot a searching inquiry into the whole subject of colonial migration, for at the beginning of the next year the Privy Council ordered the marshal of the Admiralty to hold up all vessels in the Thames bound for New England until further instructions should be prepared. On February 12, 1634, with the masters of the vessels attending the council, the new instructions were read and they were required to see to it, under bond, that all persons going to New England should take the oaths of allegiance and supremacy,

1. *Acts Privy Council, Colonial,* I, §306; Winthrop, *Journal,* I, 99, 100–101, 103, 104–105.

2. The puzzle of Endecott's laws, mentioned in a letter from Howes to Winthrop, March 25, 1633, as having been presented to the Privy Council at this time (Massachusetts Historical Society, *Collections,* 3d ser., IX, 257), has never been solved. See Phillips, *Salem,* p. 81.

3. The usual date given for the elevation of Laud to the See of Canterbury is August 6, 1633, but in the list of the privy councillors printed in the *Acts of the Privy Council, Colonial,* V, 621, Laud is entered as archbishop on May 1 of that year. In the list of the members of the second committee for New England the first name is that of the "Lord Arch Bishop of Canterbury." This committee is entered as of May 1, and it is difficult to avoid the conclusion that its chairman was not George Abbot but William Laud. If Laud was not the "Lord Arch Bishop of Canterbury," named in the records as chairman of the second committee, then he was not on that committee at all, a statement difficult to accept in view of the fact that he was on the first committee as the Lord Bishop of London, and on that of 1634 as the Archbishop of Canterbury, the chairman. Why should he have been on the committees of 1632 and 1634 and not on that of 1633? The work of the committee of 1633, which undoubtedly prepared the way for the more important committee to come and probably had a large part in drafting its instructions, is Laudian in every particular and made Laud the logical head of the committee of 1634. The matter of the date would be comparatively unimportant, were it not for the necessity of determining who was chairman of the second committee. If Laud was chairman of that committee we have an explanation of its change of attitude toward Massachusetts and the Puritans. *Acts Privy Council, Colonial,* I, §§328, 329, 341, 343; Winthrop, *Journal,* I, 127–128.

should hold service on board according to the Book of Common Prayer, and should restrain themselves from blasphemy or from "prophaning the holly name of God."

The inquiries instituted by the committee of 1633, which led to the drawing up of the instructions of February, 1634, were carried on during the first half of that year and for the first time brought into view the whole situation. The efforts of Gorges and his associates were bearing fruit and the charges against the Massachusetts Bay Company were opening up the whole question of emigration to America as a phase of national policy. Men and women of rank and respectability were going to Plymouth, Massachusetts, Bermuda, the West Indies, Old Providence, and Maryland,[1] and many thoughtful men in England were expressing the opinion that this was injurious to the best interests of the kingdom[2] as well as contrary to the well-being of the Anglican church. Archbishop Laud, in his desire to check the movement on the ground that it tended to increase non-conformity, was not alone in his opposition; there were others also who disliked the movement as taking from England hundreds of her most useful people—gentry, artisans, and laborers—from the middle and laboring classes and draining her of gold and silver and other parts of her national stock.[3] The movement was believed to be economically harmful by those who were already beginning to think in terms of mercantilism.[4]

Thus a national issue had arisen and to meet it a more powerful

1. *Calendar State Papers, Colonial*, 1574–1660, pp. 261, 266, 273, 274, 276.

2. *Acts Privy Council, Colonial*, I, §§ 326, 327, 328, 329, 381, 383, 384, 385, 387, 393.

3. *Calendar State Papers, Colonial*, 1574–1660, pp. 158, 285. The transportation of gold and silver to the plantations was prohibited.

4. We in America are too prone to think of the early settlement of our country from the point of view solely of its advantages to ourselves and to ignore the Englishman's views about it. The time was one when officials and merchants were formulating certain principles of policy that mark the beginnings of mercantilist thought. Gerald Malynes and Edward Misselden, though in opposition to each other, had both published pamphlets bearing in part on this subject (1622–1623). In the very year of the Laud commission and coincident with the issue of the Western Charter of 1634 relating to Newfoundland, Thomas Mun wrote his well-known treatise on foreign trade, which though not published until 1664 shows the working of men's minds thirty years before. Robert Powell in 1636 issued his pamphlet on *Depopulation;* Captain Lewes Roberts in 1638 his *Merchants Mappe of Commerce*, which concerned the carrying of grain and gold beyond the seas, contrary to the laws of the realm. On the other hand, we have White's *The Planters Plea* (1630), in which the value of plantations is upheld, the usual objections answered, and the settlement of New England defended; and *A Commission for the Well Governing of our People*

body, with wider authority, was necessary. On April 28, 1634, a commission was issued under the great seal to those of the Privy Council who had composed the second committee, with one exception, the addition of Sir William Alexander, Earl of Stirling. To this commission—a forerunner of the Lords of Trade of later date (1675-1696)—were granted far greater powers than had been possessed by the earlier committees, which were merely committees of council, and a body of instructions was introduced into the text of the patent which greatly extended the functions of the board. This board is the famous Laud Commission for Regulating Plantations and its legal and administrative status was the same as that of the later Lords of Trade, that is, it was a committee of council raised to the dignity, prestige, and power of an executive body, entrusted by the king with extensive jurisdictional rights for the carrying out of certain carefully defined duties. Its scope was not ecclesiastical only, but national, legal, and mercantilist, and its members were called upon to play a much more commanding part than that of arbiters in a quarrel between the Massachusetts Bay Company and its detractors, as the committee of 1632 had done.

The powers specified in the commission, which the committee of 1633 must have drawn up, represent an almost complete abdication by the Privy Council of its authority over the plantations. The board was empowered to govern and legislate for the colonies, to watch over things ecclesiastical, to remove if necessary those in office, to set up judges, ordain civil and ecclesiastical courts, change, revoke, and annul old laws and frame new ones, and hear complaints and grievances of any kind. These powers in themselves were extraordinarily comprehensive. But for Gorges and his associates, who during these months must have had the ear of the archbishop and been able to make their grievances known,[1] the all important clauses

(1633), which gives eleven rules for the proper managing of Newfoundland. On the part of the Privy Council as a whole, which was the only official body at that time interested in the plantations, there is nothing to show any particular enmity for the Puritans, but a great deal to show a desire to uphold the general welfare of the country. The order of 1632 demonstrates that. But in 1633 and 1634 larger issues were up for consideration and the attitude of the government toward the Puritans was, in part at least, determined by those issues.

1. Morton at this time wrote his *New England Canaan*, which was dedicated to the Laud Commission and was designed to influence its attitude toward New England. The work was entered at Stationers' Hall, November 18, 1633, in the name of Charles Green as publisher, showing that it was in preparation a year before the Laud Commission was created. Though some copies of the title-page were struck

came toward the end. "We empower you, or any five of you," so runs the text, "that if you shall find any of the colonies aforesaid, or any of the cheefe rulers upon the jurisdiction of others by unjust possession or usurpation . . . or withdrawing from our alegiance or our commandments" to order them either to return to England or to remove to other places assigned. And "we doe give unto you power and spetiall command over all the charters, leters patent and rescripts royale . . . to cause them to be brought before you, and the same being received, if anything surrepticiously or unduly have been obtained, or that by the same priviledges, liberties and prerogatives hurtful to us, or to our crowne, or to foraign princes have been prejudicially suffered . . . to command them according to the laws and customs of England to be revoked."[1] These were the very things that Gorges and Morton wanted the government to do. They had made no headway in their attack on Massachusetts because of the colony's harsh treatment of Morton, Ratcliffe, and Gardiner, so that it was necessary to shift their ground and to demand the recall of the charter because surreptitiously obtained and its terms unwarrantably overstepped.

No minutes of the meetings of the commission are extant and the range of its accomplishments can be discovered only by occasional references to its work. It exercised its authority to a very limited extent in Virginia and Maryland, awarding Kent Island to Baltimore in spite of Claiborne's protests, but otherwise it seems to have paid very little attention to any of the colonies outside New England. News of Gorges and Morton's plans soon crossed the water and a copy of the commission was brought over in September, 1634. Winthrop believed that the main purpose of the board was to deprive the Puritans of their charter and to compel the colony by force to accept a governor general, who, it was rumored, was to be none other than Gorges himself. He was forewarned that ships and sol-

off by Green, the work as a whole was not printed until 1637 at Amsterdam by Jacob Frederick Stam. It has been reprinted and edited by Charles Francis Adams for the Prince Society. One would like to know what Laud thought of this work, if he ever read it. There is little reason to believe that he, any more than the Massachusetts Puritans, entered into the whimsical humor of it.

1. Hazard, *State Papers*, I, 344–347; Bradford, *History*, I, 183–186; Hubbard, *History of New England*, pp. 264–268. A copy was sent to the colony in a ship which arrived September 18, 1634, bearing two ministers, Lothrop and Sims, and Mrs. Anne Hutchinson. The commission and Mrs. Hutchinson were a combination destined to make the colony considerable trouble.

diers were in preparation, ostensibly designed for Virginia—it was the time of trouble there with Governor Harvey—but as the Puritans thought for the overthrow of Massachusetts.[1] Warwick, now definitely out of the Council for New England and hostile to Gorges, showed his sympathy for the Puritan cause by writing to Winthrop congratulating him on the prosperity of the plantation, encouraging him and the colony in their determination to resist intervention, and offering to help him as best he could. The Countess of Warwick also manifested her interest by a benefaction of sufficient moment to call from the general court a letter of thankfulness to her.[2]

There is no doubt that the colony was thrown into a state of great agitation and fear at this threatened attack upon what they deemed their liberties. These apprehensions were increased by the ill-advised and intemperate act of Endecott's, who in something of a frenzy, partly religious and partly political, cut from the royal ensign at Salem the red cross or a part of it, as if it were a papal emblem, having been "given to the king of England by the pope, as an ensign of victory and so a superstitious thing and a relique of antichrist."[3] Few incidents in Puritan history are more indicative than this of the limited understanding and ineradicable prejudice of the more stiff-necked of the Puritan leaders, for coming as it did at a time when the authorities in England were stirred against the colony, it was a deliberate defiance of church and state. Winthrop

1. Winthrop, *Journal*, I, 127, 129.
2. *Ibid.*, I, 130; II, 152; *Massachusetts Colonial Records*, I, 128. In later years, as the intolerant attitude of the New Englanders became better understood in the mother country, Warwick's sympathy for the Massachusetts Puritans waned. After 1643, the commission, of which he was the head, showed in many ways its dissatisfaction with the colony. It upheld liberty of conscience; it supported Gorton in his conflict with the Massachusetts authorities; and it granted a patent to Rhode Island. The attitude in England of toleration toward the colonies found its counterpart in the Boston church, where a party arose that was strongly opposed to the Synod of 1646, fearing that its decisions would be of a coercive and intolerant character. Winthrop, *Journal*, II, 279–283.
3. *Ibid.*, I, 137. Hubbard says that Endecott acted under the influence of Roger Williams (*History of New England*, pp. 164–165; and see also Chapin, *Roger Williams and the King's Colors* [1928]), but the animosity toward the cross in the English flag was not confined to a few individuals, for the colony itself officially ordered the crosses struck from the militia flags in 1636. Samuel Gorton tells us in his *Simplicities Defence* that when Captain Cooke and his company in 1643 went to Shawomet to arrest him they shot the English colors, which the defenders hung out to show their allegiance to the "State of Old England," "many times through and through."

was well aware of the recklessness of the act, and the report of the committee appointed to investigate it must have mortified Endecott, if such a thing can be conceived as possible. The committee found the offense to be great, rash, and without discretion, a blemish upon the colony and an affront to the magistrates. More than all else the committee feared that the deed might be construed as an act of rebellion against the king. Endecott was admonished, and disabled for one year from holding any public office. That he did not receive a heavier sentence was due to the committee's belief that "he did it out of tenderness of conscience and not of any evil intent," which is only a Puritan way of saying that he let his religious convictions get the better of his discretion, a not uncommon happening in any community when men are convinced that God is controlling their moral conduct.[1]

The strain of the situation was increased by the receipt of a letter, written from England by Morton to one William Jeffrey, an old acquaintance and intimate friend, which Jeffrey, not very loyally, showed to Winthrop. In it Morton related with great satisfaction how he "had obtained his long suit and that a commission was granted for a general governor, with many railing speeches and threats against this plantation."[2] He informed Jeffrey that the king had already issued the commission on May 1; that king and council were incensed against the colony; and that Laud in a hearing before the Commissioners for Regulating Plantations had called Cradock and Humfry "a couple of preposterous knaves." Morton himself, not unnaturally in a boasting mood, uttered a Cassandra-like warning: "Repent you cruel schismatics, repent . . . I have staid long [but] I shall see my desire upon mine enemies . . . I have uncased Medusa's head and struck the brethren with astonishment." He was glad to tell them that he was not dead, as doubtless many hoped was the case, but was very much alive and proposed to come over on the ship with the governor general to bring comfort to those with grievances against the colony.

John Humfry, who with his wife Susan arrived on June 1, 1634, must have made it clear to the leaders of the colony that the situation was serious. Two months after his arrival he was chosen an assistant, and a month later the general court began its preparations

1. Winthrop, *Journal*, I, 137–138, 141–142, 143, 149–150, 174, 182.
2. *Ibid.*, I, 130; II, 194–196.

for defense, determined to resist any possible attempt on the part of king and council to interfere. It fortified Castle Island, Fort Hill, Dorchester, Charlestown and several other strategic positions, and in the next four months began the disciplining of the militia bands, ordering the captains to train their men once every four weeks and to drill new recruits at least three days in every week. It erected a war council, composed of Winthrop, Haynes, Humfry, and Endecott—later increased to nine members—with power to order and manage any resistance that might be necessary. It provided for a general survey of arms in the colony, ordered that a beacon be set up on the sentry hill to give notice to the countryside of any danger, and arranged for messengers to be sent to the towns as soon as the enemy was seen approaching.[1] It continued its preparations, rapidly and systematically, during the next two years. To emphasize its attitude of defiance, it appointed colors for every company, but left out the crosses in all of them,[2] thus laying the colonists open to the charge which was brought against them in 1636 that they were traitors and rebels. In the end the court compromised on this point —but not unanimously—by allowing the king's flag to be flown from Castle Island, because the fort there was the king's and located as it was three miles out in the harbor the flag there would be visible to all passing vessels. But it refused to use the flag elsewhere, deeming it idolatrous as an emblem of superstition and degrading as a symbol of dependence, in that its use committed them to an official recognition of the king's authority, which they were determined by every means in their power to avoid. The impression which all this warlike activity made upon others, not of the elect, was expressed by the Rev. George Burdett, former minister of Agamenticus, an antinomian and a none too savory character, who wrote to Archbishop Laud in 1638 that the Puritan government was determined "to spend their blood in maintaining their present way and humour and are using all diligence to fortify themselves."[3] To Burdett the members of the Puritan church militant were arming themselves not only for defense, but for offense also. He saw with growing

1. *Massachusetts Colonial Records*, I, 123, 124, 125, 136, 137, 138, 158, 186; Winthrop, *Journal*, I, 145, 174, 182.

2. *Ibid.*, 174.

3. *Calendar State Papers, Colonial*, 1574–1660, p. 283 (129). On Burdett, Winthrop, *Journal*, I, 279–280; II, 8; Libby, *Maine Province and Court Records*, I, 58, 70–71, 73–75, 77, 80; II, xvi, 54.

anxiety that they were threatening to become a menace to the independence of those of their neighbors who were of a different persuasion from themselves.

In the meantime important events were taking place across the water. Gorges, believing that the best way of carrying out his plans was to deal with the king and archbishop directly, now made up his mind to get rid of the Council for New England, which had proved itself wholly incompetent to meet the difficult situation in Massachusetts. He would surrender the charter, thus ending the council's existence,[1] but he would do this without letting possession of the land slip out of his hands. First he effected a general distribution of the territory among members of the council, some of whom had been admitted as patentees since the revival of activities in 1632. At a meeting held in Lord Gorges' house, St. Martin's Lane, February 3, 1635, he staged the event, though in much less dramatic fashion than in 1623, partly to secure to the patentees their share of the council's landed property and partly to enlist in his behalf some of the nobility who might be useful to him in his effort to break the Puritan hold on Massachusetts. The territory was divided into eight parts, which were assigned to Arundel (Maltravers), Lenox, Hamilton, Carlisle, Stirling, Lord Gorges, Sir Ferdinando Gorges, and Captain John Mason. Each grant was to be held of the king by knight service, that is to say, each patentee was "to find four able men armed for war to attend upon the governor of New England for the public service within fourteen days after warning given."[2] Unfortunately these deeds of feoffment, except in the one case of Gorges himself (1639), were never confirmed by the crown, as they should have been under the statute of Quia Emptores, so that the claims made in later years based on this division were without legal validity.[3] Maltravers, Stirling, and Hamilton later attempted to enforce their claims, either themselves or through their descendants, but without success, though there are today lands in America the titles to which are traceable to these grants. In 1697 the Board

1. In 1634 Gorges had two alternatives in mind, either to obtain a new charter according to the plans of 1632 (*Proceedings*, American Antiquarian Society, 1867, p. 111) or to "resign their patent to the king and so leave his Majesty the sole management of public affairs" (*Calendar State Papers, Colonial*, 1574–1660, p. 193 [36]). He chose the latter.

2. *Calendar State Papers, Colonial*, 1574–1660, pp. 195 (44), 204 (56).

3. Winthrop's comment on this circumstance is, "but the project [took] not effect. The Lord frustrated their design," *Journal*, I, 153 (June 16, 1635).

of Trade decided against the revival of these dormant patents, on the ground that to confirm them would lead to "unspeakable confusion and disturbance," a decision upon which it acted as later cases arose.[1]

On April 25, 1635, with sixteen members present at the meeting, the vote was taken to surrender the charter, and an act was read, formally adopted on June 7, resigning that document into the hands of the king. This act was accompanied by a statement, undoubtedly drawn up by Gorges and his associates, which contains the reasons for the course decided on and recounts at some length the "crosses" which the Council for New England had to bear from the beginning. "These crosses [says the document] did draw upon us such a disheartened weakness as there only remained a Carcass in a manner breathless till the end of the last Parliament in A° [1627–1629], when there were certain that desired a Patent of some Lands in the Massachusetts Bay to plant upon, who presenting the names of honest and religious men [the New England Company] easily obteyned their first desires, but those [desires] being once gotten they used other means to advance themselves a step [far] beyond their first proportions to a second grant surreptitiously gotten of other lands also," lands which had been granted to Captain Robert Gorges some years before. These intruders, the statement goes on to say, exorbitantly extending their grant from sea to sea, rode over the heads of those who had received patents in the distribution of 1623 and, "unknown to us," obtained a confirmation of their claims from the king, "by which means they did not onely enlarge their first extents . . . but wholy excluded themselves from the publique government of the Council authorized for those affairs, and made themselves a free people, whereby they did rend in peeces the first foundation of the building and so framed unto themselves both new laws and new conceipts of matters of Religion and forms of ecclesiastical and temporal orders and government, punishing divers that would approve thereof, some by whipping [Ratcliffe], others by burning their houses over their heads [Morton], and some by banishing [the Brownes and Gardiner], and the like. And all this partly under other pretences, though indeed for no other cause save onely

1. *Calendar State Papers, Colonial*, 1574–1660, pp. 282 (127, 128), 298 (25), 302 (34); 1661–1668, §735; 1696–1697, p. 579.

to make themselves absolute Masters of the Country and uncon-
scionably in their new lawes."[1]

Gorges goes on to say that he and his allies finding themselves
charged with responsibility for the misdemeanors of these Puritans
and "called for from our homes farr remote in the Country [Plym-
outh] at unseasonable times to our no small charge and trouble to
answer the same," decided to put the matter up to the king for
redress. They had no sufficient resources wherewith to give satisfaction to the persons aggrieved, and believing rectification too great
a task for themselves to perform, they "chose to resign all into his
Majesty's hands to do therein as his Majesty pleased, to whom wee
conceived it did principally belong to have a care of a business of
so high a consequence as now it is found to be." All that they asked
of the king was confirmation of the patents of land already issued
by the council and the publishing of a proclamation, the draft of
which they prepared with great care. In this proclamation the king
would announce his intention to establish a "Gen[ll] Government in
our Territory of New England," of which Gorges should be the
governor general, "a person meet and able for an Imployment of
that nature, by whose gravity, moderation, and experience" [the
king was to say] he hoped "to repair what is amisse." In thus offering himself, at the age of seventy, as a suitable candidate for the
king's service in New England for the suppression of the Puritan
government there, Gorges took occasion to speak of himself as one
who had been "an immediate mover and a principal actor to the
great prejudice of his estate, long troubles, and the losse of many his
good friends and servants in making this first discovery of those
coasts and taking the first seizure thereof."[2] There is something
very pathetic in the career of this noteworthy man, with its long
tale of disappointed hopes and failures, and something of grandeur
in this final effort to thwart the fates and to obtain a victory over
those who had taken advantage of his ill fortune to prevent the
realization of his dreams.

For the moment, however, the effort did not appear to be as hopeless as events were to show. Though the king and his advisers did
not see fit to confirm the patents or to issue the desired proclamation

1. *Proceedings,* American Antiquarian Society, 1867, pp. 123–128. Also Hutchinson, *History of Massachusetts,* I, 49–53.
2. *Proceedings,* American Antiquarian Society, 1867, pp. 119–122.

at once—inasmuch as neither was of use as long as the Massachusetts Bay charter was intact—it is more than likely that both steps would have been taken had affairs in England followed a different course. Gorges had the good will of Laud and the Privy Council, for the Puritans had antagonized the English authorities by their attempts to make good their independence of the crown and to keep themselves unspotted from the world. Laud was bound to be hostile to any Puritan organization turned Separatist, and the king in council could hardly look with favor upon an independent Puritan state in New England. Early in May, 1635, on the strength of the evidence presented to the Laud Commission, an order was prepared instructing the attorney general, Sir John Banks, to call in the Massachusetts Bay patent. Then the commission, finding that the document was not in England, authorized Banks to file in the court of king's bench charges against the company and to obtain a writ of *quo warranto* against the governor, deputy governor and assistants, that is, against all the persons named in the patent.[1] Gorges was entrusted with the duty of serving the writ upon the company in America and Morton was appointed by the Council for New England to act as solicitor in the case, not only to obtain a confirmation of the grants of 1635, but also to prosecute the suit before the court of king's bench.

The trial was prolonged from Trinity Term, 1635, to Easter Term, 1637. In Michaelmas Term, 1635, October 9 to November 28, ten members of the company in England appeared and disclaimed the charter. The governor being in default, judgment was given for the king. In Hilary Term of the next year, January 23 to February 12, Sir Henry Rosewell, and in Easter Term, April 23 to May 19, Sir John Young appeared and disclaimed, thus completing the number in England against whom the writ was directed. Except for Sir Richard Saltonstall, who having returned to England appeared and disclaimed in Hilary Term, 1637, the others who were in America, not appearing, were outlawed. Then on May 3, 1637, final judgment was given for the king "that the libertyes and ffranchises of the said Corporacon should be Seized into the king's hands and the aforesaid Mathew Cradock his body bee taken into Custody for usurping the said libertyes" and "his Maty and Councell taking into considera-

1. The writ was obtained in Trinity Term, May 27–June 15, 1635 (nineteen days from the Friday after Trinity Sunday). It is printed in *Hutchinson Papers*, I, 114.

tion the pattent granted to the Govern[r] did order that the Attorney Generall bee required to call for it and [present it to the] Board or to the [Laud] Committee for fforaigne plantations."[1] This ended the suit as far as the court of king's bench was concerned and the general understanding was that the charter had been duly brought in and cancelled.[2] Saltonstall must have taken some part in the defense, for he was afterward allotted twenty pounds "for expences incurred upon the quo warranto,"[3] and Morton, acting for the Council for New England, must have conducted his case with considerable skill, though the task was rendered relatively easy by the heavy weight of the evidence against the company. On July 23, the king, "knowing it to be his duty not to suffer such numbers of his people to run to ruin," accepted the resignation of the charter of the Council for New England, apparently assuming that the Massachusetts Bay Company's charter was already as good as vacated, and issued a declaration to the effect that he was taking the government of the colony into his own hands—as his father had that of Virginia thirteen years before—and appointing Gorges as his governor general.[4] The report spread that the charter was damned, to the great discouragement of those both in England and America who wished the Puritan experiment to succeed.

But it was one thing to obtain a verdict and another to enforce it and the situation in reality was not as bad as it looked. Laud might wax indignant at the separatistic tendencies in New England, both in church and state, but he was powerless to exercise more than a moral influence, which by itself was bound to be ineffective, and he sensed "the impolicy of forcing the church system of England upon the Massachusetts settlers,"[5] even if there were any way in which this might be done. The king was in no position to lend financial aid, for the third writ of ship-money had been issued the October before and the trial of John Hampden was in full swing. What was done must be done by Gorges himself out of his own resources and those of his friends and at this juncture these enemies of Massachu-

1. "Minutes of the Proceedings in the King's Bench agt the Gov[r] Dep[ty] Gov & Assistants of the late Colony of the Massachusetts & Judg[mt] to seize their Franchises Anno 1637." Colonial Office, I, vol. 9, no. 50; *Acts Privy Council, Colonial*, I, §366.
2. *Calendar State Papers, Colonial*, 1677–1680, p. 130.
3. *Massachusetts Colonial Records*, II, 132.
4. *Calendar State Papers, Colonial*, 1574–1660, p. 256 (60).
5. Gardiner, *History of England*, VIII, 168.

setts were practically bankrupt. The great ship that Gorges and Mason built in 1635 to carry the governor general to New England and to serve th*e quo warranto* on the colony broke in the launching, leaving Gorges with no means of transportation to his province. In the same year Mason died, already ruined by the heavy costs of the Laconia venture, and Gorges lost his most efficient ally and the prime mover, according to Winthrop, in the attack on the colony.[1] Gorges himself was not only too old now for so hazardous a venture as this promised to be but he too had been rendered penniless by the Laconia enterprise and by debts which to his great embarrassment the Privy Council, after an investigation, ordered him to discharge.

With the failure of Gorges to take advantage of the opportunity which the king and Privy Council offered him, the last serious danger to the colony was removed. Morton, as attorney, continued to press the case before the Laud Commission, which on April 4, 1638, sent a peremptory letter to Winthrop, strictly requiring and enjoining him "or any other in whose power or custody the said letters patents are" to send them back by the return of the ship which conveyed the order to him. In default of so doing the commission threatened to "cause a strict course to be taken against them and will move his Majesty to reassume into his own hands the whole plantation."[2] Two days afterward the Privy Council ordered the attorney general to prepare a proclamation forbidding all masters of vessels to carry any passengers to New England without special license from the commission, on the ground that the people of the colony were of a "factious disposition . . . unfitt and unworthie

1. Winthrop, *Journal*, I, 29, 152, 181; II, 10. Again the Lord "disappointed them and frustrated all their designs." See also, *Calendar State Papers, Colonial*, 1574–1660, p. 323 (93), and *Acts Privy Council, Colonial*, I, §§ 391, 416, 418, 422.

"Captain Mason was enthusiastic over his properties in the new world and spent time, energy, and money without limit in the effort to establish a permanent settlement that should be not only a source of wealth to himself, but a principality hereditary in his family, which should thereby forever perpetuate his name. Before his death he had sent over about seventy settlers, besides tradesmen, with an ample supply of provisions, clothing, utensils, arms and ammunition, and artillery for fortifications which were to be built. . . . Altogether [he] had expended on his province about £22,000, and . . . in 1634 he stated that he had never received a penny in return." "The Mason Title," by Otis G. Hammond in *Proceedings*, American Antiquarian Society, 1916. Also *Calendar State Papers, Colonial*, 1675–1676, §506; Burrage, *Gorges' Province of Maine*, and *Beginnings of Colonial Maine*.

2. Hubbard, *History of New England*, pp. 268–269.

. . . of any support or countenance from hence, in respect of the great disorders and want of government amongst them, whereof sundry and great complaints have been presented to the Board, and made appeare to be true by those that being well affected both for religion and government have suffered much losse in their estates by the unruly and factious partie."[1]

But Winthrop knew that nothing more was to be feared from England. The king was confronted with the Scottish revolt and Gorges, though an old man, was for the moment drawn aside into the royal service. Therefore, he answered the letter, in the name of the general court, refusing to return the charter[2] and giving a long statement of the reasons therefor. The letter is genuine and sincere and the reasons cogently and convincingly presented. It discloses, what was undoubtedly the case, that the magistrates were afraid lest a governor general might be sent, despite all their efforts to prevent it. There is reason to think that in the year 1637-1638, John Davenport and his company, who afterward went to New Haven, were unwilling to remain in Boston because they were afraid that something of the kind might happen. But events turned out quite differently. The charter had been revoked but the judgment could not be enforced and no governor general appeared until the charter was finally vacated in 1684 and Andros was sent over as governor of the Dominion of New England. The Privy Council, in a further communication, declared itself satisfied with the general court's reply and while still demanding the return of the charter and threatening penalties in case of refusal, bade the colony go on with its government until a new charter could be prepared.[3] Nothing more happened. The meeting of the Short and Long Parliaments and the approach of civil war in England were events of too pressing a nature to admit of further concern in what was going on three

1. *Acts Privy Council, Colonial*, I, §384; Winthrop, *Journal*, I, 271-272, 274-275, 278.

2. There are two original charters, one of which today is in Boston and the other in Salem. Though one is the first copy and the other a duplicate, they both bore the great seal and were equally authoritative.

3. Winthrop, *Journal*, I, 300-301, 307, 330; II, 9, 15, 42; *Calendar State Papers, Colonial*, 1677-1680, §§ 357, 358. Morton returned to New England in 1643 and tried to exculpate himself, but he was called to book by the court, imprisoned for a year, and fined £100. On being released, he went to Agamenticus and died there two years later. Winthrop, *Journal*, II, 154, 194-196; *Massachusetts Colonial Records*, II, 90.

thousand miles away. Massachusetts followed her destiny. Our interest centers in the likeness that exists between the incidents of 1635-1639 and those of 1684-1691, and between the Laud Commission and the Lords of Trade. Machinery and methods were the same in both cases, but fifty years were to make a vast difference in the power and policy of the English government. Whereas in the earlier years the judgment of the court of law in England could not be enforced in America and the attempt to coerce Massachusetts failed, in the later a similar judgment was enforced, the colony lost its charter, and a new and remodeled patent was granted it seven years afterward. In 1691 Massachusetts was finally taken into the hands of the king, and became in part a royal province.

Gorges got what he could out of the wreck of his fortunes and continued his attempts at settlement, obtaining from the king in 1639 a confirmation of his share, in the form of a charter for the province of Maine which, based as it was on the Baltimore model and probably reproducing the abortive charter of 1632, represented the kind of a colony that he wished to erect in New England. The "Province of Maine" was a diminutive copy of the great principality of his earlier dreams, and the principles underlying it were the same. At the age of seventy-four, he became the proprietor and absolute lord of a territory which, according to the boundaries given in the patent, covered one-half of New Hampshire, one-eighth of Vermont, and three-eights of Maine, constituting a feudal sovereignty with all the rights and perquisites appertaining thereto.[1]

The only occupants of the region, at the time the charter was granted, were the dwellers in a few posts and settlements at Kittery, Richmond Island, and Saco, between the Piscataqua and Casco Bay, and fishing stations at Monhegan, Pemaquid, and Damariscove. On the sluggish tidal river Agamenticus was a small group, engaged in farming rather than fishing and lumbering, at first without corporate name, but popularly known as Bristol, in which Gorges was specially interested, planning to make it the official center and capital of his province. In 1638 he issued a patent incorporating this small settlement under the name Agamenticus. There Edward Godfrey, the first settler and a Kentishman long identified with the

1. Libby, *Maine Province and Court Records*, I, vii. The only reliable printed text of the charter is in *ibid.*, pp. 9-29, from the enrollment on the Patent Rolls, 2865, 15 Charles I, 25th part, no. 6.

history of the region, had built a rough cabin in 1630 and later Gorges himself had caused a manor house to be erected at Point Christian on the river, to be the residence of his cousin and deputy governor, Thomas Gorges, who came over in 1640.[1] Under the latter's beneficent control the peace of the region, which for four years had been disturbed by the evil influence of George Burdett, was restored, and orderly government was introduced. On April 10, 1641, Gorges patented Agamenticus as a borough and market town, with mayor, aldermen, recorder, and other functionaries, upon whom he conferred the powers, legislative and judicial, possessed by "townes corporate in England." The next year, March 1, 1642, he set off a tract east of the Agamenticus river, three miles along the coast and seven from the mouth of the river northward, within which he proposed to build a city—a city in England meant an episcopal see, a cathedral town—organized on the plan of the city of Bristol, to be called after himself, Gorgeana. To this end he issued another charter of incorporation.[2] These charters serve to illustrate, quite as much as do his larger plans for colonization, the singularly conventional mind that Gorges possessed. His corporations were veritable castles in Spain, existing largely on parchment and representing his love of grandeur and his sanguine hope of a large population made up of immigrants from his own West Country. He could think in

1. Banks, *History of York*, I, ch. VIII. For Thomas Gorges see Winthrop, *Journal*, II, 8, and the entries in Banks and Libby.

2. The borough of Agamenticus was to have a mayor, eight aldermen, and a recorder, town clerk, coroner, clerk of the market, with a jail, town hall, borough courts, a borough seal, and books of record. Thomas Gorges was to be the first mayor, Edward Godfrey the first of the aldermen, and Roger Garde the recorder and town clerk. The mayor was also to be the coroner. The mayor and aldermen were to make by-laws, orders and ordinances "as are accustomed to be made in 'Townes Corporate in England.'" There were to be three sorts of courts—a court leet with view of frank pledge to be held once a year, a borough court every three weeks to hear civil causes, and a mayor's court or sessions of the peace from time to time to try criminal causes. The corporate bounds were to extend "East, West, North and South three miles every way from the Church, Chapell or place ordayned or intended" for such.

The city of Gorgeana was to have a mayor, twelve aldermen, and twenty-four common councillors, recorder, and town clerk, a court leet or "Lawe day," and a "Courte of Justice . . . to be held upon Monday in every weeke for ever and the proceedings to bee accordinge or as neere as may bee to the Courte of his Majesties Court of Chancery at Westminster," with right of appeal to the proprietor or his deputy. There were to be serjeants of the white rod, a common seal, markets, and fairs. Lands were to be held of the king as of the manor of East Greenwich in free

no other terms of civic and social life than those which followed the beaten track of the institutions familiar to him at home.

In 1639 and again in 1640 Gorges delegated powers to certain commissioners to govern the province until he could assemble free-holders and decide on a more permanent arrangement.[1] But no further change was ever made in his lifetime—he died in 1647 aged eighty-two. From June 25, 1640, when the provincial or general court, which had been in abeyance for four years, was revived, until 1649, the court sat, with periods of omission and suspension, under the leadership of the deputy governors, Thomas Gorges, Richard Vines, and Henry Jocelyn, and exercised a great variety of super-visory functions. Gorges does not appear ever to have interfered in the affairs of his province, but left the commissioners free to regu-late matters in their own way, which they did "as ny as we could according to the Lawes of England and such other ordinances as was thought meet and requisit for the better regulation thereof." In July, 1649, after the news of Gorges' death had been received, the inhabitants being "in some distraction" because of the confusion of affairs in England and the departure from the province of some of the leading men, took upon themselves to form a government of their own until "Furder order power and authorryty" should come out of England. "With one free and unius animus consent [the inhabitants of Kittery, Gorgeana (York), and possibly Wells] doe bynd themselves in a body politick and combination to see thes partes of the Cuntry and province regulated according to such lawes as formerly have bine exercised and such other as may be thought meet and not repugnant to the Fundamentall laws of our Nation and Cuntry, and to make choyse of such Governor or Governors and majestrats as by most voysses they shall thinck meet."

For three years, from 1649 to 1652, the "Province of Maine" con-

---

and common socage, and all officials were to take an oath of allegiance to the king as well as the customary oaths of office. The privileges, liberties, and freedoms were to be "(as far as in me lieth) as the Cittie of Bristol holdeth by their Charter of Incorporacon." Banks, *History of York*, I, ch. XI, pp. 435–444.

The original Agamenticus charter is in the possession of the town clerk of York; that of Gorgeana in the possession of the Massachusetts Historical Society. The Aga-menticus charter was sealed and delivered in the presence of Thomas Morton, Robert Gorges, and Richard Smithson, showing that Morton was in England and in close touch with Gorges at the time. It is natural that later he should have spent the last years of his life at Agamenticus.

1. Libby, *Maine Province and Court Records*, I, 30–41.

sisted of Kittery and York,[1] which formed a self-governing community, managing affairs and keeping the peace, with Edward Godfrey as the governor, elected "by most voysses," under the simple and effective system which the people of the province set up for themselves. At the general court, chosen by the freeholders of the two towns under the "social compact" of 1649 and held sometimes at Gorgeana and sometimes at Kittery, orders were agreed upon, laws enacted, and penalties imposed that disclose a noteworthy effort to create a law abiding community out of an honest but often unruly body of people. A measure of religious freedom and a crude form of popular government, both denied under the Massachusetts system, prevailed here as well as in Rhode Island. Governor, magistrates, and deputies were popularly chosen, jury trial was introduced, and on October 16, 1649,—oddly enough but six months after the passage of the more famous and much misunderstood Act concerning Religion by the Maryland assembly—the general court declared "That all gode people within the Jurisdiction of this province who are out of a Church [of England] way and be orthodox in Judgment and not scandalous in life, shall have full liberty to gather themselves into a Church estate, provided they do it in a Christian way: with the due observation of the rules of Christ revealed in his worde: And every Church hath Free liberty of election and ordination of all her officers from tyme to tyme provided they be able, pious and orthodox."[2] This remarkable statement is to be compared with the similar statements of Rhode Island and Maryland, though in neither Maryland nor Maine was full religious liberty recognized, as it was in Rhode Island, and it stands in striking contrast with

1. It is doubtful if Wells accepted Godfrey's authority as governor, despite the "social compact" quoted above. The independence of the "Province of Lygonia" was recognized in 1646. This province extended from Casco Bay to Cape Porpoise, had its own deputy president, general court, and officials, and lasted until 1652. It had been erected in opposition to the Gorges province, under the plough patent of Alexander Rigby, through the sharp practice of George Cleeve, deputy president in America under Rigby in England, whom Winslow calls "one of the arrantest knaves in New England" (Banks, *Col. Alexander Rigby and the Province of Lygonia;* Baxter, *The Trelawney Papers,* p. 365 note 3; Winthrop, *Journal,* II, 157–158, 266–277; *Collections,* Maine Historical Society, 3d series, I, 342–369; *Maine Genealogical and Historical Register,* II, 65–77). If Wells did not give in its adherence either to the province of Maine or to the province of Lygonia, then there were three little governments at this time between the Piscataqua and modern Portland. Libby, *Maine Province and Court Records,* I, 133.

2. *Ibid.,* I, 136. See below, page 495.

the official attitude of the Puritan colonies and their hostility toward all ways of religious thinking other than their own.

The truth is that the whole northern region from the Piscataqua to Casco Bay was occupied by a very different type of settler from that which accompanied Winthrop to Massachusetts. Both founders and permanent colonists were from the Devon country of seamen and adventurers, who cared nothing about theological dogmas and church reform. The founders were, as a rule, of the landed gentry, loyalist in sympathy and adherents of the Anglican church, with nothing in common with Puritanism. The body of the people were like their forbears, sturdy, coarse, hard-drinking, profane, none too fond of church going, and impatient of too strict an enforcement of law and order. Few aspects of the court proceedings of York County, in the years after 1652, when Massachusetts assumed jurisdiction there, are more significant than the difficulties which the court met in the effort to regulate drinking, stop swearing, enforce attendance on public worship, punish contempt of public authority, and in general keep a truly Puritan watch over morals and conduct. The region was barren of schools and education and the mention of books in wills and inventories, rare at best, shows but little in the way of literature beyond the Bible, once in a while a Book of Common Prayer, and occasionally a few old books, untitled and manifestly considered of little value. Of attempts at education there is scarcely a trace.[1]

As the government of the "Province of Maine" under the "social compact" was without authorization from England, plans were set on foot by the general court in 1651 to obtain a confirmation of its

1. *Ibid.*, II, *passim.* Libby's first volume contains the proceedings of government under Gorges and his deputy governors to 1646, under Governor Godfrey to 1652, under the younger Gorges to 1664, and under the commissioners of Charles II and their justices to 1668, when Massachusetts resumed control. The second volume contains the court proceedings of York County under Massachusetts jurisdiction, 1653 to 1664, 1668 to 1679, when by decision of the lords chief justices of king's bench and common pleas and by commission under the great seal the Maine lands were restored to the Gorges heirs and the government was resumed by the crown. The volume also contains the records of the court of associations for the county of York, 1658 to 1679, sitting at the various towns in turn and without a jury, during the intervals between the sessions of the county court, with appeals and remands to the latter. The cases that came before it were much the same as those that were acted on by the county court. No more valuable volumes for the early local history of any part of the colonial territory have ever been published. They give an amazingly vivid and realistic picture of the life of a rough, unconventional pioneer folk in the wilderness.

privileges from the parliament of the Commonwealth. But before anything could be done Massachusetts stepped in and annexed the territory. Attracted by the fir and timber bearing lands of the north and by the meadows and salt marshes lying between the Merrimac and the Piscataqua, and determined to extend to the farthest limits the boundaries of the colony, according to a literal interpretation of their meaning, that they might be well protected on all sides from settlements that could make them trouble, the Puritans effected their object partly by persuasion and partly by threats of force.[1] Not content with having set at naught the authority of the crown and courts of England, with denying the claim of the Council for New England to lands that were legally its own, and with ejecting its patentees from their grants wherever possible, they pursued Gorges even beyond the grave and took to themselves the last remnant of his territory in the north, bringing within their jurisdiction the people who had settled there under his auspices. Some of Gorges and Mason's descendants, however, were to live long enough to see the day of reckoning which the Massachusetts Bay Colony was preparing for itself.

1. Godfrey, turned out of his government by Massachusetts, went to England in 1655 and for four years endeavored, but without success, to interest Cromwell, the Rump Parliament of 1659, and Charles II in the restoration of the territory (see the documents printed in full in Banks' edition of Gardiner, *New England's Vindication,* Gorges Society, I, appendix). He was thrown into Ludgate for debt at the age of seventy-five or seventy-six, and disappears from view. Great differences of opinion appear among Maine historians as to Godfrey's character. Mr. Libby deems him "that presumptuous ass, who volunteered and recorded his own election as 'Governor' when there was no government, and his incompetence was tolerated by half the inhabitants of the two towns for three years until there was no money to pay the court's tavern scores, no one would pay taxes, and a common fellow threatened to beat him up, an incident recorded and unpunished." Dr. Banks defends Godfrey in his *History of York,* but not convincingly.

CHAPTER XX

FROM CHARTER TO COMMONWEALTH
IN MASSACHUSETTS

THE colony of Massachusetts Bay, which within less than a decade of its founding had established itself so firmly on New England soil as to defy all attempts to dislodge it, and after thirty years had extended its jurisdiction over the northern lands as far as the Kennebec, is something of a phenomenon in colonial history and calls for a careful examination of its structure and policy. It had its origin, as we have already seen, in an English company organized in the usual way for trade and colonization. Starting as an incorporated body, located in the City of London, with the usual powers and privileges of its class, it underwent a progressive transformation, without precedent or parallel, gradually changing, first into the Massachusetts Bay colony and then into the Massachusetts Bay commonwealth, a full-fledged, quasi-independent, self-governing religious community.

The dynamic agency which effected this transformation, the driving force which overrode all opposition, legal and otherwise, was the profound conviction of the Puritan leaders that they were doing the Lord's work. They looked upon themselves as instruments in the divine hand for the carrying out of a great religious mission, the object of which was the rebuilding of God's church in a land—the undefiled land of America—divinely set apart as the scene of a holy experiment that should renovate the church at large, everywhere corrupt and falling into ruins. This new and purified community was to be the home of a saving remnant delivered from the wrath to come and was to serve as an example to the mother church of a regenerated form of faith and worship. It was also to become a proselyting center for the conversion of the heathen and the extension of the true gospel among those who knew it not. In the fulfilment of this mission the Puritans counted obstacles, moral and physical, of no moment. Theirs was a religious duty to frustrate their enemies, to eradicate all inimical opinions, religious and political, and to extend the field of their influence as widely as possible. Once they had determined on their rules of polity and conduct, as laid down in the Bible and interpreted by the clergy, they had no doubts as to the justness and rightness of their course. The means employed might savor of harshness and inequity, but at all costs and under all circumstances, error, sin, and idolatry, in whatever form appearing and as determined by themselves, must be destroyed. In the process, as events were to prove, a great many very human motives played an important part in interpreting the law of God, and personal likes and dislikes, hypocrisy, prejudice, and passion got badly mixed with the higher and more spiritual impulses that were actively at work purging the church of its errors.

The period of transformation lasted from the passing of the charter to the establishment of the colony on a self-governing basis in 1634 and as an independent commonwealth in 1652. Finding its origin in the New England Company, the Massachusetts Bay Company legally entered upon its career when it received the charter, March 4, 1629, but for nearly five months after that date it is difficult to tell whether it was the one company or the other that was actually in being. At the meeting of March 23, when for the first time officials were chosen according to the tenor of the charter, the corporation is designated "the Govr and Company of the Massachusetts Bay in New England," but on May 13, when a second election took place, it is called "The New England Company." Not until the meeting on July 28 does the title "the Company of the Massachusetts Bay in New England" appear at the head of the minutes. From this time on the Massachusetts Bay Company, having completed its absorption of the New England Company, remained in England until its departure for America, regulating its own affairs and those of its infant plantation.

But with the infusion of the Puritan spirit into the body corporate and politic the transformation of the company made rapid progress. Trade and profit, though never entirely lost sight of, were relegated to the background, and the zeal of religious adventure swept through its members. The profit sought by the Puritans was chiefly of the soul not the body and the commercial interests of the original subscribers were entrusted to a subordinate group, to be furthered as something secondary and apart from the main purpose in hand. Trade and religion now went forward in separate channels, for the demands of a religious enterprise were of greater moment than the desire for dividends and wealth. They were also of greater moment than the rules of chancery and the law of England, and the Puritan leaders did not hesitate to adapt the terms of the charter to meet the imperative requirements of a divine enterprise. The charter gave them their territory and their legal right to exist and whenever they needed its aid to ward off danger they utilized it with the utmost regard for the letter of the text. But whenever its provisions interfered with or hampered the main ends they had in view they deviated from it without scruple, because there was nothing else they could do. The very election of Winthrop was irregular, because the charter required annual elections to be held on the last Wednesday in Easter term, whereas Winthrop was elected in October after only seven months of the first year had passed. His holding office for eighteen continuous months was also irregular as was also his failure to call quarterly courts at which the generality should be present as a whole or in part. These violations, though amply justified by the circumstances of departure and of the voyage across the ocean and by the want of a generality, which until new freemen were named in New England had ceased to exist, were breaches of the charter, for the simple reason that those who drafted the instrument never dreamed that the company would leave England and naturally made no provision for such an event. Winthrop, though, of course, technically but the governor of a company, had become in reality the guiding head of a large body of emigrants, not members of the company at all, but adventurers from every walk in life going to settle a plantation in the New World. Though they had the charter with them, that for which the charter had been called into being was already transmuted from a trading company into a state in the making. Leadership, under such circumstances, had to be centralized in order to be efficient, and from the time the ships left English shores government and authority were united in the hands of a very few men. There was nothing in the charter to warrant such concentration of control.

For a time after the arrival of the Puritans in New England conditions continued to be irregular and unsettled and the government assumed something of an emergency form. They reached Salem during the month of June but soon moved on to Charlestown, where perhaps a hundred people were already collected, living in houses, tents, and wigwams. There, on August 23, in the open air under a tree,[1] was held the first court of assistants, or magistrates

1. Roger Clap, *Memoirs*, p. 42.

as they were beginning to be called, at which arrangements were made for additional housing and the maintenance of the ministers, rules were laid down for court meetings every month and general court meetings every term, and justices of the peace were appointed, "in all things to have like power that justices of the peace hath in England for reformation of abuses and punishment of offenders." A second court was held at the same place on September 7, at which Endecott was chosen an assistant, Thomas Morton was ordered to be put in the bilboes, and the instruction was issued that no one should plant in any place within the limits of the patent without leave first obtained of the governor and the magistrates. This court, composed of eight or nine men, continued to sit at Charlestown until after September 28, administering affairs, imposing penalties, appointing constables, and levying assessments, until in October, because of the unhealthfulness of the place and the scarcity of water the decision was reached to move the seat of government. Winthrop at first thought of going to Watertown—the frontier plantation on the Charles—but liking "that plain Neck that was called then Black-stones-Neck, now Boston,"[1] he summoned there the first general court on October 19. The end of the long and perilous journey was now reached and the company and the charter and the hundreds of emigrants from old England found at last a resting place in the new land. A novel situation faced the Puritan leaders. In a strange and unfamiliar environment, with a body of not less than a thousand people, a number that increased steadily as the years went on, scattered up and down the coast from Salem to Weymouth and back as far as Watertown, the problems of the future were not easy to solve. The trading company, except for the remnant in England that was looking after the joint-stock, had disappeared in fact if not in law, and in its place had come an unwieldy mass of people and a congeries of plantations, the affairs of which had to be organized and administered. Local government would more or less look out for itself, for the people had come from the vills and towns of old England, but the central government for its guide had only the charter which had never been designed for any such purpose as this.

Up to this time the entire control had been in the hands of the governor, deputy governor, and assistants, who had arbitrarily, but never despotically, administered the government of the company

1. *Ibid.*, 41.

community. The charter provided for some such arrangement, when it placed the *ad interim* management in the hands of a quorum of these officials, but Winthrop, convinced that if the colony were to survive, the government must be highly centralized, continued the system much longer than the charter allowed. He was no believer in popular government. He was certain that God in his most holy and wise providence had made some rich and some poor, some high and eminent in power and dignity and others mean and in subjection, and that it was the duty of the few to rule and of the many to be ruled. He could find no warrant for any other political system in the Scriptures and could imagine no other order sanctioned by the word of God.[1] At the same time he had to reckon with the charter, which admitted a measure of popular control in providing for four general courts, meeting every quarter, at each of which "freemen" or members were to be present, constituting the generality, for the purpose of making laws and admitting other "freemen," and at the May meeting of electing the officials of the company. Thus far no such general courts had been held, for probably the only "freemen" in America were those that made up the court of assistants. If therefore the requirements of the charter were to be met, "freemen" must be created at once. The magistrates had already agreed that general courts should be summoned, and at one such court, so called, which met on October 19, the generality appear under the name "people," who are mentioned as in attendance, giving approval by "erection of hands."[2] This was clearly irregular and what we have is not a general court but a mass meeting. The "people" were not authorized by the charter to attend—an irregularity which had to be remedied. Consequently an invitation was extended to all such as desired to become "freemen" to hand in their names.

One hundred and eight men responded, most of whom had been residents of the region before Winthrop came over. The list includes Blaxton, Maverick, Jeffrey, Graves, Conant, and others, whom

1. Stanley Gray, "The Political Thought of John Winthrop," *New England Quarterly*, III, 681–705. "The divine origin of the authority of the magistrate; the ability and character required to prove his calling to office; the necessity of obeying him unquestioningly, these are the threads that run through all the political theory that we have examined . . . During [Winthrop's] life and for many years after, the aristocratic tradition of which he was the most luminous exponent in America dominated the life of Massachusetts."

2. *Massachusetts Colonial Records*, I, 79.

Winthrop wished to bring within the Puritan fold and to enlist in support of the Puritan cause. Many of these were Church of England men, particularly those from Salem and Dorchester, while others were certainly not Puritan in sympathy. As no qualification for membership was imposed at this time, except that which the word itself implies, it would look as if in this first difficult year, when death and distress were rampant and many dangers threatened the colony, the leaders were willing to do anything to ensure stability.[1] Some of the old-timers—Walford, the Normans, the Grays—refused to become freemen, and a few of them were eventually shipped back to England as undesirable persons. But before seven months had elapsed, during which time the churches in the separate towns were set up and the colony felt more sure of its own permanence, the whole idea of freemanship changed. At a general court, held on May 18, 1631, Winthrop was continued as governor and the "freemen" or "commons," as they are called in the records, or "freemen of the commons" as they appear in Winthrop's journal,[2] were confronted with an ironclad oath,[3] and the momentous decision was reached that henceforth "noe man shalbe admitted to the freedom of this body polliticke, but such as are members of some of the churches within the limitts of the same."[4]

1. Winthrop said later that these men were admitted before the churches were established and consisted of old planters. Hutchinson, *History of Massachusetts*, I, 493.

2. *Journal*, I, 63.

3. The oaths which were to be taken by the officials of the company in England, including Endecott and his councillors in the plantation, were drawn up on May 7, 1629. They begin with the promise to be good and true or faithful and loyal "unto our sovereign Lord, the King's Majesty, and to his heirs and successors" (*Massachusetts Colonial Records*, I, 37[1], 39, 349, 351; Winthrop, *Journal*, II, 99). But this form was rejected when the Puritans set up their government in New England and another substituted which omitted all reference to the king. The latter form was first drafted on May 18, 1631, and redrafted on May 14, 1634. It begins, "I, A.B. being by the Almighties most wise disposition, become a member of this body, consisting of the governor, deputy governor, assistants and a commonalty of the Mattachusetts in Newe England, doe freely and sincerely acknowledge that I am justly and lawfully subject to the government of the same." The redraft of 1634 begins, "I, A.B. being by God's providence an inhabitant and freeman, within the jurisdiction of this commonweale, doe freely acknowledge myself to be subject to the government thereof" (*Massachusetts Colonial Records*, I, 117, 353, 354). A facsimile of the original draft of the first of these, in Winthrop's handwriting, and another facsimile of the original draft of an alternative oath prepared by Dudley, are in the *Bulletin* of the Boston Public Library, July, 1894, with a brief introduction by the former librarian, Mellen Chamberlain. See also Winthrop, *Journal*, I, 293.

4. *Massachusetts Colonial Records*, I, 87.

The historian Hutchinson speaks of this as "a most extraordinary order or law," a deprivation of civil privileges which had it occurred in England by act of parliament "might very well have been the first in a roll of grievances."[1] It was probably the most flagrant violation of the charter that had occurred up to this time. The only reason assigned for it by the Puritans themselves is that "the body of the commons may be preserved of honest and good men," a statement seeming to imply that many of those already admitted did not satisfy Puritan requirements or conform to Winthrop's idea regarding those who should be allowed to take part in government. But the adoption of the qualification may well have been due to another cause—that same ever-present fear of interference and consequent defilement that led the Puritans to transfer company and charter to America in order to rid themselves of all control by a higher corporate authority in England. It was the same fear that drove them, with all the casuistry at their command, to deny the sovereign power over them of the king of England and to omit from the oath all reference to their allegiance to the crown. They were afraid that a broader suffrage might in time bring about such alteration in the personnel and principles of government as to change fundamentally the objects for which the colony was founded and the religious ends that it sought to attain. In their reply to the proposals of the lords and gentlemen in 1636, they say that they would willingly change the rule regarding freemen, if they could make it appear to their own people that such a change could "be made according to God; for to give you a true account of the grounds of our proceedings herein, it seemeth to them, and also to us to be a divine ordinance (and moral) that none should be appointed and chosen by the people of God, magistrates over them, but men fearing God (Ex. xviii, 21), chosen out of their brethren (Deut. xvii, 15), saints (1 Cor. vi, 1) . . . For, the liberties of the freemen of this commonwealth are such, as require men of faith-ful integrity to God and the state, to preserve the same . . . in case worldly men should prove the major part, as soon they might do, they would as readily set over us magistrates like themselves such as might . . . turn the edge of all authority and laws against the church and the members thereof."[2]

1. Hutchinson, *History of Massachusetts*, I, 26.
2. *Ibid.*, I, 493–495.

The infringement of the charter by the adoption of such a restriction upon freemanship at once placed the central government of the colony upon a religious foundation where it was intended to be, for the Massachusetts Bay settlement had now become no ordinary offshoot of English colonization. It formed an exception to every known condition governing England's expansion beyond the seas, for it was called into being for divine not human ends. The question naturally arises as to how broad was the religious base upon which the government of the colony rested. White, in *The Planter's Plea,* written in 1630, says that at that time "at least three parts of foure of the men there planted, are able to justifie themselves to have lived in a constant course of conformity" unto the government and orders of the Church of England,[1] but the swing toward non-conformity and separation was undoubtedly rapid as the years passed and the population increased. In time, four classes or groups appear. First, the freemen, always a minority in every town and in the colony as a whole, who alone voted for governor, magistrates, and deputies, and thus represented neither the towns nor the people but only themselves. Secondly, the church members who never offered themselves for freemanship, of whom there were a good many, though probably the total number was small. Thirdly, those of the inhabitants who were neither freemen nor church members, but who had taken the oath of fidelity and therefore were in accord with the general purpose and aims of the colony. And, lastly, those who were neither freemen nor church members and so legally were in the colony but not of it. It is impossible to conjecture, even roughly, what were the relative sizes of these four groups. Probably the third was the largest, the second the smallest, and the fourth the only one, the loyalty of which to Puritan principles can be seriously questioned. In this class were many (we may not say all) of the servants and apprentices who had come over with the Puritans in considerable numbers and who, at the beginning certainly could have had little sympathy for the Puritan ideals or have crossed the ocean with any religious purposes in their minds. In 1634 and again in 1652 all settled inhabitants were required to take the oath of fidelity, because it was found that among those who had not done

1. *The Planter's Plea,* p. 185 (ed. Massachusetts Historical Society). Gardiner, *New England's Vindication* (Gorges Society, I), pp. 36–37, and Lechford, *Plain Dealing,* p. 73, say that three-fourths of the people of the colony "remain out of the church."

so were many who were disposed to utter offensive remarks about the government.[1] This requirement, if enforced, would have eliminated the fourth class, but that it was not enforced and that this class continued to exist is unquestionably true.

The limitation upon the right to vote and hold office shows that the rule governing freemanship, as laid down in the charters of incorporated companies, had already gone by the board in Massachusetts. Yet it must be remembered that the right to vote is not an inherent right of man or one included among the liberties and immunities mentioned in these early charters as belonging to the king's free and natural subjects residing anywhere in the king's dominions. No contemporary authority or constitutional lawyer would have agreed that the exercise of the franchise was a right at all, even of Englishmen living at home. In view of their mission and of Winthrop's doctrine of government by godly men it is difficult to see how the Puritans could have done otherwise than they did if they were to adhere consistently to the purpose of their migration to America. Less excusable perhaps was the action taken the October before (October 19, 1630),[2] when it was propounded whether "it were not the best course that the freemen should have the power of chusing Assistants when they are to be chosen and the Assistants from among themselves to chuse a governor and deputy governor, who with the assistants should have the power of making laws and chusing officers to execute the same." This motion, we are told, was fully assented to by the general vote of the people and the erection of hands. This arrangement was irregular in two particulars: it took out of the hands of the generality, where the charter expressly placed it, the right of electing the governor and deputy governor; and it placed in the hands of the governor and assistants, where the charter did not place it, the making of laws and the selection of the officers who were to execute them. This reshaping of the terms of the charter was in accord with Winthrop's profound conviction that it was for the good of all that power should be kept in

---

1. *Massachusetts Colonial Records*, I, 115; III, 263. The Remonstrants, recounting the situation in 1646, said that there were at that time "many thousands in these Plantations of the English Nation free-born, quiet peaceable men, righteous in their dealings, forward with hand, heart and purse to advance the publike good . . . who are debarred from all Civil imployment (without any just cause that we know), not being permitted to beare the least office (though it cannot be denied but some are well qualified)," etc., *New England Jonas* (Marvin ed.), pp. 12–13.

2. *Ibid.*, p. 79.

the hands of those whose Christian calling it was to govern and that their number should remain as small as possible. He always stood in dread of a plebeian tyranny—control by the inferior sort—and was convinced that the "people" were not to be trusted with the election of so important an official as the governor.[1]

Again in March of the following year another violation occurred. At a court of assistants it was decided that as the number of assistants at that time was but five, and a few of these were planning to return to England, some measure should be taken to meet such an emergency. Therefore the court ordered that whenever the number fell below nine, it should be lawful for a majority to hold a court, even though the quorum should not be seven as the charter required. In so doing Winthrop and the assistants committed themselves with deliberation to the principle that they might change the charter, whenever necessity required.[2] It did not make any great difference whether the court of assistants numbered seven or five, but such a departure from the charter, spread publicly on the minutes of the court, might at some future time make them trouble, should continued infringements become known to the authorities in England.

The change from charter to commonwealth, already well advanced, finds further exemplification in an incident of the year 1632, when the pastor and elder of the church at Watertown, supported by a meeting of the people there, at which doubtless many non-freemen were present, protested against the imposition of a tax, by the court of assistants at Boston, for the purpose of making a palisade about the new town, Cambridge, amounting, in the case of Watertown, to £8 in a total of £60 assessed upon eleven of the plantations.[3] The protest was based upon the undeniable fact that, according to the charter, the governor and assistants had no author-

1. Humfry, who did not see eye to eye with Winthrop in all things, wrote him, December 12, 1630, "The Lord keep you from sin in that your too great zeal of dutie" (*Winthrop Papers*, I, 5, *Collections*, Massachusetts Historical Society). On May 18, 1631, Winthrop was chosen governor by the court of assistants "according to the meaning of the patent." The time only, not the method, was according to the patent.

2. *Massachusetts Colonial Records*, I, 84. Winthrop afterward claimed that "In those things wherein we have varied from our patent we did not touch the foundations of our government" (*Journal*, II, 171). In the main this remark is true. One can easily exaggerate the importance of these violations.

3. *Massachusetts Colonial Records*, I, 93.

ity to levy taxes of any kind, and that it was not safe to pay money under such conditions "for fear of bringing themselves and posterity into bondage."[1] The case was compromised when Winthrop explained that the colony was no longer a corporation, like an English borough, but a commonwealth, and that the body which levied the tax was of the nature of a parliament, since "no assistant could be chosen but by the freemen, who had power likewise to remove the assistants and put in others, and that at any general court (which was to be held once every year)[2] they had free liberty to consider and propound anything concerning the same." This incident discloses two things: first, that such charter provisions as were not considered suitable for a Christian commonwealth of the Puritan pattern were already thrown into the discard and that the charter itself by some metamorphosis or feat of legerdemain had ceased to be a charter and had become the frame of government for a state; and, secondly, that there were men in the colony who had regard for their parliamentary privileges and were ready to protest against the assumption of a right of taxation, which might well be construed as contrary, not only to the charter but also to the rights of Englishmen, for the question of taxation was certainly included among the liberties and immunities guaranteed by the charter. Whatever one may think of the right to vote as among an Englishman's liberties, there can be no doubt that by 1629 the House of Commons had won the right to control taxation. It may have been because of this incident that at the next general court, held on May 9, 1632, the order was agreed to "by erection of hands" that the governor, deputy governor, and assistants should be chosen by the whole body of the freemen in general court assembled, though a limitation was placed upon the freemen's choice of governor, by the requirement that he be taken from among the assistants.[3] This reversal of policy may have been induced by confidence in the godly character of the freemen under the recent law, or it may have been due to the fact that the Watertown men were looking into the charter and were finding there some powers and rights of which they had been deprived. That document could cut both ways.

There is another interesting point about this general court meet-

1. Winthrop, *Journal*, I, 74, 75.
2. Another departure from the charter.
3. *Massachusetts Colonial Records*, I, 95. The charter required that the governor be chosen from among the entire body of freemen.

ing of 1632. With the giving up of the joint-stock of the company, the colony in New England was forced to create a public or common stock of its own in order to meet the ordinary expenses of administration. The whole question of taxation had been raised by the Watertown protest and it was necessary to take some steps to put government expenses on a regular foundation. The method decided upon was this. Sixteen persons, two from each of eight plantations, were appointed (not elected) to advise with the governor and assistants at the next court "about raising a publique stock." These men were to give advice regarding the introduction of a system of taxes or assessments on the towns. Some agreement must have been arrived at, for from this time forward we meet with levies imposed and expenses incurred at the public charge. In 1634 the vote was passed that only the general court should have the right "to rayse money and taxes" and two years later, perhaps as an instruction to the towns regarding the imposing of local rates, another vote declared that "all men shalbe rated in all rates for their abilitie, wheresoever it lyes."[1] The committee of 1632 had only advisory functions and as soon as it performed that for which it was summoned, it was dismissed and did not meet again. It was only in part a representative body, but its work discloses an attempt to solve the problem of taxation and so furnishes the first instance in the history of the colony where the towns had a part in meeting an important major issue. The commonwealth was settling one difficulty after another, as it arose, particularly such as were not provided for in the charter, and in so doing was steadily enlarging its administrative limits beyond its original corporate bounds. The corporation was slowly taking on the proportions of a self-governing political community.

But one more step, and that in many ways the most important of all had yet to be taken—the proper adjustment of the position of the freemen in regard to the central administration and government and the granting to them of all the rights and privileges allowed them in the charter. Thus far they had won the right to share in the

---

1. *Ibid.*, 95, 117, 166. The imposing of taxes in Massachusetts made the retention of quit-rents unnecessary. The Puritans had no objection to quit-rents, with which they were perfectly familiar in England, and they collected them in New England when they wanted to, but they preferred a system of taxes in the towns. In 1645, for the first time, as far as we know, an auditor general was appointed to audit the common stock, *ibid.*, III, 54–55, 65.

election of the governor and in their general court to control all matters of taxation, but they had not as yet been admitted to any part in legislative or executive business or permitted to come together, in person or otherwise, four times a year, as the charter required, "to make laws and ordinances for the good and welfare of the said company." Hitherto, the governor and assistants had "made laws, distributed lands, raised money, and punished offenders" at their discretion. In 1634 Israel Stoughton wrote a long letter to his brother in England, declaring that the people at large had never seen the charter and did not know the extent of their own prerogatives, and he charged Winthrop with such arbitrary conduct of his office that he had "lost much of the applause" he had heretofore received, raising "very many hands" against himself, who were admonishing him to look a little more circumspectly into his way of doing things.[1]

The revolt against Winthrop's administration had been brewing for some time. The great Puritan believed that "the best part [of a community] is always the least and of that best part the wiser part is always the lesser." His continued retention of power in his own hands; his sharp quarrels with Roger Ludlow and Thomas Dudley, the latter of whom, though much less tolerant in many ways than himself, questioned his authority; and his characterization of his opponents as "troublers in Israel" had not served to strengthen his influence in the colony. The revolt came to a head at the meeting of the general court on May 14, 1634, at which were present freemen from each town, who chose Stoughton for their spokesman, and for three days fought the issue to a finish. Though Winthrop says in his journal that "all things were carried very peaceably," he is obliged to add, in the interest of truth, that "some of the assistants were questioned by the freemen for some errors in their government."[2]

At this meeting of the general court the whole system was placed under review. The sessions were stormy and the issues long and earnestly debated. But in the end the freemen won a notable victory. Among the many "good orders made by this court" was one for the drafting of a new freeman's oath; another declaring that none but

1. There is a brief abstract of Stoughton's letter in *Calendar State Papers, Colonial,* 1574-1660, p. 179 (115). The entire letter is printed in *Proceedings,* Massachusetts Historical Society, 58, pp. 446-458.
2. Winthrop, *Journal,* I, 125.

the general court should have authority to raise money and taxes, dispose of lands, and confirm titles; another restoring to each town certain liberties that had previously been encroached upon by the court of assistants; another instructing the towns to assess every man according to his estate and not according to the number of persons in his family; and still another to meet the discontent of the inhabitants of Newtown by granting them leave to seek out a new habitation. But the crowning order came, when the freemen in each town were empowered to choose two or three of their number as deputies to represent them in three of the four general courts, the fourth in May being the court of election at which the freemen (or later their proxies) had to be present in person.[1] The constable in each town was to give timely notice to the freemen to elect their deputies to attend upon the public service. In the performance of their duties they were to confer together and prepare such public business "as should by them be thought fit to consider of," to make and establish laws, grant lands, and "deal in all other affairs of the commonwealth wherein the freemen have to do," except the election of magistrates, in which each freeman was to vote personally or by proxy at the court of election in May.[2] The commonwealth was making progress. As far as it went the success of the freemen was complete and from this time on a limited number of men—at best a few hundreds in a total of twenty thousand inhabitants—controlled the government. A privileged class was in command, whose deputies in no way represented the colony as a whole.

To celebrate their victory the freemen, despite the ill-advised attempt of John Cotton, who in the election sermon of that year, tried to influence their decision, turned out Winthrop and elected Thomas Dudley as their governor, the more easily perhaps because the vote was taken "by papers," that is, by secret ballot, which ensured a fairer election than by show of hands. The defeat of Winthrop at this juncture, even though but temporary, is of considerable importance, in view of the ascendancy which he had attained over the assistants and over the affairs of the company since his first election, five years before, in October, 1629. Though he was, as Stoughton

1. For the number of deputies from each town see *Massachusetts Colonial Records*, I, 303–305; II, 209, 217, 231, 340. For the method of election, I, 293, 333, 341. For the manner of voting at the court of elections, II, 36, 87, 220, 286–287. These details need not be presented here.

2. *Massachusetts Colonial Records*, I, 116-121; Winthrop, *Journal*, I, 124–125.

said in his letter, "a godly man," "a man among men," and "a worthy magistrate," he was after all "but a man," who by his contemporaries and by sympathetic writers of a later date was and still is too "highly magnified." Though generous and moderate in private life he was opinionated and impatient of opposition in all that concerned affairs of a public character and was inclined to be arbitrary and self-conscious, too well aware, it may be, of his strength as one of the elect and of his place among those whom God had chosen to lead his people. For the moment, at least, even the church members were becoming tired of him. In 1635 Haynes was chosen governor and Bellingham the deputy, and in 1636 Vane was elected governor and Winthrop the deputy, largely because, as Hutchinson says, of Vane's "grave solemn deportment," although the young man was at the time only about twenty-four years of age. But the next year at a court of election held at Newtown in May, the country outside Boston, in a mood of reaction against the Vane-Hutchinson revolt and the Antinomian tendencies of the Boston church, opposed Vane and the Boston contingent and elected Winthrop again as governor. The immediate test was whether the general court should consider a petition in behalf of Wheelwright, who in February had been declared guilty of sedition and contempt, before proceeding to the election of officers. A Vane defeat and a Winthrop victory were foreshadowed when the decision was reached that the May meeting was by charter assigned for the election of officers and that the petition in Wheelwright's behalf should follow not precede the regular order of the day.[1] By these successive events the power of the freemen, exhibited in four changes of governors in as many years, received ample demonstration, and the process of transforming the company into the commonwealth came to the end of an important period in its progress. But even so the process was not yet complete.

The colony had now become to all intents and purposes a self-governing state, built up on a well proportioned but narrow constitutional foundation of governor, deputy governor, assistants or magistrates, and a general court, to which the towns sent their proxies for elections and their deputies for other affairs, all representative of the small body of freemen in the colony. This commonwealth offered

---

1. *Hutchinson Papers*, I, 74–78; *History*, I, 61–63; Winthrop, *Journal*, I, 215; *Massachusetts Colonial Records*, I, 145–146. Below, pages 482–483.

lip-service to the king, but denied his right to interfere, for, as Winthrop wrote, "we are bound to keepe off whatsoever appears to tend to our ruine or damage."[1] This matter of subjection to any body outside themselves had become a matter of frequent and anxious consideration on the part of Winthrop and others, for a long time after their arrival in America and they determined to resist the authority of any government in England, whether of Charles I, the Long Parliament, the council of state under the Commonwealth, or the king in Council after the Restoration. The motives underlying this attitude of independence offer no parallel to those that led to the Declaration of Independence in 1776, for they were religious not political and touched in no way the question of allegiance or fidelity. Their ultimate purpose was to protect "the right form of church government and discipline" as "a good part of the kingdom of Christ on earth."[2] Winthrop always argued against any recognition of authority outside the commonwealth. When in 1643 and 1644 the idea of petitioning the Long Parliament for a new charter came up for discussion, the disputants took the ground that the charter was their defense and their shield, their wall of protection against all outside encroachment, estopping the English government, whether of king or parliament, from imposing its will upon them in any respect whatever. They considered themselves free to shape their government according to their religious convictions as to what were the plans of God, revealed in the Old Testament and interpreted by the clergy of the colony. They had gone a long way off to find a place where they might build up a church-community of just this sort and they did not propose to allow anyone, not of themselves, to reverse their judgments or to disallow their laws.[3] The Puritans

1. *Hutchinson Papers.* I, 80.
2. *Massachusetts Colonial Records,* II, 154; III, 70. As late as 1643 Winthrop feared that a general governor might still be appointed.
3. Winthrop, *Journal,* I, 273, 300; II, 163, 184–187, 206, 282–284, 290–291, 314–315, 336–338. The Puritan's conviction that the charter was the palladium of their religious freedom and their warrant for "absolute power of government" (II, 290) lies at the very heart of the situation and furnishes us with the key to many phases of Massachusetts' early history. There is a very interesting paper, anonymous and without date, and printed in the *Proceedings* of the Massachusetts Historical Society (46, pp. 287–298), that sums up the arguments on each side. Eight reasons are given why the king should keep his hands off the colony. First, because the intent of the patentees could not be carried out unless they had absolute power, independent of all right of appeal to the crown, for otherwise the king might prevent them from enjoying the free exercise of their religion. Secondly, because distance had removed

were fighting for religious not political freedom and they believed that the Lord would care for his own.[1]

That which guided their policy in their relations with the mother country also determined their attitude toward affairs nearer at hand within the colony itself. Free as they were from any immediate danger of outside interference, they were able to form such government as they pleased, provided it preserved the customary rights to which Englishmen were entitled at home and followed as nearly as possible the requirements laid down in the charter. These results were not easy of accomplishment. The Puritans were called upon to square the rights of Englishmen and the terms of their charter with their own accountability to God and the rule of God's word, and with a church polity based on primitive models. They had no intention of admitting either liberty or toleration in matters of faith and worship or of popular rule in matters of government, both of which were dishonorable to religion and an affront to the Lord. There was no democracy in Israel, as Winthrop said, and, he added, among the civil nations of the world it was accounted the meanest of all forms of government, to allow which was contrary to the fifth command-

them from under the royal jurisdiction, since the common law did not extend beyond the four seas and consequently no writ or instrument of civil authority could reach them. Thirdly, because Massachusetts was not represented in parliament and hence English statutes could not bind them. Fourthly, because no duties could be imposed except such as were expressly mentioned in the charter. Fifthly, because by the charter they had liberty of making laws and of governing themselves, fully and absolutely. Sixthly, because by the same charter they had liberty to defend themselves against all desiring to do them detriment. Seventhly, because by the same charter they were secured from the consequences of any act done, and were given a sufficient discharge even against the king. Eighthly, because an acknowledgment of the king's right of jurisdiction over them would be a dangerous concession for Massachusetts to make. The arguments in this paper probably belong to the period after 1660, perhaps to the time 1664–1665 when the royal commissioners attempted to assume authority over the colony.

1. John Cotton in 1646, when delivering his Thursday lecture, just before the *Supply* sailed for England, bearing, as was suspected, appeals to the Long Parliament against the commonwealth, said, "If there bee any amongst you that have a petition to prefer to the high Court of Parliament that may conduce to the distraction, annoyance and disturbance of the peace of our Churches and weakening the government of the land where we live, let such know, the Lord will never suffer them to prosper in their subtill, malicious and desperate undertakings against his people." Winslow, *New-England Salamander*, pp. 14–17 (128–129). The cases of Captain Stagg and Captain Bayley, involving recognition of a parliamentary commission and the right of appeal to England, are excellently narrated by Miss Crump, *Colonial Admiralty Jurisdiction in the Seventeenth Century*, pp. 42–43, 46–50.

ment. Furthermore to the Puritans religion and government—their two leading and all important interests—were inextricably interlocked, admitting of no such thing as a separation of church and state. Each supplemented and aided the other, in a manner unknown to a secular corporation or to a lawyer's view of an Englishman's rights, the clergy acting as advisers in laical matters, the magistrates issuing orders regarding the maintenance of the true faith. In church polity the Puritans stood between Separatism on one side and Presbyterianism on the other; in government they sought a middle ground between popular confusion and tyrannical usurpation. There was no charitableness in their views on creed and conduct; no faith in a suffrage based on other than religious qualifications; no desire for a state system in which religion and politics should be kept widely apart.[1]

From the beginning the clergy were called upon, as a matter of course, to coöperate in the settlement of affairs of a purely secular character. Cotton in his election sermon of 1634 pleaded for the reelection of Winthrop and from that time on election sermons frequently dealt with strictly political issues.[2] Over and over again the governor and magistrates called upon the elders—the term included often the pastors and teachers also—to offer advice, draw up rules and regulations, and make recommendations whenever a troublesome political situation arose. Questions regarding land, trade, defense, the cutting out of the cross in the flag, the La Tour episode, the sow episode, relations with the Dutch, the status of the magistrates, the Hingham case, the growth of a factional spirit, the relations with England and with parliament[3]—in all of these, which were strictly of a laical or civil nature, the elders were consulted that they might "enforme us of the mind of God herein."[4] The leaders

1. But the Puritans agreed that a man could not be a civil magistrate and a ruling elder at the same time (Winthrop, *Journal,* I, 83; Hubbard, *History of New England,* p. 186). In 1637 the elders decided that the church had no power to call in question the proceedings of a civil court, because not in accordance with the practice and rule of Christ and because Scripture furnished no example of it. Winthrop said that even if the act of the civil court were unjust the church could not call the magistrate to account (*Journal,* I, 256).

2. *Ibid.,* I, 124; *Publications,* Colonial Society of Massachusetts, I, 389–390.

3. *Ibid.,* I, 116, 119, 128, 130, 141, 143, 144, 170, 171, 256; II, 108, 116, 117, 133; *Massachusetts Colonial Records,* II, 20, 232–233, 236, 294; Hubbard, *History of New England,* p. 168.

4. *Massachusetts Colonial Records,* II, 67.

—lay and clerical—were not always in accord on this point, for John Eliot, teacher at Roxbury, declared in one of his sermons that the elders made a mistake in advising peace with the Pequots, "without consent of the people" and were deserving of blame "for other failings" also, and he refused to retract this opinion even when expostulated with by Cotton, Hooker, and Welde, for stirring the people to murmur "against us for it."[1] The younger Saltonstall and Bellingham did not sympathize with so much clerical interference, for they charged the elders with invariably taking the side of the magistrates against the deputies and upholding severity and discipline. They objected strongly to a small treatise which one of the elders wrote in support of the magistrates, defending their superior place in the councils of the commonwealth, largely on the ground that the magistrates were called of God while the deputy had no such calling.[2] On the other hand when one scrutinizes carefully the part that the elders played in the affairs of the commonwealth, one easily realizes that Massachusetts was not a theocracy, as it has far too often been called, for the influence of the clergy was entirely unofficial and without the sanction of law. They never did more than offer opinions and present recommendations, either unasked or on request, and on one occasion, at least, they expressed an opinion but refused to give advice.[3]

If the elders were the sources of information as to the mind of God in secular affairs, the assistants or magistrates were the "nursing fathers of the churches."[4] There was no important issue or dispute among the congregations, no question of church doctrine or polity, no threatening heresy "tending to the subversion of the Christian and destruction of the souls of men"[5] that did not call for their active intervention. They claimed the right to exercise jurisdiction over all offenses "against the first table of the law," that is, against the first four commandments of the decalogue,[6] touching idolatry, blasphemy, and the breaking of the Sabbath—all of which were construed as offenses against God. They originated inquiries

1. Winthrop, *Journal*, I, 142.

2. *Ibid.*, II, 121, 171–172, 211–217, 218; *Massachusetts Colonial Records*, II, 20. Compare Gray, *New England Quarterly*, III, 692–693.

3. Winthrop, *Journal*, II, 296.   4. *Ibid.*, II, 279.

5. *Massachusetts Colonial Records*, II, 177.

6. "A Brief Apology" (commonly called "A Short Story") in Adams, *Antinomianism*, p. 192; *Massachusetts Colonial Records*, II, 177.

into the fitness of the clergy and into the causes of the many quarrels that arose in the churches, either among the members, between the members and the pastors, or between the pastors and the elders,[1] for it was not always smooth sailing even among the elect themselves. They took the lead in deciding where a newly arrived minister should be located, as in the case of John Cotton,[2] and whenever a heresy was suspected, as of the Anabaptists, Samuel Gorton, and Dr. Child, they were the first to open proceedings, always constituting themselves the judges in delivering the final sentence.[3] They asked the elders for their opinions and frequently gave them time in which to draw up a formal statement thereof, but they themselves sat as a secular court, which reproved, fined, imprisoned, or banished. Though the deputies raised the question as to the right of the magistrates to "command" a synod, the latter claimed the right and in 1647, during the sitting of the synod which met in 1646, the general court—governor, magistrates, and deputies—interposed and ordered the clergy to draw up a confession of faith as well as a plan of church government, which the reverend elders were apparently not intending to do.[4] Only the year before, at a postponed session held on November 4, 1646, the court itself drafted a moral code, dealing with blasphemy, idolatry, public worship, swearing, contempt of God's word and ministers, and such heresies as denying the immortality of the soul and the resurrection of the body. It decreed that, in addition to censure by the church, each person found guilty should be dealt with by the strong arm of the civil law, that is, on first offense be reproved by the magistrate and on the second to pay five pounds or "Stand two houres openly upon a block 4 foote high, on a lecture day, with a paper fixed on his breast, with A WANTON GOSPELLER, written in capital letters, that others may fear and be ashamed of breaking out into the like wickedness."[5] The church of Boston, Cotton the teacher, did not hesitate, in its turn, to draw up a code of commercial ethics for the colony, laying down in six clauses certain "false principles" in business and giving rules for the right prosecution of trade.[6] Though Cotton in his letter to Lord Saye and Sele in 1636 decried the encroachment of the one

1. Hubbard, *History of New England*, p. 143; Winthrop, *Journal*, I, 203.
2. *Ibid.*, 108.　　　　　3. *Massachusetts Colonial Records*, II, 177.
4. *Ibid.*, 176–180.　　　　5. *Ibid.*, 179.
6. Winthrop, *Journal*, I, 317, 318.

jurisdiction upon the field of the other, there are times when, in some respects, the functions of church and state would seem to have been interchangeable.[1]

On the side of civil government authority after 1634 lay in the hands of the governor, deputy governor, magistrates or assistants, and deputies, sitting as a general court, at first all together and then after 1644 as two separate houses. A trivial cause led to the separation of the two houses. This was the suit of Richard Sherman against Robert Keayne over the ownership of an ordinary white sow.[2] The plaintiff was a poor man in whose name the suit was brought by his wife, while he was in England. The defendant was comparatively wealthy,[3] and being a money lender was by many considered a hard man and a usurer. The question at issue was who owned the sow.[4] The case went first to the elders and then to the inferior court at Boston, and in each instance the verdict was for the defendant, Keayne. The latter, thus upheld, in retaliation brought suit for slander and won a favorable decision from the jury with £20 damages. These decisions were rendered on the merits of the case, for the weight of evidence is clearly on Keayne's side. But, as often happens, popular sympathy was with the woman, and the deputies, many of whom lodged under Mrs. Sherman's roof and ate at her table, were friendly toward her. When, therefore, the matter came up on appeal to the general court and the question was put, "Whether the defendant bee found to have been possest of the plaintiff's sow and converted her to his own use or not," the

1. Cotton declared that the Puritans wished to "avoide both the churches usurpation upon civill jurisdictions, *in ordine ad spiritualia,* and the commonwealth's invasion upon ecclesiasticall administrations, *in ordine* to civill peace, and conformity to the civill state," though, he added, "God's institutions (such as the government church and of commonwealth be) may be close and compact, and coordinate one to another, and yet not confounded." Hutchinson, *History of Massachusetts,* I, 497.

2. Winthrop, *Journal,* II, 64, 116–120, 164, 170; *Massachusetts Colonial Records,* II, 12, 51–52, 58–59; Rugg, "A Famous Colonial Litigation," *Transactions,* American Antiquarian Society, October, 1920, pp. 217–250.

3. See his will, 1653, *Report,* Boston Record Commissioners, 10, pp. 1–53, one of the longest wills on record.

4. Winthrop gives the details thus. "Anno 1636, there was a stray sow in Boston, which was brought to Captain Keayne: he had it cried divers times and divers came to see it, but none made claim to it for near a year. He kept it in his yard with a sow of his own. Afterwards one Sherman's wife, having lost such a sow, laid claim to it, but came not to see it, till Captain Keayne had killed his own sow. After being shown the stray sow, and finding it to have other marks than she had claimed her own sow by, she gave out that he had killed her sow." *Journal,* II, 64.

vote was two magistrates and fifteen deputies for the plaintiff and
seven magistrates and eight deputies for the defendant, with seven
neutral. On joint ballot the vote would have been for Mrs. Sherman, but as the law stood no sentence could pass without a majority
of both—magistrates and deputies—one way or the other. As it
happened a majority of the magistrates was for Captain Keayne and
a majority of the deputies for Mrs. Sherman, and a deadlock ensued.
At once the question was raised as to the right of the magistrates
to act by themselves and thus to negative the decision of the deputies, who by weight of numbers could outvote them.

The issue thus raised was not new. Under the name "The Negative Voice" or "The Negative Vote" it had been a subject of discussion since 1634, and it concerned the dominant part which the magistrates had assumed in the government of the commonwealth. The
deputies were determined to compel the magistrates to give up this
right of the negative vote, but the magistrates considering, as Winthrop says, "how dangerous it might be to the commonwealth, if
they should not keep that strength to balance the greater number
of the deputies," refused to yield and the issue continued to be debated at various times with heat and no little acrimony.[1] After the
business of the sow had been settled in Captain Keayne's favor, the
deputies raised the issue anew, and then it was that Winthrop, in
defense, wrote a small treatise, showing how the negative of the
magistrates was essential and fundamental to the government,
"which [he said] if it were taken away, would become a mere democracy." But this argument fell on deaf ears, for the deputies and
the unrepresented part of the population were not convinced that
the negative voice was fundamental to the welfare of the colony.
Despite the fact that the negative of the magistrates had been in use
for fourteen years, was upheld by the elders, one of whom wrote a

1. For the controversy over the Negative Voice, see Winthrop, *Journal*, I, 133–134,
147; II, 66, 117, 120, 121, 149, 164, 206, 223, 235, 240; Hubbard, *History of New
England*, pp. 174–175; *Massachusetts Colonial Records*, II, 40. In the colony's reply
to the proposals of the lords and gentlemen, sent over in 1636, is the following:
"Demand 5. That for facilitating and despatch of business and other reasons, the
gentlemen and freeholders should sit and hold their meetings in two distinct houses."
To which demand the answer was made, "We willingly approve the motion, only as
yet it is not so practiced among us, but in time, the variety and discrepancy of
sundry occurrences will put them upon a necessity of sitting apart." Hutchinson,
History of Massachusetts, I, 491. Thus there would appear to have been no objection
in principle to the separation into two houses.

paper on the subject, and by a majority of the leading Puritans as the only protection the colony had against plebeian rule, the deputies, supported by the younger Saltonstall, Bellingham, and Bradstreet— the three liberally minded magistrates—won the day. In 1644, upon the motion of the deputies, "it was ordered that the [general] court should be divided in their consultations, the magistrates sitting by themselves and the deputies by themselves, what the one agreed on they should send to the other, and if both agreed then to pass, etc. This order determined the great contention about the negative voice."[1] The decision marked also another step in the process of creating a commonwealth, for by it the superior power of the magistrates and the influence of the clergy were measurably reduced. Thus one of the cardinal features of the Puritan government as originally planned was permanently eliminated. To men of the Winthrop, Dudley, Wilson, Welde, and Cotton type there was no place for majority rule in "the wise administration of a civill state according to God," and they tried as long as they could to retain the sacrosanct idea of the magistrates as the mouthpieces of God that the Puritan community might not lose its character as a divinely directed institution.

The elimination of the negative voice was but one phase of a movement which had been going on from the beginning to reduce the authority of the magistrates and place it on an equality with that of the deputies. Cotton had declared early that the strength of the commonwealth lay in a threefold distribution of function—the authority of the magistrates, the purity of the clergy, and the liberty of the people—and in 1635 the magistrates by a bold stroke endeavored to checkmate the deputies and maintain their position as the custodians of authority. In order that their decisions might appear as nearly as possible the "voice of God" and their standing in the community acquire a greater dignity and permanence they proclaimed anew their right to sit as a standing council, with full executive powers, in the intervals between the sessions of the general court. Though the elders upheld the position taken by the magis-

1. Winthrop, *Journal*, II, 164; *Massachusetts Colonial Records*, II, 58–59. The house of representatives at once organized itself with speaker and rules and exercised the parliamentary privilege of determining its own membership and receiving petitions. It appointed committees and began the issue of sessional papers, *ibid.*, III, 2, 3, 7, etc.

trates[1] the deputies opposed it and became particularly outspoken in regard to it during the year that followed. Then the magistrates went a step farther. In 1636 they decided to create from among themselves a council for life, partly to retain their hold on authority and partly, it may be, to attract to the colony men of rank from England, who might look with favor upon such an oligarchic feature in the constitution. Three members, Winthrop, Dudley, and young Harry Vane, were named and the experiment tried. But the attempt proved a failure and the plan a mistake, so that despite the array of biblical precedents in its favor, it was abandoned after a trial of three years. This ill-devised scheme, contrived at a critical time in the history of the commonwealth, not only provoked the wrath of the deputies and of many from the unrepresented people at large, but aroused opposition and feelings of jealousy even among the magistrates themselves.[2]

With the disappearance of the council for life, the issue reverted to its original form. The younger Saltonstall wrote a book on the subject, in which he questioned the authority of the standing council and declared it a sinful innovation. Some passages in the book were construed by his fellow magistrates as offensive and uncalled for and a few of them, including Winthrop, proposed to hand it over to the elders for an opinion as to its soundness. But the general court would not agree and negatived the proposal, thus showing how far the deputies had gone in denying the right of the clergy to meddle in matters that were purely secular.[3] The discontent found expression in outbreaks of popular disapproval: one Shorthose was set in the bilboes for slighting the magistrates in his speeches; and Thomas Bushrod was fined for defaming the government. In 1644, with the separation into two houses, the deputies voted to create a commission composed of four magistrates, three deputies, and one elder "to order all affairs in the vacancy of the general court," but the magistrates indignantly opposed this plan as tending "to overthrow the foundations of government" and casting unjust reflections upon themselves, as if they were the ones who

1. *Hutchinson Papers*, I, 179–187. Answer of the elders to the question whether the magistrates are by patent and election of the people the standing council of the commonwealth in the vacancy of the general court.

2. Winthrop, *Journal*, I, 134, 171, 178; *Massachusetts Colonial Records*, I, 167; II, 20.

3. Winthrop, *Journal*, II, 171–172; *Massachusetts Colonial Records*, II, 20, 21.

wanted to uphold an arbitrary system in the conduct of commonwealth affairs.

The differences between the contesting groups had now become
sharply defined. Were the magistrates, by patent and election and
as Christians called to office by divine authority, justified in acting
as a standing council during vacancies of the general court or were
they not? Winthrop made a speech deprecating these altercations
and jarrings among the magistrates and between the magistrates and
the deputies and later produced his well known essay on "Arbitrary
Government," in which he laid down the principles, as he conceived
them, upon which the Puritan system rested. The elders were called
upon to reconcile the contending factions and to answer a long series
of questions, which were drawn up by Winthrop and others, covering all the points in the dispute. In their reply they upheld the
cause of the magistrates in all its aspects, and as a result the deputies
yielded for the moment to the combined pressure of magisterial and
clerical influence. But the final settlement was only postponed. Saltonstall took the part of the deputies, as he had so often done before,
and the latter, heartened, continued the struggle, to the dismay of
Winthrop, who exclaimed how hard a matter it was "to draw men
(even wise and godly) from the love of their own inventions." A
majority of the deputies remained unconvinced, and made the situation the more tense by demanding, at this juncture, the right,
hitherto exercised by the magistrates only, of selecting the preacher
of the election sermon.[1]

A truce came with the agreement to prepare and publish a body
of laws, for the purpose of safeguarding the people at large against
any undue exercise of power by the magistrates. In later days no
aspect of Puritan legislation was more surprising to the English
lawyer than the right vested in the civil and judicial authorities in
New England of inflicting punishment at will of a severity out of
all proportion to the character of the offense. The harshness of the
Puritan penal code seemed to the judicially minded Englishman of
the eighteenth century so unjust and oppressive and the authority
of the magistrates to proceed and punish as they saw fit so liable to
abuse as to constitute a menace to the community. The danger of
such magisterial license, unchecked by printed law known to all,
even though in Puritan theory magisterial judgments were always

1. Winthrop, *Journal*, II, 211–217, 226–227, 235.

divinely inspired, was unquestionably real, and the deputies were agreed that it were better for the people to know what the laws were—even though some of them might be harsh and arbitrary—than to stand in continual ignorance of the rules according to which the magistrates dispensed justice. As it happened the drafting of a legal code proved a long and difficult task.

As early as 1635 the deputies had called attention to the need of a printed code, whereby the magistrates might be curbed in their discretionary control over the liberties of the people. As a result in the same year grand and petty juries were brought into existence for the first time and a little later, without warrant from the charter, a system of inferior courts was established and local courts were set up in the towns for the trial of minor offenses.[1] The magistrates agreed to all these things, as relieving them of a heavy and exacting burden; while the deputies wanted them because they meant a distribution of judicial functions that was in conformity with the prevailing practice in all civilized communities. In 1636 Cotton was requested to aid the magistrates in compiling a body of fundamentals. This he did the following October, presenting the general court with a first compilation, called by Winthrop "a model of Moses his judicials, compiled in an exact method,"[2] a code consisting of ten chapters, covering the government, laws, and practices of Massachusetts. Despite the name given to it by Winthrop, the code is not Mosaic, even though its marginal references to the Old Testament show that its compiler believed that its provisions were in accordance therewith. As Cotton himself said in his *Subjection to Christ*, "it is foolish vanity to ask a warrant in Scripture for a [political] form of government, for human wisdom may teach this, though not in church government."[3] The "Moses his Judicials" is an epitome, not of the law of Moses but of the law of Massachusetts, based in some measure at least on the common law of England, and many of its clauses were soon after carried over to the New Haven colony and embedded in the Fundamentals there.[4]

This code was never adopted. In 1638 a committee of magistrates

1. *Ibid.*, I, 157; *Massachusetts Colonial Records*, I, 264; II, 109.
2. Winthrop, *Journal*, I, 196.
3. *Subjection to Christ* (1657), p. 64. Printed posthumously.
4. Force, *Tracts*, III, no. 9. For the influence of Cotton and his "Moses his Judicials" see Miss I. M. Calder, *The New England Quarterly*, III, 82–94, and *Transactions*, Colonial Society of Massachusetts, XXVIII, 86–94.

and elders was appointed to make another compilation, but the results were unsatisfactory and the effort came to nothing. Then in 1639 the task was turned over to Cotton and Nathaniel Ward of Ipswich—formerly a common law attorney in England—each of whom was to frame a model to be submitted to the general court. The two models were "digested with divers alterations and additions and abbreviated and sent to every town, that there might be a general discussion of the provisions." Ward's model was finally the one approved. Its clauses having been debated in the general court for three weeks, were finally reduced to one hundred items, and then adopted by the court as law.[1] They were issued, but not printed, as the Body of Liberties in 1641.[2] The code was to be in force for three years, during which time its provisions were to be tested by experience, amended if necessary, and if found satisfactory to be made perpetual.

But the deputies did not want this Body of Liberties. Ward though not a traditionalist was not a liberal, as his *Simple Cobbler of Agawam* shows,[3] and his code still left too much power in the hands of but a very small number of men, whose sympathies were not with the popular element in the colony and whose fears of popular influence were integrally bound up with their ideas of what a Puritan government should be. The deputies, who at this time were in the heat of their controversy with the magistrates, and the freemen generally, to whom had been given the opportunity of examining these laws, still not convinced that the new code sufficiently curbed the arbitrary discretion of the magistracy, renewed their agitation. After the experience of the deputies in the sow case, it became inevitable that when the three-year period had passed, the issue would be reopened by the general court and another attempt would be made to appease the discontented parties. In 1645, a new survey of the laws was ordered and continued for about two years and a half, when a careful study of the whole situation was made by a new board of compilers.[4] Even after the revised code was in the

1. Winthrop, *Journal*, II, 49; *Massachusetts Colonial Records*, I, 346.
2. Winthrop, *Journal*, I, 323–324, 362; II, 48–49. For the Body of Liberties, Gay's article, *Collections*, Massachusetts Historical Society, 3d series, VIII, 191.
3. Force, *Tracts*, III, no. 8, p. 9 for Ward's views on toleration. In 1649 Ward wrote a work entitled *Mercurius Anti-Mechanicus; or The Simple Cobblers Boy*, in which he condemns the execution of Charles I. This treatise is as well worth reading and is quite as characteristic of Ward as is the *Simple Cobbler*.
4. *Massachusetts Colonial Records*, II, 227, 239, 246, 262, 263, 286.

hands of the general court in 1647, a further scrutiny was thought necessary, and certain English law books were obtained for the purpose of aiding the court in its task. These books were: "Two of Sʳ Edwᵈ Cooke upon Littleton; two of the Books of Entryes; two of Sʳ Edwᵈ Cooke upon Magna Carta; two of the Newe Tearmes of the Lawe; two of Dalton's Justices of Peace; two of Sʳ Edwᵈ Cooks Reports."[1] For a so-called "Bible Commonwealth" the Puritan colony of Massachusetts was showing an amazing amount of interest in English law.

The progress of the revision was undoubtedly hastened because of the critical state of the colony's relations with England and its fears of a possible intervention by the parliamentary commission of 1643, of which Warwick was the head. The work was finished in the spring of 1648 and ordered sent to the printer. Six hundred copies were struck off, presumably with the intention of distributing them among the officials, private individuals, and the towns. But this plan was never carried out. Three years later, because of a desire of the court to make further alterations, the edition was apparently called in and the copies either burnt or used as waste paper. Only one specimen, recovered by almost a bibliographical miracle, has survived and has been reproduced in a faithful reprint. Its title is *The Book of the General Lawes and Libertyes concerning the Inhabitants of the Massachusetts, Collected out of the Records of the General Court for the Several Years wherein they were made and established. And now revised by the Same Court and disposed into an Alphabetical Order and published by the same Authoritie in the General Court held at Boston the fourteenth of the first month Anno 1647.*[2]

The *Lawes and Libertyes* is not a code, nor is it properly speaking a digest. It is, as the title indicates, an alphabetical arrangement or abridgement of laws which had been passed already, beginning with "Age" and ending with "Wrecks of the Sea," with a supplement of "Presidents [Precedents] and Forms of things frequently used." It was undoubtedly modeled on the familiar *Abridgements of the Statutes,* customary in England and known to every English

1. *Ibid.,* III, 232.
2. This single copy is now in the Huntington Library. A reprint of it was issued in 1929, with an introduction by the director of research, Dr. Max Farrand. The original edition bears the imprint, *Cambridge: Printed according to order of the General Court. And are to be solde at the shop of* Hezekiah Usher *in* Boston. 1648.

lawyer, for it makes no attempt to frame general rules, to lay down
principles of statute law, or to state fundamentals governing and
controlling the scope of legislation. Winthrop says that the object
was "to extract out of the whole such as should be thought fit to
be established and so reduce them into one volume to agree with
such as were already in force." In its content the *Lawes and Libertyes* is a blend of the Mosaic law, the law of the colony, and the
common law of England, the latter, which is by far the largest part,
in a form adapted to serve the peculiar needs of the colony. Except
in the section "Capital Lawes," there are no marginal references to
the Old Testament, as in the case of Cotton's "Moses his Judicials,"
and in the great majority of cases the laws follow English precedent,
for outside of ecclesiastical and capital legislation, Massachusetts had
always followed English practice, modifying and expanding it to
suit the colony. The Puritans never made the Mosaic law the source
of their own law, except in the few cases where they dealt with religious and moral conduct, for they would have found it impossible
to draw from the Old Testament the material wherewith to con-
struct a practical law code for the colony. The English common law
was the only available source for Englishmen of the seventeenth
century, whether Puritan or otherwise, who were engaged in setting
up a legislative and judicial system in a new world.

The *Lawes and Libertyes* constituted a convenient handbook of
existing legislation and became the model afterward followed in
both New Haven and Connecticut. A new edition was issued in
Massachusetts in 1660. As the laws passed at each session of the
general court were not put into print at the time and so were not
known to the great body of the colonists, the publication of such a
collection as this, showing what laws were in force and what were
not, was as great a boon and protection to the people as was the
issue of the charter to the company itself. It satisfied the freemen
and their deputies and brought to an end that long struggle over
the power of the magistrates that had been going on since the
founding of the colony. Henceforth the just rights and privileges
of every freeman were known to all, and in cases of excessive severity, should such occur, the printed law could be pleaded against the
judgment. The political privileges as well as those that were legal
are carefully defined in the code and selected sections, and if massed
together would constitute a frame of government for the colony.
These various "codes of liberty," in Massachusetts, Connecticut,

Plymouth and New Haven, embodying the law of the land and open to the knowledge of all, were bulwarks of defense against arbitrary rule and mark a definite advance in the direction of popular rights safeguarded by law. On the other hand the "liberties," thus described, were in no way conceived as analogous to any so-called natural rights of man, which to the Puritan mind, as well as to the contemporary mind in general, did not exist. They were concessions of authority not statements of right and because issued under the sanction of the general court, bore an official imprimatur. As such they represent that sense of responsibility in government which is characteristic of the political development of all English-speaking peoples.

At this very time, in 1644, when the controversy regarding arbitrary government was at its height and when certain ones in the colony—William Vassall, Dr. Robert Child, and that strange mystic, Samuel Gorton—were threatening to make trouble in England for the Puritan colony in America, a plan was set on foot to broaden the franchise and to extend some of the freemen's privileges to such as were not church members. Even with the admission of the comparatively small body of freemen to a fuller share in government by the concessions of 1634 and 1644, the affairs of the commonwealth were still controlled by very few men. Only members of churches, who had taken the freeman's oath and had been formally admitted to freemanship, could hold office or take any part in civic affairs. One exception was allowed—non-freemen who had taken the oath might hold office in the militia and vote for the minor military officers.[1] Circumstances, arising partly within the colony and partly from the fear of an English intrusion, were making necessary a modification of this rule. Every town had more non-freemen than freemen, a fact that gave rise to a number of local problems. For instance, Marblehead, before it became a town in 1649, had no freemen at all and its constable had to be chosen from among the honest and able men of the locality.[2] Even church members were no enthusiasts when it came to holding public office, and in 1647 the rule had to be adopted that if a man were a church member and refused to become a freeman in order to avoid service, he would be obliged to serve just as if he were a freeman.[3] There is no doubt

1. *Massachusetts Colonial Records*, II, 117.
2. *Ibid.*, 57, 266.
3. *Ibid.*, 208; *Lawes and Libertyes*, p. 23.

that every effort possible was made to induce church members to become freemen, but the fact that there were more church members than freemen would seem to indicate that the privileges of freemanship, at this time and at all times in colonial New England, were insufficient in the opinion of many good Puritans to outweigh the inconveniences of officeholding.

As some towns had many more non-freemen than freemen, it became necessary to admit those of the former class, who had taken the oath of fidelity, to all local franchisal privileges, in order that they might bear some of the burdens and responsibilities of local office. Therefore the local franchise was much broader than the general franchise and must have been enjoyed by hundreds not of the generality of the company and entirely outside the boundaries, strictly speaking, of the charter. In 1647, in order to make use of the "abilities of divers inhabitants amongst us, which are not freemen," the general court permitted such non-freemen, provided they had taken the oath of fidelity and were twenty-four years old, to serve as jurymen and to vote for the selectmen who looked after the prudential affairs of the town and assessed the rates.[1] In the *Lawes and Libertyes* of the next year, it was provided that every man, whether freeman or non-freeman, should have liberty to be present at any court, council, or town meeting, and either by speech or in writing to move any lawful, seasonable, or material question or to present any necessary motion, complaint, petition, bill, or information, whereof that meeting had proper cognizance, provided it were done in a convenient time and proper order and in a respectful manner.[2]

Thus before 1652, when Massachusetts declared herself an independent commonwealth, all men in the colony of mature years who had taken the oath of fidelity, possessed some share in government, either local or general. The restriction of the general franchise to church members and the disbarment of all others from holding high civil office were perhaps political hardships from a modern point of view and in course of time had to be changed to conform with practices elsewhere, but it may very well be questioned whether they worked hardships that were seriously felt to be such by the non-freeman inhabitants of the towns. The latter could vote in town-

---

1. *Ibid.*, 87, 210. The scarcity of competent jurymen is shown by the according of this privilege and by the allowing William Pynchon to use juries of six, if twelve could not be obtained. *Ibid.*, 41.

2. *Lawes and Libertyes*, p. 36.

meeting, hold office in the militia and serve on the jury, and freely present petitions and grievances to the general court. They had full rights before the law, were protected in their property and their persons, and were admitted to a full share in all the opportunities that the colony offered for profit and advancement in trade, commerce, and agriculture.[1] By 1652 the Massachusetts Bay Company had gone a long way from the path marked out for it by the charter; it had evolved into a political organism, with all the essential features, though in somewhat rudimentary form, of a modern state.[2] The Rev. Thomas Shepard, who took Thomas Hooker's place at Newtown in 1636, had some justification for the pride that he felt, when nine years later, in 1645, he gave utterance to the following: "What shall we say of the singular Providence of God bringing so many Ship-loads of his people, through so many dangers, as upon Eagles wings, with so much safety from yeare to yeare. The fatherly care of our God in feeding and clothing so many in a wildernesse, giving such healthfulnesse and great increase of posterity. What shall we say of the Worke it selfe of the Kingdom of Christ, and the form of a Common-wealth erected in a Wildernesse and in so few years brought to that state that scarce the like can be seen in any of our English Colonies in the richest places in America after many more years standing."[3]

1. Among the non-freemen, both in Massachusetts and Connecticut, were many prominent and influential men, who, unwilling to take the oath to the colony, constituted an opposition party to the government because they were not in sympathy with its limitations and restrictions. An admirable example in Massachusetts is Richard Wharton, who had come to New England, not because of any feeling of religious or political dissatisfaction but because the country offered opportunities for the acquisition of landed property and the securing of wealth through commercial enterprise. There were many others in the same class. In Connecticut Gershom Bulkeley, John Chester, Edward Palmes, Nicholas Hallam, and many others refused to become freemen, because they were opposed to the resumption of the charter government in 1689. On Wharton see Barnes in *Publications,* Colonial Society of Massachusetts, XXVI, 238–270. These men are often spoken of by New England historians as "tories" and "malcontents." Neither word is appropriate.

2. Captain Breedon, in March, 1661, told the Privy Council that Massachusetts looked on herself as "a free state . . . there being many against owning the king or having any dependence on England." He questioned their loyalty to the king, because they had not proclaimed him, did not give the oath of allegiance, but instead forced an oath of fidelity to themselves and their government (*Collections,* New York Historical Society, 1869, p. 17). Later Edward Randolph wrote, as his first impression of Massachusetts, "That government would make the world believe they are a free state and do act in all matters accordingly." *Hutchinson Papers,* II, 232.

3. *A Treatise of Liturgies* (London, 1653), pp. 7–8. The preface, in which the quoted passage appears, is dated November 28, 1645.

CHAPTER XXI

RELIGIOUS AND POLITICAL DIFFICULTIES IN THE BAY COLONY

THE Massachusetts Bay colony was founded primarily for religion and not for trade. As Emmanuel Downing wrote to Sir John Coke in 1633, "This plantation and that of Virginia went not forth upon the same reasons nor for the same end. Those of Virginia went only for profit. These went upon two other designs; some to satisfy their own curiosity in point of conscience, others (which was more general) to transport the Gospel to those heathen that never heard thereof."[1] They bore the hardships of the crossing and the settlement, remembering their calling and knowing the power of God, who as Dudley said "can support and raise us up again and useth to bring his servants low that the meek may be made glorious by deliverance."[2] Government was the structure, and trade the means of subsistence and the source of profit, but religion was the living, emotional force that gave to the community its reason for existence. It was, in the beginning at least, the "be-all" and the "end-all" of the colony's destiny. The Puritan was convinced that all forms of church polity and social conduct which had no scriptural sanction, minutely and literally interpreted, were sin and idolatry and not to be borne. To him the passages of the Bible, as he interpreted them without regard to time, place, or origin, were God's positive command and were an all sufficient authority for his purpose. Life was not a progress but a state of preparation for the life beyond and he rejected things of the earth as worldly and sought only that which the Bible showed was pleasing in the sight of God. Beauty, pleasure, and the indulgencies of the flesh, even if but moderately cultivated and enjoyed, were harmful to the soul. Righteousness was obedience—a blind obedience to God's inscrutable will—in which the individual was in direct communication with, and responsible to his Creator. Puritanism was the reawakened temper of early Christianity.

1. Historical Manuscripts Commission, *Twelfth Report*, II, 38.
2. Young, *Chronicles of Massachusetts Bay*, p. 321.

Side by side with the establishment of the political government went the organization of the churches, based on a polity that was neither wholly Separatist nor wholly Presbyterian. "The New England Way," as it came to be called, rejected the Separatist practice of putting the chief, if not the whole, church control in the hands of the congregation, whereby the influence of the elders was weakened; and it rejected the Presbyterian practice, which placed the sole power in the hands of each elder or group of elders, thus ignoring the sentiments of the people in each church or in all churches.[1] It distributed the power among the many, according to the objects sought, thus creating an evenly balanced system, for which in every part the Puritans believed they had apostolic warrant. Organized in strict conformity to what they assumed was apostolic practice, they reproduced the system of the early church, as they pictured it from a literal reading of the Bible, and so were in accord, as they profoundly believed, with the absolute word of God.[2]

In the formation of a church those concerned came together and seriously examined their spiritual condition in the desire to enter into a covenant with the Lord. Convinced of the purity of their own motives, they announced their intention to the magistrates or to some of the near-by churches and stated the time when they would make a public profession of their faith and manifest God's gracious working upon their hearts. On the day set the teaching and ruling elders of the adjacent churches gathered at the place appointed and heard the proponents confess their belief in all the principles of religion and declare their calling to Christ, professing their repentance from dead works and their trust in God and bearing testimony to the godly and approved life and conversation of each other.

After this had been done, they entered into a sacred and solemn covenant, sometimes called a profession or engagement, whereby they protested and promised, by the help of God, to walk together as became a church, in all duties of holiness before the Lord and in all brotherly love and faithfulness the one to the other. They then read the covenant, which had already been agreed upon and

1. Hubbard, *History of New England*, pp. 182–185; Richard Mather, *Journal and Life*, p. 82; Wise, *Vindication of the Government of New England Churches*, ch. V.
2. Wise, *passim;* Park, "Organization of a Colonial Church," *Publications,* Colonial Society of Massachusetts, XIII, 82–91, an admirable article, containing a luminous description of a Puritan church.

drawn up among themselves, and either subscribed it or bore witness to it by word of mouth. Then the right hand of fellowship was given the other brethren, prayers were uttered, praises offered, and hymns sung, after which the blessing was pronounced and the congregation dissolved.

Each church was organized with a pastor and a teacher, who constituted the teaching elders, with ruling elders (laymen), deacons, and sometimes, when available, deaconesses, who were usually "ancient" widows of three-score years. The duties of the pastor were to exhort, that is, to preach; of the teacher to instruct in matters of doctrine. The difference between the two was often hardly discernible. The duties of the ruling elders, who also knew their theology well,[1] were to order the assemblies, visit, and watch to see that the faithful throve in godliness; of the deacons to look after the necessities of the church, its finances, and its charities, or, as the saying was, to collect diligently, keep faithfully, and distribute carefully. The pastor was first elected by the congregation, then ordained by the imposition of hands and by prayer, either by the elders or, if there were none, by leading members of the church. When the pastor was ordained public worship followed, which consisted of reading, singing of psalms and hymns, prayer, and the monthly holding of communion or the sacrament of the supper, accompanied always by preaching. Lecture days supplemental to the Sabbath were held during the week and the particular lecture day which came before communion was called "preparatory" to that event.[2]

Members were added by solemn and formal process and dismissed

1. The whole community became a sort of church, for as the preachers knew politics so the civil leaders, ruling elders and others, knew their theology and wrote, often voluminously, upon it. The air was oversaturated with pondering on religious subjects—a condition that was characteristic of Puritan New England for many years —and the reader who wishes to sense the atmosphere of the Puritan age must study this literature as far as he can understand it. William Aspinwall contributed several writings, expository largely of Bible prophecy (Boston Record Commissioners, *Reports,* 32, ix), and Robert Keayne in his will mentions his "3 great writing bookes wch are intended as an Exposition or Interpretation of the whole Bible, as also a 4th great writing booke in which is an exposition on the Prophecy of Daniel, of the Revelations, and the Prophecy of Hosea, not long since began, all of which Bookes are written with my owne hand" etc. (*ibid.,* 10, pp. 5, 16–17).

2. Treatises by John Cotton on this subject are *The Way of Life,* which deals with the conduct of individuals and families in town and church, pp. 79–80, and *Of the Singing of Psalms,* "with a lively voyce," ch. X. In Cotton and Nichols, *Some Treasure fetched out of Rubbish* (London, secretly printed, 1660), we have

to other congregations in the same manner.[1] Delinquents were first advised, then censored by vote of the entire church, and if these methods proved ineffective were excommunicated, that is, barred from communion. In the presence of the entire body, after the necessary preliminary statements had been made, the pastor solemnly in the name of Jesus Christ delivered the obstinate and sinning member over to Satan for "the destruction of the flesh and the saving of the soul in the day of the Lord Jesus"—a dreadful sentence.

In the form thus given to the organization of the church and the manner of its worship the idea of the Puritan was "to carry all things with joynt consent of all the members, which was the practice and honour of primitive times, which Paul so much desired should be that of the church of Corinth (II Corinthians, 2.10)." Differences of opinion were met by discussion and if this failed then outside help was called in, sometimes of the clergy alone as friendly advisers and peacemakers and sometimes with the coöperation of the magistrates. Massachusetts did not establish the practice of "consociation," which later became one of the essential features of the church in Connecticut, according to which neighboring bodies voluntarily came together "for mutual affording to each other such assistance as may be requisite, upon all occasions ecclesiastical."[2] Though "synods" were held in Massachusetts as early as 1637 and continued to meet at various times and for various pur-

---

further analyses of Puritan practice, in which we are told that it was not seemly for men to pray with long hair or women bareheaded; that it was not proper for women to speak in the congregation or for many men to speak at once. The three treatises that are combined in this work largely concern the rites of the church, the third, that of Nichols, deals with the surplice, the sign of the cross in Baptism, and kneeling at the sacrament of the Lord's Supper (pp. 52–75).

In *Englishmen at Rest and Play, 1558–1714,* a book which should be read by everyone interested in New England history, there is a passage quoted at length from a Wadham College manuscript, containing the recollections and reflections of Sir William Waller, the great parliamentary general, who died in 1668. Waller's Sunday religious program was as follows: two public services, family prayers or psalm singing four times in the day, private prayer four times, and finally prayer with his wife and meditation upon and repetition of the sermons. This, says the editor, "was not penned by some desiccated hermit, but by a man of conspicuous vitality," pp. 124–125.

1. "Admission . . . was not easy, in fact it was more difficult than membership in the Anglican communion," Crouse, "The Great Migration," *New England Quarterly,* January, 1932, p. 32.

2. *Saybrook Platform,* 1708 (ed. 1838), pp. 119–120; Walker, "Why did not Massachusetts have a Saybrook Platform?" *Yale Review* (1892), pp. 68–86. Thomas

poses until 1680, and though John Cotton defends the "consociation" in his *The Way of the Churches,* as not only lawful but in some cases as necessary, and Hooker of Connecticut has a chapter on "synods" in his *Survey of Church Discipline,* yet in both colonies each church continued to remain entirely independent, many in Connecticut refusing to enter the consociations because they deemed them meddlers in their affairs.

Should an occasion arise when corrupt opinion and suspicious practice could not be eradicated by the church itself, the Massachusetts Puritans, following the rule of waiting for the hand of civil authority, would appeal to the magistrates—the "nursing fathers amongst us"—and the latter would summon a general assembly of elders to consider and find a remedy. At this gathering the matter would be propounded, the elders would declare their opinion with the reasons therefor, and any one present could express doubts and disagreements without offense. The debates were to continue until all parties were satisfied. Should the church remain delinquent then the right hand of fellowship would be withdrawn. The rules governing the management and discipline of the churches were first formulated in the Cambridge Platform of 1648, in the preface to which the compilers express the hope that "the examples of such poor outcasts as our selves" may not be without its effect upon "some or other of our brethren in England."[1]

During this period of Puritan history thoughts were centered primarily on church polity rather than on church doctrine; ecclesiastical practices were more often in the Puritan mind than were creeds; and matters of church discipline were more conspicuous than were matters of faith. In fundamental tenets there was probably little difference to be found between the Puritans' confession and the doctrinal articles of the Church of England. Persons seeking membership had to submit to a searching examination as to "their knowledge in the principles of religion, their experience in

Hooker in the preface to *A Survey of Church Discipline* (1648) declares "Consociation should be used, as occasion doth require, with allowance to counsell and admonish other churches." Massachusetts introduced the "synod," thus becoming rather synodical than "Presbyterial." Roger Williams would have considered both the "consociation" and the "synod" as a step toward the national church which he repudiated.

1. Cotton, *The Way of the Churches* (1645); Walker, *Creeds and Platforms,* pp. 196, 203–237; and *Three Phases of New England Congregational Development* (Hartford Seminary Publications, new series, no. 29).

the ways of grace, and their godly conversation among men," but one finds it difficult to determine at this stage in the history of the New England churches what exactly were the articles of doctrine to which each prospective candidate for membership was supposed to subscribe. We may assume that if asked the question, he or she would have replied somewhat in the language of the Saybrook Platform, our creed is made up of "those things which are necessary to be known, believed, and observed for salvation [and which] are so clearly propounded and opened in some place of Scripture or other, that not only the learned but the unlearned, in a due sense of the ordinary means, may attain unto a sufficient understanding of them."[1] As these words of Scripture had to be interpreted in the light of Calvinism it follows that the candidate for church membership had to know the main features of the Calvinistic theology and be prepared to accept them. The characteristic tenets of Calvinism formed the corporate and collective faith of those who belonged to these New England churches. They accepted all that Calvin taught regarding God and the Trinity, God's eternal decrees, the creation, the fall of man, Christ's mediation, free will, effectual calling, justification, adoption and sanctification, saving faith, repentance unto life and salvation, good works, assurance of grace, and the law of God as expressed in a covenant of works. These formed a fairly formidable array of doctrines for the candidate to expound, and when to them is added comprehension and acceptance of the sacraments of baptism and the Lord's supper and belief in the resurrection of the dead and the last judgment, we can understand the Puritan idea of "the saving remnant" and the Rev. Thomas Shepard's remark that it was "a tough work, a wonderful hard matter to be saved."

Before 1645 there were twenty-three churches in the colony and Winthrop tells us that there were about fifty elders. The total number of those who made up the membership of the churches was, as we have already seen, very small in comparison with the entire body of the inhabitants, but they formed the ruling element, that determined the religious integrity and political independence of the colony and made every effort to keep the faith pure. From the beginning they were engaged in purging the land of undesirable inhabitants and as early as 1631 had sent back to England or to Barbados

1. Chapter I, section vii.

many who for political, moral, or religious reasons were deemed unfit to continue within the colony's jurisdiction. Some of these were offenders against the government, as in the case of Thomas Walford who declared "his contempt of authoritie and confrontinge officers etc"; others were disrespectful of the magistrates, as in the case of one Captain Stone, who called Ludlow not a justice but a "just-ass," a play on words that was common at the time; still others were, in the eyes of the Puritans, immoral characters, seducers, and given to profanity, uttering corrupt remarks regarding churches and clergy.[1] One curious form of banishment was established by law in 1647, requiring all men and women living in Massachusetts, whose wives or husbands still remained in England, to leave the colony and go back to their consorts, because guilty of immoral conduct and loose living and given to contracting bigamous marriages.[2] But more serious and more dangerous than these were the Anabaptists, Familists, and rigid Separatists, who had "privily crept into the New England churches," the Jesuits and all spiritual or ecclesiastical persons ordained by the authority of the pope or see of Rome, and others who held erroneous and heretical doctrines, such as Henry Burt, who publicly announced his belief that he was free from original sin and that all true Christians were able to live without committing actual sin.[3] The Anabaptists were thought to be increasing and spreading in the country and they were obnoxious to the Puritans, not only for their views on baptism but also because they were deemed "incendiaries of the commonwealths," "troublers of

1. *Massachusetts Colonial Records*, I, 82–83, 86, 269 (1631); 336, 344 (William Collins and Francis Hutchinson, 1641); Captain Stone, *ibid.*, II, 108, Winthrop, *Journal*, I, 108, Hubbard, *History*, p. 156. Stone was the one whose killing at the hands of the Indians was in part responsible for bringing on the Pequot War.

2. *Massachusetts Colonial Records*, II, 211–212; III, 182. This law was enforced in York County, Maine, when under the jurisdiction of Massachusetts. There the delinquent was required to send for his wife or her husband or else to return to England. Libby, *Provincial and County Records*, II, 171, 285, etc.

3. *Massachusetts Colonial Records*, I, 266, 269, 312; Winthrop, *Journal*, II, 17; Hubbard, *History*, p. 277. For a contemporary estimate of heretics, including Familists, Antinomians, and Arminians, see a curious book by one Samuel Clarke, pastor in Bennet Fink, London, entitled *A Mirrour or Looking-Glasse both for Saints and Sinners* (3d ed. much enlarged, 1657), the preface of which is dated "From my study in Thridneedle-street, this twentieth of November, 1656," pp. 245–279. The compiler repeats the customary tale of the monsters to which Mary Dyer and Anne Hutchinson were reputed to have given birth. In his *Geographical Description of all the Countries in the Knowne World*, which follows the *Mirrour*, he has nothing to say of any of the continental colonies, an omission partly met in another of his

churches," and "infectors of persons in maine matters of religion," denying the "ordinances of magistracy and the lawfulness of making war."[1] These as well as the others were sentenced to banishment, if after due time and means of conviction they remained wilful and obstinate in their errors.[2] There was at least one Familist in the colony, Jane Hawkins, a midwife charged with being a witch and having familiarity with the devil in England, a fact believed by the Puritans to have been proved by many ministers and others who visited her there and found it true.[3] That there were ever in Massachusetts any Jesuits, who came with proselyting intent, is more than doubtful, and the reasons for the passage of the act of 1647[4] are far from clear. These reasons may be nothing more than fears of the pope and of the activities of Roman Catholics in general, who at this time seem to have been charged with designs against the Puritans as "dangerous supplanters of the Catholic cause." The court in passing the act may have been influenced by the coming of wine ships and merchants at this time from such Catholic countries as Spain, Portugal, and Madeira, or by the contacts with La Tour and the French of Acadia, where the Jesuits were always ardent missionaries in the Catholic cause. Endecott called them "those idolatrous French" and Winthrop said in 1637 that, by consent of all, Jesuits ought to be rejected. These were troublous times, full of cross pur-

works, *Four Chiefest Plantations of England in America* (1670). On the minor sects see Grant, *Truth's Victory against Heresie* (London, 1645), where ten such sects are described. Also Shepard, *New England's Lamentation for Old England's present Errours and Divisions, occasioned by the increase of Anabaptists, Rigid Separatists, Antinomians and Familists* (London, 1645).

1. For the errors of the Anabaptists and Familists see Clarke (as above), pp. 278–279. Cotton said in 1644 that there was "a generation of familists" in Boston and other towns, evidently including all Antinomians in that class, for he mentions Anne Hutchinson as one of them (*Narragansett Club Publications*, II, 80). We know that there were Familists in Maine and in Barbados. Seekers came later and Dr. Ernst (Rhode Island Historical Society *Collections* XXIV, 1; *Roger Williams*, pp. 479, 492) claims that Roger Williams was their founder and that he introduced Seekerism into England (see below, page 469, note 2). Generalists, found in Rhode Island but probably not in Massachusetts, were defined as those "who make God's mercy and justice, by wresting some Scriptures as they do our writings, to be nonsensical whimsies without any bonds or order."

2. *Massachusetts Colonial Records*, II, 85, 149, 177, 253; Winthrop, *Journal*, II, 177, 259, 260. Dr. Henry M. Dexter says that twenty persons were banished before the autumn of 1635. *As to Roger Williams*, p. 17.

3. *Massachusetts Colonial Records*, I, 329; II, 147; Winthrop, *Journal*, I, 266, 268; II, 8.

4. *Massachusetts Colonial Records*, II, 193.

poses and many suspicions, and the law may have been adopted merely as a preventive remedy.[1]

Of far more concern than any of these were the members of the Puritans own household who exhibited differences of opinion regarding some of the most cherished parts of the orthodox creed. The chief differences concerned three people or groups of people— Roger Williams, Anne Hutchinson, Dr. Robert Child and others of the Remonstrants—the offenses of whom were partly religious and partly political, and equally objectionable in either case. The effect of the prolonged struggle that ensued between 1635 and 1660, ending with the almost merciless treatment of the invading Quakers, was victory for the orthodox ruling party and the firm establishment of a rigid and schismless Puritanism as the creed of the majority in New England for nearly a century. The result of this victory was a kind of intellectual and spiritual apathy and stagnation which led eventually to the Great Awakening, a movement which shook to its foundations the entire Puritan system and affected in one way or another the religious life of all the colonies.

Roger Williams came to the colony in 1631. Of his early life we know little, beyond the fact that he was born in London in 1603, of parents belonging to the upper middle class.[2] For a time he lived in Cow Lane near Smithfield—a region of well-to-do tradesmen.[3] He entered Charterhouse (Sutton's Hospital) in 1621, was registered at Pembroke College, Cambridge in 1623, matriculated in 1624, and received the degree of B.A. in January, 1627. He became chaplain to Sir William Masham at Otes in Essex and in 1629 married Mary Barnard, maid and companion to Joan (Jug) Altham, Lady Masham's eldest daughter by her first husband.[4] A year later the newly

1. Regarding Dr. Child as a suspected Jesuit see Kittredge, "Dr. Robert Child, the Remonstrant," Colonial Society of Massachusetts, *Publications*, XXI, p. 61, note 6.

2. Williams' parentage was first discovered by Henry Waters before 1889 and the facts were printed in the *New England Historical and Genealogical Register* for that year. Additional information was afterward obtained by Walter Angell of Providence and by G. A. Moriarty, vice president of the New England Historical and Genealogical Society, some of which has never been printed.

3. For Cow Lane see Maitland's maps of the wards of London, and Agas, *Map of London*, a part of which is reproduced in *Collections*, Rhode Island Historical Society, XVI, facing p. 96.

4. He wanted to marry Jane Whalley, Lady Masham's cousin and Lady Barrington's niece, who afterward married the Rev. William Hooke of Taunton, New Haven, and England. His letters to Lady Barrington may be found in Egerton Manu-

married pair sailed from Bristol in the ship *Lyon* and reached Boston the following February. Two months later Williams was invited to assist the aged Skelton at Salem (Francis Higginson having died August 6, 1630), and on Skelton's death (August 2, 1634) he became the acting head of the Salem church, though not ordained pastor until 1635. He was temperamentally excitable—"divinely mad," as Hubbard says—was often hasty in speech and indiscreet in his efforts to enforce his own opinions, and was possessed of intensely strong convictions which he reached quickly and maintained without compromise. Sir William Martin, who knew him when in England, wrote to Winthrop expressing regret "to hear of Mr. Williams separation from you," adding that Williams was "passionate, precipitate, which may transport him into error," but hoped that "his integrity and good intentions would bring him at last into the way of truth and confirm him therein."[1] Williams was only twenty-eight years old when he came to Massachusetts, but even at that early age he was already well on his way through non-conformity to an extreme form of separatism in church polity and to an arch-individualism in matters of opinion, and was eager to stand by his views with all the impetuosity and carelessness of consequences that were born of his youthful fervor and self-confidence.

Though a landholder and a church member, Williams never became a freeman of the corporation or a resident member of any town and therefore always stood a little apart from those responsible for the government of the colony and concerned for the preservation of it as a Puritan stronghold of the orthodox faith. Hence his opinions and his public expression of them had a double significance: as the utterances of a church member and a pastor they were certain to influence others in the colony to its detriment; and as those of a non-freeman they would be unrestrained by any oath of fidelity to the commonwealth. There is nothing to show that at this early date Williams had formulated or expressed any clear cut notions—such as are customarily ascribed to him by later expositors of his place in the history of religious thought—regarding what is loosely termed "toleration" or that the question of soul liberty had

scripts, 2643 (Andrews and Davenport, *Guide*, p. 47) printed in the volume of the *New England Historical and Genealogical Register*, mentioned above, and in *Collections*, Rhode Island Historical Society, October, 1929.

1. *Hutchinson Papers*, II, 119.

any conspicuous place in the controversies that arose in Massachusetts before 1643.[1] The time had not come either in England or in
America for that burning problem to take its place as a matter of
first concern or as something uppermost in men's minds. The banishment of Roger Williams has been invested by later writers with
an importance that was not felt contemporaneously.[2]

The causes of that event were in part political and in part a matter of church polity.[3] Williams denied the validity of the Massachusetts Bay charter and the right of the colony to hold its lands by
grant from the crown.[4] Such a denial coming at about the same
time with the efforts of Gorges, Mason, Morton, and Gardiner to
bring about the recall of the charter and to procure the appointment
of a governor general over New England, was peculiarly inopportune and must have aroused an intensity of feeling that was the
greater because of the reality of the danger. From 1635 to 1637 the
commonwealth was fearful lest England should interfere in its af-

1. Williams was no advocate of toleration. He upheld religious liberty, which is
quite a different thing. There is no defense of toleration in his arguments with Cotton. He took the ground that all men were equal in the matter of religion and repudiated the notion that men of different faiths were to be tolerated, an attitude
which he thought savored of inequality, as if a superior church were condescend-
ingly tolerating one that was inferior. *Narragansett Club Publications,* III, 4; IV, 7-
8; *Collections,* Rhode Island Historical Society, VIII, 6.

2. See NOTE at the end of the chapter.

3. The efforts of Dr. Henry M. Dexter, in *As to Roger Williams* (1876), to defend
Massachusetts by demonstrating that the causes of the banishment were entirely political are a failure. Dexter's hostility for Williams and his Palfreyan attitude of apology for the Puritans, his misunderstanding of the situation in England and all that
concerns the charter, Gorges, and the English authorities, and the bitterness of his
attack on the Anabaptists and other similar groups destroys the reader's confidence
in most of his estimates. The remarks of Dr. Henry S. Burrage (*Report,* American
Historical Association, 1899, I, p. 11) are negligible.

4. "The 4 particular grounds of my sentence," in Williams' reply to Cotton,
Narragansett Club Publications, I, 324-325; Cotton's answer, *ibid.,* II, 14, 44-53,
90; *The More Bloody Tenent, ibid.,* IV, 506; Winslow, *Hypocrisie Unmasked,* pp.
65-66; Winthrop, *Journal,* I, 154, 162-163. The four reasons given by Cotton Mather
(*Magnalia,* book vii, ch. ii, §§ 2-8) are separatism, the denial of the validity of the
patent, the power of the magistrates, and the refusal to take the oath of fidelity.
Mather says nothing about liberty of conscience.

In denying the validity of the charter, Williams was controverting the doctrine,
up to this time pretty well accepted in Europe, of ownership based on the right of
discovery (letter to Mason, *Narragansett Club Publications,* VI, 348). Williams presented his ideas in a "treatise," a large book in quarto (Winthrop, *Journal,* I, 116;
Deane, *Roger Williams and the Massachusetts Charter,* 1873), which he sent to Winthrop, bidding him burn it after he had read it. Compare Cotton's reply, *Narragansett Club Publications,* II, 44.

fairs, and to have one of its own elect aiding the cause of its enemies across the water was something not to be borne. Almost equally an outrage in the eyes of the Puritan leaders was Williams' declaration that the power of the civil magistrates extended only to the bodies, goods, and outward state of men and not to offenses against the first table of the law, that is, against the first four commandments of the decalogue. To this the Rev. Thomas Shepard replied "that if the magistrate hath no power over his subjects in matters of the first table he may have also all his feathers pull'd from him."[1] In denying the right of the civil magistrates to deal with matters of conscience and religion and in vehemently asserting that in so doing they were persecuting men for actions and words that were of a spiritual and religious nature and so beyond their cognizance, Williams was entering upon that line of thought which was to lead him to his later convictions on the subjects of liberty of conscience and the separation of church and state. These subjects he eventually elaborated in his tractates on the bloody tenet of persecution for the sake of conscience.[2]

The earlier subject of dispute, which played a part less menacing perhaps to the civil peace of the community but more disturbing to the ecclesiastical peace of the churches was not liberty of conscience but separatism. On this subject Williams held strong views and he maintained them to the bitter and logical end. At his arrival in Massachusetts in 1631 he refused to join with the Boston church because he deemed it "impure" for two reasons. First, the Boston church considered it unnecessary to fellowship in Christ and the qualifications of a godly person that admitted members should all of them see and expressly bewail the pollutions with which they had been defiled in their former church contacts in England, whereas Williams demanded that they separate entirely, in mind as well as in body, from all associations and connections that represented their immediate past. Secondly, the members of the church refused to make a public declaration of their repentance for having had communion with the parish churches of England while they lived there, and after they came to Massachusetts continued to assert

---

1. *Theses Sabbaticae,* p. 311.

2. "Roger Williams his Letter to Governor Endecott," written sometime after Cotton's reply in *The Bloudy Tenent Washed* (1647), and before *The Bloudy Tenent yet more Bloody* (1652), with which, in the original issue, it is bound up, pp. 305–312.

that they separated not from the churches of old England but only from the corruptions found in them.[1] Williams went to the Salem church because he thought it "purer" than that of Boston, just as he considered the churches of Boston and other towns "purer" than the parish churches of England, and he went from Salem to Plymouth in September, 1631, in the hope of finding there a purer form of separatism than that of Salem.[2] But he discovered that the state of complete separation, at which he had inevitably and deductively arrived, was not to be found even at Plymouth, for the church there did not accept the rigid separatism that Williams demanded.[3]

So in 1634 Williams returned to Salem and from that time until the winter of 1635–1636 continued his attack on the Puritans, charging that the frame and constitution of their churches was national, since the commonweal and the church were but one, and that he who was in accord with the state must necessarily be in accord with the church also.[4] He further charged that the Massachusetts churches, while preaching against a national church in England, in reality practiced nationalism in New England, by inveighing against the practice of the Salem church, which was known to profess separatism. In this he was upheld by some of the freemen and church members and most of the non-freemen there.

The situation was aggravated by a petition which was sent in by the people of Salem for an assignment to them of a certain land "betwixte the Clifte and the Forest Ryver, neere Marblehead." This request coming at a time when the Salem church was not in good standing, because of its ordination of Williams in the face of protests from the other churches to the effect that he was spreading opinions injurious to the stability of the commonwealth, was temporarily refused by the general court.[5] Indignant at the court's ac-

1. "Mr. Cotton's Letter examined and answered" (*Narragansett Club Publications* (1644), II, 349–350, 353, 374–375, 393; and "The Answer of Cotton to Williams' Reply" (1644) are entirely taken up with this question of separatism (*ibid.*, 210, 225, 229, 234).

2. "Bradford's Dialogue" between the ancient men and the young men, printed in Morton's *New England Memorial* (ed. 1855), pp. 327–356, gives the views of the Plymouth young men that though the National Church in England was not according to the primitive order of the Gospel, there were some parish assemblies that were true churches, etc., p. 328.

3. Young, *Chronicles of the Pilgrims*, pp. 397–398. Elder Brewster neither liked Williams nor was in accord with his views.

4. *Narragansett Club Publications*, II, 298–300, 327.

5. *Massachusetts Colonial Records*, I, 147; Winthrop, *Journal*, I, 155.

tion, Williams with the consent of the Salem church sent letters of admonition in the church's name to the other churches, accusing the magistrates that were members of their respective churches "of sundry heinous offenses," and himself informing the members of his own church that unless they would separate, not only from the churches of old England, but from those of New England also he would separate from them. Salem, however, accepted the land and refused to follow Williams' extreme demand. From this time forward Williams refused to attend the church assembly or to have religious communion of any kind with his congregation, even including in his refusal his wife and children, who continued to attend. He kept a meeting in his own house, preaching to a small number, chiefly women, who came to hear him, thus carrying separatism to the extreme limit of logical application, and rejecting totally the half-way position taken by the orthodox churches of the colony.[1] In matters of both church and state Williams threw down the gauntlet and the court answered, first, on September 2, 1635, by bidding the Salem deputies go back to the freemen of the town and "fetch satisfaction for their letters sent to the several churches, wherein they have exceedingly reproached and villifyed the magistrates and deputyes of the General Court,"[2] and on October 9 it ordered that "Mr. Roger Williams, one of the elders of the church at Salem . . . shall depart out of this jurisdiction within sixe weekes now nexte ensuing . . . not to return any more without licence from the court."[3] Thus was Williams banished from the civil jurisdiction of Massachusetts; he voluntarily withdrew from the churches, "resolved not to continue in these evils."

Much more menacing from the point of view of the Puritan integrity of doctrine was the so-called Antinomian controversy, which arose from the public expression of certain ideas regarding fundamentals, during the years from 1634 to 1637, that struck into the very heart of the Puritan orthodoxy, and for a time thoroughly dis-

---

1. Hubbard, *History*, pp. 202–213. Williams claimed that the Puritans "made up a kind of national church and (as the phrase is) a Christian state, and government of Church and Commonwealth, that is, of Christ and the World together." *Tenent yet More Bloody*, pp. 40, 131.

2. *Massachusetts Colonial Records*, I, 156.

3. *Ibid.*, 160–161. *A Letter of Mr. John Cotton* (London, 1643), probably written soon after Williams left Massachusetts, in answer to the latter's complaints of the injustice of his banishment, says that he was not banished for his ideas on separation, pp. 1–2, 11–13.

rupted the peace of the community. The colony was in a state of agitation from other causes. England was threatening to interfere, to vacate the charter, and to send over a governor general; Williams was carrying his turbulent opposition to the point of sedition and was suffering banishment; Hooker and Stone were planning to remove to Connecticut and Pynchon was going also, but not to the same place; the English lords and gentlemen were making inquiries about conditions in Massachusetts and expressing dissatisfaction therewith; and John Davenport and his company were to spend a winter there and, unwilling to stay, were soon to depart for New Haven. There were differences and distractions among the magistrates also—Dudley, Haynes, Stoughton, Endecott, and Humfry—which were accompanied by the insistent demands of the deputies for a lessening of the power of the magistrates and a greater share in government for themselves. The reputation of the colony in England was suffering from the reports of those who complained of its persecuting spirit. There were dangers from the French and the Indians, which as Winthrop himself said were at that time hanging over them[1] and were to result in the Endecott expedition of 1637 against the Pequots, which probably did more harm than good, and in the very troublesome relations with La Tour and d'Aulnay when as early as 1635 La Tour, governor of Acadia, challenged the right of the Puritans to the territory upon which they were seated.[2] All these conditions disclosed weaknesses in the Puritan system that were threatening its strength and stability. With their existence as an independent colony thus menaced, with their right to their charter and their territory questioned, and with their principles of civil government facing serious modification, the Puritans were now in danger of seeing their most cherished theological doctrines and practices, guides along the way of the true religious life, denounced as worldly and materialistic, hidebound and dogmatic, and closed against the admission of the true spirit of Christ.

Anne Hutchinson, with her husband and children, arrived at

1. Winthrop, *Journal*, I, 202.
2. *Ibid.*, 146. For this famous incident, which concerned Massachusetts much less than it concerned the French in Canada, see Abbé A. Couillard Després, *Charles de Saint-Etienne de la Tour* (1930), which contains in its *avant-propos* an account of the paper-war, which has gone on in Canada from 1873 to the present time, between the defenders of d'Aulnay and those of La Tour—between the Capuchins and the Récollets, the former of whom were at Port Royal and La Hève, the latter the protégés of La Tour in Acadia.

Boston, 1634, in the ship *Griffin*. A year later came young Harry Vane, then but a youth of twenty-three. In 1636 came Anne's brother-in-law, the Rev. John Wheelwright, with his family. All of these became members of the Boston church, of which the Rev. John Wilson was the pastor and Cotton the teacher. Soon an agitation became perceptible, set in motion by the activities of Mrs. Hutchinson, who living in Lincolnshire had enjoyed Cotton's ministrations at St. Botolph's and had undoubtedly felt the influence of Wheelwright also, who dwelt nearby at Bilsby, even after these ministers had been silenced in 1632. Now in the new world of the Boston church, she gave voice to her opinions, which she expressed with all the power of a dominating personality and the skill of one naturally gifted with a love of polemical argument. She had a peculiarly magnetic temperament and an indubitable courage, and in a society that looked on a woman as an inferior creature, whose mind would not stand the strain of intellectual effort, she was deemed by the elders and magistrates something of a firebrand, an impudent dame whose tongue had got the better of her discretion and one who was in great danger of becoming a menace to the community. For a woman, who according to the dicta of the day was supposed to derive her "ideas of God from the contemplation of her husband's excellencies," she was an unexpected and unwelcome member of the Puritan body, for she no less than Roger Williams did not hesitate to speak out in private to groups of willing listeners gathered at her home and to admonish in public the elect of the colony on the error of their ways.[1]

The term "Antinomian" given to this movement was rejected by its supporters, just as the designation "Brownist" was rejected by the Pilgrims,[2] and the former retaliated by calling their opponents

1. Had Mrs. Hutchinson lived in the nineteenth century, she would hardly have become a woman's righter or the organizer of societies for the study of the Hindoo religion, as Professor Channing thinks (*History of the United States*, I, 369). Nor on the other hand does she deserve to be called "The American Jezebel," a term which one of her biographers has borrowed from Winthrop (*Journal*, I, 254), any more than Williams deserves to be called, as one of his biographers has it, "The Yankee Firebrand," even though the designation "firebrand" was used by him in speaking of Fox and Harris ("George Fox digg'd out of His Burrowes," *Narragansett Club Publications*, V, 207, 315; *Harris Papers*, pp. 77, 79, 80, 81). In each of these cases the biographer is bowing to the little gods of the new biography and using a sensational title to catch the eye of the buying and reading public. Neither work in its text carries out the title's suggestion of being flippantly ironical or portentously psychological.

2. "Bradford's Dialogue," p. 329. The non-conformist rejected the name "Puri-

"Legalists." Many a name has got attached to men and movements
of the past that represents only in scant measure the richness of
purpose and modernity of thought that underlay the original impulses, intellectual and religious, which were stirring the human
mind and soul to action. "Antinomian" was here applied to one
who refused to accept the law, that is, the requirements of the New
England way of the churches, or to conform to the practices deemed
essential to salvation that these same churches set up. The Antinomians were non-conformists, who abhorred the "vexatious legalism"
of the Puritans and declined to conform to the practices of the
model church in Massachusetts, just as the Puritans themselves had
declined to conform to many of the practices of the Church of England. They utterly denied that an outward concurrence with the
letter of the covenant was a sufficient test of true religion unless accompanied by a change in the inner life. They did not believe that
church-going, obedience to the law as laid down by the Puritan
leaders, and the doing of good works were necessary as the duties
of a Christian.[1] The Calvinistic idea was that sanctification should
precede justification, that is, that one should have performed his
religious duties—such as attendance on church worship and preaching and living in accord with the teachings of the Bible, notably of
the Decalogue—before, as a baptized person, he could be admitted
to church membership. Such obligations were accepted by the Massachusetts Puritans as an essential part of the New England system
of religious discipline.

Mrs. Hutchinson denied all this. She belonged to that group of
religious enthusiasts, of which there have been many examples in
history, known as "perfectionists" or believers in the higher life.
Such men and women held that the Holy Spirit dwells in every

tan," Henry Parker, *A Discourse concerning Puritans, A Vindication of those who
unjustly suffer by the mistake, abuse, and misapplication of that Name* (London,
1641).

1. Cotton defined these requirements or works as "secret prayer, family exercises,
conscience of Sabbaths, reverence of ministers, frequenting of sermons, diligence in
calling, honesty in dealing, and the like." *Way of the Churches*, pp. 50–51. How far
this interest in doctrine and works permeated the life of the colony may be seen
from two incidents. An individual nominated as sergeant was rejected by the company because he was "corrupt as regards the Lord's Supper"; and certain troops,
designed for service in the Pequot War, halted on their march to Connecticut in
order to discuss the question "Whether they were under a covenant of grace or of
works." Vale Smith, *History of Newburyport*, pp. 14, 15, notes; Palfrey, *History of
New England*, I, 492.

individual in such a manner as to constitute a personal union, that is, to be one with him. They denied the necessity of any other evidence of sanctification than the realization of Christ in themselves, forming a divine conjunction of Christ and the individual, consciously and exhilaratingly felt. One need only pray for the indwelling of Christ as infinitely more important than the outward manifestation of works or the possession of moral gifts and graces. To them sanctification was not required as a preliminary to justification; it was not necessary to *do* but to *be,* in order to furnish proof of Christian character and worth. One was a Christian not by "works" but by virtue of the spirit prevailing within him and of the divine power illuminating the soul, arousing a consciousness of personal reconciliation and communion with God.[1] Such consciousness exhibited itself in a willing obedience to inward impulses and voices, born of God, and in an implicit submission to his will. Not outward observance was the guaranty of salvation, but the inner light. These were the doctrines of the Mystics, the Quakers, the Evangelicals, and of the revivalist preachers of all time.[2]

The Puritan leaders—elders and magistrates—opposed all teaching of this kind because it denied their entire doctrinal system and form of church polity. They had never before come into contact with this form of religious mysticism and they not unnaturally classed its followers with the "heretical" sects—Familists, Seekers,

1. The Rev. Thomas Shepard in *The Sound Believer* (London, 1652), with a characteristic touch of humor, remarks that if good works are no proof of faith, it is because grace in them is "so little that they can scarce see it by the help of spectacles" (pp. 278–292).

2. Much of Mrs. Hutchinson's teaching is similar to the Quaker tenets of the period: morality more important than dogma; the purity demanded by the Gospel implies nothing less than self-renunciation; grace and the operation of the Holy Spirit within the souls of men overshadow all conclusions based on predestination; prayer is not to be learned by heart, but is to be the result of waiting on God, with a heart fired by love (an essential part of the Quietist belief); external worship of minor significance. In addition there were visions, the use of a kind of mystical language, and much talk of the inner light with which God illumines the soul.

Mrs. Hutchinson had much in common with James Nayler, the radical Quaker, who was associated in the popular mind with the Quaker movement, though not in good standing with Fox and his more conservative followers. Nayler took quite literally, as did also Mrs. Hutchinson, the doctrine of the indwelling of Christ, but unlike Mrs. Hutchinson he was a fanatic and belonged to the "ranter" stage of Quakerism. On this subject see Jones, *Mysticism and Democracy in the English Commonwealth,* especially the chapter on "The Seeker Movement" in which the author traces the Seeker societies in the northern counties of England, comparing them with the Seekers of New England.

Generalists, and Anabaptists—all of whom were Arminian or worse, likened by Shepard to the Manichaeans of old as believing all days equally holy and none to be observed more than another, by virtue of any command of God.[1] Just as Williams denied the validity of the patent and attacked the power of the magistrates, thus endangering the commonwealth on the civil side, so Mrs. Hutchinson, Wheelwright, Cotton (in 1635), and Vane brought into question the entire church organization and doctrine, thus endangering it on the religious side. The elders and magistrates resented this assault on themselves, their covenants, and their church institutions generally, but they resented even more the easy road to salvation that the Antinomians offered, as tending to slothfulness in religious things and the lessening of religious endeavor.[2] All responsibility was thrown on Christ. To them the Antinomian teaching seemed to relieve one of the horrors of sin and take away the obligation to lead a moral life, to exercise moral self-control, or to be bound by written covenants, by the written law of the Scriptures—the infallibility of which the Antinomians denied,[3] or by the teaching of the clergy. Perhaps worse than all else was the fact, very irritating to the Puritan who loved disputation, that the Antinomians were not open to conviction, because they would not accept as valid proofs taken from the Bible. To the latter religion was not a matter of demonstration but of feeling. Christ was their sanctification and they had no need to look to anything in life to prove justification. To be holy, they said, made no one better; to be unholy made no one worse. "He that elected me must save me" and justification came not from works or from faith but from Christ. This was all anathema to the Puritan theologians, who saw in it the canker of their peace and the ruin of their religious comfort and complacency.

At first by persuasion, preaching, and conference these theologians —both clerical and lay[4]—tried to convince the stubborn upholders of the covenant of grace of the error of their ways. Cotton, whose preaching both in old and new Boston had had a marked influence

---

1. *Theses Sabbaticae*, p. 57.

2. To the Puritans the road to salvation was hard. "It is a tough work, a wonderful hard matter to be saved," wrote Shepard, " 'Tis a thousand to one if ever there be one of that small number whom God hath picked out to escape the wrath to come." *The Sincere Convert*, pp. 98, 150.

3. To deny the inspired character of the Scriptures was made a penal offense in 1652. *Massachusetts Colonial Records*, III, 259–260.

4. See note 1, p. 464.

upon Mrs. Hutchinson's religious views, was always partly in agreement with her,[1] as he was to be later partly in agreement with Williams on the subject of liberty of conscience,[2] but he was not of the
stuff of which either rebels or martyrs are made and before the
conflict was over he had turned against the movement. Wheelwright, Vane, and a multitude of others of the Boston town and
church were Mrs. Hutchinson's chief allies and during the year
1637 the conflict raged with extraordinary intensity, surpassing in
importance and bitterness anything that had arisen up to this time.
It had more than a religious application, although that aspect of the
case was concerned with the future of Puritan orthodoxy, it was
political and regional as well. On one side as a contest between
Winthrop and Vane, it was to determine the strength of the established system of government and of the magistrates as its guardians
and defenders; on the other, as between Boston and the country
towns, it was to determine the power of the leading community to
dominate the affairs of the colony.

Three events were to decide the issue. The first concerned the
Rev. John Wheelwright. The Antinomians—Mrs. Hutchinson in
particular—put forward Wheelwright as the assistant pastor of the
Boston church, hoping to obtain for him such a position of authority as would provide an entering wedge for the reform of the whole
community. The attempt was unsuccessful and Wheelwright withdrew to the relative obscurity of the church at Mount Wollaston. Invited to be present on a fast day, January 16, 1637, at a service held
in the Boston church, where Cotton preached the principal sermon,
he gave utterance, when called upon to speak, to such a denuncia-
tory attack, from Parson Wilson's own pulpit, upon all those who
walked in a covenant of works, as to arouse the magistrates to bring
him to trial for sedition. When this decision came to the ears of the
members of the Boston church, some forty of them drew up a petition in which they begged the court to confine its judicial functions
to secular matters and not to interfere with the consciences of men,

---

1. Andrews, *Our Earliest Colonial Settlements,* pp. 115–116.
2. Cotton said that it was no prejudice to the commonwealth if liberty of conscience were suffered to such as feared God, but he made a distinction between fundamentals and circumstantials. He further added that it was not lawful to persecute
any for conscience' sake, if rightly informed, or even in the case of an erroneous and
blind conscience, until after admonition and advice. *Controversie,* pp. 6–10. All of
these points were answered by Williams in *The Bloudy Tenent,* pp. 19–42, and re-
answered in *The Bloudy Tenent Washed,* pp. 1–144.

or if that were not possible to throw open the trial to the attention of the public. The court, supported by an advisory council of the clergy drawn from the different churches of the colony, at first refused these requests and proceeded to hold the trial in secret. But in the end the anti-clerical party, which from the beginning had protested against such high-handed methods, won the day and the trial was thrown open. Just as Wheelwright's sermon, which is still extant,[1] contains nothing that can possibly be construed as contemptuous or seditious, so the trial that followed had none of the characteristics of a judicial proceeding.[2] Wheelwright was declared guilty of sedition and contempt of authority, by what appears to have been a much divided vote. William Coddington, a Hutchinson sympathizer, wrote that a majority of the magistrates and deputies were opposed to conviction, but that after two days of argument "the priests got two of the magistrates on their side and so got the major of them."[3] So intense, however, was the feeling in Boston that sentence was deferred until the court felt more sure of its position.

Governor Vane, defeated in the first encounter, not only continued to protest, but girded himself for the second round of the contest which was to come in May, when the court of election was to be held. Would he be reëlected governor and thus assure to the Antinomians continued control of the government, or would he be defeated and the old leaders returned to office? No political campaign in the colonial history of Massachusetts was ever fought with more telling effect than this one of April and May, 1637. Personal dislikes cut as deeply as political and religious antipathies and it became necessary to remove the scene of the meeting to Newtown in order to avoid serious conflict. This change of venue was Vane's first defeat. The next test of the situation concerned a matter of parliamentary procedure—should the petition presented in Wheelwright's behalf be considered before the balloting began or should the election of officers come first. Vane was for the petition and Winthrop for the election and Winthrop won, thus presaging the final result. The victory of the old guard, due in no small part to

1. First printed in the *Historical Magazine*, April, 1867, from a manuscript in the Massachusetts Historical Society. A reprint was issued later, with an introductory note by Henry B. Dawson.
2. Held, *John Wheelwright*, pp. 49–52; Adams, *Three Episodes*, II, chs. III–V.
3. Felt, *Ecclesiastical History of New England*, II, 611.

the removal to Newtown, where the influence of the Boston freemen was far less than it would have been had the court been held
at Boston, was complete and the Antinomians were effectively
routed. Vane, defeated as governor and outmaneuvered by the orthodox party, left the colony in August, a disillusioned youth, and
returned to England, after a career in Massachusetts of a little less
than two years, during which he gave expression to much boyish
petulance and emotionalism.[1] In later years, as Sir Harry Vane, and
a great leader during the Interregnum, he must have looked back,
as he penned *The Retired Mans Meditations*[2] in 1655, with feelings
of regret at the tactlessness and incivility which marked his attitude
toward his seniors in the Massachusetts Bay colony.

Vane's departure left Wheelwright without his chief protector
and the victory over the Pequots by the Connecticut men under
Captain John Mason removed from the minds of the Massachusetts
leaders the last fear of an Indian attack. Before proceeding to final
conclusions the victorious party caused a synod to be called early in
September for the purpose of settling the Antinomian heresy.
Twenty-five ministers, including Hooker and Stone from Connecticut and Davenport recently arrived from England, all the magistrates and many not in office, met at Newtown and for twenty-four
days thrashed out the whole question of heterodoxy in the colony.
Eighty-two errors were found, "some blasphemous, others erroneous, and all unsafe,"[3] and condemned by the assembly, though
not unanimously. These statements of theological hair-splitting,

1. Routledge, editor of the Calendar of *Clarendon State Papers preserved in the
Bodleian Library*, IV, 1657–1660, says of Vane (p. 222) "Among the Anabaptists
are Fleetwood and Vane; the latter's religion is really to make a party; he is led
solely by interest."

2. Sir Henry Vane, *The Retired Mans Meditations, or the Mysterie and Power of
Godliness Shining forth in the Living Word, to the unmasking of the Mysterie of
Iniquity in the most Refined and Purest Forms. . . . In which Old Light is restored,
and New Light Justified, being the Witness which is given to this Age*. London,
1655.

3. Winthrop, *Journal*, I, 232. What the Puritans thought Mrs. Hutchinson and
Wheelwright were teaching can be learned from this list of errors. Some twenty or
thirty are easy to understand, the rest are difficult. One learns nothing from Winthrop. See Adams, *Antinomians in the Colony of Massachusetts Bay*, pp. 95–124,
125–130, 218–220, 228–231; Felt, *Ecclesiastical History*, II, 313–317. The best account of the whole controversy is in Ellis, *The Puritan Age*, pp. 300–362, and in
Adams's *Three Episodes*, the latter in the author's characteristic vein. Miss Auger in
An American Jezebel has treated the subject well, better than has Miss Rugg in
Unafraid, which is only moderately successful.

though not unintelligible to the modern mind, are incomprehensible as the subject of such prolonged bitterness of feeling, provoking men to inflict such a heavy penalty as banishment upon their fellows. Nothing that took place in England under the Laudian régime can compare in its want of justification with these obscure definitions of doctrine that served as a pretext for the persecution of estimable members of a community. That behind the religious motive there lay the political necessity of control by the dominant party and, as the leaders saw it, the very security of the state itself cannot be doubted. No platform built of the material found in this list of errors could possibly become the permanent working creed of an ecclesiastical body or have been more stable than a structure erected in the shifting sands of theological controversy. So satisfactory to Winthrop, however, was the outcome of this assembly—"the Lord having been graciously present and all matters having been carried on so peaceably and concluded so comfortably in all love"—that he proposed a continuance of the gathering another year, but no steps were taken to that effect.

And so the second event came to its conclusion, and the third—the trial of "the opinionists"—followed soon after. Though the hope prevailed that the work of the synod would have a beneficial effect in pacifying the troubles and dissensions in matters of religion, the issue was otherwise. Wheelwright refused to be silenced and Anne Hutchinson—whose weekly or bi-weekly meetings of sixty or more women had been condemned in no gentle terms as disorderly and without rule—continued her exhortations, persisted in the public expression of her opinions, and denounced the clergy as violently as before. All that had really been accomplished was to wean Mr. Cotton, who must have been suffering the torments of indecision, from the side of the opposition and bring him over into the fold of the orthodox. Not one of the others—Wheelwright, Mrs. Hutchinson, Coddington, Aspinwall,[1] Hough, Coggeshall, Underhill, and the rest—swerved a hair's breadth from their convictions or from their attitude of opposition to the party in power. Fearing lest the court elected the May before would not be as amenable as they

1. For William Aspinwall at Aquidneck see Chapin's *Documentary History of Rhode Island*, II, index, and for a further account the introduction to the *Aspinwall Notarial Records*, the thirty-second volume of the publications of the Boston Record Commissioners (1903). In 1642, upon his petition and certificate of his good carriage, Aspinwall was restored to his former liberty and freedom in the colony.

desired, the leaders dissolved it early in October and ordered a new election, a gross violation of the charter. The new court, elected in the full flush of orthodox victory, was made up very differently from the old—two-thirds of the thirty-three delegates being new men and twelve only of the former court being reëlected—and its first action was to dismiss from attendance Aspinwall and Cogges-hall, two of the deputies from Boston. Thus purged, the court threw all leniency to the winds and proceeded to rid the colony of its undesirable members. Wheelwright and Aspinwall were disfran-chised and banished from the colony, Coggeshall was also disfran-chised and threatened with banishment should he persist in his ef-forts to disturb the public peace.

Then came the turn of Mrs. Hutchinson. But before final action was taken the court wished to ease its mind and to indulge its love for disputation by giving that gifted but troublesome woman an opportunity to defend her own cause. The court sat at Newtown and consisted of some forty members, with the clergy present in large numbers, and the rude church where the so-called trial was held was filled with spectators, for no event in the history of the colony had been as dramatic as this. There in the presence of Win-throp, Dudley, Wilson, Cotton, Welde, Peter, Eliot, Shepard, and many others, this frail woman, about forty-five years of age, faced her accusers, already committed—most of them—to her condemna-tion, and answered their interrogatories with the unruffled calm of a Christian martyr. By no stretch of the imagination can the proce-dure be dignified as that of a court of justice. It was an examination, a questioning, in which the inquisitors sought for answers that would convict the witness out of her own mouth, "lay open her-self" as Winthrop put it. The field of the inquiry was strictly within the domain of theology and the subjects, though not beyond the reach of the intelligent mind, were wholly out of place as part of the proceedings of a legislative session. They would better have been matters of debate in a pastor's study or in a gathering of the clergy met to discuss doctrinal differences. But the Puritans viewed the situation in a different light. Problems of theology were at this time integrally bound up with ecclesiastical uniformity. Ecclesiastical uniformity was church purity, and church purity was essential to the safety of the state. Thus the issue had a civil as well as a theo-logical bearing. More than all else it involved the preëminent position that the clergy had occupied in the commonwealth, for Mrs. Hutchinson, they said, had traduced the ministers, had denied the soundness of their judgments, and had dishonored them publicly. For that she deserved punishment. To support opinions contrary to those of the standing order was to flout authority and to pursue a course that was "greatly prejudicial to the state." She had created a disturbance, had stirred up discord, and had brought opposition parties into existence where formerly there had been none.

During the greater part of the examination Mrs. Hutchinson held her own, adroitly and with moderation, and though her questioners sought to circumvent her on the ground that she had declared their ministry to be different from that of the Gospel, in that the Puritan clergy preached a covenant of works rather than a covenant of grace, they made no progress in their somewhat ruthless manner of forcing a confession. They could obtain no adequate proof that she had "traduced the magistrates and ministers of the jurisdiction," that she had said the latter were not able ministers of the Gospel, or that she had declared that "the fear of man was a snare and therefore she would be affeared of them."[1] She eluded their charges and demanded that those who testified against her give their evidence under solemn oath, a demand that the court finally decided to refuse. Only toward the end, when in an exalted mood Mrs. Hutchinson asserted that what she had spoken was of God, "by an immediate revelation," and that what they were doing would bring a curse upon them and upon their posterity—for "the mouth of the Lord hath spoken it"—did she lay herself open to a direct attack, in declaring that all her actions were by revelations.[2] This claim put in jeopardy the foundation principles upon which the commonwealth was settled, for the Puritan leaders believed that the Massachusetts Bay colony itself was the outcome of a divine revelation. Even Cotton, who up to this time had wavered in his attitude toward Mrs. Hutchinson, now thought her deluded, and Dudley went farther and considered her deluded by the devil. Despite Coddington's vigorous plea in her behalf, in which he denied the equity

1. The report of the examination is printed in Hutchinson, *History of Massachusetts Bay* (Mayo ed.), II, appendix, ii.

2. Mrs. Hutchinson once declared, while walking with a friend through St. Paul's Churchyard, that she had always been "very inquisitive after revelation" and had never had any great thing happen to her but it was revealed to her before hand. Rugg, *Unafraid*, p. 62.

of the proceedings, and despite the opinion expressed by William Colbourn, delegate from Boston, that censure was the only reasonable penalty, the court condemned her to be "banished out of our jurisdiction as being a woman not fit for our society." When Mrs. Hutchinson asked "Wherefore am I banished," Winthrop replied, in a remark representative of all the proceedings, "Say no more, the court knows wherefore, and is satisfied."

The commonwealth had now weathered two serious attacks upon its integrity and upon the integrity of its polity and doctrine. We may not doubt that these attempts had their influence in bringing about certain important constitutional and legal changes which, as we have already seen in a previous chapter, were to take place during the ensuing ten years. The deputies in the general court, as well as many of the unprivileged inhabitants of the colony, were becoming restless under the domination of the magistrates and the clergy and were expressing their opinions in no uncertain terms. The elimination of the "negative voice," the minimizing of the influence of the clergy, the separation of the two houses, the movement toward the enlargement of the privileges of the non-freemen, and the prolonged effort to draft a body of laws that would safeguard the interests of the whole were all steps in the direction of a more evenly balanced and organized community on the governmental side. The Puritan commonwealth was the stronger for its experience and the better able to cope with its next encounter, but its very success was to prove in the long run a powerful factor leading to its own undoing.

Just as the controversies with Roger Williams and the Antinomians were partly religious and partly political, so the next disturbance was to partake of a similar dual nature. With Williams the chief issues were the validity of the patent, the power of the magistrates, and separatism; with Mrs. Hutchinson they were the doctrine of grace and factional turmoil in the state; so with the new opinionists, Dr. Robert Child and the Remonstrants, they were to be the independency of the colony and the toleration of other forms of church organization. To grasp the situation, as far as Presbyterianism was concerned, one must recall the fact that shortly after the adoption of the Grand Remonstrance by the Long Parliament in England, the Anglican members had gone over to the side of the king, leaving the Presbyterians and Independents in control, and that during the first civil war these two parties had found it impossible to work in harmony. The Independents advocated religious liberty and disliked not only the church system of the Presbyterians but their intolerance as well, and for the four years from 1643 to 1647, while the Presbyterians were a majority in parliament, the Independents were dominant in the army. The latter won their ascendancy in parliament when Pride's Purge drove out the Presbyterian leaders and brought their influence to an end. Thus during these four years Presbyterianism was in the ascendant and manifested its will in a series of measures designed to reform the church. The Presbyterians abolished episcopacy, and in the famous Westminster assembly of 1643 introduced the Westminster catechism and set up a form of ecclesiastical government after the Presbyterian plan. These events in England inevitably had their influence in Massachusetts, where religious conditions were exactly reversed. The "New England Way" was in close correspondence with that of the Independents and Presbyterianism had no official footing at all. But there were Presbyterians in Massachusetts and with their polity and catechism officially in command overseas they were not unnaturally inclined to make themselves heard.

The earliest effort in that direction, of which we have any record, was made at Newbury, when in 1643 the ministers there went about setting up some things according to the Presbyterian idea. The Puritans held an assembly or synod of a sort in 1643 and took action on the Newbury case, deciding against the polity, partly because they were afraid any recognition would serve as an entering wedge, encouraging parliament to impose Presbyterianism on the colony.[1] The next instance was at Hingham in 1645, when, as the outcome of a petty quarrel over a militia election, Hobart, the pastor, charged the government with exceeding its powers and violating the charter, declaring that the commonwealth was no more than a corporation in England. In the issue the incident brought to light parties in Hobart's church and fastened upon himself the charge of "being of a Presbyterial spirit,"[2] in that he managed church affairs without the advice of his congregation, which was not the New England way of procedure in church matters. The case ended with neither side convinced. But the most serious outbreak was that of Dr. Robert Child and the Remonstrants, who on May 16, 1646, presented a

1. Winthrop, *Journal*, II, 138–139.   2. *Ibid.*, II, 244.

"Remonstrance and humble Petition" to the general court, which involved the Puritan magistrates and deputies in a prolonged attempt to ward off intervention from England and to checkmate the schemes of those who wished to bring about important changes in the status and organization of the colony, that is, as Professor Kittredge says, "to nullify the charter and to reduce the colony to a condition of absolute dependence on the will of a Presbyterian majority in parliament."[1]

Dr. Robert Child was a young man, born in 1613, well educated, a student of medicine with a degree from Padua, widely travelled and possessed of some means. He had come to New England in 1641, possibly because of his friendship for the younger Winthrop and, returning to England, had come back in October, 1645. He was an ardent Presbyterian, and a man interested in various industrial enterprises, such as the promotion of iron works, the purchase of land, and the production of new staples. After a residence of eight months, during which time he must have been busy observing conditions in the colony and discussing these conditions with others, he succeeded in persuading six men—Burton, Smith, Fowle, Yale (the father of Elihu), Maverick, and Dand—to join with him in a protest to the general court, demanding reforms.[2] Shortly before, William Vassall, one of the original assistants named in the charter, but one whom Winthrop calls "a man of a busy and factious spirit"[3] (which is merely another way of saying that Vassall was of a different opinion with himself on such matters as liberty of conscience and independency), threatened to appeal to the Long Parliament, "that the distinctions which were maintained here, both in civil and church estate, might be taken away and that we might be wholly governed by the laws of England." On top of this and at the time of the Hingham affair, came the Remonstrance, which declared that

1. Kittredge, "Dr. Robert Child the Remonstrant," *Publications*, Colonial Society of Massachusetts, XXI, p. 86. This article is so complete, discerning, and well documented as to render it an ultimate authority on all that concerns the Child affair. Its conclusions are nearly all sound and reliable, with one exception. I can find no sufficient evidence to prove that Child ever planned to impose Presbyterianism on the colony. Samuel Maverick would hardly have joined him in any such attempt, being a strict Anglican himself. What they wanted, in all probability, was first, toleration for other churches in the colony, and, secondly, closer relations with England.

2. The Remonstrance can be found in *New England's Jonas*, pp. 8–18, and in *Hutchinson Papers*, I, 214–223. It is not printed in Kittredge.

3. Winthrop, *Journal*, II, 271. Winthrop abhorred organized opposition in government.

the conditions within the colony were bad, the people poverty stricken and discontented, the government arbitrary and tyrannical, and the whole settlement headed for ruin, unless the administration of civil affairs and of justice was changed to conform to English law, freemanship extended to all English subjects, and the Presbyterian system allowed as the polity of such of the churches as desired it. The Remonstrants threatened, in case their demands were refused, to appeal to parliament against the commonwealth.

Here was a serious situation. Parliament was controlled by a Presbyterian majority; Samuel Gorton, of whom more in a later chapter, had already, in 1645, received a favorable reply from the Warwick commission to his memorial against Massachusetts which had tried to oust him from his settlement on Massachusetts Bay; the same commissioners had granted Roger Williams a patent in 1644 that estopped Massachusetts for the time being from attempting further encroachments on Rhode Island territory; the Vassall demand for religious liberty was finding sympathizers not only in Plymouth but in Massachusetts also; and now seven leading men in the colony were preparing to put to the test the strength of the Puritans and their ability to maintain, in the face of all these perplexing conditions, their independence of English control. The danger was even greater than it had been ten years before.

The general court, not unnaturally but probably not rightly, linked together the Hobart, Vassall, and Child complaints, as parts of a common movement, and believing the peril to be more imminent than it actually was proceeded with the utmost caution and watchfulness. It endeavored to meet the complaints in part by taking into consideration the question of arbitrary government, particularly in the matter of taxation; by realizing the necessity of enlarging the liberties of the non-freemen, which resulted in the bill passed in 1647; and by hastening the revision of the laws which led eventually to the issue of the *Lawes and Libertyes* in 1648.[1] In its attitude toward the Remonstrants themselves it was the more severe because it believed that the design was wider than the mere introduction of Presbyterianism. There were but two of that persuasion among the seven and there seemed to be little reason for such a demand, inasmuch as the colony was willing to allow the formation of Presbyterian churches, however unalterably opposed it was to

1. *Massachusetts Colonial Records,* II, 197; III, 109–110.

the establishment of Presbyterianism as a state system.[1] The court was convinced that underlying the Remonstrance was a conspiracy to overthrow the Puritan government and to bring the commonwealth into a position of dependency on the mother country. Therefore it summoned the men before it, found them guilty, and fined them from ten to fifty pounds each. Three of the magistrates, Bellingham, Saltonstall, and Bradstreet, and five of the deputies opposed the verdict, but the sentence stood.[2] The Remonstrants, who had attempted to appeal to England before the decision was reached, now renewed the appeal in writing, but the court refused to accept the document or allow it to be read.

Child determined to go to England to prosecute the appeal in person. But the Puritan leaders, waiting until the last moment before taking action, because they felt sure that he was carrying incriminating papers, searched the ship on the eve of sailing and found two petitions and twenty-three queries, all of which confirmed their suspicions that the movement had a political import. One of the petitions, signed by twenty-three non-freemen, demanded liberty of conscience and the appointment of a governor general. The other, also calling for a royal governor, asked in addition for settled churches according to the Presbyterian system. Among the twenty-three queries was one inquiring whether the charter had not been violated and was therefore liable to forfeiture and whether the leaders of the colony in their acts and speeches were not guilty of high treason.[3] These were all subversive utterances and the Puritan magistrates acted quickly. Child was seized, bound over to the next court, and eventually, in 1647, fined £200. Four of the others—Smith, Maverick, Dand, and Burton—were likewise taken into custody, charged as was Child with conspiracy and heavily fined. Fowle had already got away to England and Yale is not mentioned as having had any part in this second phase of the movement.[4]

But the danger was not removed by the arrest of the conspirators. Parliament might still act favorably on the right to appeal and

1. Winslow, *Hypocrisie Unmasked*, p. 100.
2. *Massachusetts Colonial Records*, III, 94; Winthrop, *Journal*, II, 304–305.
3. *Hutchinson Papers*, I, 147–149; Winthrop, *Journal*, II, 307; *Winthrop Papers* (*Collections*, Massachusetts Historical Society), I, 381.
4. *Massachusetts Colonial Records*, III, 113–114. Professor Kittredge (pp. 53–55) prints a hitherto unknown memorial from fourteen of the deputies.

might order the Puritans to send Child to England to present his complaints, because a second copy of the Remonstrance and other papers had eluded the Puritan search and had gone over in the vessel, the *Supply*.[1] Child confidently expected parliament to act, but in the meantime Edward Winslow had sailed as the agent of Massachusetts, partly to obtain a reversal of the decision in the Gorton case and partly to prevent the commission from recognizing the right of appeal or from curtailing in any way the jurisdiction of Massachusetts. He started about the middle of December, 1646, and reached London in January, 1647, bearing a commission and instructions from the governor and company and a petition to the Warwick commissioners. He had also certain secret instructions containing answers to such objections as might be raised in England to the proceedings in the colony.[2]

Though Winslow failed to accomplish anything in the Gorton case, he was successful in carrying out the second part of his mission and in checking the efforts of the Remonstrants to obtain a review of the Massachusetts situation. He had already obtained a favorable decision from the commissioners before Robert Child, who was allowed to leave the colony in the summer of 1647, was

1. Winthrop, *Journal*, II, 309–315.

2. The presence in England of the various persons who gathered there to present their respective cases to the Warwick commissioners led to the issue of a number of important pamphlets from which are drawn many of the facts here presented regarding this controversy. Gorton, accompanied by John Greene and Randall Holden of Warwick, Rhode Island, arrived at the end of 1645 and addressed the commission in *Simplicities Defence against Seven Headed Policy* (November, 1646). Winslow answered this pamphlet, February-March, 1647, in *Hypocrisie Unmasked*, also addressed to the commissioners. In reply to Winslow, Major John Child, Robert's brother, probably acting under the direction of William Vassall, who landed from the *Supply* with many documents, in December, 1646, wrote *New England's Jonas cast up in London*, the title suggested by an incident of the voyage, when a copy of the Remonstrance was thrown overboard in the midst of a storm, but a second copy came safely through and turned up like Jonah in London. Winslow replied to Child, answering not so much Child as Vassall, in a pamphlet, *New England's Salamander recently Discovered*, May, 1647, because, as Winthrop says, Vassall was "a man never at rest, but when he was in the fire of contention." The word "salamander," like that of "firebrand," was a favorite designation at the time for a certain type of man. In a letter from Providence (probably written by Williams) to Newport, Portsmouth, and Warwick, June 10, 1667, William Harris is called "the Salamander always delighting to live in the fire of contention as witnesses his several suits of law" (*Harris Papers*, p. 78) and even as late as 1700 Gershom Bulkeley of Connecticut used a similar phrase in his *Will and Doom* (*Collections*, Connecticut Historical Society, III, 152), speaking of "factious persons (who like salamanders are out of their element when they are not in the fire)."

able to plead his case in person. On May 15 and 25 and July 22 of that year, the commissioners sent three letters, the first and second to Massachusetts alone and the third to Massachusetts, Plymouth, and Connecticut. The first forbade the Puritans to interfere with Gorton at Shawomet (Warwick), the second promised "not to encourage any appeals" from the Massachusetts jurisdiction, thus blasting Child's hope of interference from England, and the third refused to determine at so great a distance the intricate question of boundaries between the colonies of the New England Confederation and enjoined upon the Puritans the necessity of treating the Rhode Islanders with consideration and to make no effort "by an hand of power" to break up the settlements there. In all this we can see the influence of Warwick and possibly of Haselrig and Fenwick, the only members of the committee who had any knowledge of affairs in New England.[1]

With the sending of these letters the Warwick commission not only brought to an end the efforts of the Remonstrants to alter the status of the Massachusetts commonwealth but it placed its seal of approbation upon the policy of independence which the Puritan leaders had made their guiding principle for seventeen years. Child went to Ireland where he died in 1653; Vassall went to Barbados and we hear no more of him; Maverick left Massachusetts for New Netherland,[2] and was destined to play an influential part—a kind of aftermath of the Remonstrance movement—when, after the Restoration he renewed the petition (this time to the king) for the reorganization of Massachusetts. In so doing he brought upon the colony the inquisitorial visit in 1664-1665 of the royal commissioners, of which he himself was a member—a visitation that ended as unsuccessfully as had the effort of 1646-1647. Massachusetts was never stronger as a Puritan state than in the years immediately following 1647.[3] She exercised practically unlimited power, erected a

1. Winthrop, *Journal*, II, 335-338.
2. Maverick retained property in Massachusetts and continued to do business there, probably returning at times (in 1650-1651) to look after his affairs. *Report*, Boston Record Commissioners, 32, index.
3. Massachusetts was afraid, as late as 1651, that the Rump Parliament might impose a governor and magistrates upon the colonists against their wills (Hutchinson, *History*, I, appendix viii). Probably this fear was excited by the Declaratory Act of October 3, 1650, stating that all the colonies ought to be subordinate to, and dependent upon England and subject to parliamentary legislation. Firth and Rait, *Acts and Ordinances of the Interregnum*, II, 425.

mint and coined money, extended her jurisdiction over the towns
of New Hampshire and the province of Maine, performed all civil,
judicial, administrative functions, and breaking over with impunity
the bounds of her charter, took upon herself all the prerogatives of
a sovereign state.[1] Thus she remained for thirty-seven years longer,
until the ever widening circle of British expansion gradually surrounded her and new issues of trade and defense quickened the
conviction of the authorities in England that she was not a dutiful
member of the growing colonial world and needed to be disciplined
for her attitude of complete independency. In the end the Puritan
commonwealth fell, as it had to fall, as an autonomous community
having everything its own way, and became what it never wanted
to be, a subordinate colony under the British crown.

1. There was some reason for the charge which Fox brought against the colony
for its treatment of the Quakers, in his *Something in Answer to a Letter of John
Leverett Governor of Boston to William Coddington Governor of Rhode Island,*
dated 1677. "Did the king in his patent allow you that you should Hang or Burn
his Subjects with a Hot Iron and Cut off Ears and Banish upon pain of Death and
spoil their Goods, and whip such as were not of your Religion, for Religion's sake?
Look to your Patent and see if the King hath granted you that liberty or you have
gone contrary to it and contrary to the Scriptures, Christ and his Apostles." pp. 6-7.

NOTE. Though liberty of conscience as such is not mentioned by Winthrop, Cotton,
or any other contemporary writer upon the subject of Williams' banishment, it was
made a cardinal principle at Providence soon after Williams' arrival there (*Rhode
Island Colonial Records,* I, 16, 28, 377; Winthrop, *Journal,* I, 286). After Williams
went to England in 1643, he was embraced by Hugh Peter, who told him that he
(Peter) was for liberty of conscience and preached it (*Proceedings,* Massachusetts
Historical Society, 1858, p. 316). After 1642 circumstances both in England and
the colonies were bringing the issue to the front and Williams was all ready to take
a hand in the controversy. It seems that about 1637 a prisoner at Newgate had written a paper on the subject, which one Master Hall of Roxbury had sent to Cotton,
who answered it. Hall, not satisfied, sent the paper with Cotton's reply to Williams,
who while in England, answered Cotton in *The Bloudy Tenent* (1644). On December 23, 1643, parliament had issued five "Considerations," according to which the
rights of particular congregations were to be preserved and those whose consciences
could not in all things conform to the public rule were to be borne with. In a
Paraenetick or Humble Address to the Parliament and [Westminster] *Assembly for
(not loose but) Christian Liberty* (London, 1644) Williams or some one else replied
in a severe indictment of the Presbyterians for not living up to the terms of the
"Considerations" (pp. 5, 14). *The Bloudy Tenent* also was addressed to parliament
and was issued secretly and without name or imprint. It was a philippic against what
Williams conceived to be the persecuting spirit of Massachusetts in the Antinomian
controversy. Cotton replied first in *The Controversie concerning Libertie of Conscience in matters of Religion* (London, 1646) and then in *The Bloudy Tenent
Washed* (1647). This brought from Williams (when in London, 1651-1652), *The
Bloudy Tenent yet more Bloudy* (London, 1652), a further attack on persecution for
the sake of conscience, in which parliament's action of 1643 in favor of dissenting

consciences was justified. For a commentary on certain aspects of this controversy see Parkes, "John Cotton and Roger Williams debate on Toleration," *New England Quarterly,* IV, 735–756.

There is no doubt that the idea of liberty of conscience was very much in the air. In 1644 appeared the pamphlets of Thomas Parker, William Rathband, and M.S. to A.S. (a *Plea for Libertie of Conscience*), and in 1645 the pamphlet of George Gillespie (*The true Resolution of the Present Controversie concerning Liberty of Conscience*). Some time before 1645 certain people in Bermuda petitioned parliament for the privilege of religious freedom there and in October, 1645, the House of Lords ordered that they and such others as should join them were to enjoy liberty of their consciences in matters of God's worship without molestation, and instructed the committee for foreign plantations—at the head of which was Warwick, who was also governor of the Bermuda Company—to execute the order (Stock, *Debates,* I, 169–170; Lefroy, *Memorials,* I, 600–602, 609–611). In the same year Winslow reported that Massachusetts was not the only colony having trouble, as there were deputies at Plymouth who were demanding that the general court "allow and maintaine full and free tolerance of religion to all men that would preserve the civill peace and submit unto government" (*Proceedings,* Massachusetts Historical Society, first series, VI, 476–479). This was undoubtedly the work of William Vassall of Massachusetts (and possibly Samuel Gorton had a hand in it), for in the Remonstrants' appeal to the committee for foreign plantations in 1646 there is a clause calling for liberty of conscience (Winthrop, *Journal,* II, 307). The Plymouth demand was signed by twenty-five non-freemen but Governor Prence ("the only persecuting governor of the Plymouth colony") would not allow it to be brought to a vote (*Hutchinson Papers,* I, 174). "You would have admired," wrote Winslow to Winthrop (November 24, 1646), "to have seen how sweet this carrion relished to the palate of most of the deputies."

In view of all this agitation we may not be surprised that in 1649 Maryland passed her so-called act of toleration and that the province of Maine six months later ordered that "all gode people [there] shall have full liberty to gather themselves in to a church estate provided they do it in a Christian way" (Libby, *Provincial and Court Records,* I, 136). Thus not only at home but in five of the colonies was freedom of conscience and worship agitating the people. It was no mere coincidence that all these things were happening at the time of the troubles in England and that they had not happened before. Certain features of the debate which took place on the subject immediately after the restoration of Charles II are presented in *A Discourse concerning Liberty of Conscience. To which are contain'd Proposalls about what Liberty in this kind is now Politically Expedient to be given.* By R. T. (London, 1661).

On the growth of the idea of toleration "slowly and painfully out of the gradual abdication by the state of any concern with man's soul," see Jordan, *The Development of Religious Toleration from the Beginning of the Reformation to the Death of Queen Elizabeth.*

CHAPTER XXII

ASPECTS OF EARLY MASSACHUSETTS LIFE

THE growth of the colony was very rapid during the years from 1630 to 1642. In 1630 alone seventeen ships came over bringing fifteen hundred people and from that time until 1635 the numbers increased to more than eight thousand. By 1642 it is estimated that there were from sixteen to twenty thousand souls within the limits of the patent, a number too great for rapid absorption and the cause undoubtedly of many of the difficulties which arose under government during the first decade. The ebb of the tide began in 1640–1642, when in the latter year but two ships arrived, bringing not more than five or six passengers,[1] other than those of the colony who were returning to their homes. The causes for the decrease are easily discovered. The brighter prospects in England, owing to the reforming activities of the Long Parliament kept at home many of those who in the preceding decade would have left England, discouraged because of the alarming signs of the times. The coming on of civil war drew into the ranks of the army those who deemed it a religious duty to uphold the cause of the Independents, and at the same time prevented servants and laborers from leaving England and thus brought about a labor shortage in the colony. The reputation that Massachusetts had acquired as a land of intolerance and persecution was a deterrent which discouraged many who did not approve of the policy and methods of the New England authorities, while the strongly ministerial tendencies in the colony alienated such Puritans of higher rank as the lords and gentlemen, who had sympathized with and aided the Puritan cause, but now were unwilling to perpetuate, either by an increase of numbers or an enlargement of funds, a form of government and social life that departed so deliberately from the familiar and customary practices at home.

This momentary breaking of contact with the mother country threw the colony more and more upon its own resources, and in

1. Winthrop, *Journal*, II, 69.

the end proved advantageous rather than otherwise, increasing its strength and arousing a spirit of self-reliance that made for independence. But for a time the effects were depressing. The prices of land and cattle fell, foreign commodities grew scarce and very expensive, labor languished for want of workmen and artisans, little money was in circulation and men fell into debt, without the means, either in cash or corn, to meet their obligations, and the general court was compelled to regulate prices and wages by fiat of law. Surplus products available for export dwindled in variety and quantity, returns to England were insufficient to pay for the commodities received and debits accumulated across the seas as well as at home.[1] Men were losing confidence in the outlook, fearing insolvency and suffering, and were leaving the colony, some pushing farther into the interior, joining the settlements already established beyond the charter bounds; others were going to New Amsterdam, Virginia, and Barbados; many were returning to England, partly to escape the difficulties and discomforts of life in Massachusetts and partly to play their part in aiding the Puritan cause at home. Some of these rose to positions of prominence during the rule of the Puritan minority and became leaders there, particularly under the Commonwealth and the Protectorate. Among them were Hugh Peter, Israel Stoughton, Sedgwick, Desborough, William Hooke, Thomas Welde, William Aspinwall, William Pynchon, and others, either from Massachusetts, Connecticut, or New Haven. A few, unwilling to go back to England, considered the possibility of migrating to the West Indies or to Ireland and the leaders of the colony had to thwart at least four attempts from outside to persuade settlers to remove *en bloc* to other parts of the English world.

The first of these was the endeavor of the Providence Island Company to populate its settlement on the island of Santa Catalina or Old Providence in the heart of the Caribbean.[2] In 1641 about a hundred and fifty went from Massachusetts in two ships, first to England and then to the Caribbean. Among those who started was John Humfry, whose financial and domestic affairs were in bad

1. *Massachusetts Colonial Records,* I, 304, 307, 326; Winthrop, *Journal,* I, 333-335; II, 17, 19, 24, 31-32, 35, 68-69, 82, 83-84, 91, 122, 152, 154-155, 228.
2. This was a Puritan undertaking. The Earl of Warwick and his brother, the first earl of Holland—neither of them very good Puritans, though opposed to Gorges, Laud, and Strafford—Nathaniel Rich, and John Pym, treasurer and deputy governor, and others were the incorporators in 1630. A full account of this enterprise may be

condition and who had not been able to get on with either Winthrop or Endecott, because he would not accept church membership
and had been outspoken in his comments on government and the
colony generally. He accepted an appointment as governor of the
new settlement, but probably never went out at all, remaining in
England until his death in 1651.[1]

The second attempt was that of the Earl of Warwick, who in 1643
sent a vessel from Trinidad to Boston, in part to obtain provisions
and in part to induce a portion of the people to migrate to that
island, but the mission met with no success, because conditions at
home seemed to be improving and the conviction prevailed, as
Winthrop says, that it were better to stay in Massachusetts than to
go to a tropical island where life could not be better and might be
much worse.[2]

A third attempt in the same year was that of Lord Baltimore,
who offered land in Maryland to any one who would migrate
thither, promising the Puritans of New England, as later he promised the Puritans of Virginia, liberty of religion and all other privileges that the place afforded. But Baltimore had no more success
than had Warwick.[3]

The fourth, and much later attempt was that of Cromwell, who
looked on New England "only with an eye of pity, as poor, cold

---

found in Newton, *Colonizing Activities of the English Puritans*. The plantation was
governed by the company in England and exploited solely for profit as a business
venture. It failed to fulfil the expectations of its promoters, for neither soil nor climate was favorable and its location on an island in the Caribbean invited attack from
the Spaniards. The main island, Providence, was captured in 1641, and though efforts
were made later to revive the colony, partly by attracting settlers from New England, everything failed and the undertaking was permanently given up. The loss of
Old Providence was one cause of Cromwell's West Indian expedition of 1654–1655.

1. Newton, *Colonizing Activities*, ch. xiii; *Calendar State Papers, Colonial*, 1574–
1660, pp. 317–330; *Historical Collections*, Essex Institute, LXV, 293–308.

2. Winthrop, *Journal*, I, 132, 150–151. Warwick had acquired in 1638, from the
Earl of Pembroke, rights to Barbados, Trinidad, Tobago, and the mythical Fonseca—
all known as the "Montgomery Province." The purchase had validity for Trinidad and
Tobago only (Harlow, *Barbados*, p. 17; Williamson, *Caribbee Islands under the
Proprietary Patents*, ch. IX). He immediately made plans to colonize and hoped to
persuade the New Englanders to go there. He even thought of going there himself
(*Letters and Papers of the Verney Family*, Camden Society, 1853, p. 193). An ac-
count of the venture is given in Scott, "Description of Barbadoes," British Museum,
Sloane, 3662. For Warwick's efforts at Trinidad and Tobago, Historical Manuscripts
Commission, *Eighth Report*, II, no. 425; Harlow, *Colonizing Expeditions to the West
Indies and Guiana* (Hakluyt Society, second series, LVI, lv–lix, 114–119, 127–131,
141).

3. Winthrop, *Journal*, II, 150.

and useless,"[1] and wished to obtain from there settlers for the peopling of Ireland and Jamaica, two parts of the English world that had been brought under parliamentary control by force of conquest. This desire was viewed by him in the light of a benefit to the colonies there. His favorite settlement was New Haven and the one least in his good graces was Rhode Island, particularly Aquidneck. He wanted to transport the Irish elsewhere and to stock Ireland with Englishmen of the right sort and to persuade New Englanders and Barbadians to go to Jamaica.[2] To the former end, as early as 1650, he entered into correspondence with New England, and sought through intermediaries in Massachusetts and New Haven to arouse an interest in his Irish project. He seems to have had in mind a more or less systematic migration of churches with their pastors and of others under specified leaders, and the letters that were exchanged on the subject show that the suggestion was made in all seriousness. But the plan was shipwrecked on the determined opposition of the Massachusetts Bay authorities, who wrote to Cromwell begging him to desist, as "the great noise and general report of so many invited and intending to transport themselves into Ireland hath occasioned some discouragement and weakening to the whole body of the colony and necessarily brings evil report upon the land, as if defective in that which makes for a people's comfortable subsistence."[3] Failing in Massachusetts, where the colony was on the whole in a prosperous condition, Cromwell turned to New Haven, where commerce was languishing and the people were growing discouraged, and continued his efforts for a number of years. After the capture of Jamaica in 1655, these efforts became more organized and persistent and through the agency of Daniel Gookin and others he held out alluring possibilities of prosperity in this distant island. But the fears engendered by rumors that the island was unhealthful and in constant danger from the Spaniards brought the plans to naught.[4] Neither Massachusetts nor any other of the New England settlements was ever seriously weakened or its population depleted by the withdrawal of any considerable number of its inhabitants.

1. *Narragansett Club Publications*, VI, 285.
2. Harlow, *Barbados*, pp. 106–107, 112, 116, 139.
3. Hutchinson, *History*, I, appendix ix, "Letter to Cromwell, 1651."
4. Strong, "A Forgotten Danger to the New England Colonies," *Report*, American Historical Association, 1898, pp. 79–94; Steiner, *History of Guilford*, ch. v, "The Counter-Emigration"; Gookin, *Life of Daniel Gookin;* and article on the same in the *Dictionary of American Biography*.

From the very beginning of settlement the colonists had scattered widely, as was inevitable in view of the rapid immigration, and had taken up places in favorable environments about the bay and back for short distances into the interior. By 1631 not less than ten plantations and centers of religious and social activity were already in existence—Weymouth, Natascot (Hull), Salem, Charlestown, Boston, Dorchester, Medford, Watertown, Newtown, Roxbury, and Saugus (Lynn). The number had risen to twenty-one in 1642 and thirty-three in 1647,[1] with Dedham the town farthest inland. In parts of the area thus occupied men had been living for a long time, maintaining posts and plantations of a sort and engaging in fur-trading, in fishing, and to some extent in agriculture. The settlements were generally called plantations but sometimes towns, though no regular form of incorporation was adopted, it being customary to use words which indicated that the inhabitants were to enjoy the privileges of a township. These privileges were carefully defined in 1636.[2] Population was largely concentrated in the coast or near coast towns; Boston, Charlestown, Dorchester, Roxbury, Watertown, and Newtown (Cambridge) having in 1644 "near one half of the commonwealth for number of people and substance."[3]

The people were mainly of middle and lower class rank—yeomanry and tenantry—with a few of the gentry and many servants, some of whom seem to have served their masters at home in responsible positions as agents for the transaction of business in New England.[4] Among the representatives of the gentry were Winthrop himself, lord of the manor of Groton; Lady Arbella Johnson and her sister, Susan, sisters of the Earl of Lincoln; Roger and Mabel Har-

1. *Massachusetts Colonial Records*, II, 14, 224.

2. *Ibid.*, I, 84, 172 (act of March 3, 1636). As a rule the only act of incorporation during the earlier period was the entering of the names of the towns in lists of assessments and the granting, after 1634, of the right to send deputies to the general court. Yet in a few instances of later date (1642, 1644) words were used that have a corporate value, such as "Natascot being formerly made a town . . . was named Hull" (Winthrop, *Journal*, II, 178); "Wenham is granted to be a town and hath liberty to send a deputy" (*Massachusetts Colonial Records*, II, 44).

3. Winthrop, *Journal*, II, 159.

4. Francis Stiles, master carpenter, sent over by Saltonstall, was hardly a servant in the ordinary sense of the word, as he had servants under him, and his brother, Henry, is carefully distinguished from the "servants" in the Connecticut records (*Aspinwall Notarial Records*, Boston Record Commissioners' *Report*, 32, pp. 231, 250–251, 343–344; *Connecticut Colonial Records*, 1636–1665, p. 1; Stiles, *Ancient Windsor*, I, 44, 123, 544, 731). Yet Abraham Shurt, who acted as Giles Elbridge's

lakenden, of distinguished lineage from Earl's Colne in Essex, the latter the wife of John Haynes, governor first of Massachusetts and afterward of Connecticut; Sir Richard Saltonstall, son of a lord mayor of London, whose son remained in the colony, the progenitor of a line of important men; and the lady Deborah Moody, "a wise and anciently religious woman, who being taken with the error of denying baptism of infants was dealt with by the elders and admonished by the Salem church." She was afterward excommunicated and to avoid further trouble removed to New Netherland.[1] There were many of the lesser gentry, some of whom were well connected, such as Thomas Gorges, a cousin of Sir Ferdinando and the first "mayor" of York and Richard Vines, governor in Maine, 1645, whose names are closely identified with the northern province; Haynes, Bellingham, and others, men of the same type, who represented the best among the lesser professional and landowning classes in England and were possessed of no little learning and specialized skill. But the great majority were artisans, farmers, and peasants, with the coast towns containing, as the years went on, an increasing number of those associated with shipbuilding and seafaring.[2] The original homes of the settlers can be traced to one or

---

agent, is called a "covenanted servant," was to serve for five years, and to pay Elbridge a yearly annuity of three pounds lawful money as well as his passage and diet. He afterward set himself up as a merchant in Maine (Pemaquid or Bristol) and engaged in several important litigations (Aspinwall, pp. 37, 38, 107, 108; *Massachusetts Colonial Records*, III, 88; Libby, *Province and Court Records of Maine*, I, 7, 43, 48, 57, 81, 112, 118). Robert Keayne mentions a servant, who afterward became a partner with him at his farm (Boston Record Commission, *Report*, 10, p. 25).

1. Winthrop, *Journal*, II, 126; Gerard, *Lady Deborah Moody*, pp. 18–31, with an account of her son, Sir Henry Moody, pp. 31–39.

2. In 1635, of the ninety-one grantees of Newbury, two were clergymen, eight were "gentlemen," two or three had been bred as merchants, one was a maltster, one a physician, one a schoolmaster, one a sea-captain, one the mate of a ship, one a dyer, one a glover, three or four were tanners, seven or eight shoemakers, two wheelwrights, two locksmiths, two linen weavers, two weavers, one was a cooper, one a saddler, one a lawyer, and two or three were carpenters. Of the remainder only a few are styled "yeomen." Coffin, *History of Ould Newbury*, p. 368. The following list is made up from various records. Haberdashers, blacksmiths, shipwrights, shoemakers, butchers, carpenters, cardmakers, hatmakers, coopers, clothiers, sailmakers, ship carpenters, tailors, tanners, vintners, brasiers, glaziers, bakers, wheelwrights, soapboilers, bookbinders, locksmiths, plasterers, clothworkers, salters, bricklayers, gunsmiths, leather dressers, brewers, as well as merchants, shopkeepers, planters, husbandmen, and such common laborers as hoers, reapers, and ditchers. Butchers were frequently complained of as a nuisance. There were also apothecaries, physicians and "chirurgeons."

other of nearly all the English counties, the largest number coming from Suffolk and the smallest from the border shires of the north, farthest away from the Puritan influence.[1] As regards their English origin and family connections, the settlers of Massachusetts, Connecticut, and New Haven were, genealogically speaking, of fine stock and breed, even though few could claim high rank. Scores of them represented the best middle class families, intelligent, well bred, of high moral standards, and proud of their English descent.

Summing up, we find five distinct classes of people. First, a few of high rank, connected with the peerage. Secondly, a few substantial English squires, influential but not numerous, always called "Misters." Thirdly, yeomen, goodmen and their wives of the middle class but below the squires, who were as a rule small farmers or tradesmen, law abiding and religiously minded, migrating for land and homes as well as for religious reasons or, in the case of artisans and tradesmen, for freer opportunities to carry on their work. Fourthly, lesser tenantry from the English demesnes, most of whom were of peasant stock, inferior in position, intelligence, and education, living close to nature, and of the earth earthy, who had probably come in many cases as groups following a leader. Lastly, servants and apprentices, often coarse and quarrelsome, given to vicious and sometimes beastly practices, who because of drunkenness, fighting, swearing, and immoral habits made trouble for the courts. A considerable part of the Puritan penal legislation was directed against this class, which may have represented a quarter of the whole, with little or no interest in Puritan theology. In race the inhabitants were of English stock, with here and there an Irishman, a few Jews (probably from Holland), and a few negroes from Guinea or the West Indies, some of whom may have come by way of New Amsterdam, who were employed chiefly as domestic servants.[2]

For the first twenty or thirty years in the history of the colony,

1. Article by Dr. Banks in *The New York Genealogical and Biographical Record*, January, 1930.

2. *Aspinwall Notarial Records*, pp. 152–153, 300–301. A charter party of 1650 expressly forbade the captain of a vessel bound for Guinea to trade for negroes on the owner's account, though he might buy four negroes provided he paid for them with his own goods. Robert Keayne mentions his "three negars" in his will. On the general subject, Winthrop, *Journal*, I, 260, II, 26, 30, 62; *Calendar State Papers, Colonial*, 1574–1660, p. 407; *Magazine of American History*, IV, 45–46; *Massachusetts Colonial Records*, II, 136, 168 (crime of man stealing), 176; III, 45, 49.

large numbers of the settlers retained their family and property connections with England, still possessing lands[1] there as freeholders or as tenants of the lords of English manors, and having frequent occasion to employ lawyers for the transaction of legal business connected with inheritances, debts, consignments, rents, arrearages, sales, recoveries, leases, and especially legacies. There is one instance where the Rev. Ralph Smith of Ipswich and formerly of Plymouth, held title, through his wife, to a house in Leyden "uppon the uppermost graft neere the quackle brigg" (the Uiterste Gracht near the Kwakelbrug).[2] Occasionally a settler would go to England to dispose of his property rights, but more often he would send over a letter of attorney to some friend or relative, authorizing him to take charge of the business, a very common form of procedure, particularly in the case of legacies, of which there were many. Similarly English merchants or other creditors were accustomed to employ colonists to collect their debts or to transact other legal business and if necessary to sue in New England courts for moneys due,[3] so that the contacts on the business and legal sides were frequent and important.

Intellectually, the average was high, for Massachusetts contained, during these early years at one time or another, a large number of university men, or of men who though not matriculates possessed more than a smattering of knowledge. The number of university men in New England at this period could not have been less than one hundred, some of them masters of arts of either Oxford or Cambridge, the latter being the stronghold of Puritanism, offering a more sympathetic intellectual environment than did the Laudian Oxford.[4] At least two-thirds were from there, partly because of its adjacency to the East Anglian district and partly because of its congenial atmosphere, and among the Cambridge colleges Emmanuel was the favored institution—the intellectual cradle of Blaxton, Cotton, Hooker, Bradstreet, Saltonstall, Rogers, Nathaniel Ward, Thomas Shepard, Johnson, John Harvard, Samuel Stone, and others. Cotton, Hooker, and Knowles were fellows of the college

1. Such lands were exempt from taxation in the colony. *Massachusetts Colonial Records*, I, 330.

2. *Aspinwall Notarial Records, passim;* Lechford, *Note Book, passim.* For the Leyden tenement, Aspinwall, p. 331, and Plooij, *Pilgrims from a Dutch Point of View,* ch. V.

3. Aspinwall, pp. 372, 375, 377, 385.

4. Dexter, *Historical Papers*, pp. 102–115.

as well. Winthrop was a student of Trinity but did not take a degree. He, and probably others, such as the Rev. John Norton, could write letters in Latin; Endecott apparently could speak French, and there were those who could write it. Many knew their classical authors and could quote Virgil and Cicero, and others, particularly among the clergy, were familiar with parts of the Christian literature and could quote from Isidore of Seville, his summation of learning, unsystematic and uncritical as it was.[1]

These men represented one branch of the intelligentsia of England, the interests of which were dialectical and disputatious. Their learning was neither literary, scientific, nor historical, it was dedicated chiefly and primarily to theological discussion. Probably there never had been a time, when so much mental energy was expended on religious controversy and the problems of the soul, or when so many books and pamphlets were issued expounding the pros and cons of eternal salvation, as in the first half of the seventeenth century. Folios, weighty both in form and content, were in every minister's library and pamphlets in great variety issued from the presses of the English publishers. Even the layman became a proficient in the niceties of theological doctrine. The words of the Bible were construed without regard to the higher criticism and were arbitrarily adapted to the needs of the argument without any sufficient understanding of their meaning or application. Divine authority

1. Winthrop, *Journal*, II, 5, 132, 202. The pamphlets written by Massachusetts and Connecticut men during these years disclose the scope of their knowledge, and give the reader an excellent idea of the authorities—primitive, medieval, and contemporary—that were known to the Puritan clergy and laymen. The religious literature of this period is not difficult for the layman to understand, but it is at times bewildering in the dullness of its presentation, the obscurity in which the arguments are couched, and the irrelevance of the parallels cited. The Puritan must have had a strangely incurious mentality to have been satisfied with the sermons and other writings of the day. Perhaps the most extraordinary exposition of Puritan theology is to be found in John Norton's *The Orthodox Evangelist* (London, 1654). Norton was the preacher at Ipswich and his treatise is obscure even to incomprehensibility. It is designed as a complete exposition of "Ecclesiastical Truths," running to 350 pages and using a terminology and a language that is quite enigmatical. He treats of the Doctrine of the Decree, the Dominion of Sin, the Duration of Eternity, the Efficiency of God, the Distribution of the Efficiency of God, Eminental Continency, Passiveness of the Soul in Vocation, and the State of the Blessed after their Resurrection—subjects with which Norton must have wrestled in the quiet of his study and upon which he probably preached to a very long-suffering congregation. Yet he was educated at Peterhouse, Cambridge, and was influential in the colony. Sprague has a place for him in his *Annals,* that is filled with an article as humorless and solemn as was Norton himself.

was invoked for every expression of opinion, and proofs, often un-
convincing and indiscriminate, were advanced to fortify conclusions
already reached. The Puritan mind lived and labored in a world of
its own and in all that concerned man's relations with God was
lost in abstraction and unreality. Except for the history of religious
thought there is hardly a commentary of the day that has other
than a curiosity value at the present time.

Yet these men accomplished a great work in bringing a measure
of English culture to the colony, not only in the form of ideas and
practices but of books also, which though largely theological and
expository were in a few instances literary, historical, and occupa-
tional. Their libraries were constantly being added to by accessions
from England, either as purchases or gifts, the usefulness of which
was enhanced by frequent exchanges among the inhabitants themselves. Books were sold in the colony also, for Hezekiah Usher was a
bookseller in Boston, certainly in 1647 and perhaps as early as 1645.[1]
This regard for learning, derived from contacts made in the mother
country, took early form in the employment of a schoolmaster in
Boston in 1635, and the erection of schoolhouses later in Boston,
Roxbury, and Dorchester,[2] the founding of Harvard College in
1636, the setting up of a printing press in 1639—which printed the
freeman's oath first of all and then almanacs, psalm-books, and sermons—and the providing of a library in the town house, perhaps
as early as 1657.

Association with England was close during these years, for vessels were constantly going back and forth, new colonists were arriving, and knowledge of what was happening in the mother land was
easily acquired. England was home; lands, relatives, and friends
were still there and the old ties could not be easily severed. Even
the benefits and advantages of New England were not enough in
many cases to overcome the love of the land of birth and the dangers and tribulations there must have seemed at times more distress-
ing than the troubles from which the colonist had fled. Returns were

1. Usher is called a "bookseller" in 1647 and is mentioned as early as 1645,
Aspinwall Notarial Records, pp. 10, 103–104.

2. These were all free schools, as were those in the English towns, supported by
public funds. In New England these funds came from sales of town lands, rents
from lands leased on the mainlands and islands, and gifts and legacies. *Boston Town
Records,* pp. 5, 82, 95, 99, 129; *Dorchester Town Records,* pp. 39, 40, 54–57, 73–74;
and elsewhere. If to the Puritan education was a necessity, so was chastisement, for
it was a Puritan tenet of faith that "the rod of correction was an ordinance of God."

frequent. One of those who went back, the Rev. William Hooke, who had supplanted Roger Williams in the affections of Jane Whalley, gave an address at Taunton on a day of humiliation, Thursday, July 23, 1640, which was printed in London the next year, and in which appears these words: "And let us never go to our secrets without our censors in our hands for old England, deare England in divers respects, left indeed by us in our persons, but never yet forsaken in our affections."[1] Massachusetts was not isolated, as were the other New England colonies, from the world outside, and so closely knit were mother and daughter that before a score of years had passed the tide of migration, which had been setting strongly in a westward direction began to turn, and New England clergy, taught in the New England way, were wanted for service at home. New England laymen, too, were welcomed as leaders in the struggles in which the Puritan minority was engaged to establish their rule in England. Puritans were scattered widely over the colonial area, in Bermuda, Barbados and other islands of the Caribbean, in Virginia, Maryland, and New England, and it is an interesting and important fact that Puritanism, wherever found or however varied the shades of its meaning, held its followers together in a common bond of mutual sympathy and religious understanding.

The Puritan was not devoid of the spirit of inquiry and there were those both in Massachusetts and Connecticut who were anxious to know—in a semi or pseudo-scientific way—something of the phenomena of nature and to discover the causes of the woes of the flesh. Before the founding of the Royal Society, which marks a new era in the history of scientific inquiry,[2] the older generations of Puritans were largely inhibited in their quest by their belief in God's responsibility for all that went right or wrong in human affairs. They had profound faith in the intervening hand of God, who blessed his people and brought them prosperity when they obeyed his will, or who showed his displeasure and wrath when they neg-

1. *New England's Teares for Old England's Feares* (London, 1641, at the end). In a letter to Roger Williams from his brother Robert of Providence, the latter speaks of "our dear native country" (Williams Letters, Facsimiles, 1649). For old England's reciprocal affection for New England, see the preface to *New England's Teares*, written by a member of the House of Commons. This sermon is printed in Emery, *Ministry of Taunton*, I, 79–98, from the first edition of 1641. The original copy in the Yale Library is the third edition of that year.

2. Wright, *Literary Culture in Early New England;* Ornstein, *Rise of Scientific Societies in the Seventeenth Century.* Miss Ornstein does not treat of the colonies, but has an excellent chapter on the Royal Society.

lected their duty. Their God was the God of the Old Testament rather than of the New and he it was that kept watch upon scores of the incidental happenings of the Puritan's daily life. Accidents, failures, and deaths were traced not only to his disapproval of man's conduct on earth, but also to the successes of the devil, which were ascribed to God's own allowance, as a retribution for the sins of his people.[1] It was practically impossible for anyone to pursue a strictly objective investigation into the operations of nature and the phenomena of the world about him or to concern himself seriously with the prevention of disease or the curing of the sick or injured, as long as he admitted the influence of such an uncertain factor as God's miraculous providence into his calculations. Winthrop tells the story of a child's injury—a piece of the skull being driven into the brain—and adds that the advice of one of the ruling elders, a layman and "an experienced and very skilful surgeon," prevailed over the opinion of seven other surgeons (some of the country and others of the ships that lay in the harbor), and the child was left to the mercies of God and prayers of the church for a recovery which, strange as it may seem, actually took place.[2] Many other stories of the same sort could be related.

At the same time the general court could recommend to the authorities of Harvard College that such students as studied "physick or chirurgery" should have "liberty to reade anotomy and to anotomize once in four years some malefactor, in case there shall be such as the Courts allow of," and it sought to prevent epidemics by means of a quarantine at Castle Island in the harbor. In 1649 it ordered that no physician, surgeon, midwife, or others should presume to "put forth any act contrary to the knowne rules of art," in the way of using force, violence, or cruelty. Such a rule was particularly needed in the days before anesthesia was known and in cases of obstetrics, which were entirely in the hands of women,[3] and had a prominent place in family experience on account of the early and frequent marriages and the large number of children born.

1. For Hooker's belief in the power of Satan, see *Collections,* Connecticut Historical Society, I, 3.

2. Winthrop, *Journal,* II, 209–210. The date is 1644.

3. *Massachusetts Colonial Records,* II, 201, 237, 278–279; Thoms, "The Beginnings of Obstetrics in America," *Yale Journal of Biology and Medicine,* IV, pp. 665–675.

The credulity even of the intelligent leaders of the commonwealth is at all times conspicuous in the chronicles of the period, which show that belief in prodigies and portents was an everyday matter. Winthrop had no doubt that a calf was born at Ipswich with one head, three mouths, three noses, and six eyes. Mary Dyer gave birth to a woman child, so monstrous and misshapen as the like had never been seen, and even Mrs. Hutchinson was widely reported to have done the same, an event which signified to Cotton "her error in denying inherent righteousness."[1] The Rev. John Wilson had no difficulty in interpreting a combat between a mouse and a snake as an allegory in which the snake was Satan and the mouse "a poor contemptible people, which God had brought hither." As the victory lay with the mouse so would God's people overcome the devil and dispossess him of his kingdom.[2] Such analogies, allegories, and expositions had long been the stock in trade of the Puritans, whether in old or New England, and their presence in the Puritan writings does much to elucidate Puritan character and history. Once believe that the earth is the scene of an actual warfare between a personally present Christ on one side and a Satan equally present on the other, in a never ending conflict for the possession of the human soul; once become convinced that the Lord always intervenes to save his saints and to frustrate the designs of their enemies; once accept without questioning the view that the Puritan elect were the Lord's agents to carry out his purpose and to found a community and church in the place that he had chosen, and Puritan conduct becomes explicable. Under such conditions questions of toleration, liberty of thought and action, and even standards of human conduct become matters of secondary consideration, because the hand of God was everywhere and in everything.[3]

1. Winthrop, *Journal*, II, 264, 267–268, 277. A "monster" of this kind is called by Dr. Thoms a "hydatidiform mole." Winthrop and Weld spread abroad this story of the two monstrosities, and it was taken over from the latter's *A Short Story of the Antinomians* by Clarke in his *Looking Glass for Saints and Sinners*, pp. 249–250, a work of amazing credulities, anticipating some of the writings of Cotton Mather. See also Adams, *Antinomians*, pp. 88, 90, 187–190. Mrs. Hutchinson's death at the hands of the Indians was according to the Puritans a true sign of God's judgment upon a heretic. Both women were "heretics plagued by God," as Clarke puts it.

2. Winthrop, *Journal*, I, 83–84.

3. An early illustration of the Puritan's belief that God's pleasure or displeasure was manifested in the incidents of his daily life may be found in Hull, "Some Passages of God's Providence about myself and in relation to myself" (*Archaeologia Americana*, III, 141–164). One of the first acts of the general court of Connecticut,

The natural world was viewed with the eyes and understanding of a child, which is appalled at the mysteries and phenomena of the world about him. As Eggleston expresses it, "The sun, moon, and planets were flames of fire without gravity, revolved about the earth by countless angels; its God governed this our little world with mock majesty; its heaven, its horrible hell of material fire blown by the mouth of God; its chained demons, whose fetters might be loosed; its damnation of infants" were all characteristic of the medieval mind.[1] Eclipses, parhelia, and comets were danger signals hung out in the heavens as warnings, the phases of the moon were factors to be reckoned with in performing the round of daily and weekly duties, and the signs of the zodiac were a regulating influence controlling man's future and the future of his children. The phenomena of nature were to the Puritan a never ending subject of speculation: comets were meteors sent by God to awaken a morally lethargic world and earthquakes were great and terrible expressions of God's wrath. That anything could happen in the physical universe uncontrolled by God was incomprehensible to the Puritan mind. Even Roger Williams saw God in a snow storm besieging the earth "with his white legions," and wrote of the comet of 1680 as "this blazing herald from heaven [which] denounceth from the Most High wars, pestilence, famine"; [and, therefore,] "is it not then our wisdom to make and keep peace with God and man."[2] Nathaniel Morton in a lengthy essay on earthquakes, written two years after the founding of the Royal Society, could speak of them as the result of "air and windy spirits and exhalations shut up in the caverns of the earth," making it "oftimes shake and quake, and rock and rend itself, as if it shewed that he which made it, threatened by this trembling the impiety of the world and the ruin of those that dwell on the earth."[3] The seventeenth century mind in

after the adoption of the Fundamental Orders in 1639, was to appoint a committee "to ripen some orders that were left unfinished the former court," among which was the recording "spetiall passages of pᵣvidence" that had been remarkable since the "first undertaking of these plantations." Unfortunately the "ripening" if ever brought to completion was not recorded. *Connecticut Colonial Records, 1636–1665*, pp. 34, 39. This state of mind continued in New England well on into the nineteenth century.

1. Eggleston, *The Transit of Civilization*, ch. 1 (*A History of Life in the United States*, II).

2. *Narragansett Club Publications*, VI, 402–403.

3. Morton's *New England Memorial* (ed. 1855), pp. 190, 191, 198. For the earthquake at Aquidneck, Winthrop, *Journal*, I, 297.

New England, in all that concerned an understanding of nature, was still medieval, though a growing interest in scientific observations was beginning to declare itself. John Robinson, the Leyden pastor, had already said in his essays that "the highway to wisdom, divine and human," was "to observe and consider the reasons and causes of things" and the scientific attitude of John Winthrop, Jr., after the middle of the century, and of Increase Mather at its close marks a new approach to the problems of the visible and invisible worlds.[1]

So rapid had been the influx into New England of emigrants from the mother country—nearly a thousand a year on the average during the first decade after the founding of the Bay colony—that the first problems were inevitably those of land and a home. It was no easy matter for a colony, established amid unbroken forests, in a frontier wilderness, to find place for every group of new comers and to fit them in as part of a growing population. The waning of the migration was rather beneficial than otherwise, for it lessened the demand for allotments, gave time for adjustment and distribution of settlers—some removing into other parts of New England and others returning to their native land—and checked the inrush of so many leaders of strong wills and assertive dispositions that had hitherto disturbed the peace of the community. The life of the first ten years was, therefore, largely one of interest in the soil as well as in government and theology, and it is not until after 1640 that in the field of subsistence and maintenance we find indications of a more diversified industrial and commercial activity.

In the early years of all the New England towns, the distribution and allotment of land were subjects of serious and prayerful consideration on the part of those who were in charge of prudential affairs. Most of the settlers were familiar with the land arrangements of the towns, manors, and boroughs of old England, and with the open fields, enclosures, commons, meadows, pastures, and woods, amidst which they had been born and brought up, the conditions of which had changed but little for two centuries. English

1. Steiner, W. R., "Governor John Winthrop, Jr. of Connecticut as a physician" (Johns Hopkins Hospital *Bulletin*, XIV, November, 1903); Mather, *The Doctrine of Divine Providences, Opened and Applied* (Boston, 1684), and *An Essay for the Recording of Remarkable Providences* (Boston, 1684, 1690). A modern edition of the latter (1890) contains a preface by George Offor, who speaks of the work as "the dawn of light upon an enquiring mind, imbued with godly piety, leading him to penetrate the gloom with which the human intellect has been for ages shrouded."

towns were small nucleated groups of houses, surrounded by an
unfenced arable divided into fields and strips, with hedged enclosures, largely used for pasture and meadow, gradually increasing
in extent, because of the economic value of sheep-raising and better
farming methods. The New England arrangement followed the
home plan very closely. Houses and homelots formed the nucleus
of a town, with the church and later the schoolhouse nearby, while
stretching away from the center, as regularly as the lay of the land
would allow, were the fields, called by a great variety of names,
familiar to every English farmer, terriers, squadrons, shots, fur-
longs, quarters, and divisions, that were made available as need
arose. These sections were subdivided into holdings according to
various rules based on the Puritans' ideas of equity and justice.
These rules differed widely. In some towns distribution was dependent on the size of the family, as at Dedham, on the value of rateable
estate, as at Newbury, on the size of the home lots, as at Dorchester, or on all three combined, as was perhaps the more common
practice in a majority of the towns. A chief object was to prevent
engrossing and to give to every man a fair share in what the town
possessed and to encourage settlement and the improvement of the
resources of the community. Generally the grants were of different
sizes, but sometimes an equal division was made, when assignments
were determined by lot, a method which prevented bickering and
ill will, because the drawing of lots represented an appeal to the
judgment of God.[1]

As time went on and the population increased, the problems of
land distribution became more difficult of solution and the town
records are full of decisions as to when, where, and how the grants
should be made. Some of the most difficult problems concerned the
grants to servants and especially to new comers, and as early as
1635 Boston was obliged to rule that no more land should be set out
to such new arrivals as were not likely to become church members,
and the town fathers instructed all landowners not to sell any part
of their allotments to men of that kind. With the granting of land
went the care of fences, highways, and lanes, and the oversight of
stock, particularly hogs wandering about the streets and masting in

---

1. The reason that Connecticut gave in 1656 for forbidding the playing of cards,
dice, tables, etc., was that any one indulging in games of chance directly abused and
profaned the "great and sollemne ordinance of a Lott." *Connecticut Colonial Records*
1636–1665, p. 289.

the woods. These concerns occupied the time and attention of townsmen and town-meetings throughout the entire colonial period. Despite the distractions caused by Roger Williams, Anne Hutchinson, and Dr. Child, and despite the fears aroused by the attack on the charter, which were of concern only to a small part of the population, the interest of the largest number of the people was centered on the acquirement of land and the making of a living for wives and children. Men had to have soil to cultivate and crops to raise, whether their future salvation depended on a covenant of grace or a covenant of works, and in most cases the daily round of material existence was more exacting and more troublesome than the similar round of religious duties that the doctrine of works required.

As the land situation became less exigent with the dwindling of immigration, other needs pressed for recognition and industry and commerce began to find place among the interests of the inhabitants. Water mills were set up along the creeks and rivers for the grinding of corn and a "tide mill" for the same purpose appears in Dorchester in 1640. Windmills after the Dutch fashion came into use and sawmills were of necessity early employed. Shops for craftsmanship and retail selling were started, at first in private houses, then in annexes thereto authorized by vote of the town, and finally in buildings, officially approved and specially constructed for the purpose. Some of these had signs, as was the case with Joshua Foote's shop in Boston, which may have combined tavern and shop under the sign of the cock. At first designed as workshops or for the sale of certain specified products, these shops tended to take on the form of stores, where a great variety of goods, wet and dry, were offered at retail to the public. In 1657 Boston voted that no one should keep shop within the town or set up manufactures unless he were an admitted inhabitant and three years later, in an order regulating apprentices "in manufactures and sciences," decided that no person should open a shop or engage in any manufacture until he was twenty-one years old and had served as apprentice for seven years, his indenture being duly enrolled in the town records.[1]

Shipbuilding on a small scale had already begun at Plymouth, but not for sea-going purposes, and there were ship-carpenters, probably

1. *Boston Town Records*, pp. 80, 135, 156–157; *Dorchester Town Records*, p. 69; *Aspinwall Notarial Records*, p. 102; Weeden, *Economic and Social History*, I, 102–103, 168; Winthrop, *Journal*, I, 315–317. Captain Robert Keayne, of sow fame, had a shop in Boston in 1639 and got into trouble for charging extortionate prices. In

employed as house carpenters as well among those who came to Massachusetts in 1629. Winthrop's *Blessing of the Bay*, a vessel of thirty tons, built of locust wood at Malden in 1631, made a voyage to Long Island and New Amsterdam.[1] The industry thus begun in the coasting trade was continued with the building of small shallops and sloops, some broad of beam for the carrying of firewood and others designed as fishing boats with oars, sails, and anchors; and land was set apart by Boston and Salem for the construction of these vessels. In 1641 Richard Hollingsworth had a shipyard at Salem where was built "a prodigious ship of 300 Tons." In 1642 the *Trial,* a vessel of 200 tons, was built at Boston, John Cotton preaching the sermon at the meetinghouse to give the vessel its *bon voyage,* and this craft crossed the ocean to the Canaries, thence went to St. Christopher, and from there home, having had a profitable voyage. Later it went to Malaga and Bilbao, returning with a cargo of wine, fruit, iron and wool, "which [says Winthrop] was of great advantage to the country and gave encouragement to trade." After this it went to Acadia and along the eastern shore of Canada and in 1645 to London and Holland, bringing back a cargo of English and Dutch commodities. It was still in service in 1659. One of the leading shipyards was that of Benjamin Gillam & Co., located north of Copps Hill, the largest ship there recorded being the *Welcome* of 300 tons, built and owned by Valentine Hill. A still larger boat, the *Seafort* of 400 tons, is mentioned in 1645.[2]

Thus after 1640 shipbuilding and commerce became the leading

his will, 1653, he refers to the "many claymors and evill reports raised up" against him and mentions his "shops" (Boston Record Commissioners, *Report,* 10, p. 9; also pp. 27, 30–31, 35, for his defense against the extortion charge, for which he had been fined by the general court, *Massachusetts Colonial Records,* I, 280). He had formerly kept shop in London, and had served the usual term of an apprentice.

1. Winthrop, *Journal,* I, 109, 128. On the general subject, G. F. Dow, "Shipping and Trade in Early New England," *Proceedings,* Massachusetts Historical Society, 64, pp. 185–201.

2. Winthrop, *Journal,* I, 65, 109, 128; II, 70, 72–93, 157 (Winthrop gives both 160 and 200 as the tonnage of the *Trial*); Hull, *Diary,* p. 151; *Aspinwall Notarial Records,* pp. 273, 358, 365; "Book of Possessions" (Boston Record Commissioners, *Report,* 2) p. 125. It is often difficult to determine whether the vessels entered in Aspinwall's records were built in New England or were English built trading with the colony. London merchants had shares in New England built ships and New England merchants were part owners of vessels built in England. Occasionally a French or Dutch vessel entered Boston harbor and in one case a Hamburg ship was chartered in New England to go to Piscataqua. Aspinwall, pp. 22–23, 83, 207, 292–293.

activities of Boston, Charlestown, Dorchester, and Salem. Ships as small as twelve tons for the coasting trade and as large as 400 tons for ocean-going travel were gradually effecting a transformation in the character and life of these coast towns, and making them the centers of a new wealth and a new prosperity. The days when the Massachusetts Puritans had lived on a ration of acorns, clams, and Indian corn—a veritable starvation diet—were gone never to return, for from this time on all classes of the population—the lower classes to an extent never experienced in old England—were clothed, housed, and fed comfortably. There was never any extreme poverty or beggary in the colony under Puritan rule.

The waterfront of Boston and to a lesser extent of Charlestown, Dorchester, and Salem also, was gradually encircled with a line of wharves, numbering upward of thirty, amidst which stood out prominently the Dock, with its hoisting crane, at the foot of Dock Square and the market place, the predecessor of the old wharf (barricado) of 1672 and the Long Wharf of 1710. Some of these "wharves" were used as approaches to the many ferries that inter-linked the different parts of the irregular Boston peninsula with other parts of the mainland and with the islands, some fifteen in number, which were of value chiefly for pasturage or for the raising of tobacco and grain. Others were sea-walls or jetties, at which small boats might tie up, such as were used to communicate with the larger vessels lying in the capacious harbor, where, it was estimated, 500 vessels could ride at anchor in good depth of water. Wharves of one kind or another were built before 1652 by Edward Bendall, Valentine Hill, John Milom, Walter Merry, Richard Bellingham, Edward Tinge, John Anderson, Christopher Lawson, George Hal-sall, Nicholas Upsall, David Phippen, Thomas Breedon, and others, either alone or with associates, sometimes (with the permission of the town) on their own properties facing the water, rights to which extended over the flats to the channel, and sometimes on land leased for the purpose and controlled under the terms of the indenture. Owners of private wharves were allowed to charge wharfage.[1] Goods might also be landed anywhere along the shore or the banks of the rivers, and warehouses and other buildings were erected to receive them. Boston's waterfront became, as the years wore on, increasingly the center of a sea-going activity, with vessels coming

1. *Aspinwall Notarial Records*, pp. 64, 89, 110, 156.

and going, importing and exporting commodities and bringing into the community, not always to its advantage and sometimes to its discontent, a sea-faring element that often vexed the souls of the Puritan fathers. By 1650 commerce had become so important a business and the problems to which it gave rise so frequent and exacting that the general court took the matter in hand and in that year appointed a committee to examine Malynes, *Lex Mercatoria,* and extract therefrom such laws as should be applicable to the Massachusetts conditions.[1] There is nothing to show that such a maritime code was ever drawn up. Inevitably marine causes arose, such as concerned wages, bottomry, charter parties, breach of covenants and agreements, lay days and demurrage, loss of markets, "dead freighting and other dangers" (as the phrase went), all of which were settled in the common law courts of the colony.[2]

Voyages covered a wide area of profitable trading enterprise. During this period vessels went coastwise to Piscataqua, Isles of Shoals, and the Maine coast, to Plymouth, New Haven, New Amsterdam, and Virginia and quite frequently to Ferryland in Newfoundland, where planters and fishermen were still living after the abandonment by Baltimore of his Avalon grant. Overseas they went to and from England, Ireland, Holland, France, Portugal, Spain, and Italy—to London, Bristol, Dublin, Amsterdam, La Rochelle, Bordeaux, "Superdevecha," "Ourij," Marseilles, Bilbao, Lisbon, Malaga, Barcelona, Leghorn, and Malta.[3] They went occasionally to the Barbary States and Guinea, for elephants' teeth, for gold, and to a small extent for negroes, and to the Wine Islands very frequently, particularly to Madeira and the Canaries, for wines.

But their most important overseas trade was with the West Indies, chiefly Barbados, but also St. Kitts, Antigua, and Nevis. The commercial intercourse of the Barbadians with New England was one of the prime reasons for that island's prosperity in the seven-

1. *Massachusetts Colonial Records,* III, 193; IV, 69.
2. *Aspinwall Notarial Records,* pp. 253, 261, 302, 304, 364, etc.
3. There is mention also of a "Scanderone" voyage (Aspinwall, p. 253). The only Scanderoon discoverable is Iskanderun or Alexandretta in Syria. This was an important port in the Levant trade and an English vice-consul was there at this time. In its harbor Sir Kenelm Digby defeated a French fleet in June, 1628 (*Proceedings,* Massachusetts Historical Society, 59, pp. 3–25). As Digby was a friend of John Winthrop, Jr., who heard of the defeat when at Leghorn and wrote to his father about it (*Winthrop Papers,* I, 402–403), it is easy to believe that the Massachusetts merchants tried out a trading voyage there as a possibly profitable venture.

teenth and eighteenth centuries and it was equally a reason for the prosperity of Massachusetts, because of the agricultural surplus of food stuffs—fish, beef, and corn, which accumulated in the colony after 1640, and needed a market for their disposal.[1] Sometimes these vessels went on long roundabout voyages, as when a Boston boat of forty tons went to Rhode Island, to Barbados, to Guinea, back to Barbados and Antigua, and then to Boston. One charter party provided for a voyage of ten or twelve months, in a vessel of thirty tons, evidently with the intention of doing a huckstering and peddling business on the sea. Another instruction provided for a voyage along the French and Spanish coasts, with the idea of going from place to place getting the best bargains possible. These vessels were generally insured.[2]

The Massachusetts merchants exported a great variety of commodities, sometimes in their own vessels, built at their own shipyards, and sometimes in vessels hired in England, New Amsterdam, and elsewhere for freighting purposes. Sometimes they took shares in English vessels sent over by English merchants, which on their arrival in Boston harbor would take on a Massachusetts consignment, after discharging their own cargo, and go to places in Europe, the Straits, or the West Indies. A Boston, Charlestown, or Salem lading, whether to England, the Continent, the West Indies, or the Wine Islands, would consist of one part or other of the following: masts, clapboards, pipe staves and headings, treenails and bolts, props, and woodenware; wheat, pease, pork, and beef; dry fish in casks, raw fish in bulk—cod, mackerel, pilchard, etc., generally obtained from the "eastward"—Gloucester, Isles of Shoals, and the Maine coast villages—sturgeon, train oil, and oysters; bread, butter, treacle, onions, nuts, and soap; furs, chiefly moose (300 skins in one lot, 172 in another), bear, beaver, and otter; and a considerable quantity of reëxported articles, tobacco—some of which came from Barbados and Virginia in leaf, roll, and cask, some from Rhode Island and elsewhere in the nearby country, and great quantities of English goods, for Boston was a distributing center, not only for its own back country produce, but also for Connecticut and New Haven.

1. Harlow, *Barbados*, pp. 269–291, where the history of the trade with New England is narrated to 1688.
2. *Aspinwall Notarial Records*, pp. 220, 302, 313.

Imports were of infinite variety and enable us to picture the Massachusetts of that day in terms of no little luxury and abundance. Large quantities of tobacco were consumed in the colony, if we are to judge by the tobacco pipes and boxes imported from England (six hogsheads, two chests, and 500 gross are mentioned in the invoices). From Barbados came cotton, sugar, and indigo; from the Canaries and Madeira pipes and butts of wine for the colony taverns and tables; from France and Spain, fruits, oil, lemons, soap, wine, and particularly salt, which was in great demand, some of which was procured from the Isle of May among the Cape Verde group; from Malaga, raisins; from Bilbao, in return for fish and wheat, chiefly cash which was laid out in Portugal and Spain or within the Straits for European goods.¹ From England came the chief articles of dress, house furnishing, and farm work, for there is very little evidence of direct importations from any of the Continental ports of European manufactured articles. Cotton and silk cloths and many varieties of coarser and heavier cloths, hardware for house and shop, ironwork and canvas for ships, saddlers' ware, stationers' ware, shoes, stockings, caps and hats, both felt and stuff, rugs, carpeting, silk notions and threads, silver and silk buttons, window glass, pewter ware, fish lines and hooks, pots, candles, powder and shot, "arms" and fowling pieces, suits of sails, and Russia leather chairs. Also drugs, such as rhubarb, wormseed, senna, mace, nutmeg, cloves, pepper, alum, and "salve"; plants, seeds, and roots, and plenty of sack, metheglin, madeira, canary, and "strong water," that is, hard liquor.² While undoubtedly a considerable part of all these goods was reëxported, still the bulk of it must have been consumed in the colony, Boston serving as the port through which commodities were conveyed to all parts of the country behind.

1. Hull, *Diary*, p. 130.

2. From *Aspinwall Notarial Records,* "Cocquetts and Certificates," pp. 394-430. Nearly one hundred and fifty invoices are entered, of which the following is an excellent example (p. 417), "Cert[ificate] that the Speedwell of Lond[on] Dickery Carwithen Mʳ hath here Delivered for the Accᵒ of Robt Rich mer[chant] 15000 ells vittry canvas. 600 pcs lockrams. seven thousand ells linen. 6000 ells broad Germany linnen. 6000 ells narrow Germany linnen. 300 pcs Norwich stuffes. 100 pcs broad cloth. Mercery ware grocery ware haberdash ware yronmongers ware cost all two thousand pounds. twelve butts currans, Juxt. Cocqᵗ. Dat xxiijᵒ March 1649." Other invoices are even more elaborate and show a remarkable variety, quantity, and value of importations for a colony only nineteen years from its founding. These invoices help to explain the sumptuary laws passed by the colony in 1651 (*Massachusetts Colonial Records*, III, 242-243).

To take care of all this merchandise wholesale and retail shops sprang up in the coast towns and retail shops and stores in the smaller communities, for sale and barter, and the merchants themselves in Boston were often both retail and wholesale dealers. Among the English shippers were Henry Ashurst, a well-known friend of the colony, John Pocock, one of the merchant adventurers who aided the Pilgrims, William Stratton, Robert Knight, Joshua Woolnough, Joshua Foote & Co., Edward Shrimpton, whose brother Henry was a merchant in the colony, William Peake, and others; while in Massachusetts were those already noted as wharf-owners, as well as Stephen Winthrop, the governor's son, John Leverett, Henry Shrimpton, David Yale, father of Elihu, and many more, whose energies and resourcefulness were bringing confidence and strength to the colony as well as a considerable measure of covetousness and pride.

In the actual transaction of foreign business, barter, paper, and cash were all brought into use. Tobacco was exchanged for muscovado sugar, a Barbados debt was paid one-half in refuse fish, one-quarter in merchantable fish, and one-quarter in train oil; another in cash and beaver, beef and pork, and fish at market prices. In every part of the trading world debts were the rule[1] not the exception, and powers of attorney for collection were given from colony to colony. Interest was at eight per cent. Promises to pay and bills of exchange were common enough, but cash and barter were the usual means employed. There was certain amount of hard money, a good deal of which may have been brought from England, though it is equally likely that much of that which came with the settlers was in goods as well as money.[2] There were in circulation before the mint was set up in 1652, Portuguese reis and crusadoes, Spanish rials, pistoles, dollars, and pieces of eight, English "good and lawful money" mostly in silver, and occasionally Dutch guilders, French livres, and Barbary gold. Probably very little gold was in circulation; silver coin was much worn by use, sweating, washing, or clipping,

---

1. Captain Keayne had three chief debt books, one bound in vellum, a second in thin parchment, and a third in white vellum (*Report*, Boston Record Commissioners, 10, p. 39). There were others also (p. 41). Many of these debts were "desperate" or "doubtful" (p. 39). One can get a very good account of the way a prosperous man kept his books from Keayne's will. The net value of his estate in 1653 was £4000 (pp. 45, 47).

2. Keayne brought over "two or 3000 lbs in good estate" (p. 47).

and so much of it was counterfeited that the general court finally decided in 1652 to establish its own mint and to limit legal current money to its own minted coins, a witness not only to the independent attitude of the colony but to the pressing necessity also that was felt at the time for a stable currency in the transaction of commercial business. This mint was the culmination of twelve years of an expanding trading enterprise and its output took the form of the famous pine tree shillings, sixpences, threepences, and twopences, that were made from the silver plate, silver bullion, and silver coins brought for melting to the mint house of John Hull.[1] This act of sovereignty, taken in conjunction with the policy of territorial expansion to the northward and the extension of jurisdiction over the towns of New Hampshire and Maine, represents the high water mark in the assumption by the Puritan commonwealth of all the rights of independent statehood, without regard to the charter or the authorities at home.

Thus while the Puritan leaders, on the political side, were laying more soundly and broadly the constitutional and legal foundations of the commonwealth and on the religious side were preserving the faith and ecclesiastical polity of the founders from unorthodox contamination, and while the farmers of the different towns were widening the area of supply and increasing the agricultural output for purposes of export, the merchants, shipbuilders, sea-captains, and mariners were extending commerce into all parts of the north Atlantic world, were adding to the wealth and prosperity of the colony, and were raising the standard of living beyond the dreams of the early immigrants. From this time forward Massachusetts became the dominant influence in New England, the center of its trade, and the leader in the resistance to the policy of the home government in all that concerned commerce and the colonies. The very success of the Puritans was the measure of God's protecting care and as long as God was with them why should man be afraid.

1. Hull, *Diary*, pp. 185, 193; *Massachusetts Colonial Records*, III, 261–262. The mint house was located on Hull's estate, on what is now Washington Street.

INDEX